T&T CLARK HANDBOOK OF
CHRISTIAN PRAYER

Forthcoming titles in this series include

T&T Clark Handbook of Christology, *edited by Darren O. Sumner and Chris Tilling*

T&T Clark Handbook of the Early Church, *edited by Piotr Ashwin-Siejkowski, John Anthony McGuckin and Ilaria L.E. Ramelli*

T&T Clark Handbook of Public Theology, *edited by Christoph Hübenthal and Christiane Alpers*

T&T Clark Handbook of Election, *edited by Edwin Chr. van Driel*

T&T Clark Handbook of John Owen, *edited by Crawford Gribben and John W. Tweeddale*

T&T Clark Handbook of Anabaptism, *edited by, edited by Brian C. Brewer*

T&T Clark Handbook of Modern Theology, *edited by Philip G. Ziegler and R. David Nelson*

T&T Clark Handbook of the Doctrine of Creation, *edited by Jason Goroncy*

Titles already published include

T&T Clark Handbook of Christian Theology and Climate Change, *edited by Ernst M. Conradie and Hilda P. Koster*

T&T Clark Handbook of Political Theology, *edited by Rubén Rosario Rodríguez*

T&T Clark Handbook of Pneumatology, *edited by Daniel Castelo and Kenneth M. Loyer*

T&T Clark Handbook of Ecclesiology, *edited by Kimlyn J. Bender and D. Stephen Long*

T&T Clark Handbook of Christian Theology and the Modern Sciences, *edited by John P. Slattery*

T&T Clark Handbook of Christian Ethics, *edited by Tobias Winright*

T&T Clark Handbook of Analytic Theology, *edited by James M. Arcadi and James T. Turner, Jr*

T&T Clark Handbook of Theological Anthropology, *edited by Mary Ann Hinsdale and Stephen Okey*

T&T CLARK HANDBOOK OF CHRISTIAN PRAYER

Edited by
Ashley Cocksworth and John C. McDowell

t&tclark
LONDON • NEW YORK • OXFORD • NEW DELHI • SYDNEY

T&T CLARK
Bloomsbury Publishing Plc
50 Bedford Square, London, WC1B 3DP, UK
1385 Broadway, New York, NY 10018, USA
29 Earlsfort Terrace, Dublin 2, Ireland

BLOOMSBURY, T&T CLARK and the T&T Clark logo are trademarks of Bloomsbury Publishing Plc

First published in Great Britain 2022
Paperback edition published 2023

A catalogue record for this book is available from the British Library.

Library of Congress Cataloging-in-Publication Data
Names: Cocksworth, Ashley, editor. | McDowell, John C., editor.
Title: T&T Clark handbook of Christian prayer / edited by
Ashley Cocksworth and John C. McDowell.
Description: London ; New York : T&T Clark, 2021. | Series: T&T Clark
handbooks | Includes bibliographical references and index. |
Identifiers: LCCN 2021011789 (print) | LCCN 2021011790 (ebook) |
ISBN 9780567664365 (hardback) | ISBN 9780567703651 (paperback) |
ISBN 9780567664372 (adobe pdf) | ISBN 9780567664389 (epub)
Subjects: LCSH: Prayer–Christianity.
Classification: LCC BV210.3 .T32 2021 (print) | LCC BV210.3 (ebook) |
DDC 248.3/2–dc23
LC record available at https://lccn.loc.gov/2021011789
LC ebook record available at https://lccn.loc.gov/2021011790

ISBN: HB: 978-0-5676-6436-5
           PB: 978-0-5677-0365-1
           ePDF: 978-0-5676-6437-2
           eBook: 978-0-5676-6438-9

Series: T&T Clark Handbooks

Typeset by Integra Software Services Pvt. Ltd.

To find out more about our authors and books visit www.bloomsbury.com
and sign up for our newsletters.

CONTENTS

CONTRIBUTORS

Travis E. Ables is an independent scholar and former Managing Editor of the *Anglican Theological Review*. He is a theologian specializing in the thought of Augustine and its reception and transformation in mediaeval mystical movements, with particular attention to the political contexts of Christian doctrinal formation. He has taught at Vanderbilt Divinity School, Eden Theological Seminary and Regis University. He is the author of *Incarnational Realism: Trinity and the Spirit in Augustine and Barth* (T&T Clark, 2013) and *The Body of the Cross: Holy Victims and the Invention of Atonement* (2021).

James M. Arcadi is Associate Professor of Biblical and Systematic Theology at Trinity Evangelical Divinity School in Deerfield, Illinois, USA. Previously he was Postdoctoral Research Fellow in the Analytic Theology Project at Fuller Theological Seminary and Research Fellow in the Jewish Philosophical Theology Project at the Herzl Institute. His first book is *An Incarnational Model of the Eucharist* (2018). He is co-editor of *Love: Divine and Human: Contemporary Essays in Systematic and Philosophical Theology* (T&T Clark, 2019) and the *T&T Clark Handbook of Analytic Theology* (T&T Clark, 2021). Ordained in the Anglican Church in North America, he has served in parishes in Massachusetts, California and Illinois, USA.

Stephen C. Barton is a theologian with a specialism in New Testament studies. He was Tutor in Biblical Studies at Salisbury and Wells Theological College (1984–8) and Reader in New Testament in the Department of

Theology and Religion, Durham University (1988–2010). Currently, he is Honorary Fellow of Durham and Manchester Universities. Ordained priest in the Church of England in 1994, he has assisted in parishes in Durham, Newcastle and Lichfield dioceses. His publications include *The Spirituality of the Gospels* (1992), *Discipleship and Family Ties in Mark and Matthew* (1994), *Invitation to the Bible* (1997) and *Life Together: Family, Sexuality and Community in the New Testament and Today* (T&T Clark, 2001). Edited volumes include *Holiness Past and Present* (T&T Clark, 2003), *Idolatry: False Worship in the Bible, Early Judaism and Christianity* (T&T Clark, 2007) and *The Cambridge Companion to the Gospels*, 2nd edn (2021).

Tina Beattie is Professor Emerita of Catholic Studies and Director of Catherine of Siena College at the University of Roehampton. Her main research interests are in the fields of Catholic sacramental theology, psychoanalytic theory and gender, theological approaches to women's sexual and reproductive health and rights, and theology and art. She is the author of numerous journal articles and book chapters and several monographs including *Theology after Postmodernity: Divining the Void – A Lacanian Reading of Thomas Aquinas* (2013) and *New Catholic Feminism: Theology and Theory* (2006). Tina also writes for the media and contributes to a number of radio and television networks around the world. She is a regular contributor to BBC Radio 4's 'Thought for the Day'.

Stephen Burns is Professor of Liturgical and Practical Theology at Pilgrim Theological College, University of Divinity, Melbourne, Australia. His publications include *Postcolonial Practice of Ministry*, co-edited with Kwok Pui-lan (2016), *Liturgy: SCM Studyguide*, 2nd edn (2018), *Liturgy with a Difference*, co-edited with Bryan Cones (2019), *Twentieth Century Anglican Theologians*, co-edited with Bryan Cones and James Tengatenga (2020), and *Feminist Theology: Interstices and Fractures*, co-edited with Rebekah Pryor (2021), as well as a collection of Ann Loades' sermons, *Grace and Glory in One Another's Faces* (2020), and a collection of Ann Loades' work on Mary, *Grace is Not Faceless* (2021).

Cláudio Carvalhaes is a former shoe-shining boy from São Paulo, Brazil. A theologian, liturgist, artist and activist, he is Associate Professor of Worship at Union Theological Seminary in New York City. He is author of *Eucharist and Globalization: Redrawing the Borders of Eucharistic Hospitality* (2013), *What's Worship Got to Do with It? Interpreting Life Liturgically* (2018) and *Praying with Every Heart – Orienting Our Lives to the Wholeness of the*

World (2021); and editor of *Liturgy in Postcolonial Perspectives: Only One Is Holy* (2015) and *Liturgies from Below: Praying with People at the End of the World* (2020). His new book is *Eco-Liturgical Liberation Theology: Ritual At World's End* (2021).

Renie Choy is Lecturer in Church History at St Mellitus College, London. She is a historian of early mediaeval monasticism and completed her doctorate at the University of Oxford. She is the author of *Intercessory Prayer and the Monastic Ideal in the Time of the Carolingian Reforms* (2016) and *Ancestral Feeling: Postcolonial Thoughts on Western Christian Heritage* (forthcoming).

Ashley Cocksworth is Senior Lecturer in Theology and Practice at the University of Roehampton. His publications include *Karl Barth on Prayer* (T&T Clark, 2015); *Prayer: A Guide for the Perplexed* (Bloomsbury, 2018); and a volume on Karl Barth for the Classics of Western Spirituality Series forthcoming.

Ann Conway-Jones is Honorary Research Fellow at the University of Birmingham and the Queen's Foundation for Ecumenical Theological Education, Birmingham. Her research interest is early Jewish and Christian biblical interpretation, with a particular emphasis on mystical exegesis. She is the author of *Gregory of Nyssa's Tabernacle Imagery in Its Jewish and Christian Contexts* (2014).

Andrew Davison is Starbridge Senior Lecturer in Theology and Natural Sciences at the University of Cambridge, and Fellow and Dean of Chapel at Corpus Christi College. Before his appointment in the Faculty of Divinity, he taught Christian doctrine at theological colleges in Oxford and Cambridge. A priest in the Church of England, he served his curacy in South East London. Before theological studies, he read an undergraduate degree in chemistry and DPhil in biochemistry. His work ranges across topics in Christian doctrine, philosophy, natural science, apologetics, and sacramental and pastoral theology, including *Participation in God: A Study in Christian Doctrine and Metaphysics* (2019) and *Why Sacraments?* (2013). He is a regular contributor to *Church Times* and the *Times Literary Supplement*.

Elizabeth S. Dodd is Programme Leader for Postgraduate Programmes in Theology, Ministry and Mission at Sarum College, Salisbury, and Research Associate for the Oxford Centre for Religion and Culture. Her current research explores lyrical theologies and the English lyric tradition, and her work covers the areas of theology, arts and culture, theological aesthetics and poetry. Her previous publications address the metaphysical poet, Thomas Traherne, and the idea of innocence in Christian theology and literature, including *Boundless Innocence in Thomas Traherne's Poetic Theology* (2015) and *Innocence Uncovered: Literary and Theological Perspectives* (2016), edited with Carl E. Findley III.

David F. Ford is Regius Professor of Divinity Emeritus in the University of Cambridge and Fellow of Selwyn College. His publications include *The Gospel of John: A Theological Commentary* (2021); co-edited with Deborah Hardy-Ford and Ian Randall, *A Kind of Upside-Downness: Learning Disabilities and Transformational Community* (2019); *Christian Wisdom: Desiring God and Learning in Love* (2007); and *Self and Salvation: Being Transformed* (1999). He has been Church Warden of St Luke's Church, Birmingham, and is now Lay Reader in St Andrew's Church, Cherry Hinton. He co-founded the practice of Scriptural Reasoning, and co-chairs the Rose Castle Foundation in Cumbria, a centre for reconciliation, inter-faith engagement, religious literacy and conservation. In the Church of England he has served in the Urban Theology Group and the Doctrine Commission, and is a trustee of the National Society. In 2015 he was the Oxford University Bampton Lecturer. He is married to Deborah, an Anglican priest and psychotherapist.

Siobhán Garrigan is Head of the School of Religion at Trinity College Dublin, where she is Loyola Professor of Theology. She is the author of *The Real Peace Process: Worship, Politics and the End of Sectarianism* (2014) and *Beyond Ritual: Sacramental Theology after Habermas* (2004).

Tom Greggs holds the Marischal (1616) Chair of Divinity and currently serves as Head of Divinity at the University of Aberdeen. He is a Methodist Preacher and sits on the Faith and Order Commission of the Methodist Church and of the World Council of Churches, for which he convenes a subgroup on peace and pluralism. His publications include *Dogmatic Ecclesiology – Volume 1: The Priestly Catholicity of the Church* (2019), *The Breadth of Salvation* (2020), *Theology against Religion: Constructive Dialogues with Bonhoeffer and Barth* (T&T Clark, 2011), *Barth, Origen, and Universal Salvation: Restoring Particularity* (2009) and *New Perspectives for Evangelical Theology: Engaging God, Scripture and the World* (2010). He is currently working on the second volume of his three-volume ecclesiology, provisionally entitled *Encountering the Prophetic Apostolicity of the Church*.

Kevin G. Grove is Assistant Professor of Theology at the University of Notre Dame. A member of the Congregation of Holy Cross, he completed his PhD in philosophical theology at the University of Cambridge, Trinity College, in 2015. Before joining the theology faculty at Notre Dame, Grove was Research Fellow at L'Institut Catholique in Paris as well as the Notre Dame Institute for Advanced Study. His work in systematic theology engages memory, Christology and community in the writings of St Augustine as well as the treatment of the same in phenomenology. He also studies and is publishing the writings of Basil Moreau. He is the author of *Augustine on Memory* (2021).

Roy Hammerling has been Professor of Religion at Concordia College for nearly thirty years. His books include *A History of Prayer: The First to the Fifteenth Century* (2008) and *The Lord's Prayer in the Early Church: The Pearl of Great Price* (2010). He has also written articles and lectured on Martin Luther, the history of Christian spirituality, religion and film, Islam, and religion in modern culture. He travels regularly with students and alumni groups for Concordia College across Europe, Turkey and Egypt.

Mike Higton is Professor of Theology and Ministry at Durham University, where he heads up the Common Awards partnership, in which Durham validates the majority of the Church of England's ordination training (along with training for various other ministries and for various ecumenical partners) around the country. He teaches modern Christian theology and is the author of several books, including *The Life of Christian Doctrine* (T&T Clark, 2020), *A Theology of Higher Education* (2012) and *Difficult Gospel: The Theology of Rowan Williams* (2004), and, with Rachel Muers, *The Text in Play: Experiments in Reading Scripture* (2012).

Paul R. Hinlicky is Emeritus Tise Professor at Roanoke College in Salem, Virginia, and PhD Fellow at the Institute of Lutheran Theology. Previously he had been Visiting Professor of Systematic Theology at the Protestant Theological Faculty of Comenius University in Bratislava. He is the author of numerous theological studies including *Paths Not Taken: Fates of Theology from Luther through Leibniz* (2009), *Divine Simplicity: Christ the Crisis of Metaphysics* (2016), *Luther and the Beloved Community: A Path for Theology after Christendom* (2010), *Before Auschwitz: What Christian Theology Must Learn from the Rise of Nazism* (2013), *Between Humanist Philosophy and Apocalyptic Theology: The Twentieth Century Sojourn of Samuel Štefan Osuský* (T&T Clark, 2016), *Luther for Evangelicals: A Reintroduction* (2018) and a systematic theology, *Beloved Community: Critical Dogmatics after*

Christendom (2015). He is an ordained minister of the Evangelical Lutheran Church in America.

Scott A. Kirkland is John and Jeanne Stockdale Lecturer in Practical Theology and Ethics at Trinity College Theological School, University of Divinity, Melbourne, Australia. He is the author of *Into the Far Country: Karl Barth and the Modern Subject* (2016), and with John C. McDowell, *Eschatology: Christian Hope* (2018).

Travis LaCouter is Visiting Lecturer in the Department of Religious Studies at the College of the Holy Cross in Worcester, Massachusetts. He earned a doctorate from the University of Oxford in 2020 and is the author of the forthcoming monograph *Balthasar and Prayer* (T&T Clark). His current research focuses on the notion of *parrhesia* as the basis for a critical theology of protest. He is Research Associate at the Margaret Beaufort Institute of Theology (Cambridge, UK), and in addition to his scholarly work his popular criticism has appeared in *Commonweal*, *The Baffler* and *US Catholic* magazine.

Catriona Laing is Chaplain of St Martha & St Mary's Anglican Church Leuven and Associate Chaplain at the Pro-Cathedral of Holy Trinity, Brussels. Her doctoral work and previous publications explore the role of contemplative prayer in inter-faith relations. Prior to serving in Brussels, Catriona worked as a priest in Washington, DC and London before which she helped establish the Cambridge Interfaith Programme at the University of Cambridge. Her publications include 'Anglican Mission in the Middle East: 1910–1945', in *The Oxford History of Anglicanism, vol 5: Global Anglicanism, c. 1910-2000*, ed. Williams Sachs (2017); 'The Marrying Priest', in *For God's Sake: Re-Imagining Priesthood and Prayer in a Changing Church*, ed. Jessica Martin and Sarah Coakley (2017) and 'Scriptural Reasoning', in *Fear and Friendship: Anglicans Engaging with Islam*, ed. Frances Ward and Sarah Coakley (Bloomsbury, 2012). Catriona's vocation to the priesthood and her continuing academic work have been influenced by her commitment to inter-religious relations and to Christian ministry among the poor and marginalized.

Matthew Levering holds the James N. and Mary D. Perry, Jr. Chair of Theology at Mundelein Seminary. He has authored numerous books, including most recently *Did Jesus Rise from the Dead?: Historical and Theological Reflections* (2019), *Aquinas's Eschatological Ethics and the Virtue of Temperance* (2019) and *Engaging the Doctrine of Marriage*

(2020). Among his recent edited volumes are *Christian Dying: Witnesses from the Tradition* (2018), *The Reception of Vatican II* (2017) and *Reading Job with St Thomas Aquinas* (2020). He co-edits two quarterly journals, *Nova et Vetera* and *International Journal of Systematic Theology*. He directs the Center for Scriptural Exegesis, Philosophy, and Doctrine at Mundelein Seminary, and he is the co-founder of the Chicago Theological Initiative.

Andrew Louth is Professor Emeritus of Patristic and Byzantine Studies, Durham University, and was Visiting Professor of Eastern Orthodox Theology in the Faculty of Theology attached to the Amsterdam Centre of Eastern Orthodox Theology (ACEOT), Vrije Universiteit, Amsterdam. His research has largely been in patristics with monographs on *Dionysios the Areopagite* (Continuum, 1989), *Maximos the Confessor* (1996) and *St John Damascene: Tradition and Originality in Byzantine Theology* (2002). His most recent books are *Introducing Eastern Orthodox Theology* (2013) and *Modern Orthodox Thinkers: From the Philokalia to the Present* (2015). An archpriest of the Diocese of Sourozh (Moscow Patriarchate), he was elected Fellow of the British Academy in 2010.

John C. McDowell is Associate Dean at Yarra Theological Union, Melbourne, and is Professor of Philosophy, Systematic Theology and Moral Theology. Among numerous articles and book chapters on theology, higher education and popular culture, he has most recently authored *Theology and the Globalized Present: Feasting in the Presence of God* (2019) and with Scott A. Kirkland, *Eschatology: Christian Hope* (2018). He has edited a special issue of the journal *Religions* on *Hope in Dark Times* (2019), a special issue of the journal *Colloquium* on *Engaging Karl Barth* 50.1 (2018), *Kenotic Ecclesiology: Select Writings of Donald M. MacKinnon*, with Ashley Moyse and Scott A. Kirkland (2016) and *Correlating Sobornost: Conversations between Karl Barth and the Russian Orthodox Tradition*, with Ashley Moyse and Scott A. Kirkland (2016).

Gerald O'Collins received his PhD at the University of Cambridge where he was Research Fellow of Pembroke College. For thirty-three years he taught fundamental and systematic theology at the Gregorian University (Rome), and was Dean of Theology 1985–91. He is now Research Fellow of the University of Divinity, Melbourne, Australia, and Adjunct Professor of Australian Catholic University. Writer of hundreds of articles in professional and popular journals, he has authored or co-authored over seventy books. They include most recently *Revelation: Toward a Christian Theology of God's Self-Revelation in Jesus Christ* (2016), *Inspiration: Towards a Christian Interpretation of Biblical Inspiration* (2018), *Tradition: Understanding Christian Tradition* (2018), *A Christology of Religions* (2018), *A Christology of Religions* (2018), *The Beauty of Jesus Christ* (2020) and, co-authored with Daniel Kendall, *Jesuits, Theology and the American Catholic Church* (2020).

Simon Oliver is Van Mildert Professor of Divinity at Durham University and Canon Residentiary of Durham Cathedral. He was previously Head of the Department of Theology and Religious Studies at the University of Nottingham. His books include *Philosophy, God and Motion* (2005 and 2013) and *Creation: A Guide for the Perplexed* (Bloomsbury, 2017). He is editor, with John Milbank, of *The Radical Orthodoxy Reader* (2009) and is currently editing *The Oxford Handbook of Creation*. His research focuses on the doctrine of creation, theological anthropology, the work of Thomas Aquinas and the Thomist tradition, and the history of the relationship between theology and the natural sciences. His forthcoming book is an exploration of purposiveness in nature and is entitled *Creation's Ends: Teleology, Ethics and the Natural*.

Andrew Prevot is Associate Professor of Theology at Boston College. His research spans the areas of spiritual and mystical theology, philosophical theology and continental philosophy of religion, and various forms of political, liberation, black and womanist theology. He is the author of *Theology and Race: Black and Womanist Traditions in the United States* (2018) and *Thinking Prayer: Theology and Spirituality amid the Crises of Modernity* (2015) and co-editor of *Anti-Blackness and Christian Ethics* (2017). He is currently working on a book on the mysticism of ordinary life.

Christopher R. Seitz is Senior Research Professor of Biblical Interpretation at Wycliffe College, University of Toronto. He is the author of commentaries on *Isaiah 1–39* (1993), *Isaiah 40–66* (2001), *Colossians* (2014) and *Joel* (T&T Clark, 2016). His other works include *Word without End: The Old Testament as Abiding Theological Witness* (1998), *Figured Out: Typology and Providence in Christian Scripture* (2001), *Prophecy and Hermeneutics: Toward a New Introduction to the Prophets* (2007), *The Character of Christian Scripture* (2013), *Elder Testament: Canon, Theology, Trinity* (2018) and *Convergences: Canon and Catholicity* (2020). He has served parishes in the United States, Germany, Scotland, Canada and France.

Jacob Holsinger Sherman is Professor of Philosophy and Religion at the California Institute of Integral Studies. He taught previously at King's College London and the University of Cambridge and his publications include *Partakers of the Divine: Contemplation and the Practice of Philosophy* (2014).

Nicola Slee is Director of Research at the Queen's Foundation for Ecumenical Theological Education, Birmingham; Professor of Feminist Practical Theology at the Vrije Universiteit, Amsterdam; and Visiting Professor at the University of Chester. Her fields of research include qualitative research into female faith, feminist poetics, liturgy and spirituality. She is the author of *Praying Like a Woman* (2004) and several collections of poetry, prayers and liturgical material, as well as *Women's Faith Development: Patterns and Processes* (2004), *Sabbath: The Hidden Heartbeat of Our Lives* (2019) and *Fragments for Fractured Times: What Feminist Practical Theology Brings to the Table* (2020). Nicola is an Anglican laywoman, honorary vice-president of WATCH (Women and the Church) and former Chair of BIAPT (British & Irish Association for Practical Theology).

Katherine Sonderegger holds the William Meade Professorship in Systematic Theology at Virginia Theological Seminary. She is an Episcopal priest, resident in the Diocese of Virginia. Prior to her post at Virginia, she taught in the Religion Department at Middlebury College in Vermont. Her early work has focused on the dogmatic theology of Karl Barth, with a special eye for his theology of Jews, Judaism and Israel. Kate is currently at work on a systematic theology, the first and second volumes having appeared as *The Doctrine of God* (2015) and *The Doctrine of the Holy Trinity* (2020), with others to follow.

Columba Stewart is Professor of Theology at Saint John's University and Executive Director of the Hill Museum and Manuscript Library, both in Collegeville, Minnesota. He has been a Benedictine monk of Saint John's Abbey since 1981. He publishes regularly in his field of Eastern and Western Christian monastic history and is the author of *Cassian the Monk* (1998) and *Prayer and Community: The Benedictine Tradition* (1998). Most recently he has been a member in the School of Historical Studies at the Institute for Advanced Study, Princeton, New Jersey, Guggenheim Fellow and Resident Scholar at the Collegeville Institute. He was the 2019 Jefferson Lecturer for the National Endowment for the Humanities.

Jonathan D. Teubner is Research Fellow at the Institute for Religion and Critical Inquiry at the Australian Catholic University (Melbourne) and

Associate Fellow at the Institute for Advanced Studies in Culture at the University of Virginia. In 2018, Teubner was awarded an Alexander von Humboldt Research Fellowship and based at the Institut für Christentum und Antike in the Theologische Fakultät at the Humboldt-Universität zu Berlin from 2019 to 2021. His publications have examined the thought of Augustine of Hippo, early mediaeval theology and spirituality, Protestant historiographies, and theories of religion and violence, economics and secularism. His first book, *Prayer after Augustine: A Study in the Development of the Latin Tradition* (2018), won the Manfred Lautenschlaeger Award for Theological Promise in 2019.

Gabrielle Thomas is Assistant Professor of Early Christianity and Anglican Studies at Candler School of Theology of Emory University. She is a priest in the Church of England and is resident in the Diocese of Durham, UK. She completed postdoctoral work at Durham University and Yale Divinity School. Her publications include *The Image of God in the Theology of Gregory of Nazianzus* (2019), *Women and Ordination in the Orthodox Church* (2020), *For the Good of the Church: Unity, Theology and Women* (2021) and articles in the *Scottish Journal of Theology*, *Exchange*, *Ecclesiology* and *Studia Patristica*.

Susannah Ticciati is Reader in Christian Theology at King's College London. She is the author of *A New Apophaticism: Augustine and the Redemption of Signs* (2013) and *Job and the Disruption of Identity: Reading beyond Barth* (T&T Clark, 2005).

Peter Tyler is Professor of Pastoral Theology and Spirituality at St Mary's University, Twickenham, London. His most recent book is *Christian Mindfulness: Theology and Practice* (2018). Other publications include *Mystical Theology: Renewing the Contemplative Tradition*, co-edited with Christopher Cook and Julienne McLean (2018), and *The Return to the Mystical: Ludwig Wittgenstein, Teresa of Avila and the Christian Mystical Tradition* (Continuum, 2011).

Medi Ann Volpe is a Catholic moral theologian and mother of four children, including a daughter with Down Syndrome. She currently teaches theology and ethics at Durham University. Her first book, *Rethinking Christian Identity* (2013), brings contemporary theological themes into conversation with voices from the classical Christian tradition. More recently, her work has explored the intersection of ecclesiology, spiritual formation and disability. She has published in journals and handbooks, including the *International Journal of Systematic Theology*, *Modern Theology*, and the *Oxford Handbook* *of Catholic Theology* (which she co-edited with Lewis Ayres). She also serves on the board of the *Journal of Disability and Religion*. For the last several years, Volpe has been writing and speaking about the kind of church we must be if we are truly to honour the weaker members. Her current book project (*Living as the Body of Christ*) considers ecclesiology from the perspective of disability.

Frances M. Young is Emeritus Professor of Theology, University of Birmingham, where she held the Edward Cadbury Chair from 1986 to 2005. She taught New Testament and early Christian studies in Birmingham from 1971. She was ordained as a Methodist minister in 1984. She has always endeavoured to bridge academia and the life of the churches, not least by drawing from the theological insights and arguments of the early church. Amongst her many publications, she is the author of *Brokenness and Blessing: Towards a Biblical Spirituality* (2007) and *God's Presence: A Contemporary Recapitulation of Early Christianity* (2013).

Randall C. Zachman is Professor Emeritus of Reformation Studies at the University of Notre Dame, and Adjunct Instructor of Theology at Lancaster Theological Seminary. He is the author of *Image and Word in the Theology of John Calvin* (2009) and *The Assurance of Faith: Conscience in the Theology of Martin Luther and John Calvin* (2005). He has also published articles and chapters on Friedrich Schleiermacher, Soren Kierkegaard and Karl Barth.

ABBREVIATIONS

ACW	Ancient Christian Writers
ANF	Ante-Nicene Fathers
CCCM	*Corpus Christianorum Continuatio Medaevalis*
CCM	*Corpus Consuetudinum Monasticarum*
CCSG	*Corpus Christianorum, Series Graeca*
CCSL	*Corpus Christianorum, Series Latina*
CD	Karl Barth, *Church Dogmatics*, 4 vols. in 13 parts, ed. G. W. Bromiley and T. F. Torrance (Edinburgh: T&T Clark, 1956–75)
CNTC	Calvin's New Testament Commentaries
CSEL	*Corpus Scriptorum Ecclesiasticorum Latinorum*
CWS	Classics of Western Spirituality
FC	Fathers of the Church
GCS	*Griechischen Christlichen Schriftsteller*
GNO	*Gregorii Nysseni Opera*
Inst.	John Calvin, *Institutes of the Christian Religion*, trans. Ford Lewis Battles, LCC (Philadelphia, PA: Westminster John Knox Press, 1960)
LCC	Library of Christian Classics
LCL	Loeb Classical Library
LW	*Luther's Works*, ed. Jaroslav Pelikan, Helmut T. Lehmann and Christopher Boyd Brown (Philadelphia, PA: Fortress Press, 1955–)
NPNF-1	Nicene and Post Nicene Fathers – Series 1
NPNF-2	Nicene and Post Nicene Fathers – Series 2

PG   *Patrologiae Cursus Completus, Series Graeca*
PL   *Patrologiae Cursus Completus, Series Latina*
PTS   *Patristische Texte und Studien*
SC   *Sources chrétiennes*
ST   Thomas Aquinas, *Summa Theologiae*, 61 vols (London:
            Blackfriars, 1964–80)
WSA   Works of Saint Augustine

Introduction: Prayer in the School of Discipleship

ASHLEY COCKSWORTH AND JOHN C. McDOWELL

When assessing literature on prayer and praying, one might be forgiven for imagining that prayer primarily involves something of an exercising of power. Under such conditions, prayer comes to be about the manipulation of the gods being prayed to, who themselves have the power to intervene unmediatedly from their lofty heights; or the displays of the apparent machinations of the priesthood over the laity through a biopolitical tactic; or the power over the self as a form of self-help spirituality 'for the cultivation of oases of private satisfaction'; or holding the formative power over individuals and communities to shape spiritual and moral agency always for the good.[1] 'How to' manuals continue to proliferate approaches to prayer as if prayer is just another thing needing to be brought under tighter control in order to produce better 'results' that, in turn, can be tested more accurately and eventually improved. It is rare, therefore, to find this kind of literature attempting to guide readers into identifying and resisting systems of alienation and oppression through a more nuanced sense of prayer's anti-violent logic of the sort several of the chapters in this volume suggest.

---

[1]Nicholas Lash, *Easter in Ordinary: Reflections on Human Experience and the Knowledge of God* (London: SCM Press, 1988), 281. Particularly with regard to this last option, one at least needs to be sensitive to the possibility of the option being generated as something of, to use Kathryn Tanner's terms from a different context, a protest 'against its [viz., the Spirit's] domesticated captivity in rigidly controlled institutional forms'. See Kathryn Tanner, *Christ the Key* (Cambridge: Cambridge University Press, 2010), 290.

It is evident that far too little critical attention is paid in a range of articulations to the *theological* conditions of prayer. This is hardly surprising. Phenomenological studies of practices can all too little focus on the claims, assumptions, patterns of belief and meaningfulness when engaging in their work. But any claim that prayer as a 'practice' is informed by beliefs embedded within it, and that those who engage in the practices of praying have their lives shaped by those practices, would appear deeply counter-intuitive to approaches that segment elements of human life in such ways. As Stanley Hauerwas and Samuel Wells lament, frequently a practice such as prayer is regarded as 'a kind of play, a temporary escape from real life to an environment where normal rules are suspended'.[2] Such an account not only trades on distinguishing prayer from public performance (where 'public' means those practices, policies and ideas appropriate to common life), but associates the proper forms of liturgical pedagogy with matters of personal taste, private significance and communal overlaps in individuals' interests. In other words, 'prayer' here functions as more of a simply aesthetic category than as complexly noetic and political, where the aesthetic and the ethical become themselves isolatable moments of human action. Any ethical significance it may have, then, is at best limited to offering affective support for moral endeavour. In fact, it may even, at worst, function, in the words of Alexander Schmemann, as an 'esthetic and spiritual deviation from the real task' of the makings of the good common life.[3]

What would it mean, in contrast, to regard prayer in the context of theological accounts? For Hauerwas and Wells, this would order a set of activities describable as 'informed prayer'.[4] However, it is worth being a little cautious with this phrase here, lest one imagine uninformed prayer still being, in some form, 'prayer'. Moreover, theology involves – or should involve – a chastening to become a form of learned ignorance that perennially refuses to be seduced to give up its most rigorous interrogative mood and therefore its integrity as attempting to speak truthfully. As Rowan Williams observes it is the contemplative who is the most critically alert to the totalizing tendencies of system making and protecting.[5] A theology rooted in the doxological conditions of prayer is, in some important sense, necessarily

---

[2]Stanley Hauerwas and Samuel Wells, 'Christian Ethics as Informed Prayer', in *The Blackwell Companion to Christian Ethics*, ed. Stanley Hauerwas and Samuel Wells (Oxford: Blackwell, 2004), 3–12 (4).

[3]Alexander Schmemann, *The World as Sacrament* (London: Darton, Longman and Todd, 1965), 27.

[4]Hauerwas and Wells, 'Christian Ethics as Informed Prayer', 3.

[5]Rowan Williams, *On Christian Theology* (Oxford: Blackwell, 2000), xii–xvi.

an exercise in unknowing; or, at the least, involves the means of naming the fragility and brokenness of that which can be known. The first and second editions of the Prayer Book of Edward VI of 1549 and 1552 respectively open with a critical claim: 'There was never any thing by the wit of man so well devised or so surely established, which (in continuance of time) hath not been corrupted.'[6] That is an important part of the rationale for the Prayer Book's commissioning, and of the contribution of prayer to reconfiguring convictions, values, desires and practices. We are, Augustine would say, what we worship, and accordingly, 'surely the supremely important thing in religion is to model oneself on the object of one's worship'.[7] We might speak, then, of the prayerful conditions for Christian pedagogy, but only insofar that that pedagogy is as equally alert to the 'dangers' as the formative possibilities such prayerful conditions might inculcate in the lives of pray-ers and communities of prayer.[8]

This volume has its origins in a concern about the operations of a tyranny of practice that functions not only to segregate reflection on practice from consideration of theory and even belief but to displace the latter altogether. The chapters in this volume, therefore, gather around the shared conviction that prayer is irreducible to the very conditions for Christian accounts of speaking truthfully about the world and one's way within it and configuring practices conducive to supporting the necessity of mutual flourishing. Such an account may well have to claim that, in some manner, the healthiness of creaturely living has to take leave of practices uninformed by prayerful attentiveness. Moreover, there is the unease with the way the richness of the history of Christian practices of prayer can be reduced to simplified formulae, history, self-help guides and so on. In fact, there is much valuable theological work being done to interrogate how these very reductions have occurred, and what even Christian performances themselves have done to inspire or directly contribute to them. As Schmemann maintains, *leitourgia* should not be reduced 'to "cultic" categories, its definition as a sacred act of worship, different as such ... from the "profane" area of life'.[9] Prayer, it would seem, needs to be located within broader patterns of identification that even have

---

[6]*The First and Second Prayer-Books of King Edward the Sixth* (London: J. M. Dent and Sons, 1910), 3.

[7]Augustine, *The City of God*, trans. Henry Bettenson (New York: Penguin Books, 1972), VIII.17.324.

[8]See Lauren F. Winner, *The Dangers of Christian Practice: On Wayward Gifts, Characteristic Damage, and Sin* (New Haven, CT: Yale University Press, 2018). Indeed, any honest conception of prayer needs to retain a sense of the possibility of prayer going wrong – and thus becoming counter-formative, even deformative and abusive of the power it wields.

[9]Schmemann, *The World as Sacrament*, 28.

radical or subversive potential under a range of settings, renegotiating a learning-to-be that is appropriate to practices that are distinctly resistant to other sorts of description (e.g. to the functional reduction of persons to consumers or units of production of consumables). In this context, as Herbert McCabe recognizes:

> Human misery can no longer be attributed to the gods and accepted with resignation or evaded with sacrifices. The long slow process can begin of identifying the human roots of oppression and exploitation.[10]

A crucial point at which this needs to continue to happen is in resisting the reduction of prayer to the circumscribing category of 'religious' practices. There are certainly ways in which the shorthand 'religion' may be meaningfully deployed and illuminate some elements of study, behaviour, commitment and conviction. But there are multiple losses.[11] Prayer, in such a scheme, would be constrained to, at most (i.e. when it is not reduced to cultivating the individual's pious inwardness), co-opting divine agency to manifest itself in a supernaturalized in-breaking of momentarily active presence. But that would simply return us to the notion of prayer-as-power.[12]

What would prayer look like within an account that resists reducing the performance that is life itself to the brutal ebb and flow of one thing after another? The category of addressability may be of some use here. As Nicholas Lash observes, whereas Luke's disciples offer hospitality to the stranger with whom they walked and talked on the road to Emmaus, it soon becomes evident that that stranger is none other than the raised Jesus himself and that 'it is they, in fact, who are the guests, recipients of hospitality; and that it is he who is the host'.[13] As ritual action, the liturgy that makes prayer intelligible performs its witness to the worth-giving acts of the church in gratitude to the worthiness of God as *leitourgia* or human service to God, it does so only by having its ground and determination in the service that God gives, the service by God to creatures in Christ (what is known as 'grace') that creatively and re-creatively addresses them hospitably as graced and welcomed guests. In and by his life the 'fragmentary life of the world was gathered into his life' of

---

[10]Herbert McCabe, *God Matters* (London: Geoffrey Chapman, 1987), 43.

[11]See William T. Cavanaugh, 'The Invention of the Religious-Secular Distinction', in *At the Limits of the Secular: Reflections on Faith and Public Life*, ed. William A. Barbieri, Jr. (Grand Rapids: William B. Eerdmans, 2014), 105–28.

[12]Marxists would hardly feel chastened in their accounts of 'religion' as politically inefficacious by practices of offering 'thoughts and prayers' at times of trouble.

[13]Nicholas Lash, *Theology for Pilgrims* (London: Darton, Longman and Todd, 2008), 166.

embrace.[14] Prayer, then, receives its form as a responsive gesture of witness to 'the process of continuing participation in the foundational event – the forming of Christ in the corporate and individual life of believers'.[15] The purpose? For Schmemann, it is 'to fulfill the Church and that means to "re-present", to make present the One, in whom all things are at their end, and all things are at their beginning'.[16] In this context, what is needed is the lifelong therapy of a schooling in prayer, articulatable as the 'school for the production of persons in relation to the unknown God through discipleship of the crucified'.[17]

Conceiving 'religion' instead as a form of life entails that there can be no ready separation available from the secularity of things like the political, the economic and so on. In other words, there can be no separation from the demand for responsible living together as creatures without distorting what it means even to begin to use language of 'God' and 'creature'. Prayer within the liturgical ordering of the creaturely life of Christian faith cannot, then, be reduced to a 'substitute action'.[18] Instead, in following the flow of the eschatological imagination of the Lord's Supper (see Lk. 22.16, 18) since prayer takes 'its meaning and point from the sacrifice of Christ', it is rooted in the abundance of the self-giving of God.[19] Prayer, in this context, therefore, subverts itself when practised as a displacement of this world rather than an engagement in its transformation through the strange and alien figure of one crucified and on his way to raising us with him. World-loss is inseparably bound up with prayer-loss, or the loss of what is involved in the act of praying to the creatively and re-creatively self-communicative God who gives life to all things as a participation in the mystery of the very livingness of God's abundance.

The aim in this collection is to gather a series of reflections on prayer not only to inform readers about this umbrella categorizing of a set of diverse practices bound up with broader liturgical patterns and theological claims, but to challenge and provoke the deepening of consideration of the richly developed and articulated practices of prayer from within a broad family of traditions referred to as 'Christianity'. Despite its size, however, this volume makes no attempt to be exhaustive. Any familiarity with the processes of

---

[14]Schmemann, *The World as Sacrament*, 25.
[15]Williams, *On Christian Theology*, 140.
[16]Schmemann, *The World as Sacrament*, 30.
[17]Citation from Lash, *Easter in Ordinary*, 258.
[18]Dorothee Sölle, cited in Jan Milič Lochman, 'The Lord's Prayer in Our Time: Praying and Drumming', in *The Lord's Prayer: Perspectives for Reclaiming Christian Prayer*, ed. Daniel L. Migliore (Grand Rapids, MI: William B. Eerdmans, 1993), 5–19 (6).
[19]McCabe, *God Matters*, 217.

praying should be appropriately attentive to the fact that, theologically, even such a notion of exhaustive comprehensiveness is deeply problematic. There is no way that activities conducted within temporally configured conditions can close off critique, development, change and redevelopment, and it is a curse of the theological that it can be inclined to suggest that a final word can be given. This is not so much a problem of operating from an account of the revealedness of the articulable authority of God as the failure to understand that that communicativeness has an irreducible history, a history that can be spoken of appropriately only by those who appreciate the learned ignorance that comes from a chastening eschatological reticence. It is thus that when the volume does end, it ends with a prelude to prayer not as a final statement on prayer but an invitation into that irreducible history of communicativeness. Needless to say, there are omissions in each of this volume's four parts. Some of these gaps are signs of the difficult decisions made at the conception of this project as to what can and cannot be reasonably included within the limitations of a single volume. Others have emerged along the way, with some appearing too late to be filled but remain conspicuous by their absence. Then there are the many gaps we, as editors, have failed to recognize, and it is for others to notice these and hold us to account. If nothing else, the gaps speak loudly of the theological generativity and abundance of the theme of prayer.

For a volume on prayer, some might feel that the most significant gap is the apparent lack of structural attention to the actual 'practices' of prayer: petition, thanksgiving, contemplation, adoration, lamentation, glorification and so on. While many of these are taken up in the context of other chapters, for some the lack of individual chapters on particular practices of prayer may feel especially inappropriate. As mentioned above, the origins of this volume lie in part in a concern that too much discussion on prayer risks segregating the 'practice' of prayer from its complex entanglement in matters of theory and belief and doctrine. Prayer, like any practice, is not theologically neutral but depends on doctrinal assumptions and theological priorities, and often in such intensively complex ways that it becomes entirely problematic to talk about such practices apart from a consideration of the theoretical frameworks and doctrinal systems in which those practices are shaped and formed. If part of the aim of this volume, then, is to re-moor the practice of prayer, in all its rich and unending diversity, in these theological conditions, it does so by promoting a distinctively and unashamedly doctrinal agenda. This aim comes to explicit fruition in Part Two and its rethinking of the nature of Christian doctrine, and individual doctrinal loci, from the theological positionality of prayer. The volume begins, however, with an exploration of the biblical background to prayer. Prayer is, after all, a robustly biblical thing to do. Part One comprises both framing essays that trace the theme of prayer in the Hebrew Bible and then in the New Testament and more focused essays that highlight particular doxological sources and episodes in the Bible as they have been taken up in the history of Christian spirituality – Moses on Mount Sinai, the Psalms, and the central prayers of the New Testament, the Lord's Prayer and John 17. Part Two moves into an investigation of the discipline of Christian doctrine itself and then traces the 'integrity' of prayer and theology into some of the classical loci of Christian doctrine: God, creation, Christology, pneumatology, providence and eschatology. Again, these are representative examples, rather than more comprehensive, of the theological generativity of a theme such as prayer when it gets situated in more explicitly doctrinal contexts than it is sometimes used to. How can these doctrines be differently theorized when approached via prayer? And, in turn, how is prayer differently textured when it explicitly intersects with Christian doctrine? As well as its own offerings, Part Two hopes to provide some resources to reassess the doctrines it does not itself investigate in light of prayer. Then, Part Three traces and assesses the connection of theology and prayer in a select list of individual theologians and groups of theologians only some of whom might be known for their contributions to the theological thinking of prayer. All of these will be known for other contributions, but this section seeks to shed light on their sometimes overlooked writings on prayer. Again, the history of praying so presented is selective and incomplete, but the hope here, as with Part Two, is that it might mark the beginning of a conversation to enable other thinkers to be reassessed in light of their theorizing of prayer. Finally, Part Four is the host to a set of creative conversations on prayer from a variety of perspectives, including the natural sciences, analytic theology, inter-religious dialogue, poetry, conflict studies, liturgy and pastoral ministry, gender and body, black theology, liberation theology and postmodern theology. Building on the biblical beginnings of prayer (Part One), as expressed through particular doctrines (Part Two) and thinkers (Part Three), it is in these discussions (Part Four) that prayer comes fully to life. Cumulatively, what we are reaching for is an expansive view of prayer – deeply biblical, energetically doctrinal, historically rooted and relevant to a whole host of critical questions and concerns facing the world.

The final word in this introduction is one of gratitude to the many people who have brought life to this book and sustained it through its coming to be. We would like first to acknowledge with profound gratitude this volume's contributors for the expertise, thought and careful attention they have lent this project over the course of many years and for their patience in awaiting the completion of the book. Without such an inspiring and committed set of contributors, this volume would not have been possible. Bringing a project of this size to completion is complex in the best of times, let alone during a pandemic. We are especially grateful to those contributors who have been able to produce work of such searching insight in the midst of such personal and professional complexities and without easy access to the resources and support many of us have taken for granted in going about our work. Likewise, we are especially grateful to those who have had to step in, and often at unforgivably short notice, to fill some of the gaps. And we remain grateful to the several contributors who have had to withdraw from the project in order rightly to redirect attention and energy elsewhere. Without the research assistance of Dr Kirsty Borthwick, her meticulous attention to detail and her taking the lead on preparing the manuscript for delivery, it would have been difficult for this project to reach its end. Kirsty's doctoral work on prayer (in Augustine's *De Trinitate*), also completed at the same time as this volume came to an end, will make in its own right an important contribution to the kind of discussion of the theological conditions on prayer we are hoping this volume might create. At the final stage, Dr Declan Kelly, also deserving of thanks, laboured intensively and expertly to prepare the index and catch some particularly stubborn errors. Thanks are due to the team at Bloomsbury and for their nearly limitless generosity in granting the multiple extensions this project has required. We are particularly grateful to Anna Turton for commissioning the book, and Veerle Van Steenhuyse, Sinead O'Connor and, earlier, Sarah Blake for their editorial assistance.

For Ash, this project has journeyed through three institutions – from the Queen's Foundation in Birmingham, to the Department of Theology and Religion at Durham University, to its final resting place in the School of Humanities and Social Sciences at the University of Roehampton. As it has moved from place to place, each institution has left its mark on the project and especially through the support and counsel I have received from students, colleagues, friends and mentors. It is Lucy, however, and her arrival like a light during the chaos of lockdown, who created the burst of life-giving energy needed to bring this project to completion and to whom, with Hannah, I owe my greatest thanks.

John's gratitude to St Athanasius College is deep. In particular, Dr Lisa Agaiby and Fr Dr Daniel Ghabrial have been instrumental in facilitating a timely return to a Faculty leadership and lecturing position. Even during the difficult conditions of the lengthy lockdown, the move has been a productive one. As always, my family provides a considerable context for flourishing. My prayerful thanks are continually owed for the support of my wife Sandra, and our children Archie, Jonathan, Joseph, Meg and Robert.

PART ONE

Biblical Perspectives

CHAPTER ONE

Prayer in the Scriptures of Israel, the Christian Old Testament

CHRISTOPHER R. SEITZ

When we come to a topic like prayer, especially with a wide-angle lens seeking to encompass the scriptures of Israel in their entirety, it is probably important to consider what we are looking for, measured against preconceptions. What is it we are looking for, and what do we have in mind when we speak of prayer? Prayer as private devotion, prayer as spiritual exercise (Thomas Keating and 'Centering Prayer'), prayer as corporate worship (Matins), prayer as praise in hymn, prayer at a sickbed, prayer on retreat, prayer as a universal exercise undertaken by Muslim, Hindu, sailor in straits, golfer in frustration or joy? Much of this conceives of prayer as an individual exercise of some kind, deeply interiorized or private, kneeling before worship or sleep or at break of day to petition for the sick, the lonely, the grieving, for ourselves and for our loved ones.

The famous episode from Book VI of Augustine's *Confessions* comes to mind, where the worldly but searching saint-to-be encountered the spiritual hero Ambrose. Ambrose, he observed, prayed silently, and when he read, his lips did not move. He read to himself, and prayed the same way. We may forget how familiar practices like reading without reading aloud were once rare, and strangely isolated and private.

Now, as he read, his eyes glanced over the pages and his heart searched out the sense, but his voice and tongue were silent. Often when we came to his room – for no one was forbidden to enter, nor was it his custom that the arrival of visitors should be announced to him – we would see him thus reading to himself. After we had sat for a long time in silence – for who would dare interrupt one so intent? – we would then depart, realizing that he was unwilling to be distracted in the little time he could gain for the recruiting of his mind, free from the clamor of other men's business. Perhaps he was fearful lest, if the author he was studying should express himself vaguely, some doubtful and attentive hearer would ask him to expound it or discuss some of the more abstruse questions, so that he could not get over as much material as he wished, if his time was occupied with others. And even a truer reason for his reading to himself might have been the care for preserving his voice, which was very easily weakened. Whatever his motive was in so doing, it was doubtless, in such a man, a good one.[1]

This is likely how we think of prayer, too, and of a very good kind of prayer. And it is not without its biblical – Old Testament – models. Individual, silent, intent, interiorized. The scene of bereft and barren Hannah comes to mind:

As Hannah kept on praying to the Lord, Eli observed her mouth. Hannah was praying in her heart, and her lips were moving but her voice was not heard. Eli thought she was drunk and said to her, 'How long are you going to stay drunk? Put away your wine.'

'Not so, my lord', Hannah replied, 'I am a woman who is deeply troubled. I have not been drinking wine or beer; I was pouring out my soul to the Lord. Do not take your servant for a wicked woman; I have been praying here out of my great anguish and grief'.

(1 Sam. 1.12-16)

Hannah's silent prayer – her lips moved however! – was taken by Eli as a kind of drunkenness because her voice was not heard. She was 'pouring out her soul to the Lord', and 'praying out of great grief and anguish'. The same phrases describe prayer as we may mean it, and think of it today, but as we shall see is in fact not very representative.

---

[1]Augustine, *Confessions and Enchiridion*, trans. Albert C. Outler (Philadelphia, PA: Westminster Press, 1955), VI.3.3–4.

What is representative, and will need underscoring, is the uncontested fact that in her praying she had a listening ear, the Lord God of Israel. Even when seemingly silent or hiding his face, as the language goes and as sometimes happens, he is being called upon as he is. Eli did not doubt any of this, even as initially he thought she was drunk and not praying at all. Hannah was praying, and she was praying properly within the covenant life of a personal God with a personal people. She had a dial tone, and in this case, God was both listening and prepared to say yes on her terms as well as on his own. The child she prayed for she received and he would be Samuel – because the Lord God heard her.

The Character of the Old Testament Witness: The Oracles of God Entrusted to the Jews

If we are seeking to give a global account of prayer in the Old Testament, we must first ask what kind of witness this is.[2] For this literary deposit consisting of thirty-nine books does not say what it says on some neutral plane.[3] In Paul's language, the Old Testament constitutes 'the oracles of God entrusted to the Jews'. That is to say, the Old Testament is a privileged and distinctive witness to God, to God's speech to a people, and to their recording of that, stretching over a millennium. God entrusted himself and his speech and life to a people. And the canonical form bears witness to the limits of that special entrusting, so that we who are Christians, and we who are Judaism without temple, priesthood, prophet or king, and we who judge ourselves neither of these things all together look into a world not our own, yet somehow continuous with our own world. It is important to register this distance in the light of what we have said above, since praying is something we do, or claim to know something about, or at least have a preconceived hunch about just what the word means. Yet we are seeking to look over into an account that in the nature of the case has a distinctive character, inhering in what it means to speak of a 'testament' or covenant life, 'oracles of God entrusted to a people of his choosing'. If this is a truly distinctive canonical presentation, which we hold it to be, it should present us with an understanding of prayer appropriate to that character and purpose. We must be prepared to see it as odd, and to let its particular word inform us on its own terms.

---

[2]Christopher R. Seitz, *Figured Out: Typology and Providence in Christian Scripture* (Louisville, KY: Westminster John Knox Press, 2001), 159–79.
[3]See Christopher R. Seitz, *The Elder Testament: Canon, Theology, Trinity* (Waco, TX: Baylor University Press, 2018).

Consider the book of Genesis as an example. Not once is recorded a scene or act of praying as in a form familiar to us as prayer.[4] God speaks. He speaks directly. He appears. The ancestors who are part of this world of Genesis hear and speak back in response. This happens all quite naturally and without elaborate procedures for communication. God said to Abraham, 'sacrifice your son' (Gen. 22.2). God visited Abraham, Sarah, Hagar, Isaac, Jacob and Joseph. He cautioned, he aided, he directed, he allowed himself to be negotiated with, he appeared in a dream. Given the richness and directness of this reality, it is perhaps no surprise that we do not see prayer in the form we know it or see it elsewhere in the books to follow. It is important to keep this in mind in reflecting on prayer when it does appear. It is constitutive of the character of the witness we are considering that by its very form it is oracular: in it God speaks to a people. That is what makes it what it is. Prayer emerges against this backdrop. To read the Old Testament is to be initiated into a world where God is speaking directly to people, and where prayer is a subset of that basic communicative bottom line.

To be underscored here is an important consequence. The reading of this distinctive literature can be said to be a kind of praying itself, as it is a participation in the oracular life of God with a people, the reading and meditating on which involves us in this selfsame divine communication. It shapes what we know about God, and about his ways with humanity, we who share that life by virtue of the scriptures being opened to us. Genesis shows God at work with humanity both in reality and in promise, prior to the covenant at Sinai. The distinctiveness of the portrayal – direct communication, 'and God said' – portends a relationship in prayer that will follow, but also a reading and mediating – silently like Ambrose or aloud in worship – of scripture so as to be formed prayerfully by what it has to say.

This can be illustrated from another direction. Genesis reminds us in the nature of how it speaks that the God of this speech can be known as Elohim. That is, by a word that can be and will be taken on the lips of all humanity and by all creation in praise of him; a word the elect share with the generic of all his creating purposes. But this God is also giving himself to be known more personally and intimately. 'At that time humanity called on the name of the Lord', Genesis 4.26 tells us in its lapidary declaration.[5] The Lord appearing by the narrator's hand or in direct discourse to follow is at one and

---

[4]On the peculiar character of Genesis and its temporal perspective prior to Sinai, see Walter Moberly, *The Old Testament of the Old Testament: Patriarchal Narratives and Mosaic Yahwism* (Minneapolis, MN: Fortress Press, 1992).

[5]For the full discussion of this important notice, see Claus Westermann, *Genesis 1–11: A Continental Commentary* (Minneapolis, MN: Fortress Press, 1994).

the same time the God of all creation. He appears and speaks in truth and in promise to those of his choosing, and in time he will make himself known by the name more fully in fulfilment and in future faithfulness through time (Exodus 3 and 6).

Inside this strange admixture of direct divine speaking and acting, on the one side, and the more general canvas of prayer-like relating which includes those prior to or outside of the covenanted Israel alone, we can see the general shape of a contrast that will appear in sharper form subsequently. That is, 'the oracles of God entrusted to the Jews' contain descriptions of those outside the covenant life and the way in which God as Elohim is in relationship with them, including what may be called their prayerful approach.

Consider, for example, the prayer of those outside the covenant dial-tone, from the ironic example of the prophets confronting Elijah or the hired hand Balaam, to the more sympathetic portrayals of Ruth and the sailors on board ship with Jonah. The Old Testament presents Israel not in isolation in its covenant life of prayer but fully alive in the good world of his creating.

Elijah is in full-throated opposition to Israel's own king, Ahab, due to his forfeiture of the covenant life in following the Baals of Canaanite worship. Flood, rain, drought are their domain, so it is held. Elijah has Ahab gather all Israel in a contest between himself and 550 prophetic rivals. He puts the matter economically, as having to do with prayer and response: 'You call on the name of your god and I will call on the name of the Lord; and the God who answers by fire, he is God' (1 Kgs 18.24). The typographical conventions for rendering the verse into English reveal the theological substructure, itself rooted in the Hebrew. Elohim when referring to the deity/deities of the opponents rendered god/gods; YHWH, the revealed name inside the covenant life; *ha'elohim* the true God. We know the story. After a full morning of failed 'calling on the name', Elijah mocks the interceding because directed at a vain target. They are calling on someone who is asleep, in the bathroom, musing or on a journey, or non-existent, as it were. Elijah's formal petition follows, and it contains this line, 'Answer me, YHWH, answer me, that this people may know that thou, YHWH, art Elohim' (1 Kgs 18.37). YHWH Elohim responds to the prayer of Elijah, and to this the people make solemn reply, 'YHWH, he is Elohim; YHWH, he is Elohim.' Now this is a stark example because it comes in the context of life-and-death religious truth and devotion. But it shows that prayer is not about technique – we have omitted the ritual details and their elaborate nature – but about proper address and obedient life inside the solemn covenant of God's electing purposes.

That this is no simple affair of inside/outside, it is to be recalled that Ahab was himself the king of Israel, and his wife Jezebel also within that covenanted context. Here the figure of Ruth is helpful to bring alongside. Another famine, another time. Naomi and family journey to Moab. All die, tragically, save the Moabite daughters-in-law the two Judahite sons had married. Naomi's prayer is in the form of a declarative, 'May the Lord deal kindly with you ... [and] grant that you find a home, each in the house of her husband' (Ruth 1.8–9). May the Lord be true to his character, dealing kindly, on account of the kindness enacted by the Moabite wives towards her and her family. Ruth refuses to leave, declaring 'your God will be my God. ... May the Lord do so to me and more also if even death parts me from you' (Ruth 1.16-17). Ruth takes up her life within the covenant people, finds the husband's house Naomi had prayed for and in time gives birth to a son who would be the grandfather of King David. She is the woman of valour described by the final chapter of the book of Proverbs. Though not a handbook on prayer, we can see the fundamentals of calling on the name, invoking the name, living faithfully via risk in the name and by means of that faithfulness taken up into the most central chamber of God's life with his people, giving birth to a son of promise.

The book of Jonah includes a long prayer, akin to the prayers we find in the Psalter, uttered from the bottom of the sea in the belly of God's aquatic temple.[6] It is a prayer of thanksgiving, which might sound odd, but the three-day incubation has served to release him from his self-preoccupation for a moment so as to turn his mind to God, where life is. 'Deliverance belongs to the Lord' (Jon. 2.9) is the final refrain, and it triggers a vomiting up onto dry land.

Now we can back up and take in the first chapter, which proceeds Jonah's prayer, but within which we have examples of praying, this time from the outside-the-covenant sailors bound for Tarshish. Jonah had hoped this boat ride would take him 'out of the presence of the Lord' (Jon. 1.3) who had ordered him to go to Nineveh – a theological notion we are to know, from Israel's prayer book of Psalms, is an impossibility: 'If I go down to the depths of the sea, thou art there' (Ps. 139.8). Jonah is caught hiding in the boat inside his hiding from God, and he declares a truth he will come to live out, 'I fear the LORD, the God of heaven, who made the sea and the dry land' (Jon. 1.9). What is fascinating to observe is the sailors' praying each to their own gods, much like the prophets of Baal, but deducing that Jonah's God must be the true God since he alone is absent. 'What do you mean, you

---

[6]See Christopher R. Seitz, *Prophecy and Hermeneutics: Toward a New Introduction to the Prophets* (Grand Rapids, MI: Baker Academic, 2007).

sleeper? Arise, call upon your God. Perhaps the God (*ha'elohim*) will give a thought to us that we do not perish' (Jon. 1.6). Jonah does not do this and the action shifts, but the narrator tells us that Jonah had told them he was fleeing from the Lord, and so that may account for the narrative flow. His silence is adamantine, to the point of self-absorption: throw me overboard and save yourselves. At this point is triggered a different kind of prayer from the sailors. It is directed to the Lord, and it is a plea for absolution from blood guilt for throwing Jonah overboard. 'We beseech thee YHWH, let us not perish for this man's life, and lay not on us innocent blood; for thou YHWH hast done as it pleased thee' (Jon. 1.14). Their prayer to the One God, properly addressed on proper terms known to them, is heard. Now they are the ones who 'feared the Lord' indeed 'exceedingly' (Jon. 1.16). They offer a sacrifice – on ship – and make vows, prefiguring Jonah's own converted language at the end of his prayer.

In closing this section on prayer inside and outside the covenant Name, I want to bring in the figure of Job. I hope it will be clear why. Job as a book and in its constituent parts is said to date to the exilic period, and so brings us into an Israelite perspective labelled wisdom literature. Such a perspective is said to be universal in character and held by some to reflect a non-salvation-historical outlook, indeed a kind of intruder into Israel's covenantal perspective. Job is a book that, furthermore, begins a critique of clan or school wisdom that could be more easily located in that covenantal sphere, represented by the book of Proverbs. But for our purposes the important thing is not speculating about an authorial mind and audience removed from the enormously powerful depiction the book itself, in parts and as a whole, undertakes to give, but rather allowing an author at any period of time the ability to invest in Job and his age questions appropriate to them both.[7]

The book of Ezekiel ranges Job alongside Noah and the Canaanite hero Dan'el – all worthy figures operating from the perspective from which we began: the hoary days of Genesis and indeed the primordial age of Genesis 1-11 itself. The book only rarely uses – three times in the world of its direct speech ('The Lord gave, the Lord took away, blessed be the name of the Lord' [Job 1.21]) – the covenantal name YHWH, just sufficiently enough to let the reader know, in the framing narrative, that El Shaddai is indeed one and the same to-be-revealed Lord God of Israel's mature faith. In this it operates in something of the same way as Genesis 1-11 as such, with its brief notice at 4.26 that 'at that time humanity began to call on the name of

---

[7]Christopher R. Seitz, 'Job: Full Structure, Movement, and Interpretation', *Interpretation* 43 (1989): 5–15.

the Lord', and offering no further elaboration than that. Job is flying a bit blind, as it were, and to throw into the mix such an unprecedented occasion of affliction is to load the scale to the breaking point. El Shaddai is the God he demands to speak to and have respond to him, from whirlwind onto ash-heap, silencing the friends and dignifying his demand and his refusal to accept theories of causation for his plight in place of the Living God.

Not much of the book could be classified as prayer. But at its heart is the deepest question prayer poses: Is there something to our life under the sun that has to do with God and God alone? Can we speak to him and can we dare to demand that he answer by means of his own personal self, beyond rationality but consistent with it, beyond theology but not against its efforts? The book of Job says Yes, but a terrifying Yes it is, and the path to it arduous beyond measure in the hoary days of Job. When God says there is no one like him, he is not lying, before or after the affliction. He holds a particular place of honour and never relinquishes it.

As I have noted elsewhere,[8] how one judges the book's denouement and how one decides what the book is about are close to being the same thing. Satan had said no one would continue to worship/fear God for nothing but his own sake. Job had to be stripped away for Satan to be exposed as a liar and false persecutor of the human race. Job could not know what we the reader know, that this was the terrible ordeal he was undergoing, in order for God to be vindicated in his convictions about Job. Job is victorious at terrible cost. And when is that so? The divine speeches serve to silence the friends' (and in my view, Elihu's) take on things, as well as his explicit condemnation of them, and in some mysterious way Job sees in this encounter a deeper seeing than ever experienced, and one that he says suffices. But it is after the judgement over the friends that God dispatches them to the same Job on the ash-heap. And there, we are told, he prays for them. By that action of prayer, he is restored and Satan trounced. Job has become who he was at first, a righteous man who daily interceded for his children, now on the other side of an ordeal unlike any, which culminates in his prayer and so also in his restoration. Little wonder that from his angle of vision the prophet Ezekiel can point to the benchmark of true intercessory righteousness as Noah and Job. Neither are Israelites in the strict sense: Noah living before the covenant at Sinai and Job a foreigner, a man from the east. But both of them are in a life-and-death encounter with the living God who would be known as the Lord, compassionate and merciful in days ahead.

---

[8]Seitz, 'Job', 5–15.

Our point in this section is to emphasize the distinctive character of God's communication with the covenant people in respect of prayer. At the same time, this character is such that it can spill into the faithful lives of those who come into contact with Israel, or misfire within the covenant life as well. The book of Genesis and the timeframe it bespeaks allow us to see how YHWH Elohim established the ground floor of what would be the edifice of prayer such as we will encounter it later in the canonical scriptures of Israel. When Jesus teaches his disciples to pray, and encloses them in his 'our' – the Father of Jesus Christ and our Father by his agency – we see an accomplishment which is prefigured in the scriptures of Israel's own depiction. Prayer is grounded in a special gift of relation and communication for the covenant people but one which intends at the same time to extend a party-line of life and communication from the direct line operative in God's sovereign purposes through time.[9] We participate in this prayerful life through meditation on the scriptural testimony, and take our bearings on prayer from what is set forth. We turn now to examples of prayer within the covenant life which more directly illustrate what we mean by the word.

Survey

The chapters which follow in this volume dealing with prayer in the Old Testament will focus on the figures of Moses and the Psalms. Moses emerges as a critical man of prayer and given the portrayal of the book of Genesis we might rightly ask why. The prayer of Moses emerges in the context of graceful redemption and its wanton rejection by those redeemed. Moses literally rescues Israel, refusing to accept a plan that would in effect start over with a new people, much as in the days of Noah. Moses hurls himself in the breach. God relents. Moses sees in this the true character of God, 'The Lord, the Lord, gracious and merciful' (Exod. 34.6). God agrees to go with the people and not to send surrogates.

The Psalter is quintessentially the book of common prayer of the Old Testament, covering in bold fashion every aspect of human emotion: thanksgiving, praise, lament, reminiscence and the extolling of God as King and the David of his monarchical promises across the years, extending into the future and forever.

But the Psalms are not locked in this one witness only. As we have seen in the case of Jonah, they find their ways into pivotal episodes throughout God's life with his people. A 'survey' could take the form of an external

---

[9]Seitz, 'Prayer in the Old Testament', 163–5, 175.

look – an overview, a fly-over – which would seek to do justice to the full world of prayer as it arises here and there in the history of God's people. But the word can also point to something far more internal to the witness. The psalms and prayers to which we now turn appear to have been composed retrospectively to pick up, summarize and give over to God key periods in the life of Israel. That they have been secondarily inserted into narrative and prophetic texts does not make them less 'historical' but more. They lift up key figures and key moments and commend them to the one in whose hands are the times and seasons. They 'survey' providentially God's life with the covenant people, and allow major figures to remain who they are in their day and context, but also to lift that up into the superintending purposes of God.[10] Jesus' own final high priestly prayer in the Gospel of John can be fruitfully compared with this precedent testimony.

Due to the fact that prayers are often in the form of Hebrew poetry, which is set off in translated texts by distinctive printing, one can readily detect the survey structure to which I refer. Moreover, the key moments being prayerfully commended often fall at the beginnings or endings of books as these mark transitions across generations: Moses at the end of Deuteronomy, Hannah at the opening of 1 Samuel and David at the end of 2 Samuel. Solomon and Hezekiah also have key prayers, the latter appearing in both 2 Kings and Isaiah, where it serves to transition to so-called Second or Latter Isaiah chapters (40-66). The Chronicler has placed on the lips of David an extended prayer which is in fact a composite drawn from psalms we can recognize quite readily in the Psalter. Here one sees the creative principle at work whereby psalms are made to summarize in prayer form key historical seasons.

Habakkuk should be mentioned at this juncture as a good introduction to our theme. I have argued that in the final form of his book, within the context of the Twelve Minor prophets as a collection, his prayer is a model for the faithful reader of the collection as a whole.[11] It allows us to stand alongside the prophet, the theme of whose book is the perennial quest for the knowledge of God's ways in a period of hardship and waiting. That we are dealing with an explicit prayer in the final chapter of the book, indeed in the form of a psalm, is obvious in both form and content. We have the usual psalm verses of repeated phrases (first a, then b); the use of 'selah' at

---

[10]James W. Watts, *Psalm and Story: Inset Hymns in Hebrew Narrative* (Sheffield: JSOT Press, 1992). I gratefully acknowledge my indebtedness to this perspective in what follows. See also Brevard S. Childs, *Introduction to the Old Testament as Scripture* (Philadelphia, PA: Fortress Press, 1979).

[11]Seitz, *Prophecy and Hermeneutics*, 212, 244.

the end of verse 3, middle of verse 9 and end of verse 13; a superscription identifying the psalm's author/subject, and the technical musical terminology ('on the shigionoth') familiar from the Psalter, as well as a closing colophon at verse 19b. It is a psalm of trust, with historical reminiscence, trial and final confident joy.

A recent study of the book of Habakkuk seeks to resolve the problem of the identity of the vision given to Habakkuk in the pivotal scene at 2.1-3.[12] The prophet is on a watchtower, following the extended lament of chapter one, waiting for God's response. He is given a vision, plain in form. One problem for interpretation is the language of running found in verse 2. Is the idea that one running can still read it, this vision, even speeding along, so plain is its form on tablets? If so, what does that mean and what is in fact the content of the vision? Is it what follows in 2.4ff? This is far from clear.

The argument is that the language of running is similar to what we have in Isaiah 40.31: 'Those who wait on the Lord will run and not be weary.' It is an image of energized feet, mobilized because of the Lord and his faithful presence. Here the link to the psalm of Habakkuk and its final line is forged. The Lord is the prophet/pray-er's strength, we read in Habakkuk 3.19. The prayer enables the confident hope of the prophet, giving him the feet of a deer, making him run on heights. The vision given the prophet in chapter two, then, is in fact the book of Habakkuk as a whole, placed before us in its three-chapter form. It constitutes his vision, given to him by God in the midst of trial and confusion, and it enables all who now read it to be similarly encouraged and strengthened. That is the point of Habakkuk 2.2 with its image of running. The superscription of the present book of Habakkuk declares it to be the prophet's *hazon*. It is the word given to the prophet and written down by him in the form we now read it and take encouragement from it. In the present shape of the Book of the Twelve, it serves to guide the reader through the vicissitudes of history, and to find in Habakkuk a model of patience and prayer. The hermeneutical effect of the psalm's placement inside of Habakkuk coheres with the image of a vision which enables the weary to run, from Hosea to the last verses of Malachi, obediently patient before the Lord through trial and confusion.

It is the hermeneutical purpose of the psalm to enable specific prophetic declarations in time and space to gather future generations and instruct them in their day, guided by prior days. Psalms in prophetic literature, as in narrative contexts as we are about to see, serve the function of bringing

---

[12]Francis Watson, *Paul and the Hermeneutics of Faith* (London: T&T Clark, 2004). Watson has made a convincing case for the interpretation given here. See also Seitz, *Prophecy and Hermeneutics,* 112 and Seitz, *The Elder Testament,* 153–4.

future generations into instructive encounter with past generations. One could mention as well the psalms found at key moments in the book of Isaiah (12.1-6; 42.10-12; 44.23) and the depictions of praise to be enacted (51.9-11; 52.7-10; 54.1-17; 60.1-22).[13] They allow something concrete and historically specific to configure and to signify for future generations of readers. Psalms fill time with significance: the signing, the signifying from a watchtower standing over time while concretely rooted in it.

We can see a similar, though distinctive, use of a psalm to close the book of Deuteronomy, and in so doing, the Pentateuch itself. Deuteronomy 32 is a 'song' of Moses. In form it resembles the historical psalms of recital in the Psalter, even as it has a clear hermeneutical function in its present location. Blessings and curses are set before the new generation about to enter the Promise Land. Moses is about to die. His successor Joshua stands at the ready. The book of Deuteronomy does not end in a straightforward covenant form, blessings and curses attending upon obedience or disobedience, but looks ahead into the future. It assumes and indeed predicts failure. Curses will come upon an Israel which will repeat the disobedience of the wilderness generation, and so come under judgement and death. Knowing this, however, is not the end of the story. A song is written and taught to the Israelites (Deut. 31.22) because 'I know what they are disposed to do' (Deut. 31.21).

The song begins with praise of God, set against the wayward inclination of his people. The past is recalled. Jacob/Israel is God's elect out of all the nations. God has lavishly provided. In an indictment generalized so as to fit the wilderness generation but also other era, God judges his people and hands them over to the nations. The horrors of this fate are set before the generation Moses addresses now. A turning point is reached, similar to that following Moses' intervention at Sinai. God relents, forgives and protects, so that the nations will not misunderstand: his election of his people is forever and they are judged by his hand, and not because of vain power unleashed boastfully by the nations. The nations are in turn rebuked. 'Vengeance is mine, I will repay' (Deut. 32.35). At the song's conclusion an interpretative frame follows. All the words of the song are heard, are to be taught to coming generations and they reside alongside the law as a testimony. 'They are not just idle words for you – they are your life' (Deut. 32.47). Like the psalms of recital that call to mind Israel's rebellion and God's faithfulness, in Book IV of the Psalter's journey into exile and curse, the song of Moses functions as a prayer for the ages. All generations are brought before this testimony standing over time, much as on the watchtower of Habakkuk.

---

[13]See Brevard S. Childs, *Isaiah* (Louisville, KY: Westminster John Knox Press, 2001).

The next inset prayer of comparable significance returns us to the figure of Hannah, at the opening of the books of 1 and 2 Samuel. A clear counterpart, functioning like the second of two bookends, is found at the very end of 2 Samuel, in the prayer of David (2 Sam. 22). The barren Hannah's prayer is heard. When the child is born, he names him in response to the response given to her by the Lord. He is Samuel. She weans him and then delivers him to Eli, asking that he be given to the service of the Lord who gave him, all his days. Eli receives the lad. Hannah's prayer then follows. Its theme is not the election of a people and God's preservation of them through judgement at the hands of nations. Its theme is God's sovereignty. He gives, he takes away. All is in his sovereign hands. This is a more universal theme. It attaches itself to the Hannah scene specifically only at this generalized point.

> The barren has borne seven,
>   but she who has many children is forlorn.
> The Lord kills and brings to life;
>   he brings down to Sheol and raises up.
>
> (1 Sam. 2.5-6)

This is consistent with the form of prayers as inset pieces, which enable a more general application within the specific and concrete biblical episode being related.

The ending of the prayer is surprising, given this. God has quite specific plans on the horizon, beyond the days of Hannah, focused on his anointed one.

> The Lord will judge the ends of the earth;
>   he will give strength to his king,
>   and exalt the power of his anointed.
>
> (1 Sam. 2.10)

We are not prepared for this in the opening chapter of 1 Samuel, with its focus on the barren Hannah and her answered prayer. Yet the theme is calibrated all the same to the closing refrain of Judges. 'There was no king in the land. Everyone did what was right in their own eyes' (Judg. 17.6). The terrain that leads to David the anointed must cover a wrongful request from the people, that they might be like the nations, and the tragic answer to the supplication in the person of Saul. Israel was not barren or properly postured in prayer, and so the answer was premature and wrongly timed to God's purposes held up in the final line of Hannah's prayer. Much of the content of the books of Samuel plays out that fateful tension between a wrong request granted in Saul and God's own designs for a king in the person of David.

Unsurprisingly then, the next major prayer comes at the close of the books of Samuel and picks up on this point. It is a song of David, like the prior song of Moses, which David spoke to the Lord 'when the Lord delivered him from the hands of his enemies, and from Saul' (2 Sam. 22.1). This backward glance is focused but also generalized, so as to offer a retrospective summary that will also look onto a future beyond David's days, shortly to come to an end. Where in Moses' song we had a focus on the people of Israel across the generations, here the focus is on the Lord's anointed David, as bearer into the future of God's solemn promises made with him on their behalf and in relation to the nations. As for the relationship between the psalm-form and these poetic insets – we have discussed Jonah, Habakkuk, Hannah – here the association is crystal clear: 2 Samuel 22 is exactly the same prayer text as we find in Psalm 18, down to details. The adjustments, such as they are, are minor: an expanded superscription at Psalm 18 ('for the director of music') and a single introductory first-person acclamation ('I love you, Lord, my strength').

David's Song is less historically broad-ranging than Moses'. As the superscription indicates, David is speaking about God's rescue of him in all tribulations. The majority of the song is praise of God. David concludes with reference to prayer being raised amongst the nations, and of his victories making God's power known outside of Israel. David is 'head of the nations' (Ps. 18.44). David here is himself in his own lifetime, but also, as in the Psalter 'David and his descendants forever' (Ps. 18.50). 2 Samuel 22.51 echoes and brings to mind Hannah's song in 1 Samuel 2.10. David is not there named, and so 'the anointed' of Hannah's prescient praise can retain a broad reference to the Davidic promises through his entire lineage. Prayers of praise are not tied down to time, and also not to space. Moses Song at the sea fast forwards to the sanctuary of God's future intentions (Exod. 15.17). The temple is an odd intruder in the sea journeys of Jonah, and indeed right inside the belly of a great fish he will speak of his prayer rising up 'into your holy temple'. Similarly here, before the temple is constructed, David's cries call out to the Lord, 'from his temple he heard my voice; my cry came to his ears' (2 Sam. 22.7; Ps. 18.6). Yet again we get the clear hermeneutical signal that prayers and songs of praise are meant to encompass future prayers and witnesses, and are not held down by concrete historical moments but arise from them so as to guide future generations.

The next major prayer of the Deuteronomistic History's recital is indeed Solomon's, in the context of the building of that same temple sanctuary referenced in Exodus, 1 Samuel 2, 2 Samuel 22 and Jonah. It is not as long

as David's, and it takes a different form. It is more explicitly a prayer, indeed
a petition, hands spread out towards heaven (1 Kgs 8.22). It ranges more
broadly across time in an explicit sense. Not unlike the prayer of Moses in
Deuteronomy, it seeks to bring within the limited compass of the temple's
construction a much broader horizon, one of failure, assaults, defeat and
exile. Not mentioned but clearly understood is also the temple's own
destruction. Solomon repeats the refrain that the temple is an earthly reality,
whose genuine point of reference is however the highest heavens themselves,
where God dwells and, more importantly, hears (1 Kgs 8.27-30, 32, 34, 36,
39, 43, 45, 49). Unrighteous conduct, defeat because of sin, natural disasters
of all kinds, disease, sin that leads to captivity and destruction – for all of this
there is a remedy, in turning and asking for forgiveness. Even the nations who
may come because of the renown of God's name, they too have the divine
ear, 'so that all the peoples of the earth may know your name and fear you,
as do your own people Israel' (1 Kgs 8.43). Hans Walter Wolff rightly saw in
this prayer the answer to the dark portrayal of the Deuteronomistic History,
whose ending offers no glimpse of hope.[14] That dark verdict is everywhere
anticipated and seen, by Solomon and by Deuteronomy's Moses before him,
as surmounted by the divine promise to hear and forgive a repentant people,
after defeat, above curse and blessing as final integers of his more sovereign,
merciful ways.

The prayer of Solomon is nothing if not temporally and spatially
exhaustive. From highest heaven to sanctuary on earth, from a point in time
of health and peace, to times of utter forsakenness and exile. As it stands
now, Solomon's prayer has a kind of A to Z comprehensiveness. It may be
for this reason that in the material roughly shared by the Deuteronomistic
History and the book of Isaiah, the substantial prayer of Hezekiah makes no
appearance in the former. Solomon's prayer offers a first and final word. In
the larger compass of the book of Isaiah, however, the prayer of Hezekiah
functions as a kind of figural representation of Israel's own fate. The Davidic
king is himself sick until death, not unlike the Israel of Babylonian exile to
come. He prays for deliverance. His life has passed before his eyes, yet he
is restored. New life granted him is as miraculous as causing the shadow
of the sun to move backwards in reclaiming and forgiving power. Before
moving into the final and unswerving judgement of God wrought upon his
own people at the hands of the Babylonian replacements for the rebuffed

---

[14]He disputed von Rad's effort to counteract the negative verdict of Martin Noth on the
purpose of the Deuteronomistic History by reference to the kindness given to Jehoiachin in
the final scene at 2 Kings 25. See Hans Walter Wolff, 'Das Kerygma des deuteronomistischen
Geschichtswerk', *Zeitschrift für die Alttestamentliche Wissenschaft* 73, no. 2 (1961): 171–86.

Assyria of Hezekiah's day, these pivotal chapters of Isaiah help us see in the saving of Jerusalem, and the healing of her prayerful king, a figure of God's final purposes for David and Israel. Chapters 40-66 speak to that reality, including the coming of the nations who once served as God's instruments of judgement.

Conclusion

These key prayers, songs and petitions punctuate Israel's life with God, through all its contours and challenges. They permit future generations to recall, be instructed, be warned and finally be directed in hope. They find their Psalter counterparts in historical recital psalms, and on occasion are simply repeated verbatim, as in the case of 2 Samuel 22 and Psalm 8. Prayer in Israel is always individual and corporate at the same time. David is himself in the Psalter, but equally he is the monarchy in God's extensive plans, and he is everyman and everywoman.[15] To the degree to which Israel is elected to have a personal relationship with the Living God, so too the nations come to the knowledge of God through them. The scriptures of Israel are themselves prayerful vehicles. One studies them and sees in them and in the prayers they set forth a bringing near of those far off, to be guided, exhorted, instructed and put into prayerful relationship with the one Lord God.

---

[15]Christopher R. Seitz, 'Psalm 2 in the Entry Hall of the Psalter: Extended Sense in the History of Interpretation', in *Church, Society, and the Christian Common Good*, ed. Ephraim Radner (Eugene, OR: Cascade Books, 2017), 95–106.

CHAPTER TWO

Moses on Mount Sinai in the Early Christian Contemplative Tradition

ANN CONWAY-JONES

When considering the role of scripture in the development of Christian prayer, it is noteworthy that early Christian writers seeking to map out contemplation of the divine returned again and again to the Exodus account of Moses' experiences on Mount Sinai. Denys Turner has argued that the Greek theologians who brought together Plato's allegory of the cave in Book 7 of *The Republic* with the narrative of Moses encountering God on the summit of Sinai were responsible for 'a seismic shock which was still registering tremors twelve hundred years later'.[1] This chapter will focus on five key moments in Exodus as interpreted by four theologians, three from the fourth century – Gregory of Nyssa, Evagrius of Pontus and the author of *The Macarian Homilies* (referred to as Macarius) – along with the late fifth/early sixth-century anonymous Syrian monk who adopted the persona of Dionysius the Areopagite.[2] These were all influenced by the Platonic worldview of their time, as exemplified by their talk of the mind (*nous*) reaching out to God through contemplation (*theōria*). But we will concentrate on the way in which they scrutinized the biblical text, and built

---

[1]Denys Turner, *The Darkness of God: Negativity in Christian Mysticism* (Cambridge: Cambridge University Press, 1995), 11.
[2]For Dionysius the Areopagite, see Acts 17.34.

their understanding of prayer upon some of its particularities and paradoxes. These were writers who stressed the incomprehensibility of God, and the inadequacy of human language to capture anything of the divine essence, which is why they are known as mystical theologians. Scripture, however, gave them leave to speak of God, and it was above all the difficulties and peculiarities of the biblical text which fired their imaginations.

The Exodus Narrative

The book of Exodus is a compilation of originally independent traditions. The Sinai narrative in particular is full of repetitions, contradictions, disruptions and inconsistencies.[3] Moses is said to ascend the mountain eight times, sometimes in company, sometimes alone.[4] Historical–critical biblical scholarship, dominated by the documentary hypothesis of Julius Wellhausen, has attempted to identify and isolate the Pentateuchal sources, without ever reaching a consensus. Baruch Schwartz divides the Sinai narrative into three distinct stories, now intertwined. The J account, in which 'the Sinai events are essentially visual', he calls 'The Appearances of YHWH on Mount Sinai'. These passages 'are characterized by bold anthropomorphism'. He entitles the E account, which includes the episode of the golden calf, 'The Making, Breaking and Remaking of the Covenant'. And the P account he labels 'The Laws Given by God in His Earthly Abode'. Here 'the giving of the law depends on the prior establishment of the Tabernacle cult'.[5] Our early Christian authors knew nothing of such source criticism. But that does not mean that they were blind to disjunctions and inconsistencies. Indeed, as we shall see, they often focused in on them, convinced that any surface problem indicated the need for deeper understanding. As Gregory of Nyssa explains in the preface to *Homilies on the Song of Songs*:

> If something is stated in a concealed manner by way of enigmas and below-the-surface meanings, and so is void of profit in its plain sense, such passages we turn over in our minds.[6]

---

[3]For explorations of the difficulties, see Baruch Schwartz, 'What Really Happened at Mount Sinai? Four Biblical Answers to One Question', *Bible Review* 13, no. 5 (1997): 20–30, 46 and Benjamin D. Sommer, 'Revelation at Sinai in the Hebrew Bible and in Jewish Theology', *Journal of Religion* 79, no. 3 (1999): 422–51.

[4]Exodus 19.3-7, 8-14, 20-25; 20.21-24.3; 24.9-11; 24.12-32.15; 32.30-34; 34.1-29.

[5]Schwartz, 'What Really Happened at Mount Sinai?', 26–8. Schwartz's analysis should be taken as indicative of possibilities, as there is little scholarly agreement over the arrangement of sources in the Sinai narrative.

[6]Gregory of Nyssa, *Cant.* preface (GNO 6.4.18-5.3); *Gregory of Nyssa: Homilies on the Song of Songs*, trans. Richard A. Norris (Atlanta, GA: Society of Biblical Literature, 2012), 3.

We need to bear in mind that the passages turned over in this way were taken from the Greek Septuagint, which occasionally diverges significantly from the Hebrew Bible. Most of the biblical texts quoted in this chapter will therefore be translations of the LXX.[7] And in the Christian interpretative trajectory to be explored, it is taken for granted that Moses, the 'friend of God', who ascended 'the highest mount of perfection', is a fitting model for the religious elite, be that monks or bishops.[8]

The darkness of unknowing (Exod. 20.21)

After the giving of the Ten Commandments, Moses entered into 'the darkness where God was' (LXX Exod. 20.21). Exodus often depicts the manifestation of God's presence as a dazzlingly bright and dangerous light, referred to as 'glory' (*kavod* in Hebrew, *doxa* in Greek). Benjamin Sommer bluntly calls this God's body: 'something located in a particular place at a particular time'.[9] He suggests, however, that, in modern terms, it would seem to be composed of something closer to energy than matter. The Hebrew term *araphel* in MT Exodus 20.21 designates the protective cloud surrounding this deadly divine luminosity. It has been translated into English as 'thicke clowde' (Tyndale), 'thick darkness' (KJV, NRSV, NIV) or 'dark cloud' (JB, GNB); but the LXX simply uses 'darkness' (*gnophos*). Gregory of Nyssa comments on Exodus 20.21 in *Life of Moses* 2.162-164, alluding to the verse a further eight times in *Life of Moses*, and three times in *Homilies on the Song of Songs*.[10] He is aware of the oddity of God being found in darkness, especially given Moses' encounter at the burning bush: 'For what is now recorded seems somehow contrary to the first theophany; for the divine is then perceived in light, but now in darkness.'[11] He explains the darkness as symbolizing 'the

---

[7]The translation used is *A New English Translation of the Septuagint and the Other Greek Translations Traditionally Included under That Title*, trans. Albert Pietersma and Benjamin G. Wright (Oxford: Oxford University Press, 2007), abbreviated as NETS. When the Hebrew Bible (MT – Masoretic Text) is quoted, the translation used is the NRSV.

[8]Exodus 33.11. Jean Daniélou, *Grégoire de Nysse: La Vie de Moïse, ou Traité de la perfection en matière de vertu*, 3rd edn, SC 1 (Paris: Cerf, 2000), 2.319 (324) – hereafter: *Vit. Moys*; Gregory of Nyssa, *The Life of Moses*, trans. Abraham J. Malherbe and Everett Ferguson, CWS (New York: Paulist Press, 1978), 137. One exception to the early church's admiration of Moses is Eusebius of Caesarea. See Bogdan G. Bucur, '"God Never Appeared to Moses": Eusebius of Caesarea's Peculiar Exegesis of the Burning Bush Theophany', *Journal of the Bible and Its Reception* 5, no. 2 (2018): 235–57.

[9]Benjamin D. Sommer, *The Bodies of God and the World of Ancient Israel* (Cambridge: Cambridge University Press, 2009), 2.

[10]Gregory of Nyssa, *Vit. Moys*. 1.46, 56, 58; 2.152, 169, 229, 312, 315; *Cant.* 6 (GNO 6.181.6), 11 (GNO 6.322.12-323.9); 12 (GNO 6.355.12).

[11]Gregory of Nyssa, *Vit. Moys*. 2.162; author's translation.

unknown and unseen'.[12] This interpretation of Exodus 20.21 goes back to the first-century Alexandrian Jew Philo, who describes the fruitlessness of Moses' quest, out of which Moses sees 'precisely this, that [the God of real Being] is incapable of being seen'.[13] Gregory insists that what Moses seeks 'transcends all knowledge, cut off on all sides by incomprehensibility'.[14] The essence of God is beyond the grasp of human (and even angelic) intellects. Reflecting Exodus' picture of fire or glory within dark cloud, Gregory uses the oxymoron 'radiant darkness'.[15] He also quotes from LXX Psalm 17.12, saying that God 'made obscurity (*skotos*) his hideaway'.[16] And he mentions other spiritual greats, alongside Moses, who were 'initiated into ineffable mysteries in the same secret place': David, Paul and the sublime John.[17]

Dionysius, writing a little over one hundred years later, clearly draws on Gregory's work. In *Mystical Theology* he too quotes LXX Exodus 20.21 and Psalm 17.12. In a key paragraph, he collapses Moses' multifaceted experience into one archetypal ascent of Mount Sinai, culminating with Moses plunging into 'the truly mysterious darkness of unknowing'.[18] Dionysius goes further than Gregory in exploiting the interplay between overpowering brilliance and enveloping cloud. In *Epistle* 5 he states, 'The divine darkness is that "unapproachable light" where God is said to live.'[19] He has combined 'unapproachable light' from 1 Timothy 6.16 with LXX 3 Kings 8.53: '(The Lord) said that he should dwell in darkness.'[20] This darkness is not due to the absence of light, but to its excess. As Dionysius explains in *Divine Names*, 'We posit intangible and invisible darkness of that Light which is unapproachable because it so far exceeds the visible light.'[21] He has blended Moses' experience on Mount Sinai with Plato's allegory of the philosopher's ascent to knowledge, in which the prisoner who escapes from the cave emerges into blinding light. The opening prayer of *Mystical*

[12]Gregory of Nyssa, *Vit. Moys.* 2.169; author's translation. See also *Cant.* 11 (GNO 6.323.4-9), in which Gregory characterizes the darkness as 'the invisible and the incomprehensible'.
[13]Philo, *Post.* 15 (LCL 2.336-37). See also *Mut.* 7-8 (LCL 5.144-47).
[14]Gregory of Nyssa, *Vit. Moys.* 2.163; author's translation.
[15]Gregory of Nyssa, *Vit. Moys.* 2.163; author's translation.
[16]Gregory of Nyssa, *Vit. Moys.* 2.164; author's translation. LXX Psalm 17.12 corresponds to MT Psalm 18.12, and in English translations of the Hebrew Bible to Psalm 18.11.
[17]Gregory of Nyssa, *Vit. Moys.* 2.164; author's translation. See also *Vit. Moys.* 2.163, 174.
[18]Pseudo-Dionysius, *MT* 1.3 (PTS 36.144); *The Mystical Theology*, 137. The English translation of Dionysius' works, unless stated otherwise, is taken from *Pseudo-Dionysius: The Complete Works*, trans. Colm Luibheid, CWS (New York: Paulist Press, 1987).
[19]Pseudo-Dionysius, *ep.* 5 (PTS 36.162); *The Letters*, 265.
[20]LXX 3 Kingdoms 8.53 corresponds to MT 1 Kings 8.12, where the Hebrew *araphel* appears, as in Exodus 20.21. I have amended the NETS translation, because once again the Greek simply has 'darkness' (*gnophos*).
[21]Pseudo-Dionysius, *DN* 7.2 (PTS 33.196); *The Divine Names*, 107.

Theology is full of apophatic and paradoxical language. The mysteries of theology are said to lie veiled 'in the brilliant darkness of a hidden silence'.[22] For Turner, this exemplifies a 'self-subverting' utterance, 'which first says something and then, in the same image, unsays it'.[23] In Dionysius' Platonic reinterpretation, the dazzlingly dangerous glory of Exodus, surrounded by its protective cloud, is used to underline the utter failure of all human speech to describe the transcendent God.

Divine blue (Exod. 24.9-11)

Following the covenant ceremony, 'Moses and Aaron, Nadab, and Abihu, and seventy of the elders of Israel went up, and they saw the God of Israel. Under his feet there was something like a pavement of sapphire stone, like the very heaven for clearness' (MT Exod. 24.9-10). The LXX translators clearly baulked at the suggestion that the elders had seen God, and so, taking their cue from the mention of God's feet, rendered verse 10 as: 'And they saw the place, there where the God of Israel stood, and that which was beneath his feet, like something made from sapphire brick and like the appearance of the firmament of heaven in purity.'[24] Gregory of Nyssa ignores this passage, but Dionysius refers to it. He says that before plunging into the darkness of unknowing, Moses, accompanied by chosen priests, 'contemplates not him who is invisible, but the place where he stands'.[25] Dionysius interprets this 'place' as representing 'the rationale which presupposes all that lies below the Transcendent One'.[26] It corresponds, in other words, to the Platonic realm of Ideas. But in Dionysius' Christian worldview, the principles underlying creation are living heavenly beings. In *The Celestial Hierarchy*, he says that the first ranked angels are 'the divine place of the Godhead's rest'.[27] One way of reading Dionysius' description of Moses' ascent is to see it as reflecting the journey of the hierarch (bishop) during the eucharistic liturgy.[28] The 'place' of Exodus 24.10 then represents the altar, at which humans and angels join

---

[22]Pseudo-Dionysius, *MT* 1.1 (PTS 36.142); *The Mystical Theology*, 135.

[23]Turner, *The Darkness of God*, 21.

[24]I have amended the NETS translation of *sappheiros* from 'lapis lazuli' to 'sapphire', in order to conform with the NRSV and translations of Evagrius. It is probably true, however, that both the Hebrew *sapir* and the Greek *sappheiros* refer not to the clear gemstone, but to lapis lazuli, a stone prized for its deep intense blue, which often includes minute golden pyrite crystals, reminiscent of stars shimmering in the night sky.

[25]Pseudo-Dionysius, *MT* 1.3 (PTS 36.144); author's translation. Luibheid's translation – 'where he dwells' – obscures the reference to LXX Exodus 24.10.

[26]Pseudo-Dionysius, *MT* 1.3 (PTS 36.144); *The Mystical Theology*, 137.

[27]Pseudo-Dionysius, *CH* 7.4 (PTS 36.32); *The Celestial Hierarchy*, 166.

[28]See Paul Rorem, 'Moses as the Paradigm for the Liturgical Spirituality of Pseudo-Dionysius', *Studia Patristica* 18, no. 2 (1989): 275–9.

to praise 'the Cause and source beyond every source for every being', which 'transcendently draws everything into its perennial embrace'.[29]

The fourth-century author who exploited the potential of Exodus 24.10 was Evagrius of Pontus, whose life was steeped in the Bible, from copying manuscripts to reciting psalms. Biblical exegesis formed the basis of his spiritual guidance, necessitating 'a large store of biblical wisdom and a familiarity with the different levels of meaning contained in sacred scripture'.[30] He defined prayer as 'the ascent of the mind towards God'.[31] At the summit of this ascent:

> When the mind has put off the old self and shall put on the one born of grace, then it will see its own state in the time of prayer resembling sapphire or the colour of heaven; this state scripture calls the place of God that was seen by the elders on Mount Sinai.[32]

In MT Exodus 24.10, the elders 'see' (r'h) God, in the next verse they 'behold' (ḥzh) God – this stronger Hebrew verb belongs 'to the vocabulary of prophetic vision'.[33] Once again, the LXX differs, turning in verse 11 to the passive of 'to see': the elders 'appeared in the place of God'. The 'place' becomes therefore no longer what they see, but where they are. Evagrius takes the 'place of God' to represent an inner state, thus interiorizing the biblical narrative: Mount Sinai becomes 'an inner landmark, a center in the geography of the soul'.[34] The ascent is a process of detachment, symbolized by Moses being told to take the sandals off his feet before approaching the burning bush.[35] It requires the letting go not only of all passions, but also of any 'mental representations' (noēmata) – any images or conceptual thinking. Then the mind enters a state of utter simplicity, which Evagrius calls 'pure prayer'; and it sees itself shining like a star.[36] The LXX adds

---

[29]Pseudo-Dionysius, *CH* 7.4 (PTS 36.32); *The Celestial Hierarchy*, 166. See Alexander Golitzin, *Mystagogy: A Monastic Reading of Dionysius Areopagita* (Collegeville, MN: Liturgical Press, 2013), 235.

[30]Luke Dysinger, 'Evagrius Ponticus, Exegete of the Soul', in *Evagrius and His Legacy*, ed. Joel Kalvesmaki and Robin Darling Young (Notre Dame, IN: University of Notre Dame Press, 2016), 76.

[31]Evagrius, *De oratione* 36; *On Prayer*, 196. The English translation of Evagrius' works, unless stated otherwise, is taken from *Evagrius of Pontus: The Greek Ascetic Corpus*, trans. Robert E. Sinkewicz (Oxford: Oxford University Press, 2003).

[32]Evagrius, *De malignis cogitationibus* 39; *Thoughts*, 180.

[33]Nahum M. Sarna, *The JPS Torah Commentary: Exodus* (Philadelphia, PA: Jewish Publication Society, 1991), 153.

[34]William Harmless and Raymond R. Fitzgerald, 'The Sapphire Light of the Mind: The *Skemmata* of Evagrius Ponticus', *Theological Studies* 62, no. 3 (2001): 498–529 (519).

[35]See Evagrius, *De oratione* 4; *Prayer*, 193.

[36]Evagrius, *De malignis cogitationibus* 43; *Thoughts*, 182.

the word 'firmament' to the description of the sapphire blue pavement, thereby creating a link with the firmament separating the upper and lower waters (Gen. 1.6), and the firmament seen by Ezekiel over the heads of the living creatures, above which was the sapphire throne (Ezek. 1.22-26). Evagrius, however, does not use 'firmament', but the more abstract 'colour' (*chrōma*) of heaven. This indicates that, alongside the LXX, he has consulted Symmachus' Greek translation of the scriptures, where 'colour' appears.[37] Presumably he chose this as being more suitable because his interest was not cosmology, but the life of the mind. That is where, he argued, the place of God is to be found. Knowledge of God, 'essential knowledge', is not external: it is experienced through inner transformation. He writes:

> Objects are outside the intellect, whereas the contemplation concerning them is constituted inside it. This is not the case, however, with the Holy Trinity, for it is only essential knowledge.[38]

William Harmless and Raymond Fitzgerald remind us that 'in the Greek tradition, the mind (*nous*) is our intuitive side. It enables us to know and recognise the truth of things instantly, whether a friend's face or a mathematical proof.'[39] Evagrius talks of it becoming 'the temple of the Holy Trinity'.[40] He has taken over the imagery of the glory of God within the holy of holies – blinding divine radiance contained within the void of a material structure – to describe the paradox of divine light being present within a human mind. As Harmless and Fitzgerald write:

> In seeing itself as luminosity, as light like sapphire or sky-blue, the mind discovers its God-likeness. At the same time, it sees and knows by seeing – indirectly, as in a mirror – the uncreated, immaterial light that God is.

---

[37]See John William Wevers, *Notes on the Greek Text of Exodus* (Atlanta, GA: Scholars Press, 1990), 385; or Alison Salvesen, *Symmachus in the Pentateuch* (Manchester: University of Manchester, 1991), 105–6. Evagrius explicitly refers to Symmachus in *Sch. Eccl.* 50, on Ecclesiastes 6.9. See Paul Géhin, *Évagre le Pontique: Scholies à l'Ecclésiaste*, SC 397 (Paris: Cerf, 1993), 146; *Notes on Ecclesiastes* in *Evagrius of Pontus*, trans. A. M. Casiday (London: Routledge, 2006), 144. And indeed it would seem that he studied all four columns of Origen's *Tetrapla* (a digest of the *Hexapla*, without the Hebrew text or its transliteration into Greek). See Augustine Casiday, *Reconstructing the Theology of Evagrius Ponticus: Beyond Heresy* (Cambridge: Cambridge University Press, 2013), 105–7.

[38]Evagrius, *Kephalaia Gnostika* 4.77; *Evagrius's Kephalaia Gnostika: A New Translation of the Unreformed Text from the Syriac*, trans. Ilaria L. E. Ramelli (Atlanta, GA: Society of Biblical Literature, 2015), 239.

[39]Harmless and Fitzgerald, 'The Sapphire Light of the Mind', 513.

[40]Evagrius, *Skemmata* 34; *Reflections*, 214.

That is why for Evagrius prayer is at once a moment of self-discovery and an encounter with ultimate Mystery.[41]

The heavenly tabernacle (Exod. 25-28)

After the communal vision, Moses leaves the elders behind, and enters the cloud at the summit of Mount Sinai, remaining there for forty days and forty nights (Exod. 24.15-18). God shows him the 'pattern' (tavnit in Hebrew, paradeigma or tupos in Greek) of the tabernacle that the people are to build (Exod. 25.9, 40). These instructions for the tent, its furnishings, and the priestly vestments, together with the description of their subsequent manufacture, occupy a quarter of Exodus (chapters 25-28, 35-40). Gregory of Nyssa follows Exodus' lead, devoting three paragraphs of his contemplative commentary (theōria) to the darkness (2.162-164), but thirty-two to the tabernacle (2.170-201). He understands the 'pattern' shown to Moses to be the heavenly tabernacle 'not made with hands'.[42] He deciphers this in a way which resembles Dionysius' understanding of the 'place' of Exodus 24.10: as the Platonic realm of Ideas, now conceptualized as the world of angelic powers. He associates the tabernacle furniture with 'the supercosmic powers ... which undergird everything in keeping with the divine will'.[43] The altars, in particular, suggest to him 'the adoration by heavenly beings which is continuously performed in this tabernacle'.[44] But he also interprets the tabernacle as a type of Christ:

> Moses was educated beforehand by a type in the mystery of the tabernacle which encloses everything. This would be Christ, 'the power of God and the wisdom of God', which in its own nature is not made by hands, yet allows itself to be physically fashioned when this tabernacle needs to be pitched among us, so that, in a certain way, the same is both unfashioned and fashioned: uncreated in pre-existence, but becoming created in accordance with this material composition.[45]

Gregory draws on a number of biblical traditions about the tabernacle, wisdom and Christ as he reflects on the significance of calling Christ by the term 'tabernacle'. The heavenly tabernacle represents the pre-existent Christ, the one 'in whom dwells the whole fullness of divinity', which for

---

[41]Harmless and Fitzgerald, 'The Sapphire Light of the Mind', 519.
[42]Gregory of Nyssa, Vit. Moys. 2.167, 169, 170, 229.
[43]Gregory of Nyssa, Vit. Moys. 2.17; author's translation.
[44]Gregory of Nyssa, Vit. Moys. 2.182; author's translation.
[45]Gregory of Nyssa, Vit. Moys. 2.174; author's translation.

Gregory means participation in the infinity and incomprehensibility of God.[46] Christ is also the agent and pattern of creation, 'the power which encloses all existence', 'the common shelter of all'.[47] And at the incarnation, the heavenly tabernacle was, as it were, turned inside out: the infinite Christ becoming contained within the finite 'tent' of a human body. 'This is the Only-begotten God, who encloses everything within himself, yet pitched his own tabernacle among us.'[48] The earthly tabernacle also becomes a type of the body of Christ, the church – the worshipping community, which seeks to reflect the angelic liturgy of the heavenly tabernacle.

The darkness on Mount Sinai is not an endpoint for Gregory, for within it Moses receives a vision of Christ. In the words of Colin Macleod, 'The reverse side of Gregory's negative theology is Christian faith: in the very darkness which surrounds God we see the "tabernacle", Christ.'[49] But this does not undermine his apophaticism, for within the tabernacle is the holy of holies. Even Moses cannot see the mysteries hidden in the ark, shielded by the cherubim's wings. Gregory insists that 'the truth of all existence is truly a holy matter, a holy of holies, incomprehensible and unapproachable for the multitude'. 'The understanding of realities beyond apprehension must not be meddled with ... but remains ineffable in the secret spaces of the mind.'[50] He does not urge his readers to follow Moses up the mountain, but to worship in the earthly tabernacle, and, above all, to don the priestly vestments, which represent a life of virtue. Taking the blue colour of the priestly robe as his cue (MT Exod. 28.31, LXX 28.27), he writes:

> One who intends to become a priest of God ... should not damage the soul with the thick and fleshy clothing of ordinary living, but by purity of life should make all his pursuits as delicate as the thread of a spider's web, and come close to that which ascends and is light and airy.[51]

---

[46]Colossians 2.9, quoted in Gregory of Nyssa, *Vit. Moys.* 2.177. See also Exodus 40.34, John 1.16, Colossians 1.19.

[47]Gregory of Nyssa, *Vit. Moys.* 2.177; author's translation. See also Proverbs 3.19, Wisdom 1.7, John 1.3, Colossians. 1.16.

[48]Gregory of Nyssa, *Vit. Moys.* 2.175; author's translation. See also Ecclesiasticus 24.10, John 1.14. For more detail on these overlapping pictures of Christ as tabernacle, see Ann Conway-Jones, *Gregory of Nyssa's Tabernacle Imagery in Its Jewish and Christian Contexts* (Oxford: Oxford University Press, 2014), 97–104.

[49]Colin W. Macleod, 'Allegory and Mysticism in Origen and Gregory of Nyssa', *Journal of Theological Studies* 22, no. 2 (1971): 362–79 (378).

[50]Gregory of Nyssa, *Vit. Moys.* 2.188; author's translation.

[51]Gregory of Nyssa, *Vit. Moys.* 2.191; author's translation.

The cleft in the rock (Exod. 33.11-23)

After the episode of the golden calf, and the smashing of the first set of tablets, Moses asked of God, 'Show me your ways' (MT Exod. 33.13)/'Disclose yourself to me' (LXX Exod. 33.13), followed in MT Exod. 33.18 by 'Show me your glory, I pray'. Some versions of the LXX translate MT 33.18, but others, notably Codex Vaticanus, repeat the request of 33.13 in 33.18.[52] Since Gregory never refers to Moses asking to see God's glory, it would seem that he has a text in which 33.18 echoes 33.13. He notices, however, a discrepancy between 33.11 and 33.13/18:

> How does someone who Scripture says saw God clearly in such divine appearances – *face to face, as a man speaks with his friend* – require that God appear to him, as though he who is always visible had not yet been seen, as though Moses had not yet attained what Scripture testifies he had indeed attained?[53]

Historical biblical scholarship views Exodus 33 as a loose collection of separate stories, with 33.7-11, in which God speaks to Moses at the tent of meeting 'face to face', unconnected to 33.12-23, in which God declares, 'you cannot see my face; for no one shall see me and live' (33.20).[54] Gregory has no such option, but uses Moses' request and God's response to generate his distinctive conception of the spiritual quest, known as *epektasis*, from the verb *epekteinō* ('to strain ahead') in Philippians 3.13. He talks of the soul 'by its desire of the heavenly things *straining ahead for what is still to come*';[55] and argues that, despite all his achievements, Moses 'still thirsts for that with which he constantly filled himself to capacity, and he asks to attain as if he had never partaken, beseeching God to appear to him, not according to his capacity to partake, but according to God's true being'.[56] In response, 'The munificence of God assented to the fulfillment of his desire, but did not promise any cessation or satiety of the desire.'[57] In Paul Rorem's words, 'Moses does behold God but with an apophatic twist.'[58]

---

[52]See Wevers, *Notes on the Greek Text of Exodus*, 551.

[53]Gregory of Nyssa, *Vit. Moys.* 2.219; *Life of Moses*, 111-12.

[54]Maybe in order to play down this contradiction, the LXX does not translate the 'face to face' of Exodus 33.11 (Hebrew *panim el panim*) by the expected *prosōpon pros prosōpon*, but by *enōpios enōpiōi*, which is what Gregory quotes.

[55]Gregory of Nyssa, *Vit. Moys.* 2.225; *Life of Moses*, 113. There are also allusions to Philippians 3.13 in *Vit. Moys.* 1.5, 2.238, 242. Gregory uses the noun *epektasis* in *Cant.* 6 (GNO 6.174.15).

[56]Gregory of Nyssa, *Vit. Moys.* 2.230; *Life of Moses*, 114.

[57]Gregory of Nyssa, *Vit. Moys.* 2.232; *Life of Moses*, 115.

[58]Paul Rorem, 'Negative Theologies and the Cross', *Harvard Theological Review* 101, no. 3–4 (2008): 451–64 (452).

Exodus envisages the glory of God as a dangerous, blinding light. Hence the warning that human beings cannot see the face of God and live. Gregory, however, turns the meaning of the verse on its head: 'The Divine is by its nature life-giving', and therefore cannot cause death.[59] Moreover, not only is The Really Real true life, it is inaccessible to our understanding. So anyone who claims that God can be known has, by definition, turned away from The Really Real, and whatever it is they have perceived will not give them life.[60] Moses, by contrast, 'is satisfied by the very things which leave his desire unsatisfied'.[61] Gregory expands on this by producing a *reductio ad absurdum* argument for divine infinity. If the divine were finite, it would be enclosed by a boundary, and therefore necessarily surrounded by something different in nature, and larger. And so, since God is beautiful/good (*kalos*), 'those who think God is bounded conclude that he is enclosed by evil'.[62] Divine infinity has consequences for the human experience of God: 'All the desire for the beautiful which is drawn towards the upward ascent never ceases in its incessant pursuit of the lovely.'[63] And therefore, 'This truly is the vision of God: never to be satisfied in the desire to see him.'[64] Desire is forever being filled by God, and expanding in response. As Lucas Francisco Mateo-Seco phrases it, 'Every acquisition of the soul, every new progress in love, immediately turns into a new starting point towards a greater desire and greater love.'[65]

Gregory emphasizes that Moses is on a never-ending journey, each step leading to a higher one.[66] He ties the infinity of God, and the consequent relentless expansion of human desire, to the 'place' mentioned in Exodus 33.21 – the place with God, he says, 'is so great that the one running in it is never able to cease from his progress'.[67] He then contrasts this ever-expanding 'place' with the stability of the 'rock', which, following Paul, he

---

[59]Gregory of Nyssa, *Vit. Moys.* 2.234; *Life of Moses*, 115.

[60]Dionysius makes a similar argument in *ep.* 1 (PTS 36.156-7); *The Letters*, 263: 'Someone beholding God and understanding what he saw has not actually seen God himself but rather something of his which has being and which is knowable.'

[61]Gregory of Nyssa, *Vit. Moys.* 2.235; *Life of Moses*, 115.

[62]Gregory of Nyssa, *Vit. Moys.* 2.237; *Life of Moses*, 116.

[63]Gregory of Nyssa, *Vit. Moys.* 2.238; *Gregory of Nyssa*, trans. Anthony Meredith (London: Routledge, 1999), 107.

[64]Gregory of Nyssa, *Vit. Moys.* 2.239; *Life of Moses*, 116.

[65]Lucas Francisco Mateo-Seco, '*Epektasis*', in *The Brill Dictionary of Gregory of Nyssa*, ed. Lucas Francisco Mateo-Seco and Giulio Maspero (Leiden: Brill, 2010), 263.

[66]Gregory summarizes Moses' life more than once, and the details are not the same each time; but what matters to him is the unrelenting sequence, and lack of finality. See Gregory of Nyssa, *Vit. Moys.* 2.228-30; 308-14; 315-17; *Cant.* 12 (GNO 6.354-7); and *Inscr.* 1.7.51-6 (GNO 5.43.20-45.4).

[67]Gregory of Nyssa, *Vit. Moys.* 2.242; *Life of Moses*, 117.

interprets as Christ.[68] The 'rock' is 'steadfast and immovable'.[69] And so we have what Gregory designates the greatest paradox of all: 'the same thing is both a standing still and a moving. ... I mean by this that the firmer and more immovable one remains in the Good, the more [one] progresses in the course of virtue.'[70] As with his interpretation of the tabernacle, he does not dwell on theological mysteries, but emphasizes the life of virtue. He ends his commentary on Exodus 33.18-23 by contrasting the 'face' which Moses does not see with the 'back' which he does. He concludes that 'to follow God wherever he might lead is to behold God ... for good does not look good in the face, but follows it'.[71] He produces several proof texts, including 'Come, follow me' from the Gospels.[72] It is participation in virtue – discipleship – which is at the heart of standing/running in the place of God, and which leads to the ultimate prize of becoming God's friend, 'the only thing worthy of honor and desire'.[73]

Transformation (Exod. 34.29-35)

Following God's promise to pass by before him, Moses ascends Mount Sinai. When he descends again, carrying a new set of tablets, something has happened to the skin of his face (Exod. 34.29). The meaning of the Hebrew verb (qrn) is obscure, given that the root usually relates to 'horn',[74] but the LXX translates it as 'was charged with glory' – Moses had come so close to God that something of the radiance of the divine glory had been transferred onto his face. In 2 Corinthians 3.7-18, Paul draws on this episode, arguing that the glory of Moses' face has been set aside for the greater, and permanent, glory of Christ. Paul's interpretation departs from Exodus, not least when he says that 'the people of Israel could not gaze at Moses' face' (2 Cor. 3.7). According to Exodus, the Israelites did see Moses' shining face as he relayed God's commandments. Only once Moses had completed his mediatorial role would he put on the veil (Exod. 34.32-35).

---

[68]Gregory of Nyssa, *Vit. Moys.* 2.244. See also 1 Corinthians 10.4.

[69]Gregory of Nyssa, *Vit. Moys.* 2.244; *Life of Moses*, 117. See also 1 Corinthians 15.58.

[70]Gregory of Nyssa, *Vit. Moys.* 2.243; *Life of Moses*, 117.

[71]Gregory of Nyssa, *Vit. Moys.* 2.252-53; *Life of Moses*, 119-20.

[72]Gregory of Nyssa, *Vit. Moys.* 2.251. See also Luke 18.22.

[73]Gregory of Nyssa, *Vit. Moys.* 2.321; *Life of Moses*, 137.

[74]Sanders uses early first-millennium Mesopotamian sources to show that 'the need to translate the term as *either* divine radiance *or* physical protuberance is merely a side-effect of our conceptual categories'. Given the ancient understanding of light as material, 'Moses' face could, quite literally, *radiate* horns'. See Seth L. Sanders, 'Old Light on Moses' Shining Face', *Vetus Testamentum* 52, no. 3 (2002): 400–6 (405).

Gregory follows Paul in telling of Moses being transformed 'to such a degree of glory that the mortal eye could not behold him'.[75] He disrupts the biblical sequence, placing Moses' transformation before, not after, his request that God might appear to him. And rather than relating the light on Moses' countenance to his personal growth in virtue, and transformation into friend of God, Gregory takes Moses as a type of Christ, 'the true Lawgiver', who 'cut the tables of human nature for himself from our earth'.[76] Elsewhere in *Life of Moses,* Moses observes figures and types of Christ: in the transformation of his right hand, the rod's changing into a snake, manna, Joshua's fighting of the Amalekites, the tabernacle, the rock on which Moses is to stand, the bunch of grapes brought back from Canaan by the spies.[77] The only other places in the treatise where he himself becomes a type of Christ is when he stretches out his hands, taken to represent the cross.[78] Here it would seem to be the influence of Paul which causes Gregory momentarily to step aside from Moses' growth in virtue into typology and Christology. For Paul's suggestion in 2 Corinthians 3.7 that Moses' glory was fading does not easily fit Gregory's presentation of the great Moses as God's servant *par excellence.* He also follows Paul's lead in denouncing the Israelites as unworthy to gaze on the glory of Moses/Christ, taking them to represent those following 'the Judaizing heresy' (i.e. Arianism).[79] But then as he turns to the episode of the cleft in the rock, he returns to Moses as 'the ardent lover of beauty' who 'longs to be filled with the very stamp of the archetype'.[80]

The fourth-century writer who embraced the possibilities of Moses' transformation was the author of *The Macarian Homilies,* for whom 'glory' (*doxa*) was a key term. He says of Moses that, during his forty-day fast on the mountain, he was sustained by heavenly food – the Word of God. 'He went up as a mere man; he descended, carrying God with him.'[81] The glory of the Spirit 'covered his countenance upon which no one could look with steadfast gaze'.[82] This, says Macarius, 'was a figure of something else'.[83] It symbolized, firstly, 'the glory of light and the spiritual

[75]Gregory of Nyssa, *Vit. Moys.* 2.217; *Life of Moses,* 111. See also *Vit. Moys.* 2.230.

[76]Gregory of Nyssa, *Vit. Moys.* 2.216; *Life of Moses,* 111. See also Exodus 34.4.

[77]Gregory of Nyssa, *Vit. Moys.* 2.26-30, 31-3, 139-40, 147-48, 174, 243-44, 268.

[78]Gregory of Nyssa, *Vit. Moys* 2.78, 151.

[79]Gregory of Nyssa, *Vit. Moys.* 2.218; *Life of Moses,* 111.

[80]Gregory of Nyssa, *Vit. Moys.* 2.231; *Life of Moses,* 114.

[81]Pseudo-Macarius, *Hom.* II 12.14; *Pseudo-Macarius: The Fifty Spiritual Homilies and the Great Letter,* trans. George A. Maloney, CWS (New York: Paulist Press, 1992), 102 – hereafter: *Homilies.*

[82]Pseudo-Macarius, *Hom.* II 5.10; *Homilies,* 74.

[83]Pseudo-Macarius, *Hom.* II 12.14; *Homilies,* 102.

delights of the Spirit which even now [true Christians] are deemed worthy to possess interiorly'.[84] And, secondly, the resurrection, when 'what the soul now stores up within shall then be revealed as a treasure and displayed externally in the body'.[85] The glory in Christian hearts will then 'cover and clothe their naked bodies. It will sweep them into Heaven and we will at last come to rest, both body and soul, with the Lord forever.'[86] He quotes Romans 8.11 as proof text: 'He shall bring to life our mortal bodies by his Spirit that dwells in us.'[87]

Macarius also brings in Jesus' transfiguration, when 'the interior glory of Christ covered his body and shone completely'. What was inside Christ became visible. And at the resurrection, 'the interior power of Christ … will be poured out exteriorly' upon the bodies of the saints. Their bodies too will be 'glorified and shine like lightening'. But in their case, it will be a second-hand glory. 'For even now at this time they are in their minds participators of [Christ's] substance and nature.' And just 'as many lamps are lighted from the one, same fire, so also it is necessary that the bodies of the saints, which are members of Christ, become the same which Christ himself is'.[88] According to Macarius, therefore, the transformation which Moses underwent represents the interior transformation of Christians, nourished, like him, on spiritual bread – a transformation fuelled by the Holy Spirit, which involves 'reflecting as in a mirror the glory of the Lord' (2 Cor. 3.18), and which will become complete at the resurrection, when it will engulf even the body. Alexander Golitzin points out that there is a doctrinal difference between Evagrius and Macarius, concerning 'the ultimate role and eschatological destiny of the body'. For Evagrius, the body has no role in the world to come, and in pure prayer too the soul regains its primordial state of disembodied *nous*. Macarius, by contrast, works within a paradigm of bodily transformation: at the *eschaton* the transfigured human being will be 'one in whom the illumined and glorified soul shares its splendor and light with the risen body'.[89] And, as Kallistos Ware argues, his understanding of prayer 'follows from this holistic and integrated anthropology'. Prayer 'must necessarily involve the total person', including the body, with its feelings

---

[84]Pseudo-Macarius, *Hom.* II 5.11; *Homilies*, 74.

[85]Pseudo-Macarius, *Hom.* II 5.8; *Homilies*, 73.

[86]Pseudo-Macarius, *Hom.* II 5.11; *Homilies*, 74.

[87]Pseudo-Macarius, *Hom.* II 5.10; *Homilies*, 74.

[88]Pseudo-Macarius, *Hom.* II 15.38; *Homilies*, 122-23.

[89]Alexander Golitzin, 'A Testimony to Christianity as Transfiguration: The Macarian Homilies and Orthodox Spirituality', in *Orthodox and Wesleyan Spirituality*, ed. S. T. Kimbrough (Crestwood, NY: St Vladimir's Seminary Press, 2002), 129–56 (131).

and senses, and the imagination.[90] Macarius therefore revels in exuberant imagery as he describes 'the excessive love and sweetness of the hidden mysteries' revealed in prayer. But he cautions that it is not sustainable to 'sit in a corner lifted up and intoxicated' when there is work to be done, such as taking care of the community or preaching the word.[91] People embraced by the Spirit and united to the grace of Christ become 'all light, all spirit, all joy, all repose, all gladness, all love, all compassion, all goodness and kindness'.[92]

In Dionysius' *Mystical Theology,* at the climax of Moses' ascent:

> He plunges into the truly mysterious darkness of unknowing. Here, renouncing all that the mind may conceive, wrapped entirely in the intangible and the invisible, he belongs completely to him who is beyond everything. Here, being neither oneself nor someone else, one is supremely united to the completely unknown by an inactivity of all knowledge, and knows beyond the mind by knowing nothing.[93]

Dionysius' understanding of 'union' has come under intense scholarly scrutiny. There have been debates over its debt to Neoplatonism, and a recovery of its potential liturgical basis, with 'union' understood not as an intense private experience of prayer, but as an account of the corporate eucharistic mysteries – the celebrant, like Moses, emerging to bring God to the people. Little attention, however, has been paid to its scriptural roots. Despite the lack of explicit reference, Dionysius' description of Moses' union with God in the darkness of unknowing would seem to be drawing on the biblical account of Moses transcending his humanity in a private theophany so intense that he comes to take on something of the divine glory. In *Divine Names*, Dionysius says that 'the most divine knowledge of God, that which comes through unknowing, is achieved in a union far beyond mind, when mind turns away from all things, even from itself, and when it is made one with the dazzling rays, being then and there enlightened by the inscrutable depth of Wisdom'.[94] When Moses was 'charged with glory' (LXX Exod. 34.29), he was experiencing the divine by participation, rather than by human knowing.

---

[90]Kallistos Ware, 'Prayer in Evagrius of Pontus and the Macarian Homilies', in *An Introduction to Christian Spirituality*, ed. Ralph Waller and Benedicta Ward (London: SPCK, 1999), 14–30 (23).

[91]Pseudo-Macarius, *Hom.* II 8. 3–4; *Homilies*, 82.

[92]Pseudo-Macarius, *Hom.* I 13.2.4; quoted Marcus Plested, *The Macarian Legacy: The Place of Macarius-Symeon in the Eastern Christian Tradition* (Oxford: Oxford University Press, 2004), 44.

[93]Pseudo-Dionysius, *MT* 1.3 (PTS 36.144); *The Mystical Theology*, 137.

[94]Pseudo-Dionysius, *DN* 7.3 (PTS 33.198); *The Divine Names*, 109.

The only way Gregory of Nyssa could make sense of LXX Exodus 33.20 – 'for a person (*anthrōpos*) shall never see my face and live' – and still affirm God to be life-giving, was to deny that human beings ever see God. The moment of finally doing so is endlessly deferred. Perfection is continuous growth into the life of God by participation in divine virtue. There is, however, another way to solve the conundrums posed by Exodus 33-34. Maybe Moses withstood what no other human being could survive because he had transcended human nature. There are indeed hints of this in Exodus: when Moses ascended Mount Sinai to collect the second set of tablets, he stayed there for forty days and forty nights neither eating bread nor drinking water (Exod. 34.28). It was after this that he descended imbued with glory. Macarius makes Moses a type of the transformation wrought in believers as they become conformed to the glory of Christ. Turner suggests that Dionysius takes the warning of Exodus 33.20 seriously:

> Denys' is a mysticism which, as the psalmist puts it, 'seeks the face of God' (Ps. 24, 6), but under the condition imposed by Exodus: 'no one may see me and live' (Exod. 33, 20). That 'death' which is the condition of 'seeing' is Denys' 'cloud of unknowing': a death in an apophatic darkness which will rise in the knowing-unknowing vision of God.[95]

According to Dionysius, for Moses to belong completely to him who is beyond everything, he had to renounce his humanity, his very being – as it were, to die.

Conclusion

A propos of mysticism in general, Steven Katz writes:

> The role of scripture, contrary to much scholarly opinion, is essential to the major mystical traditions and to the teachings and experience(s) of their leading representatives. ... The most direct evidence of this deep mystical connection to and inextricable engagement with scripture is the literature produced by the major mystical traditions themselves. This literature is not ... primarily about an independent and individual religious experience but is, rather, more often than not, composed of esoteric commentaries on canonical texts.[96]

---

[95]Turner, *The Darkness of God*, 47.
[96]Steven T. Katz, 'Mysticism and the Interpretation of Sacred Scripture', in *Mysticism and Sacred Scripture*, ed. Steven T. Katz (Oxford: Oxford University Press, 2000), 7–67 (8).

This chapter has provided ample evidence of the importance of scripture to the earliest Christian writers on prayer. Yes, they allegorized the biblical narratives; but they read the text carefully – Evagrius consulted different Greek translations, Gregory noticed the discrepancy between Exodus 33.11 and 33.13/18. Of course, they brought their own concerns to bear, including their philosophical assumptions and doctrinal commitments. As Rorem states, 'Since the (biblical) model can be shaped according to the exegete's interpretive selectivity and embellishment, it takes on the interpreter's own imprint in the retelling.'[97] But their reliance on the biblical text was not simply a marshalling of details into pre-existing schemes; it was a two-way process. The wording and imagery of the biblical text inspired creative thinking. As Macleod recognizes:

> The biblical life of Moses offers a framework and a collection of symbols within it. It stands to the allegorist as a myth to a poet or dramatist; it can both embody and shape his thought or feeling.[98]

Shape as well as embody. And the contradictions and ambiguities of the text, in particular, proved a spur to developments in mystical theology. Among the paradoxes highlighted in this chapter are 'brilliant darkness', reflecting Exodus' depiction of dangerously bright glory surrounded by a protective cloud; the 'seeing which consists in not seeing' – Moses receiving a vision of the tabernacle while enveloped in darkness; the tabernacle (and the incarnation) being 'both unfashioned and fashioned', with the Only-begotten God, who encloses everything, pitching a tent among us; the mind, with its blue luminosity, becoming 'the temple of the Holy Trinity'; the 'place' of God as the 'unlimited and infinite'; the ascent to virtue being 'both a standing still and a moving' – never-ending progress in complete stability; interior glory 'poured out exteriorly'; and knowing 'beyond the mind by knowing nothing'.[99] Such paradoxes were taken as indications that God is not subject to the rules of human logic, and that human language can never grasp the divine. Scripture gave theologians permission to work with human language and material imagery, but, thanks above all to its enigmas, the words of scripture were used to undermine confidence that the essence of God could ever be encapsulated.

---

[97]Paul Rorem, *Pseudo-Dionysius: A Commentary on the Texts and an Introduction to Their Influence* (New York: Oxford University Press, 1993), 189.
[98]Macleod, 'Allegory and Mysticism', 376.
[99]Pseudo-Dionysius, *MT* 1.1; Gregory of Nyssa, *Vit. Moys.* 2.163, 174, 175; Evagrius, *Skemmata* 34; Gregory of Nyssa, *Vit. Moys.* 2.242, 243; Pseudo-Macarius, *Hom.* II 15.38; Pseudo-Dionysius, *MT* 1.3.

Thinking particularly of *The Macarian Homilies*, Golitzin writes, 'The whole of Israel's sacred history, of God's relations with his chosen people, becomes ... for the Christian the story of the soul's relation with Christ.'[100] As we have seen, Moses' ascent of Mount Sinai was turned into an allegory of the soul's journey towards a vision of the trinitarian God. But the four authors we have considered focus on different moments of Moses' experience, and articulate the goal of Christian prayer differently. From Exodus 24.10-11, Evagrius talks of finding the sapphire blue of heaven within the mind; from 33.21-23, Gregory describes ever-expanding desire for a vision of the divine, which is true being and true life; from 34.29, Macarius envisages the resurrection body to be the outward outpouring of the glory presently possessed interiorly; again from 34.29, Dionysius writes of a union beyond human knowledge entailing the death of self. And at the same time as early Christians were looking to Moses as an exemplar for bishops or monks, Jewish communities were developing the legacy of *Mosheh Rabbeinu* – Moses our Teacher. There were mystical currents within Judaism too, exploring such themes as ascent to the celestial sanctuary, angelic liturgy, glimpses of the enthroned divine glory and the transformation of the ascending mystic.[101] According to Elliot Wolfson, 'The problem of the visionary experience of God represents one of the major axes about which the wheel of Jewish mystical speculation in its various permutations turns.'[102] The key texts of scripture, which include the visions of Isaiah and Ezekiel as well as the narrative of Moses' ascent, have not supplied definitive answers to either community in their longings to encounter the divine in prayer, but provided endless possibilities for creative reinterpretation.

---

[100]Golitzin, 'A Testimony to Christianity as Transfiguration', 133.

[101]For the way in which motifs found in Second Temple Jewish literature re-emerge in later Jewish and Christian mystical works, see Philip Alexander, *The Mystical Texts: Songs of the Sabbath Sacrifice and Related Manuscripts* (London: T&T Clark, 2006), 121–44.

[102]Elliot R. Wolfson, *Through a Speculum That Shines: Vision and Imagination in Medieval Jewish Mysticism* (Princeton, NJ: Princeton University Press, 1994), 4.

CHAPTER THREE

Transfiguring Speech: Prayer and the Psalms

KEVIN G. GROVE

The Psalter, understood by both Judaism and Christianity to be the scriptural book of prayer *par excellence*, permeates Christian theology – liturgical, academic and pastoral. The Psalms are the language of discourse with God, providing a mirror which humans individually and communally hold up in order to see themselves, creation and their Lord more clearly. These same psalms are also medicine for broken souls groaning for God's healing as mediated through the holy writ.[1] They have given voice to liturgical practices ancient and modern of both Judaism and Christianity; mark modern spiritual journeys from Merton to Bonhoeffer to Brueggeman;[2] and serve as a point of intersection of historical, mystical, political, African, liberationist, feminist,

---

[1]The scriptures generally, and specifically the Psalms, have been called 'mirror' and 'medicine' beginning with patristic thinkers (Athanasius, Basil of Caesarea, Augustine) and continuing even unto more contemporary statements on revelation, such as *Dei Verbum (Dogmatic Constitution on Divine Revelation)*, in *Vatican Council II: The Conciliar and Post Conciliar Documents*, ed. Austin Flannery (Collegeville, MN: Liturgical Press, 1975), II.7.
[2]Thomas Merton, *Praying the Psalms* (Collegeville, MN: Liturgical Press, 1956); Dietrich Bonhoeffer, *Psalms: The Prayer Book of the Bible* (Minneapolis, MN: Fortress Press, 1970); and Walter Brueggemann, *Praying the Psalms: Engaging Scripture and the Life of the Spirit* (Eugene, OR: Wipf and Stock, 2007).

ecological and critical theologies, to name but a few.[3] On account of this kaleidoscopic influence, and because psalms thread through all aspects of the theory and practice of Judaism and Christianity, it can be difficult to know how to begin to approach such a rich and diverse set of texts.

One can productively approach the Psalms as unfolding from a single question – posed equally in times ancient and modern – which both anchors the songs in their traditions and makes them present, fresh and even arresting for the contemporary interpreter. The question is: Who is speaking? The importance of this seemingly simple question becomes clear with a prominent example from Christian prayer. Christian practices of prayer with the Psalter often begin with Psalm 51.15. In the *Book of Common Prayer,* for instance, the officiant sings: 'O Lord open thou our lips'[4] (Ps. 51.15a).[5] The gathered community responds: 'And our mouth shall show forth thy praise' (Ps. 51.15b).[6] The plain sense of the text is clear. God inspires and enables the praise which the congregants' lips offer freely in return. However, the opening of Christian prayer with Psalm 51.15 is also perplexing. This verse comes not from the opening lines of this lament of repentance and request for mercy, but from the middle of the song. Additionally, the first person singular of Israel's scriptural text – 'my lips' and 'my mouth' – has become plural in its Christian liturgical usage – 'our lips' and 'our mouth'. And so, prompted by Psalm 51.15,

---

[3]See Andrew Lincoln, J. Gordon McConville and Lloyd Pietersen, ed., *The Bible and Spirituality: Exploratory Essays in Reading Scripture Spiritually* (Eugene, OR: Wipf and Stock, 2013); Johann Baptist Metz, *Faith and History in Society: Toward a Practical Fundamental Theology,* trans. J. M. Ashley (New York: Crossroad, 2007); Gustavo Guttierez, *On Job: God-Talk and the Suffering of the Innocent,* trans. Matthew J. O'Connell (Maryknoll, NY: Orbis Books, 1987); Ernesto Cardenal, *The Psalms of Struggle and Liberation* (New York: Herder and Herder, 1971); Emmanuel Katongole, *Born from Lament: The Theology and Politics of Hope in Africa* (Grand Rapids, MI: William B. Eerdmans, 2017); Melody D. Knowles, 'Feminist Interpretation of the Psalms', in *The Oxford Handbook of the Psalms,* ed. William P. Brown (Oxford: Oxford University Press, 2014), 424–36; Arthur Walker-Jones, *The Green Psalter: Resources for an Ecological Spirituality* (Minneapolis, MN: Fortress Press, 2009); and Paul Ricoeur, 'Lamentation as Prayer?', in *Thinking Biblically: Exegetical and Hermeneutical Studies,* trans. David Pellauer (Chicago, IL: University of Chicago Press, 1998), 211–32.

[4]In the Hebrew Bible in English, it is common to differentiate between names of God. The tetragrammaton, *YHWH,* is supplied as LORD in small caps. *Elohim* is denoted 'Lord'. I follow that convention throughout. For considerations of the theological impact of the documentary hypothesis on the Psalter, see Samuel Terrien, *The Psalms: Strophic Structure and Theological Commentary* (Grand Rapids, MI: William B. Eerdmans, 2003).

[5]In the 1662 *Book of Common Prayer,* this call and response is found in both morning and evening prayer. In the Roman Catholic *Divine Office,* it marks the invitatory of the first office of the day.

[6]On account of the translation's enduring prominence in English liturgies, the psalm translations throughout are from the AV unless otherwise noted.

the question 'who is speaking?' quickly multiplies. Is it the voice of Israel reflecting on its sixth-century BCE exile? Is it the voice of the church – the call and response of officiant and congregation? Is it the voice of a solitary speaker or reader? The answer to this question, not only for Psalm 51.15 but also for the rest of psalmody, is the heart of its theology of prayer. It is a prosopological theology of prayer.

The theology of the Psalms emerges from speaking another's words as one's own.[7] In this way, psalms are 'prosopological', or personal, from the Greek word *prosopon*, meaning 'person'. *Prosopopoeia*, in Greek, or *fictiones personarum*, in Latin, is a rhetorical device through which one speaks in the voice of another. It is a form of figurative speech that classical rhetoricians like Cicero and Quintilian thought ought to be employed cautiously on account of its effects. The one who employed *prosopopoeia*, according to Cicero, in addition to needing a strong set of lungs, had to be aware of its power: to assail one's political enemies by taking up their voices, and to give speech to states, cities and peoples.[8] Quintilian went so far as to suggest that *prosopopoeia* had the power to summon down the gods from heaven and the power to raise the dead.[9] Scholars of rhetoric have long considered the Psalms as the scriptural songs where this rhetorical tool is particularly vibrant and visible. Philip Sidney, the Elizabethan poet and literary critic, wrote of David, and therein the Psalms: 'For what else is the awaking his musical instruments, the often and free changing of persons, his notable *prosopopoeias*, when he maketh you, as it were, see God coming in His majesty, his telling of the beasts' joyfulness, and hills leaping.'[10] Examining the Psalms through rhetorical *prosopopoeia* adds precision to the way in which the question 'who is speaking?' might be answered. Now, answering the question 'who is speaking?' includes in whose voice, about whom and for whom?

These questions displace the reader or speaker by presenting at least three possible voices beyond one's immediate self. To say, 'O Lord open thou our lips and our mouth shall show forth thy praise' is to speak first in the voice of Israel at prayer. Second, Christians understand the Psalms as words of Jesus Christ and so speaking the Psalms is speaking in the voice of Christ and his

---

[7]See Kevin Grove, '"The Word Spoke in Our Words That We Might Speak in His": Augustine, the Psalms and the Poetry of the Incarnate Word', in *Poetic Revelations: Power of the Word III*, ed. Mark S. Burrows, Jean Ward, and Małgorzata Grzegorzewska (London: Routledge, 2017), 29–42.

[8]Cicero, *Orator*, 25.85-87 (LCL 342).

[9]Quintilian, *Institutio Oratoria*, 9.2.29-31 (LCL 124).

[10]Philip Sidney, *An Apology for Poetry (Or the Defense of Poesy)* (Manchester: Manchester University Press, 2002), 84.22-25.

body the church. Finally, the different voices of the worshipping community remind the speaker that it is not only his or her voice which shows forth God's praise, but the voice of a single and united 'mouth'. All three of these voices require further explanation, for all of them sound simultaneously in the prosopology of psalmody.

Israel's Voice

The Psalms ensure that the voice of Israel continues to speak its relation with God. Israel's single voice is inclusive of many historical voices. Using the example of Psalm 51, the song opens with an inscription. For some psalms these inscriptions are likely to have been musical instruction for voicing during common prayer. In this instance, the first line mentions choral direction, 'for the leader', and the second is likely the work of a post-exilic redactor connecting the song explicitly with David. Together, these two lines of the psalm read 'For the leader. A psalm of David, when Nathan the prophet came to him after he had gone in to Bathsheba' (Ps. 51.1-2).[11] It might be easy for a contemporary reader to dismiss the inscription altogether, skipping ahead to the poetry. But, these inscriptions frequently identify some aspect or disposition of Israel's voice. For this reason, the church fathers considered these inscriptions as doorways or entrances to particular psalms. The value of the inscription for Psalm 51 is that it is remarkably specific. David slept with Bathsheba, had her husband Uriah the Hittite placed in battle so as to be killed and was confronted in his sin by Nathan the prophet (2 Sam. 11-12). David responded frankly to Nathan, 'I have sinned against the LORD' (2 Sam. 12.13). By this inscription opening one of the most famous of penitential psalms, the reader of Psalm 51 is directed to reflect on the voice of David: the voice of one of God's elect – the unlikely, ruddy, youngest brother – who had been the anointed leader of Israel. In considering the voice of David from the account of 2 Samuel 11-12, the post-exilic editor of Psalm 51 accomplishes three things. First, the reader can recall David's sin through the psalm. Second, in recalling the history of the anointed's plea for mercy in David, it opens the reader up to consider other examples of Israel seeking mercy, most prominently in the Babylonian exile. Thirdly, the reader can recall his or her own sin as related to both David and events like the Babylonian exile.

---

[11]In some Bibles these inscriptions are considered the first verses of the psalm, in others they appear as inscriptions without verse number.

With the voices of the inscription in place, the poetry immediately speaks multivalently. The first verses of the psalm are a request for mercy upon the admission of sin: 'Have mercy upon me, O God' (Ps. 51.1). And, the theme continues: 'For I acknowledge my transgressions: and my sin is ever before me' (Ps. 51.3). The first action of *prosopopoeia* here is the desire for God's mercy and the admission of guilt. In expressing it, the singer takes up David's voice and Israel's voice in addition to the singer's own.

The second aspect of speaking in another's voice in Psalm 51 is that the addressee is God. The intimate request of the penitential psalm is for total restoration: God's face turned from the sinner's iniquity, the blotting out of sin and a clean heart created within the speaker. The prayer of Psalm 51 is for a complete restoration of the purity of the individual penitent – offered through a sacrifice of a contrite spirit and not a burnt offering – unto a renewed life of gladness, thanksgiving and joy.

The restoration of the individual has communal consequences. The speaker of the psalm also promises: 'I teach transgressors thy ways; and sinners shall be converted unto thee' (Ps. 51.13). The one who prays Psalm 51 is not left by himself or herself. The speaker is drawn outwards to the unrighteous, to others who have sinned. The psalm ends with prayers for Zion, the rebuilding of the walls of Jerusalem, and the Lord's being pleased with the burnt offerings of the temple cult offered now by those with clean and renewed hearts (Ps. 51.18-19).

The voice of Psalm 51 takes up not only the sin of an individual speaker, but also hearkens back to the sin of David, renews the sinner, promises the teaching of others in order that they might return to God and even suggests the eventual purification of intention and acceptability of all worship in the temple cult. Thus, the voice of Israel, here demonstrated in a single psalm, is multilayered. The voice is the individual and the community praying in the present at the same time as it makes reference to persons in the tradition such as David. This voice further involves the historical redaction and prayer intentions of the communal voice in other eras such as the post-exilic period where prayers for the temple might have been added to the text.

Psalm 51 has provided but a single example of the multiplicity of voices within Israel when one speaks a psalm. There are many more voices within Israel. In other psalms these voices are the praising voices of the children of Adam (Ps. 107.8). One recalls with praise the Lord's mercies upon Abraham, Isaac, Jacob and Moses (e.g. Pss. 103, 105, 106, 115). One experiences the wicked laying snares (Ps. 119), the betrayal of friends, the conquest of enemies, exile in Egypt (e.g. Pss. 78, 105, 106), the utter darkness of sickness and death (Ps. 88), the fresh waters of repose (Ps. 23) and the heights of doxology inspired by the memory that God's goodness extends to the ends of the earth (Ps. 150).

The Psalms, then, represent a multiplicity of voices sounding at the same time, because Israel has spoken – and continues to speak – in as many voices. Inasmuch as those voices remain in relation to one another and their Lord, they further hold forth the promise that a diversity of voices across time and history might relate with intimacy to the God who journeys with them throughout.

Christ's Voice

Jesus of Nazareth spoke with yet another Jewish voice trained in the practice of psalmody. As a boy from Nazareth whom Luke the evangelist described as opening scrolls in synagogues (Lk. 4.17-21), Jesus would have grown up with the Psalms as his own prayer. In that way, Jesus himself would have experienced the various emotional intimacies and voices of the Psalms as discussed in terms of Israel's voice. Jesus, however, reshaped how Christians would take up the voices of the Psalms because of the manner of his crying out in one of them at the moment of his death.

In both the Markan (15.34) and Matthean (27.46) gospel accounts, the crucified Jesus cries out in a loud voice at the ninth hour '*Eloi eloi lama sabachtani*', that is to say, 'My God, my god, why hast thou forsaken me?' The gospel writers render this phrase first in Aramaic and then translate it into Greek, evidence already that the verses of psalmody crossed linguistic borders in Jesus' time. At the level only of the narrative itself, the citation is remarkable. At this most devastating moment, the Matthean and Markan Christ might have said other words: a more comforting phrase of psalmody, a prophecy, an evocation of his preaching, something like the Lukan account of a dialogue with the criminals at Jesus' right and left (Lk. 23.39-43), or the Johannine 'It is finished' (Jn 19.30). Or, this moment of the crucifixion would have been an excellent moment to produce an entirely original cry. But, in the Matthean and Markan texts, Jesus' final line is not an innovation. It is a quotation of the many voices of Israel: 'My God, my God, why hast thou forsaken me?' It is his cry of dereliction as it was the psalmist's and Israel's.

Jesus' citation of Psalm 22 posed a serious exegetical question of early Christians that reframed how Christians would pray the Psalms as a whole. The issue concerns the natures of Christ as fully human and fully divine. As patristic exegetes struggled to come to terms with the proper articulation of Christ's two natures, it remained problematic that one fully human and fully divine might claim to be abandoned by God. If it were the case that Jesus was not abandoned by God, as patristics scholar Michael Cameron points out, God could be cast as a divine ventriloquist.[12] Divinity would be instrumentalizing Jesus' humanity as if it were a cheap puppet, crying out in an insincere dereliction that did not reflect the full appreciation of the devastation of that moment. On the other hand, if Jesus were truly abandoned by God, then by definition he must not have been fully divine. His psalm citation just before his death presented Jesus' Christian followers in the first centuries with a charged exegetical difficulty, the explanation for which could undercut theologies of either Jesus' divinity or his humanity, respectively.

One of the ways in which Christian thinkers – famously Augustine for Latin Christianity – parsed this issue was through *prosopopoeia*. The logic works as follows: in the incarnation, the second person of the Trinity emptied himself and assumed the form of a human. Like unto other humans in all things but sin, Jesus of Nazareth had a human voice, friends, tears and emotions. In that way, Jesus also took up human life at its furthest point from God: abandonment or forsakenness on the cross. In taking up human existence in that limit experience, Jesus spoke in human words in order that humans might speak in his. No longer would the experience of abandonment be suffered alone. Those who cry out in the words of Psalm 22 are crying out in his words, in him. Jesus does not eliminate the pain and agony of the human condition of abandonment. He joins humans in it and forever changes abandonment after him such that humans who cry out in abandonment might cry out in his voice, in him.

Augustine described this as the marvellous exchange when Christ cries out in a human voice the agony of dereliction. In fact, Augustine called this high point of *prosopopoeia* an act of transfiguration: the 'marvellous exchange' in which Christ received insults but bestowed honours, drank the cup of suffering but offered salvation, and experienced death only to give life.[13] From then on, Christ the head would transfigure the cries of the members

---

[12]Michael Cameron, *Christ Meets Me Everywhere: Augustine's Early Figurative Exegesis* (New York: Oxford University Press, 2012), 185.

[13]Augustine, *En Ps.* 30, 2.3. For translations of Augustine's commentary of the Psalms, see *Expositions of the Psalms*, 6 vols., trans. Maria Boulding, WSA III/15-20 (Hyde Park, NY: New City Press, 2004). For this exchange of voices with Christ in the Psalms – called the *Christus totus* – in Augustine's writings, see Tarsicius van Bavel, 'The "Christus Totus" Idea: A Forgotten Aspect of Augustine's Spirituality', in *Studies in Patrsitic Christology*, ed. Thomas Finan and Vincent Twomey (Dublin: Four Courts Press, 1998), 84–94.

of his body by means of his own voice.[14] Christ the head and his body the members could speak with one voice, as one whole Christ. That voice, a single voice of a single body with Christ as head and human persons as members, emerged from Christ's praying a psalm at the hour of his death. The result of this exchange of voices with Christ makes possible praying with even the most difficult of the Psalms – the dark places of lament and the feeling of hopelessness in Psalm 88, the enduring intimacy of being itself as sustained by love in Psalm 139, the hymn of thanksgiving for the Exodus or the exilic tears from the rivers of Babylon of Psalm 137. One might not feel in oneself the need to lament of utter darkness. But, in some part of Christ's body, there are others in need of words of lament. And, inasmuch as one prays the Psalms in Christ – no matter how a particular image or emotion might seem distant or strange – one prays the Psalms with and in others, whose experiences and lives might be just as distant. In this dynamic exchange of prayer, the many find their voices to be one in Christ.

Once Christ had taken up this human voice, he never ceased to speak in it. Exegetes like Augustine noticed that after the ascension Christ still referred to the cry of the persecuted on earth through the referent 'me'.[15] For instance, when the voice, which identified itself as Jesus, cried out to Saul on the road to Damascus, 'Saul, Saul, why are you persecuting me?', the voice of Jesus Christ, ascended into heaven, was continuing to speak in the experience of his members, in this case their experience of persecution (Acts 9.4). Jesus does not speak of his members, his saints, his holy ones or his followers. He refers to the persecuted as 'me'.

---

[14]For foundational works on prosopological exegesis in early Christianity, including Augustine, see Andreas Andreopoulos, Augustine Casiday and Carol Harrison, ed., *Meditations of the Heart: The Psalms in Early Christian Thought and Practice* (Turnhout: Brepols, 2011); Brian Daley, 'Is Patristic Exegesis Still Usable? Reflections on Early Christian Interpretation of the Psalms', *Communio* 29, no. 1 (2002): 185–216; Brian E. Daley and Paul R. Kolbet, ed., *The Harp of Prophecy: Early Christian Interpretation of the Psalms* (Notre Dame, IN: University of Notre Dame Press, 2015); Hubertus Drobner, *Person-exegese un Christologie bei Augustinus: zur Herkunft der Formel 'Una Persona'* (Leiden: Brill, 1986); Michael Fiedrowicz, *Psalmus Vox Totius Christi: Studien zu Augustins 'Enarrationes in Psalmos'* (Freiburg: Herder, 1997); Michael McCarthy, 'An Ecclesiology of Groaning: Augustine, the Psalms, and the Making of Church', *Theological Studies* 66, no. 1 (2005): 23–48; David Meconi, 'Becoming Gods by Becoming God's: Augustine's Mystagogy of Identification', *Augustinian Studies* 39, no. 1 (2008): 61–74; David Meconi, *The One Christ: Augustine's Theology of Deification* (Washington, DC: Catholic University of America Press, 2013); Joseph Ratzinger, *Volk Und Haus Gottes in Augustins Lehre Von Der Kirche* (St Ottilioen: EOS-Verlag, 1992); Marie-Josèphe Rondeau, *Les Commentaires Patristiques du Psautier*, vols. 1–2 (Rome: Orientalium, 1982); and Rowan Williams, 'Augustine and the Psalms', *Interpretation* 58, no. 1 (2004): 17–27.

[15]Augustine, *En Ps. 30*, 2.3.

This union of voices and persons shaped early Christian life, including its social teaching and action. It is unsurprising to see, for instance, the citation of Matthew 25.21-46 alongside reflections on the members recognizing, speaking in and hearing the voice of the head who has gone before them. Taking up Christ's voice requires recognizing the need to welcome the stranger, feed the hungry, give drink to the thirsty, clothe the naked, care for the ill and visit the imprisoned. For members of the early church, the correspondence of voices spoken in prayer and sung together was to yield concrete action within the body of Christ.[16]

In this way, Christ transfigured the manner in which psalms would be interpreted by Christians who continued to pray the prayer book of Israel. In the first instance, if Christ prayed the Psalms as his own, then one can examine psalms as the voice of Christ. For this reason, scholars have looked for different prepositional voices of Jesus Christ in the Psalms. Is the voice praying in the psalm the voice of Christ the head? Is it the voice of the members among themselves? Is it Christ the head speaking through the members of his body?[17] These prepositional manifestations of relation between the head and the body, however, do not diminish but only increase the deep mysticism in psalms for Christians – that taking up the prayer of psalmody is the word by word transfiguration of the members of Christ's body by their head. In their crying out, lamenting, praising and even groaning, the members of Christ's body are becoming ever more configured both to their head who has gone before them and to one another.

The Individual and the Common Voice

Because psalms structured the prayer of Israel and marked the life and death of Jesus of Nazareth, they also structure the life of the church of Jesus Christ. One has to learn to speak, and psalms provide words of praise with multivalent meanings. Learning to speak is the work of individuals as well as communities. I will present each of these through an example which continues to have enduring impact. For the individual, I will use Augustine of Hippo, whose own confession, or speech of union with God, is presented

---

[16]In the early church one can see this sort of christological exegesis: from the third century in Ignatius of Antioch, Justin Martyr, Irenaeus, Tertullian, Cyprian, Clement of Alexandria and Origen; and, from the fourth century in Athanasius, Basil of Caesarea, Gregory of Nazianzus, Gregory of Nyssa, John Chrysostom, Hilary of Poitiers, Jerome and Ambrose of Milan. A famous twentieth-century theologian who follows a similar exegetical trajectory is Dietrich Bonhoeffer in both *Psalms: The Prayer Book of the Bible* and *Life Together* (New York: Harper and Row, 1954).

[17]See Fiedrowicz, *Psalmus Vox Totius Christi*.

to his readers in the language of psalmody.[18] Concerning the communal, I will point to Benedict of Nursia, whose rule for monks continues to shape the life of prayer for Western Christianity. Though the following treatment can only be cursory, these two thinkers represent watershed advances in Christian practice of prayer with psalmody.

One antecedent comment is necessary by way of introduction to both. Augustine and Benedict each speak extensively of humility as requisite for praying psalms.[19] For Augustine, this came in his own story, in realizing that by his own strength he could not reach God but rather that he needed to see his God grown weak at his feet and humbly cast himself down upon the flesh of Christ. Christ's rising would lift Augustine as well.[20] Benedict describes a ladder – twelve steps – of humility before he instructs his followers on the manner and method of using psalms.[21] For both of these practitioners, psalms could in no way be understood or prayed fully by the proud or the haughty. But, for the humble, both individually and communally, they became speech to, with and in God.

Augustine

Perhaps most famously on account of the continuing influence of his *Confessions*, Augustine of Hippo provides one of the most enduring examples of a life refashioned and sustained by psalmody. For, as he recounts, in his early years as a rhetorician he was repulsed by the language of scripture.[22] The Latin was simple and ordinary. Augustine, as a young man, could not speak in the words of Israel or of Jesus Christ because he found those words lacking in aesthetic and rhetorical appeal. They were unattractive and simple.

Augustine's own story is one of learning to speak the narrative of his own life as a life with and in God. This meant that he had to learn to speak a second time. It has not surpassed scholars' notice that at the time of Augustine's conversion, in a garden recalling Eden, he throws himself down under a tree, speechless on account of a voice choked with tears.[23] His

---

[18]Augustine defines 'confession' as the act of uniting oneself to Christ in *En Ps.* 75.

[19]Concerning both Augustine and Benedict on prayer and the Psalms, see Jonathan D. Teubner, *Prayer after Augustine: A Study in the Development of the Latin Tradition* (Oxford: Oxford University Press, 2018).

[20]Augustine, *Confessions*, trans. Henry Chadwick (Oxford: Oxford University Press, 1998), VII.18.24.

[21]Benedict, *Rule* 7; *The Rule of St Benedict*, ed. Timothy Fry (Collegeville, MN: Liturgical Press, 1981).

[22]Augustine, *Confessions*, III.5.9.

[23]Janet Soskice, 'Monica's Tears: Augustine on Words and Speech', *New Blackfriars* 83, no. 980 (2002): 448–58.

eventual rising and reading was to the scriptures. He would learn to speak again, anew, this time not primarily with his own words but with the very words that he had rejected when he was younger. And so, the conversion of Augustine is marked not only by learning to speak again, but specifically learning to speak the language of scripture.

From that garden in Milan, Augustine retreated with his friends to Cassiciacum where he did two things. He retired from being a 'salesman of words in the markets of rhetoric',[24] and with his friends in community he learned to speak the language of psalmody. Augustine writes: 'My God, how I cried to you when I read the Psalms of David, songs of faith, utterances of devotion which allow no pride of spirit to enter in! I was but a beginner in authentic love of you.'[25] Augustine wrote that the Psalms literally were changing him.[26] Augustine realized: 'As I read, I was set on fire, but I did not discover what to do for the deaf and dead of whom I had been one, when I was a plague, a bitter and blind critic barking at the scriptures which drip with the honey of heaven and blaze with your light.'[27]

Augustine's Cassiciacum insight bore three practical consequences for him as an individual who learned to speak the words of prayer through psalms. First, he found that the most authentic expression of his own union with God necessitated the language of the Psalter. The *Confessions* are the retelling of his own story of relation with God in terms of the scriptures. The Psalms dominate Augustine's language for this project. They are the register he chooses for exploring his relationship to God. Second, Augustine preached on psalms, or wrote commentaries on others, for nearly forty years after he was ordained and started to preach. The Psalms were his constant spiritual companion, the subject matter of his catecheses and the texts which he requested to be pasted up near his bed as he breathed his last.[28] Until modern times it was his *Expositions of the Psalms* which were his most widely reproduced and circulated works. Finally, Augustine came to describe human life – and the passing of time – like unto the recitation of a familiar psalm.[29] Augustine's restless heart searching for God (Ps. 62) had found expression not only for the angst of his unrest (Pss. 6, 35, 55, 69, 79), but also for the expectation of future peace (Pss. 4, 67, 104) in the words of psalmody. Psalms were not simply for memorization, but for

---

[24]Augustine, *Confessions*, IX.2.2.
[25]Augustine, *Confessions*, IX.4.8.
[26]See Williams, 'Augustine and the Psalms', 17–27.
[27]Augustine, *Confessions*, IX.4.11.
[28]Augustine's death is recounted by Possidius in *Vita Augustini*, 31.2; *The Life of Saint Augustine*, trans. Matthew O'Connell (Villanova, PA: Augustinian Press, 1988), 129.
[29]Augustine, *Confessions*, XI.28.38.

the life well lived.[30] In the Psalms, Augustine found one who would heal all iniquities. They provided him with the expressions for a communal life in Christ – praising and groaning,[31] labouring and resting,[32] remembering and forgetting,[33] lamenting and spiritual ascending.[34] Psalms gave Augustine the mode of confession, of the speech that unites the voices of God and humanity.

Benedict

Benedict's *Rule* for monks establishes a common life for Christians who wish to listen with the ears of their hearts to the principles of Christ. The first word of the *Rule* is an imperative form of the verb *auscultare*, 'to listen'.[35] Only a few lines later, Benedict describes what it is that the monk might hear once he has awoken and risen: he will 'hear the divine voice, calling and exhorting us daily: "Today if you shall hear his voice, harden not your hearts"' (Ps. 95.7-8).[36] In other words, once one has heeded the command to listen, the voice which one hears is speaking the language of psalmody. Of the scriptural references in the prologue to the *Rule*, psalms make eight appearances in a short segment of text.[37] In fact, the recitation of the various psalms that mark the day (what came to be known as the divine office) take up chapters 8–20 of the 73 chapters of the *Rule,* with references back to chapters 8–20 in still other places. Prayer, and specifically communal prayer composed of psalmody, is the most extensively treated aspect of Benedictine life together – more so than the selection of leadership, the apportioning of food, labour and even resolution of conflict.

Much of the *Rule* simply indicates which psalms are to be recited at various prayers throughout the day and night. For instance, Benedict writes that the versicle from Psalm 51, 'O Lord open thou our lips', is to open the night office.[38] Though many prescriptions are provided – sensitive to feria and feasts, summer and winter, saints' days and size of community – the

---

[30]Augustine, *En Ps.* 102.
[31]See Augustine's commentary on Psalms 31, 94, 95, 101, 105, and 125. See also Jason Byassee, *Understanding Praise Seeking Understanding: Reading the Psalms with Augustine* (Grand Rapids, MI: William B. Eerdmans, 2007).
[32]See Augustine's commentary on Psalms 54, 92, 93, and 114.
[33]See Augustine's commentary on Psalms 37, 39, 75, and 136.
[34]See below.
[35]Benedict, *Rule*, prologue.
[36]Benedict, *Rule*, prologue.
[37]The references come from Psalms 95, 34, 15, and 115.
[38]Benedict, *Rule* 9.

most important matter is the praying of the entire Psalter.[39] Benedict writes that all 150 psalms must be prayed during the week so that at Sunday Matins the series may start afresh. He admonishes:

> For monks who in a week's time say less than the full psalter with the customary canticles betray extreme indolence and lack of devotion in their service. We read, after all, that our holy Fathers, energetic as they were, did all this in a single day. Let us hope that we, lukewarm as we are, can achieve it in a whole week.[40]

Reciting all 150 psalms was not merely a labour among others, but the speaking as fully as possible the prayers of union with God. Benedict establishes the weekly recitation of the Psalms a minimum for those who cannot pray the psalmody in full each day.[41] He makes such provisions, however, because the *Rule*, after all, is only for beginners in the spiritual life.[42] In our time, praying 150 psalms in a week – let alone a day – might seem a great labour. For Benedict it was the foundational activity of one who sought to listen to God.

Why a community life structured by the Psalms? Benedict is convinced that God's presence is everywhere.[43] The continued prayer of psalms brings to the front of one's consciousness their place in the sight of God and of his angels.[44] Praying psalms throughout the day is precisely a lifting of one's earthly vision. The various movements of individual psalms speak to different parts of the action of praise. One may not feel like lamenting on a given Friday evening, but somewhere in horizon of creation that seeks God, another – connected in Christ – is lamenting. Inasmuch as one prays in communion in Christ, one prays in and for that other. The same is true for praising and groaning, labouring and resting. The psalms do not divide, but unite voices across experience and expression into a communion meant to be present to the vision of God. Benedict structured the communal Christian life around this union of voices earthly and divine.

---

[39]Benedict, *Rule* 18.
[40]Benedict, *Rule* 18.
[41]Benedict, *Rule* 18.
[42]Benedict, *Rule* 73.
[43]Benedict, *Rule* 19.
[44]Benedict, *Rule* 19.

Antiphonal Exercise and Increased Understanding

In the first section we considered the voices who speak – Israel, Christ and the church – in praying the Psalms. There is an additional mode of union in praying psalms that emerges from a sort of poetic dialogue.[45] It unfolds from the poetry itself and is further enacted by antiphonal prayer.

At the level of the texts themselves, the Psalms are written in a style of Hebrew poetry in which an image is repeated in a slightly altered form. This parallelism happens within couplets, and sometimes triplets. For instance, consider:

Praise ye the LORD from the heavens:
praise him in the heights.
Praise ye him, all his angels:
praise ye him, all his hosts.

(Ps. 148.1-2)

The image of heaven is seconded by heights, angels by hosts. These couplets form a liturgical and repetitive way of deepening understanding of the same idea during prayer. Another example speaks of God's action,

Except the LORD build the house,
they labour in vain that build it:
except the LORD keep the city,
the watchman waketh but in vain.

(Ps. 127.1)

The image of the house in the first phrase maps onto the city in the second. Likewise the labour of the builder is parallel to the watching of the sentinel.

This poetic structure has liturgical consequences. Couplets naturally gave rise in prayer to voices speaking with and to one another. Two persons or

---

[45]See Walter Brueggemann, 'Psalms as Subversive Practice of Dialogue', in *Diachronic and Synchronic: Reading the Psalms in Real Time*, ed. Joel S. Burnett, William H. Bellinger, Jr., and W. D. Tucker (London: T&T Clark, 2007), 3–25; Walter Brueggemann and William H. Bellinger, Jr., *Psalms, New Cambridge Bible Commentary* (Cambridge: Cambridge University Press, 2014); F. W. Dobbs-Allsopp, 'Poetry of the Psalms', in *The Oxford Handbook of the Psalms*, ed. William P. Brown (Oxford: Oxford University Press, 2014), 79–98. Sigmund Mowinckel treats metre, person and form in *The Psalms in Israel's Worship*, trans. D. R. Ap-Thomas (Grand Rapids, MI: William B. Eerdmans, 2004). Cas J. A. Vos applies this poetical construction to Christian preaching in *Theopoetry of the Psalms* (London: T&T Clark, 2005).

two groups might pray antiphonally, that is one after and in response to the other:

> Except the LORD build the house,
> they labour in vain that build it.

And then:

> except the LORD keep the city,
> the watchman waketh but in vain.

In this act, human voices praying the same song perform a dialogue – clarifying, enhancing and building on the same themes through repeated imagery. This form of recitation brings voices into harmony not through speaking in union, but speaking complementarily.

Often a deepened meaning or understanding is added by the second image of a couplet. Consider this section of Psalm 62, a song of trust:

> My soul, wait thou only upon God;
> for my expectation is from him.
> He only is my rock and my salvation:
> he is my defence; I shall not be moved.
> In God is my salvation and my glory:
> the rock of my strength, and my refuge, is in God.
> Trust in him at all times;
> ye people, pour out your heart before him:
> God is a refuge for us.

> (Ps. 62.5-8)

The parallelisms provide clarifications and additions. In verse 5 the waiting of the soul only for God is possible because of the second phrase that expectation itself comes from God. In verse 6, the consequence of God's being a rock of salvation is discovered in the next phrase when the one praying claims stability on account of God as rock. In verses 7 and 8, trust in God as a refuge is an image refined by the action of pouring out one's heart – the centre of one's self – before God.

These lines of Psalm 62 in and of themselves are powerful poetry. The addition of antiphonal recitation, which perdures in Christian practice to the present, reminds the reader not only that the Psalms' original setting was liturgical, but also that the practice of recitation is not merely a decorative afterthought but the lived performance of the structure of the songs themselves. By antiphonal recitation of psalms, those who pray together give tone and sound to the word from any variety of voices, angles and musical settings.

A striking example of the psalmody as this type of dialogical exercise is evidenced in architecture. In East Anglia, England, Ely Cathedral rises out of the fens as if a ship floating upon drained tracts of agricultural land. The cathedral, with roots in the seventh-century monastic foundation of Etheldreda, is the site of a long-standing tradition of the recitation of psalms. Notably, above the centre of the great cathedral is an eight-sided lantern, a high-medieval architectural wonder added to the building after a tragic collapse of part of the edifice in 1322. The existence of this lantern, supported by massive wooden timbers and allowing natural light to flood the centre of the church below, is not merely aesthetic. The architecture expands the horizon of prayer vertically. The panels of the lantern opened such that those standing around the oculus could look down over the centre of the church. Thus, in addition to the psalms of the cathedral office being prayed antiphonally across the centre aisle, they could also be prayed vertically with voices both high in the lantern near the windows and down on the ground below. The dialogue of the Psalms was used creatively to bridge all types of human realities, the two sides of a choir joined not only east and west, north and south, but also heaven above and earth below.

Certainly those praying the office in Ely Cathedral's lantern knew that they were not in heaven when they climbed up through the rafters and heights in order to sing strophes of psalmody antiphonally with those down below. Yet, this liturgical action was a physical performance and reminder of the transformation that psalms were bringing about in them. Their ongoing dialogue of psalmody was the speaking of prayers unto, with and in God in heaven while speaking unto, with and in one another on earth.

One cannot here treat sufficiently the manner and diversity of dialogues which the Psalms have inspired in liturgical prayer. It is only possible to mark that they do. Psalms have united voices in dialogues of lament and doxologies of praise. These voices have come from different angles, groups, sung voice parts and human conditions. But, the exercises themselves often mimic the doubled and parallel poetic structure of the Psalms. While an individual is never prevented from praying the words of a familiar psalm on his or her own, the parallel structure of psalms and various forms of their antiphonal recitation by liturgical communities have long animated and continue to inspire the prayer of Christian churches.

A Pilgrimage of Spiritual Ascent

In this final section, I draw attention to the theme of pilgrimage through a subset of psalms called the 'Songs of Ascent' (Pss. 120-134).[46] This final section integrates the two sections – unions of speaking voices and of dialogue in antiphonal performance – treated above.

The fifteen psalms of ascent were likely prayed for a particular purpose. As communities of Jewish people made their way to Jerusalem for festivals, they had to climb up the hills in order to reach the holy city. Regardless whence they came, they were ascending in order to reach their destination. As they walked, so also they sang. Physical ascent up roads and paths became the upward movement of spiritual ascent. Further, physical words gave voice to the disposition of the pilgrim's heart.

Of tantamount importance is that these psalms of ascent were enacted communally. While they might have the first person singular as a subject, the pilgrimage to Jerusalem was undertaken by families and villages of people. By singing about the steps that the psalmist was taking, the people climbing to Jerusalem were singing about their own steps. Other ascent models in the ancient world were more individuated. Examples from Hellenic philosophy include those of Plato's *Republic* or *Phaedrus* and Plotinus' *Enneads*. The one who leaves Plato's cave may have received help in order to make it up to the sun, but there is antagonism in the Platonic text between the individual who contemplates the good and the others in the cave.[47] Likewise when one contemplates the Plotinian one, having left behind earthly distraction, he or she does this alone.[48] In the psalm texts, however, the communal practice of spiritual exercise is the setting of these ascents as they were prayed.

In this way, when the psalmist prays, 'I will lift up mine eyes unto the hills, from whence cometh my help' (Ps. 121.1), the first-person voice of the psalmist is the voice of each and all of the climbers of the hills of Jerusalem. Further, their ascent is not merely to the city, but to the Lord: 'My help

---

[46]Concerning use in Christian praxis see also Paul Gavrilyuk and Sarah Coakley, ed., *The Spiritual Senses: Perceiving God in Western Christianity* (Cambridge: Cambridge University Press, 2012) and Gerard McLarney, *St Augustine's Interpretation of the Psalms of Ascent* (Washington, DC: Catholic University of America Press, 2014).

[47]This example included, for Plato, a tension between the ruler and the city. Plato, *Republic*, trans. G. M. A. Grube and C. D. C. Reeve, in *Plato: Complete Works*, ed. John M. Cooper (Indianapolis, IN: Hackett, 1997), 514a–520a.

[48]Plotinus, *Enneads* 1.6 (LCL 440). Concerning Plotinus, see Pierre Hadot, *Plotinus or The Simplicity of Vision*, trans. Michael Chase (Chicago, IL: University of Chicago Press, 1998) and Michael Wakoff, 'Awaiting the Sun: A Plotinian Form of Contemplative Prayer', in *Platonic Theories of Prayer*, ed. John M. Dillon and Andrei Timotin (Leiden: Brill, 2015), 73–87.

cometh from the Lord, which made heaven and earth' (Ps. 121.2). The ascent is at the same time both physical and spiritual. It is spoken by an individual psalmist who is journeying, but it is also the song of a people who walk together. In the days of temple festivals in Judaism the ascent marked physical pilgrimage. In Christian practice, these psalms of ascent became the regular prayer of both individuals and communities who might ascend towards the Lord in their own steps. These songs of steps, ascents or *gradua* establish those who pray the Psalms in any time and place as on the same journey to Jerusalem and seeking the same encounter with the Lord there as their ancestors.

Prosopology continues to be relevant in these songs of ascent or pilgrimage. Psalm 126 shows how such a pilgrimage of freedom might unfold. The entirety of this brief psalm is as follows:

> When the LORD turned again the captivity of Zion,
> we were like them that dream.
> Then was our mouth filled with laughter,
> and our tongue with singing:
> then said they among the heathen,
> The LORD hath done great things for them.
> The LORD hath done great things for us;
> whereof we are glad.
> Turn again our captivity, O LORD,
> as the streams in the south.
> They that sow in tears shall reap in joy.
> He that goeth forth and weepeth,
> bearing precious seed,
> shall doubtless come again with rejoicing,
> bringing his sheaves with him.

(Ps. 126.1-6)

The Babylonian exile is not a distant reality of Israel, but a captivity personally taken up by the singers of the psalm.[49] The singer gives voice to deliverance from that experience with renewed emotion: laughter on the lips, singing on the tongue and even gladness. At verse 4, however, the psalm makes an intercessory shift: 'Turn again our captivity, O Lord, as the streams in the south.' The reference is likely to dry areas in the southern part of Israel that with conditions of rain, ran with water in the wadis again. And, the psalm

---

[49]Some commentators suggest the authors may have either been in or known those in captivity. In either interpretation, the psalm clearly addresses the moment of liberation.

concludes with an agricultural image of fruitfulness that begins from sowing in tears. One might never have been to the streams of Israel's south, but the singers, and through them the community on pilgrimage whether ancient or modern, takes up this experience of liberation as their own journey. They anticipate returning to their homes carrying sheaves of divine beneficence.

The pilgrimage of the psalm, indeed of the psalms of ascent, is one that acknowledges difficulty, exile and even dryness, but is a pilgrimage taken together unto divine fruitfulness. These psalms not only give expression to hardship, but also open onto steps of prayer for peace (Pss. 122, 128), for mercy and forgiveness (Ps. 130), the commitment to pray for the good of the other (Ps. 122), for humble trust in God (Ps. 131) and to lift up one's hands to God in search for the Lord throughout the night (Ps. 134).

The psalms of ascent are the reminder that these are songs of a people together on pilgrimage. They have continued to be so even though those who sing them may not be walking the hills up to the physical city of Jerusalem. These songs give voice to memories of both blessings and exile; they express expectation and hope. They provide an example of speaking in the voice of another as one's own as well as a communal dialogue of prayer. But most importantly, they make the claim that the prayer of the Psalms is the prayer of those on pilgrimage. Psalms are the prayers which mark the steps of those who walk together unto a place they have not yet reached.

Conclusion

The biblical scholar Brevard Childs uses the term 'actualization' to describe the relationship between Israel and the Lord in his study on the Psalms, *Memory and Tradition in Israel*:

> Actualization is the process by which a past event is contemporized for a generation removed in time and space from the original event. When later Israel responded to the continuing imperative of her tradition through her memory, that moment in historical time likewise became an Exodus experience. Not in the sense that later Israel again crossed the Red Sea. This was an irreversible, once-for-all event. Rather, Israel entered the same redemptive reality of the Exodus generation. Later, Israel, removed in time and space from the original event, yet still in time and space, found in her tradition a means of transforming her history into redemptive history. Because the quality of time was the same, the barrier of chronological separation was overcome.[50]

---

[50]Brevard S. Childs, *Memory and Tradition in Israel* (London: SCM Press, 1962), 85.

Childs' definition of actualization helps us to come to terms with an important concern about theology and psalmody. The concern is historicity. One worries about appreciating the historical context of the writer of the psalm, the various voices of Israel who have taken it up as their own, the Christian claims to the same texts and finally psalms as spiritual expressions in the present. On the one hand is the concern that the one praying might appropriate wrongly all other contexts, a supersessionist interpretation by a particular historical *Sitz im Leben*. On the other hand, one could equally worry about psalms simply being a universal prayer devoid of all historical contexts so as to be universally applicable. In light of the account of prayer and psalmody in this chapter, both would be mistakes. Childs helps to present a middle way.

In Childs' definition, the Israel of the Exodus and any particular Israel after the Exodus clearly do not share the same proximity to the Exodus event. But, both are making a historical claim to time and space. Inasmuch as that time and space are shared, then in all times and spaces, there is the possibility that history – then and now – might be a part of redemptive history.

Such is the case for those who pray psalms. A particular historical memory (Ps. 51) set in an interpretive frame of David's sin with Bathsheba is not effaced but connects the modern sinner who prays the words of that psalm at the beginning of his or her own request for mercy in the Liturgy of the Hours. Christ's voice did not efface the historical cry of the exiled psalmist in Psalm 22, but Christ made Psalm 22 his own in a unique way that opened the possibility of speaking in him to those who would speak in his voice in their own times and histories. These are all actualizations of a fundamental relation to the God who relates to creation in history. Psalms keep that historical drama present just as God continues to be the source and sustainer of his creation. Thus, creative modes of prayer with these songs continue to draw out of their singers – through the prosopological union of voices, the antiphonal increase of understanding and the disposition of pilgrimage together – a hope of renewed and restored relations with God and one another. Psalms – while shirking no darkness or sin – hold forth the possibility that 'all the ends of the world' (Ps. 22.27) might become increasingly mindful that they are not their own maker, that their maker relates to them in history and that through their groaning, labouring, resting and lamenting, everything that has breath might praise the Lord (Ps. 150.6).

CHAPTER FOUR

Prayer in the New Testament

STEPHEN C. BARTON

With deep roots in the prayer of Israel and early Judaism,[1] and shaped by early Christian experience, the writings of the New Testament offer a pedagogy in prayer. Symptomatic is Luke's preamble to the Lord's Prayer: '[Jesus] was praying in a certain place, and after he had finished, one of his disciples said to him, "*Lord, teach us to pray*, as John taught his disciples". He said to them, "When you pray, say: Father, hallowed be your name"' (Lk. 11.1-2). Here, Jesus is portrayed as an exemplary pray-er whose model behaviour provokes a disciple's desire for instruction.[2] Significantly, the precedent of John the Baptist is invoked. Prayer is what prophets do. Implicit is the idea that the openness to hearing the word of God characteristic of the prophetic vocation is an openness nurtured by prayer, itself a practice transmitted by example and precept.

What follows is a selective overview of how prayer in the New Testament is understood and practised. The various texts display a rich variety of ideas,

---

[1] On this, see Samuel E. Balentine, *Prayer in the Hebrew Bible: The Drama of Divine-Human Dialogue* (Minneapolis, MN: Fortress Press, 1993); James H. Charlesworth, 'Jewish Hymns, Odes, and Prayers (ca. 167 BCE-135 CE)', in *Early Judaism and Its Modern Interpreters*, ed. Robert A. Kraft and George W. E. Nickelsburg (Atlanta, GA: Scholars Press, 1986), 411–36; and Eileen M. Schuller, 'Prayer in the Dead Sea Scrolls', in *Into God's Presence: Prayer in the New Testament*, ed. Richard N. Longenecker (Grand Rapids, MI: William B. Eerdmans, 2001), 66–88.

[2] For a separate treatment of the Lord's Prayer, see the chapter by Roy Hammerling in this volume.

itself a reflection of diversities of authorship, authorial intention, genre, historical context and cultural setting. Put summarily, prayer in the New Testament is a tradition-bearing, God-wards, communicative practice of individuals and communities shaped in life and worship by resurrection faith and experience of the eschatological Spirit.

Jesus as Pray-er

Taking our cue from the canonical gospels, we start with Jesus.[3] First, prayer was central to Jesus' prophetic-messianic vocation and mission. As the examples of Moses (Num. 14.13-23), Samuel (1 Sam. 7.5, 8-9) and Jeremiah (Jer. 32.16-25) show, prayer was characteristic of the prophetic tradition in which John the Baptist and Jesus stood. According to this tradition, the prophet not only mediates God's word to the people in proclamation, but also represents the people to God in prayer. As the prophets were *virtuosi* in prayer, so was Jesus; and the gospels give evidence of Jesus' habit of withdrawal to a solitary place to pray. Typical is Mark 6.46: 'After saying farewell to [the disciples], he went up on the mountain to pray.'

Second, Jesus' experience of the Spirit and his charismatic authority are grounded in a sense of familial – indeed, filial – relationship with God nurtured by prayer. This is expressed in Jesus' invocation of God as 'Abba, Father' (Mk 14.36), or 'Father' (e.g. Mt. 11.25-26; Lk. 10.21; Jn 11.41). Such language, rooted in the faith of Israel, expresses the dependent, trusting, but also reverential, nature of his sense of God.[4] Third, Jesus' ministry of healing and exorcism – practical expressions of his messianic battle against cosmic evil – has the discipline of prayer as its source of power and discernment. As he says to his disciples after exorcising the demonized boy: 'This kind [of evil spirit] can come out *only through prayer*' (Mk 9.29).

Fourth, the apocalyptic tenor and eschatological thrust of Jesus' mission is characteristic also of his prayer. Witness the petitions of the Lord's Prayer: 'Your kingdom come. ... [D]o not bring us to the time of trial' (Lk. 11.2, 4). Prayer, for Jesus, is armoury in the end-time battle. Fifth, teaching about prayer is a central element in Jesus' mission to revive and purify the faith

---

[3]See J. D. G. Dunn, 'Prayer', in *Dictionary of Jesus and the Gospels*, ed. Joel B. Green, et al. (Downers Grove, IL: InterVarsity Press, 1992), 617–25 and David Catchpole, *Jesus People: The Historical Jesus and the Beginnings of Community* (London: Darton, Longman and Todd, 2006), 121–68.

[4]See Dieter Zeller, 'God as Father in the Proclamation and in the Prayer of Jesus', in *Standing before God: Studies in Prayer in Scriptures and in Tradition*, ed. Asher Finkel and Lawrence Frizzell (New York: KTAV, 1981), 117–29; and James Barr, 'Abba Isn't Daddy', *Journal of Theological Studies* 39, no. 1 (1988): 28–47.

and life of Israel. In the context of the nation's subjection to Rome, the demand Jesus makes is searching: 'But I say to you, Love your enemies and *pray for those who persecute you*' (Mt. 5.44). Related to this, prayer is at the heart of Jesus' prophetic concern for the integrity of Israel's worship central to which is the continuous offering of prayer and sacrifice in the Temple in Jerusalem. This concern is clear in the justification he gives for his demonstration there: 'Is it not written, "My house shall be called *a house of prayer for all the nations*"? But you have made it a den of robbers' (Mk 11.17). Finally, recourse to prayer is how Jesus faces the suffering and death to which he is called as God's servant (Isa. 53). It is the means by which Jesus brings his will into alignment with God's, as in Gethsemane (Mk 14.32-42), on which more below. Overall, Jesus' life is a pedagogy in prayer. It is the life of the obedient Son in intimate, dependent communion with his heavenly Father, a filial relationship which Jesus invites his followers to share (Mt. 6.9).

In the light of the resurrection and in the context of early Christian experience, the tradition regarding Jesus and prayer did not remain static. We turn, therefore, to distinctive contributions from the canonical gospels.

Prayer in Matthew

First, prayer in Matthew has a distinctive theological setting. It flows from the conviction of *the divine presence*, of 'God with us' (Mt. 1.23, 28.20) bringing to a climax the judgement and renewal of Israel and the nations. It is that relationship with God the heavenly Father which gives prayer its rationale. Prayer is the essential and irresistible *response* to the divine grace revealed in Jesus the Son. Second, prayer – and pre-eminently the Lord's Prayer – along with almsgiving and fasting, is central to the way of perfection (Mt. 5.48) laid out in the Sermon on the Mount (Mt. 6.5-14).[5] As such, it is a fundamental *constitutional* practice, shaping an eschatological people in the way of righteousness – which is why it also has a role in communal discipline (Mt. 18.15-20, at 19-20). Third and related, prayer is a practice both individual and communal. Jesus himself is the model of individual prayer, as Son to Father (Mt. 26.36-46). But faith in Jesus also generates a new family of 'sons' of God and 'brothers' of one another (Mt. 23.9): and these are to call God, '*Our* Father' (Mt. 6.9).

---

[5]Strikingly, in literary as well as theological terms, the Lord's Prayer sits right at the centre of Jesus' famous sermon. See Dale C. Allison, *The Sermon on the Mount: Inspiring the Moral Imagination* (New York: Crossroad, 1999), 27–40.

Fourth, prayer and other good works give to the people of God a distinctive *identity*. They are to pray humbly, 'in secret' and trustingly, with an economy of words, demonstrating in so doing that they are like neither 'the hypocrites' nor 'the Gentiles' (Mt. 6.5-6, 7). Fifth, in terms of prayer as a soul-shaping and community-building enterprise, Matthew's Jesus places particular emphasis on *forgiveness*. Thus, as an elaboration on the petition for forgiveness in the Lord's Prayer, Matthew adds instruction on forgiveness expressive of divine reciprocity in both mercy and justice: 'For if you forgive others their trespasses, your heavenly Father will also forgive you, but if you do not forgive others, neither will your Father forgive your trespasses' (Mt. 6.14-15; see also 18.21-35).

Overall, prayer according to Matthew plays a vital role in both the 'vertical' and 'horizontal' dimensions of the people's life. It connects disciples to the heavenly domain of Father and risen Son: it also connects them to the earthly domain of brotherly and sisterly life through the practice of the spiritual disciplines. In so doing, it is likely – speaking historically – that prayer in Matthew played an important ideological and practical role in the early negotiation of the complex and challenging relations between the Matthean Jesus people and the synagogue.[6]

Prayer in Mark

Prayer in Mark is shaped theologically by belief in the sovereignty of God, for whom 'all things are possible' (Mk 9.23, 14.36); and it is shaped narratively by the confrontation, characteristic of Jewish apocalyptic eschatology, between the divine and the demonic in the Last Days (Mk 3.22-27). It is not coincidental that Jesus' first healing miracle is an exorcism, with the unclean spirit crying out percipiently, 'What have you to do with us, Jesus of Nazareth? *Have you come to destroy us?*' (Mk 1.24). Against this backdrop, the practice of prayer to God is crucial, in two distinct, but related, respects for both of which Jesus is the model.[7]

First, prayer opens access to God's power to heal, save and judge. Thus, the first reference to Jesus at prayer occurs in the immediate aftermath of the healings and exorcising in Simon's house (Mk 1.29-34) and immediately prior to an expansion of the mission to the neighbouring Galilean towns (Mk 1.38-45): 'In the morning, while it was still very dark, [Jesus] got up and

---

[6]For further on this, see Graham N. Stanton, *A Gospel for a New People: Studies in Matthew* (Edinburgh: T&T Clark, 1992).
[7]See Sharyn Echols Dowd, *Prayer, Power, and the Problem of Suffering: Mark 11: 22-25 in the Context of Markan Theology* (Atlanta, GA: Scholars Press, 1988).

went out to a deserted place, and there he prayed' (Mk 1.35; see also 6.46).
What is apparent is a pattern of public engagement to heal and exorcise,
and withdrawal in private to pray. The sense is of prayer as a practice of
alignment with the divine will and a source of divine power for both mission
and the battle with evil (Mk 9.29; see also 14.38). Especially pertinent is
Jesus' remarkable instruction (in the context of the interlinked episodes of
the cursing of the fig tree and the cleansing of the temple, in Mk 11.12-25)
on the power opened up by the prayer of faith. Here, the prayer to perform
miracles (even of the mountain-moving kind!) is promised to the one who
has faith in (the all-powerful) God – with the proviso that blocks to the flow
of power, such as a failure to practise forgiveness, have been removed (Mk
11.22-25).

There is, however, a second aspect to Markan prayer, in tension with the
first. For Mark's Gospel forces the question, If God is sovereign and all-
powerful and if, as Jesus says, 'whatever you ask for in prayer [such as healing
or deliverance], believe that you have received it, and it will be yours' (Mk
11.24), why do those who believe in God *suffer*? The question is pertinent
to Jesus' followers for whom ostracism and persecution is prophesied (Mk
13.9-13). Above all, it is pertinent to God's Messiah, the divine Son of Man,
himself. This is most evident in Mark's Gethsemane narrative (Mk 14.32-42)
where, in a scene of unprecedented distress, Jesus prays (apparently three
times), 'Abba, Father, *for you all things are possible, remove this cup from
me*; yet, not what I want, but what you want' (Mk 14.36, 39, 41). Here is
the prayer of faith. Given God's power to do 'all things', Jesus asks the One
whom he is privileged to call 'Abba, Father' to save him from the suffering
which is imminent. But, in spite of the teaching in Mark 11.24, what Jesus
asks for is *not* granted. Indeed, Jesus' subsequent experience is of divine
abandonment (Mk 15.34; see also Ps. 22.1)! Seen in this light, Markan prayer
must have a second aspect. If in the early part of the Gospel, when Jesus is
active in inaugurating the rule of God, prayer opens access to God's power
to heal and save, in the later part of the Gospel, as Jesus becomes increasingly
passive – *done to* rather than doing – prayer becomes *an engagement with the
mystery of God* central to which is the necessity of the Messiah's death (Mk
8.31-33). If there is a resolution to the tension, it lies in Mark's overarching
faith in the divine will (Mk 3.31), to which Jesus himself gestures when he
prays: 'yet, not what I want, but what you want' (Mk 14.36b).[8]

---

[8]See Dowd, *Prayer*, 164–5: 'Prayer in the Markan narrative and in the Markan community
functions as the practice in which the tension between power and suffering is faithfully
maintained. ... [H]is approach serves the pastoral function of continually bringing the
community back to the presence of God who is the source of their power and the only value
worth dying for.'

Prayer in Luke-Acts

As with Matthew and Mark, prayer in Luke-Acts has an understanding of God and salvation as its theological and existential horizon.[9] With the miraculous births of John the Baptist and Jesus, intensified in the miraculous manifestation of the Spirit on the Day of Pentecost, a new age has dawned in God's dealings with his people: it is the age of the eschatological Spirit, and a time of salvation open to all (especially the poor and marginalized) through proclamation and mission prior to the coming of the End (Lk. 4.16-30; Acts 2.14-36). Prayer, then, is joyful response to the revelation of salvation, as also a means of participation and empowerment in its progress.

In the Gospel, Jesus is portrayed throughout as a person of prayer, habitually in communion with the Father, especially at points of revelation, decision or testing. Thus, in narrating Jesus' baptism, Luke says: 'and when Jesus also had been baptised *and was praying*, the heaven was opened, and the Holy Spirit descended upon him' (Lk. 3.21-22; diff. Mk 1.9-10). Prayer as openness to the Father generates a moment of *revelation*: the Spirit descends and the heavenly voice declares Jesus to be 'my Son, the Beloved' (Lk. 3.22). Then, prior to choosing the Twelve, figures crucial for their role as witnesses in mission, Luke uniquely says that Jesus 'went out to the mountain to pray; *and he spent the night in prayer to God*' (Lk. 6.12; diff. Mk 3.13). Again, in narrating the transfiguration, a christological high-point in the story, Luke says that '*while [Jesus] was praying*, the appearance of his face changed' (Lk. 9.29; diff. Mk 9.2b). The clear inference is that the transfiguration occurs as a divine response to Jesus' deep communion with God in prayer; and once again, there is a moment of revelation: 'This is my Son, my Chosen, listen to him!' (Lk. 9.35) When the Seventy return from mission with news of their power over the demons, Luke says that 'Jesus rejoiced in the Holy Spirit' and offered a prayer of thanksgiving to the Father. Significantly, this opens the way to the sharing of an unprecedented insight into his relation with God: 'All things have been handed over to me by my Father, and no one knows who the Son is except the Father, or who the Father is except the Son' (Lk. 10.21-22). There is here an astonishing *relationality*, a profound sense of *spiritual communion*, revealed in Jesus as pray-er: joy in the Spirit, thanksgiving to the Father, and insight into the relation of Son to Father and Father to Son. Not even in suffering and cruel death does this relationship weaken. In sharp contrast with Mark's Gethsemane story, Luke's Jesus goes

---

[9]See further, Stephen C. Barton, *The Spirituality of the Gospels* (London: SPCK, 1992), 71–112 and David Crump, *Jesus the Intercessor: Prayer and Christology in Luke-Acts* (Tübingen: Mohr Siebeck, 1992).

to pray 'as was his custom' (Lk. 22.39), displays no terror,[10] kneels to pray (rather than collapsing on the ground), is reverential in his request for the cup's removal and sustains his role as teacher, twice instructing the disciples (in terms reminiscent of his teaching in the Lord's Prayer, at Lk. 11.4b), 'Pray that you may not come into the time of trial' (Lk. 22.39-46). And on the cross, we are given, not a cry of Godforsakenness (Mk 15.34), but a prayer of committal: 'Father, into your hand I commend my spirit' (Lk. 23.46a). In sum, Luke's Jesus models in life and death multiple meanings of prayer – especially prayer as transparency to God in the power of the Spirit enabling ministry to God's beleaguered people.

When we turn to prayer in Luke's second volume, the continuity between the prayer practice of Jesus and that of the apostles and the early church is noticeable.[11] This reflects Luke's conviction that the eschatological Spirit which empowered Jesus' salvific work is the *same* Spirit at work in the life and witness of the believers in Jesus now risen. The stress on continuity has a twofold function. On the one hand, it shows believers that, although ascended, Jesus is *still present* and still at work: hence the significance of invocations of 'the name [of Jesus]' (Acts 2.21; 9.15, 21), as also of prayers to 'the Lord [Jesus]' (Acts 1.24; 8.22, 24), and of reference to guidance by 'the Spirit *of Jesus*' (Acts 16.6-7). On the other hand, it offers an apologetic and a challenge to unbelievers: the disturbing novelty represented by the Christian 'way' has divine legitimation.

First, as for Jesus, prayer is a defining characteristic of the life of faith: and from the ascension onwards it is a distinguishing mark of the community (Acts 1.14; 2.42; 12.5; 14.23). Reminiscent of Jesus' baptism, the coming of the Holy Spirit to empower the church is depicted as a response to prayer (Acts 2.1-13; 4.31). Second, playing an exemplary role, the apostles and church leaders are depicted as people of prayer, enabling them to be agents of salvation. Typical is this prelude to the healing of a man lame from birth: 'One day Peter and John were going up to the temple *at the hour of prayer*, at three o'clock in the afternoon' (Acts 3.1; see also 10.9). Paul also is exemplary in this respect (Acts 13.2-3; 14.23; 16.25; 20.36; 28.8). Third, each new development in the life of the church comes in response to prayer, and each new crisis is negotiated with the help of prayer. One example, which recalls Jesus at prayer prior to the calling of the Twelve, is

---

[10]That Luke 22.43-44 are a later addition is widely (although not universally) agreed. See further, Bart D. Ehrman and Mark A. Plunkett, 'The Angel and the Agony: The Textual Problem of Luke 22.43-44', *Catholic Biblical Quarterly* 45, no. 3 (1983): 401–16.

[11]See Joel B. Green, 'Persevering Together in Prayer: The Significance of Prayer in the Acts of the Apostles', in *Into God's Presence: Prayer in the New Testament*, ed. Richard N. Longenecker (Grand Rapids, MI: William B. Eerdmans, 2001), 183–202.

the appointment of Matthias to take the place of Judas (Acts 1.24). Another, which recalls Jesus' prayers from the cross, is the depiction of the prayers of Stephen at his martyrdom (Acts 7.59-60). Prayer enables perseverance and self-transcendence. Fourth, prayer brings deliverance of various kinds, such as healing (Acts 9.40; 28.8), forgiveness (Acts 7.60; 8.22), personal salvation (Acts 8.24; 10.2, 30) and release from imprisonment (Acts 12.12; 16.25). Finally, reminiscent of Jesus' prayer of rejoicing in the Holy Spirit is the regular link in Acts between prayer, thanksgiving and joy (Acts 2.46-47; 13.48; 27.35; 28.15). In Acts overall, formation in prayerfulness through the habit of prayer offers *Spirit-inspired empowerment*. It also generates an ethos of *doxology*: for prayer is an entry into the transcendent life of the One who is prayed to.

Prayer in John

In John we find, not so much a pedagogy *in* prayer, as pedagogy *through* prayer, where the prayer of Jesus is revelatory – like the Gospel as a whole – of what is most fundamental: *the love relation between the Father and the Son* overflowing for the salvation of the world.[12] Able, perhaps, to take for granted his readers' prior knowledge of the prayer teaching of the Synoptic tradition, the Gospel of John is remarkable for its distinctiveness. Thus, the Gospel gives no picture of Jesus' characteristic withdrawal to a secluded place to pray, no parables about prayer, no offering of a model prayer such as the Lord's Prayer, no teaching about prayer and forgiveness, no reference to the Temple as a 'house of prayer' during Jesus' demonstration there, no agonizing in prayer in Gethsemane and no prayer from the cross. In fact, John's account of the public ministry offers only two prayers of Jesus, both uniquely Johannine; and what they imply is that prayer as a *vocalization* of dependence on God is all but redundant. It is as if the relation of Son to Father and Father to Son is so profound – their communion so continuous (Jn 5.19-20) – that words are hardly needed.

The first is the prayer of Jesus at the tomb of Lazarus: 'And Jesus looked upward and said, "Father, I thank you for having heard me. I knew that you always hear me, *but I have said this for the sake of the crowd standing here*, so that they may believe that you sent me"' (Jn 11.41b-42). Curiously, no account is given of what words of petition the Father heard! Instead, the prayer of thanksgiving is *prayer as witness*, testifying to the perduring

---

[12]See Andrew T. Lincoln, 'God's Name, Jesus' Name, and Prayer in the Fourth Gospel', in *Into God's Presence: Prayer in the New Testament*, ed. Richard N. Longenecker (Grand Rapids, MI: William B. Eerdmans, 2001), 155–80.

communicative relation between Father and Son, and seeking thereby to evoke in the crowd the belief that Jesus is the divine agent who, as such, has the power to raise the dead.

The second prayer comes at the climax of Jesus' public ministry, after the entry into Jerusalem and the coming of 'some Greeks' wishing to 'see' Jesus (Jn 12.20-22). In Johannine terms, this signals the fulfilment of the universal scope of Jesus' mission and provides the cue for Jesus to reveal that 'the hour' has come for his departure to the Father via the cross. It is a crucial narrative turning point, marked by the Evangelist's highly creative reworking of the Synoptic Gethsemane tradition. Thus, while there is a frank recognition of the darkness to come ('Now my soul is troubled'), there is no agonized plea to 'Abba, Father' for the removal of the cup of suffering. Instead, the tradition is turned on its head: 'And what should I say – Father, save me from this hour? No, it is for this reason that I have come to this hour. Father, glorify your name' (Jn 12.27-28a). It is as if, in the momentary struggle between the humanity and divinity of Jesus, divinity has won by invocation of the Father. And in the end, all that Jesus actually expresses in prayer are those final words, 'Father, glorify your name' (Jn 12.28a), in response to which, for the one and only time, the heavenly voice is heard: 'I have glorified it, and I will glorify it again' (Jn 12.28b). The attunement of Father and Son, expressed in petition and response, is complete and, for Gospel reader, utterly reassuring.

John's depiction of Jesus' prayer during his public ministry contributes fundamentally as *witness* to the intimate relation of Father and Son, a relation of love as the basis for saving belief (Jn 3.16). As to *teaching* on prayer, that is confined to the Farewell Discourse of John 13-16, where John tells of Jesus' *private* ministry to his disciples, the purpose of which is to prepare them for the time when he will be with them no longer.[13] The teaching comes in three pairs. In John 14.13-14, Jesus offers a twofold promise to do whatever the disciples ask in his name, the point being that this is how the disciples will be able to continue the work begun by Jesus, 'so that the Father may be glorified in the Son' (Jn 14.13). So the promise that whatever is asked for will be granted is not unqualified: it is an outworking of the Father–Son relationship now enjoyed also by the disciples. In John 15.7 and 15.16b, in the discourse on Jesus as the vine and disciples as the branches, the disciples' asking (in prayer) and receiving is predicated both on their 'abiding' in Jesus and Jesus' words 'abiding' in them (Jn 15.7), and on

---

[13]See Paul S. Minear, 'To Ask and to Receive: Some Clues to Johannine Ontology', in *Intergerini Parietis Septvm (Eph. 2:14): Essays Presented to Markus Barth on His Sixty-Fifth Birthday*, ed. Dikran Y. Hadidian (Pittsburgh, PA: Pickwick Press, 1981), 227–50.

faithfulness in (fruit-bearing) mission (Jn 15.16). Again, a disciple's prayer is not a 'wish list', nor, significantly, is it concerned with *things*. Rather, it arises in, for and out of relationship with the Father and the Son. Finally, in John 16.23-24, 26-27a, the emphasis is on prayer in Jesus' name as direct, unmediated access to the Father, access which turns mourning in the wake of Jesus' departure into joy.

This teaching on prayer in the Farewell Discourse is now modelled in Jesus' own prayer (Jn 17.1-26). Located narratively at a critical turning-point, between the Farewell Discourse (Jn 14-16) and the arrest in the garden (Jn 18.1-12), the prayer is prefaced by Jesus' words of reassurance: 'I have said this to you, so that in me you may have peace. In the world you face persecution. But take courage, *I have overcome the world!*' (Jn 16.33). Against this backdrop of eschatological victory, the prayer is a recapitulation of John's relational theology and soteriology, along with missional and pastoral concerns.

In the first part (Jn 17.1-5), Jesus prays for *his own* glorification: 'Father, the hour has come; glorify your Son so that the Son may glorify you. ... Father, glorify me in your presence with the glory that I had in your presence before the world began' (Jn 17.1b, 5). The two-part request pivots around what is to come ('the hour') interpreted in the context of the relation of Father and Son as one of mutual bestowal of honour ('glory') via the paradoxical lifting up/exaltation of Jesus on the cross and his subsequent exaltation to heaven. In sum, the prayer begins with a reiteration of *the divine relationship*, along with the revelation of 'the only true God, and Jesus Christ whom you have sent' (Jn 17.3) on which all else depends. It is as if the theological and christological foundations are being set firm.

On this basis, Jesus prays, in the second part, for *his disciples* (Jn 17.6-19). With the assurance that their faith is authentic and that their identity in God is secure (Jn 17.6-10), and out of concern for their well-being in 'the world' after his departure, Jesus makes three requests: that the disciples be kept in the divine name, 'so that they may be one' (Jn 17.11); that they be protected from the evil one (Jn 17.15); and that they be sanctified in the truth (Jn 17.17), the latter with a view to their effectiveness in continuing the work of mission begun by Jesus (Jn 17.18-19). Overall, these requests to God as 'Holy Father' (Jn 17.11) represent a practice of *prayer as pastoral care* in a hostile environment (Jn 16.1-4, 32-33; 17.15b).

In the third and final part (Jn 17.20-26), the prayer expands further to embrace *a wider circle*: those who come to faith through the mission and common life of the disciples. As in the first part, there are two requests. The first is 'that they may all be one' (Jn 17.21), a unity arising out of participation in the unity of Father and Son and a sharing in the divine glory (Jn 17.21b-23) with clear missional implications ('so that the world may know' [Jn 17.23]). The second concerns believers' future destiny: '[that they] may be with me where I am, to see my glory, which you have given me because you loved me before the foundation of the world' (Jn 17.24). To groups of believers facing persecution, such a petition is particularly pertinent. And in concluding words, the assurance of salvation it betokens is grounded, yet once more, in the intimate relationship of mutual knowledge and love between 'righteous Father' and obedient Son (Jn 17.25-26).

This momentous prayer is uniquely Johannine: but it is not a free composition. As well as elements of the Gethsemane tradition, there are also traces of the Lord's Prayer, such as the address to God as 'Father', the association of glory with God's *name* and the prayer for protection from evil/the evil one.[14] It would appear that John has taken Synoptic prayer tradition and developed it for a new context. Spoken as if from a future, post-resurrection time and a transcendent, heaven-wards place, the prayer casts Jesus as the heavenly advocate (1 Jn 2.1-2), the Son in union with the Father, offering assurance and consolation in a time of both missional opportunity and ecclesial peril.

Prayer in Paul and the Pauline Tradition

The letters of Paul and the Pauline school confirm the testimony of Acts (cited earlier) that Paul was a prayerful apostle.[15] Certainly, the practice of regular prayer, understood as personal and communal devotion to God in spaces private and public (such as the synagogue and the Temple), will have been an indelible aspect of Paul's pre-conversion piety as a Pharisee, a piety expressive of the deuteronomic command 'to love the Lord your God and to serve him *with all your heart and with all your soul*' (Deut. 11.13). Such prayer will have included adoration, thanksgiving and petition. Inspiration for prayer will have been provided by such cultural resources as the language of scripture, Temple worship, ceremonial blessings over meals, the twice-daily recitation of the *Shema* (Deut. 6.4-9; 11.13-21) and the *Shemoneh Esreh* (or 'Eighteen Benedictions'), as well as instances of sectarian prayer and piety of such as belonged to groups like the Essenes.

---

[14]See William O. Walker, 'The Lord's Prayer in Matthew and John', *New Testament Studies* 28, no. 2 (1982): 237–56.

[15]See Richard N. Longenecker, 'Prayer in the Pauline Letters', in *Into God's Presence: Prayer in the New Testament*, ed. Richard N. Longenecker (Grand Rapids, MI: William B. Eerdmans, 2001), 203–27 and W. B. Hunter, 'Prayer', in *Dictionary of Paul and His Letters*, ed. Gerald F. Hawthorne, et al. (Downers Grove, IL: InterVarsity Press, 1993), 725–34.

Nevertheless, as well as significant continuities with the piety of his Jewish co-religionists, prayer in Paul represents a major point of discontinuity. For Pauline prayer is a response to a profound religious experience which transformed his life: the revelation to/in him of God's Son, and the call to preach him among the Gentiles (Gal. 1.15-16a).[16] It is a *participation in cruciform grace*, an ongoing acknowledgement of God's gift of universal salvation and life in the Spirit made possible by Messiah's death and resurrection (Rom. 1.1-6). As such, prayer is a practice of christological monotheism, of faith in the 'one God' who rules the world through the agency of the 'one Lord', Jesus Christ (1 Cor. 8.6). Importantly, grace and faith give rise to love, such that the language of prayer expresses his heart's desire, in relation to both God and the churches (1 Cor. 16.23-24). In consequence, *prayerfulness* is a dominant mode of Pauline communication: 'What we have in Paul is ... a style of writing that is saturated by prayerful language. His gratitude, his greetings, his farewells, his hopes, his admonitions, his worries, his travel plans are all often cast in a language that borders on prayer, a language shaped and informed by his awareness of divine presence, divine activity.'[17]

Significant aspects of Pauline prayer are the following. First, as a response to grace and an expression of absolute dependence, Paul's prayer language is dominated by *thanksgiving to God*, often in his letters' introductions. Typical is the opening to his earliest extant letter, 1 Thessalonians: 'We always give thanks to God for all of you and mention you in our prayers, constantly remembering before our God and Father your work of faith and labour of love and steadfastness of hope in our Lord Jesus Christ' (1 Thess. 1.2-3; see also 1 Cor. 1.4; Rom. 1.8; Phil. 1.3; Phlm. 4; Col. 1.3; Eph. 1.16). Such introductory thanksgivings function to remind Paul's addressees of the heavenly benefactors to whom he and they owe allegiance. They also allow Paul to introduce motifs and topics upon which he will expand in what follows – in the Thessalonian case, the significant theological triad of faith, love and hope.

Second, as an expression of his apostolic vocation, including his care for the spiritual welfare of his churches, Paul offers a pedagogy in prayer. For the apostle, prayer is the believers' *identity-defining speech-act*, the ongoing acknowledgement of the sovereignty of God and the lordship of Christ.

---

[16]For a powerful account, drawing attention to analogies in traditions of Jewish mysticism, see John Ashton, *The Religion of Paul the Apostle* (New Haven, CT: Yale University Press, 2000), 73–151.

[17]Krister Stendahl, *Meanings: The Bible as Document and as Guide* (Philadelphia, PA: Fortress Press, 1984), 151–61 (151).

With their implication of prayer as a practice of *perpetual self-transcendence and abandonment to the divine will*, the following instructions are typical: 'Rejoice always, pray without ceasing, give thanks in all circumstances; for this is the will of God in Christ Jesus for you' (1 Thess. 5.16-18); 'Do not worry about anything, but in everything by prayer and supplication with thanksgiving let your requests be made known to God' (Phil. 4.6).

Third, prayer in Paul has an explicitly corporate, participatory dimension. By joining together in enlisting divine guidance and help, prayer as *shared address to God* becomes a critical means of building spiritual, emotional and material solidarity between Paul and the churches, and between the churches themselves (1 Thess. 5.25; Eph. 6.18; 1 Tim. 2.1). This is particularly pertinent in testing times – as Paul says, with reference to his experience of being under a sentence of death in Roman Asia: 'He who rescued us from so deadly a peril will continue to rescue us; on him we have set our hope that he will rescue us again, *as you also join in helping us by your prayers*, so that many will give thanks on our behalf for the blessing granted us *through the prayers of many*' (2 Cor. 1.10-11; see also Phil. 1.19; 2 Thess. 3.1-2; Rom. 15.30-32).

Fourth, Pauline prayer has a strong *eschatological* quality (1 Cor. 16.22b). It is the speech-act appropriate to believers' identity as citizens of heaven (Phil. 3.20). Stated otherwise, it is a vocal manifestation of life in the Spirit and adoption into the family of God: 'When we cry, "Abba! Father!" it is that very Spirit bearing witness with our spirit that we are children of God' (Rom. 8.15b-16; see also Gal. 4.5-6). As a gift of the Spirit for the church in God's new creation, the practice of prayer transcends boundaries of gender, class and status.[18] In the form of glossolalia – the 'tongues *of angels*' (1 Cor. 13.1) – it also transcends the bounds of mundane rationality and intelligibility. So individual and communal *prayer-discipline* is necessary if the goal of the 'building up' of the church is to be sustained, with priority in public prayer given to intelligible speech: 'Therefore one who speaks in a tongue should pray for the power to interpret. For if I pray in a tongue, my spirit prays but my mind is unproductive. What should I do then? I will pray with the spirit, but I will pray with the mind also' (1 Cor. 14.13-15).

Fifth, and related to Paul's apocalyptic eschatology, prayer is a weapon in the End-time battle with Satan. This is given profoundly paradoxical expression in Paul's autobiographical testimony (in 2 Cor. 12) to 'visions and revelations of the Lord', including an experience of mystical rapture, all qualified by a gift of a very different kind: 'A thorn was given me in the

---

[18]Note, for example, the reference to the women in the Corinthian assembly who pray and prophesy, in 1 Corinthians 11.2-16; see also 1 Corinthians 7.5.

flesh, *a messenger of Satan* to torment me, to keep me from being too elated'
(2 Cor. 12.7). Paul's response to this invasion is to counter-attack by invoking
in prayer the aid of his heavenly Lord, and doing so more than once: 'Three
times I appealed to the Lord about this, that it would leave me.' However,
instead of a gospels-like 'Ask and you will receive', his appeal is rejected:
'but he said to me, "My grace is sufficient for you, for power is made perfect
in weakness"' (2 Cor. 12.8-9). Here, prayer takes the form of an intentional
dialogue between the apostle and his heavenly Lord in the course of which,
and perhaps correlative of his persistence ('three times'!), Paul receives a
revelatory word which takes his experience – of both power and suffering – to
a deeper level: to do with the sovereignty of God, the paradoxical revelation
of the power of God in weakness, and humankind's utter dependence on
grace. It is as if key elements in Paul's theology gain clarity and resonance as
he engages in prayer, not least concerning experiences of adversity.

Finally, and related explicitly to Paul's theology of weakness, is his
remarkable acknowledgement in Romans 8 of the believer's *incapacity* when
it comes to prayer – whether how to pray or what to pray for: 'We do
not know how to pray as we ought' (Rom. 8.26). This acknowledgement
is an invitation to radical humility on the believer's part in the time of the
'not yet' of eschatological salvation. It is an invitation, at the same time, to
gratitude for the empowering support of the eschatological Spirit as divine
intercessor, who 'helps us in our weakness ... [and] intercedes with sighs too
deep for words' (Rom. 8.26). Indeed, intercession on the believer's behalf
is presented as so intrinsic to the relationship between the Spirit and God,
as also between the exalted Christ and God, as almost to be taken out of
human hands. For Paul can say both that 'the Spirit intercedes for the saints
according to the will of God' (Rom. 8.27b), and that 'it is Christ Jesus ...
who is at the right hand of God, who intercedes for us' (Rom. 8.34). Put
otherwise, to pray is to be caught up in the grace-bestowing energy of the
divine life.

Prayer in the Letter of James

James is a kind of 'round-robin' addressed to groups of Christian believers
scattered around the cities of the Mediterranean. Its main aim is to offer
instruction in the form of wisdom teaching on how to sustain Christian
faith and moral life under pressure (Jas 1.2-3).[19] In James' way of seeing

---

[19]See J. Ramsey Michaels, 'Finding Yourself an Intercessor: New Testament Prayer from Hebrews
to Jude', in *Into God's Presence: Prayer in the New Testament*, ed. Richard N. Longenecker
(Grand Rapids, MI: William B. Eerdmans, 2001), 232–40 and Robert W. Wall, *Community of
the Wise: The Letter of James* (Valley Forge, PA: Trinity Press International, 1997).

the world, there is a basic *opposition*: at the cosmic level, between God and the devil; at the social level, between those who behave in ways that unify and those whose behaviour divides; and at the individual level, it is an opposition within the human heart between 'the wisdom which is from above' and a wisdom which 'does not come down from above, but is earthly, unspiritual, devilish' (Jas 3.15). What James says about prayer presupposes this multilayered framework of belief.

First, and evoking Jesus-tradition on asking and receiving (Mt. 7.7; Jn 16.24), priority is given to asking for divine wisdom: 'Ask God, who gives to all generously and ungrudgingly, and it will be given to you' (Jas 1.5). The promise of answered prayer is not unqualified, however. In particular, asking must arise from a wholehearted faith untrammelled by doubt (Jas 1.6-7) and unsullied by selfish desires (Jas 4.2-3) or a divided spiritual allegiance (Jas 4.4-10). What is implied here is an understanding and practice of prayer appropriate to the character of the divine benefactor.

Second, and related, James' teaching on prayer is part of his teaching on the morality of speech practices as a whole. As a wisdom teacher, James is acutely aware of the power of speech ('the tongue') for good, but even more, for ill (Jas 3.1-18) – so much so that taciturnity is a virtue: 'Above all, my beloved, do not swear, either by heaven or by earth or by any other oath, but let your "Yes" be yes and your "No" be no, so that you may not fall under condemnation' (Jas 5.12-13; see also Mt. 5.33-37).[20] For James, the practice of prayer is without integrity, and therefore ineffective, if it is not of a piece with virtuous speech generally: and one imagines that James will have been in accord with the preference of the Matthean Jesus for prayers which are short in length and long on humility (Mt. 6.5-8).

Third, in bringing his letter to a climax, James turns to the practice of prayer in all of life's circumstances, and especially times of adversity: 'Are any among you suffering? They should pray. Are any cheerful? They should sing songs of praise' (Jas 5.13).[21] The implication is that there is no circumstance in life in relation to which God's presence should not be invoked. Then, having advocated prayer in response to suffering, he comes to a particular instance: 'Are any among you sick? They should call for the elders of the church and have them pray over them, anointing them with oil in the name of the Lord'

---

[20]See Luke Timothy Johnson, 'Taciturnity and True Religion: James 1: 26-27', in *Greeks, Romans, and Christians: Essays in Honor of Abraham J. Malherbe*, ed. David L. Balch, Everett Ferguson, and Wayne A. Meeks (Minneapolis, MN: Fortress Press, 1990), 329–39.

[21]As for Paul (1 Thess. 5.16-18), unceasing prayer and praise are the believer's trademark: and for James they are the essential counter-testimony to malicious talk, boasting, grumbling, anger and the like.

(Jas 5.14). In a world ever vulnerable to sickness, disease and disability, this advice is an obvious expression of James' commitment to a faith manifest in action. As such, it is of a piece with his instructions earlier about care for the poor, the widows and the orphans (Jas 1.27). In the case in point, through the engagement of the church's spiritual leaders as advocates in intercessory prayer and practitioners of ritual (in the form of the anointing with oil), the healing of the sick is made the business of the community and the business of God together. What is more, physical healing is set in parallel with *spiritual* healing: 'The prayer of faith will save the sick, and the Lord will raise them up; and anyone who has committed sins will be forgiven. *Therefore, confess your sins to one another, and pray for one another, so that you may be healed*' (Jas 5.15-16). The connection is one of analogy: sickness and sin are alike in the sense that both express a *dis-ease* in the individual, the community and the cosmos. What brings renewal of individual, communal and cosmic life is invoking the divine presence through 'the prayer of faith'. Underlying is the conviction that 'the prayer of the righteous is powerful and effective' (Jas 5.16), the exemplar for which is the prophet Elijah whose 'fervent prayer' brought eschatological blessing – represented metaphorically as rain from heaven (Jas 5.17-18; see also 1 Kgs 17-18).

Prayer in 1 Peter

Written to primarily Gentile converts in churches across Asia Minor (1 Pet. 1.1), a principal concern of 1 Peter is how to maintain a Christian faith and identity in a hostile social environment (1 Pet. 2.12; 4.4, 12). The strategy of the letter is to confirm the believers in their distinctiveness as the eschatological people of God, and at the same time offer instruction in how to live in a Christ-like way as 'aliens and exiles' (1 Pet. 2.11) bearing witness in the midst of a pagan society.[22] Prayer, therefore, is a fundamental expression of the believers' identity and calling as 'a chosen race, a royal priesthood, and holy nation' (1 Pet. 2.9-10; see also Exod. 19.5-6).

First, as members of a new family, the 'household of God' (1 Pet. 4.17), the believer has the privilege of praying to God as 'Father' (1 Pet. 1.17), a practice reminiscent of Jesus in the Gospels (e.g. Lk. 11.2) and also of Paul (Rom. 8.15b). Second, in a social context of verbal hostility and

---

[22]See Bruce W. Winter, *Seek the Welfare of the City: Christians as Benefactors and Citizens* (Grand Rapids, MI: William B. Eerdmans, 1994), 11–40; Miroslav Volf, 'Soft Difference: Theological Reflections on the Relation between Church and Culture in 1 Peter', *Ex Auditu* 10 (1994): 15–30; and David G. Horrell, *Becoming Christian: Essays on 1 Peter and the Making of Christian Identity* (London: Bloomsbury, 2013).

impoverished speech (1 Pet. 2.1; 3.16; 4.14), prayer is a witness to speech which is sanctified: 'Do not repay evil for evil or abuse for abuse; but, on the contrary, *repay with a blessing*. It is for this that you were called – that you might inherit a blessing' (1 Pet. 3.9). Doing good in this way brings God near, with scripture cited in confirmation: 'For the eyes of the Lord are on the righteous, *and his ears are open to their prayer*' (1 Pet. 3.12a; see also Ps. 34.12-15). Third, and more generally, prayer is a witness to a conversion of life, thought and feeling. Thus, in the domestic sphere, if wives and husbands relate to each other in seemly ways, their prayers will not be 'hindered' (1 Pet. 3.1-7, at v.7) – which presupposes that the practice of prayer is a joint privilege and responsibility, and also that the efficacy of their prayer is related to the character of their mutual relationship (Mt. 5.23-24; Jas 4.1-4). But, fourth, prayer is not only important in the domestic sphere. It is important also in the ecclesiological sphere. The letter's addressees are 'aliens and exiles', not in a geographical sense, but in an eschatological sense, *en route* as they are to 'eternal glory in Christ' (1 Pet. 5.10), so prayer is *a discipline of ecclesial solidarity*: 'The end of all things is near ... attend to prayers ... maintain constant love for one another ... be hospitable to one another ... [and] serve one another' (1 Pet. 4.7b-11). And, finally, with their supernatural 'adversary' prowling around, they are assured of the most important solidarity of all, connection with which is opened up by intercession: 'Cast all your anxieties on him [i.e. God], *for her cares for you*' (1 Pet. 5.7).

Prayer in Hebrews

Apart from a certain analogy with the Temple theology of the Fourth Gospel and the prayer of Jesus in John 17, Hebrews is quite distinctive in its contribution to a Christian pedagogy of prayer.[23] The distinction lies in its radical christological interpretation of Israelite worship and sacrifice as finding their fulfilment (and, indeed, supersession) in Christ as both high priest and once-for-all sacrifice (see Heb. 6.19-20; 9.11-14). With its repeated use of the terminology of 'entrance' or 'approach', Hebrews offers a christological foundation for confident access to God and to the salvation mediated by the Son of God: 'Therefore, my friends, since we have confidence to enter the sanctuary by the blood of Jesus ... and since we have a great priest over the house of God, let us approach with a true heart in full assurance of faith' (Heb. 10.19-22).

---

[23]See Michaels, 'Finding Yourself an Intercessor', 229–31.

Consistent with this, Jesus' own prayers are interpreted in sacerdotal terms. They display what qualify him for his high priestly work. Thus, in a highly creative re-appropriation of gospel tradition, Jesus' prayer in Gethsemane is given a new twist by being brought into partial alignment with the obligation on the high priest to offer sacrifice for his own sins before making sacrifice on behalf of the people (Heb. 5.3; 7.27; 9.7). The difference, of course, is that the prayer of Jesus reflects, not his sinfulness, but his humble submission to God's will: 'In the days of his flesh, Jesus offered up prayers and supplications, with loud cries and tears, to the one who was able to save him from death, and he was heard, because of his reverent submission' (Heb. 5.7).

In a wider context, and as elsewhere in the New Testament, the pattern is one of humiliation followed by exaltation (Phil. 2.5-11). This bears on Jesus' role as *heavenly intercessor*. His humiliation allows Jesus to sympathize with God's people in their weakness, having himself 'been tested in every respect'. His exaltation to heaven as high priest 'according to the order of Melchizedek' places him in a position to intercede on their behalf: 'Consequently he is able for all time to save those who approach God through him, *since he always lives to make intercession for them*' (Heb. 7.25); 'For Christ did not enter a sanctuary made by human hands ... but he entered into heaven itself, *now to appear in the presence of God on our behalf*' (Heb. 9.24).

That Jesus is the exalted high priest and heavenly intercessor has pastoral implications. In particular, it provides a basis for *parrēsia* ('boldness' or 'confidence') in prayer: 'Let us therefore approach the throne of grace *with boldness*, so that we may receive mercy and find grace to help in time of need' (Heb. 4.16).

Prayer in the Book of Revelation

The work of a Jewish Christian prophet, Revelation is a prophecy in the form of a circular letter to seven churches in the Roman province of Asia (Rev. 1.1-11).[24] Drawing creatively on the ideas and symbols of biblical prophecy and Jewish apocalyptic, its aim is to disclose an alternative space-time reality – transcendent, theocentric and christocentric – so potent that its hearers will be inspired to victorious Christian existence in their

---

[24]See Richard Bauckham, *The Theology of the Book of Revelation* (Cambridge: Cambridge University Press, 1993) and 'Prayer in the Book of Revelation', in *Into God's Presence: Prayer in the New Testament*, ed. Richard N. Longenecker (Grand Rapids, MI: William B. Eerdmans, 2001), 252–71.

respective challenging situations.[25] Against a cosmic horizon of the open heaven revealing the celestial court with God and the all-conquering Lamb enthroned (Rev. 4-5), prayer is not made a matter of pedagogy in any explicit way. Rather, it is an ingredient of the liturgy of heaven, especially in the form of *praise and thanksgiving*. Exemplary in this respect are the doxologies, as at the very beginning: 'To him who loves us and freed us from our sins by his blood, and made us to be a kingdom, priests serving his God and Father, to him be glory and dominion forever and ever. Amen' (Rev. 1.5b-6; cf. 4.8-11).

What the seer discloses in visionary form as a reality taking place in heaven in the present has as a corollary the disclosure – as a basis for perseverance in faithful discipleship – of the reality soon to be revealed on the earth:

> And I saw the holy city, the new Jerusalem, coming down out of heaven from God, prepared as a bride adorned for her husband. And I heard a loud voice from the throne saying, 'See, the home of God is among mortals. He will dwell with them as their God; they will be his peoples, and God himself will be with them'.
>
> (Rev. 21.2ff.)

This divine home-making on earth issues in an invitation: 'The Spirit and the bride say, "Come"' (Rev. 22.17a). Importantly, the initiative comes from above. It then finds an echo in the request from below: 'And let everyone who hears say, "Come"' (Rev. 22.17b). The reference to *hearing* is significant.[26] The picture is of prayer as first, hearing the divine invitation – hearing the Spirit and the exalted Christ – and then accepting. We have here a recapitulation of a motif introduced early on: '*Listen!* I am standing at the door, knocking: *if you hear my voice* and open the door, I will come in to you and eat with you, and you with me. ... Let everyone *who has an ear listen* to what the Spirit is saying to the churches' (Rev. 3.20-22).

The final words of the entire work, apart from the epistolary ending, repeat the pattern. There is divine initiative in the promise of Jesus: 'Surely, I am coming soon' (Rev. 22.20a). And there is the mirroring response in the form of the prayer of petition for the *parousia*: 'Amen. Come, Lord Jesus!' (Rev. 22.20b). The prayer is rooted in tradition: it is a Christianized

---

[25]Note the repeated promise of salvation to 'the one who conquers' which comes at the end of each of the seven 'letters' (2.7, 11, 17, 26-28; 3.5, 12, 21).

[26]See G. K. Beale, 'The Hearing Formula and the Visions of John in Revelation', in *A Vision for the Church: Studies in Early Christian Ecclesiology*, ed. Markus Bockmuehl and Michael B. Thompson (Edinburgh: T&T Clark, 1997), 167–80.

version of the second petition of the Lord's Prayer, 'Your kingdom come' (Lk. 11.2), now with the exalted, victorious Jesus as the addressee. Overall, as a prayer for the coming (or return) of Jesus, it is thoroughly characteristic of the eschatological character of early Christian prayer as a whole (1 Cor. 16.23b).

Conclusion

A brief synthesis of our subject should include the following.[27] First, in the light of the pervasive attention to prayer in the New Testament, it is reasonable to conclude that the practice of prayer and an ethos of prayerfulness were significant characteristics of the life of the early church. It is difficult to overestimate the extent to which the early church, developing its inherited scriptural and cultic traditions in creative ways, was a fellowship of prayer (Acts 2.42). Prayer was at the heart of early Christian joy and consolation.[28]

Second, prayer and belief are related, and in a reciprocal manner. On the one hand, prayer expresses belief in the sovereignty, justice, mercy, love and freedom of God, and the utter dependence of humankind (and all creation) upon God for life and salvation. Hence, New Testament prayer is invariably prayer *to God* (e.g. Acts 4.24-30), relationship with whom is mediated by the divine agency of Christ and/or the Spirit (Rom. 1.8; 8.26, 34). On the other hand, belief is shaped by experience, not least by prayer and worship. Thus, instances of prayer to 'the Lord' (*ho Kurios*) understood as the Lord *Jesus* (2 Cor. 12.8-9; Acts 7.59-60) offer evidence of a development in monotheistic faith shaped by ritual practice, mystical experience and charismatic worship (Rom. 10.9-13; 1 Cor. 12.3b; 16.22b; Phil. 2.11).[29]

Third, early Christian prayer was profoundly eschatological. It was shaped by the kingdom preaching and practice of Jesus in a context of socio-political oppression and incipient messianism. It was shaped also by the conviction of believers in Jesus that, with his crucifixion, resurrection and exaltation

---

[27]See Oscar Cullmann, *Prayer in the New Testament* (London: SCM Press, 1995), 119–42.

[28]See Stephen C. Barton, 'Spirituality and the Emotions in Early Christianity: The Case of Joy', in *The Bible and Spirituality: Exploratory Essays in Reading Scripture Spiritually*, ed. Andrew T. Lincoln, J. Gordon McConville, and Lloyd K. Pietersen (Eugene, OR: Wipf and Stock, 2013), 171–93.

[29]See Larry W. Hurtado, *At the Origins of Christian Worship: The Context and Character of Earliest Christian Devotion* (Carlisle: Paternoster Press, 1999), 63–97. See also Luke Timothy Johnson, *Religious Experience in Earliest Christianity: A Missing Dimension in New Testament Studies* (Minneapolis, MN: Fortress Press, 1998); and on mystical experience in particular, see Christopher Rowland and Christopher R. A. Morray-Jones, *The Mystery of God: Early Jewish Mysticism and the New Testament* (Leiden: Brill, 2009).

to heaven, a new creation – the age of the eschatological Spirit – had been inaugurated and that believers were living now in the overlap of the ages. Yet again, it was shaped by experiences of rejection, persecution and martyrdom (2 Cor. 1.8-11). In such a time, prayer is a participation with Christ and the Spirit in the life of heaven. It is a uniting of communities earthly and heavenly in adoration, thanksgiving and intercession (2 Cor. 4-5).

Finally, prayer is a matter of ongoing pedagogy and exhortation. This is so for a variety of reasons. Negatively, pedagogy in prayer is a prophylactic against praying wrongly (Mt. 6.5-15), losing faith and ceasing to pray (Lk. 18.1-8) and succumbing to defeat in the ongoing End-time battle against evil (Lk. 11.4b; Eph. 6.10-20). Positively, learning to pray is to follow the example of Jesus in his relation to 'Abba, Father'; it is to participate in the life of the gift-giving Spirit who makes prayer possible and effective; it is to make a connection whereby divine benefactions – power, guidance, protection, consolation, forgiveness, healing and blessing – are able to be asked for and received; it is to make a positive contribution to society's governance and well-being under God (1 Tim. 2.1-4); it is to have a means of engaging in depth with the mystery of weakness, suffering and death; and it is to practise a form of speech which is identity-forming and community-building.

CHAPTER FIVE

An Exegetical History of the Lord's Prayer: The First to the Sixth Century

ROY HAMMERLING

Early Christian authors believed that the Lord's Prayer was the truest scripture within scripture and the most succinct and complete statement of the whole of Christian theology. As a result, they held it to be an essential starting point for examining Christian thought and pious practice. This chapter offers a chronological exegetical petition-by-petition examination of the Lord's Prayer from the first to the sixth century and demonstrates that commentaries in the early church primarily understood the Lord's Prayer in the context of the distinctiveness of Christian community, worship and baptism. The introductory words, 'Our Father', said early writers, revealed how God became a parent to Christians in baptism. As a result, Jesus also became a sibling to those who emerged from the baptismal font, which was viewed as the womb of mother church. Theologians argued that the first three petitions, the so-called 'heavenly petitions', revealed that Christians honour God's name, seek the kingdom and obey God's will by leading godly lives and ultimately persevering in a desire for God. The final four, or 'earthly petitions', were directed towards the whole of life, meaning the present (praying for the needs of the day, i.e. daily bread), the past (asking for forgiveness for prior sins) and the future (seeking deliverance from temptation and evil). Hence, early commentaries suggested that the Lord's Prayer was the perfect prayer that revealed not only the true nature of God and God's love for humanity, but also the essential aspects of the Christian faith.[1]

The Lord's Prayer: Scripture within Scripture

Writers throughout the early church viewed the Lord's Prayer as the essence of scripture within scripture. Even though other biblical sayings of Jesus were also believed to be straight from the mouth of Jesus in the Bible, the Lord's Prayer had a brevity and poetic quality that the others lacked. And since the Lord's Prayer had central place in Christian worship, scholars favoured it above all other gospel texts, in part because it was easily memorized.

Still, there was a problem with the Lord's Prayer. The only two biblical passages that quote the whole of the Lord's Prayer (Mt. 6 and Lk. 11) are different. This, however, did not bother early commentators, who dismissed or explained away the discrepancies. Liturgical settings, where parishioners actually prayed the Lord's Prayer, harmonized the two accounts, blending elements of both into one communal prayer. And yet, no two versions of the Lord's Prayer in written literature or liturgies were exactly the same until liturgical practices became more widely standardized in the fourth century.[2]

Luke 11.1-4 tells how the disciples asked Jesus, 'Lord, teach us to pray, as John [the Baptist] taught his disciples'. Jesus handed over to them a five-petition prayer in the context of the Sermon on the Plain. In Matthew 6.9-13 Jesus presented a seven-petition Lord's Prayer in his Sermon on the Mount to a crowd of followers, which included the apostles.

A brief look at the two texts reveals their differences (see Table 1). Early commentators almost always assumed that the two biblical versions of the Lord's Prayer were one and the same prayer. Origen, however, stated: 'On the whole, it is better to suppose that the prayers are different, even though

---

[1]The following footnotes include representative writers down to the sixth century, who agree or echo a given point. In some instances, to highlight a particular issue, later authors will also be noted.

[2]Hans Dieter Betz, *The Sermon on the Mount* (Minneapolis, MN: Fortress Press, 1995), 372. The question of Jesus' authorship of the prayer in modern scholarship is hotly disputed. See Betz's excellent discussion of this. See also Roy Hammerling, *The Lord's Prayer in the Early Church: The Pearl of Great Price* (New York: Palgrave, 2010), chapters 1–2.

Table 1

	English		Koine Greek		Latin	
	Mt. 6.9-13	Lk. 11.1-4	Mt. 6.9-13	Lk. 11.1-4	Mt. 6.9-13	Lk. 11.1-4
Introduction	Our Father in heaven,	Father,	Πάτερ ἡμῶν ὁ ἐν τοῖς οὐρανοῖς,	Πάτερ,	Pater noster, qui es in caelis:	Pater,
First petition	holy be your name.	holy be your name.	ἁγιασθήτω τὸ ὄνομά σου.	ἁγιασθήτω τὸ ὄνομά σου·	sanctificetur nomen tuum.	sanctificetur nomen tuum.
Second petition	Your kingdom come.	Your kingdom come.	ἐλθέτω ἡ βασιλεία σου,	ἐλθέτω ἡ βασιλεία σου·	Adveniat regnum tuum.	Adveniat regnum tuum.
Third petition	Your will be done, on earth as it is in heaven.	--	γενηθήτω τὸ θέλημά σου, ὡς ἐν οὐρανῷ καὶ ἐπὶ γῆς.	--	Fiat voluntas tua, sicut in caelo, et in terra.	--
Fourth petition	Give us this day our daily (or supersubstantial) bread.	Give us each day our daily bread.	Τὸν ἄρτον ἡμῶν τὸν ἐπιούσιον δὸς ἡμῖν σήμερον·	τὸν ἄρτον ἡμῶν τὸν ἐπιούσιον δίδου ἡμῖν τὸ καθ᾽ ἡμέραν·	Panem nostrum supersubstantialem da nobis hodie.	Panem nostrum cotidianum (or quotidianum) da nobis cotidie.
Fifth petition	And forgive us our debts, as we also have forgiven our debtors.	And forgive us our sins, for we ourselves forgive everyone indebted to us.	καὶ ἄφες ἡμῖν τὰ ὀφειλήματα ἡμῶν, ὡς καὶ ἡμεῖς ἀφήκαμεν τοῖς ὀφειλέταις ἡμῶν·	καὶ ἄφες ἡμῖν τὰς ἁμαρτίας ἡμῶν, καὶ γὰρ αὐτοὶ ἀφίομεν παντὶ ὀφείλοντι ἡμῖν·	Et dimitte nobis debita nostra, sicut et nos dimittimus debitoribus nostris.	Et dimitte nobis peccata nostra, siquidem et ipsi dimittimus omni debenti nobis.
Sixth petition	And do not bring us to the time of trial (or into temptation).	And do not bring us to the time of trial (or into temptation).	καὶ μὴ εἰσενέγκῃς ἡμᾶς εἰς πειρασμόν,	καὶ μὴ εἰσενέγκῃς ἡμᾶς εἰς πειρασμόν.	Et ne nos inducas in tentationem.	Et ne nos inducas in temptationem
Seventh petition[3]	But rescue (or deliver) us from (the) evil (one).	--	ἀλλὰ ῥῦσαι ἡμᾶς ἀπὸ τοῦ πονηροῦ.	--	Sed libera nos a malo. Amen.	--

[3]This is the traditional numbering of the petitions. The English translation includes in parentheses some ambiguities of the text that exist either in translation or in manuscript variance. For another brief survey on this, see Kenneth W. Stevenson, *The Lord's Prayer: A Text in Tradition* (Minneapolis, MN: Fortress Press, 2004), 19.

they have certain parts in common.'[4] Origen noticed that Luke 11 has Jesus teaching the Lord's Prayer in a private context. His apostles did not need a longer Lord's Prayer, they knew it. Matthew, on the other hand, tells how Jesus presented the Lord's Prayer in public to a less educated audience, who required more clarity.[5]

Augustine of Hippo, unlike Origen, but like most other authors, argued the two were the same prayer. For Augustine, Luke omitted the third petition about God's will deliberately to emphasize the fact that the third petition merely repeats the same points of the first two. Similarly, Luke skipped the words, 'but deliver us from evil', to demonstrate that Christians when they are not tempted do no evil. Luke simply wanted to avoid repeating himself. Augustine assumed, as others did, that Matthew's longer Lord's Prayer is not only more complete but more authoritative and took precedence over Luke's Lord's Prayer.[6]

The Introduction to the Lord's Prayer: God 'Our Father', Jesus Our Brother, and the Church Our Mother

Early Christian writers always interpreted the words 'Our Father' and the Lord's Prayer in the context of the distinctiveness of Christian community, worship and baptism. In the two biblical versions of the Lord's Prayer, Matthew's seven-petition text (Mt. 6) starts with 'Our Father', but Luke's five-petition Lord's Prayer (Lk. 11) omits 'Our'. Nevertheless, commentators on the Lord's Prayer, like Cyprian, a bishop of a divided community in Carthage, focused upon how the communal act of praying of the Lord's Prayer in worship united God's children into one family.[7] So significant is this communal quality that early authors rarely talked about the private use of the Lord's Prayer, except in a negative way.[8] Early theologians consistently concluded that the Lord's Prayer unifies those who have been made true children of God in baptism. Paul's letters suggest that baptized Christians

---

[4]Origen, *On Prayer* 18.3; *An Exhortation to Martyrdom, Prayer and Select Works*, trans. Rowan E. Greer, CWS (New York: Paulist Press, 1979), 81–170.

[5]Origen, *On Prayer* 30.1.

[6]Augustine, *Enchiridion* 116 (WSA I/8). Augustine dealt with the problem of various versions at times. For one example of this, see his discussion of the sixth petition in Augustine, *De dono perseverantiae* 6.12 (WSA I/26).

[7]See Cyprian, *De ecclesiae Catholicae unitate* (CCSL 3) and Cyprian, *De dominica oratione* 8 (ANF 5).

[8]*Didache* 8 suggests praying the Lord's Prayer three times a day, but it is unclear whether this is simply private or in the context of family or worship or a combination of all three.

have a 'spirit of adoption' and thus not only have the right but the duty to call upon God as 'Abba, Father', or 'Our Father'.[9]

Some felt that the Lord's Prayer indicated how Christians were distinct from those who held different theological convictions or simply did not believe in Jesus; the latter most often referred to the Jews. Many argued, for example, that the Lord's Prayer revealed that the Jews had rejected Jesus as the son of God and thus had turned their backs on his and their 'Father'. Tertullian and Cyprian, quoting Isaiah 1.2 ('I have begotten sons, but they have not acknowledged me'), believed that God had been the Father of the Jews, but their 'rejection' of Jesus transformed them into children of a new father, the Devil.[10] No doubt the origins of anti-Semitic attitudes in Christianity find their roots here.

The title, 'Father', some claimed, referenced a desire by God to be known as a beloved parent in contrast to a remote Creator,[11] Judge,[12] or Lord.[13] Some New Testament passages, which include 'Abba', have been viewed by modern scholars as direct references to the Lord's Prayer because they come up in the context of baptism (Rom. 8.15; Gal. 4.6) or signify Lord's Prayer themes (Mk 11.25; John 17).[14] But all early Lord's Prayer commentaries claimed that God makes people true daughters and sons in baptism.[15]

---

[9]Romans 8.15; Galatians 4.6; see also *Didache* 8; Tertullian, *De oratione* 7 (ANF 3).

[10]Tertullian, *De oratione* 2; Cyprian, *De dominica oratione* 10; Chromatius of Aquileia, *Tractatus in Matthaeum* (CCSL 9); Origen, *On Prayer* 22.1-3.

[11]Cyprian, *De dominica oratione* 1-2; Juvencus, *Historia Evangelica*, 1.58-604 (PL 19); Augustine, *Sermon* 57 (for Augustine's sermons, see WSA III/1-11); Cassian, *Conlationes* 9-10 (*Conferences*, trans. Colm Luibheid, CWS [New York: Paulist Press, 1985]); Pseudo-Chrysostom, *Sermon* 28 (PL 4); Ildefonsus of Toledo, *Liber de cognitione baptismi* 133 (PL 96).

[12]Peter Chrysologus, *Sermon* 67 (FC 17) and *Sermon* 70 (FC 109); Pseudo-Quodvultdeus, 299 (PL 3); Coelius Sedulius, *Carmen Paschale* 2.231 (CSEL 10) and *Opus Paschale* 2.2 (PL 19); and Johann Huemer, *Sedulii Opera omnia* (Vindobonae: Apud C. Geroldi Filium Bibliopolam Academiae, 1885).

[13]Theodore of Mopsuestia, *Liber ad Baptizandos* 2.1; *Commentary of Theodore of Mopsuestia on the Lord's Prayer and on the Sacraments of Baptism and the Eucharist*, trans. A. Mingana, Woodbrooke Studies, vol. 6 (Piscataway, NJ: Gorgias Press, 1933).

[14]Mark Kiley, 'The Lord's Prayer and Matthean Theology', in *The Lord's Prayer and Other Prayer Texts from the Greco-Roman Era*, ed. James H. Charlesworth, Mark Harding and Mark Christopher Kiley (Valley Forge, PA: Trinity Press International, 1994), 15; Günter Bornkamm, 'Der Aufbau der Bergpredigt', *New Testament Studies* 24, no. 4 (1978): 419-32; Asher Finkel, 'The Prayer of Jesus in Matthew', in *Standing before God: Studies on Prayer in Scriptures and in Tradition with Essays in Honor of John M. Oesterreicher*, ed. Asher Finkel and Lawrence Frizzel (New York: KTAV, 1981), 131-70.

[15]Some notable examples include Theodore of Mopsuestia, *Liber ad Baptizandos* 2.1; Chromatius of Aquileia, *Tractatus in Matthaeum* 4; Peter Chrysologus, *Sermons* 68 and 71.

Many quoted John 1.12, 'To those who believe, he gives power to become sons (and daughters) of God,'[16] noting that those who remain slaves to sin are children of the devil, since they have only been born of their earthly parents, Adam and Eve.[17] God, the true Father, however, through the adoption of baptism, rescues people from Satan by adopting them as true daughters and sons, making them inheritors of the kingdom of heaven.[18]

Tertullian suggested, if God becomes a Father in baptism, then Christ becomes a sibling at the same time.[19] Cyprian noted that Jesus teaches his own prayer to his disciples, who in turn teach it to all baptized siblings, that is the true children of God.[20] In early liturgical ceremonies, the first prayer of the newly baptized was the Lord's Prayer, whose opening words, 'Our Father', were meant to be the first declaration of the reality that God had indeed become their heavenly parent in baptism.[21]

If God is Father and Christ brother, then the church, some reasoned, must be the mother of the baptized; also, the womb of mother church must then be the baptismal font.[22] But exactly when converts were considered to be worthy of uttering the words 'Our Father' in the baptismal-birthing process was debated. Early on Tertullian and others simply believed that catechumens became Christians only after they were born out of the font/womb during Easter morning baptisms. Therefore, in the earliest days, churches only taught the Lord's Prayer after baptism in a mystagogical manner, because to call God 'Father' before baptism would have been a lie, or a grave error.[23]

---

[16]Tertullian, *De oratione* 2; Cyprian, *De dominica oratione* 8; Chromatius of Aquileia, *Tractatus in Matthaeum* and Chromatius of Aquileia, *Praefatio Orationis Dominicae* (CCSL 9), 445; Peter Chrysologus, *Sermon* 69; Pseudo-Augustinus, *Sermon* 65 (PL 40).

[17]Cyprian, *De dominica oratione* 10; Ambrose, *De Sacramentis* 5.4 (FC 44); Theodore of Mopsuestia, *Liber ad Baptizandos* 2.1; Augustine, *De Sermone Domini in Monte* 2.4 (WSA I/15); Chromatius of Aquileia, *Tractatus in Matthaeum*; Peter Chrysologus, *Sermon* 71; Pseudo-Quodvultdeus; Pseudo-Chrysostom, *Sermon* 28; Ildefonsus of Toledo, *Liber de cognitione baptismi* 133.

[18]Augustine, *Sermons* 56, 57, 59; Augustine, *De Sermone Domini in Monte* 2.5; Cassian, *Conlationes* 9-10; John Chrysostom, *Homiliae in Matthaeum*, Homily 19 (NPNF-1 10); Cyril of Alexandria, *Homily* 71 (*Commentary on the Gospel of St Luke*, trans. R. Payne Smith [Long Island, NY: Studion Publishers, 1983]); Peter Chrysologus, *Sermon* 70; Pseudo-Quodvultdeus.

[19]Tertullian, *De oratione* 9.

[20]Cyprian, *De dominica oratione* 3.

[21]Augustine, *Sermons* 58 and 59, and in nearly all early Lord's Prayer commentaries.

[22]Tertullian, *De oratione* 8; Augustine, *Sermons* 56 and 57.

[23]Tertullian, *De oratione* 8. Joseph H. Lynch, *Godparents and Kinship: Godparents and Kinship in Early Medieval Europe* (Princeton, NJ: Princeton University Press, 2019), 115 has noted that Clement of Alexandria, *Stromata* 4.25 (ANF 2) is the first known reference to the baptismal font as a womb; see also Walter M. Bedard, *The Symbolism of the Baptismal Font in Early Christian Thought* (Washington, DC: Catholic University of America Press, 1951), 17–36; Joseph C. Plumpe, *Mater Ecclesia: An Inquiry into the Concept of the Church as Mother in Early Christianity* (Washington, DC: Catholic University of America Press, 1943); and Karl Delahaye, *Ecclesia Mater: Chez les Péres des Trois Premieres siécles* (Paris: Latour-Maubourg, 1964).

Augustine, however, handed over the Lord's Prayer to those 'still in the womb' or catechumens preparing for baptism during Lent. He was careful to state, however, that these *competentes* merely recited the Lord's Prayer before baptism and were unable truly to pray it until God had in fact become their true Father in baptism; that is they were like eggs that had not hatched yet.[24] Peter Chrysologus shortly thereafter declared that during Lent, catechumens were conceived in the womb by praying the Lord's Prayer and thus were already at that time fully God's children and rightly called upon God as Father, even though they still awaited their birth. Like other notable children in the womb, for example, John the Baptist (Lk. 1) or Jacob and Esau (Gen. 25), they participated in God's plan of salvation even before they had been baptized/born and therefore may rightly pray the Lord's Prayer even before their baptismal birth.[25] Pseudo-Quodvultdeus declared without hesitation that converts were daughters and sons of God simply by virtue of the fact that they prayed the Lord's Prayer even before baptism.[26] Thus, praying the Lord's Prayer, for some, even before their baptism, indicated that those seeking to be a part of the church were already children of God as they awaited their watery birth.

The Heavenly Petitions: Persevering in a Desire for God

Almost every Christian commentator down to the present day has understood the focus of the first three petitions to be 'heavenly', or directed towards godly concerns like making God's name holy, seeking God's kingdom and obeying God's will. Still, the actual wording of these celestial petitions proved troublesome; authors almost always began by noting the ambiguity in the idea of making God's name holy.[27] Tertullian wondered if the words 'Holy be your name', imply that God's name in some way is not holy and that humans are able to add holiness to it. He and others were quick to condemn such thinking. They concluded that God's name is always holy in and of itself, as the Bible notes (Isa. 6 and Rev. 4), and people cannot

---

[24]Augustine, *Sermon* 56.

[25]Peter Chrysologus, *Sermons* 70 and 72.

[26]Pseudo-Quodvultdeus, 299ff.

[27]Cyprian, *De dominica oratione* 12; Ambrose, *De Sacramentis* 5.4; Chromatius of Aquileia, *Tractatus in Matthaeum* 2.1; Cyril of Alexandria, *Homily* 72; see also Leviticus 11.44; 19.2; 20.7. God's name was most often understood to be 'Father', but in a few places is 'Jesus' or 'Christ' as well. See Tertullian, *De oratione* 3; Cyprian, *De dominica oratione* 12; Chromatius of Aquileia, *Tractatus in Matthaeum* 2.1; Peter Chrysologus, *Sermon* 68 and *Sermon* 70.

improve upon God's holiness.[28] Rather, almost every early scholar stated that the true meaning of the text is that God is to be made holy 'in us', that is in the lives of the faithful.[29]

Early theologians responded to the second petition in the same way by wondering if God's kingdom can be hindered from coming. Their conclusion was that God's kingdom comes in and of itself, and is indeed eternal existing in the present,[30] even though it will only come fully in the last days.[31] God always reigns, said Augustine, like a light that always shines; even if the light is unable to be seen by the blind or those who shut their eyes.[32]

The third heavenly petition raised similar questions.[33] Does praying, 'Your will be done on earth as in heaven', suggest that God's will is not done or needs prayer before it can be accomplished? All emphatically declared that God's will is always done with or without prayer.[34] What is asked in this petition again then is that God's will may be done 'in us' or believers,[35] or

---

[28]Tertullian, *De oratione* 3; see also Cyprian, *De dominica oratione* 12; Origen, *On Prayer* 24.1; Gregory of Nyssa, *De dominica oratione* 3 (ACW 18); Cyril of Jerusalem, *Mystagogic Catecheses* 5.12 (FC 64); Augustine, *De Sermone Domini in Monte* 2.5; Cyril of Alexandria, *Homily* 72.

[29]Clement of Alexandria, *Adumbrationes in Judam II* (GCS 17); Tertullian, *De oratione* 3; Cyprian, *De dominica oratione* 12; Origen, *On Prayer* 24.1; Juvencus, *Historia Evangelica* 1.58-604; Gregory of Nyssa, *De dominica oratione* 3; Ambrose, *De Sacramentis* 5.4; Theodore of Mopsuestia, *Liber ad Baptizandos* 2.1; Augustine, *ep.* 130 (WSA II/1); Augustine, *De Sermone Domini in Monte* 2.5, 2.11; Augustine, *De dono perseverantiae* 2.4; Augustine, *Sermons* 56-59; Cyril of Alexandria, *Homily* 72; Jerome, *Commentariorum in Matthaeum libri IV* 6.10 (GCS 40); Jerome, *Dialogus adversus Pelagianos* 3.15 (PL 23); Chromatius of Aquileia, *Tractatus in Matthaeum* 2.2; Peter Chrysologus, *Sermons* 67, 69 and 72; Pseudo-Quodvultdeus, 300; Coelius Sedulius, *Carmen Paschale* 2.231; *Opus Imperfectum in Matthaeum, Homily* 14 (PG 56); Caesarius of Arles, *Sermon* 147 (CCSL 103); Pseudo-Fortunatus, *Expositio orationis domincae* 14-18 (PL 88); Ildefonsus of Toledo, *Liber de cognitione baptismi* 133.

[30]Cyprian, *De dominica oratione* 13; Augustine, *Sermons* 56, 57, 59; Cyril of Alexandria, *Homily* 73; Caesarius of Arles, *Sermon* 147; Peter Chrysologus, *Sermon* 72; Pseudo-Quodvultdeus 40.4; Chromatius of Aquileia, *Praefatio Orationis Dominicae*; Cyril of Alexandria, *Homily* 73.

[31]Augustine, *De Sermone Domini in Monte* 2.6; Augustine, *Sermon* 56; Peter Chrysologus, *Sermon* 67.

[32]Augustine, *De Sermone Domini in Monte* 2.6. See Gregory of Nyssa, *De dominica oratione* 3; see also Cyril of Alexandria, *Homily* 73.

[33]Luke's version of the Lord's Prayer omitted this petition. Augustine, *Enchiridion* 116; see also Origen, *On Prayer* 18.2-3 and 26.1.

[34]Tertullian, *De oratione* 4; Cyprian, *De dominica oratione* 14; Augustine, *Sermons* 56 and 57; Chromatius of Aquileia, *Tractatus in Matthaeum*; Cyril of Alexandria, *Homily* 74; Pseudo-Augustinus, *Sermon* 65; *Opus Imperfectum in Matthaeum, Homily* 14.

[35]Tertullian, *De oratione* 4; Cyprian, *De dominica oratione* 14; Origen, *On Prayer* 26.1; Gregory of Nyssa, *De dominica oratione* 4; Augustine, *Sermon* 56; Cassian, *Conlationes* 9.20; Chromatius of Aquileia, *Tractatus in Matthaeum*; Cyril of Alexandria, *Homily* 74; *Opus Imperfectum in Matthaeum, Homily* 14; Pseudo-Fortunatus, *Expositio orationis dominicae* 30-51.

all people.[36] When the faithful pray 'your' will be done, then, noted some, they pray with the Lord's Prayer with a proper humility.[37] Christians, most writers declared, can only do God's will with the help of God's grace.[38] Augustine argued that such grace especially was required to persevere in the faith.[39] But how?

Early commentaries stated that it is primarily through baptism and the praying of the Lord's Prayer that people keep God's name holy, seek the kingdom and fulfil God's will.[40] Pseudo-Fortunatus, for example, stated that the Lord's Prayer enables Christians to remain true to the sanctity of their baptism.[41] In other words, the holiness of adoption that comes through baptism creates a desire in the faithful to persevere in seeking God in all things and the Lord's Prayer indicates how to do that.[42]

Cyprian declared that if Christians wish to persevere in their baptisms, praying and following the heavenly petitions helps them do so.[43] Augustine, echoing Cyprian, added that the first three petitions refuted Pelagian suggestions that one is able to cooperate with God in the process of salvation. Perseverance is God's gift in the same way that baptism is. Thus, the prayer for God's name to be holy, kingdom to come and will to be done is a prayer for perseverance in faith, which also is a gift of God's grace.[44] The Lord's Prayer is a daily baptism, or a baptism which may be returned to daily in order that the faithful might persevere, said Augustine.[45] The

---

[36]Tertullian, *De oratione* 4; Augustine, *De dono perseverantiae*; Augustine, *De Sermone Domini in Monte* 2.6; Cassian, *Conlationes* 9.20; Peter Chrysologus, *Sermons* 67-68; *Opus Imperfectum in Matthaeum*, Homily 14; Pseudo-Fortunatus, *Expositio orationis dominicae* 30-51.

[37]Pseudo-Fortunatus, *Expositio orationis dominicae* 30-51.

[38]Tertullian, *De oratione* 4; Gregory of Nyssa, *De dominica oratione* 4; Augustine, *Sermon* 56; John Chrysostom, *Homily* 19; Cyril of Alexandria, *Homily* 74; Pseudo-Fortunatus, *Expositio orationis dominicae* 30-51.

[39]Tertullian, *De oratione* 4; Cyprian, *De dominica oratione* 14; Augustine, *De dono perseverantiae*; Coelius Sedulius, *Carmen Paschale* 2.231.

[40]Cyprian, *De dominica oratione* 12; Augustine, *De dono perseverantiae* 2.4; Augustine, *Sermon* 59; Chromatius of Aquileia, *Tractatus in Matthaeum* 2.2; Chromatius, *Praefatio Orationis Dominicae*; Caesarius of Arles, *Sermon* 147; Pseudo-Fortunatus, *Expositio orationis domincae* 14-18.

[41]Pseudo-Fortunatus, *Expositio orationis domincae* 14-15, 18.

[42]Cyprian, *De dominica oratione* 12; Gregory of Nyssa, *De dominica oratione* 3; Augustine, *Sermon* 58.

[43]Cyprian, *De dominica oratione* 12; see also Augustine, *Sermon* 59; Caesarius of Arles, *Sermon* 147.

[44]Augustine, *De dono perseverantiae* 2.4; Augustine, *Sermon* 59; see also Chromatius, *Praefatio Orationis Dominicae*; Augustine, *In Evangelium Joannis Tractatus Centum Viginti Quatuor* 48.9 (CCL 36).

[45]Augustine, *De dono perserverantiae* 3.2.

goal of honourable Christian lives then is to honour God with prayer,[46] worship and leading holy lives within community.[47] Only in this way do people avoid dishonouring God with evil deeds or falling into heterodox beliefs.[48]

The heavenly petitions, therefore, were central in theological debates against those considered unorthodox. Augustine, for example, makes good use of them in his *On the Gift of Perseverance*, which is a polemical work directed at the so-called Semipelagians. Similarly, Cyril of Alexandria's Lord's Prayer homilies were in part targeted at Nestorians.[49]

Some held that the Jews were the first to have been promised the kingdom, just as they were the first to be the daughters and sons of God, and therefore were rightly called the chosen people. However, many authors said, the Jews 'rejected' God's name, kingdom and will when they ignored the bringer of the kingdom, Christ. Therefore, the Jews and those who cling to heterodox traditions lose the kingdom of God when they go astray from the teachings of the Lord's Prayer. The truly baptized children of God in the end, therefore, will not only be recognizably distinct from those who fail to live up to being true children, but they will also pass judgement upon them in the last days (Mt. 19.28).[50]

The Earthly Petitions: Spiritual and Physical Need in the Present, Past and Future

Interpreters of the Lord's Prayer throughout the history of the church have noted a shift of emphasis in the final four petitions of the Lord's Prayer, which move towards earthly matters.[51] These earthly petitions address the spiritual and physical needs of people in the present, past, and future. Many believed that the fourth petition was a perfect transitional petition between the heavenly and earthly petitions because it is both about a present

---

[46]Pseudo-Augustinus, *Sermon 65*.

[47]Coelius Sedulius, *Carmen Paschale* 2.231.

[48]Cyprian, *De dominica oratione* 12; Theodore of Mopsuestia, *Liber ad Baptizandos* 2.1 Augustine, *ep.* 130; Peter Chrysologus, *Sermon 67*; Jerome, *Commentariorum in Matthaeum libri IV* 6.10; Cassian, *Conlationes* 9-10; John Chrysostom, *Homily* 29; Cyril of Alexandria, *Homily* 72; Peter Chrysologus, *Sermon 67, Sermons 69-72*; Coelius Sedulius, *Opus Paschale* 2.2; Pseudo-Fortunatus, *Expositio orationis domincae* 14-18.

[49]Cyril of Alexandria, *Homily* 72.

[50]Cyprian, *De dominica oratione* 13; Origen, *On Prayer* 25.3; Gregory of Nyssa, *De dominica oratione* 3; Pseudo-Quodvultdeus.

[51]Tertullian, *De oratione* 6.

heavenly concern for spiritual bread for the soul (most often believed to be the Eucharist) and a present concern for physical bread for the body.[52]

Tertullian's threefold interpretation of the fourth petition basically became the standard. He proposed that first, bread is material food for the body;[53] second, spiritual food for the soul (John 6, i.e. Christ, the bread of life, the Eucharist); and lastly, bread for the mind (scripture and divine teaching).[54] Many equated the wording of 'supersubstantial bread', which hints more at a spiritual view of bread in Matthew 6, with Luke 11's 'daily', or a more physical bread, without explanation.[55] All authors subordinated the literal interpretation of physical bread to its spiritual meaning in some way.[56] This may have been in part because in worship the Lord's Prayer was closely positioned before the partaking of the Eucharist. In fact, it seems likely that the fourth petition may have inspired some early liturgists to place the Lord's Prayer just prior to the celebration of the Eucharist in worship.[57]

Many declared that the fourth petition avails very little unless people are set right with God through forgiveness, humanity's most basic spiritual need.[58] Early scholars often dedicated the majority of their commentaries on the Lord's Prayer to the fifth petition. When a specific petition of the Lord's Prayer came up in writings outside of commentaries on the Lord's Prayer, the vast majority of those references were to the fifth petition (e.g. Augustine

---

[52]Cyril of Alexandria, *Homily* 75; Isidore of Seville, *De ecclesiasticis officiis* 15 (ACW 61); see also Cyprian, *De dominica oratione* 18; Juvencus, *Historia Evangelica*, 1.58-604; Augustine, *De Sermone Domini in Monte* 2.7; Peter Chrysologus, *Sermon* 70.

[53]Tertullian, *De oratione* 6; Gregory of Nyssa, *De dominica oratione* 4; Augustine, *De Sermone Domini in Monte* 2.7; Augustine, *Sermons* 56-59; Chromatius of Aquileia, *Tractatus in Matthaeum* 5.1; Caesarius of Arles, *Sermon* 147.

[54]Origen, *On Prayer* 27.4; Augustine, *Sermons* 56 and 59.

[55]Tertullian, *De oratione* 6; Cyprian, *De dominica oratione* 19-21; Ambrose, *De Sacramentis* 5.4; Augustine, *De Sermone Domini in Monte* 2.7; Augustine, *Sermons* 56-59; John Chrysostom, *Homily* 19; Cassian, *Conlationes* 9.21; Chromatius of Aquileia, *Tractatus in Matthaeum* 5.1; John Chrysostom, *Homily* 19; Cyril of Alexandria, *Homily* 75; Pseudo-Quodvultdeus; Coelius Sedulius, *Opus Paschale* 2.2; Pseudo-Augustinus, *Sermon* 65; *Opus Imperfectum in Matthaeum*, *Homily* 14.

[56]Origen, *On Prayer* 27.1-2; Cyril of Jerusalem, *Mystagogic Catechesis* 5.15; for comments on the bread of the Eucharist, see Alexis James Doval, *Cyril of Jerusalem, Mystagogue: The Authorship of the 'Mystagogic Catecheses'* (Washington, DC: Catholic University of America Press, 2001), 212; Peter Chrysologus, *Sermons* 70 and 71.

[57]Ildefonsus of Toledo, *Liber de cognitione baptismi* 136; see also Cyprian, *De dominica oratione* 18; Ambrose, *De Sacramentis* 5.4; Augustine, *ep.* 130; Augustine, *De Sermone Domini in Monte* 2.7; Augustine, *Sermon* 58; Peter Chrysologus, *Sermons* 68 and 70; Caesarius of Arles, *Sermon* 147; Pseudo-Fortunatus, *Expositio orationis dominicae* 52-57.

[58]For example, Tertullian, *De oratione* 7; Cyprian, *De dominica oratione* 22.

and Caesarius of Arles).[59] Writers almost always saw the fifth petition as the most important of the seven petitions because it not only asks for but also has the ability to aid the faithful attain forgiveness.

Writers generally equated the idea of 'debts' or 'trespasses' from Matthew 6's Lord's Prayer with Luke 11's 'sins' without comment.[60] Because sins were closely identified in this way with debts, most authors noted that sins have a monetary quality.[61] Augustine suggested that humans are unable to pay their past spiritual debts in much the same way that they are incapable of paying enormous physical debts. They either do not have the means to do so, or if they do, they are unwilling to do so. Even the faithful, who have had their past debts of sin wiped out in baptism, continue to incur new debts and thus have a constant need for the help of God, who bails them out by paying their debts for them, that is offering them forgiveness by means of the generous treasure of God's grace.[62]

Some, most notably Origen, said believers owe these debts to God, others and themselves,[63] but, all held that the first step in the process of forgiveness is to acknowledge sinfulness in confession.[64] Augustine noted that since saints recognized their need and prayed the fifth petition, and so confessed daily, everyone else should do the same.[65] Every commentator noted that Jesus is always willing to forgive the debts of those who truly confess their sins by means of the fifth petition.[66] The fifth petition thus continues the work of forgiveness, which was begun in baptism, and Augustine even calls

---

[59]See, for example, the following of Augustine's sermons: 9, 16A, 17, 47, 49, 56-59, 114, 135, 155, 163, 163B, 179, 181, 211, 213, 278, 315, 352, 383, 385; and the following of Caesarius of Arles' sermons: 19, 28, 30, 35, 37-39, 60, 73, 75, 91, 107, 147, 180, 200, 202, 229, 235.

[60]Tertullian, *De oratione* 7; Cyprian, *De dominica oratione* 22; Gregory of Nyssa, *De dominica oratione* 5; Ambrose, *De Sacramentis* 5.4; Augustine, *De Sermone Domini in Monte* 2.8; Augustine, *Sermons 56-59*; Peter Chrysologus, *Sermon 68*; Pseudo-Augustinus, *Sermon 65*; Coelius Sedulius, *Carmen Paschale* 2.231ff; Coelius Sedulius, *Opus Paschale* 2.2; Prosper of Aquitaine, *Expositio Psalmorum* (CCSL 67a); Caesarius of Arles, *Sermon 147*; Pseudo-Fortunatus, *Expositio orationis dominicae* 58-61.

[61]Ambrose, *De Sacramentis* 5.4.

[62]Augustine, *De Sermone Domini in Monte* 2.8; Augustine, *Sermon 56*; see also Origen, *On Prayer* 28.4; Gregory of Nyssa, *De dominica oratione* 5.

[63]Origen, *On Prayer* 28.1-3. See especially, Irenaeus, *Adversus Haereses* 3.16, 4.9 and 4.8 (ANF 1); Tertullian, *De oratione* 7; Pseudo-Fortunatus, *Expositio orationis dominicae* 58-61.

[64]Cyprian, *De dominica oratione* 22; Chromatius of Aquileia, *Tractatus in Matthaeum*.

[65]Augustine, *Sermon 58*; Cyprian, *De dominica oratione* 22; Augustine, *In Evangelium Joannis Tractatus Centum Viginti Quatuor* 26; Augustine, *De Sermone Domini in Monte* 2.11; Augustine, *Sermons 56-59*; Chromatius of Aquileia, *Tractatus in Matthaeum* and *Praefatio Orationis Dominicae*; Coelius Sedulius, *Opus Paschale* 2.2.

[66]See Cyprian, *De dominica oratione* 22; John Chrysostom, *Homily 19*.

the Lord's Prayer, because of this petition, a 'daily baptism'.[67] Christians, said Augustine, are like a leaky boat that keeps taking on water. Unless the water is pumped out daily, the boat will sink.[68]

Augustine even considered the Lord's Prayer to be a sacrament because it bestows the grace of absolution. The Lord's Prayer, however, is sacramental in a unique way for Augustine, who believed that there was both a narrow and a broad definition of sacrament. Narrowly speaking sacraments like baptism, the Eucharist and extreme unction are unique in that they attach words to physical elements in order that God might bestow grace.[69] Broadly speaking, Augustine said, there are numerous sacraments or sacramental actions in the Old and New Testaments, the life of the church and even in other religions.[70] Augustine considered the Lord's Prayer a sacrament in both a narrow and a broad sense. The actual words of the Lord's Prayer are narrowly sacramental because they are not only a sign which points to forgiveness, but a means by which such forgiveness is accomplished. Broadly speaking, since the fifth petition in particular offers the grace of forgiveness the Lord's Prayer acts as an extension of baptism in the daily lives of the faithful and acts like a 'daily' baptism. And so, it does what baptism does not do, that is the Lord's Prayer helps forgive sins over and over again and thus can be distinguished from baptism. Since, said Augustine, Christians sustain many wounds in their war with the devil the Lord's Prayer and the fifth petition specifically serve as a daily salve, which offer regular spiritual healing for past wounds.[71]

Many commentators emphasized that the fifth petition is unique in that it also has a conditional clause, 'Forgive ... *as we forgive our debtors*'. Hence, the necessity of forgiving others, in order to be forgiven, was of paramount importance for early writers.[72] This petition came to be seen by some as a covenant between God and the faithful.[73] Augustine noted that the clause

---

[67]Augustine, *Sermon* 213; Augustine, *Enchiridion* 70-80; see also Theodore of Mopsuestia, *Liber ad Baptizandos* 2.1; Cyril of Alexandria, *Homily* 76. Bede's Sermon on John 16.23-30 in *Bedae Homiliae evangelii* and Bede's Sermon on Luke 11.9-13 (CCSL 120).

[68]Augustine, *Sermon* 56.

[69]Augustine, *In Evangelium Joannis Tractatus Centum Viginti Quatuor* 80.3; Augustine, *Contra Faustum Manichaeum* 19.13-16 (WSA I/20); Augustine, *De doctrina christiana* 3.9.13 (WSA I/11).

[70]F. Van Der Meer, *Augustine the Bishop* (London: Sheed and Ward, 1961), 280; William A. Van Roo, *The Christian Sacrament* (Rome: Pontificia Universita Gregoriana, 1992), 38. For more on Augustine's view of sacrament, see Hammerling, *The Lord's Prayer in the Early Church*, 92.

[71]Augustine, *In Evangelium Joannis Tractatus Centum Viginti Quatuor* 52.

[72]Clement of Rome, *First Epistle to the Corinthians* 13.2 (ACW 1); Tertullian, *De oratione* 7; Clement of Alexandria, *Stromata* 7.13; Cyprian, *De dominica oratione* 23; Cyril of Jerusalem, *Mystagogic Catechesis* 5.16; Ambrose, *De Sacramentis* 5.4.

[73]Augustine, *De Sermone Domini in Monte* 2.8; Peter Chrysologus, *Sermon* 68; Pseudo-Quodvultdeus; Caesarius of Arles, *Sermon* 180; Pseudo-Augustinus, *Sermon* 65.

is a 'thunderous warning'.[74] Forgive or perish![75] Ignore this part of the fifth petition and the entire Lord's Prayer becomes null and void.[76]

Cassian interestingly noted that during the prayers of the hours, some monks often went quiet during this part of Lord's Prayer, because they omitted the words '*as we forgive our debtors*'. God, said Cassian, is not deceived by such moments of silence and they will no doubt receive punishment for such simpleminded trickery. Cassian added on the contrary that this petition is also not a licence simply to overlook the debts of sinners, because an overindulgence of reprobates, or forgiveness of those who do not make a true confession, helps no one either.[77]

Gregory of Nyssa with his typical holy audacity declared that the fifth petition helps transform human into divine nature. Says Gregory, 'Be your own judge, give yourself the sentence of acquittal. Do you want your debts to be forgiven by God? Forgive them yourself, and God will ratify it.' For Gregory, if people forgive others, they imitate the divine action of God and in turn become examples to God, who imitates them by forgiving them in turn.[78]

Generally speaking, once commentators reached the sixth and seventh petitions of their Lord's Prayer commentaries, their explanations often hurried through the last two petitions, many times discussing them together and only briefly.[79] Tertullian and Augustine, however, believed that after people receive forgiveness of their past sins, they then only need two things in the future and that is to be kept from falling into temptation or being overcome by evil.[80]

---

[74]Augustine, *Enchiridion* 74; see also Augustine, *Sermons* 56-58; Augustine, *ep.* 130; Augustine, *De Sermone Domini in Monte* 2.8-11; Peter Chrysologus, *Sermons* 67-68, 70-72; John Chrysostom, *Homily* 19; Coelius Sedulius, *Carmen Paschale* 2.231; Coelius Sedulius, *Opus Paschale* 2.2; Coelius Sedulius, *Opus Imperfectum in Matthaeum*, *Homily* 14; Caesarius of Arles, *Sermons* 19, 107, 180, 187.

[75]Augustine, *De Sermone Domini in Monte* 2.8; see also Cyprian, *De dominica oratione* 24.

[76]Augustine, *De Sermone Domini in Monte* 2.8; Augustine, *Sermon* 56; see also Coelius Sedulius, *Opus Imperfectum in Matthaeum*, *Homily* 14.

[77]Cassian, *Conlationes* 9.22.

[78]Gregory of Nyssa, *De dominica oratione* 5.

[79]Tertullian, *De oratione* 8; Gregory of Nyssa, *De dominica oratione* 5; Ambrose, *De Sacramentis* 5.4; Augustine, *Enchiridion* 114-16; Augustine, *De dono perseverantiae* 116-117; Chromatius of Aquileia, *Tractatus in Matthaeum*; Pseudo-Quodvultdeus; *Opus Imperfectum in Matthaeum*, *Homily* 14; Caesarius of Arles, *Sermon* 147; Pseudo-Fortunatus, *Expositio orationis dominicae* 62; Ildefonsus of Toledo, *Liber de cognitione baptismi* 133.

[80]Tertullian, *De oratione* 8; Augustine, *Sermon* 56; Augustine, *In Evangelium Joannis Tractatus Centum Viginti Quatuor* 52.

Many wondered, 'Does the sixth petition suggest that God is a tempter?'[81] Tertullian answered, 'God forbid such a thought'. Referring to James 1, Tertullian noted, 'No one, when tempted, should say, "I am being tempted by God"; for God cannot be tempted by evil and he himself tempts no one. But one is tempted by one's own desire, being lured and enticed by it.'[82] Origen (referring to Judith 8, Psalm 34 and Acts 14) and Cyril of Jerusalem (commenting on James 1), however, did not have a problem saying that God tempts to test people in order to make them stronger in faith.[83]

Augustine distinguished two primary ways that Christians are tempted. First, they are tempted with the hope of some earthly reward or goods, or second, by the fear of bodily harm.[84] God at times withdraws from people, for divine reasons giving them up to the Devil or to their own evil desires (Rom. 1), suggested Augustine, but the sixth petition simply begs that God not abandon them in the time of temptation.[85] Others noted that God does not allow believers to be tempted beyond their abilities to resist (1 Cor. 10).[86]

The fifth petition, many suggested, healed past wounds, while the sixth and seventh petitions helped keep the Devil from doing any future harm through temptation or evil.[87] Augustine also considered daily deliverance from temptation and evil to be a gracious gift of perseverance in the faith and life.[88] To have the sixth and seventh petitions answered, noted Augustine, means that Christians are free from dread and so they may have hope that God will protect them from all future spiritual harm.[89]

---

[81]Tertullian, *De oratione* 8; Cyprian, *De dominica oratione* 25; Juvencus, *Historia Evangelica* 1.58-604; Augustine, *In Evangelium Joannis Tractatus Centum Viginti Quatuor* 52; Augustine, *ep.* 130; Augustine, *De Sermone Domini in Monte* 2.9-11; Augustine, *Sermons* 57-58; Cassian, *Conlationes* 9.23; John Chrysostom, *Homily* 19; Chromatius of Aquileia, *Tractatus in Matthaeum*; Peter Chrysologus, *Sermons* 67-68, 70-72; Pseudo-Quodvultdeus; Pseudo-Augustine, *Sermon* 65; Caesarius of Arles, *Sermon* 147; Pseudo-Fortunatus, *Expositio orationis dominicae* 62; Ildefonsus of Toledo, *Liber de cognitione baptismi* 133.
[82]Tertullian, *De oratione* 8; Cyprian, *De dominica oratione* 25; see also Chromatius of Aquileia, *Praefatio Orationis Dominicae*; Cyril of Alexandria, *Homily* 77; Peter Chrysologus, *Sermon* 70.
[83]Origen, *On Prayer* 24.3-4; Cyril of Jerusalem, *Mystagogic Catechesis* 5.17.
[84]Augustine, *Sermon* 59.
[85]Augustine, *De Sermone Domini in Monte* 2.9; Augustine, *Sermon* 57; see also Peter Chrysologus, *Sermons* 70 and 72; Origen, *On Prayer* 29.12.
[86]Ambrose, *De Sacramentis* 5.4; Origen, *On Prayer* 19.2; Chromatius of Aquileia, *Tractatus in Matthaeum*; *Opus Imperfectum in Matthaeum*, *Homily* 14.
[87]Augustine, *In Evangelium Joannis Tractatus Centum Viginti Quatuor* 52.
[88]Augustine, *In Evangelium Joannis Tractatus Centum Viginti Quatuor* 124; Cyril of Alexandria, *Homily* 77.
[89]Augustine, *De Sermone Domini in Monte* 2.9

Conclusion

Lord's Prayer commentaries from the first to the sixth century taught Christians about the nature of God and the essential and distinctive elements of Christian community, thought, and faith. Authors eventually came to believe that the act of praying Christ's own prayer was like the act of conception by which catechumens came to life in the womb of mother church. Thus, in baptism, commentaries suggested, the faithful emerged from the womb of the church, the baptismal font, as newborn, daughters and sons of God, who became their adoptive Father in the process. Likewise, at the same time, Jesus became their sibling, who out of love taught them how to pray, and by this prayer, how to lead godly lives. The heavenly petitions explained that Christians must honour God's name, seek the kingdom and obey God's will, if they hoped to persevere in faith and in desiring God until the day of judgement. The earthly petitions encompassed the whole of human life. The fourth petition showed how God provided for every present and daily need by offering daily bread. The fifth petition moved Christians to seek forgiveness for past sins. The final two petitions sought deliverance from future temptation and evil. Thus, early authors believed that Christ's words of the Lord's Prayer not only sought but provided for everything that the true children of God hoped for within their hearts, minds, and souls, that is to live out their lives as faithful daughters and sons of God, who helped them persevere in this present evil age until the glorious day when they would be united with their Father in heaven.

CHAPTER SIX

Ultimate Desire: The Prayer of Jesus in John 17

DAVID F. FORD

The prayer of Jesus in John 17, concluding his Farewell Discourses on the night before his death, can be fruitfully understood not only as the theological culmination of the Gospel of John, but also as a prayer-centred vantage point from which to re-read the rest of the New Testament and the scriptures of Israel and of Jesus, the Christian Old Testament. Even more than that, its reach extends forward through the whole tradition of prayer, liturgy, theology and Christian living that is explored in this Handbook. Even beyond all that, John 17 also reaches forward from today, opening up both an understanding and a practice of prayer that are a gift, an invitation and a radical challenge to those who pray in the name of Jesus in the twenty-first century. This chapter explores each of those dimensions of John 17.

Breath of the Spirit, Summit of Love, Place of Prayer

The Farewell Discourses (Jn 13-17) give, in characteristic Johannine style,[1] wave after wave of teaching, as Jesus prepares his disciples (*mathētai*, 'learners') for the ongoing drama of their lives after his death and resurrection.

---

[1]The opening words are a succinct example, with three waves in one verse – the third wave, as so often, the largest in terms of meaning: 'In the beginning was the Word, and the Word was with God, and the Word was God' (1.1). A more extended set of three waves is 3.1-21, in which each wave begins, 'Very truly, I tell you …'.

Love is the leading theme, signalled at the beginning: 'Having loved his own who were in the world, he loved them to the end' (13.11). The first wave of love comes in that chapter, when Jesus washes his disciples' feet, tells them to follow his example and then, after Judas departs, gives them 'a new commandment, that you love one another. Just as I have loved you, you also should love one another' (13.34). The second wave comes after the parable of the vine in John 15, moving beyond the servant imagery of foot-washing to friendship: 'This is my commandment, that you love one another as I have loved you. No one has greater love than this, to lay down one's life for one's friends. You are my friends if you do what I command you' (15.12-14). The third, overwhelming breaker comes in John 17. This is also the culmination of other waves in the Farewell Discourses besides those of love.

There have been waves of teaching on the Holy Spirit in John 14, 15 and 16. Here in John 17 the Spirit is not mentioned explicitly, but from the rest of the Gospel it is clear that the Spirit is taken for granted as present. The first mention in John 1 repeats twice that the Holy Spirit remained (the verb is *menein*, remain, abide, dwell – a key word in John) on Jesus, and so in the rest of the Gospel, and in this prayer, we are always to understand Jesus as inseparable from the Spirit. Further, Jesus says, 'As you have sent me into the world, so I have sent them into the world' (17.18), and when later, after his resurrection, he actually sends them, he breathes his Spirit into them – 'he breathed on them and said to them, "Receive the Holy Spirit"' (20.22). *So the breath of Jesus on which the words of this prayer are carried is the breath of the Spirit that is shared with his disciples.*[2] Essential to Jesus being sent is Jesus praying, and the 'as ... so ' of 17.18, repeated in 20.21, 'As the Father has sent me, so I send you', means that his disciples too are to pray as he does. And are we to imagine the risen Jesus ever ceasing to breathe his Spirit into his disciples? The utter intimacy of mutual indwelling, sealed by the concluding 'I in them' (17.26), makes that unimaginable.

The Farewell Discourses also have waves of teaching on prayer, encouraging daring petition in the name of Jesus: 'If in my name you ask me for anything, I will do it' (14.14); 'If you abide in me, and my words abide in you, ask for whatever you wish, and it will be done for you' (15.7); 'Ask and you will receive, so that your joy may be complete' (16.24). The culmination of these in John 17 is Jesus modelling such daring prayer, and what it means for those who pray to pray in his name, while abiding in him and having his words abide in them.

---

[2]See the rich reflections on the theme of breath and prayer in Elizabeth Dodd's chapter in this volume.

So in John 17 the teaching on both the Holy Spirit and on prayer reaches a culmination in the form of actual prayer in the Spirit – a demonstration, enactment or incarnation of what has been taught. It is teaching by doing. This is intensified by the occasion, what John's Gospel calls 'the hour', towards which the drama of Jesus' life has been heading since the beginning of his ministry (2.4), the time of his passion, death and resurrection. It is happening at Passover, the annual Jewish re-enactment of the Exodus, the key event in Israel's history – in this Gospel, Jesus dies at the same time as the Passover lambs. And this whole history is a drama of loving, as headlined in the first explicit mention of love in this Gospel, 'for God so loved the world that he gave his only son, so that everyone who believes in him may not perish but may have eternal life' (3.16).

In the Farewell Discourses, the enactment of this love by Jesus is first in washing his disciples' feet, and in the second wave Jesus affirms his disciples as friends for whom he is laying down his life. But this third wave in his final prayer goes even further. It opens up the 'space' of the intimate relationship between Jesus and his Father in prayer, marked by the intensity of mutual glorification: 'Father, the hour has come; glorify your Son so that the Son may glorify you' (17.1). This is the embracing 'place of prayer', soon described as mutual indwelling, with the repeated use of 'in' in verses 21, 23 and 26. Readers of the earlier chapters already know that this Father–Son relationship is one of love (3.35, 10.17, 14.31, 15.9). The 'time' of this glory is that of eternal life, 'the glory that I had in your presence before the world existed' (17.5) – and this eternal life has been linked to love since 3.16. The prayer for his disciples that follows emphasizes their belonging to Jesus and to the Father: 'They were yours, and you gave them to me. ... All mine are yours and yours are mine ... so that they may be one, as we are one' (17.6, 10, 11). This is a culmination of covenantal belonging, the historic and continuing 'place of prayer', and the Farewell Discourses have made clear that its key mark is love.

But love has not yet been made explicit in the prayer. This comes in the climactic final verses which look ahead to the ongoing drama of discipleship, as Jesus prays 'on behalf of those who will believe in me through their word' (17.20). It is a stupendous vision of mutual indwelling in unity, of communion with God and with each other that overflows towards the world: 'As you, Father, are in me and I am in you, may they also be in us, so that the world may believe that you have sent me' (17.21). The very glory of God, with which the prayer opened, is shared with this community: 'The glory that you have given me I have given them, so that they may be one as we are one, I in them and you in me, that they may become completely one' (17.22-23a). The verb in the phrase 'may become completely (*or* perfectly) one' (*teteleiômenoi eis hen*) has been used in 4.34, 5.36 and 17.4 about Jesus completing what the Father has given him to do, suggesting his forthcoming death. Its noun, *telos*, 'end', was used in 13.1, the love-centred headline for all the Farewell Discourses, likewise pointing to his death. And a related verb, *telein*, will be the last word Jesus speaks on the cross, 'It is finished' (19.28). This is a completeness or perfection that is about sacrificial loving, even to the point of dying, and the rest of verse 23 makes the source of this love explicit: 'so that the world may know that you have sent me and have loved them even as you have loved me.' *We have arrived at the summit, where God's glory and God's love are shared.* This is what the opening verses of the prayer summed up as 'eternal life' (17.2, 3), and the middle part expressed as mutual belonging, complete joy (17.13), and being 'sanctified in truth' (17.17–19).

But there is yet more: 'Father, I desire that those also, whom you have given me, may be with me where I am, to see my glory, which you have given me because you loved me before the foundation of the world' (17.24). This characteristically Johannine repetition with variation takes the earlier themes of belonging, glory and the eternal love of God, and connects them with the desire of Jesus, the 'I am' of him being present as God is present, and the seeing of his glory. The verse can be read as the summary distillation of where this Gospel's three fundamental questions, as raised in John 1, are intended to lead readers.

The first is 'Who are you?' (1.19). This is first addressed to John the Baptist, but immediately redirected by John towards who Jesus is, and that remains the core question throughout John's Gospel. The most distinctive answer is in the 'I am' statements of Jesus through the Gospel, but every chapter gives answers in narrative form. 'With me where I am' is a further 'I am' statement that is not only about the ultimate future, beyond death, but also, as the theme of mutual indwelling makes clear, about life now. *This is the place of prayer and worship, the place of the glory and love of God, inseparable from who Jesus is.* Prayer in the name of Jesus means prayer and worship that recognizes who Jesus is, trusting and receiving his love, giving love in response and letting the 'I desire' of 17.24 shape the desires of the one who prays and acts, as he or she inhabits this relationship.

This answers a second fundamental question from the beginning of the Gospel, the first words of Jesus' first disciples: 'Rabbi ... where are you staying?' (1.38 – the verb is *menein*, abide, dwell). Readers of the Prologue were already aware that the ultimate, eternal answer to that question is 'close to the Father's heart' (1.18), but for the disciples in the story this answer only comes as the drama unfolds and reaches its theological climax here in the Farewell Discourses. It is signalled strongly in John 15, where the verb *menein* comes ten times in ten verses – variously translated as 'abide', 'dwell', 'live', 'be vitally united to', 'remain', 'make your home', 'intimately join with', and (of fruit) 'last', 'be lasting', 'not spoil'. In John 17 it is usually signalled by the little but infinitely capacious word 'in'.

Then there is the third question, the first words of Jesus in this Gospel, spoken to his first disciples: 'What are you looking for?' (1.38 – *ti zēteite*; 'What are you seeking, searching for, wanting, desiring, expecting, striving for?'). That is a strong verb, occurring many times in John. The whole Gospel can be read as an education of desire, an invitation to readers to align their desires with the desire of Jesus. *The prayer of Jesus in John 17 is the fullest expression of his desire for human beings: for our union in love with God and each other – and also, as I will suggest, with the whole of creation.*

The prayer continues with a renewed emphasis on who God is ('Righteous Father … your name …'), and concludes with the love-centred, desired purpose of the life, death and resurrection of Jesus: 'so that the love with which you have loved me may be in them, and I in them' (17.26).

The View from this Summit

This summit of love is a prayerful vantage point from where we can look back and see paths of convergent meaning. A great deal more could be said about how it resonates not only with the Farewell Discourses and John 1,[3] but also with all the rest of the Gospel of John. A fruitful practice is to read and pray it alongside each chapter in turn (see further below). This can also be done with the Synoptic Gospels, the Pauline letters and other New Testament writings, and also, of course, with the one set of intertexts that we know for certain that John knew, the scriptures of Israel. I take here as examples the Lord's Prayer, the prayer in Ephesians 3.14-21 and the Psalms. They can

---

[3]In particular, there is a fascinating relationship with the Prologue. John 17 has the Prologue themes of the word, God, creation, life, the world, believing, trusting and receiving, knowing and not knowing, truth, the name, power or authority (*exousia*), the community of disciples, and perhaps the two most important of all: glory; and the relationship between the Father and Jesus the Son. But John 17 also goes beyond the Prologue, reaching back even before creation, reaching forward to a vision of ultimate fulfilment in joy, reaching outwards to a vision of ultimate reconciliation and unity, and above all going deeper into glory, into love, into the dynamics of community with God and each other and creation, and into who God is. They are both expressed in straightforward language, basic words, simple Greek, but they have that strange, striking characteristic that applies to the whole Gospel: on the one hand, it is accessible to almost anyone, and its words make sense on first reading or hearing; on the other hand, the more one re-reads it, let alone tries to live it, it becomes more and more challenging, more and more mysterious, more and more stretching – imaginatively, intellectually, spiritually, practically.

only be discussed cursorily, and the aim is not at all to give a full account of their intertextual relationships with John 17, but rather to encourage readers to explore the relationships for themselves. But first I draw on Stephen C. Barton's chapter in this volume in the New Testament in order to connect John 17 with the key dimensions of prayer that he describes.

John 17 and the rest of the New Testament

'Put summarily, prayer in the New Testament is a tradition-bearing, God-ward, communicative practice of individuals and communities shaped in life and worship by resurrection faith and experience of the eschatological Spirit.'[4] Barton's description fits John 17 well.

In particular, 'resurrection faith' is important for the way John 17 combines both pre-resurrection and post-resurrection perspectives, as does the whole of the Gospel of John. Jesus in John 17 speaks to his disciples both in order to prepare them for his coming death and from an eternal standpoint beyond his resurrection. This horizon is first opened up by John's Prologue, which culminates in Jesus, the Word made flesh who is identified with God, in the intimate, permanent relationship of being 'close to the Father's heart' (1.18). John's combination of historical testimony and post-resurrection experience and reflection has been the topic of a great deal of debate, and it is especially relevant to John 17. Lesslie Newbigin writes:

> The prayer is not a free invention of the evangelist; nor is it a tape recording of the words of Jesus. It is a representation of what Jesus was doing when he prayed in the presence of his disciples during the supper, a re-presentation which rests upon the authority of the beloved disciple guided by the Holy Spirit in and through the continuous experience of the community which gathers week by week to rehearse again the words and action of Jesus on that night when he was betrayed.[5]

There are many other ways of construing this example of what Rudolf Schnackenburg calls 'theological history-writing' in John. John wants both to give reliable testimony to people (above all, to who Jesus is) and events (above all, to the crucifixion and resurrection of Jesus) and also to open up the theological depth that comes through ongoing, Spirit-led, post-resurrection relationship with Jesus. In doing this he, like other ancient

---

[4] See Stephen C. Barton's chapter in this volume.
[5] Lesslie Newbigin, *The Light Has Come: An Exposition of the Fourth Gospel* (Edinburgh: Handsel Press, 1982), 224.

biblical and non-biblical authors, often shapes the details to make the fuller meaning clearer, testifying to both pre- and post-resurrection truth.

The 'eschatological Spirit' is also very important for John. He has more on the Holy Spirit than any of the other Gospels, and, as already discussed, the Spirit as Paraclete, *paraklētos* (comforter, strengthener, advocate, helper, 'one who cries out alongside') plays a key role in the teaching of the Farewell Discourses. John relates the Spirit as closely as possible to Jesus, beginning in John 1 and culminating in the risen Jesus breathing the Spirit into his disciples (see above). His eschatology is also utterly centred on Jesus. The final saying of the risen Jesus to Peter about the disciple Jesus loved, 'If it is my will (*or* desire) that he remain (*or* abide) until I come, what is that to you? Follow me!' (21.22), is an exquisitely succinct distillation of it: the desire and the personal presence of Jesus are key to the future; those who are his followers do not have access, nor do they need to have access, to future events or to any privileged overview of the future of other people (or of themselves), about which they should be content to remain agnostic; what they are to do is to abide, to which this Gospel has given deep content, culminating in John 17;[6] and, in abiding, the leading imperative is to follow the risen Jesus, living in line with what he desires – and his communication of what he desires also culminates in John 17.

Barton helpfully describes John's pedagogy of prayer being given less through what Jesus says than through how he prays, especially in John 17. It is also striking how many of key elements of prayer identified in other New Testament writings also figure in John, giving a sense of the fourth Gospel as the recapitulation and maturing of a tradition. To select just some of the elements, there are: Matthew's emphases on divine presence, 'God with us', identity, and the coming together of earth and heaven; Mark's on the sovereignty of God, the mystery of God, and the divine will; Luke's on participation, empowerment, the communion of Jesus, 'the beloved', with his Father, and the 'Johannine thunderbolt' in Luke 10.21-22 (paralleled in

---

[6]This final scene also describes 'the disciple whom Jesus loved' as 'the one who had reclined next to Jesus at the supper and had said, "Lord, who is it that is going to betray you?"' (21.20 NRSV); '… next to …' is a weak translation of *epi to stēthos* – literally 'on the breast', which is repeated from the account in John 13.25. The parallel phrase in 13.23 is *en tō kolpō*, literally 'in the bosom', recalling the Prologue's phrase in 1.18 about Jesus being *eis ton kolpon tou patrou*, literally 'into the bosom of the Father' (NRSV, 'close to the Father's heart'). The imagery, which is missed by the NRSV, suggests the interconnection of Jesus being utterly intimate with his Father, the beloved disciple being utterly intimate with Jesus, and, in the light of the prayer in John 17 and the sending of the disciples as Jesus was sent, the same relationship of utter intimacy being opened to all who are drawn to Jesus ('And I, when I am lifted up from the earth, will draw all people [some manuscripts read, "all things"] to myself' – 12.32) and come to trust Jesus. One reason for the anonymity of the beloved disciple may be to leave open any disciple's self-identification as beloved.

Mt. 11.25-27); the Acts of the Apostles on the Holy Spirit and the continuing presence of the risen Jesus, joy, and glory; the Pauline letters on God as Father and 'christological monotheism', life in the Spirit, participation in Christ and cruciform grace, a community of love, pedagogy through praying, and how power and suffering come together; 1 Peter on God as Father and witnessing; Hebrews on the prayer of Jesus and boldness in prayer; and Revelation on theocentricity combined with christocentricity, victorious Christian existence inseparable from suffering, the Lamb of God, divine home-making on earth, and prayer as first of all about listening, hearing and responding to the voice of Jesus Christ.

Out of those writings I now focus on just two exemplary prayers as intertexts with John 17.

John 17 and the Lord's Prayer

The echoes of the Lord's Prayer in John 17 are so many that the latter can be read as an improvisation on the former.[7] Both begin by invoking God as Father in heaven: 'He looked up to heaven and said, "Father"' (17.1). There are further obvious parallels, such as glorifying and hallowing; the name; on earth; giving; and protection from the evil one. John's equivalent of the Synoptic kingdom of God, or kingdom of heaven, is 'eternal life',[8] introduced in 17.2,–3. In 17.2 the association of eternal life with the kingship of God is strengthened by the mention of authority over all people (literally, all flesh). Doing the will of God is also present in John 17: the will is done by Jesus – 'finishing the work that you gave me to do'; and by the disciples – 'they have kept your word'. Since the main imperative of the will of God is to love, the emphasis on love later in the prayer is another rich resonance. And the Greek word for 'will' (*thelēma*, Mt. 6.10) is echoed by Jesus about himself in 17.24, 'I desire ...' (*thelô*).[9] Forgiveness is not explicit in John 17, but is surely implied by the vision of unity with God and each other. The daily bread of the Lord's Prayer might be read in the light both of John 4.34, 'My food is to do the will of him who sent me and to complete his work', and of Jesus himself as the bread from heaven, the bread of life (6.22-71).

---

[7]I will focus just on Matthew 6.9-13; one could do a parallel study with Luke 11.2-4.

[8]This is signalled in John 3.1-21, where the first two waves of teaching speak of the kingdom of God, but the third (3.11-21) speaks of eternal life (together with love and light), and no further mention is made of the kingdom of God in the remainder of this Gospel.

[9]The breadth of meaning of *thelō*, *thelēma*, embracing both willing and desiring, is important. The narrowing of focus on God's will, understood in terms of command and the demand for obedience to the imperatives of an omnipotent divine will, has been fateful for much Christian theology, spirituality and exercise of authority. 'Your desire be done on earth as in heaven' can lead to these being shaped very differently.

Perhaps the most embracing parallel from the Lord's Prayer is 'on earth as in heaven'. Both 'as' and 'in' are repeated again and again in the climactic final prayer for unity in love (17.20-26), whose themes of mutual indwelling and shared glory intimately interrelate 'earth' and 'heaven'. There is a future dimension to heaven, but primarily (as throughout the Bible) it is, as here, simultaneous with earth, and heaven in John is not so much a spatial term as the reality of fullest, eternal relationship in love, centred on the Father and the Son. In John 17 the focus is simultaneously and inseparably on the Father in heaven and on life on earth – the Father is addressed throughout; 'world' occurs no less than sixteen times.

If the context of each prayer is considered, the illuminating richness of their interrelation is intensified. Matthew's 'Our Father' comes exactly in the centre of the most substantial body of direct teaching by Jesus in this Gospel, the Sermon on the Mount; just as John's chapter 17 comes as the culmination of his most substantial body of Jesus' teaching in chapters 13–16. Once one connects the two, there is a further opening, beyond reading the two prayers alongside each other, into reading each body of teaching in the light of its prayer, and vice versa. The Sermon on the Mount is perhaps the single text that most illuminates the Lord's Prayer – it is well worth reflecting on each of the prayer's petitions in relation to its teachings. Likewise, the single text that most illuminates John 17 is that of the Farewell Discourses, as already suggested. Each prayer distils into address to God the body of teaching in which it is set. And so, beyond this, the resonances between the Lord's Prayer and John 17 invite readers to interrelate the bodies of teaching. These are mutually illuminating in profound and challenging ways. They cannot be explored here, but the fruitfulness of the practice of such intertextual reading and praying needs to be noted. *The Lord's Prayer is deepened immeasurably when understood and prayed as an intertext with John 17, and the interconnection of prayer and action is both illuminated and strengthened when the Sermon on the Mount and the Farewell Discourses are read in conversation with each other.* Such practical exercises ideally develop into habits of intertextual reading and praying with other texts, as further explored below in relation to the letter to the Ephesians and the Psalms.

The studies of the Lord's Prayer by Roy Hammerling and Medi Ann Volpe elsewhere in this volume show the remarkable authority and scope that this prayer has had across the millennia. It has been seen as the truest scripture, a distillation of the whole of theology, a summary of the Gospel, a formation in discipleship that enables a community of forgiveness, an encouragement to resist temptation and to persevere in desiring and seeking God, an orientation for mission, a way to partake of the divine nature, a way into prayer without ceasing, an invitation into prayer and love for the whole world, a sign of citizenship in heaven, a bulwark of church unity – and more. Each of those elements can be enhanced and deepened if it is understood and prayed in the light of John 17.[10] Indeed, given the pervasive influence of the Gospel of John on the whole tradition of theology, liturgy and prayer, a hypothesis worth testing is that John 17 was a significant ingredient in shaping the wisdom of a tradition that came to grant such broad significance to the Lord's Prayer.

John 17 and Ephesians 3.14-21

It is arguable that the letter to the Ephesians represents a late stage of the Pauline tradition just as the Gospel of John is often held to be the fourth and culminating canonical Gospel. If so, each can be read as a mature expression of a fundamental New Testament theological stream. Thomas Brodie makes a strong case for John 17 as an intertext not only with the Lord's Prayer but also with the whole letter to the Ephesians, especially with the prayer in Ephesians 3.14-21 together with the early part of Ephesians 4 on unity.[11]

So we can add to the reciprocal interplay between the Lord's Prayer (together with the Sermon on the Mount) and John 17 (together with the Farewell Discourses) a further interplay with Ephesians 3.14-21 (together

---

[10]I am not at all making an exclusive claim for John 17, or the Gospel of John. On the contrary, John's intertextuality is extraordinarily hospitable to a wide range of other texts, just as the Lord's Prayer could never have been understood as described by Hammerling and Volpe had it not likewise been read in intertextual relationship with other texts across the whole of scripture and beyond it.

[11]See Thomas Brodie, *The Quest for the Origin of John's Gospel: A Source-Oriented Approach* (Oxford: Oxford University Press, 1993), chapter 12. The chapter opens: 'Thus far John 17 has been linked, at least in passing, or through appendices, with a wide variety of texts – the pre-death prayer in Gethsemane (Mk 14.32-42; cf. Mt. 26.36-46), the Our Father (Mt. 6.9-13), the shepherd-like care for the little ones (Mt. 18.10-14), the Zacchaeus incident (Lk. 19.1-10), and Moses' final discourse (Deut. 29-30). But despite the apparently genuine contribution of each of these component parts, John's climactic chapter appears to depend even more on yet another source – the epistle to the Ephesians. Ephesians is concerned with how Christ brings the fragmenting world back to God. It is as though God's creation had come apart, riven by dark demonic sin, yet through an age-old plan of God – an eternal love, which comes from within God and which is manifested in Christ's self-giving – there is at work, even amid the world's darkness, a greater force for unity. Through this unifying power – a power which shows itself in the holiness and unity of the church – Christ is bringing creation to a new fullness. This picture of God – as working through Christ to bring everything back to a greater unity – is central to John 17.' See Brodie, *The Quest for the Origin of John's Gospel*, 128. Whether or not the scholarly case is agreed, an acceptance of both John and Ephesians as part of the Christian canon of scripture lends theological legitimacy to reading them together like this.

with the rest of the letter to the Ephesians). *Here the three main streams of New Testament witness to Jesus Christ – the Synoptic Gospels, the Gospel of John and the Pauline letters – come together in prayer; and this prayer is set in the context of three of the richest distillations of New Testament teaching.* Their interplay sets up a dynamic that can inspire ever-deeper prayer, wisdom-seeking and discipleship.

Some of the depths to be sounded in themes shared by the Ephesians prayer and John 17 include: heaven and earth, glory, love, indwelling, faith/belief/trust, knowledge, the community of believers, abundance, and eternity; and if one moves on into the opening of Ephesians 4 there is also the climactic John 17 theme of unity. This is 'christological monotheism' being performed in the sort of prayer that eventually fed into the doctrine of the Trinity.

Vital to that development, as to many others, is the invitation into what Gregory of Nyssa called '*epektasis*' – the inexhaustible stretching of desire, mind, imagination, heart and action into the superabundant knowledge, love and glory of God.[12] In Ephesians this is signalled by 'the riches of his glory' (3.15); by 'the power to comprehend, with all the saints, what is the breadth and length and height and depth, and to know the love of Christ that surpasses knowledge, so that you may be filled with all the fullness of God' (3.18-19); and, above all, by the culminating invocation, which hyperbolically suggests that there is more even beyond the fullness of God that has just been asked for: 'Now to him who by the power at work within us is able to accomplish abundantly far more than all we can ask or imagine, to him be glory in the church and in Christ Jesus to all generations, for ever and ever. Amen' (3.20-21).

John's Farewell Discourses open up a similarly daring horizon for desiring, believing, comprehending, loving, glorifying and praying, culminating in 17.20-26. There, the intensity of mutual glorifying between the Father and the Son, with which the prayer opens, is not only identified with the love between them, but their whole relationship is opened up fully to the disciples: 'The glory that you have given me I have given them, so that they may be one as we are one, I in them and you in me, that they may become completely one, so that the world may know that you have sent me and have loved them even as you have loved me.' Here, in the sharing of the glory, life and love of God, the pervasive Johannine theme of abundance – expressed in a dazzling variety of ways – reaches its God-centred climax. It is as if the expansive dimensions of breadth, length, height and depth in Ephesians

---

[12]Richly expounded by Gabrielle Thomas in her chapter in this volume.

are concentrated into the intensive, multidimensional unity of John, as each attempts to do justice to the overwhelming glory and love of God.[13]

Yet for neither is this an experience of God in which to rest. Each goes on to work out the implications of prayer in ongoing life. Prayer is the depth of action, and the shaper of life in community. Ephesians 4-6 is about the sort of life that is in line with the prayer in 3.14-21. John 17 leads into the passion, death and resurrection of Jesus, and then into the ongoing drama of discipleship. The statement of Jesus, 'As you have sent me into the world, so I have sent them into the world' (17.18), is pivotal between this prayer (as he approaches the climax of his own drama) and the ongoing drama of the community, initiated by him commissioning the disciples after his resurrection: 'As the Father sent me, so I send you' (20.21).

'Into the world' is where the prayer and life in community lead. The final chapter of John gives three vivid pictures of what this might mean. There is a return to the ordinary daily work of fishing, but with a surprise catch, and then a meal with Jesus – 'Come and have breakfast' (21.12); there is Peter's vocation in pastoral ministry – loving Jesus, doing what Jesus desires ('Feed my lambs', 'Tend my sheep', 'Feed my sheep' – 21.15, 16, 17), and being taken 'where you do not wish to go', even to the point of suffering, glorifying God by his death (21.18-19); and there is the ministry of meaning of the disciple Jesus loved – 'This is the disciple who is testifying to these things and has written them, and we know that his testimony is true' (21.24). The Ephesians prayer too overflows into the shaping of community life, with its ongoing drama of struggle against sin and evil in the church and in the world.

John 17, the Septuagint and the Psalms

John's Gospel (and the rest of the New Testament) is marinated in the Septuagint, the translation of the Hebrew Scriptures into Greek done by Jews in Alexandria a couple of centuries before the New Testament was written in Greek. John has fewer direct quotations from it than the Synoptic Gospels have, but more pervasive allusions and echoes. The intertextuality of John with the Septuagint is a large topic which cannot be dealt with here, and even the resonances in John 17 would far exceed the space available.[14] I want simply to note the fruitfulness of this intertextual relationship through the way John 17 echoes the Psalms, and I would encourage readers

---

[13]The supporting imagery is of abundant wine (Jn 2), water (Jn 4, 7), wind (Jn 3), bread (Jn 6), light (Jn 1, 8), fish and books (Jn 21).

[14]For a superb treatment of all four Gospels in relation to the Septuagint and Hebrew scriptures, which addresses scholarly, literary and theological questions, see Richard Hays, *Echoes of Scripture in the Gospels* (Waco, TX: Baylor University Press, 2016).

who wish to go deeper into John 17 to immerse themselves simultaneously in the Psalms.

The Psalms are the prayer book of the Bible and are also John's most explicit intertext, the biblical book to which John directly refers most frequently. Margaret Daly-Denton's thorough study, *David in the Fourth Gospel: The Johannine Reception of the Psalms*,[15] gives a master class in intertextual reading and reflection. She not only discusses in detail, and with alertness to theological depth, what the quotations from Psalms 2, 8, 22, 31, 34, 41, 69, 78, 82, 91, 102 and 118 contribute to the meaning of John; she also attunes our ears to a remarkable range of nuances, variations and enrichments that are implicit, and mostly missed.

> As we moved to a less explicit form of intertextual reference, we found that hearing the harmonics and noting the sympathetic vibrations which certain combinations of texts set in motion requires attuning the ear to what is often no more than a single word or a particular turn of phrase. We saw that Fourth Gospel allusion to the scriptures is frequently thematic, rather than dictional. Thus we found that verbal allusions to the psalms can be quite fragmentary and elusive. ... [T]here is no doubt that the book [i.e. the Psalms] of *hē graphē* [scripture] which the fourth evangelist favours most as a witness to Jesus has exerted a profound influence on his entire composition.[16]

Readers of John 17, who have been trained by Daly-Denton, Richard Hays and others (stretching right back to the biblical authors, and down the centuries, and including the often-anonymous authors of liturgies, collects and hymns) who teach, whether explicitly or by example, the habit of reading intertextually, will find there, especially if they are steeped in the Psalms, layer beneath layer of fresh meaning. This includes what Kevin Grove in his chapter in this volume discusses,[17] and more. The Psalms themselves are intertextual, and distil in the mode of prayer and worship a great deal of the rest of Israel's scriptures, so that John 17, when read through the lens of the Psalms, gives a prayerful vantage point on much of the Old Testament as well as the New Testament. Themes that are opened up include glory and glorifying (and the kindred practices of blessing, praising, rejoicing,

---

[15]Margaret Daly-Denton, *David in the Fourth Gospel: The Johannine Reception of the Psalms* (Leiden: Brill, 2000).

[16]Daly-Denton, *David in the Fourth Gospel*, 287.

[17]Especially relevant are Grove's discussions in this volume of who is speaking in the Psalms, of individual and community, of pedagogy, and of the vertical and horizontal.

delighting, exalting, magnifying and honouring), eternity, life, the name, the word, knowing, belonging, sending, giving, receiving, holiness, protection, evil, the world, joy, asking, truth, believing and trusting, dwelling, unity, community, righteousness, desire and love. Above all, John's intertextual relationship with the Psalms has the effect of engaging with who God is inseparably from who Jesus is.

Alan Ecclestone has drawn a provocative lesson from the kinship between the Gospel of John and the Psalms:

> One purpose has shaped this book. It is a plea for learning to read the Gospel according to St John with the kind of attention that can best be described as praying it. In doing that, I believe, we come nearest to the mind and intention of its author. In that way we latch on to what he himself did. He wrote that others might join him. I hope to suggest some ways of setting about it. Here I simply remind myself that it calls for selfless attention, unwearying patience, passionate commitment, honesty of purpose, hunger for truth. Reading in this way is not foreign to Jewish and Christian traditions of prayer. In just such deliberate fashion Torah was studied and Psalms were recited from time immemorial. They will go on being used in that way for generations to come. My plea is for doing that kind of prayer-reading of the Fourth Gospel. It would be like turning it into a Christian Psalter. Such use of it is greatly needed and long overdue.[18]

For such 'prayer-reading', John 17 can be both paradigm and inspiration.

John 17, Christian Prayer down the Centuries and Twenty-First-Century Challenges

I have given a mere taster menu that points to the nourishing of prayer that this one chapter of John can provide. The main concentration has been on its interplay with the Farewell Discourses, the Sermon on the Mount, the letter to the Ephesians and the Psalms; but other chapters in this volume help to show its relevance to other parts of the Bible and to Christian prayer down the centuries.

That relevance could be further illustrated through the rest of this volume, ranging from Christopher Seitz on the Old Testament, through

---

[18]Alan Ecclestone, *The Scaffolding of Spirit: Reflections on the Gospel of John* (London: Darton, Longman and Todd, 1987), 2. In an appendix, Ecclestone lays out a three-month lectionary cycle of daily readings covering all of John.

the early church, the Middle Ages and the Reformation, to the array of contemporary perspectives – from prayer and natural science to prayer and gender, the body and race. In conclusion, I want now to assume all those, and to point up just three interrelated invitational challenges (selected from a great many), one personal, one ecclesial and one global, that John 17 poses in the twenty-first century.

John 17 and personal prayer: Desire

Given the unique role that the Lord's Prayer and the Psalms play in the prayer of so many Christians, it may be that the single most generative, personal invitation and challenge is to pray those daily in the light of John 17.[19] To do that year after year, following the ramifications into the rest of John, the rest of the New Testament, the rest of the Old Testament, and the whole tradition of Christian prayer and contemporary issues that this volume opens up, carries immense potential for personal formation and transformation.

Out of all that, I choose just one theme, discussed above, that is essential to the Lord's Prayer, the Psalms and John 17: desire. Desire is something that pervades both the Gospel of John and our culture, with its intensified dimensions of expectation and disappointment, challenges to self-worth and dignity, pervasive advertising, consumerism, participation in social media, addiction and more. John 17 expresses the desire of Jesus, and invites others to let their desires be shaped in line with his, and in continual intimate relationship with him. The radicality of this challenge is only matched by the comprehensiveness of the love that makes it possible to follow this way, 'so that', as the prayer concludes, 'the love with which you have loved me may be in them, and I in them' (17.26).

John 17 and the church: Desire for unity

The desire of Jesus is above all for a unity of mutual indwelling in love between his Father, himself and those who respond to them in trust and love. This prayer, especially 17.20-26, was at the heart of the remarkable ecumenism among many Christian churches in the twentieth century. In a movement probably without parallel in history, churches with hundreds of

---

[19]For those praying in traditions in which the Eucharist (which usually includes both the Lord's Prayer and Psalms) is central, a further regular setting is given to face this challenge. A fascinating dimension here is the location of John 17 at the end of a Last Supper in which the main symbolic action of Jesus has been to wash the feet of his disciples, while John's discourse most relevant to the Eucharist is in chapter 6. A key connection between John 6 and 17 is the introduction for the first time in John 6 of mutual indwelling: 'Those who eat my flesh and drink my blood abide in me, and I in them' (6.56).

millions of members moved from relationships of alienation, conflict and sometimes violence into conversation, collaboration and sometimes organic unity. The movement has had many problems and disappointments, as well as inspiring new initiatives, institutions and practices,[20] and John 17 remains as a continuing radical challenge to it, and to all Christians. But, as with the invitation to desire in line with the desire of Jesus, this is good news, and not an impossible demand, because it is a gift before it is an invitation – the gift of Jesus himself, his love and his Spirit.

It may be that by the time the Gospel of John was completed the community within which it was written was itself experiencing division and conflict (the letters of John later in the New Testament suggest this) and that this influenced the way climactic prominence is given to the desire of Jesus for unity. Indeed, the whole of John's Gospel can be read as crafted to enable profound unity within diversity. For example, its central emphasis on who Jesus is is hospitable to a broad range of other New Testament and Old Testament strands, and has classically been the leading integrator of thinking about Jesus; and in ethics it avoids going into the sort of detail on controversial topics found in the Synoptic Gospels and Pauline letters, preferring to trust its readers to work out what practices might, in their various contexts, be in line with the narrative of Jesus and with its basic invitational imperatives of washing feet as Jesus did, loving one another as Jesus did and following Jesus. If John's Gospel is one's leading criterion for Christian belonging then there is room for a good deal of diversity. John severely limits the number and character of issues that could be argued to be church-dividing. It would be hard, for instance, to advocate that even deep differences on issues of church organization, sexuality or pacifism should be more important than the desire of Jesus for unity in love. That passionate desire, leading to him laying down his life, becomes the radical model to follow in the face of divisive community issues.

John 17 and the world: Desire for the flourishing of all creation

The unity of the Christian community is not an end in itself. The horizon of John 17 and the rest of the Gospel of John is the whole world, as announced in the Prologue. The community follows one who was sent by his Father

---

[20]I see the movement of Receptive Ecumenism as the most profound theological and practical element in the current ecumenical context: see David F. Ford, 'Mature Ecumenism's Daring Future: Learning from the Gospel of John for the Twenty-First Century', in Paul D. Murray, Paul Lakeland and Gregory A. Ryan, ed., *Receptive Ecumenism as Ecclesial Learning: Principles, Practices, and Perspectives* (Oxford: Oxford University Press, forthcoming).

in costly love for the world (3.16). This can inspire a passionate desire for peace, reconciliation, love and unity, with unlimited practical implications.

But, even beyond this, there is a vision of the unity of all creation. In the Prologue the Word of God, soon identified with Jesus Christ, is the one through whom all things, and all life, have come into being. So unity with him is unity with one to whom everything in creation matters. Margaret Daly-Denton, in her Earth Bible commentary on John, *Supposing Him to Be the Gardener*,[21] deeply and convincingly connects John's Gospel and the environmental crisis. She not only takes readers deeper simultaneously into the truth of Jesus and into the truth of the crisis, but also challenges them to act in line with that truth and gives suggestions for how to do so. In the light of this Gospel, how could any Christians ever think Jesus is indifferent to how we treat our environment and every species of life? How could Christians not be passionately earth-conscious and active for the flourishing of life in all its abundance (10.10)? The unity desired in John 17 embraces unity not only with God, all Christians and all people, but also all creation. Daly-Denton's decisive conclusion is: 'Jesus' prayer, "that they may all be one", invites us today to rethink faith in the light of an ecological crisis that calls for a whole new way of being Christian.'[22]

So this prayer expresses the ultimate desire of Jesus. It is ultimate for each person, for the community of those who trust, love and follow him, for all humanity and for all creation. It is also ultimate for himself. He is about to lay down his life in love for his friends, present and future, 'finishing the work that you gave me to do' (17.4). He asks, 'So now, Father, glorify me in your own presence with the glory that I had in your presence before the world existed' (17.5). This ultimate, abundant intensity of life, love, joy and glory is what the climax of the prayer throws open to all – 'The glory that you have given me I have given them' (17.22). The deepest secret of his desire is to be revealed in the events of the coming days: '"And I, when I am lifted up from the earth, will draw all people [or, in a very significant alternative reading in well-attested ancient authorities, pointing in the direction of Daly-Denton's reading of John 17: all things] to myself." He said this to indicate the kind of death he was to die' (12.32-33). No boundaries are set around the scope of this attractive, sacrificial love; no time limits are laid down for responding to it; and the stories in all the Gospels teach us to expect immense surprises. The drama of the desire of Jesus continues.

---

[21]Margaret Daly-Denton, *John: An Earth Bible Commentary – Supposing Him to Be the Gardener* (London: Bloomsbury, 2017).
[22]Daly-Denton, *John*, 199.

PART TWO

Doctrinal Perspectives

CHAPTER SEVEN

Doctrine and Prayer

MIKE HIGTON

The work of doctrinal theology is inseparable from prayer. Doctrinal theology hazards articulations of the knowledge of God that lives in prayer, it does so in the hope that it might enrich and sometimes guide lives of prayerful discipleship, and its precarious work of articulation itself needs to be offered to God in prayer.

This chapter has three sections. I begin by exploring the relationship between prayer and the knowledge of God, arguing that knowledge of God is intimately related to knowledge of how to go on praying in all circumstances. In the second section, I ask why Christians have attempted the articulation of this prayerful knowledge of God in doctrinal terms, and what benefit they have hoped for from such attempts. Finally, in the third section, I argue that this work of articulation is fraught with possibilities of harm as well as possibilities of benefit, and that it therefore needs to be accompanied by prayer and to be offered as a form of prayer.[1]

---

[1]There are many ways of approaching the relationship between doctrine and prayer. Two excellent recent studies, taking approaches that differ significantly from, but are compatible with mine, are Ashley Cocksworth, 'Theorizing the (Anglican) *lex orandi*: A Theological Account', *Modern Theology* 36, no. 2 (2020): 298–316 and Andrew Prevot, *Thinking Prayer: Theology and Spirituality amid the Crises of Modernity* (Notre Dame, IN: University of Notre Dame Press, 2015). I have also been challenged to think about the relationship of doctrinal theology and prayer by long conversations with Lam Swee Sum, whose thesis, 'Kerygmatic Hermeneutics: A Theology and Practice of Theological Interpretation for the Tabernacle Church and Missions' (Durham University, 2018), tackles the relationship between prayer and biblical interpretation. My approach draws on material I develop in Mike Higton, *The Life of Christian Doctrine* (London: Bloomsbury, 2020).

A word about definitions is in order. Beginning from one side, one can take 'doctrine' to refer to those brief statements of core Christian beliefs, especially about God and God's ways with the world, that appear as articles of classic creeds and confessions, or as numbered paragraphs in the doctrinal bases of various Christian organizations. 'Doctrinal theology' is then the name for the various practices in which these claims are discussed, elaborated upon and argued about. Alternatively, one can begin with 'doctrinal theology' as a name for the whole tangle of activities of discussion, elaboration and argument by which Christians explore what they should say and think about God and God's ways with the world. That whole unruly flow of conversation turns out to eddy around various key loci, and 'doctrine' can be the name of those eddies. The 'doctrine of creation' is, for instance, a name for the eddy of claims about God being the source and sustainer of everything that is, claims that keep turning up in the flow of Christian conversation, and keep turning out to be important.

One last definitional point: I use the term 'doctrinal theologian' to refer to anyone who commits time and energy to engaging with others in these practices of discussion, elaboration and argument. I certainly do not see it as synonymous with 'academic theologian' or 'professional theologian'. Doctrinal theology happens in all sorts of ways and all sorts of locations across the life of the church.

Knowing God in Prayer

To know God is 'to comprehend, with all the saints, what is the breadth and length and height and depth, and to know the love of Christ that surpasses knowledge, so that you may be filled with all the fullness of God' (Eph. 3.18). That is, to know God is to know the love of God by which one is held, and the love of God to which one is called. To grow deeper in knowledge of God is to discover more of this divine love.[2]

This knowledge of God is intimately related to prayer. There are many ways in which one could explore this connection, but one route in is to consider the role of thanking and asking. One may learn what the word 'God' means by learning to thank God in prayer: learning to thank God

---

[2]My reading of Ephesians has been shaped by Ester Petrenko, *Created in Christ Jesus for Good Works: The Integration of Soteriology and Ethics in Ephesians* (Milton Keynes: Paternoster Press, 2011). My account of the knowledge of God draws, in part, on Mark A. McIntosh, *Mystical Theology* (Oxford: Blackwell, 1998); David Ford, *Christian Wisdom: Desiring God and Learning in Love* (Cambridge: Cambridge University Press, 2007); and Sarah Coakley, *God, Sexuality, and the Self: An Essay 'On the Trinity'* (Cambridge: Cambridge University Press, 2013).

for all that God has done, learning to thank God for all good things. In thankfulness, one refers all this good to a source, a source to which one can and must respond in gratitude. 'God' is the name of this source – and this is not some preliminary understanding of what 'God' means, to be surpassed once one has reached a higher level of intellectual and spiritual maturity. Fuller comprehension comes not with a transition to some other kind of knowing, but with knowing how to thank God more fully: learning how to thank God for all that God has done, supremely for the love of Christ; learning how to thank God for the whole of creation; learning how to thank God together and individually for everything good. This thanking tips over into adoring, because thankfulness by its nature draws one's attention not just to the gifts in which one rejoices but to the good giver from whom they come, the one whose goodness is communicated in the goodness of these gifts, the one whose generosity is never exhausted by any one gift or by all of them together, but the one from whose unending abundance they all flow. This knowledge, in thankfulness that tips over into adoration, is knowledge that one can inhabit; it is knowledge that can fill one up.[3]

One also knows God in asking. One turns to God in the midst of a world that does not reflect the goodness of God, desiring to see more of God's gifts in the world. One knows God more fully the more one knows how to cry out, the more one can identify what in the world is closed off against God's gracious giving. And this asking includes the confession of one's sins as one identifies what in oneself, too, is closed off against the gracious giving of God. In asking and confessing, one expresses one's desire for more of God. To go deeper in knowledge of God is to go further into such asking and confessing, further into the ordering of one's desire towards God. This, too, is knowledge that one can inhabit, and that can fill one up.

One learns to comprehend God more deeply the more one learns how to give thanks, and how to cry out, in all circumstances. It might be better, however, to say that knowledge of God involves learning how to give thanks, how to cry out, in *each* circumstance. Knowledge of God is not a blanket of prayer thrown over all the particularities of one's life, smothering them in a generalized piety. To know how to pray – how to give thanks, how to cry out – always involves knowing how to pray just here, just now. One learns to know God more deeply the more one learns to name what is good, and what resists the good, in each particular situation, learning, in effect, how to name God again in this moment. The knowledge of God grows deeper (one inhabits it more deeply, is filled by it more fully) the more these particular

---

[3]For an account of creation as gift, see Simon Oliver, *Creation: A Guide for the Perplexed* (London: Bloomsbury, 2017).

namings are simmered together. Prayer is the primary space in one's life in which this simmering takes place.

All of this means that knowledge of God is inseparable from the life of prayerful discipleship. To know how to pray in any given situation is inseparable from knowing how to go on as followers of Jesus in that situation: knowing what to love, knowing what to cry out against – how to act prayerfully, and pray actively, in these specific circumstances. This knowledge is never complete. Each situation is different, resembling past situations in countless ways but differing from them in countless ways too. Discipleship is unavoidably improvisatory, and the knowledge of God that takes the form of prayer and discipleship is therefore, necessarily, a form of wisdom.

Prayer therefore enters this picture of the knowledge of God again, in a second way. This wisdom, this knowledge of how to go on as praying followers of Jesus in the midst of each new situation, is not something that one can produce by an act of will, nor even by a determined pattern of habit-forming action. It demands more than determination and diligence; it demands creative insight; it demands improvisatory discovery – and these can only come as gifts. One's effort is not enough. That effort has to be accompanied by, and offered as, a prayer; a prayer that God will enable one to live faithfully here and now, which is both a prayer that one will be enabled to live what one already knows of God, and a prayer that one will discover what more one needs to know. To pray for strength and to pray for wisdom are therefore the proper foundation for all of one's endeavours at discipleship. If prayer in general is the form taken by one's knowledge of God, these elements of praying are the form taken by one's knowledge of one's knowledge of God: one's knowledge that one's knowledge of God depends upon God's grace; one's knowledge that whatever one knows of God is itself a gift of God to be received in thankfulness, and that one's misunderstandings are a darkness from which one must cry out for help.

The Role of Doctrine

To ask how doctrine and doctrinal theology relate to all this, I find it unhelpful to focus on prayer in isolation. It is more fruitful to ask how doctrine and doctrinal theology relate to the life of prayerful discipleship in all its complexity.

The starting point for an answer is the simple fact that, as Christians have lived lives of prayerful discipleship together, they have in various ways tried to articulate, and have gone on trying to articulate, what they think they know of God and of God's ways with the world. That articulation has sometimes taken the form of doctrinal theology, and of doctrinal claims or statements. One should not, however, think that this is simply an obvious or natural process. Don't think, for instance, that the knowledge of God grasped in a life of prayerful discipleship is obviously inadequate, and that doctrinal theology is the natural response to that inadequacy. The knowledge of God grasped in a life of prayerful discipleship is not inherently vague and indirect. It does not inherently call out for the kind of conceptual articulation that doctrinal theology provides.

In order to understand the roles that doctrinal theology can play in relation to the life of prayerful discipleship, it is worth turning to some of the pressures that shaped this contingent emergence in the early church. There is only space here for a brief and impressionistic description, but I highlight four contexts in which something like doctrine and doctrinal theology emerged within Christian life: proclamation, teaching, controversy and confession.[4]

Proclamation

The Christian church begins with the women at the tomb on Easter morning, hearing the news of the resurrection and being commissioned to pass it on. It continues with the wider community of apostles gathered in Jerusalem, hearing these women's voices, witnessing the risen Christ and then being impelled by the Spirit to tell all those around them about God's mighty acts. From the beginning, the Christian community was involved in proclamation, and that proclamation took the form of telling the story of God's ways with the world, and of inviting the world to respond. One might say that in their proclamation Christians tell the world what it is that they are grateful for; they find words to express to others what they praise and thank God for in prayer. Those who hear the proclamation are, in turn, invited to make it their own in prayer: they are invited to confess, to give thanks, to praise.

---

[4]I am offering reflections on the history of the emergence of doctrine, rather than attempting to write that history myself. For that history, see (among many others), Morwenna Ludlow, *The Early Church* (London: I.B. Tauris, 2009); Frances M. Young, *The Making of the Creeds* (London: SCM Press, 1991); Jaroslav Pelikan, *Credo: Historical and Theological Guide to Creeds and Confessions of Faith in the Christian Tradition* (New Haven, CT: Yale University Press, 2003); Christoph Markschies, *Christian Theology and Its Institutions in the Early Roman Empire: Prolegomena to a History of Early Christian Theology* (Waco, TX: Baylor University Press, 2015); Larry Hurtado, 'Interactive Diversity: A Proposed Model of Christian Origins', *Journal of Theological Studies* 64, no. 2 (2013): 445–62; and Rowan Williams, 'Does It Make Sense to Speak of Pre-Nicene Orthodoxy?', in *The Making of Orthodoxy: Essays in Honour of Henry Chadwick*, ed. Rowan Williams (Cambridge: Cambridge University Press, 1989), 1–23.

There is no prior necessity built in to the way that religious communities work, or built in to the story-telling propensities of human beings, or built in to the universal dynamics of prayer, that dictated that the church's expression of its message should take this form. The community could well have been gathered by some other form of dominant discourse: a pattern of legal reasoning, say, in which narrative accounts of the events of Jesus' life played a decidedly subordinate role; or communication that focused on depicting the cosmic backdrop against which the events of Jesus' life had played out, and in relation to which those events, and his teachings, would become cryptic signs. But the early Christian community found itself impelled into story-telling, weaving together the story of Jesus, the story of God's dealings with Israel, the story of God's making and remaking of the world, the story of their own community and the stories of their own lives.

There was no one form in which this story was told. Rather, when we look at the proclamation of the early church, we see multiple different tellings of the story, always different, related by dense nets of family resemblance but always being adapted to new audiences and new settings. In the midst of this mobile and creative practice of story-telling, however, we do hear a stock of common elements beginning to emerge. As the initial explosion of proclamation settled into an ongoing practice – a practice in which people might receive instruction, a practice that could be passed on and developed – it became possible for practitioners to notice these stock elements, to name them and talk about them, and to explore how they connected. It became possible for people to summarize and articulate the content of Christian proclamation, and to do so deliberately and deliberatively.

An articulated summary is, however, never the whole story. It is, precisely, a summary; it works by leaving material out, by cutting flesh away to reveal bones. And summarizing, as an activity, does not come first; it is an activity that follows the story-telling to which it attends. The process of articulating and summarizing the content of proclamation is no more than a prop for the practice of proclamation itself; an aid, precisely in its sparseness and regularity, to the richly improvisatory process of proclaiming the faith in specific new situations, to specific audiences.

Doctrinal theology is, then, in part a form of service to proclamation, and that proclamation is itself a service to the life of prayerful discipleship. Doctrinal theology aids (or should aid) Christians in learning how to speak from what they know in prayer, and to call others into that life of prayer; it aids (or should aid) Christians in speaking from gratitude and calling to gratitude. As such, doctrinal theology is not the primary home of Christian knowledge of God; it is a form of service supporting that life of prayerful discipleship which is the form properly taken by the Christian knowledge of God.

Teaching

Alongside the proclamation of the good news to those who had not yet heard and responded to it, the church was from the beginning shaped by practices of teaching – that is, by forms of communication within the Body, by which some member sought to help other members participate more fully and deeply in the Body's life. In the light of my first section above, we might say that all Christian teaching is both instruction in discipleship and instruction in prayer.

In the early church, some Christian teaching took the form of setting out the backdrop against which Christian action and Christian prayer should take place, in any given situation. That is, it involved teachers articulating truth claims about God and God's ways with the world, telling the story of how God had acted, and calling for thanksgiving, petition and acts of service that would respond to and fit with that story. Think, for instance, of the form of many of the epistles, in which a rehearsal of the acts of God (a rehearsal often framed as a prayer of thanksgiving) precedes a body of ethical instruction – the two parts joined together by a 'therefore'.

Once again, there was no antecedent necessity that Christian teaching should take this form. It could, say, have become and remained a matter of learning at the feet of the apostles and their successors, imitating their lives, joining in their prayers, listening to their wisdom sayings and parables, without any intensive investment in the development of an articulated canopy of truth claims.

One of the factors that pushed Christian teaching in the direction of doctrinal theology, however, was Christianity's polycentricity.[5] In a process that could have gone quite otherwise (and that has often since been betrayed), the Christian faith, as it spread, was (sometimes, and to a degree) allowed to take root differently in different locations. All of those who became Christians were understood to be called to follow the same Jesus in the power of the same Spirit, but they understood differently what discipleship demanded in their various locations. Most strikingly, the early church came eventually to agree that the development of discipleship amongst the Gentiles need not look the same as it had come to look amongst Jews. Those who responded to Christian proclamation were asked not so much to take on an already formed way of life as to be converted by the same word that had converted

---

[5]My account in this paragraph is heavily influenced by Willie James Jennings, *Acts* (Louisville, KY: Westminster John Knox Press, 2017); Andrew Walls, 'Converts or Proselytes? The Crisis over Conversion in the Early Church', *International Bulletin of Missionary Research* 28, no. 1 (2004): 2–6; and John G. Flett, *Apostolicity: The Ecumenical Question in World Christian Perspective* (Downers Grove, IL: IVP Academic 2016).

those who were witnessing to them. They were asked what this word would make of their lives – how it would convert their histories, their cultures, their habits of mind and body. They were asked, in effect, how they might learn to offer all of their particularity to the God of Jesus Christ in prayer. And as that conversion happened, reports of its yield flowed back to the existing centres of the church's life, challenging and transforming them – the conversion of new populations to Christianity itself continuing to convert those who were already Christians.

The invention or discovery of this polycentric form of life involved the invention or discovery of a distinction between the converting word and the converted life. That is, it involved the invention or discovery of a distinction between the proclamation of the truth about God's ways with the world and the working out of the implications of that truth in the midst of ordinary life. It is hard to think polycentricity without thinking some such distinction, even if one also insists that the working out of the implications is always deepening, challenging and extending one's understanding of the proclaimed truth.

The invention or discovery of that distinction was also bound up with the development of one of the characteristic forms of early Christian teaching: the ministry of itinerant apostles. If your teacher is no longer present, so that learning the ways of the faith cannot any longer be a matter of sitting day-by-day at his or her feet, then he or she must find some other means of enabling your continued growth. One response to that situation was for the teacher to insist that members of the community already know all they need in order to discover how to respond to whatever new situation or controversy they are facing. The answers to the community's questions about the shape of day-by-day faithfulness flow from the teaching they have already received; they know the storyline of the faith, and that should be enough to enable them to know how to go on in the present.

The development of Christian polycentricity was, then, the development of a form of life in which the same faith was understood to be taking root differently in different locations, in each of which the local faithful were understood to be responding to the demands of their particular situation in response to the same acts of God. That development was at the same time the emergence of the idea that these diverse forms of life were rooted in common teaching about the one gift that enabled all of them: the story of God and God's ways with the world. Or, to put it differently, we might say that the emergence of polycentricity involved the emergence of the idea that the diverse forms of Christian life should be rooted in, and grow from, a common practice of thanksgiving. And the fundamental form of the knowledge of God that Christian teaching can help generate is the knowledge of how to live lives more firmly rooted in this thanksgiving.

Controversy

As the Christian faith spread, and communities sprang up in different locations living this faith differently, the question was bound to arise as to whether they were indeed following the same Jesus in the power of the same Spirit. Christianity had, in significant part, developed in such a way that it was held together – or was supposed to be held together – by common allegiance to the same claims about God and God's ways with the world, but the diverse forms that lives of prayerful discipleship took in different places, and the diverse ways in which Christians articulated what they knew, made the question of unity unavoidable.

The same articulated summaries that emerged from and shaped proclamation, and that were used as means of Christian teaching, therefore became fodder for controversy. The question of the unity between scattered Christian communities became, in part, a question of the mutual recognizability of their doctrinal teachings, and scrutiny of these doctrinal teachings became one of the means by which Christians held one another to account, or called one another's faith into question.

Discussions of the relationship between doctrine and prayer often focus here, on the content of Christian controversy, and scour our records of those controversies on the lookout for occasions when the participants referred to the practice or content of prayer in the course of their arguments. It is, however, precisely in the context of such controversy that doctrinal theology can detach most easily from the life of prayer, and the very fact that we can look for specific moments when prayer is referred to in the course of arguments that otherwise function quite differently is perhaps itself already a sign of that detachment.

Those engaged in such controversy worked with articulated summaries of the faith that have been squeezed into recognizable and reproducible forms by the pressures of controversy, by the demands of catechesis or (as we shall see) by the repetitions of liturgy. Under these pressures, and especially the pressures of controversy, their language began to become a technical language – that is, a language with explicitly stated rules and a circumscribed vocabulary. Once that has happened, it is all too easy to play the game of manipulating such language without any more than an occasional backward glance at the much messier, much livelier, much less controllable language of ordinary belief and ordinary prayer. And as the game of manipulating such language becomes more elaborate, it is all too easy for some to think that the findings of doctrinal theology are where the deepest knowledge of God is to be found, rather than in the apparently far less sophisticated language of ordinary prayerful discipleship.

It is better to see these controversies – however abstruse they sometimes become – as all, at root, controversies about how best to resource and guide the practice of prayerful discipleship. A highly developed ability, say, to deploy the language of technical trinitarian theology does not in and of itself mean that the doctrinal theologian knows God better than the ordinary prayerful believer for whom such language is unfamiliar or incomprehensible. It might, however, mean that the doctrinal theologian has access to resources for informing and to guidance for shaping the practice of ordinary prayerful discipleship which is the proper form of the knowledge of God. Doctrinal theology serves prayerful discipleship, not the other way around.

Confession

There is one final aspect of the emergence of doctrinal theology that I want to mention, because it has a specific relationship to the practice of prayer.

In the early church, Christian identity was not simply given by location; it was not simply a natural concomitant of being one of the people in this place. Christian communities were marked out from their surroundings in various ways. It came to be the case that one of the central forms that such marking took was a declaration of allegiance to the central claims of the faith, a public owning of the story that was henceforth to be the story within which one's own story took place.

The act of confession (here meaning not the act of identifying one's sins and repenting of them, but the act of declaring one's faith) is both a public declaration of allegiance and an act of worship: an act of commitment to the God of Jesus Christ, offered to God in prayer. In both respects, there is a pressure towards a certain terseness and repeatability, a pressure towards the formulaic. Confession of faith is therefore one of the places where, from very early on, we see the development of summary articulations of the faith that begin to look like creeds.[6]

One of the central locations for this development was the development of baptismal confession. This was both a pedagogical form – an epitome of the catechesis that the new Christian had undergone, now summarized, articulated and made memorable for educational reasons – and a confessional form – formulaic precisely in order to indicate that new Christians were declaring the same faith as their teachers, declaring their membership of

---

[6]On confession, see John Webster, 'Confession and Confessions', in *Nicene Christianity: The Future for a New Ecumenism*, ed. Christopher R. Seitz (Grand Rapids, MI: Brazos Press, 2001), 119–31 and Edmund Schlink, *The Coming Christ and the Coming Church*, trans. I. H. Neilson, et al. (Edinburgh: Oliver and Boyd, 1967), 16–95.

the community of this shared confession. And that dual nature seems to be visible in the dual location of these confessions: on the one hand, in the engagement prior to baptism between catechist and catechumen, offered from teacher to pupil and then pupil to teacher as a marker of the passing on of the faith; on the other, in the emerging liturgy of baptism itself, offered as an element of the catechumens' prayers, the beginning of a lifelong journey deeper into prayer, and so deeper into knowledge of God.

Other forms of confession, even when they originated in other contexts, catechetical or controversial, often migrated into the liturgy, becoming a distinctive form of prayer in their own right. And whilst the presence of such formulae in the language of prayer is by no means central to the relationship between doctrine and prayer, it is a telling sign of the deeper relationship that I have been exploring.

Doctrine and prayer

It was by the combination of the pressures shaping proclamation, teaching, controversy and confession that Christianity became, in many of its most visible forms, a doctrinal faith: a faith concerned with orthodoxy, expressing that orthodoxy in terse formulae, and endlessly exploring, elaborating and debating the ideas captured in those formulae. And although some of these practices, especially the practices of debate, sometimes allowed for a certain distance to grow between the discussion of doctrine and the practice of prayer, that distancing is not an inevitable part of the picture. Properly understood, the practices of doctrinal theology (the practices within which these summary articulations of the faith are proposed, explored, elaborated upon and argued over) are practices that should serve and support the life of prayer. In particular, and as I have said repeatedly, the Christian knowledge of God is not a matter of doctrinal proficiency, but of prayerful discipleship.

At their best, the practices of doctrinal theology are a reminder of the shape of the story that prayer inhabits, and of some of the motifs on which prayer can feed as it explores this story. Doctrine can, for instance, remind the praying person that all good things come from God, and that whatever we offer back to God was ours only because it was first God's gift to us. This might, at times, be a helpful, even a necessary reminder. But that reminder is no more than an outline, an abstraction. It is only as people learn in practice to thank God for all good things, including all that is good in themselves, that this outline is filled in and becomes living knowledge of God – and the filling in is always more than a neat colouring between the lines. Christians learn how to thank, how to move from thanksgiving to lament, to petition, to adoration, in ways that outstrip their articulations, and that can always call them to think again and to think more deeply. Doctrinal theology supports prayer, but it is always also supported by it; it properly feeds on it and remains dependent upon it, because the life of prayer is where the knowledge of God transpires.

Praying for Better Doctrinal Theology

There is one last aspect of the connection between doctrine and prayer that I want to explore. The pursuit of doctrinal theology is itself, for many of its practitioners, one of the practices of faith, rather than something that stands on its own. For these practitioners, it is in its own way a form of discipleship – and it demands the same animation by prayer as any form of discipleship. Whatever is good in it comes from God, and should elicit one's thanks; whatever is distorted or broken in it should elicit one's penitence, and one's petitions for the grace to amend one's ways. No less than any other form of discipleship, it should be pursued in prayerful acknowledgement of one's insufficiency for the task. No form of diligence or effort on the part of the doctrinal theologian can guarantee that what she offers will in fact build up the Body; no form of diligence or effort on the part of the doctrinal theologian can securely prevent her from doing harm. The doctrinal theologian can only offer her diligence and effort accompanied by prayer, and as a form of prayer, relying upon God's gracious help.

This section of the chapter is more tentative than the first two. It is also a section where I can't sustain the apparent neutrality of the voice in which I have written the first two sections. To explore what it might mean for doctrinal theology to be a form of prayer, I am going to explore what it might mean for someone like me, working in a context like mine. I write from a position of significant privilege: an affluent, white, Western, middle-class, cis-gendered, heterosexual man, who has a secure job in a research-intensive university and who has been granted a voice in the affairs of my church (the Church of England) that has as much to do with that identity and position as with what I happen to have done with them. I am encouraged, in all sorts of ways, to speak with a theological voice that sounds authoritative, stable and dependable – to make an authoritative, stable and dependable name for myself. What it means for me to learn to see the work of doctrinal theology as prayer might be rather different from what it means for others.

It may sound at this point as if I have switched to a different set of topics from those that I was exploring earlier in the chapter. The articulated summaries that doctrinal theologians produce, elaborate and argue about are, however, always no more than proposals – proposals for making sense of the wider life of discipleship and prayer. That is, they are always no more (and no less) than creative and contingent construals, generated with the help of specific resources of imagination and insight, and always produced from some particular vantage point, the product of some particular history, disseminated from a particular position by means of particular structures and relationships. They tend, for good and ill, to reproduce something of the life that has enabled them: for good, because they might pass on whatever inheritance of faith, whatever accumulated wisdom, whatever refinements of insight the doctrinal theologian in question has received; for ill, because they will also tend to pass on the distortions and the exclusions, the inattentiveness and misprisions that mark that inheritance, and to reinforce the patterns of unearned and unexamined privilege that have made the doctrinal theologian's work possible.

Yet doctrinal theology is not, or need not be, entirely imprisoned by the contexts and histories from which it is produced. One could consider the ways in which those engaged in doctrinal theology are likely to have been taught to read scripture and to engage with voices from the tradition in ways that, however much they are entangled in these dynamics of reproduction, might nevertheless also allow them to hear a disrupting and enlivening challenge. One could consider the ways in which doctrinal theologians are likely to have been taught practices of reasoning that might also, on a good day, help them to reach disrupting and enlivening conclusions. I want to focus, however, on a different and more direct possibility for enlivening disruption, for being called beyond what one has already received and already knows, beyond the current pattern of one's prayers. I want to focus on the possibility of enlivening disruption by the voices of those who – in our polycentric, improvisatory faith – have learnt to live the faith differently, in the midst of different histories. And I want to focus in particular on those who one might think, misleadingly, stand at or beyond the margins of the life of one's church.

To hear the prayers of others who pray differently – to hear what they rejoice in, what they ask for, what makes them cry out – and to hear their articulations of what they know of God in those prayers, can be a means of God's grace. It can, by the grace of God, call one to hear or see differently the faith that one has received; it can prompt one to construe differently – to see different possibilities for articulating and summarizing the faith, to see different forms that the practices of articulation and discussion might take, or simply to see different ways in which one might pray.[7]

---

[7]For a picture of the way in which prayer can be caught up in, for instance, the dynamics of racism, see Lauren F. Winner, *The Dangers of Christian Practice: On Wayward Gifts, Characteristic Damage, and Sin* (New Haven, CT: Yale University Press, 2018), 57–94. Imagine bringing the prayers that Winner describes into conversation with the patterns of prayer explored in Andrew Prevot's discussion of James Cone in *Thinking Prayer*, chapter 6.

There are, however, two layers of reception involved in such a process of change. Most obviously, there is the reception of the different substantive possibilities represented by those voices: different ways of construing and inhabiting the faith; different ways of thanking, asking and confessing. Beneath that, however, there is the reception of the very openness that might make such learning possible. One's openness to this kind of enlivening disruption is itself something that one receives and needs to go on receiving. Prompted by whatever words of scripture, whatever strands of the tradition, whatever conversations, whatever processes of reasoning have tipped one towards them, one might begin to listen to different voices. Yet one of the things one might hear is precisely that one's forms of openness are themselves inadequate. One might hear, perhaps, that one has so far been listening in ways that subtly reinforce or protect one's privilege; one might hear that what one has taken for openness is just another form of self-congratulation. One might be challenged to listen differently, to rethink the stance one is taking, to learn new practices of engagement and attentiveness.[8]

The enlivening disruption made possible by hearing the voices of others is, then, not something that one can predict or control. It is not something that can be guaranteed by any effort, any form of diligence, even the effort and diligence of listening. One does not and cannot know when and how one will hear the voice that sends one back to read differently the scriptures one thought one knew; to see connections one had missed; to recognize the political and personal entanglements of claims one had thought calmly reasonable. And even one's receptivity to the possibility of this enlivening disruption – to the extent that this means more than a generalized attitude of openness, and means instead the specific practices of engagement, attention and deliberation that can drive real learning – is also not within one's power to produce, or to will into existence. One receives this, too, at the hand of others. To whatever extent one is made genuinely open, one receives that openness by the grace of God, breathing through the voices of others.

This is why the work of doctrinal theologians itself has to be accompanied by prayer, and to be offered as a form of prayer.

First, doctrinal theology is a work wholly dependent upon the grace of God for any good service it can do to the Body of Christ. Specifically, it is dependent upon grace that is mediated to the doctrinal theologian in part through the voices of those who inhabit that Body differently. Doctrinal

---

[8]I am grateful to Jenny Leith for helping me think through this point. I have also learnt from Romand Coles, *Beyond Gated Politics: Reflections for the Possibility of Democracy* (Minneapolis, MN: University of Minnesota Press, 2005) and Al Barrett, 'Interrupting the Church's Flow: Hearing "Other" Voices on an Outer Urban Estate', *Practical Theology* 11, no. 1 (2018): 79–92.

theologians can do all in their power to pursue the forms of engagement, attentiveness and deliberation that they already know – but they cannot pursue the forms that they do not yet know. Their work is surrounded by grace that they do not yet know how to recognize, yet that grace is needed for their work to be fruitful. Their work – my work – makes sense only as an earnest petition for that grace.

Second, doctrinal theology is a work that should be characterized by gratitude, for whatever is good in it is received from others. This might mean, especially for someone like me, that much more of it than hitherto will take the form of recognizing, acknowledging, celebrating and amplifying the voices of those through whom one has been and is receiving grace: not so much making a name for oneself as praising God for the names of others. It is work that should be accompanied by, and should express, prayers of thanksgiving.

Third, doctrinal theology is a work that should be characterized by penitence, by working through deliberately and visibly the ways in which the enlivening disruption one receives through others can question and reorder the patterns of life, thought and prayer into which one had settled. It may be that, especially in a context like mine, *Retractationes* should be a far more central form of doctrinal work than it has tended to be.

It is not, of course, that doctrinal theology that is prayerful in these ways is itself guaranteed to be good theology, or that the prayerful theologian will necessarily be a better theologian than the prayerless. And, of course, thinking of doctrinal theology in this way can bring with it specific dangers of its own: we are familiar with the temptation to treat prayer, even (or perhaps especially) penitential prayer, as a form of self-aggrandizing display. These prayers can only be offered in the hope that God might act through one's doctrinal theological work, but also in the knowledge that this work remains fallible, broken and potentially harmful, and so in trust that God will also act despite and even against one's work – and despite and even against the distortion in one's prayers.

Doctrinal theology, then, lives by prayer. It is sustained by petition, by thanksgiving and by confession; it feeds on the knowledge of God that lives in prayer, and gives whatever gifts it receives back to the life of prayer. Doctrinal theology and prayer belong together, and without this entanglement with prayer the pursuit of doctrinal theology makes little sense.

CHAPTER EIGHT

The Act of Prayer and the Doctrine of God

KATHERINE SONDEREGGER

'Let my prayer be set forth before thee as incense; and the lifting up of my hands as the evening sacrifice' (Ps. 141.2). This verse from the Psalter places prayer in the heart of Israel's worship of God. As incense ascending from the smoking brazier, and as the pleasing savour of the evening sacrifice rises up before the Holy LORD of the Covenant, prayer joins Heaven and earth. This psalm has found its way into the Evening Office of Christian worship, evoking prayer as a vesper sacrifice to the Living God.[1] It marks the descent of the day into night, and, as the note of sacrifice suggests, the slow or sudden descent of life into death. King David is the traditional author of Psalm 141, and in its brief compass, the ten verses of this psalm embrace the lament over suffering and wrong, the confident trust in God in the face of injury and danger, and the delicate interplay of the individual and the collective, so characteristic of Israel's piety – all of it constituting the sturdy realism of prayer as act before Almighty God. The creaturely act of prayer and the Doctrine of God belong together; they are a natural pair.

Of course, some in the Christian tradition have not considered these natural companions: in the natural knowledge of God, for example, the

---

[1]As an example, see the Evening Prayer service in Episcopal Church, *The Book of Common Prayer and Administration of the Sacraments and Other Rites and Ceremonies of the Church: Together with the Psalter or Psalms of David According to the Use of the Episcopal Church* (New York: Seabury Press, 1979), 115–26.

Doctrine of God may be thought a conceptual and speculative domain, logically independent of – Sovereign over – the human cries and calls upon the Holy One; and in our era, the moral problems that attend the act of prayer – the overwhelming evidence of evil in this sorry world, the painful reality of prayers that go unanswered, or those that receive an answer only in the coinage of silence, the teeming, disparate ends of human prayer that cannot coincide and cannot make peace – all these make the relation between an Omnipotent and Benevolent God and creaturely prayer an uneasy, disjointed, even broken one. I do not want to dismiss these objections out of hand: in truth, how could anyone who has studied these conceptual and moral problems for more than a moment make light of the obstacles they present? My conviction, rather, is that the invocations and laments of the world's creatures, their prayers of many kinds, and the God who is known, addressed, feared and provoked by these petitions, belong together, as natural pair, and in a specific pattern – that of ascent and descent.

It will take some complex scaffolding to build this pattern of ascent and descent as a natural pair, and this chapter will attempt to put those pieces together with care. But, as with many building projects, we might begin with a bit of ground clearing. Does the entire aim of prayer as compatible relation to Almighty God reduce this entire enterprise to a debased form of subjectivism or relationalism?[2] Can we have a Doctrine of God without the creature, and her prayers? Have I posed the question that will animate the whole in such a way that the sturdy Objectivity of the One God can no longer be praised, conceptually specified or intellectually worshipped? In prayer, is God only and always known merely as the One turned to us, the Spiritual Phenomenon of our own inmost desires? These questions are not idle ones, for the proper defence of the Objectivity and Aseity of God is certainly one of the deep problematics of the modern era in theology. To link the One God to creaturely acts of inwardness threatens to return Christian theology to a form of subjectivism Karl Barth always labelled 'Cartesianism'.[3]

It seemed, in the early modern era of European letters, that knowledge could be had only from within: that metaphysics, to express this in alternative idiom, could be had only through epistemology. Certainly, students of modern Protestant dogmatics associate this problem directly with the Critical Philosophy of Immanuel Kant. But in truth the roots lie much further back, further down into the Augustinianism that was received and

---

[2]For a sophisticated account of 'Relationalism' as a major alternative among Protestant academic theologians in the modern period, see Hans Frei's unpublished doctoral dissertation, 'The Doctrine of Revelation in the Thought of Karl Barth, 1909–1922' (Yale University, 1956).
[3]For an example of this analysis in Barth's extensive corpus, see Barth, *CD* I/1, 198-227.

re-worked in the particular form of Idealism advocated by René Descartes. The remarkable genius of Descartes – for Christian theology, at least – was to transmute Augustine's God, the *Interior intimo meo*, by the alchemy of the *cogito* into the modern Infinite and Perfect Being, grasped by the human intellect in its clear and distinct idea of infinity. Now, Descartes has some stunning argument – persuasive in my mind – to demonstrate that our concept of infinity must rest upon an Infinite who cannot be contained by nor be made dependent upon the human intellect.[4] (Descartes, I say, was a Realist in the Doctrine of God.) But it is a small step from the *Meditations* to an epistemology that cannot successfully break out of its own inwardness, to a metaphysical realm beyond the self. Indeed, if Descartes is right, no non-theist could ever hope to do so.

Descartes' legacy led to a 'turn to the subject' in Christian theology, making the believing creature a centrepiece of dogmatic reflection. And this inward move is not simply Schleiermacher's alone! Modern theology, Catholic and Protestant, has demonstrated a singular devotion to the 'economy' of the triune God's presence among creatures, and a heightened preoccupation with apophatic or negative predication of God.[5] Such themes in Christian theology are not new! But they take on novel forms under the impress of 'Cartesianism' (not to be confused with Cartesian thought itself); and the threat to proper knowledge of God, and affirmation of His Sovereign Aseity, is very real indeed. One need only consult briefly the profound conceptual struggle Karl Barth undertakes in his *Fides Quaerens Intellectum* to sample what it cost a theologian to put Cartesianism behind him.[6]

In such a theological world, the natural pairing of creaturely prayer and the Doctrine of God might seem an unmistakably clear instance of Subjectivism or Cartesianism in theology: the God of prayer and the creaturely act of prayer, locked together in a single, epistemic, and thereby, metaphysical whole. There is much to say about this primal sub-structure of modern theology; much more than can be said in a brief chapter. But here at least we want to address a certain form of this Subjectivism directly: is the knowledge of God possible only by the intellect at prayer? Is God the glorious Reality who can be thought only by an intellect that has given itself

---

[4]All this can be found in Descartes, *Meditations on First Philosophy*, in *Philosophical Works of Descartes*, vol. 1, trans. E. Haldane and G. R. T. Ross (Cambridge: Cambridge University Press, 1931), especially the great Meditation III, 157–71.

[5]For two instances, consider Karl Rahner's treatment of the Dogma of Trinity in his essay, *Trinity*, trans. Joseph Donceel (New York: Crossroad, 1997) and Jürgen Moltmann, *The Crucified God: The Cross of Christ as the Foundation and Criticism of Christian Theology*, trans. R. A. Wilson and John Bowden (New York: Harper and Row, 1974).

[6]Karl Barth, *Anselm: Fides Quaerens Intellectum*, trans. Ian W. Robertson (London: SCM Press, 2012).

over to contemplation and adoration? It may well be that Descartes hoped
to persuade his readers that this was so. His most profound demonstration
of God's Formal Causality – Meditation III – breaks into an apostrophe
on God's glory and sublimity. The majestic pace of the *Meditations* halts
while Descartes contemplates in prayer. Though it does not seem to follow
directly from Descartes' own account of clear and distinct ideas, this pairing
of knowledge and prayer is a very attractive position for a Christian to hold,
and indeed many modern theologians affirm this form of Subjectivism.
The knowledge of God is 'self-involving', as some post-liberal theologians
express it.[7] As we think the thought of God we are transformed: in the
Summa, Thomas says that the intellect is made 'Deiform' as it receives the
intellectual light by which it knows God.[8] But as the very *Summa Theologiae*
makes clear in other Questions, the Reality of God has not always been
thought to be linked inextricably to prayer.

Enter 'natural knowledge of God'. This opens an avenue to the concept
of Deity that was famously affirmed by Vatican I in its Articles of Faith.[9]
Students of modern Protestant theology will know that Karl Barth considered
this a grave danger and mis-step in proper confession of God; they will know
that Barth considered the 'Deity' known by natural powers little but an idol,
a rarefied projection of intellectual ideals.[10] But they will also know that
the sort of Natural Theology practised in the *Prima Pars* of the *Summa*,
for example, does not fall necessarily under Barth's proscription. Indeed,
the opening Questions of the *Summa* are themselves hardly uncontested or
uniformly interpreted, even among Thomists. Still we can say, in the midst
of all this, that what appears to be claimed in such natural knowledge is an
ability, connatural with the human intellect, that allows the human mind
to reach the truth that God exists, yet to hold that truth in the form of
other natural knowledge – without 'self-involvement' or 'Deiformity', or
prayer. God can be known, that is, under the mode of ordinary knowledge,
though the Object known may be considered unique, even strongly so.
The principles of higher mathematics or of Quantum Mechanics might be

---

[7]For an early expression of this conviction, see Donald Evans, *The Logic of Self-Involvement:
A Philosophical Study of Everyday Language with Special Reference to the Christian Use of
Language about God as Creator* (London: SCM Press, 1963).

[8]Aquinas, *ST* I, q. 12, a. 5, ad. 3; Natural Theology is thought to begin in q. 2 (the famous Five
Ways) and extend through the Treatise, *De Deo Uno*, q. 26.

[9]See the First Vatican Council in Norman Tanner, *Decrees of the Ecumenical Councils*
(Washington, DC: Georgetown Press, 1990).

[10]Classically expressed in *Natural Theology: Comprising 'Nature and Grace' by Professor Dr
Emil Brunner and the Reply by Dr Karl Barth, 'No!'*, trans. Peter Fraenkel (London: Geoffrey
Bles, 1946).

parallel here: remarkable, perhaps unique facts, dazzling in complexity and explanatory scope, occupying the far reaches of the human intellect, yet learned, comprehended and recalled as are the humble facts of addition and the mechanism of levers.

In scholastic theology, a distinction is usually drawn here, between the truths that can be known in a worldly, natural fashion, and the truths that belong properly to the Christian mystery – the God who dwells among us, full of grace and truth. Trinity, Incarnation, Redemption, Eucharistic Presence: these are among the high mysteries of the Christian faith that can be known only through prayer, only in faith, only by grace. They claim a whole human life, and they transform the knower. In contrast, the natural knower recognizes a Primal Source, a Cause that simply Is, a Unicity that cannot be divided or compounded, an Intellect and Will that are perfect, complete and unbounded in themselves. These are truths, so the Natural Theologian holds, that can be known by the 'unaided intellect' and seem to transform the knower as little as does the knowledge of the specific weight of hydrogen. Yet the Deity known by unaided reason, these theologians argue, is no idol. The natural Divinity is held to be rational *and* worthy of worship, so Natural Theologians say, because the True God is *both* Idea and Person, both metaphysical, substantial Truth and the True, Faithful One. Made to know God, the human intellect can think Deity as Concept and Cause, that primal category in Natural Theology. The relation between these Divine abstractions and the living God of Holy Scripture was one marked off by grace: the Covenant LORD is present to the intellect only by a gracious elevation and healing. But the Divine Idea is simply known by a rational creature by reflection on first things: there is no full knowledge of 'substance', say, nor of 'motion' that does not lead the rigorous intellect to the Idea of Necessary Being or Prime Mover. As the final destination of the scientific mind, the Idea of God makes a world out of chaos or random principles (so Kant claimed),[11] and teaches the complete meaning of contingency or finitude. Unaided, our minds can know God as Final and Necessary – and these properties are true of God, absolutely, in the realm of both nature and grace.

Now, such natural knowledge appears to lessen the threat of an all-consuming Subjectivism in the Doctrine of God. God is simply known and

---

[11]This is the Critical form of the cosmological argument advanced by Kant in *Critique of Pure Reason*, trans. Norman Kemp Smith (New York: St Martin's Press, 1965), Book II, chapter 2, especially Sections 7–9, and Solutions I and II, and given an intriguing Thomistic parallel in R. Van De Velde, *Aquinas on God: The 'Divine Science' of the Summa Theologiae* (Aldershot: Ashgate, 2006).

referred to as Object, a Reality independent of our relation to it. This familiar form of sturdy Realism underlies much scientific knowledge and logical argument, within theology and beyond it. The objectivity of primary scientific knowledge, for example, is rarely contested; though not invariably. (Radical irrealism in the philosophy of science is not unknown in some circles.[12]) But on the whole, the scientists at work in their laboratories quietly assume the metaphysical sturdiness of their objects of study, and although the very large and the very small seem poised on the edge of irrealism, the world of objective physical knowledge appears to hold. The foundational category of cause takes centre stage here in rational knowledge: a real object possesses, at the very least, causal powers. If Almighty God, in His Necessity and Originating Power, can be known in a natural manner – a 'scientific' one – we might assume also a firm Objectivity to this Reality that undergirds and makes possible our small creaturely insights. And so it seems that natural knowledge of God might be a bulwark against the reductive down-rush of prayer as the sole avenue to proper knowledge of God.

But is that so? Here I want to begin a proper investigation into the pattern of ascent that is ingredient in the act of prayer, and in the proper knowledge of God. In this pattern we join together a creaturely inwardness and a motion *upwards* towards the Reality of God. What we seek to explore here is whether there is *any* intellectual or spiritual movement towards God that could be otherwise than an ascent, lifting upwards, as does the incense of prayer. Might prayer, that is, form the sole *relatio* between the creaturely *mens* and the Object of our desire, whether we consider it a kind of rational or natural knowing, a kind of adoration or a kind of petition and invocation? I do not want to propose a form of *reductionism* here – a suppressing and delimiting and reducing of all form of God–world relation into a single one of prayer. Rather I propose we examine how prayer might be *expanded* to encompass many, divergent forms of Creator–creature *relatio*, an expanded pattern I have called, the pattern of ascent. The Platonists of the ancient world gave Hellenistic Christians the language of ascent to God, and we see that pronounced motion upwards in figures as diverse as Augustine, Dionysius, Gregory of Nyssa and the mystagogues, Plotinus and Proclus. The significant pattern for us here is the union of all knowledge, all virtuous

---

[12]Such 'constructivism' has been traditionally traced to Thomas S. Kuhn, *The Structure of Scientific Revolutions* (Chicago, IL: University of Chicago Press, 1962). But the extent of the irrealism in such a view is not settled. For a broad discussion of varying schools of anti-realism and constructivism in scientific knowledge, see André Kukla, *Social Constructivism and the Philosophy of Science* (London: Routledge, 2000).

striving, all confession and petition and mystical longing, under the common language of ascent.

This pattern, to be sure, seems to connote a restless and searching human creature, striving under its own agency and powers, to raise itself upwards by its own moral and rational will, into the knowledge – and mastery? – of the Transcendent. All Christian writers seem neuralgic on this very point, seeking again and again to underscore God's utter Mystery, even to the adept, and the Luminous Darkness that awaits the climber when she ascends the last peak into the Holy Reality. The idiom of knowledge and ignorance, of grasping and losing all control, of sight and utter blindness, in this pattern of ascent seems to comb together creaturely agency and creaturely nescience into a single fabric. From this rich mixture stem the later tradition of a 'learned ignorance' and a 'cloud of unknowing' that appear ready to combine human striving with a strict limit and powerlessness before the Object of one's desire. In this neighbourhood, too, we might locate the pronounced distinction between the Transcendent God's Essence, wrapped in utter Mystery, and His Works or 'Energies' that alone can be perceived in this sphere of Divine Economy. The pattern of ascent, then, is a complex heritage, a weighty one, for a Christian Doctrine of Prayer, a tradition that must be sorted through with care.

First, we can ask: Might it be that the pattern of ascent is in truth a pattern of descent? This is the sketch I would like to explore in the proper relation of prayer to a full and Objective Doctrine of God. Might it be the case that God alone gives Himself to be known by creatures, both in worship and in rational knowledge? Might it be possible that the only reason a rigorous intellect can reach a full knowledge of substance or change or cosmology as a whole is because God Himself *permits* such a thought? This possibility or proposal would take a step beyond the traditional claim that the human intellect has been made for God – the *inquietus* of Augustine – and the exegetical tradition of the *Imago Dei* developed in Late Antiquity.[13] My expanded notion of prayer – the pattern of ascent, both rational and confessional – would demand that the One, Triune LORD act decidedly and specifically to welcome proper knowledge of Him, as well as invocations of His Holy Name. The very thought of God would be itself a manifestation of God's decisive Self-disclosure. This would not rule out natural knowledge of God; indeed it would license it. But it would suggest that all rigorous argument for the Reality of God in one, virtuous sense, always already

---

[13]Augustine, *The Confessions*, trans. Maria Boulding (Hyde Park, NY: New City Press, 1997). See also Basil the Great, *On the Human Condition*, trans. Nonna Verna Harrison (Crestwood, NY: St Vladimir's Seminary Press, 2005).

assume the Objective Reality of the Self-Revealer. (Just so, I think, Barth read Anselm's *Proslogion*.) All relationship with God would be contingent utterly upon God as Self-Giver, both in rational thought and in petition and adoration. This would have the effect of broadening the Doctrine of Grace to the proper and final use of the scientific intellect: 'unaided reason' would receive still the gift of permission, the full exercise of its powers. In this limited but specific sense, all knowledge of God would be by prayer, by ascent to the Heavenly Throne.

Some unusual consequences would flow from such an experiment. Let me take the example of God as the Highest Good. We might take this as a species of natural knowledge of God, a Divine Property or Identity known by the ancients, and affirmed in Christian teaching. On my proposal, God Himself permitted and made possible the metaphysical insights of the *Phaedrus* and the *Metaphysics* – indeed of the *Enneads* and *Critique of Practical Reason* – and disclosed to the human intellect the Truth that God is the Good Itself. Now, this being so, the God who is loved and adored and called upon in prayer is also the True God, and to give Himself in this way is the greatest Gift. God's Self-disclosure in prayer thus uncovers two central attributes of God Himself: His Humility and His Constancy or Immutability.

Divine Humility is an Attribute or Perfection that can be easily overlooked – perhaps from the nature of the case. God is the Humble One not simply in His great kindness: His condescension to creatures, as theologians from Chrysostom to Calvin have noted,[14] can be seen throughout the saving Economy of Grace. But Humility as a Divine Predicate belongs to God's Aseity, His Sovereign Independence and Nature. God is Humble in this sense, above all: that He is Immaterial, Unbodied, and in just this way, Invisible to His creatures. The Lofty LORD is the One who does not require the proud borders of a material object; does not demand a place to occupy; is not extended nor need be; is Luminous Self-Presence in quiet Immateriality. Such a God can be known as the Good without protest or Self-assertion. The Humble God can be known *as*. Augustine records in his *Confessions* and *Soliloquies* the startling recognition that God is known *as* Truth; this insight unmade him.[15] The True God is content, it seems, to be known under the categories of the Transcendentals, and recognized only by

---

[14]For Chrysostom and Calvin, see John Chrysostom, *Homilies on Genesis 1-17*, trans. R. Hill, FC 74 (Washington, DC: Catholic University of America Press, 1986) and Calvin, *Inst.*, 1.8 and 1.9.

[15]For the *Confessions*, see Book VII; for the *Soliloquies*, see *Writings of St Augustine – vol 1*, trans. Thomas F. Gilligan, FC 5 (New York: Cima Publishing, 1948), especially Book II.

The God known in the pattern of ascent is also the Constant, Immutable One. This Divine Perfection undergirds natural ascent to God in striking fashion. We may offer a warm welcome to the notion of Divine Humility, and perhaps even to the proposal that all ascent to God presupposes a prior Divine Descent: But! Is there not an air of Occasionalism that hangs over the whole? To say that all knowledge of God is by Divine Permission is to suggest – does it not? – that God grants, to this one and to that, a concept or ideal that can name the True, Good and Humble Lord. It appears that all true knowledge of God is an event of God's own doing, His making of the creaturely thought that, on occasion, He bestows upon seekers after the infinite and the good. Occasionalism of this sort makes creaturely knowledge, at base, unstable and unreliable. On some canons of knowledge it would fail to pass muster. (Do we really know the object that flashes before us, an object that, like Eliot's mystery in the orchard, is here then gone, then here again, randomly and without measure?) The sturdy Objectivity of God that underwrites Natural Theology, and seemed one of its great assets in the natural pairing of theology and prayer, appears now scattered and dissipated by the God who permits and reveals – or might we say, Veils and Unveils? In such straits I think we might justify a brief appeal to a kind of transcendental argument in which we locate the condition of possibility for natural knowledge of God in the Constancy and Immutability of Almighty God. That knowledge of Prime Cause or the First Good or the Absolute Infinite is genuine knowledge, permanent and sturdy and reliable, rests on an Attribute of God: He is Constant, Unshakable. When we speak of a Divine Permission in the Pattern of Ascent and Descent, then, it cannot consist in a Voluntarism that makes the Divine movement us-wards occasional, random or seemingly without rational foundation. Rather it must be true that our seeking after God meets with a God who offers Himself to thought as a *Substance*, as That which Is, and underlies all motion or predication. This will have the unusual effect of making Immutability one of the so-called Personal Attributes of God: His Humble Will to be known by us in our rational ascent will be utterly Immovable, Permanent and Peaceable, at rest, Sabbath rest. In this way, the demand for a strong counter-factual account of Divine freedom is muted: God's Constancy is a Personal Freedom, and thereby a Freedom simply to be utterly Thus. So, the Objectivity and Aseity of the True God is preserved in the natural pairing of the Doctrine of God and prayer – though not, to be sure, without some surprisingly correlates.

Yet in all this we have not said the most important thing about prayer and natural knowledge of God. If God is known truly as the First or Highest Good, why is that knowledge itself not the answer to *all* prayer? I have underscored the natural compatibilism of prayer and the Doctrine of God;

but here it seems that the Doctrine of God – and only one of its many Attributes – will in the end *erase* prayer itself. When we consider the many other forms of prayer – what we might call the 'religious forms' – we may well wonder whether my account of God as Good and True, the Humble One, might make all petition, lament and intercession otiose. After all, if God is the Highest God, why is not simply the Self-Offer of God, the very thought of Him, not the highest gift, the greatest good, the most lavish gift and blessing? This is a deep problem at the heart of religious prayer; but one that is often over-looked. Why would a creature ask for anything other than God? If God is the Final Good, why would not God's own Self-disclosure be simply the answer to any and all prayer? As God is Benevolent, He would will only to give the best gift, the truest and highest form of benefit to the creature. And that, we know, is simply God Himself. It may well be that God could grant or permit or endow the creature with many worldly goods – our first parents' garments of skin; Job's new kith and kin; Lazarus' life which he hoped to lay down for his Saviour – but they would not constitute His best gift, but only a secondary, finite and utterly inferior bestowal, one that worms will only destroy. It seems then that our proper knowledge of God's Attributes, and God's own Matchless Benevolence, demand that prayer seek and receive only the highest Gift, God Himself. Let grace come, and the world pass away, the *Didache* says. Perhaps for the one who prays, we might say, Let Almighty God come, and prayer itself pass away. Why does prayer seem to circle around other forms of ascent to the Heavenly Realm: protests and laments, requests and sighings, beseechings and callings upon the Name, demands for intervention or healing or deliverance, revenge upon enemies and hardships? Why all these? Is God not what we creatures all desire, in our hearts and in our minds? Why is the pattern of ascent not simply the unfettered and unmeasured drive to know the Presence of God, to receive the matchless Gift of His own Self-giving?

Holy Scripture at axial moments appears to teach just this austere Doctrine of Prayer. When Moses encounters the Almighty, learns His Name and receives the commission that puts slavery to flight, he calls upon God to have mercy upon him in this terrifying task. 'Who am I, that I should go to Pharaoh, and that I should bring forth the children of Israel out of Egypt?' The LORD God answers: 'I will be with you.' Secondary signs and tokens are given to Moses, certainly; some are used and some set aside. But the principal gift it seems that the Almighty One gives Moses is simply His own Presence: The LORD Himself. When Abram is called in a vision by the LORD, he receives promises, yes, and descendants like the stars in the inky sky, and signs in the midst of a deep and terrifying sleep – but his first gift is this: 'I am your shield and your exceedingly great reward.' 'Be not afraid of them', the Commanding God tells Jeremiah, 'for I am with you to deliver you, says the LORD.' And will we not think immediately of Maid Mary, who hears the Archangel Gabriel, drawing near to a remote village in the Galilee: Hail, Full of Grace: the LORD is with you? And at the end of every trial, every ministry and healing, at the end of an expected and terrible death, the Risen Lord ascending from his disciples, and speaking now as does Almighty God: Lo I am with you always, even unto the end of world? It seems that Holy Scripture, even in its most 'narrative', most human-scale and intimate scenes, reflects this riddle posed by the natural knowledge of God as Highest Good. The answer to the deepest human struggle and searching is simply, God Himself, His Presence. In His Goodness, His Humility and Self-Offering, the LORD God gives the answer to each and every prayer – the surpassing value of God as the Present One.

Now, we might be tempted to stretch such a pattern of human ascent and Divine descent into the ceaseless and painful question about unanswered prayer, especially those sent Heavenward in evil days. Might the problems of unanswered prayer, even the problem of evil, be properly addressed by this conviction that God Himself, in His Majestic Presence, is the Constant Answer and Blessing? It is true that the Apostle Paul could count the whole world dross in the dazzling Presence of the Risen Christ, to know and be known by Him: but could the whole religious enterprise of entreaty and lament be encompassed by such a Promise and Gift? Saints and martyrs in the long church tradition appear to add lustre to this idea, abandoning their worldly goods and their lives simply to attain God, to know that He is with them, and in life and also in death. True, this is the radicality of the very concept of God: the world is sharply relativized and made next to nothing, compared to the Reality of God. And it is the testimony of the great spiritual masters that even in the darkest hour of abandonment and silence, God stands Present, Hidden yet Real behind that impenetrable barrier. Were we to follow this line of analysis to the end, then, we would once again consider all prayers answered, even at the gravest crisis and greatest cost, by God simply giving Himself, to thought and to creaturely inwardness. Might not this be the inner dynamism of Calvin's powerful treatment in Book III of the *Institutes* of the Christian act of trusting in God as Fatherly Provider?[17] To trust that the slender ray of light that penetrates even an upper window in a prison cell is still wholly and fully light – that is the confidence of the heart that, in trial and terror, trusts that the Father is with him, despite all and everything; nothing can snatch the creature from His Hand. These

---

[17]See the treatment of King David as exemplar, Calvin, *Inst.* 3.11.17.

are powerful testimonies, and the temptation is strong to say that God's Omnipresence is simply the answer to prayer, all of it.

And yet. We have not reckoned yet with the most striking element of prayer as natural pair to the Doctrine of God: the Scriptural command to ask, to seek, to knock, to plead. When the disciples ask the Lord to teach them to pray, Christ gives them a compressed litany of *petitions*: to hallow, to bring justice on the earth, to feed, to pardon and to deliver from evil. Nor are these petitions new. The characteristic patterns Jesus lays down in parable and example to his followers can be found throughout Israel's scriptures. The prayers of David ring the changes on these petitions, as does the prayer of his son, Solomon, as do the Psalms, from imprecation to contrition; Hannah pours out her bitter heart to the LORD, desperate for a son; Hagar weeping for Ishmael, that he might be spared a cruel death. Everywhere in Israel's covenant history we read of prayers of invocation, of petition, of sacrifice and hallowing, all of them specific, earth-bound, temporal. To His disciples, Jesus continues this practice of calling upon the LORD. They are not to tire, not to back down, not to fear; rather they are to *ask*, to cry out, to entreat. In the hour of greatest danger, Jesus Himself in Gethsemane prays a petition that we are permitted to overhear: if it be Your will, let this cup pass. (It seems that this is the *great* example of prayer unanswered, or answered only in the coinage of silence.) And from the cross, in the Lukan account, Jesus prays that His Father forgive, an intercession pled even at that bitter hour. Indeed, Jesus is portrayed, especially in the Third Gospel, as a Man of Prayer, spending long nights in prayer, alone. We cannot evade the impression that the Bible is a book of petition, a covenant history of prayer for earthly gifts of healing, of deliverance, of child-birth, of blessing. Such petitions are answered *in kind*, if they be answered at all, and scripture sings with the joy of health returned, death delayed, children given, enemies routed and put to flight. What should we say about all this?

It seems that God wills to give not only the Highest Good, but also the lowly, and secondary, and lesser gifts of creaturely desires. It seems that the Lord of Heaven and earth is eager to bestow on His children – or on some of His children – the ends that *they* desire, the creaturely aims *they* define and insist upon. It seems that the Good God is content to speak in the idiom of creatures, and to realize for them the healings, security, victory, daily bread and pardon that they crave. Now, if prayer and the Doctrine of God are a natural pair, such petitions, granted or no, must disclose to us something of the Perfections of God that He Himself permits us to conceive. Perhaps it is here that we should recognize the profound reach of the Apostle Paul's hymn to *lowliness*, the descent of the One in the Form of God who empties and humbles Himself to take our lot and assume our dust. Though to be sure this Hymn of Christ, the *Carmen Christi*, concerns the Incarnation of the Son, we might hear in this text also a disclosure of the Divine Nature, the *Forma Dei*. Might the astonishing Humility of God also encompass His intent to enter down into our needs and longings, to speak in our idiom, and to give in our currency? It seems that the very idea of prayer as petition demands that we know the Holy One in this way, too. We might say, then, that the Transcendent God has a *disposition*, a metaphysical 'readiness' for living among us, and sharing our nature. Prayer might be best understood, then, as the correlate to this Divine Property, the Disposition of Lowliness, that stoops down to hear our cries.

A metaphysical disposition is a *structure* or *capacity* that inheres in an object, whether enacted or not. Think: fragility. A glass ornament is fragile *in itself*, so to say; it need not be broken for us to learn that its structure is delicate and friable.[18] I propose that we consider the Divine Nature as *disposed* in this metaphysical and structural sense: from Eternity God is the Humble and Lowly One, not proud, not serenely indifferent and turned inwards, but always, eternally Radiant, Self-Giving, Invisible and thereby perfectly Self-Present. Creaturely prayer does not awaken a responsiveness in God, far less compel or entail a reply. No, the God who answers prayer is the One who is Eternally Ready, Eternally Disposed to enter down into the world of His creatures and to meet their own ends.

But what of those left unanswered, lifted up in the night season, but met only by the dark sky and by silence? There will be no complete answer to this agonizing question that can be given by mere creatures; by the nature of the case we can only propose, only tentatively suggest, only trust that some word, too, might be said about this final struggle in the natural pairing of God and prayer. Perhaps we might say that the Disposition of Lowliness is enacted in our world under our conditions: our temporality, our development and obstacle, our historicity and innovation. God speaks and inhabits this framework, this densely human arena of expectation and futility, this chaos tamed by retrospection and inwards reflection. God is present there. His mode is not of His own High Goodness and Sovereign Deity, but rather of ours, our needs and fears and deep uncertainties about the path ahead. Prayers that are answered not by God's own Self-Presence, His Truest Gift, conform instead to the conditions of our human lot – a gift given but perhaps unseen or refused; a gift long delayed, perhaps because it must be; a complex weave of human deeds and national purposes; the veil drawn across the future; the rescue that cannot be recognized until all danger

---

[18]For a classic and influential philosophical treatment of dispositions, see Nelson Goodman, *Fact, Fiction and Forecast* (Cambridge, MA: Harvard University Press, 1954).

is past; the ambiguity of history itself. The LORD God enters and assumes these. I think it is too strong – too bold and confident – for a creature to say that all prayers are answered. But I think these secondary answers are always in the human key, and attended by the development, the form and the dissonance of that fleshly art. It may well be that God has in His Goodness determined to give only His Highest Gift, His Presence, and not the earthly aim and need. But it may be too that those who greet the Promise from afar but do not enter into it will be saved in some future generation, not apart from us, but rather shoulder-to-shoulder with us, their answer in God's own Mystery, tied up in ours and more astonishingly still, in us.

King David prays in our Psalm 141:

As when the earth is cleft and broken up
our bones are scattered at the mouth of Sheol.
My eyes are fixed upon You, O GOD my Lord;
I seek refuge in You, do not put me in jeopardy.

Perhaps his prayer is our last word, for there the trust, the lament, the urgency and the deep confidence are mingled in this hero of Israel. The Doctrine of God and prayer are a natural pair, correlative and deeply instructive; yet what a complex, demanding and unexpected pairing it turns out to be! Almighty God, it seems, is always more than we can think or imagine.

CHAPTER NINE

Creation and Prayer

SIMON OLIVER

Whilst prayer is often a passionate act – an expression of our concerns, desires and laments – it is also, for the Christian tradition, a profoundly intellectual act. According to Evagrius Ponticus, the fourth-century master of the spiritual life, prayer is 'the mind's conversation with God', 'undistracted prayer is the highest function of the mind' and 'prayer is the mind's ascent to God'.[1] For Evagrius, impediments to prayer are principally impediments of the mind and the first stage of prayer is therefore the mind's purification. Similarly, for Thomas Aquinas 'prayer is an act, not of the appetitive, but of the intellective power'.[2] He quotes Cassiodorus to the effect that 'prayer (*oratio*) is spoken reason'.[3] Prayer, for Aquinas, is an act of practical rather than speculative reason. Whereas speculative reason is concerned with the apprehension of truth, practical reason apprehends truth for the attainment of some end, and ultimately for the attainment of our final end, which is God himself. Prayer, therefore, is an act of the practical reason in the sense that

---

[1]Evagrius Ponticus, *De oratione* 3, 34, 36. The English translation of *De oratione* is taken from *Evagrius of Pontus*, trans. Augustine Casiday (London: Routledge, 2006). See also B. Bitton-Ashkelony, 'The Limit of the Mind (νοῦς): Pure Prayer According to Evagrius Ponticus and Isaac of Nineveh', *Zeitschrift für Antikes Christentum/Journal of Ancient Christianity* 15, no. 2 (2011): 291–321.

[2]Thomas Aquinas, *Summa Theologiae*, trans. Laurence Shapcote (Lander, WY: The Aquinas Institute, 2012), II-II, q. 83, a. 1. 'On the contrary, Isidore says (*Etymologiae* x) that "to pray is to speak." Now speech belongs to the intellect. Therefore prayer is an act, not of the appetitive, but of the intellective power.' All translations of Aquinas' *Summa Theologiae* are from this edition – hereafter: *ST*.

[3]Cassiodorus, *Expositio Psalmorum*, 38.14 (PL 285C): '*Oratio est oris ratio, quam proni allegamus vota nostra pandentes.*'

prayer attempts to set things in order by petitioning or beseeching God for that which is fitting for the attainment of our final end. This is not to say that will or desire are absent from prayer, for 'the will moves reason to its end'.[4] Aquinas suggests that the will, in desiring God above all things, moves the intellect towards the divine. In prayer, the intellect discerns what to ask of God through the aid of the Holy Spirit (Rom. 8.26) and is informed through charitable friendship with the divine.[5] The intellectual practice of prayer is therefore entwined with the desire for God, and all things as they tend towards God.[6] For Aquinas, following Dionysius the Areopogite, prayer is the unveiling and raising up of our minds to God through the motive power of the will.[7]

The emphasis on the mind, intellect and reason belongs within the long tradition of mental and vocal prayer evoked by teachers of the Christian spiritual life. In trying to understand the relation of prayer to wider creation, however, its mental and intellectual character presents a particular challenge for modern thought influenced by Cartesian understandings of mind and matter. If prayer belongs to the mind and is characterized by reason and intention, and if mind and reason are fundamentally distinct from matter and non-human nature, it seems that prayer is an exclusively *human* phenomenon which has little to do with wider creation. In what sense, other than the purely metaphorical, can one claim that creatures other than human beings (never mind inanimate nature) have anything to do with the intellectual and petitionary act of prayer? For the modern imagination, it seems that prayer, just like mind and reason, is a strange aberration in an otherwise inert and directionless universe.

This question gains a further dimension when one considers another dualism characteristic of modernity, namely the apparent separation of nature and culture.[8] According to philosophers such as Bruno Latour, in the modern imagination culture is characterized by freedom, reason and human

---

[4]Aquinas, *ST* II-II, q. 83, a. 1, ad. 2.

[5]See Rik Van Nieuwenhove, *Thomas Aquinas and Contemplation* (Oxford: Oxford University Press, 2021), 148–54.

[6]Aquinas, *ST* II-II, q. 83, a. 3, ad. 1: 'The will moves the other powers of the soul to its end, as stated above (q. 82, a. 1, ad. 1), and therefore religion, which is in the will, directs the acts of the other powers to the reverence of God. Now among the other powers of the soul the intellect is the highest, and the nearest to the will; and consequently after devotion, which belongs to the will, prayer, which belongs to the intellective part, is the chief of the acts of religion, since by it religion directs man's intellect to God.'

[7]Aquinas, *ST* II-II, q. 83, a. 1, ad. 2 and *ST* II-II, q. 83, a. 3, ad. 3.

[8]Bruno Latour, *We Have Never Been Modern*, trans. Catherine Porter (London: Harvester Wheatsheaf, 1991); Louis Dupré, *Passage to Modernity: An Essay in the Hermeneutics of Nature and Culture* (New Haven, CT: Yale University Press, 1993).

creativity. It includes literature, music, art, business, commerce, reason and values. Nature, by contrast, is the non-human realm of base animal instinct and determinism. Nature provides resources for culture; through the natural sciences and technology, nature is manipulated and harvested for culture's ends. The modern university is divided according to this dualism of culture (the humanities) and nature (the natural sciences), with the social sciences suspended in the middle. If religion is identified as a cultural phenomenon and prayer is the defining religious act, as for modern thinkers such as Novalis and Feuerbach, prayer is an exclusively human cultural practice which has little or nothing to do with wider nature.[9] Indeed, for Feuerbach prayer is a kind of 'technology', a means of the manipulation of nature by the culture of religion which turns the human heart not outwards towards creation, but inwards towards itself.

> Prayer alters the course of Nature; it determines God to bring forth an effect in contradiction with the laws of Nature. Prayer is the absolute relation of the human heart to itself, to its own nature; in prayer, man forgets that there exists a limit to his wishes, and is happy in this forgetfulness.[10]

Against this modern background in which prayer belongs to mind and culture, as distinct from matter and nature, it is not obvious that prayer has anything to do with the order of creation beyond the human. For the theologian, it is easy to imagine prayer as an aspect of theological anthropology (prayer as a human practice), Christology (we are instructed in prayer by Christ, chiefly through the Lord's Prayer), pneumatology (the Holy Spirit inspires and guides prayer) or providence (God directs and provides for creatures by means of prayer). But how are we to imagine prayer with respect to the doctrine of creation?

This chapter will explore three ways in which one might consider prayer as an aspect of the doctrine of creation. The first follows the long Christian tradition in viewing prayer as a human act of the practical reason motivated by our natural desire for God, focusing specifically on the human person *as created*. Examining prayer as the action of the human creature will be our initial task with particular reference to the doctrine of creation

---

[9]See, for example, Ludwig Feuerbach, *The Essence of Christianity*, trans. George Eliot (Cambridge: Cambridge University Press, 2012), 121: 'The ultimate essence of religion is revealed by the simplest act of religion – prayer.' For Novalis, praying is to religion what thinking is to philosophy. See Friedrich Heiler, *Prayer: A Study in the History and Psychology of Religion*, trans. Samuel McComb (Oxford: Oxford University Press, 1932), v–ix.
[10]Feuerbach, *The Essence of Christianity*, 122.

ex nihilo. In the context of this fundamental doctrine, we find the fount of thankful prayer in the creature's identity as gift, and petitionary prayer in the creature's desire for God and its constant need of all that sustains life and flourishing. With reference to the account of prayer provided by the Catholic phenomenologist Jean-Louis Chrétien, I will examine both the aporetic character of prayer and the necessity of prayer for the human creature's fulfilment and self-manifestation.

In the second section of this chapter, I will move from a particular focus on the human *as* created to focus on the human *in* creation through the ancient and medieval image of the human person as a microcosm of creation. The human gathers into a unity the material natures below and the spiritual natures above. In turn, this gives rise to the human voice of prayer as the expression of intellectual desire. We will see that the voice of prayer is anticipated in the 'breathing' of creation and at the same time it is transformed in the incarnation as God 'breathes' and teaches the church to pray with a voice that is divine and human.

In the third section of this chapter, I will move from the human as microcosm to focus more exclusively on creation as a school of liturgy and prayer. I will explore the way in which creation, in its symbols and structures, forms and instructs liturgy which, in turn, provides the context for prayer. This is evident in the account of creation's liturgical structure in the opening chapters of Genesis. Creation instructs prayer in the sense that its order and cycles are also the order and cycles of the Temple and the church. This tradition is developed in patristic and medieval theology and I will examine one example of prayer instructed by creation in the work of Bede. In prayer, the human heart and mind bring to fruition and offer to God what is embedded in the prayerful order of creation. Prayer, after all, is cosmic and not merely cultural. In the voice of the human practical intellect, it brings to fruition what is always anticipated in the fabric of creation.

Creation *ex nihilo* and Prayer

Within Christian theology, creation *ex nihilo* is a 'distributed doctrine' in the sense that its meaning and implications are realized throughout Christian teaching.[11] For patristic and high medieval theology, creation *ex nihilo* – which Janet Soskice labels 'a *biblically compelled* piece of metaphysical

---

[11]John Webster, '"Love is Also a Lover of Life": *Creatio ex nihilo* and Creaturely Goodness', *Modern Theology* 29, no. 2 (2013): 156–71.

theology' – finds its basis in the doctrine of God.[12] If God is *ipsum esse per se subsistens* – self-subsistent being itself – then God exists essentially and simply; there is no composition in God, for essence and existence are one.[13] As being itself, God is therefore the source of the existence of everything that is not God. According to Aquinas' classic expression of the doctrine of creation, God is 'the principle and cause of being to other things'.[14] There is nothing that exists without God bringing it to be, so we must not speak of God creating the universe from some always-present material stuff. The act of creation is not an act of manufacture or change; it is not an instance of one thing being made into something else. We might say that, according to creation *ex nihilo*, the universe does not have a material cause. God is the source not only of particular things, but of created being per se. The defining characteristic of creation, as opposed to the making of something, is the instantiation of created being absolutely, not simply this or that particular being.[15] The consequence of viewing God as the ultimate source and principle of created existence is that we must speak of God creating 'out of nothing', because there is no thing whose existence is not caused by God.[16]

Creation *ex nihilo* establishes a radical asymmetry between God who exists by his essence (*ens per essentiam*) and creatures who exist by participation in God (*ens per participationem*).[17] It is concerned not simply with an act of creation in an unimaginably distant past, but with God's sustaining of creation in existence at every moment. This moment is just as much *ex nihilo* as the first moment, for creation is continually in receipt of its being through participation in God. In itself creation is nothing, for existence is not *proper* to creatures; it is given.

At every moment, therefore, the creature is in receipt of its being and everything that sustains its life. This is expressed in narrative and poetic style in scripture when the Genesis account of creation describes God's first gift of the being of creatures (Gen. 1.24-28) and the second gift of food to sustain creaturely life (Gen. 1.29-30). The radical asymmetry between God and creatures, described metaphysically in the doctrine of creation *ex nihilo*,

---

[12]Janet M. Soskice, '*Creatio ex nihilo*: Its Jewish and Christian Foundations', in *Creation and the God of Abraham*, ed. David Burrell, et al. (Cambridge: Cambridge University Press, 2010), 25; emphasis original.

[13]Aquinas, *ST* Ia, q. 3 and *ST* Ia, q. 4.

[14]Aquinas, *Summa contra Gentiles* (Notre Dame, IN: University of Notre Dame Press, 1975), II.6.1.

[15]Aquinas, *ST* Ia, q. 45, a. 4, c.

[16]Aquinas, *Compendium of Theology*, trans. Richard J. Regan (Oxford: Oxford University Press, 2009), §68: 'God's first effect in things is existence itself, which all other effects presuppose, and on which they are founded. And everything that exists in any way is necessarily from God.'

[17]Aquinas, *Summa contra Gentiles*, I.22.9; *ST* Ia, q. 3, a. 4, c.

establishes the fundamental context for prayer: the creature's receipt of the gift of being invites thanksgiving, and its continual need of all that sustains life prompts petition. As Jean-Louis Chrétien puts it in his phenomenology of prayer:

> To ask is actively to acknowledge that we are not the origin of every good and every gift, and it is actively to acknowledge that the one whom we address is what he is. All prayer confesses God as giver, by dispossessing us of our self-centredness, in a speech that at every instance the addressee alone, in our eyes, makes possible.[18]

To pray, therefore, particularly in the mode of thanksgiving and petition, is to realize the fundamental truth that one is *created*. The one who prays in thanksgiving acknowledges the gift of created being. The one who petitions in prayer acknowledges the creature's continual need of all that sustains life. As Aquinas puts it, 'We need to pray to God, not in order to make known to Him our needs or desires but that we ourselves may be reminded of the necessity of having recourse to God's help in these matters.'[19]

To this insight we can add that prayer is the self-manifestation of the creature *as creature* in the presence of God, principally in the expression of thanksgiving and petition.[20] The person praying addresses another and makes herself present to God as his creature. 'If prayer is the response to a theophany', writes Chrétien, 'it is first and foremost an anthropophany, a manifestation of man.'[21] Thus prayer is the manifestation of the whole human person as a material and spiritual creature, the union of body and soul, both to God and herself. The anthropophany before the divine concerns the intellect and, at the same time, it is expressed through the body in practices such as ritual ablution, in the covering of the head and distinctive vesture, in posture such as kneeling or prostration, in gesture such as the sign of the cross or the lifting of hands, in movement such as dance, and in the body's orientation in certain directions, for example eastwards towards the rising sun.

> Written into the body, this presence to the invisible and this appearance before it comprise, essentially, acts by which the person praying declares to God or the gods his desires, his thoughts, his needs, his love, his

---

[18]Jean-Louis Chrétien, *The Ark of Speech*, trans. Andrew Brown (London: Routledge, 2013), 21–2.
[19]Aquinas, *ST* II-II, q. 83, a. 2, ad. 1.
[20]For Chrétien, prayer 'inhabits an act of presence to the invisible'. See Chrétien, *The Ark of Speech*, 19.
[21]Chrétien, *The Ark of Speech*, 19.

repentance. ... The person praying before God is in his very being an active manifestation of himself to God. All modes of prayer are forms of this self-manifestation, whether individual or collective.[22]

Understanding prayer as anthropophany implies its necessity for the realization of the most profound truth about the human: that it is created. Yet the doctrine of creation *ex nihilo*, as well as pointing to the necessity of prayer, also reveals it aporetic character. This aporia is more profound than the apparent futility of addressing even our most secret desires to an omniscient God, or the temerity of the sinner's prayer directed to the divine holiness. The irreducibly asymmetric relation of creature to God means that there can be no common measure or common ground between them. The act of prayer, the familiar address of 'thou', assumes the possibility of the creature addressing, not merely naming, the infinite ground of its own being from within the confines of finitude. It presupposes a measure between creature and creator as the basis of a dialogic address. Creation *ex nihilo*, however, establishes that there can be no common ground and no exchange, no negotiation, for all that the creature has, including the voice of prayer, is already *from* the one to whom the prayer is addressed. This implies that the practice of prayer finds its possibility not in any creaturely power or claim on the divine attention, but in the gracious gift of God who awaits the creature's response with an eternal and silent attention. The grace which enables prayer as the creature's presence and self-manifestation before the divine is expressed in scripture when Paul writes, 'Likewise the Spirit helps us in our weakness; for we do not know how to pray as we ought, but that very Spirit intercedes with sighs too deep for words' (Rom. 8.26; see also Gal. 4.6-7). Prayer is already the Spirit's moving and prompting from within the depths of the human person's created being.

Whilst the doctrine of creation *ex nihilo* establishes the aporia of prayer and the need of grace, at the same time it points to the natural desire to pray which is grounded in the natural desire for God. This desire is prompted by the realization that the human creature is insufficient unto itself, not simply in terms of what is required to sustain life, but in its very being. Creation is radically contingent and exists only through participation in God, so at every moment the creature receives the gift of its own being. All that the human person can return to God in prayer has already arrived as a gift from an infinite and eternal plenitude. Yet for created being to realize its true nature as gift, it must receive and recognize itself *as gift* lest

---

[22]Chrétien, *The Ark of Speech*, 19.

its nature become a meaningless brute fact. To give thanks is to receive one's life as a gift to oneself and therefore to realize the full meaning of one's humanity. Thanksgiving is crucial to the life of prayer understood as a relation of I–Thou because gift establishes and mediates a relationship. A gift conveys something of the giver to the recipient and awaits a return gift in response.[23] Whilst the creature can offer nothing to God that it has not already received, its recognition of its own gifted nature, and the prayer of gratitude which accompanies that recognition, *is* the reciprocal gift offered in response to God's gratuitous gift of creation *ex nihilo* which prompts the further donation of lives of service. At the heart of prayer, therefore, is the recognition that the human creature is not sufficient unto itself; its very being points to a source which is its own eternal ground and towards which prayer is directed. The proper receipt and fulfilment of human creaturely existence as gift is fundamentally eucharistic – the prayer of thanksgiving.

The aporia of prayer also exceeds the problem of theological language more generally, for prayer is not simply speech *about* God but speech *to* God. It therefore carries with it the danger of a too easy familiarity in which the transcendent addressee of prayer, called upon as 'thou', becomes the object of one's own creaturely imagining. For Chrétien, however, the familiarity of such address and the use of the vocative helps to preserve divine transcendence: 'For it is only in familiar address that objectification comes up against an uncrossable limit, it is only in the hymn in which we sing for the one we sing that "the abyss of transcendence" can be really recognized and confessed.'[24] For Christian theology, it is certainly the case that the transcendence and immanence of God are two aspects of a single doctrine. The otherness of God, expressed in the irreducible asymmetry of God and creation, is at once the ground of God's radical immanence. Only in being wholly other than the creature can God be wholly immanent to sustain the creature's being from within, as it were. In prayer, we address as 'thou' the God who is irreducibly transcendent yet 'more inward than the most

---

[23]See Marcel Mauss, *The Gift: The Form and Reason for Exchange in Archaic Societies*, trans. W. D. Halls (London: Routledge, 2007); Simon Oliver, *Creation: A Guide for the Perplexed* (London: Bloomsbury, 2017), 143–57. See particularly John Milbank's seminal contributions to debates concerning the theology and philosophy of gift, including: John Milbank, *Being Reconciled: Ontology and Pardon* (London: Routledge, 2003) and 'Can a Gift Be Given? Prolegomena to a Future Trinitarian Metaphysic', *Modern Theology* 11, no. 1 (1995): 119–61.

[24]Chrétien, *The Ark of Speech*, 26. Carl Kerényi points out that, in antiquity, only with Jews and Christians is *theos* used in the vocative: 'On the other hand, in the whole Greek language, so far as it is not spoken by Jews or Christians, *theos* has no vocative – for one does not address an event.' See Carl Kerényi, *Zeus and Hera: Archetypal Image of Father, Husband, and Wife*, trans. Christopher Holme (Princeton, NJ: Princeton University Press, 1975), 11.

inward place of my heart'.[25] Nevertheless, only through a lifetime of learning how to pray in a manner which addresses truthfully the transcendence *and* immanence of the divine can the tendency towards idolatry be confessed and eroded. This mode of address cannot be learned in advance of the practice of prayer, but only in the midst of prayer. Even the disciple's request to Jesus, 'teach us to pray' (Lk. 11.1), is itself a prayer. Whilst it is the case that one can only pray by turning to God and one can only turn to God in prayer, the human creature's natural desire for God in the most inward place of the heart prompts the most immediate response to itself *as a creature*, namely the prayer of gratitude and petition addressed to the transcendent and immanent source of its being. This is why the psalmist prays that *God* will open our lips as the act of grace which begins prayer. Thus begins the church's daily prayer: 'O Lord, open thou our lips, and our mouth shall shew forth thy praise' (Ps. 51.15).

In Chrétien's phenomenology, prayer is further characterized as agonistic in the sense that the impossibility of prayer – that is, a personal address to the fount of the creature's being across the abyss of transcendence – is only learned in the act of praying. In prayer, the human creature suffers 'the ordeal of the transcendence'. Prayer is a 'theopathy' in the following sense:

> To have God listening to you is an ordeal, a testing of speech incomparable with any other, for our speech is incomparably stripped bare by it, in all it seeks to hide, to excuse, to justify, to obtain in real terms. Speech appears in the attentive light of silence, the voice is really naked.[26]

This means that, for the human person created *ex nihilo*, all prayer is *de profundis* – from the depths of its non-being in the face of a divine plenitude which 'strips bare' the speech of a creature whose need and desire in the presence of the divine are absolute.[27] In the prayer of gratitude and petition which is the profession of the supplicant's creatureliness, the pretence to be self-standing and the fantasy that one is 'a god' (Gen. 3.5) are laid waste. At the same time, the true nature of the human creature is luminously clear in this prayer: an absolute desire for God as humanity's final end, to which all other desires and ends are ordered and discerned through the practical reason of prayer.

---

[25]Augustine, *Confessions*, trans. F. J. Sheed (Indianapolis, IN: Hackett Publishing, 2006), III.6.11: 'Yet all the time You were more inward than the most inward place of my heart and loftier than the highest.'
[26]Chrétien, *The Ark of Speech*, 27.
[27]Chrétien, *The Ark of Speech*, 24.

So the naked cry of the human voice emerges *de profundis* (Ps. 130) and it is vocal prayer that, for Chrétien, is 'the index of religious existence'.[28] The various forms of silent and contemplative prayer are defined in relation to vocal prayer because 'only the voice can fall silent, and only speech can stop talking'.[29] Silent (or mental) prayer, as appropriate and profound as it may often be, is always the suspension or interiorization of the voice. The complexities of the voice, from murmured chants to exultant song, lend prayer the rich textures which allow the manifestation of the human creature in the intensities of its passion and the depth of its need.[30] The voice finds its origin in the creative voice of God from above and its anticipation in the breath of life gifted to creatures from below. Life is breathing.[31] Into the dust of the earth God breathes the breath of life and 'the man became a living being' (Gen. 2.7) with a voice to name the creatures that are formed out of the ground (Gen. 2.19). With breath come voice, speech and the possibility of prayerful address. God breathes life into creation as Christ breathes the Spirit onto his disciples. Prayer is breathing with the Spirit – the *exitus* and *reditus* of life. Indeed, for patristic theology prayer does not belong exclusively to the human creature; creaturely breathing bears the promise of prayer. In the early third century, the Carthaginian theologian Tertullian concluded his treatise *De oratione* as follows:

> The angels, likewise, all pray; every creature prays [*orat omnis creatura*]; cattle and wild beasts pray and bend their knees; and when they issue from their layers and lairs, they look up heavenward with no idle mouth, making their breath vibrate after their own manner. Nay, the birds too, rising out of the nest, upraise themselves heavenward, and, instead of hands, expand the cross of their wings, and say somewhat to seem like prayer.[32]

For patristic and medieval theologians, prayer, understood as a turning towards God the creator in witness, praise and petition, was regarded as a characteristic of the whole creation. Prayer is not exclusively human or

---

[28]Chrétien, *The Ark of Speech*, 37.

[29]Chrétien, *The Ark of Speech*, 37.

[30]The distinction between vocal and mental prayer, whilst commonplace, is less clear in instances of ecstasy and distress. For example, the prayer of Hannah, even though her voice is not heard by Levi, does not fit obviously into either category (1 Sam. 1.9-17).

[31]This is emphasized in the flood narrative in Genesis 6-9: the breath of life is extinguished by the deluge.

[32]Tertullian, *De oratione*, in *Latin Christianity: Its Founder, Tertullian*, ed. Alexander Roberts and James Donaldson, ANF 3 (Grand Rapids, MI: William B. Eerdmans, 1985), 691. See also Chrétien, *The Ark of Speech*, 36.

cultural. Creatures are invested with allegorical significance, for God is the author of the book of nature as well as the book of Scripture, and creatures point to the creator in a fashion that could be described as 'prayerful'.[33] This is entirely consistent with the Jewish liturgical tradition which regards creation as a panoply of divine praise and blessing.[34] Ancient liturgical texts such as the *Benedicite*, which places humanity in the midst of God's creatures rather than simply at its apex, refer to creation's praise of the creator. Humanity gives voice and reason to creaturely praise and petition; in the voice, anticipated in creatures and called forth by the divine Word, creation is gathered and addressed to the creator.

The human voice gathering the voice of creation points to the ancient and medieval understanding of the human as a microcosmos. We now turn to this tradition to examine the way in which prayer is offered for, and on behalf of, the whole of creation.

The Human as Microcosm

The Christian understanding of the human person as a microcosm or 'small world' finds its origins in the Greek view of the human as a 'middle' or 'frontier' being situated between the transcendent and immanent.[35] The soul, in particular, lies at this boundary. For Plato, in his cosmology *Timaeus*, the corporeal is fabricated within the World Soul which 'being woven throughout the Heaven every way from the centre to the extremity, and enveloping it in a circle from without, and herself revolving within herself, began a divine beginning of unceasing and intelligent life lasting throughout all time'.[36] The World Soul, which is the frontier of transcendent and immanent, rationally orders the material realm. The human soul partakes of that ordered motion in its contemplation and knowledge of the living cosmos. In turn, through the soul's gathering and ordering of the body, the human is a likeness of

---

[33]On the two books tradition, see Peter Harrison, *The Bible, Protestantism and the Rise of Natural Science* (Cambridge: Cambridge University Press, 1998) and Oliver, *Creation*, 98–109.

[34]To offer just two examples: Psalms 19.1-4 and 145.15-16.

[35]I am indebted to the overview of the human person as microcosm in W. Norris Clarke, *The Creative Retrieval of Saint Thomas Aquinas: Essays in Thomistic Philosophy, New and Old* (New York: Fordham University Press, 2009), 132–51. I demur somewhat from Clarke's reading of the Platonic approach to the body–soul relationship. For a fascinating account of the development of the human as microcosm in the high Middle Ages, see Marie-Dominique Chenu, *Nature, Man, and Society in the Twelfth Century: Essays on New Theological Perspectives in the Latin West*, trans. Jerome Taylor and Lester K. Little (Toronto: University of Toronto Press, 1997), 24–37. A particularly fecund idea for the development of natural philosophy is that, in coming to know nature, man comes to know himself.

[36]Plato, *Timaeus* 36e (LCL 234).

the cosmic living creature. The soul, therefore, is an intermediary in the sense that it gathers to itself the entire cosmos as it contemplates creaturely becoming in relation to the realm of being.[37] For Aristotle, the soul is 'in a sense all existing things' because it can gather within itself the forms of all things and thereby be en-formed by them.[38] This does not preclude the body, for the soul is the form of the body and it is through the body that the intellective soul operates. The soul, therefore, is an intermediary in the sense that it gathers to itself the entire cosmos in the acquisition of knowledge, and contemplates nature (*physis*) in relation to the pure actuality of *theos* as the final end of all things. An important aspect of this Platonic and Aristotelian view of the human person is that the wider cosmos *instructs* the soul through the body in the literal sense of 'informing' the speculative and practical intellect. The forms of things come to reside in the soul.

The Christian theological tradition developed the pagan Greek notion of the human as an intermediary being and proposed more explicitly the human person, body and soul, as a microcosm. Gregory of Nyssa, for example, in his treatises 'On the Making of Man' and 'On the Soul and the Resurrection', writes of humanity as a 'little world' uniting the divine and rational with the brutish and irrational.[39] Developing this cosmic anthropology, Maximus the Confessor writes:

> Man, who is above all – like a most capacious workshop containing all things, naturally mediating through himself all the divided extremes, and who by design has been beneficially placed amid beings – is divided into male and female, manifestly possessing by nature the full potential to draw all the extremes into unity through their means, by virtue of his characteristic attribute of being related to the divided extremes through his own parts. ... This was why man was introduced last among beings – like a kind of natural bond mediating between the universal extremes through his parts and unifying through himself things that by nature are separated from each other by a great distance – so that, by making of his own division a beginning of the unity which gathers up all things to God

---

[37]See Simon Oliver, *Philosophy, God and Motion* (London: Routledge, 2013), chapter 1.
[38]Aristotle, *De Anima* 431b20 (LCL 288). See Aristotle, *Physics* 8.2.252b (LCL 288) for reference to a creature as 'microcosm'. See also George Perrigo Conger, *Theories of Macrocosms and Microcosms in the History of Philosophy* (New York: Columbia University Press, 1950), xiv. Conger regards this latter passage from the *Physics* as the first indisputable occurrence of the term *mikros kosmos*, although the origin of the term is earlier.
[39]Gregory of Nyssa, 'On the Making of Man' and 'On the Soul and the Resurrection', in *The Select Writings and Letters of Gregory, Bishop of Nyssa*, trans. William Moore, NPNF-2 5 (Edinburgh: T&T Clark, 1994), 386–426 and 427–67.

their Author ... he might reach the limit of the sublime ascent that comes about through the union of all things in God.[40]

This image was adopted by a host of later medieval theologians, including Robert Grosseteste,[41] Bonaventure[42] and Nicholas of Cusa.[43] For Aquinas:

The order of the universe is the end of all creation. But in man there is a kind of likeness of the order of the universe, and that is why man is called a little world [*minor mundus*], because all natures flow together [*confluunt*], as it were, in man. Therefore, it seems that man is in some way the end of all things.[44]

The image of humanity as a microcosm implies that the whole creation 'flows together' in the human where it finds a profound unity in consciousness. Indeed, for Gregory of Nyssa this is the heart of the theological teaching that humanity is made in the *imago Dei*: humanity images the transcendent goodness of God by gathering together the full goodness of creation in sharing in the divine and rational as well as the brutish and irrational.[45] In the compound nature of the human we can behold 'in micro' every aspect of God's creation brought to unity, from sottish matter to angelic intellect.

The notion of the human as microcosm, in which creation attains a certain *telos* in the unity of consciousness and speech, suggests that creatures find a

---

[40]Maximos the Confessor, *Ambiguum* 41, in *On Difficulties in the Church Fathers: The Ambigua*, vol. 2, trans. and ed. Nicholas Constas (Cambridge, MA: Harvard University Press, 2014), 104–5. See also Maximus the Confessor, *The Church's Mystagogy*, in Maximus the Confessor, *Selected Writings*, trans. George C. Berthold, CWS (New York: Paulist Press, 1985), 196.

[41]See James McEvoy, *The Philosophy of Robert Grosseteste* (Oxford: Oxford University Press, 1982), chapter 6, especially 371–2, for a translation of a fragment of Grosseteste's treatise *Quod homo sit minor mundus*.

[42]See James McEvoy, 'Microcosm and Macrocosm in the Writings of St Bonaventure', in *Sancta Bonaventura 1274–1974*, vol. 2, ed. Jacques Guy Bougerol (Grottaferrata: Collegio San Bonaventura), 1974), 309–43.

[43]Nicholas of Cusa, *De Docta Ignorantia*, in *Complete Philosophical and Theological Treatises of Nicholas of Cusa*, vol. 1, trans. Jasper Hopkins (Minneapolis, MN: The Arthur J. Banning Press, 2001), III.3.198: 'Now, human nature is that [nature] which, though created a little lower that the angels, is elevated above all the [other] works of God; it enfolds intellectual and sensible nature and encloses all things within itself, so that the ancients were right in calling it a microcosm, or a small world.'

[44]Aquinas, *Scriptum Super Libros Sententiarum Magistri Petri Lombardi Episcopi Parisiensis*, vol. 2, ed. R. P. Mandonnet (Paris: P. Lethielleux, 1929), II.1, q. 2, a. 3; author's translation. See also Aquinas, *ST* Ia, q. 77, a. 2 and *Commentary on the Book of Causes*, trans. Vincent A. Guagliardo (Washington, DC: Catholic University of America Press, 1996), 2.16: 'The soul is the last boundary of eternity and the starting point of time.'

[45]Gregory of Nyssa, *On the Making of Man* 16.9.

rational voice in the human. It also reflects the view that mind and reason are not alien to material creation, but its fulfilment. The multifarious song of creation, its groans of labour and longing for freedom (Rom. 8.22) reach a conscious intentional pitch, ordered to the infinite, in the voice of human prayer. Creation flows together in the human (to use Aquinas' phrase) and flows out again, to be returned to God in the sacrifice of prayer. Whilst Aquinas is clear that 'man is *in some way* [*quodammodo*] the end of all things' because their ultimate end is God, this intermediate end in the human microcosm nevertheless forms part of the pattern of divine providence. In the order of divine providence, established in creation *ex nihilo*, God is the universal primary cause who is 'the principle and cause of being to other things'.[46] As part of that universal providence, God ordains real, potent and free secondary causes thorough which he brings to fruition his loving purposes.[47] Amongst those secondary causes, which are efficacious through their participation in the primary causal power of God, is human prayer:

> For, since all things naturally desire the good … and since it pertains to the supereminence of divine goodness to assign being, and well-being, to all in accord with a definite order, the result is that, in accord with His goodness, He fulfils the holy desires which are brought to completion by means of prayer.[48]

This is to say that God ordains that his providence may operate through created secondary causes, including prayerful petitions. Whilst God particularly desires the fulfilment of the petitions of the rational creature because it participates most fully in divine goodness and providence, God desires the fulfilment of all creatures because they are 'by way of likeness a certain participation of His being'.[49] The proper object of God's will and love is his own essence and perfection; in willing his own essence he wills the good and perfection of all creaturely participants in that essence. In the prayer of the human microcosm, towards which all creatures flow, the needs and desires not only of the human person but, in a certain manner, of all creation, are offered to God. The human voice can petition for creation because in so doing it is responding to the divine desire for the well-being and perfection of all creatures. The cosmic anthropology of the microcosm, however, suggests that the prayer of humanity is not simply prayer *for* creation, it is the prayer *of* creation, a prayer which is part of the eternal

---

[46]Aquinas, *Summa Contra Gentiles*, II.6.1.
[47]On the metaphysics of primary and secondary causes, see Oliver, *Creation*, 75–80.
[48]Aquinas, *Summa contra Gentiles*, III.95.2.
[49]Aquinas, *Summa contra Gentiles*, I.75.4. See also *Summa Contra Gentiles*, III.95.5.

divine providence. That prayer expresses all creatures' desire for God as their final end, yet only in the human, whose conscious intention is open to the infinite, is that desire expressed as a desire for God *as God*, the source of all being and goodness, rather than simply a creature's *particular* goodness or perfection. Following a hint in Aquinas, we might say that prayer is 'the interpreter of that desire' and the bringing forth into voice of creation's longing for its divine source and goal.[50]

For Christian theology, the image of humanity as microcosm is further transformed by the theology of the incarnation and the mystery of Christ. The incarnation reveals the dignity of the human in soul and body, and with it the dignity of all creation, both material and spiritual. If material nature, sanctified in the Word made flesh, is hypostatically united to divine nature to manifest the full glory of God, there can be, in principle, no limits to what material nature might reveal; it can shimmer with an eternal light, as at the transfiguration; it can overcome death in resurrection; it can ascend in glory. God takes a human voice in the incarnation of the Word, in whom, through whom and for whom all things are created (Jn 1.1-4; Col. 1.15-17; Heb. 1.1-3). By incorporation into the mystical body of Christ, the voice and breathing of the human person joins the voice and breathing of Christ. As Augustine puts it in his commentary on Psalm 86.1:

> Therefore we pray to Him, through Him, in Him; and we speak with Him, and He speaks with us; we speak in Him, He speaks in us the prayer of this Psalm, which is entitled, 'A Prayer of David'.[51]

If human nature, towards which flows the whole creation to form a microcosm, is assumed by the Word, this suggests that Christ gathers creation into his life and prayer. Being grafted into Christ through baptism and eucharist, creation's voice of gratitude and petition is joined to the voice of Christ by the power of the Spirit who cries 'Abba! Father!' (Gal. 4.6).

The Christian tradition commonly cites humanity's place in the middle of the cosmic hierarchy as the reason for the Word taking human flesh: from the middle, the 'microcosm', the grace of Christ touches all creation. This cosmic dimension suggests that the catholicity of the church as the body of Christ is not confined to the global; it is a catholicity that extends to all creation (Eph. 1.22-23). At the same time, in being joined to Christ through the human's incorporation into the mystical body of Christ, creation's voice

---

[50]*ST* II-II, q. 83, a. 1, ad. 1: 'a petition is like the interpreter of a desire' (*petitio sit quodammodo desiderii interpres*).

[51]Augustine, 'Psalm 86', in *Expositions on the Book of Psalms*, trans. A. Cleveland Coxe, NPNF-1 8 (Edinburgh: T&T Clark, 2007), 409–19, quoted in Chrétien, *The Ark of Speech*, 30.

is assimilated to the prayer of that mystical body which is the church. This points to an important feature of prayer to which Chrétien alludes. The person praying does not borrow the prayers of the church to express their desires and needs in the way that one might quote a poet or a song. Rather, it is the other way around: the human, and with the human, creation, is assimilated to the prayers of the church (e.g. the Psalms) and therefore the prayer of Christ. Individual prayer and collective prayer can be distinguished, but only as modes of the one prayer of the church which, by the power of the Spirit, prays with the mind of Christ who is the head of the body (Col. 1.18). So Chrétien writes:

> The highest intimacy with God is expressed in words that we do not invent but that, rather, invent us, in that they find us and discover us where we were without knowing it. And formulary prayer, prayer that uses the traditional or scriptural formulae, is not a constrained prayer but the most free of all.[52]

Whilst the breathing of creation which gives rise to the human voice is assimilated to the prayer of Christ in and through the church, this is not an arbitrary or violent assimilation because all things are created in, through, and for Christ. In him, all things hold together (Col. 1.17). The Eastern tradition expresses this scriptural teaching and the presence of the Word throughout creation in terms of the *logoi* – the scattered rational principles which order creation according to the *Logos*.[53] Augustine refers to the *rationes seminales*, the rational seeds sown at the moment of creation which are expressions of the Word.[54] Those scattered seeds are brought to life and fruition in creation's prayer as it is assimilated through the church to the prayer of Christ, the incarnate *Logos*.

Creation is not, however, passive in this process. A long scriptural tradition, beginning with Genesis, suggests that creation informs and enables human prayer and participation in the divine life. Creation is structured for worship and forms the liturgy of the Temple and the church. To this tradition, we now turn.

---

[52]Chrétien, *The Ark of Speech*, 35.

[53]See Torstein Tollefsen, *The Christocentric Cosmology of St Maximus the Confessor* (Oxford: Oxford University Press, 2008), chapter 3.

[54]Augustine, *De Trinitate*, III.2.13: 'Thus it is the creator of all these invisible seeds who is the creator of all things, since whatever comes into our ken by a process of birth received the beginnings of its course from hidden seeds, and derives its due growth and final distinction of shape and parts from the as it were original rules'. Translation adapted from *The Trinity*, trans. Edmund Hill (New York: New City Press, 1991). See also Simon Oliver, 'Augustine on Creation, Providence and Motion', *International Journal of Systematic Theology* 18, no. 4 (2016): 379–98.

Creation Instructs Prayer

The scriptural account of creation that we find in the opening chapters of Genesis is often thought to be the work of two writers, even though the text may have been the work of a single editor. Genesis 1.1 to 2.4a is attributed to the Priestly writer and the remainder of Genesis 2 and Genesis 3 are attributed to the Yahwist writer. The text may be exilic or early post-exilic, although it could include much older textual influences. The writer of the opening chapter is named Priestly because of an apparent concern with the cosmic cycles and the Sabbath rest which structure the ritual life of the Temple in Jerusalem. For example, in Genesis 1.14 the lights in the dome of the sky that separate day from night are 'for signs and for seasons and for days and years'. They mark the ritual religious calendar according to solar and lunar cycles. The completion of creation – the unity of the universe – is expressed in the Sabbath rest through which creatures participate in the divine life. The Sabbath worship and the sacrifice of prayer offered to God in praise and thanksgiving are ritual expressions of the unity and completeness of creation.

The 'hexameral' period of creation – the pattern of six days followed by a day of rest – is one of the distinguishing features of the Genesis narrative when compared to ancient Babylonian creation myths such as *Enuma Elish* or *Atrahasis*. It connects the pattern of Temple worship with the created order. Before the Temple in Jerusalem, God provided the Temple of his creation. The two Temples can be connected in the figure of Moses through whom the Law was gifted to the Israelites. The book of Exodus reports Moses' encounter with God on Mount Sinai when a cloud covered the mountain for six days and on the seventh day God called to Moses out of the cloud (Exod. 24.15-18). This six-day encounter has been interpreted as God's revelation of the six days of creation to Moses.[55] After Moses' encounter with God on Mount Sinai, he is commanded to receive an offering from the people for the building of a sanctuary so that God may dwell amongst them. The construction of the tabernacle and its furnishings

---

[55]This connection is made explicit in the book of Jubilees, a Hebrew text dated to around the second century BCE. This is a retelling of Genesis and the opening of Exodus, hence later Hellenistic tradition referred to it as 'Little Genesis'. In the second chapter of Jubilees, which recounts Moses' encounter with God on Sinai, we read that 'the angel of the presence spoke to Moses by the words of the Lord, saying, "Write the whole account of creation, that in six days the Lord God completed all his works and all that he created. And he observed a Sabbath the seventh day, and he sanctified it for all ages. And he set it as a sign for all his works"'. See *Jubilees* 2.1, in *The Old Testament Pseudepigrapha*, vol. 2, ed. James H. Charlesworth (London: Darton, Longman and Todd, 1985) and Margaret Barker, *Creation: A Biblical Vision for the Environment* (London: T&T Clark, 2010), chapter 1.

reflect the ordering of creation.[56] We read the details of that ordering in
Exodus 40.16-33. The work begins on the first day of the first month and
is therefore representative of the new year and the renewal of creation. The
ordering of the tabernacle is a seven-stage process reflecting God's creation,
each stage being punctuated by the phrase 'as the Lord had commanded to
Moses'. Moses sets up the tabernacle on the first day, covering it with a tent
(Exod. 40.17-19). As on the first day of creation when there is no distinction
except light and dark, so in the tabernacle the various spaces are not yet
distinct, as they will be later when each space gains its particular meaning
in relation to the others. On the second day, Moses takes the covenant and
places it into the ark and places the mercy seat over the ark. He places the
ark in the tabernacle and sets up the curtain which separates the Ark of the
Covenant from the remainder of the tabernacle (Exod. 40.20-21). Moses
therefore distinguishes between different spatial regions: that which is holy
and that which is the holy of holies. Thus the tabernacle is now divided in
two, just as creation is divided into the sky above and the waters beneath the
dome on the second day (Gen. 1.6-9). So the pattern continues until Moses
completes his work on the seventh day, a cloud covers the tent, and the glory
of the Lord comes to fill the tabernacle (Exod. 40.33-34).

The structure and cycles of creation described in Genesis therefore
constitute the structure and cycles of the tabernacle. This pattern is seen in
other Old Testament texts, notably the seven-day inauguration of Solomon's
Temple described in 1 Kings 8.65 and 2 Chronicles 7.8-9. The idea that
creation is God's first Temple and the place of his dwelling is also seen in
other texts, for example Isaiah 66.1-2 ('Heaven is my throne and the earth
is my footstool') and Psalm 104 ('You stretch out the heavens like a tent. ...
You set the earth on its foundations, so that it shall never be shaken'). The
psalmist tells of the presence of God in every corner of creation. God is
present in the Temple of his creation as he promised to be present to his
people in the tabernacle and Temple.

> Where can I go from your spirit? Or where can I flee from your presence?
> If I ascend to heaven, you are there; if I make my bed in Sheol, you are
> there. If I take the wings of the morning and settle at the farthest limits
> of the sea, even there your hand shall lead me, and your right hand shall
> hold me fast.
>
> (Ps. 139.7-10)

---

[56]See Joseph Blenkinsopp, 'The Structure of P', *Catholic Biblical Quarterly* 38, no. 3 (1976):
275–92 and Peter J. Kearney, 'Creation and Liturgy: The P Redaction of Ex 25-40', *Zeitschrift
für die alttestameutliche Wissenschaft* 89, no. 3 (1977): 375–87.

As creation instructs the structure and liturgy of the tabernacle and Temple, so too it forms the praise and prayer of the church. I suggested above that prayer is not truly individual or solitary, but is part of the prayer of the church as the body of Christ. Under the inspiration of the Holy Spirit, the church prays with the mind of Christ. Like the patterns of the Temple, the church's prayer is liturgically ordered in feasts, fasts and ordinary time so that its arrangements proclaim God and God's dealings with his people: thanks for creation, lament over the fall, remembrance of the first covenant, witness to prophecy, wonder at the Incarnation, joy at redemption in Christ and the new covenant, and hope for the eschaton. That proclamation of God's goodness and grace also belongs to creation as God's gift, so creation instructs liturgy and prayer for the telling of God's story. As creation is God's dwelling place, so too is the Jerusalem Temple and, by the Holy Spirit, the church as the body of Christ. This implies that liturgy and prayer are not concerned with escaping the material elements of God's creation to reach an immaterial spiritual realm. Quite the reverse: liturgy and prayer in Temple and church concern the assimilation of creation's deepest structures, symbols and cycles.

The tradition of creation instructing prayer and liturgy became particularly evident in patristic and medieval Christianity. One clear example is the work of Bede the Venerable, monk, doctor of the church and one of its greatest historians, biblical translator and commentator, mathematician and astronomer. Bede's learning was prodigious, not least in the field of natural philosophy. Amongst his many concerns was time and what became known as the *computus* – the science of time-reckoning and the fixing of liturgical feasts such as Easter.[57] A brief description of Bede's understanding of time and the dating of Easter indicates the way in which creation instructs prayer.

In two treatises on time composed in the early eighth century, *De Temporibus Ratione* and *De Temporibus*, Bede describes a threefold division of time.[58] First, there is natural time such as the solar year and the lunar month. Secondly, there is customary time – the kind of dates we set to structure our cultural life. Thirdly, there is time given by authorities, either human or divine. For example, the division of the week into seven days is

---

[57]See, for example, Máirín MacCarron, *Bede and Time: Computus, Theology and History in the Early Medieval World* (London: Routledge, 2020).

[58]See Carolyn G. Hartz, 'Bede and the Grammar of Time', *British Journal for the History of Philosophy* 15, no. 4 (2007): 625–40. For Bede's several treatises on time, see Bede, *Bedae Opera de Temporibus*, ed. Charles W. Jones (Cambridge, MA: Mediaeval Academy of America, 1943).

not a matter of custom but of divine authority because the seven-day week is given in the creation story in Genesis. The first day of the week marks the first day of creation, the creation of light. Could the dating of liturgical festivals such as Easter be a matter of customary time (e.g. fixing the date of Easter on the first Sunday in April) or is the dating a matter of natural time and time given by divine authority?

In his writings on time and in *The Ecclesiastical History of the English People*, Bede's concern over the dating of Easter is very clear.[59] In the generation before Bede the so-called 'paschal controversy' had been fierce: Should Easter be dated according to the Irish or Roman method? Having a single method for dating Easter, the principal Christian festival, would ensure the unity of the kingdom and the unity of the church. The calculation of the date of Easter was extremely complex and the mathematical tables used in the science of *computus*, including those produced by Bede, were extraordinarily intricate. So how was the dating of Easter resolved? Put very simply, we take the spring equinox, when day and night are the same length, then calculate the first full moon after the spring equinox, and Easter falls on the Sunday after that full moon. That first full moon is known as the Paschal Moon and it determines the date of the Jewish Passover. Because Christ was crucified and rose during the Passover festival, maintaining the link between Easter and Passover was clearly important. For Bede, however, it is crucial for wider theological reasons which concern the allegorical significance of the book of nature. First, at the spring equinox, the day and night are the same length; after the equinox, the days become longer into the summer. The spring equinox is the time when light begins to overcome darkness. Secondly, the first full moon is the time when the world is illuminated for a full twenty-four hours – during the day by the sun and during the night by the brilliance of the full moon. Again, the light triumphs over darkness, Christ over the shadow of sin, life over death. This puts the festival of Easter into a cosmic context. Easter is not like a saint's day for Bede; it is not an anniversary. Nor is it a matter of customary time. It is a festival with a full cosmic setting which brings together natural time and the time established by divine authority. These are, in a sense, one and the same, or at least in harmony, because natural time is God's creation and bears his authority. The natural time of the cosmos helps us tell the story of light overcoming darkness in Christ. Easter is both our festival *and* creation's festival – the first day of the week is creation's beginning and the day of Christ's new life is humanity's new beginning. Indeed, the date of Christmas, apparently

---

[59]Bede, *The Ecclesiastical History of the English People*, ed. Judith McClure and Roger Collins (Oxford: Oxford University Press, 1994), 3.25.

an anniversary or a matter of customary time, is similarly concerned with darkness turning to light. Its proximity to the winter solstice – the shortest day – marks the turning of the year. Light increases as the light of the world is born.

The intimate links between creation and Temple, as well as cosmic time and ecclesiastical time, indicate the way in which creation instructs and orders liturgy and prayer. Prayer is not, after all, a purely human cultural enterprise or arranged according to custom. The practice of prayer is ordered, enabled and instructed by the deepest symbols and structures of God's creation. The liturgical feasts which order prayer are both natural and cultural.

Conclusion

This chapter began with the observation that it is not obvious how prayer can be an aspect of the doctrine of creation, if prayer is understood as a practice of practical reason which is confined to the realm of culture. Whilst preserving the intellectual character of prayer described by figures such as Evagrius and Aquinas, the doctrine of creation in fact provides the fundamental context for understanding the nature and practice of prayer. This begins with creation *ex nihilo* which establishes the human creature as a gift to itself. The realization of the creature's gifted being and its consequent need of all that sustains life are eucharistically expressed in thanksgiving and petition. Understanding the person praying as a microcosm, we can see that all creation 'flows towards' the human. Creation's breathing gives rise to the human voice which offers creation back to God who, in the Incarnation, takes to himself a human voice. Finally, creation is not passive in its assimilation to the human microcosm and its gathering into Christ 'in whom all things hold together' and 'who fills all in all'. Creation instructs prayer and prayer, through the liturgical cycles of feast and fast, becomes cosmic.

The view of prayer in the context of creation offered in this chapter challenges the naturalism and materialism which is prevalent in many strands of modern thought. The human person understood as microcosm is not confined to a cultural domain which stands over and against the natural; culture and nature are united under the more fundamental category of 'creation'. Mind, to which belongs the intellectual practice of prayer, is not alien to nature but is anticipated in material creation. Material creation is teleologically ordered to mind, and therefore to prayer. Similarly, the life of creation – its 'breathing' – gives rise to the human voice which, in prayer and praise, offers creation back to God as instructed by Christ through the Spirit. Creation is, after all, a mode of prayer.

CHAPTER TEN

The Christology of Prayer: Praying in Christ Who is Priest, Prophet and King

TOM GREGGS

As Jesus teaches us in the Lord's Prayer, when we pray, we pray to the God who is *Our* Father (Mt. 6.9-13; Lk. 11.2-4) – the Father of Christ and the Father of us all. We share with Christ in calling upon God as Father, and join with Christ in doing so. When we pray, therefore, we come before the Father in and with Christ who is our sole mediator. God does not leave us to pray on our own unaided or alone, but graces us with the gift that – even in our sinful state – we come as humans in prayer before God in Jesus Christ who is our salvation. Put otherwise, one might say that, since Christ is the one who mediates God's salvation to humanity, Christ's mediatorial saving graces also involve the mediation of our prayer and worship to God.[1]

Indeed, in the Pastoral Epistles, the connection between the mediation of Christ and our prayer is made clear. Following Timothy's instructions to pray is the reminder: 'For there is one God; there is also one mediator between God and humankind, Christ Jesus, himself human, who gave

---

[1]Geoffrey Wainwright, *Doxology: The Praise of God in Worship, Doctrine and Life* (New York: Oxford University Press, 1980), 66.

himself a ransom for all' (1 Tim. 2.5-6). As fallen humans, we come before the holiness of God in prayer in Christ who makes us justified (Rom. 3.24, 5.1, 8.30; 1 Cor. 6.11; Tit. 3.7), holy (1 Cor. 1.30, 6.11; Heb. 10.1-2, 10, 14) and acceptable to God (Eph. 1.6; 1 Pet. 2.5; Col. 2.13) in him and the reconciliation Christ uniquely and singularly achieves. Calvin writes:

> Since no man is worthy to present himself to God and come into his sight, the Heavenly Father himself, to free us at once from shame and fear, which might well have thrown our hearts into despair, has given us his Son, Jesus Christ our Lord, to be our advocate (1 Jn 2.1) and mediator with him (1 Tim. 2.5; cf. Heb. 8.6 and 9.15), by whose guidance we may confidently come to him, and with such an intercessor, trusting nothing we ask in his name will be denied us, as nothing can be denied to him by the Father.[2]

Or else, in the more positive terms in which Alan Torrance helpfully puts the matter, it might be said:

> The Son has taken what is ours (our confused, tempted, struggling humanity that is unable to pray and worship in truth) and has sanctified it in himself so that we might have what is his (healed, cleansed, perfected humanity). So now we are given to share, by the Spirit, in *his* worship, in *his* prayer, in *his* intercessions for us and for the world, and of course, in *his* ongoing mission from the Father to the world.[3]

Any theology of prayer is, therefore, innately related to Christology as a doctrine: if we pray in Christ, Christ's own person is foundational for our understanding of the nature of Christian prayer.

Of course, this does not mean that we somehow take the place of Christ or that our own praying is synonymous with or identical to his, or even an independent repetition of his. His prayer is the perfect prayer of his perfect mediation. One way to consider this perfect mediation might be in relation to the perfect humanity of Christ compared to our sinful humanity. Christ's perfect prayerful relation to the Father is an expression of his true and perfect humanity: Christ in his true humanity prays perfectly, and it is *in his prayer* that our prayers can be brought before the holy throne of God. In relating

---

[2]Calvin, *Inst.*, 3.20.17.
[3]Alan J. Torrance, 'Reclaiming the Continuing Priesthood of Christ: Implications and Challenges', in *Christology, Ancient and Modern: Explorations in Constructive Dogmatics*, ed. Oliver Crisp and Fred Sanders (Grand Rapids, MI: Zondervan, 2013), 184–204 (193).

Christ's prayer to his humanity, it is not the case, therefore, that – since we pray and Jesus prays – he shares in our 'true' humanity; it is, instead, rather the case that – since Jesus prays and we pray – in our praying we share in his true humanity. We anticipate and express our true humanity, which awaits us fully in redemption,[4] proleptically when we pray, since in praying we join with, in and through Jesus' humanity in calling God 'Abba'. Barth puts this well when he states about the final three petitions of the Lord's Prayer: 'The *us* refers to the brotherhood of those who are with Jesus Christ, God and Man, who allows and commands them to join with him in his own intercession with God, that is, to pray with him.'[5]

Our own prayer in the mediator is in and of itself mediated, however. It is not that we are subsumed into Christ, but that through the Spirit we are enabled actively to participate in the objective reality of that which Christ has achieved for our humanity. When we pray, we come objectively in, with and through Christ to share actively in his perfect humanity in calling God '*our* Father' in prayer. We do not do this as if the church or the Christian *were* himself or herself Christ, but only as those who *in* Christ share by an event of the act of the Spirit in Christ's true humanity as one of constant prayer.[6] Paul puts it thus in Romans 8: 'When we cry, "Abba! Father!" it is that very Spirit bearing witness with our spirit that we are children of God' (Rom. 8.15b-16).[7] In sharing in the same Spirit who rested completely and fully on Christ God's only Son, we are freed through God's turning to us in the reconciling grace of God in Christ to turn our hearts towards God as Father; and – in so doing – to share in and with Christ in calling God '*Abba*', becoming children of God. As those who call God *Our Father*, we are, therefore, 'joint heirs with Christ' (Rom. 8.17a); and in this way, our humanity subsists in his perfect humanity, becoming truly human as he is truly human. We learn to pray as we learn by the event of the Spirit's act to pray in Christ and actively to *share* and *participate* in his prayer. Barth's words are wise here:

Christian prayer is participation in Jesus Christ; participation, basically, in the grace which is revealed and active in Him, in the Son of God; and

---

[4] I have at times discussed this theme in terms of a parallel to *theosis*, which might be thought of as *anthroposis*. See, for example, Tom Greggs, *Dogmatic Ecclesiology: Volume 1 – The Priestly Catholicity of the Church* (Grand Rapids, MI: Baker Academic, 2019), chapters 1–3.

[5] Karl Barth, *Prayer and Preaching* (London: SCM Press, 1964), 43.

[6] Non-identification between Christ and the church or the Christian is a particular concern of my ecclesiology.

[7] 'It is the *us* of those who, being united with Jesus Christ crucified, are able to pray with him as members of God's family'. See Barth, *Prayer and Preaching*, 44.

then only, and in this basis, participation in the asking of the Son of Man. Christian prayer is life in and with the community of Jesus Christ; life primarily and basically out of and in the fullness of the Spirit and the hope which Jesus Christ imparted and continually imparts to them.[8]

It is incumbent upon any theology of prayer, therefore, to consider who the Christ is in whom by the Spirit we pray, and what benefits come for the creature in light of who the Christ is. In considering how Christ is the great mediator of God to humanity and our humanity to God, unpacking his mediatorial office has often been done in the Magisterial Protestant traditions' relation to the *munus triplex* – the threefold office of Christ as prophet, priest and king.[9] The idea that rests behind this threefold office is that Christ as the one who is 'anointed' (as the name *Christos* indicates) is anointed in his own person and mission to the offices and services which had, in the Hebrew Bible, been variously located with different groups of people. In the Hebrew Bible, individuals and groups of people received anointing from God and for a purpose, and this anointing was to the office of priest, prophet or king (though in some, such as David or Moses, there was a twofold uniting of these offices). Heinrich Heppe writes, therefore: 'Since then, the truth of ancient unction is to be sought in Christ, just as prophets, priests and kings were consecrated to their office by outward unctions, so Christ had to exist anointed by God Himself to be prophet, priest and king.'[10] As the anointed one, Christ's own person and work incorporates all of the offices to which God had called people to be anointed. These various offices are one in Christ in their interrelation, and only manifold in others as 'types' or forerunners of Christ, and (potentially) successors of him.[11]

This chapter will, therefore, consider how Christology relates to prayer by unpacking Christ's mediating work through expounding Christ's threefold office. It will highlight how each of Christ's mediating offices highlights aspects of Christian prayer which are made in him. In the expounding of the

---

[8]See Barth, *CD* III/3, 282–3.

[9]However, it should be noted that most Lutheran theologians until Wendelin tended only to speak of two offices – that of Christ as priest and Christ as king.

[10]Heinrich Heppe, *Reformed Dogmatics*, trans. G. T. Thomson (Eugene, OR: Wipf and Stock, 1950), 453.

[11]Care here is needed over the issue of supersession. It is in the eternal and pre-existent Christ that the prophets have their own prophetic life, the priests theirs, the kings theirs. It is not that there are prophets, priests and kings, and Christ supersedes them and makes them redundant; it is rather that Christ is the true prophet, priest and king who is the Word at the beginning of creation, and prophets, priests and kings share in his vocation. Christ does not supersede the prophets, priests and kings but precedes them and is the basis on which and content of their calling.

prophetic office of Christ, the chapter will consider what it means for the Christian and the church to confess sin and hear the promise of forgiveness in prayer in Christ: we encounter Christ the true prophet who speaks God's truth to us, convicting us by his Spirit of our sin and giving us the deposit of salvation in the forgiveness he declares. In discussing the priesthood of Christ, the chapter will examine what it means for the church and the Christian to participate actively in prayer in Christ's priestly mediation and intercession: we participate in Christ as priest when in him we bring intercession to the Father for others and to respond in thankfulness. In examining Christ's kingly office, the chapter will consider the church and the believer's active engagement in Christ's glorification of God in worship: in Christ who is the eternal and sovereign king, our prayers are transformed into offerings of adoration and worship which glorify the God who is enthroned in heaven and lives world without end.[12]

Christ as Prophet: Encountering the Truth and Holiness of God in Confession

Christ as prophet is the one whom we encounter as he speaks the Word of God in truth to creation. Christ is the Word of God whom the prophets not only foretell, but also in truth tell forth. As the one who is the Word, it is Jesus Christ and his truth which is the content of the prophets' teachings. Christ *is* the way, truth and life (Jn 16.6) of which the prophets speak. He is the one who not only is the greatest of the prophets, but whose Word is the very basis of the words the prophets speak. When the prophets called the people away from sin and back towards God, they were offering an anticipatory echo of the ministry and office of Christ as the true prophet who calls the people to repentance and faith in God.

It is a feature of the opening chapter of Mark's Gospel that Jesus is introduced as the completion of the prophets. Not only is Jesus seen as the one whom the prophets testified to and the fulfilment of their promises (Mk 1.2-3); Jesus is also seen as the one who succeeds the last of the prophets with whom John the Baptist identifies in his message and his clothing (Mk 1.4-8). Indeed, even in the resonances of going into the wilderness for forty days, Jesus is compared to Moses (the greatest of the prophets) and is clearly considered by Mark greater still (Mk 1.9-11). Even Jesus' public message is reminiscent of the call of the prophets for Israel to turn from its sins and

---

[12]In these three sections, there is a summary of positions I hold (or plan to hold) in the chapters on prayer in the volumes of my ecclesiology.

to place faith in God and the kingdom God is bringing about (Mk 1.15). This trope of Christ the prophet is one which finds its place in the earliest theological literature. Justin Martyr, for example, speaks of Jesus Christ as the content of the message of Moses.[13] It is not so much the case that Christ is the completion of prophecy. It is, rather, the case that Christ as the Word of God is the *basis* of all prophecy. It is Christ who is the content of the truth and the call of the prophets.

As the prophet who not only speaks but also *is* truth, our encounter with Christ in prayer is one which leads us *both* to encounter the truth of our sinfulness *and* to encounter the truth of the good news of salvation in God's forgiving and saving grace. Through the inward convicting grace of the Holy Spirit who brings us into all truth (Jn 16.15), we come to know the truth that Christ discloses to us (Jn 16.14) as prophet. Heppe puts this well when he states:

> Christ's 'prophecy' is on the one hand a *prophetia legalis*, since Christ did not come forward at all as a new legislator. In order to found the true knowledge of salvation of grace imparted through him he teaches us to recognise the true righteousness which the Law demands. ... On the other hand Christ's prophetic office is likewise a *prophetia evangelica*, since Christ arouses the most blessed knowledge of the gracious salvation extended to the world.[14]

There is a twofold dynamic to prayer considered from the perspective of Christ as prophet. In this prayer, we encounter God who is the source of all truth. First, as we approach God in prayer through Jesus Christ, his truth brings to light our lies – to others, ourselves and about ourselves. We discover the penultimate truth about ourselves – that we are sinners in whom there is no health. In this, we confess our sins to God, beautifully captured in the first half of the General Confession in the *Book of Common Prayer*:

> Almighty and most merciful Father; We have erred, and strayed from thy ways like lost sheep. We have followed too much the devices and desires of our own hearts. We have offended against thy holy laws. We have left undone those things which we ought to have done; And we have done those things which we ought not to have done; And there is no health in us.

---

[13]Justin Martyr, *First Apology*, trans. Thomas B. Falls, FC 6 (Washington, DC: Catholic University of America Press, 1948), 63.
[14]Heppe, *Reformed Dogmatics*, 453–4.

Coming to the throne of grace in prayer through Christ who is prophet, we are called – as the prophets have always called the people – to turn from our sins and return to the Lord who is the source of all truth. Our confession arises from encounter in prayer with the one who is the source of all law and truth; knowing him and his perfect standard, we learn in encounter with him what it means to be a sinner.[15] But crucially, second, in Christ's words of absolution, we learn that we are children of God who are forgiven and redeemed. Christ, who is prophet, speaks healing words of grace to us, assuring us through his resurrection words of the peace and restoration he brings (Jn 20.19), and continuing to speak these words to us in forgiveness. Our confession tells us the truth of our penultimate reality – that we are sinners; but our absolution and assurance of forgiveness in prayer tells the ultimate truth of our status as those who are simultaneously forgiven of sin and restored to all righteousness through grace. Christ the prophet speaks the truth of our reality of being sinners saved by grace, and in our prayer in him we confess and are absolved. Through the inward assurance of the Spirit, we are convicted of sin and assured of our complete restoration in Christ.

This restoration involves knowing the reality that our 'sins are forgiven on account of his [Christ's] name' (1 Jn 2.12b). But having been restored to righteousness in him, through the forgiveness of our sins, we share prayerfully in the reality of the kingdom whose coming we pray for. Having put away all falsehood, and been forgiven and assured of salvation, we are called to forgive as we have been forgiven. The letter to the Ephesians expands this aspect of the prayer of Jesus in which we join, when it states that turning from our sin, we are to be 'be kind to one another, tender-hearted, forgiving one another, as God in Christ has forgiven you' (Eph. 4.32). In this way, we encounter the reality of the Word of God that in Christ we are 'a chosen race, a royal priesthood, a holy nation, God's own people, in order that you may proclaim the mighty acts of him who called you out of darkness into his marvellous light' (1 Pet. 2.9).

Christ as Priest: Intercession in the Great Intercessor

Christ's priesthood arises from the uniqueness of Christ's person. As the one who is fully human and fully divine in one person, Christ perfectly mediates

---

[15]'Only when we know Jesus Christ do we really know that man is the man of sin, and what sin is, and what it means for man'. See Barth, CD IV/1, 389.

God to humanity and humanity to God in his own perfect life through the hypostatic union.[16] As Graham Tomlin puts it:

> Christ is priest because he is the Mediator – the one who binds together both humanity and divinity in one. The incarnate Son is not a third party who reconciles humanity and God. Instead, Christ's mediation between God and humanity is dependent on his sharing the full nature of both. Christ is Mediator precisely as both human and divine. The priesthood of Christ refers ... in particular to his unique divine-human nature.[17]

For the church in relation to prayer, this priesthood is of particular significance in terms of Christ's continuing life as our everlasting intercessor. As mediator between humanity and God, Christ in his heavenly session (following the ascension) is the Great Intercessor for humanity. There, he pleads for humanity and also offers the oblation of humanity to the Father. T. F. Torrance helpfully asserts: 'After His ascension He ever lives before the face of the Father as our *Leitourgos* and Intercessor, for there he confesses us before the face of God as those for whom He died, as those whose names He has entered as members of His Body.'[18] In his life and work as our *Leitourgos* and Intercession, Christ fulfils that which as humans we cannot.[19] He is the representative of our humanity to God, and in this representation as our high priest brings to God both our worship and our intercession – appearing perfectly before the throne of grace to bring those who are within his body (and their adoration and their pleas) to the Father.

As those who, in our sin, are unworthy to appear before the throne of God in prayer, Christ is our mediator and our advocate, ever interceding for us. Prayer is not something to which as humans we have a right in our sinful condition, or something which is a natural activity for humans: desperate calling to a *deus ex machina* might well be; but that in itself might well be an expression of a sinful desire for self-preservation rather

---

[16]'We must think of Jesus Christ as the Mediator of divine revelation and reconciliation in virtue of what he is in his own Identity and Reality. He does not mediate a revelation or a reconciliation that is other than what he is, as though he were only the agent or instrument of that mediation to [hu]mankind. He embodies what he mediates in himself, for what he mediates and what he is are one and the same. He constitutes in his own incarnate person the content and the reality of what he mediates.' See T. F. Torrance, *The Mediation of Christ* (Edinburgh: T&T Clark, 1992), 67.

[17]Graham Tomlin, *The Widening Circle: Priesthood as God's Way of Blessing the World* (London: SPCK, 2014), 25.

[18]T. F. Torrance, *Royal Priesthood: A Theology of Ordained Ministry* (Edinburgh: T&T Clark, 1993), 13.

[19]See Barth, *CD* IV/1, 276.

than any shared calling upon the God and Father of the Lord Jesus Christ by the Holy Spirit. It is only because of divine grace that we might pray. This is something John Wesley recognizes well when he states that prayer 'whether in secret or with the great congregation' is the *chief means of grace* by which he means 'outward signs, words or actions, ordained by God, and appointed for this end – to be the *ordinary channels* whereby he might convey to men preventing, justifying, or sanctifying grace'.[20] This grace is given to us only in Christ who is our mediator and high priest. Put otherwise, we might say: only in the great intercession of its high priest, Jesus Christ, can the church offer its oblation and intercessions to the Father.

When we pray and offer oblation and intercession, we as Christians actively participate in the grace of Christ as the everlasting and perfect high priest. It is in Christ, therefore, that as those who call upon *Our* Father, Christians bring their oblation and intercession to God. Only through the mediation of Christ's priesthood is this made possible. But it is also the case that as those who participate in the body of Christ, if we wish to be the body of Christ, prayerful intercession and oblation is a necessary condition of the Christian life. In discussing Paul on this topic, Calvin writes:

> And he [Paul] does not make himself mediator between the people and God, but he asks that all members of Christ's body mutually pray for one another, 'since the members are concerned for one another, and if one member suffers, the rest suffer with it' (1 Cor. 12.25-26; cf. Vg.). And thus the mutual prayers for one another of all the members yet laboring on earth rise to the Head, who has gone before them into heaven, in whom 'is propitiation of sins' (1 Jn 2.2, Vg).[21]

In doing this, through the event of the Spirit's act in constituting us as the body of Christ, we actively participate *de facto* in the life we already possess *de jure* in Christ. In praying in Christ our high priest, we display and embody, in the words of Barth that:

> Jesus Christ is not an isolated form or figure. To Him there belong those who are elected in and with Him, His own people, who by the Spirit of His Word are called by faith in Him, and by faith to obedience to Him. ... This body of His is the community, His community, the Christian

---

[20]John Wesley, 'The Means of Grace', in *The Works of John Wesley: Sermons I (1–33)*, ed. Albert C. Outler (Nashville, TN: Abingdon Press, 1984), 381.

[21]Calvin, *Inst.* 3.20.20.

community, His people. He has given Himself to this people as Lord, and revealed Himself as the Lord.[22]

When we pray, we form ourselves actively into the body in which we passively participate, and grow to understand what it means to be the body of him who is our head.

It is perhaps Luther above all others who has drawn theological attention to the significance of Christ's priesthood and our sharing in it in prayer. It is – along with our ability to speak the Word of God to one another – our capacity to intercede for each other that makes us Christ's 'fellow-priests' according to Luther. For him, 'As priests we are worthy to appear before God and to pray for others and to teach one another divine things.'[23] Therefore, for Luther, to pray to God for others is at the heart of priestly identity. In its intercessions, the *church* takes the priestly form of Christ in whom it participates and in which the individual subsists: the whole body is conformed into the likeness of him whom is its head. This idea is at the heart of what is later considered to be Luther's doctrine of the priesthood of all believers. Luther unpacks the themes associated with this idea in his 'The Freedom of a Christian' in which he discusses the priesthood of Christ and relates this to believers in the church.[24] In this work, Luther unpacks the priesthood of Christ in terms of Christ's status as first-born and the discussion in Hebrews about Melchizedeck. It is this which then determines the priesthood of each member of the church, as those who receive the benefits of Christ, who are able to speak the Word of God to and intercede on behalf of others. Luther writes: 'Now just as Christ by his birthright obtained these two prerogatives, so he imparts them to and shares them with everyone who believes in him. ... Hence all of us who believe in Christ are priests and kings in Christ.'[25] For him, 'As priests we are worthy to appear before God to pray for others and to teach one another divine things.'[26] By actively undertaking what Christ undertakes as priest in interceding and speaking the Word of God, believers fulfil the priesthood they have in Christ. This is a sharing in Christ's own priestly life and priestly prayer. Barth puts this matter thus:

---

[22]Barth, CD III/3, 271.

[23]Luther, 'The Freedom of a Christian', in *Career of the Reformer I*, ed. Harold John Grimm and Helmut T. Lehmann, LW 31 (Philadelphia, PA: Fortress Press, 1957), 355. What is more, as Althaus makes clear, it is not just for Luther the case that Christians can approach God on their own behalf, but also the case that the Christian can approach God on behalf of others and the creation. See Paul Althaus, *Theology of Luther* (Minneapolis, MN: Fortress Press, 1966), 302–3.

[24]On the priesthood of Christ, see Luther, 'The Freedom of a Christian', 353–4.

[25]Luther, 'The Freedom of a Christian', 354.

[26]Luther, 'The Freedom of a Christian', 355.

[The community] will not allow its Lord to be alone in prayer, but it will be at His side with its own asking, however imperfect and perverted and impotent this may be compared with His. And both with heart and mouth the asking of the community which is elected together with Him will be a true and genuine asking, because and in the very fact that it is merely a repetition of His petition, that it is enclosed in His asking, that it is associated with it, that it lives by its seriousness and power, that it is related to the gift and answer of God present within it. ... It is in this that the community participates in Him, in His life as the Lord. It is in this that it really is His community.[27]

However, it is not only in our interceding that we participate in Christ's priesthood and priestly prayer. We do so also as we bring our oblation. The priest does not only offer petitions on behalf of the people but oblations on behalf of the people also. In bringing worship to God in Christ, our *Leitourgos*, the weak and inadequate sacrifices of thanksgiving that Christians offer are transformed into 'spiritual sacrifices' to God. Although these do not in any way repeat or enhance the unique, complete and once-for-all sacrifice of Christ upon the cross, our worship is nevertheless *within Christ's priestly self-sacrifice* an offering fitting to God. In Christ's priestly life, our prayers participate in time in that which is already complete such that they become through the Spirit freed from the dead actions of work-based righteousness and are instead the living worship of those who worship in spirit and in truth (Jn 4.22ff.). In Christ's perfect obedient priestly humanity is included by divine grace *enhypostatically* our imperfect offerings of oblation.

Christ as King: Glorifying the Glorious One

Christ's priesthood is one which is royal. The closest parallel to his priestly life is the *kingly* priest Melchizedek (and also David). Christ is the one to whom the Magi bring gold in adoration (Mt. 2.11); to whom one day every knee will bow (Phil. 2.10); and before whom every king or queen will one day cast their crown. He is executed as king of the Jews (Mt. 27.37), but is in fact so much more as well – king of the Jews and High King of Heaven. He is the king of kings and the lord of lords (1 Tim. 6.15; Rev. 17.14, 19.16). Frequently, throughout the history of the church, Christ's kingship has been the means by which to speak of his sovereign providential grace. This is a theme which emphasizes the spiritual nature of Christ's kingly office, Heppe

---

[27]Barth, CD III/3, 277.

highlights,[28] and which Calvin describes in the following terms: 'Our king will never leave us destitute, but will provide for our needs until, our warfare ended, we are called to triumph. Such is the nature of his rule, that he shares with us all that he has received from the Father.'[29] But Calvin goes on to link the kingship of Christ with his glory and our capacity to give glory to him and to the Father in him and his kingship. For Calvin, the benefits of Christ's kingship give us 'the most fruitful occasion' to give glory to God and to 'bring forth fruit to his glory'.[30] As the one who is king, Christ is both the object of our glory and the one in whom we give glory to the Father.

This glory of God is known to us in the manifestation of Jesus Christ the Son, who reveals to creation the reality of the eternal triune Creator's glorifying and loving dynamic both in God's own eternal life *in se* and in God's glory *ad extra* in the context of creation. John tells us that Christ is the one who has glory in the presence of God before the world existed (Jn 17.5) and who also glorifies God on earth (Jn 17.4). This Son is the one who glorifies the Father as the reflection of God's glory, 'light from light' as the Nicene symbol puts it, in God's eternal immanent life, and in the effulgence of God's Light in the economy.[31] The Son is the one eternally destined to be for creation's salvation and redemption, as an expression of the Father's love for creation in the eternal love of the Father and Son (Jn 17.23). Kingly glory bespeaks God's twofold movement in the Son of God: God's internal immanent life of paternity and filiation; and God's manifestation in the realm of God's creation of God's own presence in the effulgence of God's glory in the person of Jesus – the very One who is eternally self-determined to be for the creation which was created through him and reconciled by him. When we give glory to Christ our king and to the Father in Christ our king, we fulfil Jesus' prayer to the Father: 'All mine are yours, and yours are mine; and I have been glorified in them' (Jn 17.10). In Christ the king, we are glorified in bringing glory to God. Our humanity and its vain worship and adoration joins with eternal heavenly glorification of the Son by the Father and the Father by the Son. In giving glory to God in Christ the king, humanity is taken up into the act of the Father and the Son's relationship of glorification, and their glorifying is

---

[28]Heppe, *Reformed Dogmatics*, 481–2.
[29]Calvin, *Inst.* 2.15.3.
[30]Calvin, *Inst.* 2.15.3.
[31]Regarding the Son's filiation, Origen writes: 'This is an eternal and everlasting beginning, as brightness is begotten from light'. See *On First Principles*, trans. G. W. Butterworth (New York: Harper and Row, 1966), I.2.4.

transformed thereby – 'changed from glory into glory' (to quote Charles Wesley in his hymn, *Love Divine*).[32]

This act of human glorifying does not add anything to God who is already in God's self perfectly glorious. When we give an account of glorifying God in Christ the king, we do not in any way through our worship and adoration add anything to God who is already complete in God's self. In acknowledging that Christ *is* king, we bring our glorying of God to, in and through him who eternally glorifies the Father as Son and is glorified by the Father. We offer an account of the recognition by the Christian in prayer of the divine Creator's qualities and perfections, such that we acknowledge that God's glory would not exist, be diminished or would exist in a changed manner, did God not have a life *ad extra*. Christ is the king. He is *Pantokrator*. He is the one who through all eternity is the king of kings. When in Christ we bring glory to God, we adore and worship the one who *is* perfectly and completely glorious. In glorifying God in the one who – without us – is king, we are saying in prayer that God is perfectly and fully glorious in God's eternal life in and of itself. It is proper to God to be glorious. God's glory is a glory which has existed in the eternal triune life as the Father eternally glorifies the Son so that the Son may glorify the Father (Jn 17.1) in the unity of the Holy Spirit. This is a glory which the presence of God had 'before the world existed' (Jn 17.5), and is, therefore, not a glory which is dependent on creation or the Christian giving glory. When in prayer we give glory to God, we do not add anything to the divine life which God lacked before our glorifying of God, but we simply acknowledge the perfection of glory in the eternal glorification of the Father, Son and Holy Spirit. The *Gloria* reminds us of this:

> Glory to the Father and to the Son and to the Holy Spirit,
> *As it was in the beginning, is now, and shall be forever.*

In offering this glory, we do so in the king of all glory who is already perfectly glorious as the eternal Son.

As the king, however, Christ is the one who is supremely regnal in humility – as an infant to whom the Magi come; as the one who rides a colt; as the crucified one who reigns from the tree. Our glory in prayer is not the glory of the world, but a glory which is transformed by grace as it is a glory found in the face of Jesus Christ, the knowledge of which we possess in clay jars (2 Cor. 4.6-7). When we offer glory to, in and through Christ who is king, we do as the widow offering her mite (Lk. 21.1-4) not as the Pharisees

---

[32]See Wolfhart Pannenberg, *Systematic Theology: Volume 3*, trans. Geoffrey W. Bromiley (Grand Rapids, MI: William B. Eerdmans, 1997), 625.

with their wordy and public prayer (Mt. 6.2; Lk. 18.9-14). There is humility in coming into the presence of the king and coming in the king to glorify his Father. The mode of Christ's kingship reveals to us the mode of our prayer of glorification in Christ. It shows us that we are to kneel at the foot of the cross of Christ who is king, and our glorification is one which is transformed from its earthly glory to the eternal glory of the lamb who was slain before the foundation of the world (Rev. 13.8). To glorify God in our prayers of worship and adoration is to allow those prayers to be transformed such that they take the form fitting of the king who is our servant in, through and to whom all glory belongs.

CHAPTER ELEVEN

The Intercession of the Holy Spirit: Pneumatology and Prayer

MATTHEW LEVERING

I have chosen to centre this chapter around a set of problems and insights deriving from Romans 8.26-27, a central biblical text for understanding the relationship of prayer and the doctrine of the Holy Spirit. Paul states in Romans 8.26-27:

> Likewise the Spirit helps us in our weakness; for we do not know how to pray as we ought, but the Spirit himself intercedes (ὑπερεντυγχάνει)[1] for us with sighs too deep for words. And he who searches the hearts of men knows what is the mind of the Spirit, because the Spirit intercedes (ἐντυγχάνει) for the saints according to the will of God.

Shortly after he discusses the Spirit's intercession for us, Paul affirms that Jesus, too, intercedes for us. Paul praises 'Christ Jesus, who died, yes, who was raised from the dead, who is at the right hand of God, who indeed

---

[1] For the English text of Romans 8.26-27, I employ the RSV. The RSV's 'for us' in Romans 8.26, however, may likely be a scribal addition. See the manuscript variants noted in *The Greek New Testament*, ed. Barbara Aland, Kurt Aland, Johannes Karavidopoulos, Carlo M. Martini and Bruce M. Metzger, 4th edn (Stuttgart: Deutsche Bibelgesellschaft, 1993), 540. The editors choose 'ὑπερεντυγχάνει' rather than 'ὑπερεντυγχάνει ὑπὲρ ἡμῶν'.

intercedes (ἐντυγχάνει) for us' (Rom. 8.34). In his humanity, Christ mediates between God and the human race; thus Paul proclaims that 'there is one mediator between God and men, the man Christ Jesus' (1 Tim. 2.5). As human, Christ intercedes on behalf of his fellow humans; as God, Christ bestows divine gifts.

Augustine clarifies the nature of the Son's intercession. On the one hand, Augustine affirms that the 'Mediator in whom we can participate, and by this participation reach our felicity, is the uncreated Word of God, by whom all things were created'.[2] Jesus Christ is none other than the incarnate Word. On the other hand, however, Augustine remarks that Christ 'is not the Mediator in that he is the Word; for the Word, being pre-eminently immortal and blessed, is far removed from wretched mortals. He is the Mediator in that he is man.'[3] Building upon this teaching, Thomas Aquinas comments that as God, the Son cannot communicate to the Father and the Spirit anything that they are not already. The Son cannot change the Father's will, because the Father's will is none other than his own eternal will. Aquinas says of Christ: 'As God, He does not differ from the Father and the Holy Spirit in nature and power of dominion.'[4]

We should now be able to see why, for the early Christians, the suggestion that the Spirit 'intercedes' for us (Rom. 8.26-27) posed a problem regarding the doctrine of co-equal divinity of the Holy Spirit. If the Spirit is fully God, how can the Spirit (as God) 'intercede' with God? After all, the Spirit's will is the same as the Father's. The Spirit's role in divine action is not to intercede with God the Father; rather the Spirit is the divine benefactor, even though the benefaction is a trinitarian act in which the Persons act in accord with their personal property.[5] The three divine Persons cannot be differentiated by the possession of diverse wills and intellects, because this would make them into three gods.[6] Rather, divine intellect and will pertain to what is common to the Persons, to what belongs to their utterly simple divine nature.[7]

---

[2]Augustine, *The City of God*, trans. Henry Bettenson (New York: Penguin Books, 1984), 9.15 (361).
[3]Augustine, *The City of God*, 9.15 (361).
[4]Aquinas, *ST* III, q. 26, a. 2.
[5]For discussion see Gilles Emery, *The Trinitarian Theology of Saint Thomas Aquinas*, trans. Francesca Aran Murphy (Oxford: Oxford University Press, 2007).
[6]Thus we cannot suppose that the Father's infinite divine will and intellect – which is none other than the infinite knowing and loving common to the three divine Persons – reaches a finite limit where the other two Persons' wills and intellects supposedly begin.
[7]See Steven J. Duby, *Divine Simplicity: A Dogmatic Account* (London: Bloomsbury, 2016), 207–34; see also Gilles Emery, *Trinity in Aquinas*, trans. Matthew Levering, et al., 2nd edn (Naples: Sapientia Press, 2006).

To address in a brief compass the topic of the relationship of Christian prayer to the doctrine of the Holy Spirit, Romans 8.26-27 provides an intriguing point of entry. This is so even if one relies only upon modern commentaries, which generally do not mention the seeming problem posed for the Spirit's co-equal divinity. In N. T. Wright's theologically rich commentary on Romans, for example, he proposes that the Spirit's helping us 'in our weakness' (Rom. 8.26) involves ensuring that in our prayer, we raise our minds to the eschatological future: 'Those who cannot see that for which they eagerly hope need assistance to peer into the darkness ahead and to pray God's future into the present.'[8] Wright argues that the problem faced by Paul is quite simply that weak human beings (Christians), subject to disease and death, 'do not even know what to pray for, how it is that God will work through them to bring about the redemption of the world'.[9] The Spirit therefore intercedes – but not, as Christ does at the right hand of the Father, by interceding with the Father (Rom. 8.34). Rather, in Wright's view, the interceding of the Spirit has to do with impenetrating and elevating the Christian's (and the church's) very act of prayer.

Wright explains that 'the Spirit's own very self intercedes within the Christian precisely at the point where he or she, faced with the ruin and misery of the world, finds that there are no words left to express in God's presence the sense of futility (v.20) and the longing for redemption'.[10] In other words, the Spirit himself does not intercede with the Father; rather, the Spirit's intercession consists in aiding the church in its intercessory prayer for the final redemption of the world. The Spirit's intercession is efficacious because the Spirit 'is in intimate touch' with the Father, with the result that our 'inarticulate but Spirit-assisted groanings come before God as true prayer, true intercession'.[11] Wright sums up: 'What Paul is saying is that the Spirit, active within the innermost being of the Christian, is doing the very interceding the Christian longs to do, even though the only evidence that can be produced is inarticulate groanings.'[12] What might seem to be the Spirit's intercession with God the Father is in fact the Spirit's intercession within Christians to enable the prayer of Christians truly to be intercessory on behalf of a church and world deeply in need of the eschatological consummation.

---

[8]N. T. Wright, 'The Letter to the Romans: Introduction, Commentary, and Reflections', in *The New Interpreter's Bible*, ed. Leander E. Keck, vol. 10 (Nashville, TN: Abingdon Press, 2002), 393–770 (598).
[9]Wright, 'The Letter to the Romans', 599.
[10]Wright, 'The Letter to the Romans', 599.
[11]Wright, 'The Letter to the Romans', 599.
[12]Wright, 'The Letter to the Romans', 599.

Wright recognizes that this elevation of our interior prayer by the Spirit requires, for its efficacious power, that 'God, the living, transcendent God, is in intimate touch with the Spirit'.[13] Through the Spirit's intercession 'according to the will of God' (Rom. 8.27), Wright notes, 'God's own life, love, and energy are involved in the process' of Christian prayer.[14] He thereby suggests that the Spirit's co-equal divinity is implied here, though neither he nor Paul says this explicitly. Once the Spirit's intercession is taken to mean aiding our prayer (rather than interceding directly for us with the Father), of course, the problem of potential subordination of the Spirit is much reduced. As we will see, this is how patristic and medieval interpreters also address the problem, though, unlike Wright, they make explicit the issue of whether the Spirit is fully divine.

Ben Witherington III's commentary makes the problem more evident. Without saying that the Spirit is divine, he suggests that this is implied, and he also suggests that Paul is envisioning the Spirit as a distinct personal agent. Aware that the 'Spirit' is sometimes thought by scholars to be (even in the New Testament) simply another way of naming God's presence, rather than being a distinct agent, Witherington notes that 'in all of this discussion the Spirit is spoken of in profoundly personal terms' and that 'Paul does not see the Spirit as merely some sort of force or power or even just the presence of God'.[15] The implication is that Paul sees the Spirit as a personal divine agent, distinct from the Father and yet fully divine. Witherington concludes his treatment of Romans 8.27 by stating: 'The Spirit prays, which is a profoundly personal act, and we are told here the Spirit intercedes for the saints.'[16] The question, then, is whether the Spirit intercedes with the Father in the way

---

[13]Wright, 'The Letter to the Romans', 599.

[14]Wright, 'The Letter to the Romans', 600.

[15]Ben Witherington III and Darlene Hyatt, *Paul's Letter to the Romans: A Socio-Rhetorical Commentary* (Grand Rapids, MI: William B. Eerdmans, 2004), 226.

[16]Witherington and Hyatt, *Paul's Letter to the Romans*, 226. Witherington directs attention to James D. G. Dunn, 'Spirit Speech: Reflections on Romans 8:12-27', in *Romans and the People of God: Essays in Honor of Gordon D. Fee on the Occasion of His 65th Birthday*, ed. Sven K. Soderlund and N. T. Wright (Grand Rapids, MI: William B. Eerdmans, 1999), 82–91. Dunn emphasizes that Christians, in their weakness, experience 'confusion and frustration' because 'they just do not know what God's will is for them; they do not know what to want'. See Dunn, 'Spirit Speech', 89. On this view, the Spirit intercedes by working 'deep at the root of creation's futility and the believer's frustration. ... Because the heart is where the inner reality of the person is, the openness and opening of the heart to God is an effective communication with God and succeeds in keeping open the channels of grace between believers and God. At this point Spirit speech and heart language are one'. See Dunn, 'Spirit Speech', 89–90. See also James D. G. Dunn, *Did the First Christians Worship Jesus?: The New Testament Evidence* (Louisville, KY: Westminster John Knox Press, 2010), 116–17, 129 and John R. Levison, *The Spirit in First-Century Judaism* (Leiden: Brill, 1997).

that Christ, in his glorified humanity (as a human mediator), intercedes with the Father. If the Spirit prays and intercedes for the saints, is the Spirit requesting a favour that only God can grant, and thereby showing himself to be somehow less than God (the Father)? The problem is still clearer in James Dunn's discussion of the passage, since he thinks that Paul's appeal to the Spirit's intercession 'draws on the Jewish tradition of angelic intercessors', although Dunn also holds that 'the Spirit is ... with God' and that 'the Spirit working deep at the root of human inarticulateness ... is working with God, as part of and in accordance with God's will'.[17]

In what follows, I give particular attention to commentaries on Romans 8.26-27 from the crucial fourth century, in which Christian trinitarian doctrine was formulated. The contemporary trinitarian theologian Gilles Emery has rightly noted the perennial relevance of the '"Trinitarian Christian culture" that was formed at the end of antiquity, as much in the East as in the West. This culture retains, even today, a decisive importance in orienting our reflection.'[18] For this reason, my approach to the topic of prayer and the Holy Spirit devotes a large amount of attention to this patristic trinitarian inheritance. Emphasizing that this inheritance flowed from a lengthy exegetical debate about the meaning of scripture, the patristics scholar Robert Wilken highlights the 'fervent and prolonged debate that occupied the church's most gifted thinkers for two centuries'.[19]

My first section examines various patristic interpretations of Romans 8.26-27 in light of the question of whether the Holy Spirit is divine. My second section argues that something of a shift occurs through Augustine's trinitarian theology. Whereas the earlier Fathers whom I treat understand the Spirit as teaching the intellect so that we can pray more fruitfully, Augustine's focus on the Spirit as *love* leads later theologians to understand the Spirit especially (though not exclusively) as moving the will so that we can love God more fully in our prayer. By recourse to Thomas Aquinas as a representative later theologian, I try to indicate the impact that the Augustinian doctrine of the Holy Spirit has upon the way that we understand the Spirit's role in Christian prayer.

---

[17]Dunn, 'Spirit Speech', 89.

[18]Gilles Emery, *The Trinity: An Introduction to Catholic Doctrine on the Triune God*, trans. Matthew Levering (Washington, DC: Catholic University of America Press, 2011), xvi. For historical background, see Lewis Ayres, *Nicaea and Its Legacy: An Approach to Fourth-Century Trinitarian Theology* (Oxford: Oxford University Press, 2004), chapters 8–10.

[19]Robert Louis Wilken, *The Spirit of Early Christian Thought: Seeking the Face of God* (New Haven, CT: Yale University Press, 2003), 83. See also Khaled Anatolios, *Retrieving Nicaea: The Development and Meaning of Trinitarian Doctrine* (Grand Rapids, MI: Baker Academic, 2011).

Patristic Commentators on Romans 8.26-27

During the intense fourth-century conflict over whether the Holy Spirit should be understood to be a divine Person, those who denied the Holy Spirit's divinity challenged Basil of Caesarea sharply with respect to Romans 8.26-27. Basil recounts their argument in his *On the Holy Spirit*, written when the controversy over whether the Spirit was fully divine was raging in the Christian East, prior to the definition at the Council of Constantinople (381) of the Spirit's divinity. According to Basil, those who subordinated the Spirit (making the Spirit less than divine) argued that the fact that 'the Spirit intercedes' (Rom. 8.27) indicates the Spirit's inferiority. The point is that if one has to intercede for something, then one is not the benefactor. The benefactor is the one who has the power to grant the petition, whereas the petitioner lacks the power. Summarizing the case of those who deny the Spirit's divinity, Basil states that 'to the extent that the suppliant is inferior to the benefactor, the Spirit falls short of the dignity of God'.[20]

In response, Basil argues that 'intercedes' in Romans 8.26-27 means 'teaches and guides'.[21] He does not claim that the verb strictly has this meaning – as indeed modern dictionaries of New Testament Greek confirm it does not. But even if the verb does not strictly have this meaning, Basil suggests that in the context of the passage we can safely infer that the meaning has to do with the Spirit's interior teaching and guiding of the believer. Specifically, the Spirit meets us in our condition of not 'know[ing] how to pray as we ought', and the Spirit re-orients our prayer. We need the Spirit's teaching, says Basil, because sin has 'blinded' us and deprived us of the full ability 'to choose what profits us'.[22] Thus the Spirit 'intercedes' for us by enabling us to pray for what is truly best for us. The Spirit is thereby our divine 'benefactor' who shows the divine love for us.[23] This emphasis on the Spirit as guiding and teaching reflects Romans 8.14, 'for all who are led by the Spirit of God are sons of God' and Romans 8.16, 'it is the Spirit himself bearing witness with our spirit that we are children of God'.

For Basil, then, the Spirit is above all 'the Spirit of truth' (Jn 14.17; 15.26; 16.13). The Spirit of Christ testifies within us and thereby overcomes our ignorance and guides our prayer towards what is best for us, so that we set our 'minds on the things of the Spirit' and 'live according to the Spirit' (Rom. 8.5). Basil credits the Holy Spirit with being an 'illuminating power'

---

[20]Basil the Great, *On the Holy Spirit*, trans. Stephen Hildebrand (Crestwood, NY: St Vladimir's Seminary Press, 2011), 86.
[21]Basil the Great, *On the Holy Spirit*, 86.
[22]Basil the Great, *On the Holy Spirit*, 86.
[23]Basil the Great, *On the Holy Spirit*, 86.

that 'leads to knowledge' and that 'supplies to those who love to see the truth the power to see the image [the Son] in himself [i.e. in the Spirit]'.[24] The main emphasis in Basil is on the fact that 'creation receives the revelation of mysteries through the Spirit'.[25]

John Chrysostom argues along similar lines. He interprets Paul's phrase 'the Spirit helps us in our weakness' (Rom. 8.26) to mean that, as we 'groan inwardly as we wait for adoption as sons, the redemption of our bodies' (Rom. 8.23), we will be sustained by God's 'grace' (see Rom. 5.2). This is what Paul calls 'the new life of the Spirit' (Rom. 7.6). Having emphasized grace as the key help given to us by the Spirit in our weakness, Chrysostom finds in the next part of the sentence a specification of what grace does for us. Namely, grace helps us to 'pray as we ought' (Rom. 8.26). Chrysostom reasons that what Paul means by not knowing 'how to pray as we ought' is that we, in our fallen condition, choose to pray for the wrong things. In other words, we do not know what is truly good for us. What seems most desirable to us is what we pray to obtain, but the blessings that we seek are actually not the ones that God knows will benefit us. Chrysostom bemoans our inability to perceive our own good: 'So feeble is man, and such a nothing by himself.'[26] Even Paul prays for the removal of his 'thorn' (2 Cor. 12.8), until God teaches him that God wills to work through the 'thorn'.

However, Chrysostom gets rather tripped up by the claim that 'the Spirit himself intercedes for us with sighs too deep for words' (Rom. 8.26). He proposes that these 'sighs' or groanings (στεναγμοῖς ἀλαλήτοις) are gifts of the Spirit, gifts that he calls 'spirits'.[27] Discussing the statement 'the Spirit himself intercedes for us with sighs too deep for words', he remarks that 'this statement is not clear, owing to the cessation of many of the wonders which then used to take place' among the early Christians – such as prophecy, curing of the sick, miraculous raisings of the dead, and the sudden ability to speak different languages (see 1 Cor. 12.4-11).[28] Chrysostom supposes that in addition to these gifts of the Spirit, 'there was also a gift of prayer, which also was called a spirit, and he that had this prayed for all the people'.[29]

---

[24]Basil the Great, *On the Holy Spirit*, 82.

[25]Basil the Great, *On the Holy Spirit*, 94.

[26]John Chrysostom, *The Homilies of St John Chrysostom on the Epistle of St Paul the Apostle*, Homily XIV, in *Chrysostom: Homilies on the Acts of the Apostles and the Epistle to the Romans*, trans. J. B. Morris and W. H. Simcox, NPNF-1 11 (Peabody, MA: Hendrickson, 1995), 329–564 (447).

[27]John Chrysostom, *Homily* 14, 447.

[28]John Chrysostom, *Homily* 14, 447.

[29]John Chrysostom, *Homily* 14, 447.

For Chrysostom, then, Paul in Romans 8.26 is speaking not about the Holy Spirit but about the person within the community who received the Spirit's gift of prayer. He explains that this person 'was the appointed person to ask for in behalf of all, and the instructor of the rest. Spirit then is the name that he gives here to the grace of this character, and the soul that receives the grace, and intercedes to God, and groans.'[30] This interpretation avoids a subordinationist interpretation of the Spirit's work, but at the cost of a lack of plausibility.

Another interpretation of Romans 8.26 is offered by the theologian known to scholars as Ambrosiaster. The precise identity of 'Ambrosiaster' is unknown, although scholars have been able to determine he 'was writing during the pontificate of Damasus I (366-384)'.[31] Ambrosiaster, like Basil, first comments that 'our weakness' (Rom. 8.26) consists in the fact that we pray for the wrong things, due to our fallen condition. What the Holy Spirit does to help us is to elevate our mind, so that we can pray for the right things at the right time. Ambrosiaster specifies that the Holy Spirit overcomes our ignorance regarding the will of God for us. The Spirit helps us in our prayer by showing us what God wills. In this way, the Spirit enables us to accept suffering as part of God's plan for our salvation and therefore as a blessing for us. Here Ambrosiaster quotes 2 Corinthians 12.9, where Paul learns from God that he should not pray for the removal of his 'thorn'.

If the Holy Spirit helps us to avoid 'arrogant and stupid' prayer,[32] how does this fit with the Spirit's *interceding* for us? Ambrosiaster's answer is simple: 'Paul says that the Spirit intercedes for us not with human words but according to his own nature.'[33] Certainly, the Spirit 'speaks to God', but not in the anthropomorphic, let alone tritheistic, way that we might imagine.[34] Instead, the Spirit's speech is the same as the Father's speech; and their speech is the wisdom of God. Ambrosiaster explains, 'The Spirit given to us overflows with our prayers, in order to make up for our inadequacy and lack of foresight by his actions, and to ask God for the things which will be of benefit to us.'[35] Present in us, the Spirit ensures that our prayer serves its purpose. As God, fully possessed of the 'substance' of the Father,[36] the

---

[30]John Chrysostom, *Homily* 14, 447.

[31]Gerald L. Bray, 'Translator's Introduction', in Ambrosiaster, *Commentaries on Romans and 1–2 Corinthians*, trans. and ed. Gerald L. Bray (Downers Grove, IL: IVP Academic, 2009), xv–xxiii (xvi).

[32]Ambrosiaster, *Commentaries on Romans and 1–2 Corinthians*, 69.

[33]Ambrosiaster, *Commentaries on Romans and 1–2 Corinthians*, 69.

[34]Ambrosiaster, *Commentaries on Romans and 1–2 Corinthians*, 69.

[35]Ambrosiaster, *Commentaries on Romans and 1–2 Corinthians*, 69.

[36]Ambrosiaster, *Commentaries on Romans and 1–2 Corinthians*, 69.

indwelling Spirit knows what God's wise plan for us is, and the Spirit acts to ensure that we receive what truly benefits us.

For Ambrosiaster, then, the indwelling Spirit, by a kind of divine overflowing, enables the prayer of weak humans such as ourselves to be united to God's wisdom. Only if the Spirit is fully God could the Spirit's intercession be effective in surmounting our weakness and uniting us to the divine plan. The divine Spirit does not intercede with the Father through any kind of creaturely speech, but in a manner that depends upon his divine knowledge and that overcomes our ignorance. Ambrosiaster emphasizes that 'the Spirit intervenes on our behalf, because he knows that we are asking for things in ignorance, not because we deliberately want the opposite'.[37] We pray for temporal blessings, whereas the Spirit (as God) knows that the true blessing for us, in this fallen world, may even be to suffer. In Ambrosiaster's view, this is what Paul means by saying that 'the Spirit intercedes for the saints according to the will of God' (Rom. 8.27), and it also explains Paul's observation in the next verse that 'in everything God works for good with those who love him, who are called according to his purpose' (Rom. 8.28).

In sum, Basil, Chrysostom and Ambrosiaster emphasize our ignorance as the fundamental problem. They conceive of the Spirit as a teacher who helps us to avoid foolish prayer. They think that our tendency to pray for the wrong things – to 'set the mind on the flesh' (Rom. 8.6) – is rooted in a fallen condition that makes us ignorant of our true good and makes us unable to recognize how suffering can be a good for us. The Spirit's co-equal divinity gives him the power to reorient our minds so that we are able 'to pray as we ought', namely in accord with 'the will of God' (Rom. 8.27).

Further Developments: Augustine and Aquinas

By comparison to these earlier church Fathers, Augustine shifts the theology of the Holy Spirit from wisdom to love, from intellect to will. Building in part upon Hilary of Poitiers' connection of the Spirit with 'gift', but even more upon Paul's statement that 'the love of God has been poured into our hearts through the Holy Spirit who has been given to us' (Rom. 5.5)[38] and upon John's identification of the Son as the divine 'Word' (Jn 1.1), Augustine associates the Spirit with love, which is the greatest gift. Augustine's doctrine

---

[37]Ambrosiaster, *Commentaries on Romans and 1–2 Corinthians*, 70.
[38]For a succinct history of the translation of the Greek genitive here, see Robert Louis Wilken, '*Fides Caritate Formata*: Faith Formed by Love', *Nova et Vetera* 9, no. 4 (2011): 1089–100.

of the Holy Spirit draws out the fact that in the economy of salvation, the Spirit is identified as the one who 'proceeds from the Father' (Jn 15.26) and who is sent also by the Son (Jn 15.26; 16.7). The Spirit is the 'Spirit of God' and the 'Spirit of Christ' (Rom. 8.9), thereby signalling that the Spirit comes forth from the Father and the Son. The Spirit is also 'Christ's gift' (Eph. 4.7) and the Spirit is uniquely 'gift' in the Book of Acts (2.38; 8.20; 11.17).

Augustine concludes that when the Spirit is 'poured into our hearts', the 'love of God' – of God the Father and of God the Son – is poured into our hearts. The Spirit proceeds as this 'love' of the Father and the Son; and this love is 'given to us' and 'given' by the Father and the Son in the intra-trinitarian life as supreme 'gift'. Whereas the Son is begotten, the Spirit is given; and since the Spirit is given by the Father and Son as love, 'the Holy Spirit is a kind of inexpressible communion or fellowship of Father and Son'.[39]

Biblically speaking, then, Augustine holds that the Holy Spirit is the love of the Father and the Son, associated more properly with love than with truth – truth being more associated with the divine Word, as in Christ's statement that 'I am the way, and the truth, and the life' (Jn 14.6) and as in his later prayer to his Father, 'Sanctify them in the truth; your word is truth' (Jn 17.17). Augustine also approaches the doctrine of the Holy Spirit through the trinitarian analogy that he develops upon the basis of the Son's name 'Word' – the analogy of the mind, its knowledge and its love.[40] Augustine shows that 'in a wonderful way ... these three are inseparable from each other, and yet each one of them is substance, and all together they are one substance or being, while they are also posited with reference to one another'.[41] The Father, in knowing himself, begets his consubstantial Word; and when the Father knows himself in and through his Word, he loves himself, spirating his consubstantial Love (the Holy Spirit). Augustine knows that this analogy has many weaknesses, but he nonetheless considers it the best one for gaining a glimpse of how it is that the divine Trinity does not negate the divine unity and for how it is that the Son and Spirit come forth from the Father as truly distinct divine Persons. The Spirit is not another Word because he comes forth not as generated by the Father, but as spirated by the Father and Son. The Father gives all that he is to the Son, including a share in his spirative power.[42]

---

[39]Augustine, *The Trinity*, trans. Edmund Hill (Brooklyn, NY: New City Press, 1991), V.12; see also XV.27–39.
[40]See Augustine, *The Trinity*, IX.4.
[41]Augustine, *The Trinity*, IX.8.
[42]Augustine, *The Trinity*, XV.47.

Much more could be said about Augustine's doctrinal approach to the Spirit.[43] But my purpose here is simply to indicate the shift from connecting the Holy Spirit mainly with truth to connecting the Holy Spirit mainly with love.[44] Admittedly, Ambrosiaster also connects the Holy Spirit with the gift of love, though not with love as the personal property of the Spirit. Commenting on Romans 5.5, Ambrosiaster states that 'we have in us the pledge of God's love through the Holy Spirit, who has been given to us'.[45] Likewise, Chrysostom comments on Romans 5.5 by stating that the 'greatest gift' is the Holy Spirit and adding that the fact that God gives us this divine gift shows us the power of God's love for us – although Chrysostom does not identify the Spirit as hypostatic love.[46]

By contrast, in commenting on Romans 5.5, Thomas Aquinas agrees with Augustine and, indeed, extends Augustine's insight. Aquinas notes that the 'love of God' described in this verse can either be 'the love by which God loves us' or 'the love by which we love God'.[47] Either way, this love is connected distinctively with the Holy Spirit. Aquinas explains, 'For the Holy Spirit, who is the love of the Father and of the Son, to be given to us is our being brought to participate in the love who is the Holy Spirit, and by this participation we are made lovers of God.'[48] The Spirit is not given to us by coming forth from the Trinity, as though God were spatial. Rather, the gift of the Spirit to us involves a change in the creature: the human being gains a new participation in the distinct Person of the Holy Spirit, a participation that unites the human being not only to the Spirit but also, through the Spirit, to the Son and the Father.

---

[43]For further discussion, see Lewis Ayres, *Augustine and the Trinity* (Cambridge: Cambridge University Press, 2010), chapter 10; Rowan Williams, *On Augustine* (London: Bloomsbury, 2016), chapters 9 and 10. See also my *Engaging the Doctrine of the Holy Spirit: Love and Gift in the Trinity and in the Church* (Grand Rapids, MI: Baker Academic, 2016), chapter 1.

[44]I am not advancing an exhaustive claim, of course, since in this chapter I am focusing only on a few examples of early Christian writing about the Spirit. Notably, Gregory Palamas and more recent Eastern Orthodox theologians such as Dumitru Stăniloae adopt the Augustinian insight into the Spirit as love, without thereby concurring with the *filioque*. See Gregory Palamas, *The One Hundred and Fifty Chapters: A Critical Edition, Translation, and Study*, ed. Robert E. Sinkewicz (Toronto: Pontifical Institute of Medieval Studies, 1988); Dumitru Stăniloae, *The Experience of God*, trans. and ed. Ioan Ionita and Robert Barringer (Brookline, MA: Holy Cross Orthodox Press, 1994).

[45]Ambrosiaster, *Commentaries on Romans and 1-2 Corinthians*, 38.

[46]John Chrysostom, *Homily* IX, 398.

[47]Thomas Aquinas, *Commentary on the Letter of Saint Paul to the Romans*, trans. Fabian R. Larcher, ed. John Mortensen and Enrique Alarcón (Lander, WY: Aquinas Institute for the Study of Sacred Doctrine, 2012), 132 – hereafter: *Romans*.

[48]Aquinas, *Romans*, 132.

Interpreting Romans 8.26-27, Aquinas focuses primarily on the Holy Spirit's action upon the human will. He argues that the word translated as 'intercedes' – which in his Latin Vulgate version is *postulat* – does not mean to imply that the Holy Spirit himself intercedes for us. Rather, what Paul means here is that the Holy Spirit makes us pray to God in the right way. In other words, the Holy Spirit intercedes or asks God for a favour only in the sense that the Spirit causes us to ask God for the favour. Aquinas explains that 'the Holy Spirit makes us ask, inasmuch as he causes right desires in us, because to ask is to make desires known'.[49] Thus, Aquinas holds that the Spirit's intercession consists in his elevating our will or our desires, so that we love (and pray for) what we ought to love. Aquinas rules out any notion of a creaturely intercession, which always 'is the role of a lesser person' asking for a favour from a greater person.[50] Aquinas points out that if we insisted upon taking literally the Spirit's intercession, we would also have to take literally the image of the Spirit interceding with 'sighs' (Rom. 8.26) or groanings.

Instead, what is changed is our will, and this change makes all the difference for our prayer. God, who knows our hearts, knows whether or not our prayer is sincerely rooted in love and thus whether or not we are truly praying in accord with God's will. Aquinas quotes Psalm 7.9's reference to God trying 'the minds and hearts' of the righteous. When we are united with the Spirit – when the Spirit, who is love, has been given to us – we will pray with sighing and desire until we receive the good things that we most desire, namely the 'heavenly things' that God has promised us.[51] Indeed, these sighs will be 'too deep for words' because they concern the true blessings for which the just yearn in charity. These blessings consist in a deep sharing in the life of God in the fully established communion of saints. Aquinas states that the sighs are 'too deep for words' (or unspeakable) either because they concern divine mysteries or because these 'movements of the heart cannot be sufficiently described, inasmuch as they proceed from the Holy Spirit'.[52] Thus, when the Holy Spirit helps us to pray, he does so by moving our will to desire rightly, and this love is inexpressibly sweet because it flows forth in us by the indwelling activity of the Spirit. This is the delightfulness and sweetness of Christian prayer.

Yet, Aquinas also recognizes that the Spirit helps us to know 'what we should ask for in prayer and the manner in which we ought to ask'.[53] The

---

[49]Aquinas, *Romans*, 229.
[50]Aquinas, *Romans*, 229.
[51]Aquinas, *Romans*, 229.
[52]Aquinas, *Romans*, 229.
[53]Aquinas, *Romans*, 228.

Spirit's helping us 'in our weakness' includes the instruction of our minds. Not surprisingly, there is no opposition in Aquinas' view between the Spirit moving our hearts and the Spirit illuminating our minds; the Spirit does both in assisting us in prayer.

It might seem, however, that Christians do not need the Spirit's help in elevating our minds and hearts in prayer. In the Lord's Prayer (Mt. 6.9-15), Jesus Christ himself teaches us for what to pray. Furthermore, James cogently addresses the question of what we should do when we do not know for what to pray: 'If any of you lacks wisdom, let him ask God, who gives to all men generously and without reproaching, and it will be given him. But let him ask in faith, with no doubting' (Jas 1.5-6). In response to this seeming problem, Aquinas points out that even if we know generally what we should pray for (following the instructions of the Lord's Prayer), we do not know specifically what to pray for. For example, we might desire our 'daily bread' (Mt. 6.11) and therefore pray to be able to earn a good living, whereas God knows that if we become too rich it will be a spiritual snare for us.

Through the Spirit, then, God teaches us what we should pray for specifically, given our personality and circumstances. The same point applies to our prayer for freedom from suffering. As with Paul's 'thorn', God sometimes permits us to suffer for the sake of the spiritual good of humility, and the Spirit will teach us to pray in accord with the will of God in such matters. Likewise, we know that we are supposed to pray in a virtuous spirit, but in special cases we may need the Holy Spirit's help to show us which virtues should come into play. If we pray for retribution on behalf of innocent victims of oppression, for instance, the Spirit will ensure that we are praying from zeal for justice rather than from unrighteous anger.[54]

A final step can be taken when we recall that for Aquinas, the mission of the Holy Spirit in us means that we 'participate in the love who is the Holy Spirit, and by this participation we are made lovers of God'.[55] This participation signals the trinitarian nature of prayer. Our participation in the Holy Spirit gives us a share in the love of the Father and the Son. It draws us into the trinitarian communion, the trinitarian life. In this regard, rightly ordered prayer – in which our healed and elevated desires are directed to divine things as our ultimate end – is already a sharing in trinitarian wisdom and love. Most notably, this sharing describes the prayer of the whole church, that is, the liturgy. Paul's words in Romans 8 are directed not simply to individuals but to all Christians as 'children' and 'heirs' of God, and the

---

[54]Aquinas, *Romans*, 229.
[55]Aquinas, *Romans*, 132.

Spirit intercedes not simply for individuals but for the whole church: 'The Spirit intercedes for the saints according to the will of God' (Rom. 8.27).

Conclusion

We have seen that Aquinas' recognition that the Spirit heals and elevates our rational desires by moving our wills goes hand-in-hand with his equal awareness that the Spirit teaches our minds what to pray for and when. Furthermore, Aquinas understands the activity of the Spirit in the believer as united synergistically with our will so that the Spirit works by working through our free will.[56] The Spirit's intercession so that we can 'pray as we ought' ensures that in *our* prayers the Spirit himself speaks.

Contemporary trinitarian theologies of Christian prayer recognize this same synergistic point. For example, Hans Urs von Balthasar comments that in prayer it makes a great difference when 'I have the conviction that my inadequate attempt to understand is supported by the wisdom of the Holy Spirit dwelling within me, that my acts of worship, petition and thanksgiving are borne along and remodeled by the Spirit's infinite and eternal acts, in that ineffable union by which all human doing and being has been lifted up'.[57] It is this synergy that Balthasar considers to be the meaning of Romans 8.26-27. He quotes these verses as evidence that 'human inadequacy and ignorance are outbalanced by divine omnipotence and omniscience'.[58] Note that he presents the Spirit here as aiding both our will and our intellect, so that we can 'pray as we ought'. Balthasar goes on to say that 'the Spirit breaks forth out of the very core of the believer's spiritual life, showing him the way, stirring him to action, thinking, willing and praying with him'.[59] Balthasar also characterizes this Spirit-filled prayer as already a participation in the trinitarian life. He contends that 'through the Spirit of grace, we are drawn into the mystery of divine sonship. That is, we are actually brought to participate, by grace, in the begetting of the Son from the Father.'[60]

---

[56]Thus, the Christian's graced actions are condignly meritorious because – although fully the Christian's own actions – they are primarily grounded in the Holy Spirit's work. See Aquinas, *ST* I–II, q. 114, a. 3. For discussion, see Joseph P. Wawrykow, *God's Grace and Human Action: 'Merit' in the Theology of Thomas Aquinas* (Notre Dame, IN: University of Notre Dame Press, 1995) and my *Jesus and the Demise of Death: Resurrection, Afterlife, and the Fate of the Christian* (Waco, TX: Baylor University Press, 2012), chapter 5.

[57]Hans Urs von Balthasar, *Prayer*, trans. Graham Harrison (San Francisco, CA: Ignatius Press, 1986), 76.

[58]Balthasar, *Prayer*, 76.

[59]Balthasar, *Prayer*, 77.

[60]Balthasar, *Prayer*, 70.

The greatest twentieth-century theologian of the Holy Spirit, Yves Congar, comments on Romans 8.26 by highlighting the synergy between God and the human being, in which God plays the pre-eminent role. He states that what Romans 8.26 means is that the Holy Spirit 'prays in us'.[61] But he hastens to add, 'This is not a case of God replacing us ... There is a communication of dynamism or of an active faculty and we continue to act.'[62] He goes on to argue that 'prayer is essentially communion with God and with his will'.[63] Along Augustinian lines, he holds that what the Holy Spirit does is to enable us to desire God and to desire God's will, because indeed the Holy Spirit is the hypostatic love or 'desire' of God.[64] Again reflecting upon Romans 8.26 – though without citing it directly – Congar states that prayer, through the Spirit, makes of our soul 'a place where God encounters himself and where there is consequently an inexpressible relationship between the divine Persons'.[65] Christian prayer is a participation in the trinitarian communion. It is so because the Spirit transforms and elevates our desire (our will) and our knowledge of what is good for us. Yet, the Spirit does this in a manner that goes beyond the limits of our conscious activity. Congar speaks of 'the desire or longing of God himself interceding for the saints at a deeper level than their own expressed or expressible prayer'.[66] Paul certainly indicates in Romans 8.26-27 that this is the case.

It is evident, therefore, that the concerns and insights of the Fathers have a significant place in contemporary theology of the Holy Spirit and Christian prayer. I hope to have shown that Augustine's shift towards the will and towards love in his theology of the Spirit had an impact on later theologies of Christian prayer. But more than this, I hope to have given some indication of the biblical expectations that believers rightly have regarding the Spirit's transforming of our prayer so as to unite it, despite our weakness, with God's salvific will.

---

[61]Yves Congar, *I Believe in the Holy Spirit*, trans. David Smith (New York: Crossroad, 1997), vol. 1, 32.
[62]Congar, *I Believe in the Holy Spirit*, vol. 1, 32.
[63]Congar, *I Believe in the Holy Spirit*, vol. 2, 116.
[64]See Congar, *I Believe in the Holy Spirit*, vol. 2, 116; citing Jean-Claude Sagne, 'L'Esprit-Saint ou le désir de Dieu', *Concilium* 99 (1974): 85–95.
[65]Congar, *I Believe in the Holy Spirit*, vol. 2, 117.
[66]Congar, *I Believe in the Holy Spirit*, vol. 2, 117.

CHAPTER TWELVE

The Hiddenness of Providence: Praying to a God beyond Speech

SUSANNAH TICCIATI

I begin this chapter by putting before you two quotations, which together, in their apparent contradiction, set up the problem I attempt to address in what follows.

> Then Moses stretched his hand over the sea, and the LORD drove the sea back by a strong east wind all night and made the sea dry land, and the waters were divided.
>
> (Exod. 14.21, ESV)

> Let us suppose, however, that God does not make any particular difference (in the sense that there is no event or occurrence for which the best explanation would be: God did it).[1]

If there is any event that, within a doctrine of providence, is to be ascribed to God, then the parting of the red sea is surely such an event. As pivotal in the liberation of the people of Israel, it is a quintessential example of God's saving 'provision' for that people, just as earlier God 'provided' Abraham a

---

[1]Nicholas Lash, *Easter in Ordinary: Reflections on Human Experience and Knowledge of God* (Notre Dame, IN: University of Notre Dame Press, 1988), 224–5.

ram to offer in place of Isaac.[2] But if Nicholas Lash is correct to suppose that God 'does not make any particular difference' – that no particular event, as distinguished from any other, can be ascribed to God rather than to another – then a serious challenge is posed to any doctrine of providence worthy of the name. If nothing in particular can be singled out as a providential act of God, then it would seem that the doctrine of providence has nothing to distinguish it from the doctrine of creation. And this, in turn, would seem to undermine the practice of Christian prayer as one in which the Christian both prays for God to act in specific ways and thanks God for so acting.

Conversely, biblical speech as exemplified by Exodus 14.21 poses a serious challenge to Lash's theologically (and philosophically) derived position. The dilemma before us is the familiar one of 'the God of the Bible' versus 'the God of the philosophers'. In this chapter, I will plot a course through the dilemma – with particular reference to providence and prayer – informed by the Aquinas-inspired apophaticism of Herbert McCabe, and in keeping with Lash's dictum.

An apophatic theology is a 'theology done in the acknowledgment of the failure of all language with respect to God'.[3] Such a failure results, in McCabe's terms, from the fact that God, as the creator of the whole universe, is not included in that universe as an item within it.[4] This insight is traditionally worked out in terms of the classical doctrines of divine simpleness, immutability and impassibility, and has implications for the whole of Christian doctrine. While to those who pit the God of the Bible against the God of the philosophers these 'classical attributes' imply God's indifference to and aloofness from 'his' creatures, for thoroughgoing apophaticists such as McCabe or Lash, they define divine transcendence in a way that sets it in complementary rather than oppositional relation with divine immanence – indeed as entailing God's inconceivably intimate presence to all creatures. Among other things, it is just such a non-oppositional account of divine transcendence that makes possible a coherent account of the incarnation.[5]

---

[2]Genesis 22.8 and Genesis 22.14. The Hebrew is *ra'ah*, literally 'to see'. In *The Cambridge Dictionary of Christian Theology*, ed. Ian McFarland, et al. (Cambridge: Cambridge University Press, 2011), David Fergusson suggests that the meaning of providence comes from both senses of the Latin *providere*, 'to foresee' and 'to provide' (entry under 'Providence').

[3]Susannah Ticciati, *A New Apophaticism: Augustine and the Redemption of Signs* (Leiden: Brill, 2013), 1.

[4]Herbert McCabe, 'God and Creation', *New Blackfriars* 95, no. 1052 (2013): 385–95 (388). See also Herbert McCabe, *God Matters* (London: Continuum, 2005), 58. I am indebted to my former PhD student, Franco Manni, for introduction to the scope and depth of McCabe's thought. See Franco Manni, *Herbert McCabe: Recollecting a Fragmented Legacy* (Eugene, OR: Wipf and Stock, 2020), for his published thesis.

[5]See McCabe, *God Matters*, part 2, 'Incarnation', 53–74.

Framed in these terms, the account of providence and prayer I offer in what follows eschews the opposition of the dilemma. This sets it apart, on the one hand, from 'open theistic' accounts that embrace the God of the Bible in critique of a tradition that has remained, or so it is argued, too closely yoked to ancient philosophical accounts of the divine.[6] But it equally sets it apart, on the other hand, from the Calvinism to which open theistic accounts are opposed,[7] according to which God is sovereignly in control of every last detail of creation, directing it in accordance with the mysterious but definite divine purpose.[8] From an apophatic perspective, this sovereignly managerial God is no less anthropomorphic than a God who is dynamically affected by God's creatures.

My account is also – although more subtly – to be distinguished from accounts that take up the trajectory of Karl Barth and Hans Frei.[9] These appeal to a figural imagination which (however fragmentarily) traces patterns within history in which God's purposes (again, however dimly) can be discerned. I argue for the hiddenness of providence in a stricter sense, concluding that

---

[6]Clark H. Pinnock, et al., *The Openness of God: A Biblical Challenge to the Traditional Understanding of God* (Downers Grove, IL: InterVarsity Press, 1994). An important source for open theism is the work of Abraham Joshua Heschel, and especially his *The Prophets* (New York: Harper and Row, 1962). Heschel's thought is modulated, however, by being transposed from a Jewish to a Christian context. It is beyond the scope of this chapter, which argues within a Christian framework, to engage with Heschel in his own right. For an approach to divine naming that invites complementary engagement with Jewish and Christian perspectives, see Janet Martin Soskice, 'The Gift of the Name: Moses and the Burning Bush', in *Silence and the Work: Negative Theology and Incarnation*, ed. Oliver Davies and Denys Turner (Cambridge: Cambridge University Press, 2002), 61–75. This essay, also invoking Augustine, arrives at a similar conclusion to my own regarding the character of divine transcendence and the role of prayer.

[7]Terrence Tiessen, in *Providence and Prayer: How Does God Work in the World?* (Downers Grove, IL: InterVarsity Press, 2000), places Calvinism at one end of a spectrum near the other end of which he places open theism. He argues for an intermediate view. For a proponent of the Calvinist position in this context, see Paul Helm, *The Providence of God* (Downers Grove, IL: InterVarsity Press, 1994).

[8]Whether such a rendition is true to Calvin is another question. For a balanced account of Calvin's doctrine of providence in a wider Reformed context, see David Fergusson, 'Providence in the Reformed Tradition: From Calvin to Barth', in *Van God gesproken: over religieuze taal en relationele theologie*, ed. Theodoor Adriaan Boer (Zoetermeer: Boekencentrum Academic, 2011), 233–45. However, Molinist or Arminian accounts that modify a strict Calvinist position in order to find more room for creaturely freedom presuppose the opposition that an apophatic theology denies. See Kathryn Tanner, *God and Creation in Christian Theology: Tyranny or Empowerment?* (Oxford: Blackwell, 1988), and more recently, David Bentley Hart, 'Providence and Causality: On Divine Innocence', in *The Providence of God: Deus Habet Consilium*, ed. Philip G. Ziegler and Francesca Murphy (London: T&T Clark, 2009), 34–56.

[9]For example, Mike Higton, *Christ, Providence and History: Hans W. Frei's Public Theology* (London: T&T Clark, 2004) and Vernon White, *Purpose and Providence: Taking Soundings in Western Thought, Literature and History* (London: T&T Clark, 2015).

the purpose of ascribing something to God's providence is less to trace in it the patterning of a divinely ordered history, and more to ask how, in its inextricable connectedness with God's other creatures, it can be used for their common good – or, in other words, with a view to its end in God.

I will begin with a brief elaboration of McCabe's apophaticism, from which I will derive two rules for a doctrine of providence that will inform the chapter throughout. For McCabe, to recall, God, as creator of the world, is not an item within it, ranged alongside (other) creatures. Unlike created causes, 'God's creative and sustaining activity does not make the world different from what it is – how could it? It makes the world what it is.'[10] It follows, McCabe argues, that 'God cannot *interfere* with the universe, not because he has not the power but because, so to speak, he has too much; to interfere you have to be an alternative to, or alongside, what you are interfering with. If God is the cause of everything, there is nothing that he is alongside'.[11] McCabe also gives positive expression to the non-oppositional character of God's agency: 'Every action in the world is an action of God; not because it is not an action of a creature but because it is by God's action that the creature is *itself* and has its *own* activity.'[12]

McCabe's grammar of the relationship between creator and creation yields two rules for speech about providence. First, providential divine agency is not restricted to certain special moments by contrast with others: it does not abide by a 'this not that' grammar. Negatively, the logic of providence is *non-contrastive*; positively, providence is *ubiquitous*. Second, where providential divine agency is operative it does not supplant the creature. Negatively, its logic is *non-competitive*; positively, because what one sees is the creature and its activity, providence is *hidden*.

The aim of the chapter is to articulate a grammar of appropriate ascription to God that both abides by these apophatic rules and does justice to scripture's robust speech about divine action. To that end I draw on two contrasting but complementary works of Augustine of Hippo, each of which in its own way is a significant lesson in providence: the *City of God* and

---

[10]Herbert McCabe, *Faith Within Reason*, ed. Brian Davies (London: Continuum, 2007), 75.

[11]McCabe, *God Matters*, 6.

[12]McCabe, *God Matters*, 7. Tanner develops a similar account of the relationship between divine and creaturely agency, according to which divine agency, being 'beyond both identity and opposition' with creaturely agency, is by the same token 'immediate and universally extensive' in creation. See Tanner, *God and Creation*, 47. To the same end, Webster argues that the theological task for a doctrine of providence is to apply belief in providence precisely to cases in which we naturally shy away from doing so, to reconcile 'providence and horrors'. The implication is that providence must apply everywhere or not at all. See John Webster, 'On the Theology of Providence', in *The Providence of God: Deus Habet Consilium* ed. Philip G. Ziegler and Francesca Murphy (London: T&T Clark, 2009), 158–75 (158).

the *Confessions*. The *City of God*'s account is austere and ascetical, while the *Confessions* could not be more rich and effusive in its appeal to divine providence. I hypothesize that the difference can be accounted for above all by the fact that the *Confessions*, as a whole and in every detail, is framed as an utterance to God in prayer. I argue, more specifically, that prayer as a form of speech wards off contrastive and competitive conclusions about divine agency, and thereby gives licence for the kind of profusion and liberality of appeal to divine providence exhibited in the *Confessions*. Prayer thus models a grammar of ascription to God from which other forms of speech about God may take their cue. My account of prayer is normative rather than straightforwardly empirical, and it will be counterintuitive for those who argue from the apparently give-and-take character of (especially petitionary) prayer to a give-and-take understanding of God's providence.[13]

The chapter is structured as follows. I begin with the *City of God*, which situates and fleshes out the two rules of providential ascription eschatologically. The chapter's pivot is a normative analysis of the grammar of prayer: it is here that the dilemma of the God of the Bible versus the God of the philosophers finds a logical response. Finally, I turn to the *Confessions* to trace the grammar of prayer in action, culminating in an analysis of illustrative passages from the *Confessions* that exhibit robust and unabashed appeal to divine providence, showing how these at the same time conform to the austere framework established in the *City of God*.

The *City of God*

The *City of God* is, on the one hand, an epic testimony to the omnipresent providence of God, from which no event however great or small is exempted. With the sack of Rome centrally before his eyes, Augustine understands *everything* to be a display of divine providence. In response to those who ask of the righteous when they suffer, 'Where is thy God?', Augustine answers: 'Our God is present everywhere, wholly everywhere, nowhere confined. ... When He subjects me to adversity, this is either to test my merits or chastise my sins'.[14] On the other hand, divine providence is by definition hidden. This is evidenced not only by Augustine's assertions

---

[13]As, typically, do open theists. For example, John Sanders, *The God Who Risks: A Theology of Providence* (Downers Grove, IL: InterVarsity Press, 1998), 268–74. An alternative approach to prayer, which transcends the terms of the debate as framed by Sanders, is offered by McCabe in 'Prayer', *God Matters*, 215–25, in which he argues that it is *God* who prays, and that we only pray insofar as by the grace of Christ we share in the sonship of God.

[14]*civ.* 1.29 (for the Latin, see LCL 411-17); *The City of God against the Pagans*, trans. and ed. R. W. Dyson (Cambridge: Cambridge University Press, 1988).

to that effect,[15] but perhaps more powerfully by his analytic use of 'hidden' (*occulta*) to qualify 'providence'.[16] In sum, 'All these things are ruled [*regit*] and governed [*gubernat*] as it pleases the one true God. Though the causes be hidden [*occultis causis*], are they unjust?'[17]

The *City of God*'s register is different from the grammatical and logical register of our rules derived from McCabe. In its elaboration of the ubiquity and hiddenness of providence it is theologically freighted in a way that those rules are not. It is thus able (in a way that the rules alone are not) to deliver a framework for thinking positively about the purpose of ascription to God in prayer. Nevertheless, I proceed according to the assumption that its 'ubiquity' and 'hiddenness', while doing more theological work, also minimally correspond to the 'non-contrastiveness' and 'non-competitiveness' of our two rules, in the way outlined above. The purpose of the present section is to display that theological work without losing sight of its underlying grammar.

Framing the simultaneous ubiquity and hiddenness of providence is the *City of God*'s orientation towards the eschaton. In Book 19, towards the culmination of the work, Augustine argues against those philosophers who hold that true happiness can be had in this life that the Supreme Good, from which alone issues happiness, is eternal life. He concludes that happiness amidst the evils of this age can only be had 'in the hope of the world to come'. It is not yet possessed, but must be awaited 'with patience'.[18] All that he has said about providence in the earlier parts of the work is shaped by this insight: what God 'provides for' is not earthly happiness but eternal happiness. To ascribe something to providence is thus to refer it beyond this life to its contribution to eternal happiness.

One has to wait until the final two chapters of the final book of the *City of God* for Augustine's description of the eternal felicity that lies in store for the city of God. The Supreme Good – the 'reward of virtue' and 'the end of our desires' – is God himself. Moreover, this Good will be 'common to all [*omnibus communis*]', as God becomes 'all in all' (1 Cor. 15.28).[19] God is the common, eschatological end of all things. To ascribe to providence, we infer more precisely, is to refer something beyond itself to its communal end in God. If it is the commonness of this end that underlies the ubiquity of providence (as God provides all things with a share in the common good), it is its eschatological character that underlies the hiddenness of providence in the time of earthly pilgrimage.

---

[15]For example, *civ.* 1.28, 4.33.
[16]For example, *civ.* 2.23, 7.35.
[17]*civ.* 5.21.
[18]*civ.* 19.4.
[19]*civ.* 22.30.

Augustine's dazzling description of eschatological manifestation throws that hiddenness into sharp relief. Having spent some time discussing the possibility and the mechanics of the resurrection of the body, Augustine comes to the question of the vision the saints will have of God in the world to come, 'vision' being used both metaphorically and literally.[20] He reaches the following remarkable surmise: 'It may well be … that in the world to come, we shall see the bodily forms of the new heaven and the new earth in such a way as to perceive God with total clarity and distinctness, everywhere present and governing [*gubernantem*] all things, both material and spiritual.' And he continues a little later: 'In the world to come, wherever we shall look with the spiritual eyes of our bodies, we shall then, by means of our bodies, behold the incorporeal God ruling [*regentem*] all things.'[21] This clarity and transparency of vision is contrasted with our present mode of apprehension, 'darkly and in part, as in a glass', by faith not by sight, and in which 'the invisible things of God' must be inferred from what is made.[22] The directness of our vision of God's rule at the eschaton is to be contrasted with the indirectness of our knowledge of God's providential rule in this passing age.[23] In short, divine providence may be ubiquitous, but it cannot be seen, only inferred in faith.[24]

But what exactly is it that is now hidden and will become manifest? The short answer is God, but insofar as God will be 'all in all', our vision of God will include all creatures as they have their place in this common end. Speaking ostensibly of the individual body, but with tantalizing resonance with the corporate body of Christ, Augustine says that 'those harmonies which are now hidden, will then be hidden no longer', as 'all the members and inward parts … will join together in praising God'.[25] What is hidden in

---

[20]*civ.* 22.29.

[21]*civ.* 22.29. Note that the same verbs are used of God here as when Augustine is speaking about divine providence in *civ.* 5.21.

[22]*civ.* 22.29, alluding to Romans 1.10 and 1 Corinthians 13.12.

[23]For a contemporary account of eschatological life redolent of Augustine's, see Katherine Sonderegger, 'Towards a Doctrine of Resurrection', in *Eternal God, Eternal Life: Theological Investigations into the Concept of Immortality*, ed. Philip G. Ziegler (London: T&T Clark, 2016), 115–30. See also McCabe, *God Matters*, 116–29, who contrasts the unlimited communicativity of the resurrection body with the relative opacity of present earthly bodiliness.

[24]Karl Barth establishes right at the outset of his doctrine of providence that belief in providence is a matter of faith (and not sight). This insight is twinned with an emphasis on the hiddenness of providence. God's lordship, Barth claims, 'takes place in the world, but is concealed in world-occurrence as such, and therefore cannot be perceived or read off from this.' 'The history of God's glory … is a hidden history.' He thus cautions against 'the equation of belief in providence and its confession with a philosophy of history'. See Barth, *CD* III/3, 19-21.

[25]*civ.* 22.30.

the present age and manifest at the eschaton, I suggest, is the connectedness of all things in God.[26] To ascribe something to providence, therefore, is at once to refer it to its end in God, and to place it in its connectedness with all things for their mutual good in God.

But it follows that the point of ascription to providence has to do less with a detached discernment of the divine purpose and more with the transformation of the creature doing the ascribing: to refer something to its end in God is to enter into right relation with that thing, which is at the same time to place it in right relation with its fellow creatures. In short, it is to relate to other creatures for the sake of God as their common good. In order to characterize this creaturely stance more fully, Augustine draws on the *uti/frui* (use/enjoyment) distinction he first fully developed in his *De doctrina christiana*.[27] As he recapitulates it pithily in the *City of God*: 'For the good make use of this world in order to enjoy God; but the evil, by contrast, wish to make use of God in order to enjoy this world.'[28] What is significant in respect of God's providence is not what is received – whether good or bad – but how it is used. Indeed, Augustine does not tire of underlining the indiscriminacy of God's distribution of good and evil (often with an accompanying citation of Mt. 5.45).[29] This rules out any attempt to descry an earthly calculus – in which fortune and adversity are equated with reward and punishment, or in which adversity is reduced to its function of warding off pride. While Augustine allows for all these possibilities, his more basic appeal is to the hiddenness of providence.[30] God 'acts in accordance with an order of things and times which is hidden from us, but entirely known to Him'.[31] He concludes:

> Of the highest importance here is the use made of those things which are deemed fortunate and those which are called adverse. ... [U]nder the

---

[26]See Sonderegger, 'Resurrection', 125, who offers a vision of eschatological life as one in which the interrelatedness of all creation becomes luminously transparent.

[27]Augustine, *doctr. chr.* I (CCSL 32). See Oliver O'Donovan, '*Usus* and *Fruitio* in Augustine, *De Doctrina Christiana* I', *Journal of Theological Studies* 33, no. 2 (1982), 361–97, for an account of the history of this pairing in Augustine's writings. O'Donovan argues that it drops away after *De doctrina christiana* ('*Usus* and *Fruitio* in Augustine', 397), and more strongly that Augustine's conclusion in *doctr. chr.* I.22.20 – that the neighbour is to be used rather than enjoyed – must be regarded as a mistake which Augustine does not repeat (O'Donovan, '*Usus* and *Fruitio* in Augustine', 390). I depart from O'Donovan in the present chapter, emphasizing the continuity between Augustine's usage in *De doctrina christiana* and in the *City of God*.

[28]*civ.* 15.7.

[29]For example, *civ.* 1.8, 4.2.

[30]For example, *civ.* 1.28, where he begins by appealing to Romans 11.33, before going on to speculate about the correction of latent pride.

[31]*civ.* 4.33.

same affliction, the wicked hate and blaspheme God while the good pray and praise Him. What is important, then, is not what is suffered, but by whom[.][32]

Let us sum up the emergent picture. Divine providence is the presently hidden directedness of all things to their common end in God, which will become manifest at the eschaton as the connectedness of all things in God. We are as far as could be from an account of providence that singles out specific worldly occurrences (by contrast with others) as interventions of God (in usurpation of creatures). Negatively: hiddenness entails non-competition, since God operates hiddenly in what is made without supplanting it; and ubiquity requires a non-contrastive grammar, since God is operative everywhere. Positively: to ascribe to providence is to refer something beyond this life to the eternal felicity of the city of God, which is to refer something beyond itself to its end in God; and this is to place something in its connectedness with all things, which is to *use* it for the common good.

In this light, let us return to an appeal to providence in the context of the Exodus story with which the chapter opened. To ascribe to God the closing of the red sea upon the Egyptians for the sake of Israel's salvation (Exod. 14.26-30) fails, in the terms of the *City of God*, to be a responsible appeal to providence if the meaning of the event for other creatures is neglected: it would be to use God for a private (in this case Israelite) rather than common good. In other words, one must simultaneously ask how that closing was a 'good' for the Egyptians, too. To ask the question (even if an answer cannot be provided) is to seek the connectedness of the Israelites and Egyptians in God. It is to treat the red sea's closing as something to be 'used' for the common good.

The Grammar of Prayer

The *City of God* has given us an austere framework for thinking about providence that guards against two dangers attending ascription to God. In the first place, it tells us that divine providence is ubiquitous, warding off the otherwise natural grammatical conclusion that when we ascribe *this* to God we are implying that *that* is not to be ascribed to God. While a 'this not that', or contrastive, grammar predominates in our ordinary (creaturely) speech, it is not appropriate (so the *City of God* teaches us, in keeping with the apophaticists above) in the context of ascription to God.

---

[32]*civ.* 1.8.

Take the ordinary speech example, uttered in the context of a building project, 'It was Mary who fixed the door handle to the door'. Depending on the more precise context, we are likely to assume that it was someone else who, for example, fixed the door on its hinges, or who made the door handle in the first place. We might be surprised to be told that it was also Mary who made the door, and even more so to discover that Mary built the house, let alone all the houses in the village, etc. Without further qualification, the initial claim will be understood to be singling out the affixing of the door handle from other acts in order to ascribe it (in distinction from those other acts) to Mary. Were there nothing left with which to contrast Mary's work, ascription to Mary would lose its meaning.

While we learn from the *City of God* that the 'this not that' grammar of creaturely ascription is not operative in the case of God, we are not told how, linguistically, such a grammar is to be circumvented in divine ascription. I will argue in the present section that prayer models for us a grammar of ascription to God that successfully blocks the 'not that' implication of the creaturely grammar.

In the second place, the *City of God* tells us that divine providence is hidden, warding off the otherwise natural grammatical conclusion that when we ascribe something to *God* we do so at the expense of some creaturely agent (to whom it might otherwise have been ascribed), the implication being that God did it *rather than* someone or something else. God's agency is hidden in the sense that God is not an agent alongside creatures that might be manipulated for a particular end. God's agency, in other words, does not usurp creaturely agency, thus evacuating the creation of its creaturely integrity. It is hidden, rather, within creaturely causes, upholding them in their manifold connectedness.

A competitive logic prevails in creaturely ascription. Saying that Mary affixed the door handle implies that Paul did not (the contrast, this time, being between agents rather than actions). The implication of non-ascription to someone or something else must therefore be blocked in the practice of divine ascription. Again, I will argue that prayer models a practice of ascription to God that undermines a competitive logic. In this section I will consider the grammar of prayer in general, normatively understood, before turning to the *Confessions* to flesh out the argument by way of illustrative examples of divine ascription in the context of prayer.

In prayer actions are ascribed to God in the context, for example, of thanks, praise, lament, complaint and (by anticipation) petition. When, to take our initial biblical example, I thank God for driving back the red sea, I do not imply that Moses had nothing to do with it, nor that God was not also, say, responsible for the pursuit of the Egyptians that had in the first place made necessary the parting of the red sea. Why not?

Let us start with the circumvention of the 'this not that' grammar. My grateful singling out of the parting of the red sea for ascription to God does not gain its meaning from the contrast between the parting as ascribed to God and, say, the Egyptian pursuit as something not ascribed to God (but in response to which God had intervened).[33] Rather, it is singled out as something I am grateful for. Ascription to God is mediated in this prayer by the expression of my relationship (gratitude) to the matter in question (the parting). I may not feel grateful for everything God has done (e.g. the pursuit). Thus, the prayer is not evacuated of meaning when it is acknowledged that God is responsible for everything else as well, since the contrast that lends it specificity is between my attitude here and my attitude there (not between divine agency here and not there). Moreover, insofar as prayer refers something (the parting) to its end in God, and thus seeks (if only imperfectly) to place it in the context of the common good, it cannot thank God for that something without inviting the question of how it is related, in the context of the common good, to other things (e.g. the Egyptian pursuit and subsequent drowning) for which I am not presently thankful. My gratitude for the Israelite rescue must not ultimately be at the expense of my indifference to the Egyptians' demise – even if I may legitimately start there.[34]

But what about competitive agency? To find out how prayer circumvents that, too, I turn to an example treated in Augustine's late, anti-Semipelagian work, *On the Gift of Perseverance*. The so-called Semipelagians deny that perseverance in faith is a gift of God in order to safeguard human free choice at least in this delimited sphere of the Christian life. Augustine, by contrast, interpreting the sixth petition of the Lord's Prayer as a prayer for perseverance, argues on that basis that perseverance must be God's to give.[35] He does not conclude from that, however, that it is not also in the power of

---

[33]Scripture (in a different way from prayer) circumvents this implication by the sheer promiscuity of its ascription to God. Specifically, God's responsibility for the Egyptian pursuit is made clear in Exodus 1.4 and 8.

[34]More strongly, McCabe argues that we *must* start there: 'We must pray for what we *want*, and not for what we just think we *ought* to want'. Only if we come to God as we are, without pretence, can our desires be changed in the course of prayer: 'If a child is treated as though she were already an adult, she will never become an adult.' See Herbert McCabe, *God, Christ and Us*, ed. Brian Davies (London: Continuum, 2005), 105. See also Denys Turner, *God, Mystery and Mystification* (Notre Dame, IN: University of Notre Dame Press, 2019), chapter 2, where he argues that the point of prayer is to place our desires honestly before God so that, in having them interpreted to us, we discover what we really want.

[35]Augustine, *persev.* 23.63 (PL 45).

human beings to enact. Rather, embodying a non-competitive grammar, the prayer for perseverance presupposes that perseverance is 'at once something that God gives and something that I do'.[36] What God grants me is precisely my agency in perseverance. The non-competitive logic is not one that can be conceived, but it is one that can be put to work in prayer.[37] Moreover, insofar as my prayer for perseverance situates my agency in perseverance in the context of divine agency, it invites me to view that agency in its orientation to the common good. Such petitionary prayer should thus subject to critique any action for which I ask to be empowered that clearly stands at odds with the good of others.

In sum, the grammar of prayer is both *non-contrastive*, warding off a 'this not that' grammar, and *non-competitive*, not pitting divine agency against creaturely agency, but enacting their asymmetrical coinherence. Insofar as prayer is oriented to the common good, moreover, it will accomplish two complementary things. First, it will invite me to search for the connectedness of 'this and that' in the common good, thus, for example, expanding my gratitude to areas of life which I could previously only regret. Second, it will invite me to place my own agency in the context of the common good, and thus to seek not only to be empowered but to be empowered for the good of others.

The *Confessions*

I turn, now, to Augustine's *Confessions* to look at this grammar of prayer in action. Unlike the *City of God*, the *Confessions* is liberal and profuse in its appeal to divine providence, and is so in connection with the minutest of events in Augustine's life. To be sure, the *City of God* underlined the ubiquity of providence; but its emphasis on its hiddenness would seem *prima facie* to be in contrast with the manifest character of God's dealings with Augustine as narrated in the *Confessions*. I hope to show that this contrast is a superficial one, and indeed that the *Confessions* precisely takes up the invitation implicitly issued by the *City of God*'s doctrine of providence – to use each creature in relation to its end in God. It does so in the mode of prayer. As we shall see, its prayerful use is both non-contrastive in its ascription of everything to God, and non-competitive in its acknowledgement and even celebration of the creaturely agency in and through which God acts.

---

[36]Ticciati, *A New Apophaticism*, 96.

[37]That scripture presupposes a non-competitive logic is implied by the fact that it has no problem, for example, ascribing the parting of the red sea to both God *and* Moses (Exod. 14.21). It thus circumvents the need to choose between them.

Confessions begins with a soliloquy, addressed to God, on the possibility and character of speech addressed to God, culminating in the petition 'let me speak [*sine me loqui*] in the presence of your mercy'.[38] It is, more specifically, a discourse on prayer uttered in prayer. Augustine's questions shift from being about the mechanics of prayer in respect of the divine nature – 'What place is there in me where my God may enter in, where that same God who made heaven and earth may enter into me?'[39] – to being about the transformation that is wrought by prayer in Augustine – 'Who will allow me to find rest in you? Who will allow me to let you enter my heart and intoxicate it so that I forget my troubles and embrace my one and only good, namely yourself?'[40] More briefly, Augustine moves from the question 'so what are you, my God [*quis es ergo, deus meus*]?'[41] to 'what are you to me [*quid mihi es*]?'[42] And Augustine's answer is that the invocation of God requires an enlargement of Augustine's soul: 'The house of my soul is too narrow for you to enter it: it needs you to widen it. It is in ruins: rebuild it. It contains things that will displease your eyes: I admit it, I know it. But who will cleanse it?'[43] We might not be far off if we understood the *Confessions* itself as this enlargement – the rebuilding of Augustine's house that is at once its cleansing.

On the basis of this initial framing, and before turning to some illustrative passages, I hypothesize that the *Confessions* is the ascription of Augustine's life – in all its details and including all with which it comes into contact – to God in prayer. It circumvents a 'this not that' grammar insofar as it singles out those details, not in respect of their contrast with other details not ascribed to God, but in respect of the attitude which Augustine takes up towards them (of confession, of thanksgiving, of repentance, etc.). It circumvents a competitive logic in the fact that Augustine's confessions are precisely the narration of his own life as ascribed to God. Furthermore, God's entering Augustine by way of this prayerful ascription is precisely Augustine's enlargement rather than his displacement.

I turn now to some specific passages to put this hypothesis to the test. There are some moments in the *Confessions* where it is tempting to read Augustine according to a 'this not that' grammar.[44] I will look at two such moments, at the beginning and end of Book VIII respectively, first rehearsing

---

[38]*conf*. I.6.7 (for the Latin and for the English translation, see LCL 26-27).
[39]*conf*. I.2.2.
[40]*conf*. I.5.5.
[41]*conf*. I.5.5.
[42]*conf*. I.5.5.
[43]*conf*. I.6.6.
[44]While the first set of examples highlights the challenge of a 'this not that' grammar, we will see that it brings a competitive logic in its wake.

a contrastive reading, and then offering an alternative, and in my judgement more persuasive, reading. At the beginning of Book VIII Augustine finds himself at an important crossroads, already being intellectually converted to the God of the Christian scriptures, but prevaricating about the commitment of his whole self to God, being still bound by the sinful desires and habits of his former life – a state he describes in terms of two conflicting wills.[45] The sequence of events that make up the narrative of the book begins, amidst his prevarication, with a specific event: 'Then you put an idea in my mind, and it seemed good in my sight: to make my way to Simplicianus.'[46] It is easy to read this, without sufficient attention to the fuller context, as a moment of divine intervention. On his own Augustine is stuck. God must step in to set off a train of events that leads to his full conversion – the integration and healing of his two wills.

Moreover, for this end to be accomplished, God must intervene again – and this time decisively. To be sure, God has (on this reading) not been idle in between, and Augustine alerts us to moments when his steering hand has been operative. But the crucial moment comes at that famous scene in the garden in which Augustine hears the chanting of children from next door, 'pick it up and read it'. 'Understanding it as nothing short of divine providence [*nihil aliud interpretans divinitus*]', Augustine returns to his Bible, and opening it, understands the first passage he alights upon to be addressed by God directly to him.[47]

On this reading, divine providence is occasional (rather than ubiquitous) and extrinsic (rather than hiddenly mediated by creaturely agency). In other words, it has a contrastive *and* competitive logic. The extrinsic character of providence is accentuated by Augustine's remark that the children's chant is not one that he otherwise recognizes. In other words, its providentiality appears to be connected with its extraordinary character – God's interruption of the normal flow of creaturely events. By analogy, the idea God puts in his mind at the beginning of the book must be understood as an alien intrusion into the natural course of his thoughts.

This is an enticing reading, but it is one that must be resisted, for reasons that will unfold in the course of my analysis. I will begin in Book VIII, before turning to passages elsewhere in the *Confessions* that point in another direction. Book VIII opens in a series of jussives that frame the whole book as a confession of thanks to God: 'You have torn away my bonds: let me offer to you a sacrifice of thanksgiving. How you tore them away, I shall

---

[45]*conf*. VIII.5.10.
[46]*conf*. VIII.1.1.
[47]*conf*. VIII.12.29.

now recount, and let everyone who worships you say, when they hear these things, "Blessed is the Lord"'.[48] Everything that Augustine goes on to narrate, in other words, is to be understood as the effect of divine agency, and thus as the cause for praise and thanksgiving. In that context, Augustine's ascription to God of specific events within that narrative is to be understood as the making explicit of what is always the case – a punctuation of the narrative with reminders of its confessional frame. To say 'then you put an idea in my mind' is simply to say 'then I had an idea', but with the acknowledgement built in that everything that Augustine is narrating is due to God.

Later in the book, in the course of puzzling over the apparent complementarity of joy and hardship, Augustine asks:

> Or is this their proper sphere, and this only have you allotted them, since from the heights of heaven down to the depths of the earth, from the beginning to the end of the ages, from the angels to the smallest worm, from the first action to the last, you set all kinds of good things, and all your just works, each in its proper place and activate each one at its proper time? Alas for me! How high you are in the heights, and how unfathomable in the depths! You are nowhere absent, yet we struggle to return to you.[49]

This is a clear expression of the ubiquity he espouses in the *City of God*, but with interrogative and vocative inflection. As second-order discourse it tells us not to read Augustine's divine ascription within the narrative contrastively, instead inviting us to read Book VIII as Augustine's attempt to 'return' the events of his life as narrated there to God (who is nowhere absent). As confession, it is itself an attempt of return, one that sets Augustine's life in the context of the whole of creation, thereby acknowledging the limits of Augustine's insight even into his own life – whose connectedness with the rest of God's creation he can only begin to plumb. Nevertheless, the return his narrative enacts can be understood, in keeping with the opening of Book I, as his enlargement and cleansing, as he retrospectively discovers God at work in the recesses of his sinful life.

In this light, the children's chant during the scene in the garden cannot be read in contrast with all the other events narrated as a special act of divine providence. What, then, are we to make of Augustine's apparent singling it out as such? Unlike the earlier moment of ascription I have examined, it should be noted that this later one is not made by Augustine as narrator,

---

[48]*conf.* VIII.1.1.
[49]*conf.* VIII.2.8; translation slightly modified.

but by Augustine as a character in the narrative. What is special about the event, we can infer, is that Augustine attributed it to God at the time, when God's providential agency was otherwise hidden to him. Retrospectively, Augustine can attribute everything to that agency, and thus read that event as part of a larger, God-given narrative. His attribution at the time says something about the contours of his own journey rather than about God's involvement. It may indeed have been that moment that began to unlock Augustine's ability to see God at work throughout – to reread his whole life as ascribed to God. That the chant is not one that he recognized may have helped him 'see through' the creaturely agency to God, but a later discovery that the chant was in fact a well-known one would not undermine the significance of the event in Augustine's life, nor its ascription to God.

The main target of the foregoing rereading has been a contrastive logic, although a competitive logic also crept in. I now turn to some passages in the *Confessions* in which a competitive logic is what is primarily at stake. In Book VI Augustine narrates an incident in which Alypius, one of Augustine's former students who in Carthage had become ensnared by love of the circus games, happened to be in attendance at one of Augustine's classes in rhetoric, at which Augustine's use of an analogy with the games was understood by Alypius as a reproof directed specifically at him. Augustine, not having had Alypius in mind at all, praises God in the following words:

> It was not I who had reproached him, though, but you: you use [*utens*] everyone, whether we know it or not, in the order that you alone comprehend, and that order is just. You fashioned my heart and tongue into burning coals by which you kindled his diseased mind into a good hope, and cured it.[50]

A competitive reading, 'not I, but you', is immediately undermined by the way in which Augustine continues. God's providence is precisely God's 'use' of creatures for the common good, which itself provides for good *creaturely* use – in this case, Alypius' reception of Augustine's words as rebuke. In other words, Augustine's competitive language must be understood, rather, as setting Augustine's action in its divine context, which is not to undermine it as Augustine's action, but to see its wider ramifications for the common good. The significance of the fact that Augustine did not himself intend rebuke is interpreted by him as another layer of divine 'use': 'To ensure that his amendment should be rightly attributed to you, you brought it about

---

[50]*conf.* VI.7.12.

through me but without my being aware of it.'[51] God provides not only for mere events, but also for our interpretation of them. Indeed, this is what the *City of God* was, on one level, all about: good creaturely use *is* proper ascription of earthly things to God.

The next example comes from Book VII, amidst his wrestlings over the nature of the divine substance and the origin of evil. The narrower context is his narration of how he was freed from his stubborn belief in astrology.

> For it was you, only you – for who else calls us back from all our deadly error except the Life itself that does not know how to die, and the Wisdom that enlightens our needy minds while needing no light itself, and which arranges the affairs of the world even down to the changing of leaves on the trees – you who dealt with my stubbornness.[52]

Here, divine ubiquity ('the affairs of the world, etc.') appears to be conjoined with a competitive logic ('only you'). However, what Augustine goes on to narrate is an entirely creaturely narrative about Augustine's exchange with a friend Firminius, who, having come to consult Augustine on business matters, ended up sharing a story with Augustine about two simultaneous births with very different outcomes, a story that succeeded in entirely dispelling Augustine's belief in the powers of astrological prediction.

'Only you' cannot, therefore, be understood to rule out creaturely agency; indeed, it seems precisely to invite Augustine's detailed exploration of it. What, then, is the force of 'only you'? In the *City of God*, Augustine contrasts divine providence with chance on the one hand and fate on the other, going on to identify fate with the determination of creaturely destiny by the position of the stars.[53] To say that things happen by chance is (he explains) to say that they have no ultimate rational order, which would undermine belief in the coherence or connectedness of all creation in God. To say that they are determined by fate (the stars) would be to posit a creaturely calculus that exhausts the meaning of creaturely events, preventing them from signifying their eschatological end in God. In other words, it posits a reductive connectedness that forestalls the search for their deeper connectedness in God. By contrast with attribution to chance or fate, attribution to God ('only you') frees one for a proper attentiveness to creaturely contingency in its manifold and (presently) hidden connectedness. It is no coincidence that Augustine is, in the *Confessions*, discussing how

---

[51]*conf.* VI.7.12.
[52]*conf.* VII.6.8.
[53]*civ.* 5.1.

God overcame his belief in astrology. 'Only you' gains particular purchase in this context: Augustine cannot put his change of mind down to the stars as a cause that would competitively rule out the significance of any other story he might tell. 'Only you', by contrast, is fundamentally non-competitive.

This reading is confirmed by other moments in the *Confessions* in which Augustine's ascription to God is immediately followed by detailed narration of the attending creaturely circumstances. For example, after the introductory sentence, 'You guided me into a conviction that I should set out for Rome', he continues: 'I shall not neglect to confess to you why I was persuaded to do this, for in these actions both your deepest secrets and your most immanent mercy toward us demand that we reflect on them and proclaim them.'[54] What he proclaims is precisely the creaturely factors, internal and external, that led to his decision. At another point, Augustine confesses, 'so too you brought me to an awareness of my own wretchedness', and goes on to narrate his encounter with a beggar whose relative carefree-ness brought Augustine to a realization of how embroiled in cares and far from joy he really was.[55]

What all the above examples cumulatively show is how Augustine's ascription to God is the context for his attentive exploration of the internal and external connections of his creaturely life. On the one hand, his narrative is a patchwork of his formative relationships and encounters with other people – Simplicianus, Firminius, Alypius, the children overheard in the garden and so on. And these are shot through with stories of yet further people whose lives give cause for reflection.[56] On the other hand, these intersections with the lives of other people are complemented by Augustine's intensive scrutiny of his interior life. Both are laid bare before God. If the narration of the *Confessions* is Augustine's enlargement of the house of his soul, as I surmised above, then that enlargement would seem to consist in his making manifest before God the multiple connections (interior and exterior) in which his life subsists – which is precisely to tell his life as an integrated story.[57] Augustine's life is a unity in its ultimate directedness towards eschatological rest in God, a unity he can begin to see in retrospect after a series of conversions to that end. In the language of the *City of God*, Augustine *uses* the creaturely events of his life for their end in God – which is precisely to find their connectedness in the common good.

---

[54] *conf.* V.8.14.

[55] *conf.* VI.5.8.

[56] Simplicianus tells the story of Victorinus' conversion, Firminius of his father's astrological investigations, Ponticianus of the life of Anthony of Egypt (*conf.* VIII.6.14), etc.

[57] His ability to do so might be understood to be a consequence of the integration of his two conflicting wills, as powerfully dramatized in the garden scene. See *conf.* VIII.8.9-VIII.12.30.

But this immediately gives rise to a challenge. The common good is that in which *all* things are connected. Augustine's story is only a partial 'whole': the connections he explores do not exhaust all those he might have explored, nor those that might have come to light from a vantage point later in time. More bluntly, his life as told in the *Confessions* is an unfinished one, and it will remain unfinished until its eschatological consummation (when its connectedness with all the creatures of God's creation will be made transparent). If, on the one hand, to make manifest before God is to tell an integrated narrative, then, on the other hand, it is to resist any premature closure that replaces the common good with a partial whole.

How does the *Confessions* resist such closure? Again, we may appeal to its character as prayer. We have already seen how prayer resists both a contrastive and a competitive logic, and specifically how it does so in the *Confessions*. Its resistance of what we might call a reductive logic follows. Insofar as the God to whom a prayer has implicitly ascribed 'this' is also responsible for 'that', the pray-er cannot stop at a prayer in respect of 'this', but is invited to seek the connection between 'this' and 'that', so that 'that' can also become the subject of prayer. More specifically, to pray for 'this' means to begin, even if only incipiently and falteringly, to place 'this' in its relation to God as the common good, and therefore in its manifold connectedness with all things.

As a prayer the *Confessions* casts Augustine's life as a 'this' that seeks to be brought into connection with manifold 'that's. Negatively, its non-reductive logic, or grammar of non-closure, is signalled by Augustine's appeal at key junctures to the unfathomability of God's providence, indicating that he has only begun to plumb the connections into which his life enters.[58] This side of the eschaton, the connections we discover are inferred rather than seen directly; they will tend, moreover, to occlude other connections left uninferred, thus making partial wholes (such as Augustine's life) that can only be provisional in relation to the unity of the common good. Positively, the *Confessions*' grammar of non-closure is powerfully evident at the end of Book VIII, where Augustine narrates how he and Alypius go to tell Augustine's mother, Monica, what has happened: 'And she began to bless you, who have power to act beyond what we ask and conceive, because she could see that you had granted her so much more for me than she regularly asked for with her pitiful crying and groaning.'[59] Not only is Augustine's life cast here as the fulfilment of the prayers of another, but it is so in ways beyond expectation. Monica's prayers for the 'partial whole' of Augustine's

---

[58]For example, *conf.* V.7.13, VI.7.12, VIII.2.8.
[59]*conf.* VIII.12.30.

conversion are exceeded in a good beyond what she had desired – a good not only for Augustine but for the many others into connection with whom his life would come.

It would take another essay to explore how this grammar of non-closure is amplified in Books X–XIII. Suffice it to say that the contexts in which we are to hear his confessions are successively broken open. In Book X we are brought from the apparent closure of his past life into the openness of his present, and are invited to become 'fellow travelers'[60] who pray for him,[61] and together with him reflect on the character of the memory that has both made possible and been made manifest in the foregoing narrative. Through the musings on time in Book XI Augustine finally takes us to the creation in Books XII and XIII. This is the ultimate and final context for his own autobiographical narrative – one that holds it open to the many connections in which it already hiddenly subsists.

Conclusion

In this chapter I have sought a grammar of ascription to divine providence that abides by McCabe's apophatic logic, while being able to accommodate scripture's robust speech about God. I have done so by drawing on what we might call the apophaticism of the *City of God* and the robust God-talk of the *Confessions*, mediated by the grammar of prayer. On the one hand, the former gave theological, and specifically eschatological, embodiment to McCabe's logic, with the result that it became possible, beyond the negative proscriptions of the apophatic grammatical rules, to give a positive account of the purpose of ascription to divine providence. To ascribe something to providence, I concluded, is to seek its connectedness with other things in God; or more briefly, to use it for the common good. On the other hand, the *Confessions* took up the robustness of scriptural speech in prayer. Prayer was shown, minimally, to operate with an apophatic grammar, and maximally, to enact the use of the object of prayer for the common good. The *Confessions* was understood as Augustine's use of his life for the common good – his search for its connectedness with other things, and ultimately all creation, in God. The ultimate (eschatological) horizon of the *Confessions*, and implicitly of all prayer, drew attention to a third, non-reductive logic, to be unfolded from the first two (non-contrastive and non-competitive) logics specifically in the context of this passing age of divine hiddenness – in which

---

[60]*conf.* X.4.6.
[61]*conf.* X.3.5.

the connectedness of all things is obscured as well as illuminated by the partial connections we infer in prayer.

It remains to say something specifically about scriptural speech about God. I suggest that the grammar of prayer embeds the logic by which we are also to read scriptural speech: *lex orandi, lex credendi.* The first two logics (non-contrastive and non-competitive) rule out a closed account of the purpose of scriptural ascription to God: its purpose is not to single out 'this' act as divine by contrast with 'that' one, nor to affirm a divine cause at the expense of a creaturely cause. They thus make way, open-endedly, for a deeper exploration of the significance of that which has been ascribed to God in its wider context – that context ultimately being the whole of creation. The third (non-reductive) logic forestalls the conclusion that in any one reading we have got to the bottom of its significance, inviting us to read and reread the scriptural verses in which it figures in the new contexts in which we find ourselves – in which new (previously obscured) connections may come to light.

We have learnt from Augustine, furthermore, to frame such open-ended exploration of something ascribed to providence in terms of its use for the common good. To bring that something into connection either with the subject matter of other scriptural verses or with events, people and situations beyond scripture (including within our own lives) is, on this account, less about discerning the patterns of a divinely ordered history, and more about being transformed within the midst of a history to which one is contributing, now in this way and now in that way, by prayerful search for, and invocation of, the common good.[62]

---

[62]The difference from the figural imagination articulated by Barth and Frei, and others in their wake, may be more a matter of emphasis than of principle. The difference is important nevertheless. On my account, ethical transformation is the overarching purpose of ascription to providence – which is as such necessarily self-involving and indexed to local context, and need not yield any glimpse of broader patterns in history.

CHAPTER THIRTEEN

Eschatology and Prayer

GERALD O'COLLINS

The first proven occurrence of 'eschatology' in English theological literature came in an 1845 work by an American biblical scholar, George Bush. In line with its previous usage in German (*Eschatologie*) and Latin (*eschatologia*), Bush referred the term to 'the doctrine of the last things' (the *eschata*).[1]

Through the nineteenth into the twentieth century, eschatology often continued to be reduced to a minor subject taught in seminaries or university departments towards the end of a theological course. It involved studying death, individual judgement, purgatory, the last (universal) judgement, hell, heaven and, occasionally, questions concerning the resurrection of the body. Many theologians of different schools forgot that eschatology, far from being a mere branch of their discipline, denotes the future orientation and destiny of our entire present existence as Christians and human beings. They needed to share the conviction of Jürgen Moltmann: 'From first to last, and not merely in the epilogue, Christianity is eschatology.'[2]

---

[1]George Bush, *Anastasis* (London: Wiley and Putnam, 1845), ix; see v, 275, 300, 348, 365.

[2]Jürgen Moltmann, *The Theology of Hope: On the Ground and Implications of a Christian Eschatology*, trans. James W. Leitch (London: SCM Press, 1967), 16. Some have heard in Moltmann's statement an echo of Karl Barth's *The Epistle to the Romans*, trans. Edwin C. Hoskyns (London: Oxford University Press, 1933), 314 (trans. corrected): 'Christianity which is not utterly and entirely eschatological has utterly and entirely nothing to do with Christ.' In the same book Barth remarked ironically on the 'short and perfectly harmless chapter' entitled 'eschatology', which puts us comfortably to sleep at the conclusion of Christian dogmatics. See Barth, *Romans*, 500. The early Barth interpreted the *Parousia* as a timeless symbol for an immediate relationship with God that is always possible. But the later Barth, like Moltmann, recovered the futurity of eschatology and its political resonances – a recovery that underpinned Barth's support for the 'Confessing Church' in its struggle against the National Socialism of Adolf Hitler. On Barth's eschatology, see John C. McDowell, *Hope in Barth's Eschatology: Interrogations and Transformations beyond Tragedy* (Aldershot: Ashgate, 2000).

In constructing his now-classic study of divine promise grounding human hope, Moltmann appealed to Gerhard von Rad's summary of the Old Testament as a 'book of ever-increasing expectation' and to Ernst Käsemann's identification of apocalyptic hope 'as the mother of Christian theology'.[3] We should add that this ever-increasing, eschatological expectation was also disclosed in collective and individual prayer, while the apocalyptic hope was supremely embodied in the prayerful expectation of the final coming of the crucified and risen Jesus (1 Cor. 11.26, 16.22; Rev. 22.20). Moltmann's landmark study of eschatology would have been strengthened if Rad and Käsemann had encouraged him to appeal to *the eschatological expectation expressed in hopeful prayer*.

The views of Melchior Cano on the principal places or sources for Christian theology, the *loci theologici*, exercised an unfortunate influence among Roman Catholics and beyond – not least by failing to incorporate the theme of liturgy and, for that matter, sacred music. His scheme did not make room for the principle of Prosper of Aquitaine: '*lex orandi, lex credendi* (the law of praying is the law of believing)', or, in its fuller form, '*legem credendi lex statuat supplicandi* (let the law of supplication establish the law of believing)'. Prosper knew that prayer, especially liturgical prayer, should shape and inform the interpretation of Christian faith, as Eastern theology has always recognized. Western theology often followed Cano by omitting liturgy and, in general, prayer as a key place or source for reflection and discussion.

From first to last, and especially at liturgical services for the dead, Christian prayer is eschatological. The eschatological faith and hope that prompt such future-directed prayer shine through the Lord's Prayer, found in a shorter version (Lk. 11.2-4) and a longer version (Mt. 6.9-13). The central, eschatological petition in both versions is the same: 'Your kingdom come.' This amounts to praying: 'come and rule as king'. John P. Meier describes the meaning of 'the whole first part of the Lord's Prayer' in Matthew's version: 'Father, reveal yourself in all your power and glory [= hallowed by your name] by coming to rule as king [= your kingdom come].'[4]

The 'only prayer he [Jesus] ever taught his disciples' supports the conclusion 'that Jesus' message was focused on a future coming of God to rule as king, a time when he would manifest himself in all his transcendent

---

[3]Gerhard von Rad, *Old Testament Theology*, trans. David M. G. Stalker, vol. 2 (Edinburgh: Oliver and Boyd, 1965), 319, and Ernst Käsemann, *New Testament Questions of Today*, trans. W. J. Montague (London: SCM Press, 1969), 83–137.

[4]John P. Meier, *A Marginal Jew: Rethinking the Historical Jesus*, vol. 2 (New York: Doubleday, 1994), 299.

glory and power'.[5] This eschatological hope, expressed in what remains the central prayer for all Christians, is rooted in the Jewish people's memory and prayer life.[6]

David Crump, summing up the biblical witness, has written: 'Eschatology is the grammar of prayer. Prayer is the language of eschatology.'[7] Nowadays eschatology is frequently understood in a christological perspective, but rarely from a prayerful perspective. Calvin Roetzel, to name only one example, describes biblical eschatology, but manages to do so without mentioning prayer.[8] Let us examine the support which Crump's claim about eschatological prayer receives from the Old Testament and then from the New Testament.

The Prayerful Eschatology of Jews

The Jewish, eschatological liturgy that looked forward to a future good was *par excellence* the festival of the Passover and the associated festival of the Unleavened Bread (Exod. 12.1-28; 13.1-16). Those prayerful feasts memorialized the events of the deliverance from Egypt, the divine covenant with the people (Exod. 19.5-6; 24.7-8) and the entrance into the promised land. Their religious narratives constituted a collective prayer of continuing hope founded on the memory of God's saving promises and actions. The prayer of memory was the prayer of hope, and vice versa.[9]

---

[5]Meier, *A Marginal Jew*, vol. 2, 300. On the Lord's Prayer, see Hans Klein, 'Das Vaterunser: Seine Geschichte und sein Verständnis bei Jesus und im fruhen Christentum', in *Das Gebet im Neuen Testament*, ed. Hans Klein, et al. (Tübingen: Mohr Siebeck, 2009), 77–114.

[6]See Gregory Glazov, 'Eschatology', in *Encyclopedia of the Bible and Its Reception*, vol. 7 (Berlin: De Gruyter, 2013), 1154–98; Jerry L. Walls, ed., *The Oxford Handbook of Eschatology* (Oxford: Oxford University Press, 2008); Alexa F. Wilkes, 'Hope', in *Encyclopedia of the Bible and Its Reception*, vol. 12 (Berlin: De Gruyter, 2016), 372–83; Pierluigi Piovanelli, 'Eschatology', in *The New Interpreter's Dictionary of the Bible*, vol. 2, ed. Katharine Doob Sakenfeld (Nashville, TN: Abingdon Press, 2007), 290–308.

[7]David Crump, *Knocking on Heaven's Door: New Testament Theology of Petitionary Prayer* (Grand Rapids, MI: Baker Academic, 2006), 299.

[8]Calvin J. Roetzel, 'Eschatology', in *The Oxford Encyclopedia of the Bible and Theology*, ed. Samuel E. Balentine, vol. 1 (New York: Oxford University Press, 2015), 262–73. A work by E. P. Sanders of over 850 pages, *Paul: The Apostle's Life, Letters, and Thought* (Minneapolis, MN: Fortress Press, 2015), so far from ever linking eschatology and prayer, contains nothing about prayer; it does not feature in the index of subjects.

[9]See Baruch M. Bokser, 'Unleavened Bread and Passover, Feasts of', in *Anchor Bible Dictionary*, ed. David Noel Freedman, vol. 6 (New York: Doubleday, 1992), 755–65; on the feasts of the Passover, Unleavened Bread, and Weeks, see Roland De Vaux, *Ancient Israel: Its Life and Institutions*, trans. John McHugh (London: Darton, Longman and Todd, 1965), 484–95.

Christian liturgies were to take over songs in which Moses and Miriam led the people in praising God for liberating them from slavery and giving them a new life of freedom (Exod. 15.1-21). The Easter Vigil would include a classic hymn of thanks and hope with which the Israelites remembered their deliverance from Egypt: 'I will sing to the Lord, glorious his triumph! Horse and rider he has thrown into the sea. ... The Lord is a warrior! The Lord is his name. The chariots of Pharaoh he hurled into the sea. ... Your right hand, Lord, glorious in power, your right hand, Lord, has shattered the enemy' (Exod. 15.1, 3-4, 6).

Paul led the way in understanding the festivals of the Passover and the Unleavened Bread as Christians putting aside corruption ('the old yeast' of leavened bread) and celebrating prayerfully the Passover feast of the crucified and risen Christ: 'Clean out the old yeast so that you may be a new batch, as you really are unleavened. For Christ, our paschal lamb, has been sacrificed' (1 Cor. 5.7). Paul pressed on to emphasize the 'new covenant' in the Lord's blood (which recalls the blood with which the people were pledged to God [Exod. 24.8]), and to describe the liturgy of the Eucharist in a future-directed way – as 'proclaiming the death of the Lord until he comes' (1 Cor. 11.25).

An ancient creed, which recalls the family of Abraham and Sarah ('a wandering Aramean was my ancestor; he went down to Egypt and lived there as an alien') and their liberation by God (Deut. 26.5-11), shaped Jewish worship for the festival of the weeks (Deut. 16.9-12). The people remembered liturgically the divine bounty, which brought them into 'a land flowing with milk and honey', and presented at a central sanctuary the first fruits of the harvest. A festive meal eaten at the sanctuary supported the hope that God's bounty would continue. Paul was to name the risen Jesus as 'the first fruits of those who had died' (1 Cor. 15.20, 23), whose resurrection inaugurated the final resurrection of the dead to which Christians looked forward in hope. By evoking the festival of the weeks, the apostle gave his eschatological hope a liturgical setting formed by a confession of God's bountiful gifts being remembered as a pledge of the blessings to come.

An eschatological hope for the final coming of the Lord, drawn from a common memory and rooted firmly in liturgical prayer, strikingly coloured the eucharistic tradition of the Lord's Supper transmitted by Paul. The bread saying was completed by the instruction 'do this in remembrance of me'. The cup saying, 'this cup is the new covenant in my blood', was likewise followed by the instruction: 'Do this, as often as you drink it, in remembrance of me' (1 Cor. 11.24). The liturgical 'remembrance of me' supported hope for the final coming of the Lord (1 Cor. 11.26) and the end of human history. A collective, eschatological hope was founded in a liturgically enacted memory.

Around one-third of the Psalms are psalms of lamentation, prayers which face the future and are regularly characterized by a lively hope that God will act to end present crises and suffering (e.g. Ps. 7.6). The most famous of these psalms of lamentation is undoubtedly Psalm 22, which opens with the poignant cry of abandonment: 'My God, my God, why have you abandoned me?' (Ps. 22.1). The New Testament was to make this psalm one of key texts for understanding and interpreting the passion and death of Jesus. At the end, the psalmist looks to 'all the families of the nations' who will turn to the Lord and worship before him (Ps. 22.27). 'Future generations' will be told about the Lord and serve him (Ps. 22.30). The divine rule will also extend to the dead (Ps. 22.29). Thus the psalm that begins with the cry of a suffering individual ends with an eschatological vision of God's universal rule. The repeated 'my God' (Ps. 22.1, 2, 10) rather than 'our God' supports a very personal note in the first section of the psalm. But the psalm concludes with a vision of the universal divine rule. Over and over again the Psalms of lament prayerfully express human hope in the faithful God who will provide deliverance and a blessed future.[10]

The New Testament cited 129 psalms out of the 150 that constitute the complete Psalter. The psalms were repeatedly used in prayer to focus the messianic lordship of the crucified and risen Jesus that established Christian, eschatological hope. To him God said: 'You are my son; today I have begotten you' (Ps. 2.7). Along with this verse, Psalm 110.1 proved the other most widely quoted verse that illuminated the status of Jesus and the promise conveyed by his resurrection from the dead: 'The Lord says to my lord, "Sit at my right hand until I make your enemies my footstool"' (e.g. Acts 2.34).

The psalms drew authority from a widespread belief that King David was their author. Hence Peter is pictured at Pentecost as citing David's testimony in Psalm 16 to the resurrection of Jesus: 'He was not abandoned to Hades, nor did his flesh experience corruption' (Acts 2.31). The prayerful and poetic language of the Psalms conveyed and nourished faith in Christ's resurrection and the eschatological hope it embodied.

Where the direction of the Psalms, precisely as prayers, is from human beings to God, prophetic oracles and, in particular, oracles of promise moved in the opposite direction. In one way or another, prophets were called to make known the divine mind and will. Their personal judgement and human words became invested with divine authority. In the Old

---

[10]See David Starling, 'The Messianic Hope in the Psalms', *Reformed Theological Review* 58, no. 3 (1999): 121–34. At times prophetic texts appeal to God in ways that resemble the psalms of lament: for instance, 'O that you would tear open the heavens and come down' (Isa. 64.1).

Testament, the expression 'the word of the Lord/God' occurs 241 times, and in 225 of these cases we deal with prophetic utterance. The prophets, while meeting at times opposition and rejection, were usually understood to be mouthpieces of the divine Word and, specifically, the divine promises. Their language raises, of course, questions about the nature of the prophetic experience and the need to discern carefully what we may recover from their historical testimony.[11] But the prophets' words and subsequent writings were characteristically received with religious reverence and elicited hopes for new life within history and, eventually for new life beyond history, as prophetic oracles became more apocalyptic, and the proto-apocalyptic of exilic and post-exilic times (e.g. Isa. 55-66; Ezek. 38; Zech. 9-14) gave way to full-blooded apocalyptic (e.g. Dan. 7.1-12.13).[12]

With the book of Isaiah, we find prophets reaching the pinnacle of their powers and subsequently enjoying an inspiring impact on the origins and history of Christianity. Isaiah proved a deep reservoir from which Christians drew fresh hope in God and the divine promises. In picturing an ideal, anointed ruler, Isaiah used lyric language that entered the New Testament, Christmas carols and Handel's *Messiah*: 'A child has been born for us, a son given us; authority rests upon his shoulders; and he is named Wonderful Counsellor, Mighty God, Everlasting Father, Prince of Peace' (Isa. 9.6).[13] Within a poem that pictured the coming, peaceful kingdom, three pairs of attributes expressed the charismatic endowments of the future king: 'The Spirit of the Lord shall rest on him, the spirit of wisdom and understanding, the spirit of counsel and might, the spirit of knowledge and the fear of the Lord' (Isa. 11.2).

Down to about 700 BCE, Isaiah son of Amoz was active in Judah during the reign of four kings – a prophetic career reflected in Isaiah 1–39. Chapters 40–66 cannot be earlier than the sixth century, since they address situations that reflect the fall of Jerusalem in 586 BCE (with the city in ruins in Isa. 44.26), the deportation of much of Judah's population to Babylon (with the people in exile in Isa. 43.5-6) and the return from exile. Chapters 40–48 may well have been composed in or near Babylon, and Isaiah 49–55 in

---

[11]See Gerald O'Collins, *Rethinking Fundamental Theology: Toward a New Fundamental Theology* (Oxford: Oxford University Press, 2011), 87–92.

[12]See John J. Collins, 'Daniel', in *The Oxford Handbook of the Reception History of the Bible*, ed. Michael Lieb, Emma Mason and Jonathan Roberts (Oxford: Oxford University Press, 2010), 77–88; and Stephen L. Cook, 'Prophecy and Apocalyptic', in *The Oxford Handbook of the Prophets*, ed. Carolyn J. Sharp (Oxford: Oxford University Press, 2016), 67–83.

[13]See John Butt, 'George Friedric Handel and *The Messiah*', in *Oxford Handbook of the Reception History of the Bible*, ed. Michael Lieb, Emma Mason and Jonathan Roberts (Oxford: Oxford University Press, 2010), 294–306.

Jerusalem. Chapters 55 (or possibly 56) to 66 reflect what happened later, when some of the exiles had returned to Jerusalem. Both Isaiah 1–39 and, even more, 40–66 incorporate end-time prophecy, with the promise of God 'coming' to save and create a new beginning (Isa. 35.4; 40.9-10; 59.19-20; 66.15, 18).

The prophet Isaiah son of Amoz and then numerous authors and editors were responsible for the final form of the book of Isaiah. The later contributors brought about a striking unity. An initial vision of all nations streaming to Jerusalem when universal disarmament and peace come (Isa. 2.1-4) is retrieved and expanded at the end (Isa. 56.1-8; 60.1-22; 66.18-24). Jerusalem becomes a place of final salvation for the just ones from the nations, as well as for the righteous Israelites. The Temple will become 'a house of prayer for all people' (Isa. 56.7). Both at the beginning and at the end, Isaiah highlights God's universal sovereignty, the final gathering of a worshipping community, and the centrality of Jerusalem. These themes would reach their New Testament climax in the book of Revelation. The imaginative and eschatological language of Isaiah has continued to encourage believers, Christian and Jewish, to maintain a trusting and prayerful hope in their faithful God. It is appropriate that passages from Isaiah permeate the liturgy and divine office of Advent and serve to evoke the second coming or *Parousia*, Christ's return in glory at the end of history to judge the world and complete the final kingdom.[14]

This will be 'the Day of the Lord' (1 Cor. 1.8; Phil. 1.10), the second coming of Jesus Christ expressed in an eschatological term derived from the Old Testament prophets. The seventh-century book of Zephaniah is nothing less than a collection of oracles concerned with 'the Day of the Lord'. It elaborates the message of Amos (5.18-20; 8.9-14) about that fearful day pictured in the language of divine warfare:

> The great day of the Lord is near, near and hastening fast; the sound of the day of the Lord is bitter, the warrior cries aloud there. That day will be a day of wrath, a day of distress and anguish, a day of ruin and devastation, a day of darkness and gloom, a day of clouds and thick darkness, a day of trumpet blast and battle cry against the fortified cities and against the lofty battlements.
>
> (Zeph. 1.14-16)

---

[14]On Isaiah, see Ulrich Berges, 'Isaiah: Structures, Themes, and Contested Issues', in *Oxford Handbook of the Prophets*, 153–70 and John F. A. Sawyer, 'Isaiah', in *Oxford Handbook of the Reception History of the Bible*, ed. Michael Lieb, Emma Mason and Jonathan Roberts (Oxford: Oxford University Press, 2010), 52–63.

Many Christian hymns picked up language from the Vulgate translation of this passage in Zephaniah. 'The most famous of its offspring is the *Dies irae*, whose language, metre and music combine to make it the most majestic of all the hymns.'[15] After six verses describing the eschatological judgement, the writer puts himself into the scene of judgement. He appeals for the divine mercy, which prompted the incarnation, the toil of the ministry and the crucifixion: '*recordare, Jesu pie, quod sum causa tuae viae, ne me perdas illa die. quaerens me sedisti lassus; redemisti crucem passus, tantus labor non sit cassus.*'[16] 'The final verse is a cry of humble hope which sums up the whole hymn – *gere curam mei finis* (take care of me when my end comes)'.[17]

The classical (Latin) hymns for Advent, such as the seventh-century *Creator alme siderum* (Loving Creator of the stars), are filled with eschatological hope when they face the coming Day of the Lord. But, unlike the *Dies irae*, the *Creator alme siderum* avoids individualism and prays in the plural: '*te deprecamur ultimae magnum diei judicem, armis supernae gratiae defende nos ab hostibus.*'[18] Another early hymn used in Advent, *Verbum supernum prodeuns* (Heavenly Word coming forth [from the Father]), likewise expresses a common hope: '*ut, cum tribunal judicis damnabit igni noxios et vox amica debitum vocabit ad caelum pios, non esca flammarum nigros volvamur inter turbines, vultu Dei sed compotes caeli fruamur gaudiis.*'[19]

These hymns and, in general, the Advent liturgy understand the coming of Christ to be threefold: a past coming in flesh and weakness, a present coming in spirit and power, and a future coming in majesty and glory. The hymn *Verbum supernum prodeuns* dedicates one stanza to the first coming, one stanza to the present coming, but its third and fourth stanzas (just quoted) to the future coming. All three comings are honoured and become themes for sacred music, but the final coming is emphasized.[20]

Thus far I have sampled major items from Jewish festivals, the Psalms, and the prophets to illustrate how prayer regularly framed eschatological hope and how such prayerful Old Testament hope fed into Christian liturgy.

[15]Joseph Connelly, *Hymns of the Roman Liturgy* (London: Longmans, 1957), 253–6.

[16]'Remember, faithful Jesus, that I am the reason for [your human] journey. Do not lose me on that day. Seeking me, you sat weary [by the well]. [It was me] you redeemed when you endured the cross. May such toil not be in vain.'

[17]Connelly, *Hymns of the Roman Liturgy*, 253–6.

[18]'We pray you, great Judge of the last day, defend us with the arms of heavenly grace from [our] enemies.'

[19]'And thus, when the throne of the Judge will condemn the guilty to the fire and a loving voice calls the faithful to heaven, may we not be cast into the dark whirlpools as food for the flames, but share in the vision of God and enjoy the happiness of heaven.'

[20]For the Advent hymns, see Connelly, *Hymns of the Roman Liturgy*, 49–53.

A book-length treatment would need to examine, for instance, Daniel 12.1-3 (which clearly features resurrection, final judgement and everlasting life) and further apocalyptic expectations found in non-canonical books, as well as studying Isaiah 26.19 and Ezekiel 37. Let us turn now to sample the New Testament for its witness to eschatology fashioned in and through prayer.

Jesus and Prayerful Eschatology

The central message of Jesus proclaimed the kingdom of God (e.g. Mk 1.15), the divine act of salvation which is coming not as a reward for human merits but as sheer gift from God's loving kindness. Jesus invited his hearers to 'enter' the kingdom or receive it joyfully as a child does a gift. Jesus gave himself totally to the service of the present (Mt. 12.28) and future (Mt. 8.11) divine rule. To 'repent' and 'believe' in the 'good news' of the kingdom (Mk 1.15) obviously involved receiving this eschatological promise prayerfully. Repentance and faith are inconceivable without prayer.

The final, saving kingdom was anticipated through the preaching, teaching and miraculous deeds of Jesus: 'He went throughout Galilee, *teaching* in their synagogues and *proclaiming* the good news of the kingdom and *curing* every disease and every sickness among the people' (Mt. 4.23; see 9.35). Accepting that teaching and proclamation clearly implied an openly prayerful attitude. Such an attitude was also required if the sick were to profit spiritually when their bodies were healed. Here the healing of Peter's mother-in-law proves exemplary. As soon as she was physically healed, she began 'to serve' Jesus and his companions (Mk 1.29-31), and may well have belonged to the women who 'followed Jesus in Galilee, served him', and courageously attended his crucifixion (Mk 15.41). Responding to the preaching, teaching and healing ministry with which Jesus initiated the eschatological kingdom of God obviously called for prayer and faith. The evangelists note both the prayer of petition which could precede a healing (e.g. Mk 1.40) and the praise of God and thanksgiving that could follow a healing (e.g. Mk 1.12; Lk. 17.15-16).

The beatitudes, both in Matthew's version and Luke's version, begin by promising 'the kingdom of God' to 'the poor' (Lk. 6.20) or 'the poor in spirit' (Mt. 5.3). It goes without saying that those to whom the blessings of God's final kingdom are promised, the 'poor', the 'merciful', 'the pure of heart', 'the peacemakers' and so forth, are people who adore and thank God, petition their Creator and Lord, and in other ways live lives of prayer. The eschatological blessings are prepared in and through prayer.[21]

---

[21]On beatitudes, see Meier, *A Marginal Jew*, vol. 2, 317–36.

The parables of Jesus indicated that the final kingdom of God was taking shape now and already making claims in the present. Thus the story of the marriage feast illuminated the coming kingdom and its demands by inculcating the need to answer God's invitation to the final feast and to live appropriately holy lives (Mt. 22.1-14). The parable of the ten bridesmaids highlighted the call to be vigilant and ready when waiting for the coming of Christ, the radiantly beautiful Bridegroom (Mt. 25.1-13). Other parables of Jesus underlined the need for his followers to show vigilance and faithfulness as they wait for the end. In one place he did this by introducing the image of a great household and its master who is out for the night (Lk. 12.35-48). In another place he used the picture of a watchful householder who is constantly on the alert against a possible break-in from robbers (Lk. 12.39-40). In yet another place Jesus focused on a manager whom the master puts in charge while he goes off somewhere for some unspecified purpose and also for an unspecified amount of time. This individual is expected to perform his ordinary duties, above all that of providing a regular amount of food for the other servants (Lk. 12.42). Through these and further parables, Jesus stressed the vigilant and prayerful responsibility elicited by the eschatological promise of God's final kingdom.

Jesus did not tell his stories simply 'to point a moral and adorn a tale'. Much more than mere picturesque illustrations, his parables questioned his hearers, challenged their normal standards and securities, invited their reflection and called on them to walk in radically different ways. His eschatologically directed parables looked for the response of prayerful engagement and subsequent action.

The Gospels recall Jesus' 'meals with sinners and the disreputable', meals that celebrated 'God's eschatological mercy' and were 'a preparation and foretaste of the coming banquet in the kingdom of God' (e.g. Mk 2.19). At the end he spoke of a final, heavenly banquet to come (Mk 14.25; Mt. 8.11).[22] The coming kingdom of God will be revealed and, as John's Gospel pictures that future, Jesus' disciples will finally be at home with him in the house of the Father (Jn 14.1-3). In the meantime, he expected his followers to serve the hungry, the thirsty, strangers, the naked, the sick and prisoners. The parable of the Last Judgement encouraged nothing less than such action (Mt. 25.31-46).

Jesus knew how vulnerable his followers were, and asked them to 'keep awake and pray' so that they would not fail in the coming crises (Mk 14.38;

---

[22]See Meier, *A Marginal Jew*, vol. 1, 302–17, on Matthew 8.11-12. On Mark 14.25, see Joel Marcus, *Mark 8–16* (New Haven, CT: Yale University Press, 2009), 956–68.

see Mt. 6.13; Lk. 21.36; 22.39-46). They were 'to pray always, and not lose heart', crying out to God 'day and night', until the Son of Man came (Lk. 18.1, 7).

Post-Easter Prayerful Eschatology

In his first surviving letter Paul prayed that believers persevere in holy expectation of the end: 'May he [the Lord Jesus] so strengthen your hearts in holiness that you may be blameless before our God and Father at the coming of our Lord Jesus Christ with all his saints' (1 Thess. 3.13). The letter ended with a similar prayer: 'May the God of peace himself sanctify you entirely; and may your spirit, mind and body be kept sound and blameless at the coming of our Lord Jesus Christ' (1 Thess. 5.23). Later, in his masterpiece, Paul summed up Christian life: 'rejoice in hope, be patient in suffering, persevere in prayer' (Rom. 12.12). The Letter to the Philippians put this more fully, and emphasized prayer: 'The Lord is near. Do not worry about anything, but in everything by prayer and supplication with thanksgiving, let your requests be known to God. And the peace of God which surpasses all understanding will guard your hearts and your minds in Christ Jesus' (Phil. 4.5-7). Ephesians, while briefer on the topic, stressed prayer in expectation of the end ('pray in the Spirit at all times in every prayer and supplication'; Eph. 6.18). Colossians likewise highlighted alert perseverance in prayer: 'Devote yourself to prayer, keeping alert in it with thanksgiving' (Col. 4.2; see 1 Tim. 5.5).

New Testament authors followed up Jesus' language about the coming Son of Man (e.g. Mk 13.24) by promising the final manifestation of the glorified Christ at the end of history (e.g. Phil. 3.20; Tit. 2.13; Heb. 9.28). Paul expected that, when we come to God at the end, 'we will see face to face' and 'will know fully even as we have been fully known' (1 Cor. 13.12). First John consoles its readers with the hope that they will enjoy the divine presence when they will 'see' God disclosed 'as he is' (1 Jn 3.2).

Such eschatological hopes of Jesus' followers were embodied and founded in the prayerful rite of baptism. It was central to the great commission, presented as coming from the risen Jesus and summarizing the central ministry of the Matthean church: 'Go therefore and make disciples of all nations, baptizing them in the name of the Father, and of the Son, and of the Holy Spirit, and teaching them to obey everything that I have commanded you. And remember, I am with you always, to the end of the age' (Mt. 28.19-20). The 'end of the age' recalled how the actions and prayers with which baptism was conferred were directed towards the close of human history and the final future. Baptism entailed public prayer and prayerful symbolism, both concerned with the promise of final life with God.

Paul expresses the eschatological thrust of baptism by speaking of dying with Christ, being buried with him, living a new life and eventually sharing in his resurrection from the dead:

> Do you not know that all of us who have been baptized into Christ Jesus were baptized into his death? Therefore, we have been buried with him by baptism into death, so that, just as Christ was raised from the dead by the glory of the Father, so we too might walk in newness of life. For if we have been buried with him in death like his, we will certainly be united with him in a resurrection like his.
>
> (Rom. 6.3-5)

Baptism, in these terms, is a sacrament of prayerful hope that anticipates the fullness of bodily resurrection. Subsequently in Romans, it is within a cosmic vision of a renewed creation that the apostle sums up the new life in the Holy Spirit (Rom. 8.1-39). The Spirit is at work in the whole creation and in human beings as they 'groan', suffer and pray in expectation of the end.

Paul quotes one of the oldest (and briefest) Christian prayers of eschatological expectation in a benediction that closes one of his letters: 'Maranatha' (1 Cor. 16.22).[23] Transliterated into Greek from two Aramaic words, in this context 'Maranatha' probably means 'Our Lord, come!' rather than 'Our Lord has come'. The New Testament ends with the same prayer (but in Greek): 'Come, Lord Jesus!' (Rev. 22.29). Thus Christians expressed in prayer the hope that the risen and exalted Jesus would come to them in his post-Easter glory. Jesus was remembered as speaking of himself as the Son of Man who was to come in glory at the end to judge the human race. Yet the early Christians did not pray 'come, Son of Man', but 'come, Lord Jesus'.

The glorious, final coming of Jesus will bring the resurrection of the dead and eternal life with God – the central Christian hope prayerfully celebrated in Revelation. Replete with visions, from the inaugural vision of the exalted Christ (Rev. 1.9-20) to the final vision of the new Jerusalem (Rev. 22.1-22.5), this 'Apocalypse of Jesus Christ' (Rev. 1.1), without explicitly saying so, draws much of its vivid language and prayer from earlier scriptures and transforms earlier images through the visionary's hope and imagination. Of

---

[23]On this verse, see Anthony C. Thiselton, *The First Epistle to the Corinthians* (Grand Rapids, MI: William B. Eerdmans, 2000), 1348–53.

its 404 verses, well over half (275 verses) contain one or more quotations from (or allusions to) the Hebrew Bible or its Greek translation (the Septuagint) – above all, from Isaiah, Ezekiel and Daniel.[24] In the New Testament, no other book draws more on the inherited scriptures, is more saturated by prayer and contains such a wealth of prophetic and apocalyptic visions to be communicated to the author's audience. It is the only visionary book among the twenty-seven books of the New Testament.

Seeing the 'face' of God (Rev. 22.4), the community of all who have reached a blessed fulfilment will live forever in the heavenly Jerusalem. This 'beatific vision' is pictured primarily as a collective transformation rather than an individual, self-sufficient completion of the salvation to come. Using images of angels, thrones, trumpets, heavenly music and similar apocalyptic and prayerful language, Revelation provides a scenario for a final manifestation of God at the resurrection of the dead and the renewal of the cosmos.

None of this testimony (from Revelation or other books of the New Testament) to the eschatological disclosure of God constitutes reports derived, as it were, from 'eyewitness accounts of a future which is still outstanding'.[25] Christians continue to pray 'your kingdom come', but do not enjoy testimony that might tell them clearly what that final kingdom will reveal itself to be. Daniel, Ezekiel, the Psalms and other Old Testament sources provided Mark 13 and Revelation with rich symbolic imagery. This apocalyptic language aimed to evoke religious feelings in prayer rather than provide descriptions of what will be revealed at the end. The beatific vision of God to come remains mysteriously hidden, an experience that, through faith, hope and love, we can glimpse only 'dimly' (1 Cor. 13.12).

The book of Revelation encourages us to 'locate' God in the future: '"I am the Alpha and the Omega", says the Lord God, who is and who was and who is to come' (Rev. 1.8). God is not described here, as one might expect, as the One who is and who was and who *will be* – that is to say, as equally related to past, present and future. Revelation highlights the coming God, the God of the eschatological future.

In this connection Rudolf Otto's classic account of the Holy as the *mysterium tremendum et fascinans* (the frightening and fascinating mystery)

---

[24]See Garrick V. Allen, Ian Paul and Simon P. Woodman, ed., *The Book of Revelation: Currents in British Research on the Apocalypse* (Tübingen: Mohr Siebeck, 2015); Jan Fekkes, *Isaiah and Prophetic Traditions in the Book of Revelation: Visionary Antecedents and Their Development* (Sheffield: JSOT Press, 1992); and Steve Moyise, *The Old Testament in the Book of Revelation* (Sheffield: Sheffield Academic Press, 1995).
[25]Karl Rahner, *Foundations of Christian Faith: An Introduction to the Idea of Christianity*, trans. William V. Dych (New York: Seabury Press, 1966), 431.

enjoys a fresh application. The God to whom we pray is the unpredictable mystery of the future that is both terrifying and enthralling. The future engages and attracts us with the seemingly unlimited possibilities that it holds out. It is at the same time fearful because it is unknown and in many ways incontrollable. God is this numinous power of the future, the One who will not be fully our God until the final kingdom comes.

Prayerful Eschatology in Post-New Testament Christianity

With its images and symbols, the book of Revelation enjoyed a widespread impact on the prayerful imagination of Christians down through the ages.[26] Sculpture, illuminated manuscripts, stained glass, mosaics, engravings, paintings, hymns and literature spread images from Revelation and inspired future-directed prayer and reflection. The altarpiece in Ghent completed in 1432 by Jan van Eych, for instance, drew on Revelation 7.9-17 to depict a multitude of the blessed worshipping the Lamb. The triumphal arch mosaics in the church of Cosmas and Damian in Rome exemplified a straightforward adoption of the symbol of the slain Lamb. Like the altarpiece in Ghent, these mosaics elicited an eschatological response from those gathered to celebrate prayerfully the eucharistic liturgy.

A sequence of fifteen woodcuts by Albrecht Dürer have popularized for lasting audiences some of Revelation's apocalyptic images.[27] *The Light of the World* by Holman Hunt inspired prayer by bringing alive for millions of viewers the words of Jesus: 'I am standing at the door, knocking; if you hear my voice and open the door, I will come in to you and eat with you and you with me' (Rev. 3.20). Radiant elements in the extraordinary popular image of the Virgin Mary in the Basilica of Our Lady of Guadalupe, Mexico (coming from a vision of 1531 reported by St Juan Diego), recall the woman clothed with the sun (Rev. 12.1-4). The image has prompted prayer from innumerable pilgrims to that shrine.

Addressing Jesus Christ by the eschatological title, 'the Alpha and the Omega, the first and the last, the beginning and the end' (Rev. 22.13; see also

---

[26]See Ian Boxall and Richard Tresley, ed., *The Book of Revelation and Its Interpreters: Short Studies and an Annotated Bibliography* (Lanham, MD: Rowman and Littlefield, 2016) and Judith L. Kovacs and Christopher Rowland, *Revelation through the Centuries* (Oxford: Blackwell, 2004).

[27]On the work and biblical interpretation of Dürer, see David H. Price, 'Dürer, Albrecht', in *The Oxford Encyclopedia of the Bible and the Arts*, ed. Timothy K. Beal, vol. 1 (New York: Oxford University Press, 2015), 280–5.

1.8; 21.6), fed into a hymn, *Corde natus*, by Aurelius Prudentius Clemens, still sung in the popular version by J. M. Neale:

> Of the Father's love begotten,
> Ere the worlds began to be,
> He is Alpha and Omega,
> He the source, the ending be.

From ancient times, religious art drew on Revelation to symbolize Christ by the letters 'alpha' and 'omega'. A hymn by Charles Wesley, 'Love Divine, All Loves Excelling', culminates in praise as worshippers cast their crowns before the throne of God – a gesture that recalls what the four elders do in Revelation 4.10.[28]

As well as being blatantly eschatological with its division into the *Inferno*, *Purgatorio* and *Paradiso*, the *Divine Comedy* of Dante was deeply influenced by the book of Revelation and its eschatology. As Ronald B. Herzman has written, 'No work of medieval literature draws so directly and comprehensively from the Book of the Apocalypse as do the last cantos of *Purgatorio*, wherein the pageant of church history presented there for the pilgrim and the reader would be unintelligible without some knowledge of the Apocalypse.' The pilgrimage to the New Jerusalem of the 'scribe and visionary' who, as 'both exile and even a kind of martyr', wrote Revelation, proved a model for Dante, who is 'both poet and pilgrim'.[29]

Recognizing the impact of the book of Revelation on Dante's *Comedy* should not gloss over the way he has absorbed and re-elaborated Revelation and other books of the Bible. He creatively 'bends' the biblical text 'to his own needs and aims'.[30] We can see this, for instance, in his version of the Lord's Prayer (*Purgatorio*, canto XI), which Dante takes from Matthew 6.9-13, expands with such themes as angels, love and peace, and puts into the mouths of those who have sinned through pride. In the case of the eschatological petition, 'Thy kingdom come', Dante adds a qualification,

---

[28]Over the centuries, the interpretation of Revelation has also involved conflicts over such matters as the thousand-year reign of the saints on earth (Rev. 20.1-6). But this apocalyptic work has also exercised a widely positive impact on Christian prayer and life. See Craig R. Koester, *Revelation: New Translation with Introduction and Commentary* (New Haven, CT: Yale University Press, 2014), 29–65.

[29]Ronald B. Herzman, 'Dante and the Apocalypse', in *The Apocalypse in the Middle Ages*, ed. Richard K. Emmerson and Bernard McGinn (Ithaca, NY: Cornell University Press, 1992), 398–413.

[30]Piero Boitani, 'Dante and the Bible: A Sketch', *Oxford Handbook of the Reception History of the Bible* ed. Michael Lieb, Emma Mason and Jonathan Roberts (Oxford: Oxford University Press, 2010), 281–93 (282).

'the peace of thy kingdom come'. This joins the eschatological prayer, which Jesus taught his disciples, with the messianic hope for peace that threads through the scriptures from Isaiah 9.6 (see above) to Philippians 4.7, and beyond. The prayer of eschatological hope is a prayer for full and lasting peace, a prayer that led early Christians to put on the graves of their beloved dead the words 'in peace (*en eirēnē*)' and that still leads Christians to pray 'may he/she rest in peace (*requiescat in pace*)'.

It was Thomas Aquinas who provided Dante with much 'food for verse'. Aquinas presented his eschatological hope not only through doctrinal teaching on the sacraments but also through hymns and prayers prepared for the feast of Corpus Christi instituted in 1264.[31] He himself was probably the author of the sequence or chant sung at Mass before the Alleluia verse for the feast (*Lauda Sion*), a hymn (*Adoro te devote*) and other texts composed for the newly instituted feast. The *Lauda Sion* ends by praying to Jesus as 'good shepherd' and 'true bread': 'You know all things and can do all things. You feed us mortals here [in this life]. Make us your table guests there [in the life to come]. Make us co-heirs with you and companions of the holy citizens [of heaven].'[32] The *Adoro te devote* also ends with a future-directed petition, albeit expressing an individual ('I') rather than a collective ('us') hope: 'Jesus, you are veiled as I look now on you. I pray that what I long for may come about, that, seeing you with your face disclosed, I may be blessed in the vision of your glory.'[33] In an antiphon prepared for Corpus Christi, Aquinas ended with the eschatological hope (in the plural) aroused and enlivened by the Eucharist: 'O sacred banquet in which Christ is received, his suffering is remembered [from the past], our mind is filled with grace [present experience], and there is given to us a pledge of future glory [hope].'[34]

---

[31]See Barbara R. Walters, Vincent Corrigan, and Peter T. Ricketts, *The Feast of Corpus Christi* (University Park, PA: Pennsylvania State University Press, 2006).

[32]'*Tu qui cuncta scis et vales,*
qui nos pascis hic mortales,
tuos ibi commensales,
cohaeredes et sodales
fac sanctorum civium.'

[33]'*Jesu, quem velatum nunc aspicio,*
oro fiat illud quod tam sitio;
ut te revelata cernens facie,
visu sim beatus tuae gloriae.'
After a period of serious doubts, scholars now seem ready to attribute the 'Adoro te devote' to Dante; see Mary Isaac Jogues Rousseau, 'Adoro te devote', in *New Catholic Encyclopedia*, vol. 1, ed. Catholic University of America (Detroit, MI: Thomson Gale, 2003), 120.

[34]'*O sacrum convivium, in quo Christus sumitur: recolitur memoria passionis, mens impletur gratia et futurae gloriae nobis pignus datur.*'

Conclusion

Many possibilities open up for those who wish to explore more fully the ways in which prayer maintained and evoked the eschatological hopes of Christians, and vice versa. First, a book-length study could examine, for instance, the notable writers who have expounded the Our Father and, specifically, its petition, 'Thy kingdom come': from Tertullian, Origen, and Cyprian, through Martin Luther, Teresa of Avila, and Lancelot Andrewes, down to Kenneth Stevenson, and various modern biblical scholars. Second, we could examine the eschatological hopes expressed in the prayers, readings and music of Masses for the dead. As Sven Rune Havsteen writes, the Requiem Mass 'provided a textual basis for the most prominent musical interpretation of eschatological themes in Western history'.[35] An 'acoustic' examination of eschatology would include the liturgical use of the triple *Sanctus* (Isa. 6.3; Rev. 4.8) and of *Alleluia* or *Hallelujah*, found four times in Revelation (19.1, 3, 4, 6) and nowhere else in the New Testament. After its sumptuous use in Revelation (8, 9, 11), the trumpet became the musical instrument *par excellence* in musical interpretation of eschatological texts.

Third, what has already been said about the visual arts as handing on eschatological hopes could be greatly expanded. Representations in (or outside) churches of 'the last things' have stirred and accompanied collective and individual prayers that depict our final future with God. Eschatology articulated in sculpture and painting – for instance, Michelangelo's *Last Judgement* in the Sistine Chapel – have undoubtedly done more to transmit prayerful, eschatological expectations than any number of theological treatises on the topic.

Fourth, Christian experience has shown how easily so many biblical texts turn into prayer or are in fact prayers. This pervasive characteristic of the Bible suggests investigating the prayer which shaped and produced the relevant texts. Take, for example, the eschatological prayer of Paul: 'May he [the Lord Jesus] so strengthen your hearts in holiness that you may be blameless before our God and Father at the coming of our Lord Jesus with all his saints' (1 Thess. 3.13). Over and over again, such verses in Paul, 1 Peter, Revelation and other New Testament books are, in fact, prayers or else revert very easily into prayer. This particular text in 1 Thessalonians regularly draws useful comments from biblical scholars about the early Christian conviction, shared for some years by Paul, about the *Parousia* or second coming of the Risen Christ being imminent. But

---

[35]Sven Rune Havsteen, 'Eschatology', in *Encyclopedia of the Bible and Its Reception*, vol. 7 (Berlin: De Gruyter, 2013), 1154–93 (1187).

the scholars might also reflect on such eschatological texts being rooted in the prayer life of the apostle.

This chapter has set itself to suggest ways of reading Christian eschatology from the perspective of the eschatological prayer that identified the first followers of Jesus and gave meaning to their lives. There are, unquestionably, other valuable ways of reading this eschatology. But failure to recall prayer, both individual and collective, will leave substantially impoverished any account of Christian eschatological faith and hope in the risen and ascended Christ. Likewise, I have become more aware than ever that any account of Christian eschatology requires the recovery of the political resonances of Christian hope. Eschatological hope calls for eschatological prayer *and* eschatological practice/politics. The hope of Christians inspires and shapes their activity not only in prayer but also in political engagement.

This conviction means dissenting from those who treat the Christian message as more 'spiritual' than 'material'. In a book that enjoyed a wide influence in the twentieth century, Rudolf Schnackenburg wrote: 'The salvation proclaimed and promised by Jesus in the reign and kingdom of God is purely religious in character.'[36] Did Jesus take no stand on social and political issues? In putting this question, one must insist that 'political' is not to be reduced to national, still less nationalistic, issues. It refers to all matters of public and civic concern.

Without going as far as Schnackenburg, John Meier assures his readers: 'Jesus was not interested in and did not issue pronouncements about *concrete* social and political reforms, either for the world in general or for Israel in *particular.* He was not proclaiming the reform of the world; he was proclaiming the end of the world.'[37] But do pronouncements of a social and political character (about ills to be corrected and reforms to be introduced) always have to be concrete and particular? Can the agenda for social and political reform also be broad and general? Elsewhere I have critiqued in detail Meier's vision of a non-reforming Jesus.[38] I much prefer what Pope John Paul II taught in *Redemptoris Missio* (7 December 1990) about Christian hope for the future kingdom proclaimed by Jesus involving not only prayer but also eschatological activity: 'Working for the kingdom means acknowledging and promoting God's activity, which is present in human history and transforms it. Building the kingdom means working for liberation from evil in all its forms.'

---

[36]Rudolf Schnackenburg, *God's Rule and Kingdom*, trans. John Murray (London: Burns and Oates, 1968), 95.

[37]Meier, *A Marginal Jew*, vol. 2, 335.

[38]See Gerald O'Collins, 'Jesus Christ the Liberator: In the Context of Human Progress', *Studia Missionalia* 47 (1998): 23–35.

PART THREE

Historical Perspectives

CHAPTER FOURTEEN

Christian Prayer in the Pre-Nicene Period

FRANCES M. YOUNG

'Thanks be to God, the Almighty, the King of the universe, for all His mercies, and heartfelt thanks to the Saviour and Redeemer of our souls, Jesus Christ, through whom we pray that peace, from troubles outside and troubles in the heart, may be kept for us stable and unshaken for ever.'[1] That is how Eusebius of Caesarea opened the last book of his *Church History*. It must have been around 325 (the year of the Nicene Council) that the old bishop finally completed Book 10 of a project which had engaged him for some twenty years. Having lived through the years of the final Great Persecution, Eusebius gives thanks for Constantine's victory and the recovery of the church.

This is almost the only prayer text in Eusebius' history – indeed, prayer figures surprisingly little as he reviews the church's past, perhaps because it appeared rarely controversial. Now and again in his narrative we find, especially in material he quotes, a backdrop of hymn-singing, praise and thanksgiving,[2] but prior to Book 10 prayer is principally associated with tales of miracle and martyrdom,[3] and the same may be said of other early

---

[1] Eusebius, *Historia Ecclesiastica* 10.1 (GCS 9); G. A. Williamson, *Eusebius: The History of the Church* (New York: Penguin Books, 1963) – hereafter: *HE*.
[2] Eusebius, *HE* 5.3; 7.9 (in a quotation from Dionysius' letters); 9.1; 9.8; 9.9.
[3] Eusebius, *HE* 4.15 (quoting the *Martyrdom of Polycarp*); 5.1; 5.5; 5.7 (quoting Irenaeus); 6.8; 6.9; 8.7.

Christian narrative material, such as the Apocryphal Acts. In Book 10, however, we are introduced to richer dimensions of Christian worship, with that opening prayer and a transcription of Eusebius' celebratory address at the dedication of the new church building at Tyre. We finally begin to sense that the struggles of the pre-Nicene church had actually been about right prayer and worship – to whom it should be offered and by what means.

So despite the paucity of references to prayer in Eusebius' history, we may pick up from across his work some, often interconnected, themes around which to organize a trawl for clues; for, apart from several third-century treatises on prayer, the evidence is largely embedded in texts with other priorities. Just as Eusebius reconstructed the past from resources in his library, so we depend on deductions from what happens to be extant, whether patristic classics or recently rediscovered documents.

Theme 1

Prayer is to be offered on behalf of all to the one God, Creator of the universe, by contrast with calling on the gods many and lords many of the Greeks and Romans.

For Eusebius this was fundamental: it was the providence of this one and only 'Master of the Universe' which had brought about the situation for which he gives thanks in that opening prayer. This perspective is found right back in the earliest post-New Testament texts we have.

Towards the end of the letter known as *1 Clement*, sent sometime in the late first century from Rome to Corinth, the author slips into prayer: God is addressed as the God of all flesh, the one who sees everything and helps those in danger, the Creator and Overseer of everyone. The prayer seeks not only the good of Christians, but prays:

> Let all the nations of the earth know that thou art God alone. ... Thou, O Lord, by thine operations didst bring to light the everlasting fabric of the universe, and didst create the world of men. From generation to generation thou art faithful, righteous in judgement, wondrous in might and majesty. Wisely hast thou created, prudently hast thou established, all things that are.[4]

Here the creative activity of the one God, taken for granted in the writings of the New Testament, is a truth, at one level still axiomatic, yet at another

---

[4]*1 Clement* 59–61 (LCL 24); Maxwell Staniforth and Andrew Louth, *Early Christian Writings: The Apostolic Fathers* (London: Penguin Books, 1987).

needing to be rubbed home; and, not just in this prayer-text but across the whole letter, it is both a key characterization of the God to whom prayer is offered, and the warrant for ethical advice. It is reinforced by repeated reference to 'the one who made us',[5] to the *Pantokrator* (Almighty), the *Despotes* (Master) of the universe, the *Demiurge* (Artisan), the Father, the King, the all-seeing God. According to *1 Clement* the all-embracing, all-encompassing power and greatness of the one source of all existence lies at the heart of Christian belief and practice. As Paul put it in 1 Thessalonians, conversion meant turning from idols to serve the living and true God (1 Thess. 1.9).

This God is the *episcopos*, the one with oversight over everything and to whom all will be accountable in the end. True, Jesus Christ appears as the agent of this God, bringing salvation and initiating resurrection, but the title 'Lord' is ambiguous and the dominant focus is on the Master and Lord of all, the one Creator God.

> Let us turn our eyes to the Father and Creator of the universe, and when we consider how precious and peerless are His gifts of peace, let us embrace them eagerly for ourselves. Let us contemplate Him with understanding, noting with the eyes of the spirit the patient forebearance that is everywhere willed by Him, and the total absence of any friction that marks the ordering of His whole creation.[6]

> *The Spirit of the Lord*, as the Bible tells us, *is a candle searching the inward parts of the body*; so let us keep in mind this nearness of His presence, remembering that not a single one of our thoughts or reasonings can ever be hid from Him. ... For He is the searcher of our thoughts and desires.[7]

> Therefore, since there is nothing He does not see and hear, let us approach Him with awe. ... [W]e must approach him in holiness of spirit, lifting up pure and undefiled hands to him in love for the gracious and compassionate Father who has chosen us to be His own.[8]

That 'lifting up of hands' signifies adopting the appropriate stance for prayer. In the final prayer, then, it is acknowledged that everything is in God's hands, and we find petitions for help and protection, not just for

---

[5] *1 Clement* 7.3; 20.11; 26-28; 32; 33; 35; 59.2; 61.2; 62; 64.
[6] *1 Clement* 19.
[7] *1 Clement* 21.
[8] *1 Clement* 28, 29.

'us', but for the afflicted, the lowly, the fallen, the needy, the sick, and a request 'to bring home thy wandering people', to 'feed the hungry, ransom the captive, support the weak, comfort the faint-hearted', and let all nations know this God is God alone.

Other texts from this earliest period also enjoin praying for all humankind, and affirm that nothing is hidden from the Creator of everything.[9] To find these perspectives in material so close to the New Testament period is significant: clearly they set out certain red lines ahead of creation becoming a bone of contention in the second century.[10] The Apologists would persistently challenge the myths and gods of traditional culture, contrasting idolatry with worship of the one true Creator God, and some of them,[11] defending the absolute sovereignty of the Creator, reinforced the red lines by arguing, in dialogue with philosophers, that God was the sole first principle, able to create from nothing, unlike a mere human sculptor, or indeed Plato's Demiurge who needed pre-existing material stuff from which to create. Meanwhile, prayer to the creator would hardly be offered by so-called 'Gnostic' groups, given their belief that the maker of the material universe was a being who had fallen from the spiritual world and trapped them in flesh, escape from which came through knowledge of their true, spiritual being. For Irenaeus the issue about creation was central to his argument with these heretics. The outcome of these second-century debates would be crucial for future articulation of the identity of the Christian God,[12] and, I suggest, was profoundly shaped by the attitude of mind fostered by the type of prayer found in *1 Clement* and other early second-century texts.

Theme 2

On the basis of those principles Christians refused to engage in Emperor-worship by offering sacrifice or incense, but did offer prayers to the Supreme God of the universe on behalf of the Emperor.

---

[9]*The Shepherd of Hermas* 1.1 (LCL 25); Ignatius, *Ephesians* 10 and 15 (LCL 24). See also Justin, *1 Apology* 12 (FC 6).

[10]Third-century authors occasionally include I Clement or The Shepherd of Hermas among the New Testament books. On the doctrine of creation, see Frances M. Young, '*Creation ex Nihilo*: A Context for the Emergence of the Christian Doctrine of Creation', *Scottish Journal of Theology* 44, no. 2 (1991): 139–51.

[11]Justin Martyr and others took a Platonic perspective, but Tatian and Theophilus anticipated Irenaeus and Tertullian in adopting the notion of creation out of nothing.

[12]See Frances M. Young, 'Creation: A Catalyst Shaping Early Christian Life and Thought', in *Schools of Faith: Essays on Theology, Ethics and Education in Honour of Iain R. Torrance*, ed. David Fergusson and Bruce McCormack (London: T&T Clark, 2019), 23–33.

For Eusebius the martyrs were those who 'showed magnificent enthusiasm for the worship of the God of the universe' by refusing to offer 'disgusting, unholy sacrifices'.[13] The martyrologies he quotes indicate that even offering incense to the emperor was a mark of disloyalty to Christ. Yet he also quotes a remarkable letter from Dionysius concerning the way the Emperor Gallus made the same mistake as his predecessor Decius, the notorious mid-third-century persecutor:

> When his reign was proceeding smoothly and things were going to his liking, he drove away the holy men who were praying God to grant him peace and health. In banishing them, he banished their supplications on his behalf.[14]

In other words, because Christians prayed for the emperor, it was to his own detriment that Gallus turned against them.

Already in the prayer text found in *1 Clement* there is petition for the authorities:

> Grant unto them then, O Lord, health and peace, harmony and security, that they may exercise without offence the dominion which thou hast accorded them. And forasmuch, O heavenly Master and Monarch eternal, as thou dost thus give to the sons of men glory and honour and power over the dwellers upon earth, vouchsafe so to direct their counsels as may be good and pleasing in thy sight, that in peace and mildness they may put to godly use the authority thou hast given them, and so find mercy with thee.[15]

The one God, Creator of all, had established those authorities. So not only did they deserve prayer support, but also obedience and loyalty, as is clear from the immediately preceding request to 'deliver us from such as hate us without a cause' and to 'make us obedient both to thine own almighty and glorious Name and to all who have the rule and governance over us upon earth.'[16]

Consistently the Apologists affirm that the refusal of Christians to participate in conventional religious rites is not because they are atheists;

---

[13] Eusebius, *HE* 8.3-4.
[14] Eusebius, *HE* 7.1.
[15] *1 Clement* 61.
[16] *1 Clement* 60.

rather, the church offers prayers for the emperor to the one God who governs everything on earth. Athenagoras sums up his defence on that point:

> Proof has now been offered to show to the best of my ability, if not as it deserves, that we are not atheists when we recognise the Maker of the universe and the Word proceeding from him as God.[17]

He has already affirmed the loyalty of Christians to the emperor and the rule of law, expecting a fair hearing;[18] addressing the emperor in his conclusion, he asks:

> Who ought more justly to receive what they request than men like ourselves, who pray for your reign that the succession to the kingdom may proceed from father to son, as is most just, and that your reign may grow and increase as all men become subject to you.[19]

Likewise, Theophilus asserts: 'I will pay honour to the emperor not by worshipping him but praying for him', and directs his reader to 'honour the Emperor by wishing him well, by obeying him, by praying for him, for by doing so you will perform the will of God.'[20]

Theme 3

Sacrifices and material offerings, the universal way of worship in Antiquity, were rejected altogether as inappropriate to worshipping this one Creator God, and replaced by the offering of spiritual sacrifices: prayer, praise, thanksgiving, fasting, holy living, and martyrdom.

Eusebius, preaching at the dedication of the cathedral in Tyre, states:

> The great High Priest of the universe, Jesus Himself, the only begotten of God, receives with shining eyes and upturned hands the sweet-smelling incense of all the worshippers, and the bloodless and immaterial prayer-sacrifices, and transmits them to the Father in heaven, the God of the universe.[21]

---

[17]Athenagoras, *Legatio* 30.6; *Legatio and De Resurrectione*, trans. and ed. William R. Schoedel (Oxford: Clarendon Press, 1972).
[18]Athenagoras, *Legatio* 1.2; 2.2-6.
[19]Athenagoras, *Legatio* 37.2.
[20]Theophilus, *Ad Autolycum* 11; *Theophilus of Antioch: Ad Autolycum*, trans. and ed. Robert M. Grant (Oxford: Clarendon Press, 1970).
[21]Eusebius, *HE* 10.4.

This turning away from sacrifice to spiritual offerings goes right back into our earliest texts, often exploiting psalms and prophetic texts to justify this approach. *1 Clement*, for example, uses Psalm texts to show that God needs nothing except 'confessions of his name', 'sacrifices of praise' and 'a humble spirit'.[22]

Eusebius mentions a second epistle 'said to be from Clement's pen'; modern scholars are equally sceptical on the question of authorship.[23] This text, however, does appear to be the earliest extant Christian sermon. By God's mercy 'we do not sacrifice to dead gods', it suggests, but through Christ 'have come to know the Father of truth'.[24]

> How do we acknowledge him? By doing what he says and not disobeying his commands; by honouring him not only with our lips, but with our heart and mind.[25]

The author urges his hearers to repent with their whole hearts, to turn to God. Charity, like repentance, is good; but 'fasting is better than prayer, and charity than both'.[26] It is all about serving God with a pure heart, loving and doing what is right, leading 'a holy and upright life' and seeking to repay Jesus Christ for the 'suffering he endured for us'.[27]

In other early texts fasting is described as 'a sacrifice acceptable to God', especially if what you would have eaten is given to someone in want.[28] Similar lists of acceptable spiritual sacrifices occur in the Apologists. Justin, for example, insists:

> The Maker of the universe has no need of blood and libations and incense, but praising him by the word of thanksgiving for all that he has given us ...; honor worthy of him is, not to consume by fire the things he has made for our nourishment, but to devote them to our use and those in need, in thankfulness to him sending up solemn prayers and hymns for our creation and all the means of health.[29]

The anti-sacrificial passages in the prophets were exploited by the Apologists, Irenaeus and many others to show that sacrifices were not required by

---

[22]*1 Clement* 52.
[23]Eusebius, *HE* 3.38.
[24]*2 Clement* 3.3 (LCL 24).
[25]*2 Clement* 3.4; see also 5.1 and 10.1.
[26]*2 Clement* 16-17.
[27]*2 Clement* 11.1; 12.1; 5.6; 1 3.
[28]*The Shepherd of Hermas*, 5.3.
[29]Justin, *1 Apology* 13.

God.[30] Indeed, Malachi 1.10-11 was a favourite text for showing that God would not accept sacrifice; but 'from the rising of the sun to its setting my name is great among the nations, and in every place incense is offered to my name, and a pure offering; for my name is great among the nations, says the Lord of hosts'.

Citing that Malachi text, Irenaeus states that directions were given to the disciples to 'offer to God the first-fruits of His own created things'; so now in the Eucharist the Gentiles glorify the name of the Son, who glorifies the Father. For Irenaeus the eucharistic offering is not made because God needs it, but as the way of rendering thanks for God's gifts, and so sanctifying what has been created.[31] Elsewhere in early Christian texts we find material offerings, such as first-fruits, may accompany thanksgiving, and are used to support clergy or the poor.[32] But from *1 Clement* on there was a strong sense that God needs nothing but 'sacrifices of praise' and 'a broken and contrite heart'.[33]

Tertullian, towards the end of his treatise *De oratione*, states that prayer 'is the spiritual oblation which has wiped out the ancient sacrifices', quoting Isaiah's prophetic questions implying the purposelessness of sacrifice (Isa. 1.11-12), as well as the saying from John's Gospel (Jn 4.23-24) that the hour will come when true worshippers will worship the Father in spirit and truth.[34] Origen of Alexandria, the first great Christian scholar and scriptural exegete, is the one who most extensively turns sacrifice into spiritual offerings – for God is to be worshipped in spirit.[35] The spiritual cult of the church is the offering of prayers; the spiritual altar is the mind of faithful Christians; spiritual images of God are the virtues implanted in people by the *Logos/Word*.[36] The Body of Christ is a spiritual Temple, and Christians continually celebrate spiritual feasts and fasts by constant prayer and abstention from wickedness.[37] Above all Christ offered the perfect sacrifice, and is the High Priest through whom Christian prayers are offered.[38] Such was the picture of Christian worship he spelt out in answer to the pagan critic, Celsus.

---

[30]For example, Justin, *1 Apology* 10, 13.

[31]Irenaeus, *Adversus Haereses* 4.17-18, in *The Apostolic Fathers, Justin Martyr, Irenaeus*, ed. Alexander Roberts and James Donaldson, ANF 1 (Peabody, MA: Hendrickson, 2004).

[32]For example, *Didache* 13 (LCL 24) and *The Apostolic Tradition* 28.

[33]*1 Clement* 52, quoting Psalms 60, 50 and 51.

[34]Tertullian, *De oratione*; *Tertullian's Tract on the Prayer*, trans. Ernest Evans (London: SPCK, 1953).

[35]Origen, *Contra Celsum* 6.70 (GCS); *Origen: Contra Celsum*, trans. Henry Chadwick (Cambridge: Cambridge University Press, 1953).

[36]Origen, *Contra Celsum* 1.69; 3.34, 81; 5.4; 7.44, 46; 8.13, 17, 26.

[37]Origen, *Contra Celsum* 8.19; 8.22.

[38]Origen, *Contra Celsum* 1.69; 3.34; 5.4; 8.13, 26.

Furthermore, in his *Homilies on Leviticus* he turned all the directions about sacrifices into foreshadowings of Christ's sacrifice or the spiritual sacrifices now offered by his followers.

Martyrs, above all, embodied sacrifice as self-offering. The narrative concerning the martyrdom of Polycarp keeps mentioning his persistence in prayer as he faces the inevitable,[39] including the pre-vision of his end granted while praying. It is, however, the prayer-text found at the point of death that captures its sacrificial dimension:

> O Lord God Almighty, Father of thy blessed and beloved Son, Jesus Christ, through whom we have been given knowledge of thyself; Thou art the God of angels and powers, of the whole creation, and of all the generations of the righteous who live in Thy sight. I bless Thee for granting me this day and hour, that I may be numbered amongst the martyrs, to share the cup of thine Anointed and to rise again unto life everlasting, both in body and soul, in the immortality of the Holy Spirit. May I be received among them this day in thy presence, a sacrifice rich and acceptable, even as thou didst appoint and foreshow, and dost now bring it to pass, for thou art the God of truth and in thee is no falsehood. For this, and for all else besides, I praise thee, I bless thee, I glorify thee; through our eternal High Priest in Heaven, thy beloved Son Jesus Christ, by whom and with whom be glory to thee and the Holy Ghost, now and for all ages to come. Amen.[40]

Theme 4

The powerful prayer of Christians, especially saints and martyrs, proved the sovereignty of the one Creator God.

Eusebius tells an extraordinary story of answer to prayer. Marcus Aurelius was about to engage his forces in battle with the Germans and Sarmatians, but they were parched with thirst. The soldiers of the Melitene Legion

> knelt on the ground, our normal attitude when praying, and turned to God in supplication. The enemy was astonished at the sight, but the record goes on to say that something more astonishing followed a moment

---

[39]The prayers, hymn-singing and praise of martyrs is a recurrent theme: for example, Eusebius, *HE* 5.1, 8.7, 9.1.

[40]*The Martyrdom of Polycarp* 14; quoted by Eusebius, *HE* 4.15. See also the account of the martyrs of Lyons and Vienne, quoted by Eusebius, *HE* 5.1, where Blandina 'looked as if she was hanging from a cross, and through her ardent prayers she stimulated great enthusiasm in those undergoing their ordeal'; they saw 'the One who was crucified for them' in the person of their sister. Eventually she 'was sacrificed'.

later: a thunderbolt drove the enemy to flight and destruction, while rain fell on the army which had called on the Almighty, reviving it when the entire force was on the point of perishing from thirst.[41]

Eusebius claims the story is to be found in non-Christian as well as Christian sources, one of which stated that the legion was renamed by the emperor, 'the Thundering Legion'; while Tertullian, in his *Apology*, refers to letters from Marcus Aurelius in which he testified that in Germany his army 'on the verge of destruction through lack of water' had been 'saved by the Christians' prayers'.[42] The story is all the more remarkable given the fact that Christians were discouraged from military service, not least by Tertullian.[43] Indeed, Eusebius would soon be telling the story of how the martyr, Potamiaena, would be led to execution by the soldier, Basilides, who would be converted by her prayer and, as a Christian, would then refuse to take the oath and be himself beheaded for his faith.[44]

References to the miraculous power of prayer occur elsewhere in Eusebius' narrative.[45] For example, 'many stories of miracles wrought by Narcissus, handed down by generations of Christians, are told by members of the community' of the Jerusalem church where he was bishop. 'Once during the great all-night-long vigil of Easter, the deacons ran out of oil.' Narcissus asked for water, 'said a prayer over the water, and instructed them to pour it into the lamps with absolute faith in the Lord'. 'In defiance of natural law, by the miraculous power of God the substance of the liquid was physically changed from water into oil,' and many 'preserved a little of it, as proof of that wonderful event.'[46]

In Antiquity a religion was proved by its power, and to martyrs and apostles particularly powerful and converting prayers are attributed,[47] not just in Eusebius but in many other texts, notably the Apocryphal Acts of the Apostles. In the *Acts of Peter*, people were 'astonished by the power of a man that called upon his Lord by his word; and they accepted it to their sanctification': Peter had prayed and raised a widow's son.[48] In the *Acts of*

---

[41]Eusebius, *HE* 5.5.

[42]That Eusebius correctly reports what Tertullian wrote is confirmed by Tertullian, *Apology* 5 (LCL 250).

[43]He wrote a whole treatise on the matter, Tertullian, *De Corona* (CCSL 2).

[44]Eusebius, *HE* 6.6.

[45]For example, Eusebius, *HE* 7.18 – the banishment of a demon.

[46]Eusebius, *HE* 6.9.

[47]For example, Eusebius, *HE* 3.23, quoting Clement of Alexandria; Eusebius, *HE* 5.7, quoting Irenaeus.

[48]*Acts of Peter* 27; Edgar Hennecke, *New Testament Apocrypha – Volume 2*, trans. R. McL. Wilson (London: Lutterworth Press, 1965).

John, the apostle heals a woman and raises her husband, who had failed to pray to the Lord for her and by his lamentation collapsed and died. He had begged the apostle to 'glorify your God by healing her'; but now his death made it look as if the cause was lost.[49] John prays:

> Now is the time of refreshment and of confidence in thee, O Christ. Now is the time for us who are sick to have help from thee, O physician that healest freely. Keep my entrance to this place free from derision. I pray thee, Jesus, help this great multitude to come to thee who art Lord of the universe. ... We therefore ask of thee, O King, ... two souls, through whom thou shalt convert <those who are present> to thy way (and) to thy teaching.[50]

In the same work conflict with the worship of Artemis in Ephesus is graphically depicted, with prayer causing her altar and seven images to split and half the temple to fall down.[51] It is impossible to instance here all the miraculous, curious and converting results of prayer, or indeed the frequent prayer-texts, to be found in such apocryphal material.[52] We conclude this theme with praises offered for healing in the *Acts of Thomas*:

> Glory be to thee, Jesus, who (to all) alike hast granted healing through thy servant and apostle Thomas! And being in health and rejoicing we beseech thee that we may become (members) of thy flock and be numbered among the sheep. Receive us therefore, Lord, do not reckon unto us our transgressions and our <former> errors which we committed while in ignorance.[53]

Theme 5

Prayer meant corporate liturgy, but also private thanksgivings and petitions, or personal communion with God.

In Book 10 of his *Ecclesiastical History* Eusebius celebrates 'dedication festivals in the cities and consecrations of newly built places of worship ...,' friendly intercourse between congregation and congregation, unification of

---

[49]*Acts of John* 19-25.
[50]*Acts of John* 22.
[51]*Acts of John* 38-44.
[52]See also for example, *Acts of Thomas* 51; 68; and Peter's thanksgiving on his martyr's cross in *Acts of Peter* 39.
[53]*Acts of Thomas* 59.

the members of Christ's body conjoint in one harmony'. There was 'one hymn of praise on all their lips', 'ceremonies with full pomp', 'the sacraments and majestic rites of the Church', 'with the singing of psalms and intoning of the prayers given us from God'; and

> Together, the people of every age, male and female alike, with all their powers of mind, rejoicing in heart and soul, gave glory through prayers and thanksgivings to the Author of their happiness, God Himself.

This picture of corporate prayer includes the 'carrying out of divine and mystical ministrations; while over all were the ineffable symbols of the Saviour's Passion' – celebration of the Eucharist is clearly implied.

Gathering for the Eucharist on the Lord's Day appears in the earliest manual of Christian practice, the *Didache*, along with outlines of procedure and accompanying prayers.[54] Other early liturgical material is found in Justin's *1 Apology*, for example, and in *The Apostolic Tradition* attributed to Hippolytus.[55] There is hardly space here to do justice to the pre-Nicene material which liturgiologists have trawled to reconstruct early forms of eucharistic and baptismal prayers: the results can be found elsewhere.[56]

In Book 5 of Eusebius' *Ecclesiastical History*, however, in the quoted account of the martyrs of Lyon and Vienne, we are told that the martyr Alexander 'uttered no cry, not so much as a groan, but communed with God in his heart'. The narrative thus acknowledges prayer as personal and private, not just public and corporate. It is remarkable, however, that this prayer is recorded as silent; like reading, even personal prayer would generally be spoken.

For it was communal prayer which spilled over into everyday life. The *Didache* suggests praying the Lord's Prayer three times a day, as do Origen[57] and Tertullian;[58] both the latter set this requirement within Paul's injunctions to 'pray constantly' or 'pray at every time and place' (1 Thess. 5.17; Eph. 6.18; 1 Tim. 2.8). Insofar as we have access to it, private prayer was largely rooted in the same patterns of posture, gesture and language as corporate, liturgical prayer; this is clear from the treatises on prayer by Origen and Tertullian. Personal petitions and individual circumstances, however, clearly figured, and in the earliest texts visions are sometimes associated with such

---

[54]*Didache* 9-10, 14.
[55]Justin, *1 Apology* 65-67; and *The Apostolic Tradition* attributed to Hippolytus.
[56]For example, Paul F. Bradshaw, *The Search for the Origins of Christian Worship: Sources and Methods for the Study of Early Liturgy*, 2nd edn (Oxford: Oxford University Press, 2002).
[57]Origen, *On Prayer* 12.2; *An Exhortation to Martyrdom, Prayer and Select Works*, trans. Rowan E. Greer, CWS (New York: Paulist Press, 1979).
[58]Tertullian, *De oratione* 24-25.

prayer: Polycarp, while praying for churches all over the world, has a vision anticipating his own way of martyrdom – being burnt alive,[59] and Hermas receives his visions when walking and praying.[60]

Examples of prayer as personal communion with God are hard to find, and mostly appear in texts later regarded as barely orthodox. The *Odes of Solomon* give some access to a sense of mystical communion with the divine, for example:

> My heart was cloven [= circumcised] and its flower appeared; and grace sprang up in it: and it brought forth fruit to the Lord, for the Most High clave my heart by His Holy Spirit and searched my affection towards Him: and filled me with His love. ... I was established upon the rock of truth, where He had set me up: and speaking waters touched my lips from the fountain of the Lord plenteously: and I drank and was inebriated with the living water that doth not die; and my inebriation was not one without knowledge, but I forsook vanity and turned to the Most High my God, and I was enriched by His bounty.[61]

Two prayer texts have appeared in the Nag Hammadi library, one a prayer of thanksgiving from the Hermetic Corpus, the other is *The Prayer of the Apostle Paul*, which opens the Jung Codex, and includes:

> [My] Redeemer, redeem me, for [I am] yours: from you have I come forth.
> You are [my] mind: bring me forth!
> You are my treasure-house: open for me!
> You [are] my fullness: take me to you!
> You are <my> repose: give me [the] perfection that cannot be grasped![62]

Theme 6

Though the language and forms of prayer drew principally from the Psalms and the Lord's Prayer, the influence of other patterns of invocation gradually had an impact.

---

[59]*Martyrdom of Polycarp* 5 (LCL 24).
[60]*The Shepherd of Hermas*, introducing each vision.
[61]From Ode 11; *The Odes and Psalms of Solomon*, ed. Rendel Harris (Cambridge: Cambridge University Press, 1911).
[62]*The Nag Hammadi Library in English*, trans. Coptic Gnostic Library Project of the Institute for Antiquity and Christianity (Leiden: Brill, 1977).

The importance and use of the Psalms is evident from the wealth of quotations in Eusebius' *Ecclesiastical History* Book 10; while the fact that Origen, Tertullian and Cyprian all composed treatises on the Lord's Prayer indicates its central importance in both corporate and personal prayer life. For Origen the Lord's Prayer provided a model;[63] while Tertullian presupposes that people will use the Lord's Prayer, then add their own petitions, a pattern actually reflected in the narrative of the *Acts of Thomas*.[64] Jewish prayer forms are reflected in the majority of the early texts we can trace, such as the prayer in *1 Clement* cited earlier. The *Odes and Psalms of Solomon* were largely modelled on the biblical Psalter – we may contrast the previous quotation from Ode 11 with the following from Ode 5:

> I will give thanks unto thee, O Lord, because I love thee; O most High, thou wilt not forsake me, for thou art my hope: freely I have received thy grace, I shall live thereby. ... For my hope is upon the Lord, and I will not fear, and because the Lord is my salvation, I will not fear: ... even if everything should be shaken, I stand firm: and if all things visible should perish, I shall not die: because the Lord is with me and I am with Him. Hallelujah.

However, enculturation was probably bound to happen eventually, and the influence of Hellenistic religious invocation, its forms and terminology, can be observed, at least by the third century. The most notorious example is the prayer found in the *Paedagogus* of Clement of Alexandria:

> King of saints,
> all-taking word
> of the most high Father,
> ruler of wisdom,
> ever joyful support
> for the mortal race
> in toil and pain.
> Saviour Jesus,
> shepherd, ploughman,
> helm, bridle,
> heavenly wing,
> of the most holy flock,
> fisher of men,

---

[63] Origen, *On Prayer* 18.1.
[64] Origen, *On Prayer* 10.

of those saved
from the sea of evil,
luring with sweet life
the chaste fish
from the hostile tide.
Holy shepherd
of sheep of the *Logos*,
lead, O king,
the unharmed children;
the footprints of Christ,
are the path to heaven.[65]

That is approximately one-third of the prayer. What is striking is the piling up of epithets to celebrate the nature and deeds of the one celebrated, just as is found in hymns to Artemis or Isis.[66] It is also noticeable that the object of this prayer-form is Christ rather than the Creator God and Father of all. Prayers found in the narratives of the *Acts of Thomas* take similar forms – for example:

My Lord and my God, the companion of his servants, who doth guide and direct those who believe in him, the refuge and rest of the oppressed, the hope of the poor and redeemer of the captives, the physician of the soul laid low in sickness and saviour of all creation, who dost quicken the world to life and strengthen the souls, thou knowest what is to be, who dost also accomplish it through us; thou, Lord, who dost reveal hidden mysteries and make manifest words that are secret; thou, Lord, art the planter of the good tree, and by thy hands are all good works engendered. … I pray thee, Lord Jesus.[67]

Theme 7

Jesus Christ, and often also the Holy Spirit, were associated with God the Father in prayer.

---

[65]Clement of Alexandria, 'Pedagogue', trans. Annewies Van Den Hoek, in *Prayer from Alexander to Constantine: A Critical Anthology*, ed. Mark Kiley, et al. (London: Routledge, 1997), 296–303 (3.12.101).
[66]Even more notorious is Cyril of Alexandria's homily on the virgin Mary, delivered at Ephesus, the home of the great temple to Artemis; but that is to stray into the post-Nicene period.
[67]*Acts of Thomas* 8.

The prayer of Eusebius, with which this chapter opened, clearly associates Jesus Christ with God the Almighty, King of the universe, including him in the thanksgiving and directing prayer to him. Eusebius was himself reluctant to accept the Nicene *homoousion*; yet that is what would ultimately legitimate prayer directly offered to the Son alongside the Father.

Earlier, Origen, in his treatise *On Prayer*, specifically states that prayer in its strict sense should only be offered to the God and Father of all, not 'to anyone begotten, not even to Christ'. However, Origen is clear that 'when the saints give thanks to God in their prayers, they acknowledge through Christ Jesus the favors He has done', and 'no prayer should be offered to the Father without Him', or 'without the High Priest' through whom and in whose name prayers are offered.[68] Christ has a mediatorial role. The question is to what extent and how early prayer was directly addressed to Christ.

If we return to the prayer in *1 Clement* we find exactly what Origen affirms – the association of Jesus Christ with God the Father as the one through whom prayers are offered. The prayer ends thus:

> To thee, [O heavenly Master and Monarch eternal], who alone canst grant to us these and other yet more excellent benefits, we offer up our praises through Jesus Christ, the High Priest and Guardian of our souls; through whom be glory and majesty unto thee now and for all generations and unto ages of ages. Amen.[69]

Ignatius, in his letter to the Romans, asks them to 'form a loving choir … and sing hymns of praise in Jesus Christ to the Father';[70] being 'in Jesus Christ' and so in unity with God and one another is a frequent expression.[71] Polycarp's prayer as he faces martyrdom addresses God as 'Father of Jesus Christ', and its climax is:

> I praise you, I bless you, I glorify you for everything, through the everlasting and heavenly High Priest, Jesus Christ, your beloved Child, through whom be glory to you with him and the Holy Spirit, both now and for ever. Amen

In *1 Apology* Justin describes the president taking a cup of wine mixed with water and giving 'praise and glory to the Father of the universe, through the name of the Son and of the Holy Ghost'.[72] The prayers in the *Apostolic*

---

[68]Origen, *On Prayer* 15.
[69]*1 Clement* 61; see also 64.
[70]Ignatius, *Romans* 2 (LCL 24) and *Ephesians* 4 (LCL 24).
[71]Ignatius, *Magnesians* 7 (LCL 24), *Ephesians* 10; *Philadelphians* 10 (LCL 24).
[72]*1 Apology* 65.

Tradition ascribed to Hippolytus follow the same pattern. All this second-and third-century material seems to support Origen's careful specification: prayer is offered through, not to, Jesus Christ. This also accords with our first theme: the insistence on the one true God, Creator of all, over against multiple divine beings.

However, prayers to Jesus Christ are certainly found away from formal liturgical material; the *Acts of Thomas* providing many examples of such direct pleas, especially for help in healing.[73] According to the *Acts of John*, John's final prayer before his death was directed to 'the Lord', 'our gracious God', 'our God Jesus Christ' and also to 'Lord Jesus', 'Christ Jesus, God, Lord'.[74] The long prayer of Clement of Alexandria, partially quoted earlier, is clearly an invocation of Christ.

Nor is this tendency entirely absent from liturgical material, even at very early dates. Melito's *Peri Pascha*, probably a Passover Haggadah for Christians in Asia Minor in the second century,[75] concludes by celebrating Christ:

It is he that made heaven and earth
and fashioned man in the beginning,
who is proclaimed through the law and prophets,
who was enfleshed upon a virgin,
who was hung upon a tree,
who was buried in the earth,
who was raised from the dead
    and went up to the heights of heaven,
who sits at the Father's right hand,
who has power to save every man,
through whom the Father did his works from beginning to eternity.
He is *the Alpha and the Omega*;
he is *beginning and end*,
    beginning inexpressible and end incomprehensible;
he is the Christ;
he is the king;
he is Jesus;
he is the captain;
he is the Lord;

---

[73]For example, *Acts of Thomas* 39, 60, 72, etc.
[74]*Acts of John* 106-10.
[75]Alistair Stewart-Sykes, *The Lamb's High Feast: Melito, Peri Pascha and the Quartodeciman Paschal Liturgy at Sardis* (Leiden: Brill, 1998).

he is the one who rose from the dead;
he is the one who sits at the Father's right hand;
he carries the Father and is carried by the Father.
To him be glory and power for ever. Amen.[76]

There is also a prayer, which could go back to the second or early third century, later incorporated into the Liturgy of Addai and Mari, which is clearly addressed to Christ:

> And with these heavenly powers we give Thee thanks, O my Lord, we also, Thy unworthy, frail and miserable servants, because Thou hast dealt graciously with us in a way that cannot be repaid, in that Thou didst assume our humanity that Thou mightest restore us to life by Thy divinity. And didst exalt our low estate, and raise up our fallen state, and resurrect our mortality, forgive our sins, and acquit our sinfulness, and enlighten our understanding, and, our Lord and God, overcome our adversaries, and give victory to the unworthiness of our frail nature in the overflowing mercies of Thy grace.[77]

Finally, there is good reason to believe that already in the third century the *Phōs Hilaron* was sung at vespers as lamps were lit.[78] Largely biblical in its language, the use of the word '*hilaron*' nevertheless suggests that Christ is presented as a challenge to the mystery-cults of Isis and Cybele. This hymn has been continuously used in the Eastern Orthodox churches ever since, and, from the seventeenth century, entered Western church traditions, where it is best known in John Keble's translation:

> Hail, gladdening Light of his pure glory poured
> Who is the immortal Father, heavenly, blest,
> Holiest of holies, Jesus Christ our Lord!
> Now we are come to the sun's hour of rest;
> The lights of evening round us shine;
> We hymn the Father, Son and Holy Spirit divine.

---

[76]Melito, *Peri Pascha*; *Melito of Sardis: On Pascha and Fragments*, ed. Stuart George Hall (Oxford: Clarendon Press, 1979).

[77]Anthony A. Gelston, *The Eucharistic Prayer of Addai and Mari* (Oxford: Clarendon Press, 1992), 51. Gelston argues that this is probably the earliest extant anaphora with a relatively fixed form, and could go back to the second or early third century, though a definite date cannot be proved.

[78]See R. Garland Young, 'The Phos Hilaron', in *Prayer from Alexander to Constantine*, 315.

Worthiest art thou at all times to be sung
With undefiled tongue, Son of our God, giver of life alone;
Therefore in all the world thy glories, Lord, they own.

Conclusion

So looking behind Eusebius into the range of sources available to us we have been able to tease out some of the most important themes in the understanding and practice of prayer in the pre-Nicene period, as well as some examples of actual prayer texts. Perhaps one of the most striking overall features is the extent to which the corporate prayer of the gathered community shaped personal prayer, at least as far as we can tell. Also implicit in what we have found is the influence of prayer habits on the gradual articulation of the characteristic theology of early Christianity.

CHAPTER FIFTEEN

Following an Arc of Prayer: Clement, Origen, Evagrius and John Cassian

COLUMBA STEWART

From at least the end of the second Christian century there was a sustained use of Greek philosophy to interpret Christian experience of prayer and biblical texts. The original locus of this project was the Hellenistic city of Alexandria on the Mediterranean coast of Egypt, a marketplace of ideas and religions where Jewish thinkers such as Philo had already begun a dialogue between their tradition with its sacred texts and Greek intellectual culture. The Jewish effort would not survive the first- and second-century devastations of the Roman-Jewish wars. The Christian version, necessitated by internal theological developments and apologetic responses to external critiques, developed over the centuries into one of the principal streams of Christian spirituality.

Whenever we try to understand the prayer of early Christians, we face the challenge of sources: lacking the voices of the great mass of believers, we rely on the writings of teachers of prayer and biblical interpretation. Even that evidence is incomplete, as only some of their writings have survived, especially from the earliest stages of the tradition. As theological fashions changed, or developed beyond the doctrinal frameworks of earlier literature, many texts were no longer copied.

Our access to this particular tradition of Christian prayer begins with texts from around 200. In them we already see the essential traits of what we may call an Alexandrian theology of prayer. This tradition can be traced from Clement of Alexandria to Origen, Evagrius of Pontus and the Latin author John Cassian. At each stage there were shifts in emphasis, new philosophical and theological influences, and what were presumably the marks of the personal experience of the author. Terminology appears, recedes and reappears; controversies leave their mark.

Clement of Alexandria (c. 200): The Christian Gnostic

The story as we know it begins with Clement, a widely travelled teacher of Christianity who settled in Alexandria in the later second century. A former pagan and assiduous student of philosophy, Clement learned his philosophy and theology from a variety of teachers throughout the Eastern Mediterranean. His claim to be summarizing the wisdom of his masters evokes an era of Christian theological ferment otherwise almost entirely lost to us.

Clement addressed his case for Christianity to educated people whose intellectual worldview was entirely shaped by Hellenistic philosophy. He – and his teachers before him – needed to craft a theology that made sense philosophically and was faithful to the Bible and basic Christian doctrines. Had they not, Christianity would have been marginal to the intellectual circles of Greek cities throughout the Mediterranean world. The parallels between Clement's teaching on prayer and that of his philosophical predecessors reveal their common challenge of interpreting traditional religious texts and practices in a manner consistent with an intellectual framework informed by centuries of Greek thought.

Clement was also refuting those who claimed to be Christian but, in his view, had distorted the Gospel in ways that vitiated essential elements of the faith. His application of the term 'knower' (*gnōstikos*) to the perfect Christian was both Platonic in origin and a tactical move, deployed against those who claimed to be 'knowers' through esoteric revelation rather than the common teachings of Christianity. Early Christian theologians were consumed by the battle against the dualism and false knowledge of what is commonly called 'Gnosticism'. The label covers a wide array of writings, sects and teachers, including some who considered themselves to be Christian.

Clement left no formal treatise on prayer akin to Origen's, but the seventh book of his *Stromateis* ('Miscellanies') refers frequently to prayer

as it describes the life of one who has become a 'knower' of divine truths.[1]
The book is organized as an apologetic manual with responses to the typical
critiques of Christianity by 'Greeks', i.e. pagans: Christians are atheists, their
religion does not foster human perfection, they are a confusing muddle of
warring factions. The teaching on prayer comes in the section where Clement
refutes claims of atheism with assertions that Christians believe in the true
God, worshipped truly.[2] Though Clement is often characterized as a Stoic
because of his emphasis on self-control, the term 'knower' would suggest that
his teaching on prayer owes much to Platonic epistemology and metaphysics
with their emphasis on the intellect (*nous*) as the human spiritual faculty.[3]
The questions he explores were also addressed by philosophers seeking to
make traditional Greek religion accord with a spiritual worldview. Clement's
answers often echo theirs on problems such as the value of petitionary
prayer.[4]

As Lorenzo Perrone writes, Clement 'attributes to prayer an importance …
of context or spiritual atmosphere more than equating it in the strict sense
with the action of prayer'.[5] This requires stilling the passions that war against
the intellectual part of the soul. Through disciplines both intellectual and
physical, one may reach a state of *apatheia*, freedom from the tyranny of
unruly drives and emotions, becoming capable of intimacy with God.[6] It is
the activity of knowing that forms the bond with God, not the possession of
knowledge as if it were an object.[7] All Christians pray from time to time, but
the knower prays continually, in 'conversation' (*homilia*) with God, always

---

[1]The Greek text of the *Stromateis* is available both by Otto Stählin (GCS 17) and the more
recent edition by Alain Le Boulluec (SC 428) with French translation and notes – hereafter:
Strom. An English translation can be found in J. E. L. Oulton and Henry Chadwick, *Alexandrian
Christianity: Selected Translations of Clement and Origen*, LCC (Philadelphia, PA: Westminster
John Knox Press, 1954), 93–165. That translation is a revision of J. B. Mayor's 1902 version.
[2]Clement, *Strom.* 7.1-54.
[3]Note that 'intellect' should not be construed in the way it is commonly understood today.
These theologians correlated the philosophical word 'intellect' (*nous*) with the biblical term
'heart'. See Columba Stewart, 'Evagrius Ponticus and the "Eight Generic Logismoi"', in *In the
Garden of Evil: The Vices and Culture in the Middle Ages*, ed. Richard Newhauser (Toronto:
Pontifical Institute of Medieval Studies, 2005), 3–34 (21–22).
[4]For a survey, see Gilles Dorival, 'Modes of Prayer in the Hellenic Tradition', in *Platonic
Theories of Prayer*, ed. John Dillon and Alexei Timotin (Leiden: Brill, 2016), 26–45.
[5]*La preghiera secondo Origene: l'impossibilità donata*, Letteratura Cristiana Antica, N.S. 24
(Brescia: Morcelliana, 2011), 537.
[6]Clement, *Strom.* 7.10.1; see also 7.1.1-4; 7.3.17; 7.84.2.
[7]Clement, *Strom.* 7.35.4 and 38.2.

present to God just as God is always present to us.[8] Clement emphasizes the silent aspect of such prayer, since God is aware of thoughts and does not need the human voice to communicate them. Instead, the 'intelligible voice' is produced by turning towards God.[9]

Clement echoes the grammar of prayer so central to Christian practice in that the knower honours the *Logos* (Son), and through the *Logos* honours the Father. For him, however, it describes a way of life, not a liturgical formulation.[10] Similarly, while the knower follows the prescribed times of individual and communal prayer,[11] and adopts the customary postures of turning to the east and raising the hands towards heaven, these practices unsurprisingly have a deeper signification. One should stand on tiptoe as the prayer concludes, as if the human spirit flying towards 'the intelligible being' were lifting the body from the earth. He writes that the soul now 'winged' by desire for better things can approach the 'holy place',[12] melding the Platonic image of the winged soul (*Phaedrus*) with the biblical one of the High Priest entering the Holy of Holies (Heb. 9.25). We see in Clement's writings one of the first Christian examples of the synthesis previously crafted by Philo and other Alexandrian Jews striving to render the Hebrew Bible (in its Greek Septuagint form) intelligible to those able to read it. This Hellenistic cultural ambit was inhabited by pagans, Jews and Christians often united by language and philosophical perspectives while being divided on matters of religion.

As the focus on Gnosticism faded and new controversies arose, especially in the course of the fourth century, Clement's writings became passé. The *Stromateis* survive in a single eleventh-century manuscript now in Florence (with a sixteenth-century copy of it in Paris). Despite his later obscurity, Clement played a crucial role in developing a theological understanding of the Christian life. His emphasis on silent communion with God, which he understood as fulfilling the precept of unceasing prayer, was a key contribution. That he did so without disdaining verbal prayer and other

---

[8]Clement, *Strom.* 7.39.6 and 7.35.4. This famous definition is also found in the writings of Clement's non-Christian contemporary Maximus of Tyre, further indication of a broadly shared philosophical approach to prayer. See Brouria Bitton-Ashkelony, 'Theories of Prayer in Late Antiquity: Doubts and Practices from Maximos of Tyre to Isaac of Nineveh', in *Prayer and Worship in Eastern Christianities, 5th to 11th Centuries*, ed. Brouria Bitton-Ashkelony and Derek Krueger (London: Routledge, 2017), 10–33.

[9]Clement, *Strom.* 7.43.1-5.

[10]Clement, *Strom.* 7.35.1.

[11]Clement mentions prayer at the third, sixth and ninth hours of the day (*Strom.* 7.40.3-4), at meals, bedtime and during the night (*Strom.* 7.49.3-4).

[12]Clement, *Strom.* 7.40.1.

observances was crucial. Following the lead of Philo and anticipating Origen, he knew that the spiritual meaning of the Bible or of a religious practice must be based on a literal text or an enacted deed to be authentic. He thereby avoided the pitfall of his Gnostic adversaries whose dualism could not sustain a union of the material and the spiritual.

Origen (c. 185–253): Ascetic Biblical Interpretation

Origen was a native of Alexandria and a famed catechist. Unlike the married householder Clement, Origen was an unmarried ascetic, and thus a transitional figure in this survey. His primary interest was exegesis and biblical commentary, applying the tools of spiritual interpretation honed by Philo and evident in Clement's writings.[13]

Both Clement and Origen lived in a time of sporadic Roman persecution of Christians. Persecution came close to Origen when his father was executed in 202 and again when he himself was arrested and tortured during the Decian persecution of 250. These events remind us that the seemingly other-worldly spirituality of Clement and Origen was not only a matter of their philosophical assumptions but also a response to experiences of extreme contingency, with the usual perils of life in the ancient world compounded by waves of persecution that grew in frequency during the third century.

Origen was a prolific writer. The bulk of his surviving works are biblical commentaries and homilies, but he also wrote an ambitious theological compendium (*On First Principles*), a long response to the vehement critique of Christianity by the second-century philosopher Celsus, and treatises on martyrdom and prayer. The treatise on prayer was addressed to a pair of educated Christians, Ambrose and Tatiana.[14] It was one of Origen's later works, dating from the 330s during his years in Caesarea, the Roman administrative capital of Palestine.

When Clement wrote to the 'Greeks' about prayer, he led with philosophical language and concepts rather than with biblical citations. Origen, writing to devout Christians, used a catechetical approach, fashioning his teaching

---

[13]As outlined in Book IV of his treatise, *On First Principles*, trans. G. W. Butterworth (New York: Harper and Row, 1966).

[14]The Greek text of *On Prayer* is available in Paul Koetschau, *Origenes Werke – Volume 2*, GCS (Leipzig: Hinrichs, 1899), 295–403. For the English translation, see Origen, *An Exhortation to Martyrdom, Prayer and Select Works*, trans. Rowan E. Greer, CWS (New York: Paulist Press, 1979), 81–170.

around key biblical texts about prayer.[15] Origen explores two principal issues. (1) How to pray 'in the manner required', i.e. with the proper ethical and intellectual disposition. The key text is 1 Timothy 2.8: 'I desire, then, that in every place the men should pray, lifting up holy hands without anger or argument.'[16] (2) What to pray, both in terms of types of prayer and the verbal content of prayer. Central to the former is 1 Timothy 2.1: 'I urge that supplications, prayers, intercessions, and thanksgivings be made for everyone.' For the verbal content of prayer, Origen provides an extended commentary on the Lord's Prayer. Both of these expositions are suffused with Origen's Middle Platonism and incorporate the Stoic psychology used by Clement and other writers of the era. Origen draws upon these resources as he addresses these basic topics. Throughout the treatise he maintains a strongly trinitarian focus, evident in the prologue, which concludes: 'to discuss prayer requires the Father to bring it to light, his first-born Word to teach it, and the work of the Holy Spirit to understand and speak rightly of it'.[17] He begins the treatise proper as he often does, with a philological analysis of the two Greek words commonly used for prayer (*euchē* and *proseuchē*), tracing their use throughout the Bible.

The linking of human prayer to God's response sets up a discussion of objections to prayer.[18] A few decades earlier, Clement had responded to objections from followers of a (false) gnostic, Prodikos, who argued that God's providence made prayer superfluous. Origen, addressing Christians struggling to reconcile human prayer and divine omniscience, offers a much more sophisticated response. By placing God's foreknowledge outside of created, sequential time, Origen can claim that providence is a response to the human exercise of free will. Prayer is efficacious because God is able to hold request and result together as if in the same moment in a manner beyond human understandings of cause and effect. Origen then returns to his main topic, starting with how to pray 'in the manner required'.[19] Much of his language echoes Clement's Stoic ideal, though he avoids the term *apatheia*, emphasizing instead a 'harmonizing' of the mind for prayer through moral

---

[15]For Clement and Origen compared, see Lorenzo Perrone, 'Clemens von Alexandrien und Origenes zum Gebet: Versuch eines Paradigmenvergleichs anhand ihrer Schriftstellen', in *The Seventh Book of the Stromateis: Proceedings of the Colloquium on Clement of Alexandria (Olomouc, October 21–23, 2010)*, Supplements to Vigiliae Christianae 117, ed. Matyáš Havrda, Vít Hušek and Jana Plátová (Leiden: Brill, 2012), 143–64.

[16]The text goes on to speak about the proper attitude of women; Origen is primarily interested in what it means to pray 'with holy hands'.

[17]Origen, *On Prayer* 2.6.

[18]Origen, *On Prayer* 5-7.

[19]Origen, *On Prayer* 8-13.

purification. He later describes this as 'a sound mind, a healthy soul, and well-managed thoughts'.[20]

Origen focuses particularly on the need to purge anger, following the lead of his chosen biblical text, 'lifting up holy hands without anger or argument'.[21] Though he does not go into great detail here, one of his signal contributions to Christian spirituality was his astute psychology, which brilliantly wove biblical teaching, particularly that of Jesus, into a conceptual framework shaped by philosophy. The result was a sophisticated analysis of the psychodynamics of sinful thoughts, relating them to the demonic forces prominent in Pseudepigraphal literature and in the Gospels.[22] The monastic author Evagrius of Pontus would repackage Origen's teaching in his schema of eight 'generic thoughts' (see below).

Along with the pure hands, 'the eyes of the mind' and the soul too are also lifted up (Ps. 123.1 and Ps. 25.1), leaving behind earthly and material things to contemplate God alone, the 'one who listens' in intimate conversation. Shifting the metaphor slightly, the soul separates from the body as it follows the lead of the Spirit, even surrendering its own existence so as to be in the Spirit.[23] Thus far Origen is echoing Clement, but then he goes deeper theologically by anchoring prayer in the 'Word of God', the divine *Logos* himself: '[The one praying] participates in the Word of God who stands even with those who do not know him, never absent from prayer, praying to the Father along with the person for whom he is the mediator.'[24] Such praying with the Spirit and the Word transforms the mind, which becomes like 'light rising from the understanding (*dianoia*) of the one who prays'.[25] The whole of life then becomes 'a single great prayer', fulfilling the apostolic injunction to pray without ceasing (1 Thess. 5.17). Following Clement's lead, Origen explains, 'part of this prayer is what is usually called prayer, which ought to be done at least three times a day'.[26] With this broader and more elevated understanding of prayer, the one who prays will look beyond 'insignificant and earthly things' to the spiritual mysteries that are the proper object of prayer.[27] Here Origen refers explicitly to his teaching on

---

[20]Origen, *On Prayer* 17.1.

[21]Origen, *On Prayer* 9.1.

[22]See Columba Stewart, 'Evagrius Ponticus and the "Eight Generic Logismoi"', 7–12.

[23]Origen, *On Prayer* 9.2.

[24]Origen, *On Prayer* 10.2. He also writes of the role of angels, who pray with us and serve as a communication channel with God (*On Prayer* 11.3-5).

[25]Origen, *On Prayer* 12.1; see 2 Peter 1.19.

[26]Origen, *On Prayer* 12.2.

[27]Origen, *On Prayer* 13.4; see also 16.2-17.2.

the spiritual interpretation of scripture, comparing prayer for material things to the purely literal reading of the Bible.[28] Such prayer is not wrong, but it is incomplete.

After some musing on the kinds of prayer (the 'supplications, prayers, intercessions, and thanksgivings' of 1 Tim. 2.1), Origen explains the grammar of prayer. It is always addressed to the Father through the Son, and never without him; but prayer should not be made *to* the Son instead of the Father.[29] Origen's rationale is that the Son is 'other' than the Father in nature (*ousia*) and existence (*hypokeimenon*). Although this pre-Nicene understanding of the relationship between the Father and the Son was later deemed an insufficiently robust affirmation of the divinity of the Son, this remains the standard formula for liturgical prayer. As noted above, Origen is careful throughout the treatise to provide a thoroughly trinitarian ethos for his teaching, emphasizing also the presence and working of the Holy Spirit.

The bulk of the treatise is a commentary on the Lord's Prayer, prefaced by a review of Jesus' teaching on prayer. Origen understands the two versions of the prayer in the Gospels of Matthew and Luke to have been taught by Jesus on different occasions. This allows him to comment on points of slight divergence to creative effect. Throughout the exposition, Origen's Platonic metaphysics and sophisticated theology are fully in play. The privilege of calling upon God as 'Father' is possible for faithful Christians who imitate the Only Begotten Word,

> [Who] forms their deeds, words, and thoughts according to himself, imitating the Image of 'the invisible God' (Col. 1.15, 2 Cor. 4.4) ... so that there comes to be in them 'the image of the heavenly man' (1 Cor. 15.49) who is himself the Image of God. The saints therefore are an image of an Image, the Image being the Son. ... They become conformed to the One in a glorious body (cf. Phil. 3.21), transformed by 'the renewal of the mind' (Rom. 12.2).[30]

Commenting on 'your kingdom come', Origen writes of the kingdom internalized in the perfected soul: 'I think that the kingdom of God may be understood as the blessed condition of the ruling faculty (*hēgemonikon*) and

---

[28]Origen, *On Prayer* 23.1, 27.5. As outlined in Book IV of the treatise *On First Principles*.
[29]Origen, *On Prayer* 15.1-4.
[30]Origen, *On Prayer* 22.4.

the [right] ordering of wise thoughts.'[31] And once that kingdom is established, 'the mind is occupied with intelligible things without sense perception, "face to face"'.[32]

Like Clement, Origen offers some practical directions for prayer. The posture is the usual one: standing, hands raised, facing east. As Clement had done, Origen spiritualizes the stance: 'before the hands, extend the soul; before the eyes, raise the mind to God; before standing, raise the governing faculty (*hēgemonikon*) from the ground and place it before the Lord of all things'. Praying in such a manner makes the body 'the image in prayer of the fitting characteristics of the soul'.[33] The treatise ends with a template for personal prayer:

1. Praise of God through Christ and in the Holy Spirit.

2. Thanksgiving for benefits received.

3. Confession of sins and prayer for forgiveness.

4. Petitions for self, family and general society.

5. A closing doxology to God through Christ, in the Holy Spirit.

As we have seen, Origen's further development of Clement's teaching is firmly embedded in the Christian scriptures, astute in its psychology and grounded in practice. The influence of nascent Neoplatonism, further developed from the metaphysics of Clement's time, is pervasive.

Origen's *On Prayer*, as crucial as it was for the development of a central tradition of monastic spirituality, is extant in a single fifteenth-century manuscript.[34] This puzzling fact can be explained by the damage done to Origen's reputation in the late fourth century. Writing more than a hundred years before the ecumenical councils that established theological parameters still accepted by most Christian churches, Origen's theological imagination could roam widely. He explored the cosmos (like many ancient thinkers, he believed that stars had their own kind of soul) and elaborated ingenious theories to explain how rational beings fell away from their Creator and how they might return. These theories involved speculations about the pre-existence of souls and successive 'worlds' or phases of existence. By later standards, these theories were highly problematic. When combined with his

---

[31]Origen, *On Prayer* 25.1.

[32]Origen, *On Prayer* 25.2; 1 Corinthians 13.9-12.

[33]Origen, *On Prayer* 31.2.

[34]At Trinity College, Cambridge, MS. B.8.10, now missing two leaves at the end; fortunately, one of its previous owners had commissioned a copy when it was still complete.

pre-Nicene Christology and a large dose of ecclesiastical politics in the late fourth century, the result was toxic. Many of his works in Greek were lost. Fortunately, *On Prayer* survived.

Origen is often criticized for a kind of escapism that devalues the body by over-emphasizing the intellectual aspect of human existence. His spiritualizing approach was always in conversation with the literal text, the human body and emotions. The philosophers of Antiquity and the theologians of Late Antiquity lived in a highly contingent world in which death was never very far. For Origen it came particularly close because of persecution. The Christian promise of resurrection spoke powerfully in such an environment, as did the philosophical emphasis on a higher plane of existence. We should not judge them without taking up their challenge to hold together the temporal and the eternal, the mortal and the immortal.

Evagrius of Pontus (c. 345–99): The Alexandrian Tradition in a Post-Nicene Monastic Context

Clement wrote for educated pagans (and perhaps for catechumens). Origen wrote for educated Christians. Evagrius wrote for monks. This trajectory illustrates the spread of Christianity and the emergence of the monastic form of asceticism. Because Evagrius' path to monastic life was indirect, he bridged the philosophy of the schools and the philosophy of the desert.[35] He was a talented young man from Pontus (northern Asia Minor) who received an excellent philosophical and theological education. Among his teachers were Basil the Great and Gregory Nazianzen, both lovers of Origen's writings. In 379, Gregory took Evagrius with him to Constantinople. The young deacon flourished in the capital city and remained there after Gregory returned home in 381. Shortly thereafter, a doomed love affair led him to depart the capital in haste. He found refuge with learned friends in Jerusalem, Melania and Rufinus, westerners who, like Evagrius, were part of an international network of theologians strongly influenced by Origen's writings. Still unsettled, Evagrius was sent by Melania to Egypt, where he began to practice the monastic life in the famed desert colony of Nitria, withdrawing later to the greater solitude of the Cells (Kellia). He was able to synthesize his intellectual formation and his monastic experience, becoming a prolific author and spiritual guide with a keen interest in a monastic

---

[35]See Antoine Guillaumont, *Un philosophe au désert: Évagre le Pontique*, Textes et Traditions 8 (Paris: Vrin, 2004).

pedagogy informed by philosophical models, Origen's views on biblical interpretation, and the wisdom of the elders he met in the desert.

The monastic theology of Evagrius shows the clear influence of both Clement and Origen. Evagrius retrieved the terms *apatheia* and 'knower' (*gnostikos*) from Clement. He also borrowed from him the classic definition of prayer as 'conversation with God'. From Origen, Evagrius inherited an interest in the activity of disturbing passions or demonic instigations, repackaging Origen's analysis in a schema of the eight 'generic thoughts' that a monk must address to attain *apatheia*. Evagrius also mapped the eight thoughts (gluttony, lust, avarice, anger, sadness, accidie, vainglory and pride) onto a version of the widely used Platonic tripartite model of the soul with faculties of reason, desire and aversion.[36]

Evagrius used elements of Origen's approach to biblical interpretation to craft a curriculum for monastic instruction consisting of two stages, asceticism (*praktikē*) and contemplative knowledge (*theōria* and *gnōsis*). The first was devoted to recognizing and managing the eight thoughts through ascetic practices. The latter was subdivided into 'natural' contemplation, which considered created things (*theōria physikē*), and 'theology', the contemplation of uncreated being, that is, the Holy Trinity (*theōria theologikē*). In Evagrius' view, the perfect monk would be both *praktikos* and *gnōstikos*, becoming able to instruct others in the interpretation of scripture and the correct understanding of prayer.

Evagrius lays out this programme in three fundamental works: the *Praktikos*, on the eight thoughts and *apatheia*; *Gnōstikos*, a manual for monastic teachers; and *Kephalaia Gnōstika* ('Chapters on Knowledge'), an often-cryptic collection of maxims. While these texts present his ascetic and theological system, one must consult three other works for his teaching on prayer: *On Thoughts*, which explores mental activity and the eight thoughts in depth; the *Chapters on Prayer*, which will be the focus here; and the *Skemmata* ('Reflections'), a collection of brief chapters on various topics, including prayer.[37] Taken together, they help us understand Evagrius' emphasis on imageless prayer as a corollary to ascending forms of knowledge and the meanings of biblical texts. These texts were obviously found useful

---

[36]This is best outlined in *Praktikos* 89 (SC 171), modified from a Peripatetic manual, among other things substituting an allusion to Gregory Nazianzus ('our wise teacher') for the 'Plato' of his source.

[37]Antoine and Claire Guillaumont, followed by their student Paul Géhin, have published most of the Evagrian corpus with a French translation in the *Sources chrétiennes* series, including *On Thoughts* (SC 438) and *On Prayer* (SC 589). An English translation of both can be found in *Evagrius of Pontus: The Greek Ascetic Corpus*, trans. Robert E. Sinkewicz (Oxford: Oxford University Press, 2003). Note that after chapter 34 of *On Prayer* Géhin's and Sinkewicz's numberings differ by one. I follow Géhin here.

by later monks; unlike some of Evagrius' writings, they continued to be copied in Greek.[38]

In typical monastic fashion, Evagrius recited memorized biblical texts while working or travelling. He chanted the psalms of the early morning and evening liturgies prescribed even for hermits. He also wrote a series of brief commentaries (scholia) on the Psalms and other frequently recited texts. We see his knowledge of the Bible and his monastic practice on display in the *Antirrhētikos* ('talking back'), a compendium of biblical phrases to be deployed against various manifestations of the eight thoughts. As with Clement and Origen, for Evagrius 'prayer' is related to, but distinct from, such routine monastic psalmody and biblical recitation. Psalmody calms the passions and hones ascetic attention, but it pertains to the 'wisdom of variety' (Eph. 3.10) and is replete with 'representations' or 'depictions' (*noēmata*) that form lingering 'impressions' on the mind. Even *apatheia* is not a sufficient condition for true prayer, for someone no longer controlled by disorderly passions 'can still be among simple representations and distracted by their information, and thus far from God'.[39] Such representations may be biblically inspired and edifying, but they keep the mind in the realm of variety and multiplicity when the ultimate goal is 'immaterial and single knowledge', 'the activity befitting the dignity of the mind, its best and purest activity and use'.[40] Evagrius thus modifies Clement's definition to emphasize the intellectual aspect: 'prayer is a conversation (*homilia*) of the mind with God'.[41] This seemingly cool intellectualism nonetheless has an intimacy, for 'God approaches the mind directly and puts into it knowledge of the things he wills, soothing the intemperance (*akrasia*) of the body through the mind'.[42]

The task, then, is to work through the various meanings of a biblical text to reach the 'place of prayer' where knowledge of God no longer requires mediation by word or symbol.[43] Evagrius was emphatic about the danger of mental depictions of God, which are easily distorted by the passions or manipulated by demons: 'Do not give form to the divine in yourself when you pray, nor let your mind be imprinted by any form, but advance immaterially to the immaterial and you will understand.'[44] If the mind can attain such

---

[38]For an overview of Evagrius' teaching, see Columba Stewart, 'Imageless Prayer and the Theological Vision of Evagrius Ponticus', *Journal of Early Christian Studies* 9, no. 2 (2001): 173–204.

[39]Evagrius, *On Prayer* 56.

[40]Evagrius, *On Prayer* 35-36: 'Prayer without distraction is the highest understanding of the mind. Prayer is the ascent of the mind toward God.'

[41]Evagrius, *On Prayer* 3.

[42]Evagrius, *On Prayer* 64.

[43]Evagrius, *On Prayer* 83-86.

[44]Evagrius, *On Prayer* 67.

simplicity and freedom, it may even see its own natural light, or perhaps the light of the Holy Trinity as seen by Moses when he beheld the 'place of God' atop Sinai.[45] The angels encourage and protect the one who ascends, and can even ensure that the light of the mind operates properly, without wavering.[46]

Evagrius' Christian form of neo-Platonic mysticism appealed to those trained in the same philosophical tradition. Beyond that necessarily limited circle, his teaching could provoke consternation. Around the time of his death in 399 a controversy arose among the monks of Egypt about whether God may be imagined in human form during prayer (anthropomorphism). Evagrius' adamantine position may have caused the controversy or been his response to it, though much about this conflict remains obscure. It was also a time when 'Origenism' was under attack by the heresiologist Epiphanius of Salamis (Cyprus), Jerome in Bethlehem and others. The precise relationship between these two controversies is now impossible to know. The anthropomorphite issue may have been how the larger Origenist controversy came home to the monasteries or may have precipitated it. One of Evagrius' disciples, John Cassian, provides a glimpse of how it cut through Egyptian monasticism. Cassian's *Conferences* 10 opens with a poignant story of an experienced monk (with the Egyptian name Serapion) who learns from a deacon imported from Cappadocia (named Photinus, 'bright one') that the way he had prayed throughout his long monastic life was fruitless because he had prayed to a God in human form.[47] Cassian writes as a partisan for the Evagrian position, but one cannot help but feel sympathy for the crushed old monk.

In the end, the Anthropomorphites won in Egypt. The Origenist controversy devastated Egyptian monasticism. Shortly after the death of Evagrius, the type of monks who read his writings – and those of Origen – were forced to leave Egypt. Ironically, their dispersal spread Evagrius' understanding of monastic spirituality throughout the Mediterranean basin. Evagrius' clear formulation of the Alexandrian tradition of prayer would also prove decisive for its survival and later popularity in Syriac Christianity. Though some of his writings in Greek were lost, the most important ones continued to be copied, even if they were attributed to someone else.[48] The

---

[45]Evagrius' interpretation is based on the Septuagint text of Exodus. See Stewart, 'Imageless Prayer Imageless Prayer and the Theological Vision of Evagrius Ponticus', 195–8.

[46]Evagrius, *On Prayer* 75.

[47]Cassian, *Conf.* 10.1-5 (CSEL 13); *John Cassian: The Conferences*, trans. Boniface Ramsey, ACW 57 (New York: Paulist Press, 1997). See Columba Stewart, *Cassian the Monk* (New York: Oxford University Press, 1998), 86–90.

[48]See Columba Stewart, 'Evagrius beyond Byzantium: The Latin and Syriac Receptions', in *Evagrius and His Legacy*, ed. Joel Kalvesmaki and Robin Darling Young (Notre Dame, IN: University of Notre Dame Press, 2016), 206–35.

writings on prayer were among the survivors, a testament to their reception by at least a portion of the monastic world.[49]

John Cassian (c. 365–c. 435): The Tradition Comes to the Latin West

John Cassian's *Institutes* and *Conferences* are imbued with the teachings of Origen and Evagrius and served as the principal conduit of their theologies of prayer to the Latin world.[50] These monastic compendia written in the 410s and 420s reveal Cassian's knowledge of Greek and deep familiarity with the Septuagint. They contain a number of Greek words, many of them attributable to his reading of Evagrius.[51] The eight thoughts (rechristened 'vices') are the core of his ascetic instruction. Several of the *Conferences* echo themes from Origen's *On First Principles*;[52] the ninth shows a clear debt to Origen's *On Prayer*. The fourteenth is based on the spiritual interpretation of the Bible as taught by both Origen and Evagrius. By the time Cassian wrote, it had become dangerous to name either of them or to use terminology such as *apatheia* (which became 'purity of heart' in a tactical shift from Stoic to biblical vocabulary). The superficial concealment of Cassian's sources cannot hide their impact on his thought. While his understanding of prayer follows theirs closely, he also weaves in a strand of his own spiritual experience in his teachings on compunction and ecstatic 'fiery prayer'.

After several years spent in monasteries in Palestine and Egypt, Cassian left Egypt around 400 with the monks exiled because of the Origenist controversy. We know that he worked for John Chrysostom in Constantinople before the latter's downfall in 404 and visited Rome to plead Chrysostom's case. At some point Cassian settled in Massilia (Marseilles) on the southern coast of Gaul, founded a monastery for men and another for women, and began to advise bishops how to foster authentic monasticism in their dioceses. His writings grew out of that work.[53]

---

[49]According to Paul Géhin (SC 514, 73), there are more than 120 known manuscripts of *De oratione*.

[50]Cassian, *Inst.* (CSEL 17); *John Cassian: The Institutes*, trans. Boniface Ramsey, ACW 58 (New York: Paulist Press, 2000).

[51]Columba Stewart, 'From λόγος to *verbum*: John Cassian's Use of Greek in the Development of a Latin Monastic Vocabulary', in *The Joy of Learning and the Love of God: Studies in Honor of Jean Leclercq*, ed. E. Rozanne Elder (Kalamazoo, MI: Cistercian Publications, 1995), 5–31.

[52]Columba Stewart, 'John Cassian's Scheme of Eight Principal Faults and His Debt to Origen and Evagrius', in *Jean Cassien entre l'Orient et l'Occident*, ed. Cristian Badilita and Attila Jakab (Paris: Beauchesne, 2003), 205–19.

[53]For a review of his life, writings and teaching on prayer, see Stewart, *Cassian the Monk*.

In the *Institutes*, which were devoted to asceticism and the practices of the 'outer self', Cassian specifies how 'canonical' prayer (the standard times of psalmody and prayer) should be celebrated by monks. In the *Conferences*, he turns to the problem of how to pray unceasingly. He begins in *Conferences* 9 with a general overview of basic aspects of prayer, clearly modelled on Origen's *On Prayer*. Cassian writes about the proper disposition for prayer, the four types of prayer and the spiritual meaning of the Lord's Prayer. When he turns to the practice of unceasing prayer in *Conferences* 10, he interrupts the narrative with the story about Abba Serapion and the heresy of anthropomorphic prayer described above. His actual method of unceasing prayer is anchored in the traditional monastic practice of reciting memorized biblical texts. A monk struggling to focus the mind or facing temptation should use the opening verse of Psalm 69.70, 'God, come to my assistance; Lord, make haste to help me', as a 'formula' for prayer. He linked this to the broader recitation of biblical texts, which provide wholesome material for mind and heart, as well as to ascending interpretations of them from literal to moral to spiritual meaning.[54] He quaintly compares the novice monk to a hedgehog hiding behind the rock of the Gospel, and the more advanced monk to the 'reasoning deer' roaming the higher pastures of the Bible to feed on the 'highest and most sublime mysteries' (*sacramenta*) of the Prophets and Apostles. Over time, he writes, the Bible becomes so internalized that a monk recites the words as if they were his own, intuiting the meaning even before speaking.[55]

Like Evagrius, Cassian taught that prayer should be free of mental depictions of God, even of the human Christ, lest these trap the monk in his own thoughts or lead to a false interpretation of anthropomorphizing biblical texts.[56] Unlike Origen and Evagrius, however, Cassian wrote of another kind of prayer. Equally beyond word and image, this prayer is exhilarating and ecstatic, a 'transport of the mind' (*excessus mentis*). Cassian uses language of longing, desire and rapture as he writes about the mind on fire in prayer.[57] This is far in tone from Evagrius' descriptions though not in contradiction to them. Cassian claims for his teaching the endorsement of the most famous of monks, Antony the Great, whom Cassian says was known for his frequent prayer *in excessu mentis*. He attributes to Antony the dictum 'it is not a perfect prayer when a monk understands himself or what he prays'.[58]

---

[54]Cassian, *Conf.* 14.8-11.
[55]Cassian, *Conf.* 10.11.
[56]Cassian, *Inst.* 8.4.3; *Conf.* 9.1-5.
[57]For example, Cassian, *Inst.* 2.10.1; *Conf.* 3.7.3, 4.2, 4.5, 6.10.2, 9.14-15, 9.25-29, 10.10-11, 12.12, 19.4-6.
[58]Cassian, *Conf.* 9.31.

Cassian's interest in spiritual experience is also evident in his analysis of what he calls 'compunction', a generic term for a range of intense spiritual states ranging from the enstatic to the ecstatic, and in his discussion of the gift of tears in prayer.[59] Whether this interest reflects simply his own experiences or suggests other literary influences is impossible to know. There were writings such as the fourth-century Ps-Macarian *Homilies* that presented a more affective view of prayer, and some scholars have speculated about their influence on Cassian.[60] Intriguingly, the mid-fifth-century Greek spiritual author Diadochus of Photike creates an explicit synthesis of Ps-Macarian and Evagrian motifs in his hundred *Chapters on Knowledge*. Cassian had explored an analogous reconciliation some decades earlier. In both cases their work was important in bringing two strands of teaching together into a new form. In the West, it would have a strong influence on Gregory the Great, most beloved of authors in early medieval Europe. In the East, it would be the foundation for later Byzantine spirituality as evident in the writings of Maximus the Confessor (seventh century) and Symeon the New Theologian (tenth to eleventh century). It is fortunate that despite the later theological and political disputes between the Greek and Latin churches, their monastic spirituality remained in harmony.

Conclusion

Throughout this survey we have seen the common traits of the Alexandrian understanding of Christian prayer. First, a fundamentally Platonic metaphysic in which the immaterial and spiritual aspect of existence is privileged over the physical and material. The human reasoning faculty or intellect (Gk. *nous*, Lat. *mens*) has access to that spiritual level of existence. In Christian terms, because the intellect is understood to be the image of God in which human beings were made (Gen. 1.26), it can serve as the medium between the earthly and human realm and the heavenly and divine one. Second, a hybrid Stoic-Platonic psychology which prizes equanimity as evidence of the management of unruly passions and readiness for prayer. Third, a multifaceted understanding of prayer consisting of both communal and individual practices. In its most essential form, however, prayer is a spiritual and intellectual state, the means of communion with the divine.

Their view of prayer seems far removed from our experience and understanding. Setting aside the philosophical construct behind it, the

---

[59]Cassian, *Conf.* 9.27-29.
[60]See Stewart, *Cassian the Monk*, chapter 7, on 'Experience of Prayer', 114–30.

core emphasis on what is typically called apophatic prayer (imageless, non-conceptual) became a central strand of Christian spirituality that endures today. The added dimensions of contemplation of light and descriptions of ecstatic prayer temper the emphasis on negation, suggesting a wide range of what would later be termed religious experiences. In assessing their writings, we can admire their effort to use the linguistic and intellectual resources at hand to interpret Christianity within the Hellenistic world in which Christianity took shape. They also challenge us to equal their achievement.

CHAPTER SIXTEEN

The Cappadocians on the Beauty and Efficacy of Prayer

GABRIELLE THOMAS

The efficacy of prayer is summarized exquisitely by Gregory of Nyssa in the first of his five sermons on the Lord's Prayer:

> Prayer is intimacy with God and contemplation [*theoria*] of the invisible. It satisfies our yearnings and makes us equal with angels. Through it good prospers, evil is destroyed, and sinners will be converted. Prayer is the enjoyment of things present and the substance of things to come. ... Now I think that, even if we spent our whole life in constant communion with God in prayer and thanksgiving, we should be as far from having made God an adequate return as if we had not even begun to desire making the Giver of all good things such a return.[1]

Gregory of Nyssa belongs to the group of theologians, known as 'The Cappadocians', along with his older brother, Basil of Caesarea, their sister, Macrina the Younger, and their friend, Gregory of Nazianzus. Belonging to noble and wealthy families, the three men became bishops who wrote myriad

---

[1]Gregory of Nyssa, *Sermon* 1; *The Lord's Prayer, The Beatitudes*, trans. Hilda C. Graef, ACW 18 (New York: Paulist Press, 1954), 24–5.

letters, sermons, poems and prayers, most of which address contemporary pastoral and doctrinal issues. Macrina's thought is represented in Nyssen's work, in which she is depicted as a woman who exerts a great influence upon the development of fourth-century monasticism.[2] Whilst Basil is best known for his efforts in establishing monastic communities, in which a rigorous life of prayer and service was practised, the Cappadocians were all involved in community life at different periods of their lives. In addition to their pastoral work, each of the bishops took an active role in the theological controversies of their time, including the Second Ecumenical Council in Constantinople in 381.

Best known for his 'Theological Orations', through which he aimed to delineate the doctrine of God, Nazianzen also wrote hundreds of prayers in poetic form.[3] Basil, too, wrote complex theological treatises alongside the Divine Liturgy, which continues to be prayed in the Orthodox Church.[4] Whilst Nyssen is known traditionally as the most mystical and speculative of these theologians, he also taught on practical concerns, many of which arise in his five sermons on the Lord's Prayer. For our bishops, all prayer is communal, since even the personal prayers have been written down for other believers to pray themselves.

Each Cappadocian, in his or her own way, contributes a timeless message about the beauty of prayer and its integrity to the Christian life. They lived and prayed their theology centuries before it became convention to treat spirituality and theology as separate disciplines; hence, for the Cappadocians, prayer and theology are constantly integrated. They taught that a person could not become a good theologian without praying; at the same time, no one is able to pray well without knowledge of correct doctrine.[5] Due to the way they integrated prayer and theology, their writing about prayer is scattered throughout orations, letters and poems, which are dedicated to doctrinal and pastoral issues. Through instruction on prayer and the prayers themselves, the Cappadocians grapple with such doctrines as creation, the Holy Spirit, the incarnation and the Trinity, to name but a few. It is important to note that for the Cappadocians, prayer does not exist in a vacuum, but

---

[2]On Macrina's influence, see Susanna Elm, 'Virgins of God': The Making of Asceticism in Late Antiquity (Oxford: Clarendon Press, 1994), 78–105.

[3]For the poems, see J.-P. Migne, ed., Patrologia cursus completes: series Graeca (Paris: Petit-Montrouge, 1857–83), vol. 37, 1240–430. Much of Nazianzen's work does not exist in published English translations. For English translations of selected prayers, see Gregory of Nazianzus, Selected Poems, trans, John A. McGuckin (Oxford: SLG Press, 1986).

[4]Olga A. Druzhinina, The Ecclesiology of St Basil the Great: A Trinitarian Approach to the Life of the Church (Eugene, OR: Wipf and Stock, 2016), 80.

[5]This forms the theme of Gregory of Nazianzus, Oration 27; On God and Christ: The Five Theological Orations and Two Letters of Cledonius, trans. Lionel Wickham and Frederick Williams (Crestwood, NY: St Vladimir's Seminary Press, 2002), 25–35.

in a world inhabited by spiritual beings. Thus, prayer is an incontrovertible means for the baptized to equip themselves in resisting the spiritual powers of darkness; namely the devil and demons.

Since the theme of prayer in the writings of the Cappadocians is too vast to explore in a single chapter, this chapter will focus on select themes which exemplify how the Cappadocians view spirituality, prayer and theology as one and the same.[6] These include the unity of body and soul; purification and illumination for knowledge of God; the divinity of the Holy Spirit; Nyssen's teaching on *epektasis*; and the role of angels and demons. First, let us briefly explore the prevalent teaching in Nyssen's sermons on the Lord's Prayer. These sermons draw together confession of God; Father, Son and Holy Spirit, the moral life of the believer, and intimacy with God.

The Lord's Prayer

The present congregation needs instruction not so much on how to pray, as on the necessity of praying at all, a necessity that has not been grasped by most people. In fact, the majority of people grievously neglect in their life this sacred and divine work which is prayer.[7]

In the first of his five sermons on the Lord's Prayer, Nyssen laments how few people appreciate the value and purpose of prayer. His comments are as applicable today as they were over fifteen hundred years ago. Due to the general lack of appreciation for prayer, in his first sermon, Gregory explains why prayer matters. He reminds his readers that they are made in the image of God, but that this image has been tarnished. Prayer, then, is a means through which the image can be restored, because prayer draws believers into union with God.

The second sermon reflects upon 'Our Father who art in heaven'. Through this, Gregory stipulates the importance of Christian identity; namely the significance of being called children of God. Christians owe their identity to Christ, since through Christ's life and teachings they can call God 'Father'. This demands a response from the baptized, to which we shall return when we discuss purification.

---

[6]It is worth noting that despite the extensive treatment of prayer in the writing of the Cappadocians, this is an under-researched area of their thought. For a thorough consideration of prayer which incorporates the Cappadocians, see Tomaš Špidlík, *Prayer: The Spirituality of the Christian East – Volume 2*, trans. Anthony P. Gythiel (Kalamazoo, MI: Cistercian Publications, 2005).

[7]Gregory of Nyssa, *Sermon* 1; *The Lord's Prayer*, 21.

The third sermon expounds upon 'Hallowed be Thy Name, Thy Kingdom come'. Gregory's sermon draws upon a text of Luke 11.2 which reads 'May thy Holy Spirit come upon us and purify us' instead of 'Thy kingdom come'. As Anthony Meredith has identified, this text is not found anywhere else, apart from, possibly Marcion.[8] Much of the sermon is devoted to defending the deity of the Holy Spirit. Gregory's logic follows that since the Spirit purifies the believer then the Spirit must be God, because only God purifies. He argues this at length to oppose those who, at the time, were arguing against the deity of the Spirit.[9] As we shall see throughout this chapter, the deity of the third person of the Trinity is key to all Cappadocian teaching on prayer.

In his fourth sermon, Gregory connects the concept of God's will with 'give us our daily bread'. Gregory explains the kind of blessings followers of Christ should seek, if they truly want to know God and live an authentic Christian life. He argues that there is little value in desiring physical bread if Christians do not first desire the true bread of life, Christ.

The fifth sermon reflects upon 'forgive us our debts as we forgive our debtors'. Since God alone forgives, the human act of forgiveness demonstrates the human propensity to become like God. Nyssen teaches that through imitating the divine attribute of forgiveness, humans become like God. This resonates with Nazianzen's teaching on *theosis*, although Nyssen does not use *theosis* here.[10] The sermon concludes with a discussion of 'lead us not into temptation, but deliver us from the Evil One'. Nyssen observes the different ways that the devil tempts believers to sin. For him, as for the other Cappadocians, the devil is not a symbol of evil; rather, the devil is a real spiritual enemy, as we shall discuss later.

With seamless grace, the sermons blend contemporary doctrinal issues with concerns about how to pray. These reach from the divinity of the Holy Spirit through to ways in which the baptized may avoid becoming distracted from prayer. Each sermon reflects in different ways how believers might become more like Christ through prayer. As Carol Harrison comments, 'It would not be an exaggeration to say that for Gregory, saying the Lord's Prayer effectively begins the transformation of the speaker into the image of his immutable, internal, divine hearer.'[11]

---

[8]Anthony Meredith, 'Origen and Gregory of Nyssa on the Lord's Prayer', *Heythrop Journal* 43, no. 3 (2002): 344–56 (349–50).

[9]R. P. C. Hanson, *The Search For the Christian Doctrine of God: The Arian Controversy 318–381* (Edinburgh: T&T Clark, 1988), 760.

[10]For variation in Cappadocian teaching on *theosis*, see Norman Russell, *The Doctrine of Deification in the Greek Patristic Tradition* (Oxford: Oxford University Press, 2004), 206–34.

[11]Carol Harrison, *The Art of Listening in the Early Church* (Oxford: Oxford University Press, 2013), 194.

Praying as a Whole Human Person

Turning our attention to Basil, we shall see that his teaching on prayer exemplifies unity of theology and spirituality, as we saw with Nyssen. Basil understands that the body plays an important role in prayer, since his vision of the human person is one in which body and soul form a unity. Thus, he teaches that a person does not only know God through their soul, but through body and soul.

Basil laments that those attending church do not know when they should pray. Based upon his reading of scripture, he recommends following a set pattern of prayer, which consists of praying no less than seven times a day. Inspired by Psalm 119, Basil writes, 'since David says: "Seven times a day I praise You, because of Your righteous judgments (Ps. 119.164)"'.[12] Added to this, Basil shows great concern that those in church do not understand the significance of the movements they make during prayer, such as why they stand, sit or kneel. Through his exhortation, it becomes clear that every move signifies a particular meaning. More importantly, the moves made in prayer help the person praying to remember significant events in the biblical narrative:

> We all pray facing East, but few realise that we do this because we are seeking Paradise, our old fatherland, which God planted in the East of Eden. We all stand for prayer on Sunday, but not everyone knows why. We stand for prayer on the day of the Resurrection to remind ourselves of the graces we have been given: not only because we have been raised with Christ and are obliged to seek the things that are above, but also because Sunday seems to be an image of the age to come. ... Every time we bend our knees for prayer and then rise again, we show by this action that through sin we fell down to earth, but our Creator the Lover of Humankind, had called us back to heaven.[13]

Through his reflection on the various moves made in prayer, Basil calls our attention to the importance of the whole human person, and particularly the role of the body in prayer. In short, a life of prayer is not about abstract piety. In the passage above, the body plays an important role in enabling the person praying to remember key events, such as Christ's resurrection. The

---

[12]Basil of Caesarea, 'An Ascetical Discourse', in *Ascetical Works*, trans. Monica M. Wagner, FC 9 (Washington, DC: Catholic University of America Press, 1962), 207–22 (212–13).

[13]Basil of Caesarea, *De Spiritu Sancto* 27.66; *On the Holy Spirit*, trans. David Anderson (Crestwood, NY: St Vladimir's Seminary Press, 1997), 99.

act of remembering through the body draws believers into union with God, which Basil explicates in a letter to his friend, Gregory Nazianzen:

> Prayers, too, after reading, find the soul fresher, and more vigorously stirred by love towards God. Prayer is to be commended, for it engenders in the soul a distinct conception of God. And the indwelling of God is this – to have God set firm within oneself through the process of memory. We thus become a temple of God whenever earthly cares cease to interrupt the continuity of our memory of him.[14]

Throughout their work Basil and his fellow Cappadocians highlight the unity of body and soul. Through this unity, the human person is created with capacity to remember God and to know God through prayer. For each Cappadocian, knowing God, vis-à-vis becoming a theologian, requires purification and illumination. Let us turn now to Gregory Nazianzen, who is one of only three theologians on whom the title 'Theologos' has been conferred univocally in the Eastern Christian tradition. Whilst it is not clear precisely how the title came about, it was in use by the time of the Council of Chalcedon in 451, which referred to Gregory as 'Blessed Gregory, the Theologian'.[15] We shall see that for Gregory, no one should think of themselves as a theologian if they are not willing to commit to a life of prayerful purification and illumination, but even then no one can know God fully.

Purification and Illumination

Do we not travel towards God through prayer?[16]

In the first of his five 'Theological Orations', Nazianzen begins by explaining the prerequisites for those who wish to become theologians, or, said another way, those who long to know God. However, whilst our theologian teaches on how to know God, ultimately, he believes that complete knowledge of

---

[14]Basil of Caesarea, 'Letter 2', *Basil of Caesarea*, trans. Philip Rousseau (Berkeley, CA: University of California Press, 1995), 80.

[15]For a full translation and commentary of the council, see Richard Price and Michael Gaddis, *The Acts of the Council of Chalcedon* (Liverpool: Liverpool University Press, 2005).

[16]Gregory of Nazianzus, *Oration* 27.7; author's translation. For a published translation, see Gregory of Nazianzus, *On God and Christ*, 30–1. Where I have cited my own translations, I have used the French, critically edited *Sources chrétiennes* series for the Greek text: *Discours 27–31* (SC 250) and *Discours 38–41* (SC 358). On purification and illumination in Nazianzen's work, see Christopher A. Beeley, *Gregory of Nazianzus on the Trinity and the Knowledge of God: In Your Light We Shall See Light* (Oxford: Oxford University Press, 2008), 63–113.

God is impossible. In the work of the Cappadocians, the figure of Moses is used as a means of expressing intimacy with God, whilst affirming that no one can truly know God. At the beginning of *Oration* 28, Nazianzen puts himself in the place of Moses. He ascends through the heights of Mount Sinai and on reaching the top of the mountain Gregory enters the cloud. His purpose in penetrating the cloud is to contemplate God. Whilst sheltering in the rock, which is Christ, however, Gregory explains that he can only see God in the way that one sees 'shadowy reflections of the Sun in water'.[17] As close as Gregory comes to God, ultimately, he finds that God is unknowable, from which he concludes: 'to tell of God is not possible ... but to know him is even less possible'.[18] Whilst they teach that knowledge of God is apophatic, the desire for God compels the Cappadocians to continue to seek God. This entails purification, as Nazianzen explains in the first of his 'Theological Orations':

> Discussion of theology is not for everyone, I tell you, not for everyone – it is no such inexpensive or effortless pursuit. Nor, I would add, is it for every occasion, or every audience; neither are all its aspects open to inquiry. It must be reserved for certain occasions, for certain audiences, and certain limits must be observed. It is not for all people, but only for those who have been tested and found a sound footing in contemplation [*theoria*], and more importantly, have undergone, or at least are undergoing, purification of body and soul.[19]

The Cappadocians teach that purification is necessary because knowledge of God is not simply about dogmatics. Knowledge of God involves the spiritual progress of theologians themselves, since correct doctrine and spiritual progress work together in every instance. For each Cappadocian, purification and right living are serious concerns. Nyssen, for example, in his second sermon on the Lord's Prayer, teaches that the person praying must live in light of their prayer:

> If therefore the Lord teaches us in his prayer to call God Father, it seems to me that he is doing nothing else but to set the most sublime life before us as our law. ... But if we call our Father [the One] who is incorruptible and just and good, we must prove by our life that the kinship is real.[20]

---

[17]Gregory of Nazianzus, *Oration* 28.3; *On God and Christ*, 39.
[18]Gregory of Nazianzus, *Oration* 28.4; *On God and Christ*, 40.
[19]Gregory of Nazianzus, *Oration* 27.3; *On God and Christ*, 26–27, with amendments.
[20]Gregory of Nyssa, *Sermon* 2; *The Lord's Prayer*, 39–40, with amendments.

Nyssen moves on to argue that if anyone prays 'Our Father' whilst preoccupied with money or other deceits offered by the world, they are in danger of hypocrisy. Thus, purification is essential so that prayer mirrors how a person lives. As Nyssen warns, 'It is dangerous to use this prayer and call God one's Father before one's life has been purified.'[21] Neither Nyssen nor the others suggest that the purity can be earned simply through human effort, since the purification itself comes from God. This prompts the question, 'how, then, does purification occur'?

The Cappadocians teach that when embarking upon the road to purification, baptism is essential. Amongst its many virtues, baptism is a gift, grace and bath.[22] The depiction of baptism as a bath relates to the purification, which takes place through the sacrament. In an allegorical reading of Luke 17.14, Nazianzen reimagines Christ's healing of the ten lepers occurring at baptism. He relates the purification of the lepers to Genesis 1.26, in which the human person is created as an image of God. He writes, 'If you were covered head to toe with leprosy (that formless evil), after you had been scraped clean from the evil matter and received the healed image, show the purification to me as your priest.'[23] Nazianzen's point is that baptism initiates purification. This leads to the important doctrine concerning the divinity of the Holy Spirit.

The Holy Spirit

As we saw earlier, Nyssen explains in his third sermon on the Lord's Prayer that true purification and illumination can occur only if it is God who purifies. Nazianzen explains this further in his oration *On Baptism*:

> The cleansing is double; through water, I say, and the Spirit. Whilst being received bodily the one is seen and the other encounters it apart from the body and is invisible. Whilst the one is symbolic, the other is true and cleanses the depths.[24]

Nazianzen explains that baptism is at once both symbolic and true, because it consists of both water and the Spirit. Since the Spirit makes no physical mark on a person's body, an invisible or metaphysical reality is impressed on the image of the person who receives it. The extent of the purification

---

[21]Gregory of Nyssa, *Sermon 2*; *The Lord's Prayer*, 40.
[22]Gregory of Nazianzus, *Oration* 40.4; *Festal Orations*, trans. Nonna Verna Harrison (Crestwood, NY: St Vladimir's Seminary Press, 2008), 100–2.
[23]Gregory of Nazianzus, *Oration* 40.34; author's translation.
[24]Gregory of Nazianzus, *Oration* 40.8; author's translation.

and renewal which occurs at baptism is only possible if the Holy Spirit is confessed as God. Yet again, in the Cappadocian pursuit of purification we encounter a unity of theology and spirituality. Purification depends upon a correct profession of the Holy Spirit at baptism. In the same way, a person cannot hope to profess true doctrine, if she is not being purified.

For all the Cappadocians, purification continues through to illumination, which is a metaphor the bishops frequently use to describe knowledge of God. Once more, it is the Spirit who illumines the believer. Through the Spirit the 'Father is known and ... the Son is glorified and known'.[25] Nazianzen uses the concept of knowledge to describe the Spirit's revelation of the Father and the Son. He also connects both knowledge and illumination to life in the Spirit. We see this through his use of Psalm 13, which he applies in order to explain that those who do not know God are in danger of death: 'If you are blind and without illumination, "illumine your eyes, so that you may never sleep in death".'[26] Thus, Gregory links illumination to life, since those who are illumined become spiritually alive. The person who is spiritually alive is the one who recognizes the truth of Jesus Christ. In his oration *On the Holy Spirit*, Basil explains that the Spirit enables believers to say, 'Jesus is Lord'. After this, he moves on to teach that through the illumination of the Holy Spirit believers recognize 'the true light that enlightens every man comes into the world'.[27] Thus, the Spirit purifies and illumines the baptized so that they might recognize Jesus as Lord and receive life.

As we have already observed, whilst the Cappadocians teach that the Spirit gives life to and illumines the baptized, ultimately full knowledge of God is not possible because God is limitless. For this reason, the soul leans towards God throughout life on earth and beyond. Nyssen develops this belief quite distinctly, through his doctrine '*epektasis*'.

Epektasis

Taking the Spirit as companion and ally, one is inflamed towards a love of the lord and seethes with longing, not finding satiety in prayer, but always inflamed towards a love of the good and enkindling the soul with desire.[28]

---

[25]Gregory of Nazianzus, *Oration* 41.9; author's translation.
[26]Gregory of Nazianzus, *Oration* 40.34; author's translation.
[27]Basil of Caesarea, *De Spiritu Sancto* 18.47; *On the Holy Spirit*, 74.
[28]Gregory of Nyssa, 'On the Christian Mode of Life', in *Ascetical Works*, trans. Victoria Woods Callahan, FC 58 (Washington, DC: Catholic University of America Press, 1967), 125–60 (152).

Nyssen teaches that even prayer cannot wholly satisfy the soul, due to the limitlessness of God. Because God has no limit, the soul continually stretches towards God even after death, and throughout eternity. Nyssen develops the concept of *epektasis* to describe this perpetual movement of the soul towards God. Like all the theological work of the Cappadocians, Nyssen's development of *epektasis* is the fruit of much reflection on scripture. His inspiration for this particular doctrine is Paul who, in his letter to the Philippians, writes, 'beloved, I do not consider that I have made it my own, but this one thing I do: forgetting what lies behind and straining forward (*epekteinomenon*) to what lies ahead' (Phil. 3.13). In *The Life of Moses*, in which he develops at length an allegorical interpretation of the ascent of Moses up Mount Sinai, Gregory reflects upon Paul's concept of straining forward:

> But in the case of virtue we have learned from the Apostle that its one limit of perfection is the fact that it has no limit. For that divine Apostle, great and lofty in understanding, ever running the course of virtue, never ceased straining toward those things that are still to come. Coming to a stop in the race was not safe for him. Why? Because Good has no limit in its own nature but is limited by the presence of its opposite, as life is limited by death and light by darkness.[29]

Jean Daniélou, the French Jesuit writer, has shown that *epektasis* is foundational to Gregory's spirituality. It overlaps with key doctrines in Gregory's work, for example, divine ineffability.[30] Further to this, *epektasis* establishes a crucial difference between Creator and created: God's perfection consists in immutability. This contrasts with the perfection of the human person, which exists in mutability. It is significant that Gregory does not consider human mutability as negative, but as wholly positive. This contrasts with contemporary Greek thought, which was a proponent of the belief that final perfection after death belongs to a static state. Gregory achieves his depiction of human mutability as good, because mutability means that the soul possesses the potential to move ever closer to God.[31]

[29]Gregory of Nyssa, *The Life of Moses*, trans. Abraham J. Malherbe and Everett Ferguson, CWS (New York: Paulist Press, 1978), 30.

[30]See Jean Daniélou, *Platonisme et théologie mystique: Essai sur la doctrine spirituelle de saint Grégoire de Nysse* (Paris: Aubier, 1944). Daniélou's work on *epektasis* established the doctrine within Western Christian thought.

[31]For an excellent literature review of Nyssen's doctrine of *epektasis*, see Morwenna Ludlow, *Gregory of Nyssa, Ancient and (Post)modern* (Oxford: Oxford University Press, 2007), 125–34. See also Paul M. Blowers, 'Maximus the Confessor, Gregory of Nyssa, and the Concept of "Perpetual Progress"', *Vigiliae Christianae* 46, no. 2 (1992): 151–71.

It is important to note that *epektasis* is established through the belief that God is Love. The soul constantly desires to know God more clearly, but reaches no point of satisfaction because God's love is limitless, a theme which Gregory develops in a number of texts, such as *Homilies on the Song of Songs* and *On the Christian Mode of Life*. Gregory does not set out a clear path consisting of varying degrees of ascetical effort; rather, he presents a life lived through falling more and more in love with the Word. Christ is central to Gregory's thought about perpetual progress, since he writes, 'the one who finds any good finds it in Christ who contains all good'.[32] By virtue of being created according to the Image, who is Christ, all human persons participate in the incarnation of Christ. Through this, they have the potential to know God to some degree.

As we observed at the beginning of this chapter, the Christian life is not lived out easily. The Cappadocians teach that creation consists of not only that which is visible, but also invisible spirits; namely angels, the devil and demons. These invisible spirits influence the extent to which a person can know God through prayer in both positive and negative ways. Again, observe the unity of spirituality and theology; the Cappadocians account for invisible spirits theologically at the same time as describing how these spirits are present during the prayers of the baptized.

Angels and Demons

The Cappadocians, following Christian tradition, 'accepted the reality of the spiritual world'.[33] They lived, following an age, in which the importance of angels had increased significantly through the influence of mystical Judaism, along with Apocryphal and Pseudepigraphical traditions. For the Cappadocians, neither angels nor demons are peripheral to Christian experience. Rather, angels and demons appear so frequently in Cappadocian writing on prayer that it could be said they are integral to Cappadocian spirituality. This involves a radically different approach to the cosmos from the worldview which developed through modernity. Catholic philosopher Charles Taylor explicates the change in the landscape. He summarizes the pre-modern world as one of 'enchantment',[34] within which existed 'spirits, demons and moral forces'.[35] In the enchanted world the human being is

---

[32]Gregory of Nyssa, *The Life of Moses*, 118.

[33]Everett Ferguson, *Demonology of the Early Christian World* (New York: Edwin Mellen Press, 1984), 133.

[34]Charles Taylor, *A Secular Age* (Cambridge, MA: Harvard University Press, 2007), 446.

[35]Taylor, *A Secular Age*, 29.

'open and porous and vulnerable to a world of spirits and powers'.[36] Taylor argues that through modernity and the rise of humanism, this was displaced by a 'disenchanted' view of the world.[37] In the disenchanted world, humans have no need to be concerned with spiritual beings. When thinking about the ways in which the Cappadocians view prayer we should remember that they understand their world to be 'enchanted'. They do not consider themselves as either distant from or invulnerable to spiritual powers, such as angels and demons. Consequently, angels are invoked frequently in prayer. Furthermore, prayer often serves the purpose of resisting various kinds of demons, which we shall discuss shortly.

Regarding the nature attributed to these invisible spirits, Nazianzen describes them as 'second lights', observing that whilst they are brilliant, angels are creatures and therefore distinct from their Creator:

> First, while [God] conceived the angelic and heavenly powers … in this way the secondary splendours came about, servants of the first Splendour; one must consider them as intellectual spirits or fire as such immaterial and incorporeal, or as another nature, which is closest to that of which has been spoken.[38]

For the Cappadocians, angels are the closest to God in creation. The implications of this for human persons are that angels are worthy of imitation, as Basil writes in a letter to Nazianzen, 'What, then is more blessed than to imitate on earth the choirs of angels; hastening at break of day to pray, to glorify the Creator with hymns and songs?'[39] In addition to singing hymns to God, angels have multiple functions, each in a particular rank according to their brilliance.[40] They serve the Trinity by executing God's commands in heaven, continuing on earth as Christ's entourage.[41] Angels are characterized as co-workers alongside humans, active in the life of the church and present at baptism.[42] They play a key role as guardians, both of church communities and of individual believers.[43] For this reason, angels feature regularly in prayers for those who are sick or dying. Nazianzen, for example, even speaks to his own angel when he is ill, 'But where is my angel? I am here, may you

---

[36]Taylor, *A Secular Age*, 27.

[37]Taylor, *A Secular Age*, 27.

[38]Gregory of Nazianzus, *Oration* 38.9; author's translation.

[39]Basil of Caesarea, *Saint Basil: Letters 1–185 – Volume 1*, trans. Agnes Clare Way, FC 13 (Washington, DC: Catholic University of America Press, 1951), 7.

[40]Gregory of Nazianzus, *Oration* 28.31; author's translation.

[41]Gregory of Nazianzus, *Oration* 38.14; author's translation.

[42]Gregory of Nazianzus, *Oration* 40.36; author's translation.

[43]Gregory of Nazianzus, *Oration* 42.9; author's translation. See also Brian Daley, *Gregory of Nazianzus* (London: Taylor and Francis, 2006), 144–5.

cool the water.'[44] Also, in a beautiful prayer, which Macrina prays on facing her own death, angels are shown to accompany human beings not only in life, but also through death: 'Put down beside me a shining angel to lead me by the hand to the place of refreshment.'[45] Thus, present from the beginning of the Christian life at baptism, through to the end of life on earth and beyond, angels play important roles in the lives of believers. Unfortunately, as Basil warns, not all angels work towards the welfare of the church. Some angels have fallen from heaven, and consequently they endeavour to inhibit a life of prayer: 'For it is the way of the devils to urge us to be absent during the time of prayer on the pretext of a seemingly worthy reason, so that they may plausibly draw us away from saving prayer.'[46]

The prevalence of prayers and warnings against demons indicate that the Cappadocians considered them to be real spiritual enemies.[47] Following Christian tradition, the Cappadocians refer interchangeably to the devil, Satan, the fallen angel Lucifer and the serpent. This follows a common patristic reading of Isaiah 14.12 which understands Lucifer, the Morning Star, to speak of both Satan, who appears in Job, and the serpent in Genesis 3. The prayers prayed by the Cappadocians relate most often to the ways that the devil works through the world, the flesh or the passions in order to draw believers from Christ. In no less than thirteen consecutive prayers, Nazianzen depicts the devil's assault upon the human person using vivid language.[48] Six of the thirteen prayers are entitled *Against the Evil One*, which offers an indication of his preoccupation with the work of the devil. In these poems, Gregory describes the devil's attempts to destroy him (and, by extension, all those baptized) by continual provocation to sin. 'And if the destroyer of the image trips me up, who might become my guardian, save you, Lord?'[49] In response to these attacks Nazianzen advises the church to pray constantly, since prayer serves as a shield against the devil:

Keep yourself inaccessible, both in word and deed and life and thought and movement. The Evil One interferes with you from every side, he

---

[44]Gregory of Nazianzus, *Carm.* 2.1.89 (PG 37, 1443, 8); author's translation.

[45]Gregory of Nyssa, *The Life of Saint Macrina*, trans. Kevin Corrigan (Toronto, Ontario: Peregrina Publishing, 1997), 41.

[46]Basil of Caesarea, 'On Renunciation of the World', in *Ascetical Works*, 15–32 (28–9).

[47]Morwenna Ludlow, 'Demons, Evil and Liminality in Cappadocian Theology', *Journal of Early Christian Studies* 20, no. 2 (2012): 179–211.

[48]Gregory of Nazianzus, *Carm.* 2.1.54–2.1.67 (PG 37, 1397, 11–1407, 8). Translations of all the prayers are not available in English. For translations of eight prayers, see Dayna Kalleres, 'Demons and Divine Illumination: A Consideration of Eight Prayers by Gregory of Nazianzus', *Vigilae Christianae* 61, no. 2 (2007): 157–88.

[49]Gregory of Nazianzus, *Carm.* 2.1.65 (PG 37, 1407, 6–7). 'The image' refers to Genesis 1.26.

scopes you out everywhere, where he may strike, where he may wound. Do not let him find any corner laid open and ready for his blow.[50]

To know God and become like God it is imperative that followers of Christ protect themselves through prayer. Through their writing on spiritual warfare, the Cappadocians proclaim the victory, lordship and divinity of Christ. Christ is the first to rule over the evil powers because he is God's Son.[51] Thus, uttering the name of Christ in prayer is one of the greatest weapons against the devil. It is only through participation in Christ that the devil can be resisted, 'resist him (the devil) with the saving Word, who is the bread sent from heaven and giving graciously life to the world'.[52]

Throughout the various challenges with demons, it is not only Christ's divinity which is recognized, but also the divinity of the Holy Spirit. Since the Holy Spirit is God, the Spirit is able to protect the believer and furthermore enable those attacked by demons to become victorious over them: 'Don't be afraid of the battle. Protect yourself with water, protect yourself with the Spirit, in whom every single burning missile of the Enemy is put out.'[53] In sum, whilst the battle is fierce, through the victory of Christ and the protection of the Spirit, hope of overcoming prevails.

Conclusion

Our brief sojourn through Cappadocian prayer has shown that the person who prays must do so in light of correct doctrine; likewise, no one can hope to confess correct doctrine if they do not live a life of prayer. In light of this, we might describe a Cappadocian view of prayer as a dynamic web which connects together myriad important doctrines, practices and beliefs.

The overwhelming theme running through Cappadocian teaching on prayer concerns knowledge of God: if anyone longs to know God, to experience intimacy with God, and even to become like God, then they must pray. Since the body and soul work together as a unity, prayer encompasses the whole human person. Each movement made in prayer enables those praying to remember important truths, all of which build faith and draw believers closer to God. That said, whilst those who commit themselves to a life of prayerful purification and illumination may comprehend God, they will never know God completely, since God is limitless. In response to this,

---

[50]Gregory of Nyssa, *Sermon* 1; *The Lord's Prayer*, 31.
[51]Gregory of Nazianzus, *Oration* 40.10; author's translation.
[52]Gregory of Nazianzus, *Oration* 40.10; author's translation.
[53]Gregory of Nazianzus, *Oration* 40.10; author's translation.

the soul yearns continually for God, and stretches out towards Love, which Nyssen describes as '*epektasis*'.

A full appreciation of Cappadocian prayer must account for the reality of angels and demons in their world, since these invisible spirits appear in both teaching on prayer and the prayers themselves. Whether helping or hindering the baptized, spiritual beings are prevalent in the texts, pointing in different ways to important truths, such as the divinity of Christ and the Spirit.

In sum, prayer is essential to the Christian life, the goal of which is to know and glorify God; Father, Son and Holy Spirit. This is summarized in the following prayer by Nazianzen, which draws together the themes we have discussed:

Glory to God the Father
And to the Son who reigns over all.
Glory to the all-holy Spirit
to whom all praise is due.
This is the One God, the Trinity,
who created all existence
who filled the heavens with spiritual beings,
the land with creatures of earth,
the oceans, rivers and streams
with water's living things.
From God's own Spirit, God gives life to all that lives
so that all creatures can sing out praise
to the wisdom of the Creator,
the solitary cause of their life, and their enduring.
But more than all others,
and in all things,
rational nature shall sing out
that God is the great king, the good father.
And so, Father, grant to me,
by spirit and soul,
by mouth and mind,
in purity of heart,
to give you glory. Amen.[54]

---

[54]Gregory of Nazianzus, *Carm.* 1.1.31 (PG 37), 510–11; *Selected Poems*, trans. John A. McGuckin, Fairacres Publication (Oxford: SLG Press, 1986), 10, with amendments.

CHAPTER SEVENTEEN

Augustine on Prayer: Sin, Desire and the Form of Life

JONATHAN D. TEUBNER

'We do not know Augustine if we do not recognize the praying person in him,' wrote the late T. J. van Bavel.[1] For Augustine, prayer was not a task set apart: the walls of his cathedral did not cleanly separate 'church' from 'world'. Rather, prayer is intimately entangled with all his efforts to understand himself, God as Trinity, and his corporate existence within the church. In short, Augustine's understanding of prayer informs his account of Christian existence as it plays out in this world. Many today connect Augustine's totalizing vision for prayer with his *Confessions*. But placing our focus there can distort our understanding of prayer's place in Augustine's life, for *Confessions* is only one snapshot of his prayerful pursuit of God. For Augustine, prayer is always *in via*, not only in the sense of spiritual development, but in the sense of always being on the way to something else. When Augustine talks about prayer he is also often speaking about something else as well. To understand Augustine on prayer is, then, to appreciate prayer not as a distinct practice that is started and stopped at will. Rather, it is to see prayer as a life form that manifests in all facets of his individual and communal existence.

In this chapter, I shall not attempt to report, even in summary form, on such a totalizing vision.[2] Instead, I will organize Augustine's understanding

---

[1]Tarsicius J. Van Bavel, *The Longing of the Heart: Augustine's Doctrine on Prayer* (Leuven: Peeters, 2009), 1.

[2]For a more developed account, see my *Prayer after Augustine: A Study in the Development of the Latin Tradition* (Oxford: Oxford University Press, 2018).

of prayer around his developing sense of what it means to 'pray without ceasing' as is commanded by 1 Thessalonians 5.17. Augustine's response to this Pauline command develops in concert with his thinking about the soul's desire for God. Augustine famously proclaimed, 'Your desire is your prayer, your prayer is your desire.'[3] How and why this is the case took Augustine decades to specify. And, contrary to the Pelagian suspicion of the Bishop of Hippo, Augustine is far from willing to let one's will and its desires pass without inspection, rebuke and correction. To pray without ceasing is, for Augustine, hard-won through a lifelong struggle to desire rightly. But it is precisely in its intimate connection with desire that prayer is liable to go wrong – to deform us and our relationships with others. Our desires are, to say the least, wayward. For this reason, Augustine insisted that such desire-led prayer must always be embedded within a community that continually tests one's desires against the holy petitions of the Lord's Prayer. But even this model has its limits, for there is nothing guaranteeing that the community as a whole is not deformed in some fundamental way. In short, community-tested prayer cannot save us any more than our own desire-led prayer can.

Augustine's early attempts to think about prayer's formative role in one's pursuit of finding rest in wisdom take on seminal formulation in the so-called ascents of the soul, psycho-dramatic exercises of refining and directing one's intellectual and moral life. Prayer is not a theme commonly connected with the 'ascents', for they are more obviously bound up with the process of ratiocination, of cultural and intellectual *Bildung*. But when we re-focus our understanding of Augustine's evolving thinking on the ascent around the theory and practice of prayer, a different trajectory of Augustinian *Bildung* emerges, one that finds Augustine counter-posing certain doctrinal and moral perplexities. By reading Augustine's reflections on ascent through his evolving thoughts on prayer we can see that they are not abandoned as some kind of Platonist juvenilia, but are rather refracted through a deep and persistent engagement with the Lord's Prayer. Therefore, I shall draw Augustine's ascents of the soul together with his reflections on the Lord's Prayer to frame how Augustine proposes that we might fulfil the Pauline command to pray without ceasing. In short, Augustine thinks of prayer as not one task among many but as a life form that all Christians ought to take on. In a final part of this chapter, I shall reflect on how the *Rule of St Benedict* institutionalizes a certain understanding of prayer as a life form. To appreciate how Latin monasticism struggled to *legislate* a life of 'unceasing prayer' is to capture the tension within an Augustinian vision of Christian desire caught between this world and the next.

---

[3]Augustine, *En Ps.* 37.14 (CCSL 38); *Expositions of the Psalms – Volume 2: 33–50*, trans. Maria Boulding, WSA III/16 (Hyde Park, NY: New City Press, 2000).

Locating *our* Augustine

As I have already suggested, we make a mistake when we jump straight to Augustine's self-representation as a practitioner of prayer in his *Confessions*. Today, the focus on the *Confessions* often comes at the expense of the *Enarrationes in Psalmos,* a series of sermons that were widely circulated before the emergence of our modern fascination with Augustine as a kind of spiritual 'genius'. This modern line of inquiry found seminal expression in Adolf von Harnack's 1887 lecture on the *Confessions*.[4] Harnack commends Augustine for turning inwards and seeking a direct and immediate connection with the divine. This implied, for Harnack, a turning *away* from popular forms of piety, from what the pre-eminent *Wissenschaftler* of his day took to be the crass supernaturalism of the mass and our feeble attempts to call God to act in this world.[5] Harnack might seem a surprising champion of Augustine, as the great church historian famously decried the influence of 'Hellenism' on Christian thought and practice. But for Harnack – a man indelibly stamped by the intellectual imagination of the nineteenth century, Goethe's above all – Augustine represented a man set apart, as if he were wandering above a sea of fog. In the *Enarrationes*, by contrast, we find Augustine embedded within the day-to-day life of the church that refuses to give up on its received forms of popular piety. Augustine endorses those supposedly crass practices – praying for your crops as well as your sick and dying loved ones – that are thought to be holdovers from 'naturalistic religion'. For this reason, Harnack judged that Augustine's reformation of Christian piety is only half-complete, that the Neoplatonist wisdom-seeker is ultimately overwhelmed by the tasks of the church.[6]

Between the *Confessions* and the *Enarrationes* we have, then, an almost-schizophrenic portrait of Augustine: he is either striving for a more intellectually honest (if a bit self-obsessed) form of prayer or a man ineluctably formed by the traditional piety of the Roman African Church. Today, scholars are, on the whole, more inclined towards accounts that embed Augustine within communal forms of prayer that reveal the moral formational aspects of such an activity. Where a certain modern sensibility sought to capture Augustine-the-individual, our age attempts to discover an Augustine that might challenge an individualism whose inner curvature sinks into a

---

[4]Adolf von Harnack, *Augustins Konfessionen: Ein Vortrag* (Giessen: De Gruyter, 1887). See also Adolph von Harnack 'Die Höhepunkte in Augustins Konfessionen', in *Aus der Friedens- und Kriegsarbeit* (Giessen: De Gruyter, 1916), 69–99 and *Augustine: Reflexionen und Maximen* (Tübingen: Mohr Siebeck, 1922).
[5]Adolph von Harnack, *Lehrbuch der Dogmengeschichte – Volume 3: Die Entwicklung des kirchlichen Dogmas II/III*, 4th edn (Tübingen: J. C. B. Mohr, 1909), 62–5.
[6]Harnack, *Lehrbuch der Dogmengeschichte*, 77.

spiritual narcissism. In this sense, contemporary scholarship on Augustine's 'spirituality' can be seen as a response to Hannah Arendt's criticism, initially laid out in her 1929 Heidelberg Dissertation *Der Liebesbegriff bei Augustin*, that Augustine induces Christians to withdraw from the political or public realm.[7] While very few would defend Arendt's reading of Augustine, which largely accepts Harnack's interpretation of Augustine, a substantial portion of scholarship on what Harnack called Augustine's 'piety' attempts to fashion an Augustine one would be proud to introduce to Arendt. It is instructive to see how Augustine was able to conjure out of the day-to-day practices of the Christian life a compelling theological construct that would secure him a place in the Romantic pantheon (and elicit rebuke from one of the twentieth century's most perceptive critics).

Augustine's account of prayer is perplexing precisely because it refuses to be pinned down by one text or line of argumentation. This becomes all the more obvious when we turn to reflect on Augustine's unique approach to the Pauline command to 'pray without ceasing'. But Augustine was not the first to reflect on the apparent impossibility of such a command. The third-century Greek theologian and ascetic Origen of Alexandria proposed that 'the entire life of the saint taken as a whole is a single great prayer, [and] prayer in the ordinary sense ought to be made no less than three times a day'.[8] The fifth-century Latin theologian and monastic theorist John Cassian suggested that monks would in effect celebrate 'the offices' spontaneously throughout the whole day: 'For they are constantly doing manual labour alone in their cells in such a way that they almost never omit meditating on the psalms and on other parts of Scripture.'[9] For both Origen and Cassian, the Pauline command necessitated an entirely different form of life, one that is distinguished from both the laity and secular clerics. In contrast to this potentially 'elitist' rendition, Augustine simultaneously grounds unceasing prayer in a psychology that foregrounds desire and the practices of common prayer. But as in so many other areas of his thought and practice, Augustine arrives at this position slowly and painstakingly, reversing in parts and modifying in others. In sum, Augustine's understanding of prayer is a product of his propensity 'to think as he writes and writes as he thinks'.[10]

---

[7]Hannah Arendt, *Der Liebesbegriff bei Augustin: Versuch einer philosophischen Interpretation* (Hamburg: Felix Meiner Verlag, 1996), 93.

[8]Origen, *On Prayer* 12.1; *An Exhortation to Martyrdom, Prayer and Select Works*, trans. Rowan E. Greer, CWS (New York: Paulist Press, 1979), 81–170.

[9]Cassian, *Inst.* 3.2 (CSEL 17); *John Cassian: The Institutes*, trans. Boniface Ramsey, ACW 58 (New York: Paulist Press, 2000), 59.

[10]Augustine, *ep.* 143 (CSEL 44); *Letters – Volume 2: 100–105*, trans. Roland J. Teske, WSA II/2 (Hyde Park, NY: New City Press, 2002).

Prayer and the Ascent of the Soul

On his return to Africa sometime around 388, Augustine made a short stop in Rome. There he encountered a group of what we can only call monks. 'Dwelling in the most desolate places', Augustine records in *De moribus ecclesiae catholicae*, 'they enjoy conversation with God, to whom with pure minds they adhere and are completely happy in the contemplation of his beauty'.[11] For Augustine, this represented an ideal of prayer.[12] The language Augustine uses – 'with pure minds' (*cui puris mentibus*), 'adhere' (*inhaerere*) and 'contemplation' (*contemplatio*) – is reminiscent of the approach to the divine that we have come to call the 'ascent of the soul', the process through which Augustine climbs from material to immaterial understandings of God. The most developed example of this is his 'vision' at Ostia in the *Confessions*. Augustine and his mother Monica begin by conversing over what scripture says about the eternal life, leading their joint exploration from material to immaterial, from 'outer things' to 'inner things', finally to a fleeting encounter with eternity itself: 'We touched it in some small degree by a moment of total concentration of the heart.'[13] Though highly debated, the order of the ascents of the soul in the *Confessions*, from the early frustrated efforts in *Confessions* 7 to the fleeting 'success' at Ostia, could be read as a salutary reminder that ascent is not to be entered into lightly, that to achieve the divine is a hard-won accomplishment and, as Augustine would later articulate more explicitly, ultimately an unmerited gift.

Caution is in order when using the concept of 'ascent' to frame Augustine's thinking about prayer, for it picked out a particular set of practices in late antique intellectual culture. Lewis Ayres has helpfully outlined two senses of ascent that Neoplatonist authors in particular used. In the first, Ayres sees such authors using ascent 'to describe the process that results in immediate vision' (but not necessarily of the One).[14] And in the second, ascent is 'the long process of learning the intellectual disciplines that train the mind to distinguish the character of intelligible reality, the necessary preliminary to resting in *Nous*'.[15] It is tempting to see these as alternatives: either ascent is an escape hatch from this world, or it is the very process of *using* this world.

---

[11]Augustine, *Mor.* 1.31.66 (CSEL 90); *On the Catholic and the Manichean Ways of Life*, trans. Donald A. Gallagher, FC 56 (Washington, DC: Catholic University of America Press, 1966).
[12]Augustine, *Mor.* 1.31.66.
[13]Augustine, *Confessions*, trans. Henry Chadwick (Oxford: Oxford University Press, 1991), XI.10.23. For the whole passage, see *Confessions*, XI.10.23-26.
[14]Lewis Ayres, *Augustine and the Trinity* (Cambridge: Cambridge University Press, 2010), 122.
[15]Ayres, *Augustine and the Trinity*, 123.

But this division is misleading. Where ascent as immediate vision is a kind of desirable objective that the aspirant exists with and in synchronically, ascent as the pedagogical process of rightly desiring the object is indispensably diachronic. The synchronic and diachronic aspects are mutually dependent in the same way that the goal and the process of any task or skill are mutually dependent. But for Augustine, the coordination of desire and the desired object is only achieved through a process of *reformation* or 'ascesis' of the very desire that composes the steps of the ascent.

A passage in *De ordine* 2 is instructive for appreciating the centrality of the ascetical or reformational dynamic in the ascent. In this context, Augustine is at pains to establish how reason (*ratio*) creates its own degrees or steps (*gradus*) by which it can ascend to contemplate its own structure: as *ratio* emerges from speech to dialectic it attains self-awareness through which it can find delight or pleasure in the disciplines of poetry, geometry and astronomy by discovering their 'ideal proportions born of reason' – their rhythm or number.[16] When Augustine's aspirant reflects on rhythm or number she begins to discover *ratio* itself as that which is most pleasing. This movement from shapes, sounds and formations to the internal structure of such phenomena is a movement from the material to immaterial. Yet it would be improper to conceive of this as a 'flight' from materiality. Instead, we might better understand it as a movement into and through the materiality of the disciplines to the immaterial reality that structures them. For the material to be retained the affective relationship one has with it must undergo reformation. In other words, without the ascesis of desire the ascent from material to immaterial cannot be anything but a rejection of the material.

The monks Augustine encountered in Rome in 388 might seem to be models of successful ascent. But such a reading would obscure the ways in which prayer complicates ascent. Indeed, in Augustine's last dialogue *De magistro* (391), we can see a hint of how prayer *heightens* the tension between materiality and immateriality. *De magistro*, a work that has been mined for Augustine's theory of language, is structured as a dialogue between 'Augustine' and his son 'Adeodatus'. But their dialogue also fundamentally alters Augustine's thinking about prayer. The digression on prayer is sparked by the question 'Augustine' poses to 'Adeodatus': Is speaking done for the sake of teaching or reminding? 'Adeodatus' responds with the example of prayer. The purpose of prayer is neither to teach God something nor to remind God of anything, for the simple reason that God is omniscient and impassable. In other words, God already knows everything we desire and is

---

[16]Augustine, *Ord.* 2.15.43 (CCSL 29); author's translation.

unmoved by such desires. But why would a God so conceived expect people to pray to him? Augustine's response reveals how he comes to understand prayer's materiality:

> I dare say you don't know that we are instructed to pray 'in closed chambers' – a phrase that signifies the inner recesses of the mind – precisely because God does not seek to be taught or reminded by our speaking in order to provide us what we want. Anyone who speaks gives an external sign of his will by means of an articulated sound. Yet God is to be sought and entreated in the hidden parts of the rational soul, which is called the 'inner person'; for He wanted those parts to be His temples.[17]

The monks' prayer that Augustine witnessed in Rome was, as he can now see, a 'conversation' that is inwardly directed – to the *interior homo*, the 'inner person'. Augustine's answer to the quandary about why one might pray to an omniscient God recapitulates *ratio*'s movement from phenomena to their structure in *De ordine:* we pray in order to be led into the interior recesses of our thinking soul (the 'closed chambers'). In other words, the monks' 'endless conversation' is not proof-positive of a successfully completed ascent, but an exhibition of such an undertaking *in process*.

Prayer as the Tutor of Desire

But what do we do about the *words* of prayers, of the persistence of *saying* prayers? Is this simply the vestiges of a crass supernaturalism of the masses? Or is there a more intimate connection between the movement of the soul and the language of prayer? Augustine's brief reflection on the Lord's Prayer in *De magistro* indicates an important ligature between a 'philosophical' account of prayer that eschews the centrality of prayer as speech and the more-routine Christian practice of saying or reading prayers. 'Adeodatus' glosses the indispensably *linguistic* quality of the Lord's Prayer by suggesting that '[Christ] did not teach them words, but the things themselves by the use of words'. Prayer is not so much a sign, like speech, but an action, for words are the *means* not the act of prayer. In this context, the words of prayer are an irreducible part of the act. As we will see, the words of the Lord's Prayer are especially critical for directing human thoughts to those things one ought to desire.

---

[17]Augustine, *Mag.* 1.2; modified translation from *Against the Academicians and The Teacher*, trans. Peter King (Indianapolis, IN: Hackett Publishing, 1995), 95–6.

In his commentary on the Sermon on the Mount, Augustine embeds *ratio*'s ascent through its own powers in the traditional practices of prayer. By petitioning God with the lines of the Lord's Prayer the aspirant participates in the same process that *De ordine* outlined. It is, however, a *petitionary* ascent into divine mysteries. In keeping with the strictures established in *De magistro*, Augustine here reiterates that the petitioner offers God no new knowledge. Rather, the *act* of petitioning is the occasion for moral transformation of the very desires necessary for the ascent. The awkwardness of prayer as *speech* does not disappear. To the contrary, it is intensified in Augustine's commentary on the Lord's Prayer. Augustine is no longer considering petitions that might arise in our experience of want, need, depravity, thanksgiving, joy or worship. Rather, the petitions are the very words given by Christ. The linguistic or oral nature of prayer would thus seem to be indispensable. But by repeating Christ's petitions Augustine's desires will be formed by those very petitions over time. While Augustine never states it outright, the Lord's Prayer is a kind of gift that initiates the very possibility of praying rightly.

Here the underlying theological anthropology of prayer is important. The pray-er must be capable of transformation and change, remaining open to the very possibility of receiving a gift that fundamentally shifts how they exchange petitions with the source of the gift. But this is not, for Augustine, an automatic or guaranteed process: '[God] is always ready to give us His light, not that which strikes the eye, but that of the intellect and spirit. But we are not always prepared to receive, attracted as we are to other things and benighted by our desire for temporal things.'[18] If there is a 'process' for turning the potentiality of receiving a gift into an actuality it is praying the Lord's Prayer, as Augustine describes it:

> Hence there takes place in prayer a turning of the heart to Him who is ever ready to give if we will but accept what He gives. And in this turning there is effected a cleansing of the inner eye, consisting in the exclusion of those things which filled our earth-bound desires so that the vision of a pure heart may be able to bear the pure light, radiating from God without diminution or setting; and not only bear it, but also to remain in it, not merely without discomfort but with the unspeakable joy whereby truly and unequivocally a blessed life is perfected.[19]

---

[18]Augustine, *S. dom. m.* 2.3.14 (CCSL 35); *On the Lord's Sermon on the Mount*, trans. John J. Epson, ACW 5 (New York: Paulist Press, 1978).
[19]Augustine, *S. dom. m.* 2.3.14.

Augustine does not fully spell out the psychology of this process. But Augustine's language of 'vision' and 'heart' suggests that prayer plays a central role in what we might today call 'passional reasoning'.[20] For Augustine, the transformations of desire cleanse reason, and the cleansing that reasoning undergoes in turn reforms desires. Augustine here envisions prayer as the form in which the mutual ascesis of reason and desire occur, driving the Christian progressively towards the vision of God, the full achievement of which remains, for Augustine, outside or beyond this world. Augustine's pray-er, like the monks he encountered in Rome, are always in the process of becoming a pray-er.

Despite the decidedly philosophical bent of Augustine's account, it would be wrong to read the Lord's Prayer as a kind of 'elite' programme for spiritual adepts who are making progress toward the *beata vita*, the blessed life. Augustine's account should not be read as an elitist interpretation of an otherwise popular practice, a way of making the vulgar respectable. Instead, the Lord's Prayer is unequivocally necessary for all, as Augustine would assure the laywoman Hilary in 'Letter 157'.[21] It is for this reason that the Lord's Prayer is not some kind of ladder one climbs that can be kicked away when they reach the top. On the contrary, no one ever transcends their need to pray the petitions of the Lord's Prayer. In his strife with the Pelagians, this is crystalized by the constant need to pray, 'Forgive us our debts, as we also forgive our debtors' (Mt. 6.12). As Augustine stresses to the same Hilary, 'After all, one for whom these words in the prayer will not be necessary would have to claim to live without sin.'[22] This same claim was at stake in Augustine's strife with the Donatists that unfolded most intensely in the first decade of the fifth century. At the end of the fourth century the Donatists were still the majority church, having represented themselves as the 'true' or 'pure' church in Roman Africa for persevering in the face of persecution in the late third century.[23] For Augustine, the error at the bottom of the Donatist self-identity as the 'true church' is, as Robert Dodaro has pointed out, a claim to possess absolute justice here and now.[24] Accordingly, this

---

[20]See Jonathan D. Teubner, 'The Failure of *affectus*: *Affectiones* and *constantiae* in Augustine of Hippo', in *Before Emotion: The Language of Feeling, 400–1800*, ed. Juanita Feros Ruys, Michael W. Champion, and Kirk Essary (London: Routledge, 2019), 9–25.

[21]Augustine, *ep.* 157.2 (CSEL 44); *Letters – Volume 3: 156–210*, trans. Roland J. Teske, WSA II/3 (Hyde Park, NY: New City Press, 2004).

[22]Augustine, *ep.* 157.2.

[23]Peter Iver Kaufman, *Augustine's Leaders* (Eugene, OR: Cascade Books, 2017), 137.

[24]Robert Dodaro, *Christ and the Just Society in the Thought of Augustine* (Cambridge: Cambridge University Press, 2004), 200–1.

makes them incapable of practising true penitence and hence they cannot pray, 'Forgive us our debts, as we also forgive our debtors.'[25] In both the Donatist and Pelagian controversies, the Lord's Prayer is a consistent, daily refrain that is meant to remind Christians that they cannot save themselves, that no one, not even the Apostles, ever transcended the need for practising penitence and reconciliation.

The enduring need to pray the Lord's Prayer is also bound up with the very process of desiring the *beata vita* rightly. In 'Letter 130' written around 410 that is his most developed account of prayer, Augustine implores the widow Proba, 'Always pray with a continuous desire filled with faith, hope, and love.'[26] Augustine opposes this to what he reports about certain Egyptian monks who are 'said to say frequent prayers, but very brief ones that are tossed off in a rush, so that a vigilant and keen intention ... may not fade away'.[27] The issue here hinges on the use of the Lord's Prayer. As Augustine reminds Proba, the petitions of the Lord's Prayer encompass every 'holy petition'.[28] For Proba's desire to be filled with faith, hope and love her desire must have already been formed by and through the Lord's Prayer, which Augustine sums up for Proba in the single petition, 'not as I will but as you will, Father'.[29] Proba's desire, issued forth in and through her prayers, ought to be chastened and moulded by the petitions of the Lord's Prayer. As Augustine suggests in *Sermon 56*, preached around the same time as he wrote to Proba, 'The words our Lord Jesus has taught us in his prayer give us the framework of true desires.'[30]

While it is clear that Augustine thinks one ought actually to *say* the Lord's Prayer, his emphasis is not on the speech act of prayer, but rather on what these speech acts *do*. But one must not lose sight of the shifting sense of agency in prayer itself: *Who* is actually performing the act? The petitions of the Lord's Prayer are primarily those of the Son for the Father, and any human participation in it will necessarily fall short. Again, Augustine thinks that we are always in the process of learning to pray. To this end, Augustine describes all human efforts at prayer as failed in 'Letter 130'. He takes this from a reading of Paul's 'failed' prayer in 2 Corinthians 12 to relieve him of his 'thorn in the flesh'. Augustine highlights that even Paul did not know how to pray because the object of his prayer is such that 'we cannot think of

---

[25]Augustine, *ep.* 185.39.
[26]Augustine, *ep.* 130.18.
[27]Augustine, *ep.* 130.20.
[28]Augustine, *ep.* 130.20.
[29]Augustine, *ep.* 130.24-26.
[30]Augustine, *Sermon 56*; *Sermons 51-94*, trans. Edmund Hill, WSA III/3 (Hyde Park, NY: New City Press, 1991).

it as it is'.[31] Paul's prayer for his 'thorn of the flesh' to be removed improperly expressed prayer's desire for the *beata vita*, just as any human supplication would. But in the failure to desire the *beata vita* correctly the Holy Spirit emerges to 'intercede for us with inexpressible groans'. The Holy Spirit is not providing some divine version of intercessory prayer, for the Spirit is 'immutable God in the Trinity' and thus does not intercede from outside the Godhead as humans do. Rather, for Augustine, the Holy Spirit is that which transforms human prayer.[32] Only in the Holy Spirit can humans pray for the *beata vita*; only by virtue of the Holy Spirit's groaning and weeping are humans' sighs and weeping directed towards the *beata vita*. Augustine wants, in short, to disabuse his listeners and readers of any illusion that they might be able to manipulate or tinker their way to desiring God rightly.

Prayer as Life Form

There is a persistent temptation in theological interpretations of prayer to unhook prayer from the contingencies of human existence, to think that it is some method of rising above or transcending day-to-day life. It would seem rather easier to pray unceasingly if it were elevated above the warp and woof of daily life that can get in our way. But prayer is not, for Augustine, a practice of a solitary individual, an 'alone to the alone'. Rather, it is a practice that gathers together the body of Christ in union with its head. For this reason, the rehabilitation of desire occurs through the continual give-and-take of life lived with others. Those others with whom we share our lives have their own desires, and enjoying life with them is not simply a matter of waiting for them to properly reform their desires. On the contrary, the formation of the desire for the *beata vita* results from patiently living with others' desires, holy and otherwise, trusting that just as yours are being transformed, so too are theirs. In this sense, prayer is, for Augustine, not simply a task but a communal or corporate form of life. Learning to pray for the *beata vita* is thus forged in and through the mutual give and take of community life.

The form of life that most immediately shapes Augustine is his own monastic community. But he shares this vision with the wider church community through his homiletic practices, chief of which is his famed *totus Christus*. Augustine developed the rhetorical motif of the *totus Christus* – the 'whole Christ', both Christ as 'head' and the church as 'body' – over

---

[31]Augustine, *ep.* 130.27; *Letters – Volume 2*, 197.
[32]Augustine, *ep.* 15.28 (CSEL 34/1); *Letters – Volume 1: 1–99*, trans. Roland J. Teske, WSA II/1 (Hyde Park, NY: New City Press, 2001), 198.

a long period of time. Augustine's earliest uses of this motif emerge in his efforts to puzzle through the question 'who is speaking?' in the Psalms. This is crystalized, for Augustine, in the phrase from Psalm 21 'My God, my God, look upon me, why have you forsaken me?' that the Gospel of Matthew put in Jesus' mouth (Mt. 27.46), and becomes a kind of hermeneutical key for understanding a wide range of perplexing voices and tenses in the Psalms. Recent work has shown how central Augustine's *Expositions of the Psalms* are to the development of his Christology.[33] This christological focus has also opened up new avenues to think about the Psalms as redemptively significant prayers. As Michael Fiedrowicz pointed out, all the voices of Christ are understood by Augustine as prayer.[34] In fact, all of the Psalms are read as prayers, whether of exaltation or lamentation, praise or weeping, joy or anguish. For Augustine, the *totus Christus* sits at the intersection of Christology and soteriology, doctrine and practice, informing how we ought to pray and live as the body of Christ.

The rhetorical motif of the *totus Christus* can, however, seem like an abstraction that is unrelated to the problems and crises of day-to-day existence: a kind of manipulation of language that is divorced from the messy reality of instructing, correcting, leading and forming Christian desire. But when this rhetorical motif is understood through his monastic life, the *totus Christus* takes on a thoroughly ethical valence that extends far beyond the walls of the monastery. For Augustine, the monks' regular prayer provides the basis for living 'harmoniously' with 'one heart and one soul seeking God'.[35] It is no coincidence that he structures the monastic day around praying the Psalms, for in them the brothers would voice the full range of their social and affective experience. Within the monastic context, the vision of dwelling together in unity is always already caught up in the realities of disappointment and suffering. The harmony of voices in the chapel must be heard against the bickering coming from the refectory.

In his exposition of Psalm 123, which is one of his most extensive commentaries on the monastic life, Augustine draws on the image of the *totus*

---

[33]See, for example, Michael Cameron, *Christ Meets Me Everywhere: Augustine's Early Figurative Exegesis* (Oxford: Oxford University Press, 2012); Dominic Keech, *The Anti-Pelagian Christology of Augustine of Hippo, 396–430* (Oxford: Oxford University Press, 2012); and Michael Fiedrowicz, *Psalmus vox totius Christi: Studien zu Augustins 'Enarrationes in Psalmos'* (Freiburg: Herder, 1997).

[34]Fiedrowicz, *Psalmus vox totius Christi*, 178.

[35]Augustine, *Reg.* 3.1.2; *The Rule: Monastic Order*, in *Augustine of Hippo and his Monastic Rule*, trans. George Lawless (Oxford: Clarendon Press, 1987). See also George Lawless, 'Augustine's Decentering of Asceticism', in *Augustine and His Critics: Essays in Honour of Gerald Bonner*, ed. Robert Dodaro and George Lawless (London: Routledge, 2000), 80.

Christus to inform a kind of existence that seeks to inhabit the inevitably non-ideal nature of community. Augustine associates the oil flowing down from the beard to the opening of the tunic as the union of the head and body. Augustine draws these together in his reflection on Stephen's prayer for those who persecute him:

> But when the stones rained upon him his charity was not conquered, because fragrant oil had run down from head to beard, and he had heard the head saying, *Love your enemies, and pray for those who persecute you* (Mt. 5.44). From that same head he had heard something else; from Christ hanging on the cross he had heard the prayer, *Father, forgive them, for they do not know what they are doing* (Lk. 23.34). The oil that had flowed from the head to the beard produced a similar effect, for as Stephen was being stoned he knelt and prayed, *Lord, do not hold this sin against them* (Acts 7.60).[36]

Augustine goes on to clarify that the beard is Christ the 'head', oil is the Spirit and the edge of the tunic is those brothers who 'bear one another's burdens' (Gal. 6.2).[37] In this image, the head is bonded to the body through the work of the Spirit. It is, however, a body that is united with itself – dwelling together in unity – through active care and forbearance of one another, even those who persecute them. In this context, the *totus Christus* is not some final, perfected state, but that in which Christians find themselves whenever they 'bear one another's burdens'. The *totus Christus* is the form through which Augustine and his monastic *confrères* assimilate the Son's cry to the Father. It is, in short, one way that they come to terms with a form of life that is shot through with struggle and suffering.

Just as the Lord's Prayer catches up the petitioner in the Son's prayer to the Father, so too does the *totus Christus* draw the pray-er into the Son's cry of dereliction. But, as we have already seen, when such a theological rendition finds expression in the life of struggle the trinitarian shape of all prayer is made evident. In the image of oil flowing down from Aaron's beard in Psalm 132, it is the Spirit as oil that bonds the head to the body that bears one another's burdens. Here, the Spirit's work in and through human 'failure' is unmistakably communal: the life of communal prayer is actualized in and through the messy reality of learning to dwell together in unity.[38] It is

---

[36]Augustine, *En Ps.* 132.8 (CCSL 40); *Expositions of the Psalms – Volume 6: 121–150*, trans. Maria Boulding, WSA III/20 (Hyde Park, NY: New City Press, 2004).
[37]Augustine, *En Ps.* 132.9.
[38]Augustine, *En Ps.* 132.12.

through the give and take of words and gestures that the conflicting claims of desire are encountered and, to a certain extent, momentarily overcome. The exchange of voices, both with each other and with Christ, is thus central to the process of 'deepening human relations' that Augustine thinks should be characteristic of all forms of Christian community.[39] When Augustine invites his congregation to learn to pray the Psalms as the 'whole Christ', he is not just inviting them to take a brief 'moral holiday' from their lives, but to turn to others to shape and reform their desire. It is, in sum, an invitation to participate in a mutualism that is, no doubt, irritating and exasperating but nonetheless salutary and salvific. It is this life form of prayer that is, no doubt, unceasing here in this age.

Prayer after Augustine

Augustine's understanding of prayer was very much born out of his own experiences – intellectual, moral and spiritual. Augustine never envisioned himself as having a 'doctrine' or even an authoritative practice of prayer. We must therefore resist the temptation to tidy up Augustine's understanding of prayer in such a way that we erase the very person at its centre. We can, however, locate a consistent line of inquiry – or better perplexity – with the Pauline command to 'pray without ceasing'. Through this focus on unceasing prayer, desire emerges as central to Augustine's understanding of prayer. Indeed, we can learn much about what Augustine thought about desire and the role it plays within the Christian life by reflecting on his understanding of prayer.

It was ultimately not Augustine who provided the institutional structure for such an approach to prayer, but those Latin monastic legislators of the fifth and sixth centuries. Cassian is foremost in this institutional process. Influenced by some theological trends emanating from the Greek East, Cassian provided a detailed account of the nuances and theological intricacies of the life of prayer in his *Institutes* and *Conferences*. But it was ultimately Benedict of Nursia, a murky and largely unknowable figure, who provided a 'little rule for monks' that shaped Latin Christianity's understanding of a *life* of prayer. Within the institutional structure of formalized monasticism that we find in Benedict's age, the command to 'pray without ceasing' is, in one sense, resolved. Those who profess a religious vocation have dedicated their entire lives to the life of prayer. But the tension between the command and human limitations is, in another sense, made all the more intense. Within

---

[39]Lawless, 'Augustine's Decentering of Asceticism', 142–63.

the life of the Benedictine monk, only a portion – albeit a privileged one – of the day is dedicated to prayer. The rest is filled with eating, working, sleeping and other sundry activities. In his own subtle and laconic way, Benedict recognized that prayer had to be re-envisioned to encompass all these activities as prayer.

Our construct of the 'life of prayer' can thus sit oddly with the practice of *legislating* such a life. If prayer is, indeed, wrapped up with the very movements of the soul, would not the legislation to pray in specific places and specific times suggest that it is a circumscribed practice? Benedict, in fact, specifically discusses prayer in relation to the regulation of the liturgy (*Rule* 8-19), personal prayer (*Rule* 20), daily reading and work (*Rule* 48), observance of lent (*Rule* 49) and rules regulating the oratory (*Rule* 52). Benedict even goes so far as to suggest that prayer should be 'short and pure'. But for Benedict such commands support and give coherence to the structure of the way of life (*conversatio*). To take one example, the regulation of the oratory as a place strictly for prayer serves as a constant reminder of the ideal community life in this world.[40] To pray the Psalms in the chapel, to have one voice lifting up in unison, is to exemplify the unity brothers are to have in the refectory, field and library. But the oratory is also a geographical centre of communal life, as brothers and sisters are always coming to and going from the oratory. It is in this sense that an empty oratory can play an equally vital role to an oratory filled with prayer and song. Just as the prayer could not be reduced to an interior movement of the soul in Augustine, so too cannot it not be reduced to a communal task that happens then not now in the Benedictine life.

The most fundamental tasks are often those that are taken most for granted. For Augustine, the spiritual life is primed and paced by the continual sighing of prayer, for it embodies and gives formation to our desires that fundamentally shape who we have been, are, and are becoming. This totalizing vision for prayer must, however, never be deracinated from its ritual formations, whether found in weekly gatherings of the faithful or in the monks' hours. It is in these contexts, where prayer is at times legislated and controlled, that the faithful's desires are tested and refined by the Lord's Prayer, that which provides for Augustine the framework of true desire.

Yet even the ritualized testing and perfecting of desires in community does not guarantee against the risk that our desires are not only deformed in their individual manifestation – as products of *my* sin – but are also being further deformed when tested and refined in community – as products of *our*

---

[40]Augustine, *Reg.* 2.1-4; *Regula Benedicti* 52.1 (SC 181).

sin. We must always be wise to the possibility that our prayers, as heartfelt and genuine as they may have been, as tested and refined as they may be becoming, are nevertheless liable to distort and misdirect our desire for the *beata vita*. We can, in short, never presume that our prayer has been perfected, for it always exists with and in the realities of earthly existence. It is precisely in this recognition of prayer's incompleteness that, for Augustine as well as for Benedict, prayer exposes the self as utterly dependent on God. Far from ripping us away from the regrettable compromises of life, and resolving for them the tensions and dilemmas of life, reflecting on prayer reminds us that there is never a moment when the self is not in a dependent relation to God. To pray without ceasing is to live, consciously or not, with the awareness that what I want might not be what I should want.

CHAPTER EIGHTEEN

The Formulation of Prayer for the Formation of Faith in the Early Middle Ages, *c.* 700–900

RENIE CHOY

What characterizes prayer? Spontaneity and freedom, the intuitive and unguarded outpouring of human feeling, or care and consideration, thoughtful and studied speech? Perhaps nothing makes the definition of 'prayer' so difficult to pin down as divergent assumptions about the form by which prayer is recognized – what, in other words, prayer looks or sounds like, and when and where it happens. In the seventeenth century, the Anglican divine Thomas Pittis chided those who refused to use the *Book of Common Prayer*. Extempore invocations, he wrote, are a 'very rude indigested heap, rashly conceived and uttered', 'fraught too frequently with impertinency and nonsense' which too often become 'the cause of blasphemy also'.[1] The main recipient of his attacks was the Puritan John Owen, whose justification of the

---

[1]Thomas Pittis, *A Discourse of Prayer: Wherein This Great Duty Is Stated, so As to Oppose Some Principles and Practices of Papists and Fanaticks; As They Are Contrary to the Publick Forms of the Church of England, Established by Her Ecclesiastical Canons, and Confirmed by the Acts of Parliament* (London: B. White, 1683), 296.

use of extempore prayer in public worship rested in part on the following interpretation of history. In early Christianity, he wrote:

> The Orthodox and the Arians composed Prayers, Hymns and Doxologies, the one against the other, inserting in them passages confirming their own profession, and condemning that of their Adversaries. Now however this Invention might be approved whilest it kept within bounds, yet it proved the Trojan Horse that brought in all evils into the City of God in its Belly. For he who was then at work in the Mystery of Iniquity, laid hold on the Engine and occasion to corrupt those Prayers, which by the constitution of them who had obtained Power in them, the Churches were obliged and confined unto. And this took place effectually in the constitution of the Worship of the second Race of Christians, or the Nations that were converted unto the Christian Faith after they had destroyed the Western Roman Empire. To speak briefly and plainly, it was by this means alone, namely, of the necessary Use of devised Forms of Prayer in the Assemblies of the Church, and of them alone, that the Mass, with its Transubstantiation and Sacrifice, and all the Idolatrous Worship wherewith they were accompanied, were introduced, until the World inflamed with those Idols, drench'd it self in the bloud of the Saints and Martyrs of Christ for their Testimony against those abominations. And if it had been sooner discovered, that no Church was intrusted with Power from Christ to frame and impose such devised Forms of Worship, as are not warranted by the Scripture, innumerable Evils might have been prevented.[2]

The early Middle Ages feature centrally in Owen's explanation about why people mistake the use of 'devised forms' for true prayer. In the effort to assert a unified and powerful Christendom, post-Roman ecclesiastics and rulers established ritual and liturgy as the forms by which prayer was to be recognized; this Owen laments as contradictory with prayer 'in the Spirit'. Yet, we must observe that this 'second Race of Christians' also equally invoked Ephesians 6.18: they believed that to pray in the Spirit was to pray correctly and beautifully. Why? In this chapter, we shall attempt to understand the rationale and spirituality behind the firm establishment of set forms by which prayer was recognized during the early Middle Ages.

---

[2]John Owen, *A Discourse of the Work of the Holy Spirit in Prayer with a Brief Enquiry into the Nature and Use of Mental Prayer and Forms* (London: printed for Nathanael Ponder, 1682), preface.

Learning to Pray as Jesus Taught

Much anti-Catholic rhetoric – Puritan and otherwise – rests on the notion of deviation from earliest Christianity. As John Owen pointed out, the use of set forms of prayer 'is not warranted by the scriptures, nor is of Apostolical Example, nor is countenanced by the practice of the primitive Churches'.[3] Indeed, Allan Bouley has argued that early Christian assemblies gave prominence to improvised prayers in the Spirit.[4] The *Didache*, for example, permits prophets to give thanks 'as they will' because they speak in the Spirit, and the *Shepherd of Hermas* refers to prophets as having the power in the Spirit to utter prophecies to the assembly.[5] But the charism of the Spirit for prayer was also, by the time Clement of Rome wrote his letter in the second century, attached to the ministerial and specifically liturgical role of the bishop, whose particular duty was to offer the improvised prayer of the Eucharist.[6] In Justin Martyr's *First Apology*, the bishop improvises his prayer 'at length', addressing to God 'prayers and thanksgivings to the best of his ability'.[7] Yet the improvisations of the bishop were not subject to his whim and moods; they were guided by conventions regarding the structure, content and characteristic vocabulary of eucharistic prayer.[8] As John Owen himself admitted, such conventions became increasingly important in the church's encounter with doctrinal heresies. In North Africa, the primary concern of bishops at the Third Council of Carthage in 397 was that only those prayers, orations, prefaces and blessings which had been approved by the synod be used, 'lest perhaps something against faith be composed either through ignorance or through insufficient care'.[9] Augustine reports that the prayers of many presidents required correction because 'much against catholic faith is found in them' and many had been composed 'not only by unskilled babblers but even by heretics'. The simplicity of many celebrants meant that they 'cannot evaluate the prayers and think them good'.[10] The stage, it would appear, was set for Owen's 'Trojan Horse'.

Indeed, the appearance of our first prayer books – showing heightened interest in correct forms and phrasing of prayer – coincides with the

---

[3]Owen, *A Discourse of the Work of the Holy Spirit in Prayer*, preface.
[4]Allan Bouley, *From Freedom to Formula: The Evolution of the Eucharistic Prayer from Oral Improvisation to Written Texts* (Washington, DC: Catholic University of America Press, 1981).
[5]Bouley, *From Freedom to Formula*, 90–9 (with reference to *Didache* 9.1 and 10.1), 103–4 (with reference to Shepherd of Hermas, *Book of Mandates* 11).
[6]Bouley, *From Freedom to Formula*, 103.
[7]Bouley, *From Freedom to Formula*, 110–12.
[8]Bouley, *From Freedom to Formula*, 255.
[9]Bouley, *From Freedom to Formula*, 163–4 (quoting Mansi, *Sacrorum conciliorum nova et amplissima collectio* IV, col. 330).
[10]Bouley, *Freedom*, 165 (quoting Augustine, *De baptismo contra Donatistas* 6.47).

assertion of catholicity by post-Roman successor kingdoms. In this context, the establishment in the West of various 'liturgical families' from the fifth and sixth centuries (e.g. the Roman, Ambrosian, Hispanic, Gallican and the Celtic) can be understood *à propos* missionary efforts to promote and preserve orthodox doctrine among the converts from paganism and Arianism.[11] Yet, though John Owen would see in this formalization of prayer the introduction of 'innumerable Evils', it was precisely the guarding *against* evil which motivated bishops and rulers to legislate set forms of prayer. For them, prayer, as an expression of correct belief, should be recognizable by certain exterior forms, and such forms in fact played an important didactic role in the formation of faith itself.

The instructive nature of prayer to nurture faith is an idea which early Christian writers already present in the context of catechesis, preparing candidates for baptism. Tertullian and Cyprian linked the Lord's Prayer to the so-called 'discipline of the secret' (*disciplina arcani*), a term which refers to the mysteries of Christian doctrine which ought deliberately to be protected from the heathen in order to safeguard its venerable and sublime nature.[12] The conception that prayer, as the verbal expression of faith, must be especially taught to authentic initiates is an altogether important concept to grasp, without which misunderstandings arise about the entrenchment of ritualized formulae in medieval prayer. A sixth-century text ascribed to Jerome and purporting to record the life of Pachomius, the founder of coenobitic monasticism, makes the point explicit. Whilst a pagan, Pachomius encounters an angel who instructs him to pray. Pachomius' response? 'I do not know how to pray, I do not even know what I ought to say.' Later, a newly converted Pachomius reflects: 'For you know, Lord, that I knew nothing about speech, and you deigned to grant that I would speak to you, and you taught me with what words I should address you.'[13] The text here

---

[11]In contrast with the development of the Eastern liturgies: the liturgy of Jerusalem, the East Syrian (Nestorian) liturgy, the West Syrian (Antiochean) liturgy, the Alexandrian, Ethiopian and Byzantine liturgies.

[12]See C. Ricci, '*Disciplina Arcani* (Discipline of the Secret)', in *Encyclopedia of Ancient Christianity*, ed. Angelo Di Berardino, Thomas C. Oden, and Joel C. Elowsky (Downers Grove, IL: InterVarsity Press, 2014), vol. 1, 725–6 and Roy Hammerling, *The Lord's Prayer in the Early Church: The Pearl of Great Price* (New York: Palgrave, 2010).

[13]Albrecht Diem and Hildegund A. Müller, 'Vita, Regula, Sermo: Eine unbekannte lateinische Vita Pacomii als Lehrtext für ungebildete Mönche und als Traktat über das Sprechen', in *Zwischen Niederschrift und Wiederschrift: Frühmittelalterliche Hagiographie und Historiographie im Spannungsfeld von Kompendienüberlieferung und Editionstechnik*, ed. Richard Corradini, Max Diesenberger and Meta Niederkorn-Bruck (Vienna: Verlag der Österreichische Akademie der Wissenschaften 2010), 223–72 (261–2). See also Renie Choy, *Intercessory Prayer and the Monastic Ideal in the Time of the Carolingian Reforms* (Oxford: Oxford University Press, 2016), 26–32.

insists on the distinction between the prayer of Christians and the paganism of Pachomius' past, and in the ninth century, Paschasius similarly writes that the Lord's Prayer must be learned because by it Christians signal how their prayers differ from the *ethnici* (pagans). What is meant by Jesus' words, 'Thus therefore shall you pray'?, Paschasius asks:

> Not as the hypocrites to be seen, or as the pagans in much speaking, but you shall pray as I teach you and what I teach you and how I teach you, who are my people. Therefore not only the effect of prayer is considered, but truly also the posture of the body and the tone of voice, besides the gentleness of Christ's discipline and the decorum of humility. For this reason, he inserts, 'Thus therefore shall you pray', as if to say, '[Do] as I instruct and as I teach and as I prescribe'.[14]

Various legislative decrees promulgated by the Franks made the Lord's Prayer, in addition to the Apostles' Creed, the foundation for Christian formation. The Council of Frankfurt in 794 decreed that the 'catholic faith' as expressed in the Lord's Prayer and the Creed be the priority of a priests' teaching, and the Council of Friuli in 796 further specified:

> Every Christian of every age, every sex and every condition, male, female, young, old, slave, free, boys, married and unmarried women ought to know by heart the Creed, certainly, and the Lord's Prayer, because without this blessing no one will be able to gain a portion of the kingdom of heaven.[15]

The emperor Charlemagne showed a particular concern that godparents – responsible as they were for the spiritual formation of children – be able to recite and understand the Lord's Prayer.[16] Given the concerns of church leaders about the limited education of the laity and the threat of pagan superstition and doctrinal heresy, the Lord's Prayer represented the tool by which all could reliably learn and express the content of faith.

This connection between prayer and the formation of faith helps us understand why, to a large extent, theologians of the early medieval West

---

[14]Paschius, *Expositio in Matheo Libri XII*, IV.6.9 (CCCM 41), 378.

[15]*Capitulare Francofurtense* c. 33 and *Concilium Foroiuliense, MGH Concilia aevi karolini I* (Hannover: Hahnsche, 1906), 169 and 189; Owen Phelan, *The Formation of Christian Europe: The Carolingians, Baptism, and the Imperium Christianum* (Oxford: Oxford University Press, 2014), 152.

[16]See Joseph Lynch, *Godparents and Kinship in Early Medieval Europe* (Princeton, NJ: Princeton University Press, 1986), 312–19.

were not interested in invention and improvisation; the image of 'culling from the flowers of the Fathers' so ubiquitous in Carolingian texts shows a spirituality which valued the reception and transmission of instruction. Selections drawn from the historic treasury of prayers were assembled in order to preserve the best orations as regards both orthodoxy and quality. A significant development in the practice of prayer in the early Middle Ages was the production of prayer books, manuscripts which represent an essential source for understanding medieval piety. I shall therefore turn to some important aspects of the standardization of prayer that become apparent through these rich textual sources, especially noting the characteristic language and attitudes about prayer which accompanied this standardization between *c*. 700 and 800. We shall first discuss eucharistic orations, then note some significant principles of prayer inherited from the monastic tradition, before finally observing the specific vocabulary of personal and public prayer. In these areas, we shall retain our goal of understanding why early medieval Christians viewed set prayers as essential for instruction in the way of faith.

Praying Rightly and Justly

The eighth and ninth centuries saw the intensive production of the first liturgical books organized as such.[17] The family of books known as the *Gelasian Sacramentaries* reflects the early romanization of the Frankish liturgy: the Roman rite had been in use in the presbyterial churches of Rome and must have reached Gaul in the course of the eighth century, whence we have a surviving witness in the form of Manuscript Vat. Reg. 316, copied in the eighth century in a scriptorium in the nunnery of Chelles near Paris.[18] The manuscript comprises prayers for Masses over the church year and on saints' feast days, as well as Masses for particular occasions and intentions ('votive masses'). It presents the formularies structuring the Mass in the form many would recognize today, including collects, the secret, the proper preface, the postcommunion and the prayer over the people. The consistent iteration of clauses beginning with '*qui*' (for invoking God's power through naming

---

[17]A good survey from which I have drawn for the basic information about the development of liturgical books which follows is Eric Palazzo, *A History of Liturgical Books from the Beginning to the Thirteenth Century*, trans. Madeleine Beaumont (Collegeville, MN: Liturgical Press, 1998).

[18]L. C. Mohlberg, L. Eizenhöfer and P. Siffrin, ed., *Liber sacramentorum Romanae aecclesiae ordinis anni circuli (Sacramentarium Gelasianum)* (Cod. Vat. Reg. Lat. 316/Paris Bibl. nat. 7193, 41/56), Rerum Ecclesiasticarum Documenta, Series Maior, Fontes 4 (Rome: Casa Editrice Herder, 1960).

his character and acts), '*ut*' (to present appeals and petitions) and '*per*' (to signal the mediation of Christ and the Holy Spirit) show the deliberateness with which the prayers were composed. In the ninth century, this type of Mass book, along with the intermediary eighth-century (Frankish) Gelasian, was supplanted by what is known as the Gregorian Sacramentaries, the introduction of which represented Charlemagne's attempt to bring unity to the ecclesiastical – as with the political – situation in Western Europe. Responding to Charlemagne's request for a sacramentary, Pope Hadrian in the late eighth century sent him one from Rome which he claimed was a copy of the very Mass book composed by Gregory the Great, and Charlemagne set about disseminating this throughout his empire. To further liturgical reform, a 'supplement' was appended to this sacramentary to provide even more prayers for use in Christian worship. Together, the *Hadrianum* and its *Supplement* represent a profound source for examining the language of Latin Christian prayer, drawing its language, formulae, and styles from Hebrew forms, post-biblical tradition, hymnody and many other sources. As Daniel Sheerin writes, these are 'a peculiar and very imitable hieratic style built up upon a strict choice and collocation of words for particular effects, including propriety and dogmatic precision, allusive catechesis, compression and pleonasm, emphasis, balance and antithesis, periodicity, and rhythmical endings'.[19]

The word 'hieratic' has been attached to the study of liturgical languages through a well-established body of scholarly literature, and in this case relates to the fact that the texts for the canon of the Mass are clearly intended for the use of a clerical elite: by these liturgical texts and the particular wording of the prayers, people were served by ritual specialists who brought them into a proper relationship with God.[20] Thus the voice of the medieval church at prayer, in the words of Uwe Michael Lang, was 'a highly stylized medium of worship'.[21] Articulating the characteristics of God which allow one to approach him, acknowledging why and how he may be approached, identifying the petitions desired, explaining the reasons for the petition and so on, all demand great care in phrasing. For example, a prayer for a Mass for those going on a journey illustrates the disciplined, methodical and well-

---

[19]Daniel Sheerin, 'The Liturgy', in *Medieval Latin: An Introduction and Bibliographical Guide*, ed. F. A. C. Mantello and A. G. Rigg (Washington, DC: Catholic University of America Press, 1996), 157–82 (170), with reference to Friedrich Stummer, 'Vom Satzrhythmus in der Bibel und in der Liturgie der lateinischen Christenheit', *Archiv für Liturgiewissenshcaft* 3, no. 2 (1954): 233–83.

[20]See the helpful overview by Uwe Michael Lang, 'The Liturgy and Sacred Language', in *T&T Clark Companion to Liturgy*, ed. Alcuin Reid (London: Bloomsbury, 2016), 365–82.

[21]Uwe Michael Lang, *The Voice of the Church at Prayer: Reflections on Liturgy and Language* (San Francisco, CA: Ignatius Press, 2012), 54.

considered approach to prayer. The turns of phrases are thoughtful and compact, the composition poetic:

> God of infinite mercy and immense majesty, whom neither the expanse of places nor the interval of time removes from those whom you guard, attend to your servants N. and N. trusting in you everywhere, and through the whole journey which they are about to take, deign to be a leader and companion to them. May nothing of adversity harm, may no difficulty obstruct, may all be health to them, may all be prosperity, and by the power of your right hand, may they attain by swift effect what they ask by just desire.[22]

Benedict of Aniane devoted particular attention to the composition of new prefaces for Masses, which he appended as part of his *Supplement*. They show the compositional priorities of prayer: brevity and density. The prefaces invite close analysis, for often the phrases hold together seeming paradoxes which are resolved in faith. Some rely on typological readings, as here in Benedict of Aniane's preface for the finding of the Holy Cross, which engages in word plays even as it follows the basic structure we have seen of '*qui*', '*ut*' and '*per*':

> VD (It is truly right and just …). You who redeemed the world by the passion of the cross, and sweetened the bitter taste of the ancient tree by the medicine of the cross, and overcame the death which had come through the forbidden tree by the trophy of the tree, so that by the marvelous bestowal of his affection, we, who had departed from our flowery seat through the eating of the tree, may return to the joys of paradise through the tree of the cross.[23]

Other prefaces exploit to rhetorical and theological effect the contrast between earthly life and the life to come, as in one of the five prefaces that Benedict of Aniane included for the Masses for the dead:

> VD (It is truly right and just …). Although the condition of death having been brought upon the race of man saddens our hearts, yet by the gift of your mercy we are raised with the hope of future immortality, and, mindful of eternal salvation, we are not afraid to sustain the loss of

---

[22]Jean Deshusses, ed., *Le sacramentaire Grégorien*, Spicilegium Friburgense 16, 24, 28 (Fribourg: Éditions Universitaires, 1971–82), vol. 1, 438–9.
[23]*Le sacramentaire Grégorien*, vol. 1, 530.

this light. For to the faithful, by the blessing of your grace, life is not destroyed but changed; and souls, being liberated from the prison of the body, abhor mortal things while they obtain the immortal. Thus we that your servant N. being placed in the tabernacles of the blessed, may be glad that he has escaped fleshly chains, and by the promise of glorification may anticipate the day of judgment with confidence. Through Christ.[24]

Such careful and intricate design marked the composition of these prefaces that Antoine Dumas, in the twentieth-century liturgical reforms associated with Vatican II, believed he could in fact retrieve the fundamental character of the 'Roman preface' and with it the principles for guiding contemporary revision: the preface, he argued, ought primarily to reflect thanksgiving, and by clearly recalling the wonderful mysteries of God and salvation, present the intentions of the Mass to be celebrated.[25] Equally specific principles characterize the other components of the prayers at Mass; nothing of eucharistic prayer should be meandering but all elements should serve a pronounced purpose.

Seeking Pure Prayer

This emphasis on the ritual and formulaic prayer of priests is not to say that early medieval Christians had no concept of contemplative, mystical prayer. In fact, by the ninth century, a strong notion had emerged of a particular group of people in society whose primary duty was to engage in the contemplative life through unceasing prayer. The fourth-century Egyptian monk Evagrius set an important trajectory when he articulated his theory about the 'ascent of the soul' through stages: purification from vice, contemplation of God through creation, and the pinnacle of union in which one holds converse with the Divine free from words, images, or concepts derived from the world or from discursive thought.[26] At the hands of Cassian who transmitted the tradition of Egyptian monasticism to the West, this 'pure prayer' (oratio pura) was reconceived as something which should specifically be pursued within the regulated and communal life of a monastery. Ecstatic contemplation – characterized by fervour, intensity, wordlessness, interior

---

[24]*Le sacramentaire Grégorien,* vol. 1, 573.
[25]See Nathaniel Marx, 'The Revision of the Prefaces in the Missal of Paul VI', in *Issues in Eucharistic Praying in East and West: Essays in Liturgical and Theological Analysis,* ed. Maxwell E. Johnson (Collegeville, MN: Liturgical Press, 2010), 349–82 (362–4).
[26]Andrew Louth, *The Origins of the Christian Mystical Tradition: From Plato to Denys* (Oxford: Clarendon Press, 1981), 100–13 and Columba Stewart, 'Imageless Prayer and the Theological Vision of Evagrius Ponticus', *Journal of Early Christian Studies* 9, no. 2 (2001): 173–204.

conviction, a sublime experience, the profusion of tears or an experience of light and fire – may be a wonderful foretaste of the beatific life and certainly represents the apex of the ascetic experience, but the way there is a narrow path and a long ascent, mounted with help by the discipline of monastic profession.[27] Thus, crucial for establishing the connection between monastic life and prayer which would so characterize the European Middle Ages was Cassian's insistence that most of prayer is discipline, learning the words of prayer – words provided, most crucially, by the Psalms. Essential to this discipline of prayer is regularity and repetition, and both specific phrases from the Psalms (such as the oft-repeated 'O God, make speed to save me; O Lord, make haste to help me', Ps. 70.1) as well as the entire run of 150 psalms constitute the monk's primary language of prayer. In the words of Stephanie Clark, Cassian does not leave space for 'personal creativity (in the sense of creating prayers)'. The continued repetition of the formula 'O God, make speed (etc.)', for example, serves to 'blot out "the rich and full resources of all thoughts", erase that distracting interior monologue, lead to a radical unmaking of the psyche, and remould it according to the form of the Psalms'.[28] Clark goes on to observe that this idea is the 'exact opposite of the modern ideals of genuineness and sincerity in prayer' such as that which we have seen insinuated by John Owen:

> Ideally, the Egyptian ascetic does not pray from his own experience and does not pray his own words but begins to adopt the words and experience of someone else, the Psalmist. Spontaneous prayer, in its endless iteration and re-representation of the self to the self (or, if you will, the self to God) would be powerless to effect the kind of transformation the ascetics sought.[29]

Following the model of Cassian who collected the wisdom of the desert fathers into writing, early medieval writers produced several collections of material from the tradition of cenobitic monasticism. Benedict of Aniane in the ninth century bound together over twenty-five rules spanning five centuries from Eastern and Western fathers into his *Codex Regularum,* and in his *Concordia Regularum* sought to demonstrate how each of these geographically varied rules cohered with the most important rule of them

---

[27]See, for example, the prologue by Smaragdus of Saint-Mihiel to his *Expositio in regulam sancti Benedicti* (CCM 8); *Commentary on the Rule of St Benedict*, trans. David Barry (Kalamazoo, MI: Cistercian Publications, 2007).

[28]Stephanie Clark, *Compelling God: Theories of Prayer in Anglo-Saxon England* (Toronto: University of Toronto Press, 2018), 88 (with reference to Cassian, *Conf.* 10).

[29]Clark, *Compelling God*, 89.

all – the *Rule of St Benedict*.[30] In the *Rule of St Benedict*, the 'pure prayer' of Cassian reappears, but now with the added qualification of brevity: '*Et ideo brebis debet esse et pura oratio* (Therefore, prayer should be brief and pure)'.[31] Benedict of Aniane offers commentary on this instruction about how to show reverence in prayer via the *Rule of St Basil* (as translated and transmitted by Rufinus), the *Rule of the Master* and the *Rule of the Fathers*.[32] Then he quotes from the *Regula Cassiani*, an eighth-century anonymous compilation drawn from Cassian's *Institutes*. The first excerpt explains that the person who is 'lukewarm of mind' but nevertheless prays outloud, clears his throat, spits or yawns sins twice, first by carelessly offering his own prayer, and second by disturbing the prayers of another.[33] Another excerpt underscores the necessity of engaging the mind with the words of prayer through psalms:

> because we ought to take pleasure not in the multitude of verses, but in the understanding of the mind, following this excellently: 'I will sing with the spirit, I will sing also with the understanding'. Therefore it is more useful to sing ten verses with the attention of reason than to pour forth a whole psalm with confusion of mind. And the confusion of the mind is produced by this, namely that when we realize the remainder and measure of the number of psalms, we seek not understanding of the mind or the perception of the senses, but with the disgrace of lukewarmness we strain to rush to the end.[34]

Though monks by the time of Benedict of Aniane were obliged to pray an extensive number of psalms through the eight Offices each day (plus seven penitential psalms to be recited for the dead as well as the occasional Office of the Dead), the understanding was that this pattern represented prayer 'short and pure': psalms were divided into shorter sections, the dismissal upon completion was to be swift, nothing prolix or extraneous was to be admitted in order to allow for maximum attention and alertness. Carolingian writers emphasized that mind and spirit must be engaged through the liturgy of the hours, and by the phrase 'praying at all times in the Spirit' (Eph. 6.16),

---

[30]See Renie Choy, 'The Deposit of Monastic Faith: The Carolingians on the Essence of Monasticism', in *The Church on Its Past*, ed. Peter D. Clarke and Charlotte Methuen (Woodbridge: Boydell and Brewer, 2013), 71–83.

[31]*Regula Benedicti* 20 (SC 181); *The Rule of Saint Benedict*, ed. and trans. Bruce L. Venarde (Cambridge, MA: Harvard University Press, 2011), 92–3.

[32]Benedict of Aniane, *Concordia Regularum* c. 26 (CCCM 168a), 207–11.

[33]Benedict of Aniane, *Concordia Regularum*, 212 (quoting *Regula Cassiani* c. 6).

[34]Benedict of Aniane, *Concordia Regularum*, 213 (quoting *Regula Cassiani* c. 7 and 1 Cor. 14.15).

the monk Smaragdus meant something rather specific.[35] The reading of scripture, he writes, quoting Isidore:

> is always associated with prayer, and must always be joined to prayer. For prayer cleanses us, while reading instructs us. And therefore he who wishes to be always with God must frequently pray and frequently read. For when we pray, we speak with God; but when we read, God speaks with us. All progress, then, proceeds from reading, prayer and meditation. What we do not know we learn by reading; what we have learned we retain by meditations; and by prayer we reach the fulfillment of what we have retained. ... Prayer is not opposed to reading, nor is reading foreign to prayer.[36]

Smaragdus derives this link between reading (*lectio*) and prayer (*oratio*) from earlier monastic fathers. For our purposes here, the adage underscores the importance of words: the physical (and usually audible) task of repeating words to produce an internal effect, the 'chewing' (*ruminatio*) of scripture by which the meaning of a text was absorbed and appropriated until it becomes one's own personal prayer.[37] Such constitutes prayer 'in the Spirit', which is not necessarily an emotional or ecstatic experience. For Smaragdus, the soul's longed-for contemplative union with the Lord results from this diligent and disciplined process. 'For Christ the beloved', he writes using an intimate image, 'is not found in the bed of carnal pleasures, but is found in holy labors, in sacred watches and frequent prayers'.[38] The mystical union with God might ultimately inspire wordless prayer, but words – the disciplined and correct use of them, the hearing and repetition of them, the personal appropriation of them from scripture – direct the individual to this state.

Asking to be Heard

In noting the formulaic utterances of priests and the disciplined meditations of monks, we confront an essential complexity in the early medieval conception of prayer. On the one hand, the terse, repeated, premeditated and indeed

---

[35]Smaragdus, *Expositio in regulam sancti Benedicti* (CCM 8), 135.

[36]Smaragdus, *Expositio in regulam sancti Benedicti* 4, 134–5 (quoting Isidore, *Sententiae* III.8.1-4).

[37]See *The Prayers and Meditations of Saint Anselm with the Proslogion*, trans. Benedicta Ward (New York: Penguin Books, 1973), 43 and Bernard McGinn, *The Growth of Mysticism: From Gregory the Great to the Twelfth Century* (New York: Crossroad, 1994), 134.

[38]Smaragdus, *Expositio in regulam sancti Benedicti*, 195; *Commentary on the Rule of St Benedict*, 313.

borrowed articulation of words and phrases represented opportunities for rhetorical flourish and oratorical style; on the other, they also reveal deep personal engagement and reflection about the mysteries of Christian doctrine. Set prayers through formulae and the Psalms expressed faith at both a personal and public, individual and societal level. In this final section, I wish to attend more closely to the phrases typical of early medieval prayer, by which Christians addressed their worship, confession and petitions to God, and by which they felt they might be heard.

The first kind of phrasing which we shall note characterize many of the prayers found in *libelli precum*, collections reflecting Anglo-Saxon and Celtic influence which seem predominantly to feature prayers of private devotion but are by no means limited to such use. The texts are often deeply penitential and reveal penetrating introspection. One fine example is the 'Prayer in the morning of the priest Saint Jerome' found in the *Book of Cerne*, a volume reflecting Insular culture and produced in southern England during the ninth century:

> Be with me (O Lord God) Sabbaoth when I arise in the morning. Attend to me Lord and govern all my acts and my words and my thoughts. Direct me in the right way, so that I may pass the whole day in your will. Give to me Lord the fear of you, compunction of the heart, humility of the mind, a pure conscience, so that I may understand the world, aspire to heaven, hate sin, love justice. Remove from me Lord the concerns of the world, greedy appetite, the longing for fornication, love of money, the disease of anger, worldly sadness, murder, vain joy, earthly pride. And plant in me Lord good virtues: denial of flesh and chastity of body, patience, humility which is not false but true fraternal charity. Guard my mouth that I might speak neither vain nor worldly tales. May I neither by absence withhold nor by presence speak evil wrongly, but on the contrary, let the blessing of the Lord at all times and his praise always be on my mouth.[39]

The prayer continues with a so-called 'lorica', the listing of parts of the body for physical and spiritual health. Equally brief and repetitive, but containing phrasing which shows a different concern, is the prayer which comes next in the *Book of Cerne*. This prayer – also for the morning – illustrates another way of praying for the attainment of virtue:

> Let us walk in the abundant light of this day, in the great strength of the Lord most high, in the good kindness of Christ, in the light of the Holy

---

[39]*The Prayer Book of Aedeluald the Bishop, Commonly Called the Book of Cerne*, ed. A. B. Kuypers (Cambridge: Cambridge University Press, 1902), 89–90.

Spirit, in the faith of the patriarchs, in the merits of the prophets, in the peace of the apostles, in the joy of angels, in the splendor of the saints, in the works of the monks, in the power of the just, in the witness of the martyrs, in the chastity of virgins, in the wisdom of God, in much patience, in the denial of the flesh, in the control of the tongue, in abundance of peace, in praise of the Trinity, in the sharpness of senses, in constant good deeds, in spiritual thought, in divine words, in blessings. In this is the way of all labouring for Christ, who led the saints after death into everlasting joy, so that I might hear the voice of the angels praising God and saying 'Holy, holy, holy'.[40]

The repeated dative phrase 'in' emphasizes not only the alignment of the precator with those virtues he desires, but also his participation in the power of those saints who have gone before, and helps explain the regular invocation of saints and of Mary, as in this prayer from another ninth-century Anglo-Saxon volume, the *Book of Nunnaminster*:

Guard me, through the prayers of the patriarchs, through the merits of the prophets, through the suffrages of the apostles, through the victories of the martyrs, through the faith of the confessors who have pleased you from the beginning of the world.[41]

Prayers of this sort reveal why people invoked the assistance of saints and angels: the special deeds, faith and triumphs of holy individuals cannot, as it were, be for nought, but achieve good for those still living: 'Let Holy Abel pray for me, who was first crowned martyr, let Holy Enoch pray for me, who walked with God and was translated out of this world,' and so forth for the apostles and confessors.[42] The recollection of what a saint achieved on earth which allows him or her to be heard in heaven inspired beautiful stylistic phrasing, and nowhere is this better seen than in prayers addressing

---

[40]*The Prayer Book of Aedeluald the Bishop*, 91–2. See also H. A. Wilson, 'On a Rhythmical Prayer in the Book Of Cerne', *The Journal of Theological Studies* 5, no. 18 (1904): 263–5.

[41]'Incipit Oratio sancti Gregorii Papae Urbis Romae', *An Ancient Manuscript of the Eighth or Ninth Century: Formerly Belonging to St Mary's Abbey, or Nunnaminster, Winchester*, ed. Walter de Gray Birch (London: Simpkin and Marshall, 1889), 58. On this prayer, see Marie Schilling Grogan, 'The Book of Nunnaminster', in *A Benedictine Reader: 530–1530*, ed. Hugh Feiss, Ronald Pepin and Maureen M. O'Brien (Collegeville, MN: Liturgical Press, 2019), 78–93.

[42]'Incipit Oratio sancti Gregorii Papae Urbis Romae', *An Ancient Manuscript of the Eighth or Ninth Century*, 58.

Mary and reflecting on the mystery of the incarnation. In this example, Bede seeks the intercession of Mary:

> And you, Virgin Mary, glorious mother of God, blessed above all women, favour our praises. … Whose chaste womb, consecrated to the Holy Spirit, brought forth the king of the world, born from the seed of David. Whose blessed breasts, filled with the highest gift, nourished for the world the unique glory of earth and sky.[43]

Yet, appeals addressed directly to God also occasioned vibrant and poetic phrasing, as, for example, this ninth-century 'Prayer on the Holy Trinity' from the *Libellus Trecensis*:

> Holy Trinity, You are my helper. Hear me, hear me my God. You are my living and true God. You are my holy father. You are my pious lord. You are my great king. You are my just judge. You are my one teacher. You are my timely helper. You are my most powerful doctor. You are my most beautiful beloved. You are my living bread. You are my priest in eternity. You are my clear wisdom. You are my pure simplicity. You are my catholic unity. You are my peaceful concord. You are my complete protection. You are my good portion. You are my eternal salvation. You are my great mercy. You are my most robust wisdom, Saviour of the world who lives and reigns, world without end, Amen.[44]

The insistent use of the first personal possessive pronoun turns the prayer into something entirely personal and self-aware; the force behind this deeply personal and rich grammatical construction is the will rather than emotion, a reasoned determination to accept the totality of Christ. Here the operative word is 'my', to denote a strong sense of personal resolve. This type of phrasing shows prayer as an expression of intent and even self-persuasion in the way of faith.[45]

These prayers, though usually classified as 'private', draw from biblical language and employ rhymes and repetitions typical of liturgical assemblies. For this reason, no emphatic distinction should be made between prayers for

---

[43]*Liber hymnorum, rhythmi, variae preces* (CCSL 122), 433; trans. Mary Clayton, *The Cult of the Virgin Mary in Anglo-Saxon England* (Cambridge: Cambridge University Press, 1990), 92.

[44]Troyes, 'Bibliothèque municipale, MS 1742', in *Precum libelli quattuor aevi Karolini*, ed. André Wilmart (Rome: Ephemerides Liturgicae, 1940), 13.

[45]See Renie S. Choy, '"The Brother Who May Wish to Pray by Himself": Sense of Self in Carolingian Prayers of Private Devotion', in *Prayer and Thought in Monastic Tradition: Essays in Honour of Sr Benedicta Ward*, ed. Santha Bhattacharji, Rowan Williams and Dominic Mattos (London: Bloomsbury, 2014), 101–20.

private use and those for public liturgical processions: the litany of saints, for example, was equally employed for both.[46] In public processions, the structured, brief and repetitive manner of prayer becomes a particularly effective means of including the participation of all people and classes. Angilbert's order for the solemn processions on Rogations Days, part of his liturgical instruction for the monks at St Riquier, reflects the Carolingian policy of including all members of society into these events of prayer. He prescribed an elaborate three-day ritual that involved monks and the local people of Centula, as well as participants from seven neighbouring towns. Priests, deacons, subdeacons, acolytes, exorcists, lectors, porters and monks, as well as the lay scolae bearing red standards, noble men and women, boys and girls, and a mixed population of the old and infirm were all to form a procession seven persons wide. While monks chanted psalms, all the people sang the three creeds (Apostles', Constantinopolitan and Athanasian), the Lord's Prayer and a litany of saints. Walahfrid Strabo states that the Synod of Orléans ordered that people take a holiday from servile work during the Rogations to ensure that the litanies were celebrated fully by all in society.[47] The prayers which were chanted during processions such as these might be suggested in the Sacramentary of Gellone. The *ordo baptisterii* includes a brief litany of the saints to be sung during the procession from the church to the baptistery in the service of Holy Saturday.[48] The litany begins 'Christ hear us', and all repeat this phrase. Then the litany of saints: 'Holy Mary, pray for us. St Peter, pray for us. St Andrew, pray for us. ... Let all the saints pray for us'. Then the suffrages:

Be merciful; deliver us, O Lord. From all evil, deliver us, O Lord. We sinners ask you, hear us. That you may give peace, we ask you, hear us. That you may give rain, we ask you, hear us. That you may give serenity, we ask you, hear us. That you may give seasonable weather, we ask you, hear us. Son of God, we ask you, hear us. Lamb of God who takes away the sins of the world, have mercy on us. Christ hear us.[49]

---

[46]See the remarks of Susan Boynton in *Shaping a Monastic Identity: Liturgy and History at the Imperial Abbey of Farfa, 1000–1125* (Ithaca, NY: Cornell University Press, 2006), 89–90. By the early ninth century, the litany of the saints was a well-established feature of continental prayer, both used in liturgical processions and found in prayer collections for private or semi-private use.

[47]Walahfrid Strabo, 'De exordiis et incrementis quarundam in observationibus ecclesiasticis rerum 29', *Walahfrid Strabo's libellus de exordiis et incrementis quarundam in observationibus ecclesiasticis rerum*, trans. Alice Harting-Correa (Leiden: Brill, 1996), 184–7.

[48]Michael Lapidge, ed., *Anglo-Saxon Litanies of the Saints* (London: Boydell Press, 1991), 33–4.

[49]Ordo Baptisterii, *Liber Sacramentorum Gellonensis*(CCSL 159), 332–3.

Conclusion

In this chapter, we have observed the words assimilated, appropriated, learned and performed for prayer: the Lord's Prayer, eucharistic formulae, the Psalter, penitential prayers and litanies for private use and public processions. The critical importance of words brings us to a final but pressing question: how could set prayers possibly be considered the expression of the genuine prayer of the people if it was couched in Latin, a language used and understood only by a small group of literate, clerical elite? The evidence only throws up more questions for interpretation and debate.[50] Intriguingly, the first extant texts on the Continent documenting Romance vernaculars coincide with the intensive development of liturgical books in Carolingian Europe in the eighth and ninth centuries. In some of the earliest texts, vernacular language is added 'in-scriptural' to Latin manuscripts and clearly represent spontaneous and expressive speech, the scribes invariably returning to Latin when formally addressing God.[51] One of these texts is the 'Veronese Riddle' scribbled on the front page of the *Libellus Orationum*, an eighth-century Visigothic prayer book. This riddle, written in a mix of vulgar Latin and Romance dialect, reads: 'He pushed oxen in front of him, ploughed white fields, carried a white plough, and sowed a black seed' (the answer: a scribe). But Latin is used for the prayer formula which immediately follows: '*gratias tibi agimus omnipotens sempiterne deus* (We give you thanks, almighty eternal God)'.[52] In another example, on the front page of a Latin manuscript produced at around 1000 at the monastery of St Gall, a scribe begins with prayer and a scriptural citation in Latin ('This is my God. *My God, why hast Thou forsaken me*') but breaks into vernacular to test a new pen ('Diderros should earn a fly from it').[53] In both these examples, the use of the vernacular is reserved for non-religious light-hearted interjections. But there is also evidence of bilingual ecclesiastical texts which employ

---

[50]See Rosamond McKitterick, 'Latin and Romance: An Historian's Perspective', in *Latin and the Roman Languages in the Early Middle Ages*, ed. Roger Wright (London: Routledge, 1991), 130–45.

[51]See Barbara Frank-Job and Maria Selig, 'Early Evidence and Sources', in *The Oxford Guide to the Romance Languages*, ed. Adam Ledgeway and Martin Maiden (Oxford: Oxford University Press, 2016), 24–36.

[52]Pio Rajna, 'Un Indovinello Volgare Scritto alla Fine del Secolo VIII o al Principio del IX', *Speculum* 3, no. 3 (1928): 291–313. See also Francesca Guerra D'Antoni, 'A New Perspective on the Veronese Riddle', *Romance Philology* 36, no. 2 (1982): 185–200. This translation from Claudia Baldoli, *A History of Italy* (London: Palgrave, 2009), 25.

[53]Frank-Job and Selig, 'Early Evidence and Sources', 26; Barbara Frank and Jörg Hartmann, ed., *Inventaire systématique des premiers documents des langues romanes* (Tübingen: Narr, 1997), vol. 2, 126.

both Latin for liturgical prayer and vernacular languages for expressions of
religious devotion. Perhaps the most famous example from the early Middle
Ages is the Old English gloss of Caedmon's *Hymn* from Bede's *Ecclesiastical
History*, preserved in a mid-eighth- or early ninth-century manuscript.[54]
Other examples from the period seem to correspond with the goals of
Carolingian reform, in particular to foster the formation of faith among the
laity and heighten their participation in Christian worship. A Montpellier
psalter transmits eighth-century *Laudes regiae* (liturgical acclamations of
prayer for rulers) written in the vernacular within a litany of saints written in
Latin. The Romance parts of the text name the Carolingian rulers followed
by a collective '*tu lo(s) iuva* (May you bless him/them)', suggesting special
concern to encourage lay participation and to heighten the sense of collective
participation.[55] Perhaps the acceptance of vernacular languages for prayer is
most clearly seen in the permission granted by John VIII to Methodius to
perform the Mass and say the Offices in Slavic in the recently converted
regions of Moravia and Dalmatia: 'For we are instructed by sacred authority
that the Lord should not be praised in only three languages but rather in all
languages.'[56] Yet this open-mindedness about non-Latin liturgy soon seemed
a step too far; soon afterward in the ninth century Pope Steven V overturned
this decision and enforced the exclusive use of Latin.

These cases demonstrate a certain tension in the linguistic approach to
early medieval prayer: a tendency, on the one hand, to retain and heighten
the quality and prestige of Christian latinity, and a willingness to embrace,
on the other, elements of everyday language. Early medieval Christians
honoured Latin, as with the two other languages of Hebrew and Greek,
not because of some inherently superior quality, but because, as the use of
these three languages on the cross upon which Christ died made clear, they
communicated the Gospel to the Jews, pagans and Romans. In the words of
Hilary of Poitiers, in these languages was 'preached above all the mystery of

---

[54] Elliot V. K. Dobbie, *The Manuscripts of Caedmon's Hymn and Bede's Death Song* (New York:
Columbia University Press, 1937); Katherine O'Keeffe, 'Orality and the Developing Text of
Caedmon's Hymn', *Speculum* 62, no. 1 (1987): 1–20.
[55] Barbara Frank-Job, 'Les traditions des textes paraliturgiques', in *The Church and Vernacular
Literature in Medieval France*, ed. Dorothea Kullmann (Toronto: Pontifical Institute of Medieval
Studies, 2009), 35–62 (46–7); Gabriele Kaps, *Zweisprachigkeit im paraliturgischen Text des
Mittelalters* (Frankfurt am Main: Peter Lang, 2005), 27–43.
[56] Patrick Geary, *Language and Power in the Early Middle Ages* (Waltham, MA: Brandeis
University Press, 2013), 50–1.

the will of God and the expectation of the coming Kingdom of God'.[57] In other words, Latin had fulfilled a special function in conveying the Gospel to those who dominated the world and its people, and was thus essential as a schoolmaster in the way of faith. *Lectio* and *oratio* in Latin therefore represented an act of meditative learning, in receiving the Gospel and acknowledging how it forms the Christian mind and a Christian church. Yet close inspection also reveals the admission of 'popular' components drawn from everyday speech and, importantly, the influence of socially diverse and even non-Christian environments. Els Rose has demonstrated, for example, that the Gothic Missal, produced in Gaul around 700, contains many vulgar traits alongside the opulent and splendid constructions expected in liturgical Latin. Neologisms, fluctuations in orthography, the adoption of loan words, and even the admission of archaic or pagan lexical and semantic elements dispel the notion that liturgical Latin was comprehensively immune from the influence of everyday speech and people.[58] It was not stylistic perfection per se which was the aim of prayer, but what the effort to achieve it represented. Formulaic prayers were costly because they represented time spent learning, transmitting and memorizing the vocabulary and phraseology of faith. And like the precious bones of saints encased in reliquaries, the expensive wax required for lighting lamps and candles, the costly oils and incense used in ritual ceremonies, the texts of prayers were often contained in books elaborately decorated with expensive materials like ivories, gems and ink. Thus one phrase from the *Gothic Missal* seems a fitting way to summarize the aim of early medieval Christians at prayer: 'May our prayer be as fragrant as the precious ointment which [Mary] poured over Your sacred feet.'[59]

---

[57]*Tractatus super psalmos*, prol. 15, quoted in Lang, 'The Liturgy and Sacred Language', 366–7.

[58]See *Missale Gothicum* (CCSL 159d), 23–187.

[59]*The Gothic Missal*, trans. Els Rose (Turnhout: Brepols, 2017), 197.

CHAPTER NINETEEN

Anselm on Prayer: Lament of Self and Contemplation of God

TRAVIS E. ABLES

There are two Anselms. Or so one would be tempted to think, upon reading a little about him. On the one hand is the Anselm of philosophy and theology textbooks – excerpted and anthologized, his texts often decontextualized and reduced to a set of logical formulae. Here his major contributions are two: a logically perturbing, stubbornly persistent proof of the existence of God, known as the 'ontological argument'; a 'satisfaction' theory of atonement, one of the (supposed) three main strands of Western Christian atonement thinking, distinguished largely for being the progenitor of later doctrines of penal substitution. Both are characterized by his programme of *fides quaerens intellectum* and are among the first texts of medieval Scholasticism to explicate rationally the mysteries of the faith. The second Anselm is lesser known, except to historians: he is the author of a slim volume of *Prayers and Meditations* that stands at the origins of the tradition of affective meditation in the Middle Ages, the practice of prayerful devotion stressing penitence and self-formation by the imaginative portrayal of the life of Christ and emotive identification with his sufferings.[1] Anselm's precise location in this

---

[1] On this movement, see Caroline Walker Bynum, *Jesus as Mother: Studies in the Spirituality of the High Middle Ages* (Berkeley, CA: University of California Press, 1982), 129–46; Denise Despres, *Ghostly Sights: Visual Meditation in Late-Medieval Literature* (Norman: Pilgrim Books, 1989), 5–54; Sarah McNamer, *Affective Meditation and the Invention of Medieval Compassion* (Philadelphia, PA: University of Pennsylvania Press, 2010), 1–14; and Michelle Karnes, *Imagination, Meditation and Cognition in the Middle Ages* (Chicago, IL: University of Chicago Press, 2011), 111–20.

tradition is debated, but once again he stands at or near the origins of a distinct trajectory in medieval Christianity.

Of course, the dualism is ours, not Anselm's. It is difficult for us to reconcile the abstractions of necessary and contingent existences, feudal-penitential models of divine propitiation, and imaginary islands with the vocabularies of spiritual formation and devotional prayer. All these were of a piece, for Anselm; but even if he rejects this dichotomy, he is still not done alienating modern readers. For if we turn to his prayers, we find them strange, even repellent. Even for the medieval monastic worldview, hung upon the twin Augustinian poles of original sin and the corruption of the will, they are extreme. Liberally employing a rhetoric of shame, self-abasement and the terror of divine judgement, there is little in them to commend them to modern concerns for self-care and spiritual formation. It is difficult to imagine a passage like the following being used in a contemporary devotional or *lectio divina* service:

Miserable little man, throw yourselves in the dark depths of boundless grief, for of your will you fell into the dark depths of horrible iniquity. Unhappy man, let the weight of terrible sorrow bury you, for you freely sank into the mud of stinking hell. Wrap yourself round, wretch, in the horrible darkness of inconsolable mourning, for you were willing to roll into the pit of sordid lust. Plunge into the whirlpool of bitterness – you have wallowed in the trough of moral corruption.[2]

Premodern prayers emerge from technologies of devotional practice grounded in theological assumptions and sociocultural contexts distant from our own, and to assimilate uncritically such scripts would be to drain them of their particularity and insight (it might also be to gloss over their dangers). Therefore, in this chapter I will first lean into the 'strange' elements of Anselm's *Prayers and Meditations* in order to identify their theological framing and rhetorical programme. Mindful of my opening dilemma, I will then analyse the relationship of the *Prayers* and Anselm's famous theological texts *Proslogion* and *Cur Deus Homo*. I conclude by broadening the range of this discussion and placing Anselm within his broader sociocultural context.

---

[2]Anselm, 'Meditation 2: A Lament for Virginity Unhappily Lost', in *The Prayers and Meditations of Saint Anselm with the Proslogion*, trans. Benedict Ward (New York: Penguin Books, 1973), 226.

The Context of the *Prayers and Meditations*

The first version of the *Prayers and Meditations* appeared in 1072, when Anselm sent a set of seven prayers and a cover letter to Adelaide, daughter of William the Conqueror; he sent a later edition to Countess Matilda of Tuscany in 1104, but the bulk of the prayers were written by 1075, when he had substantially finished his three prayers to Mary – without question the most theologically significant and innovative pieces in the collection. Only after he had written *Cur Deus Homo* late in life did he pen a 'Meditation on Human Redemption' recasting its argument in devotional terms, followed by the brief prayers to God and for the Eucharist, which effectively serve as cover letters or prefaces for the *Prayers*; these completed the collection he sent to Matilda.[3] Thus the majority of the *Prayers and Meditations* are relatively early, but their revision and expansion span the major years of his authorship: the *Monologion* and *Proslogion* were written 1075–8, and *Cur Deus Homo* was completed in 1098. The only completed work to postdate this period is *De Concordia* ('The Compatibility of God's Foreknowledge, Predestination, and Grace with Human Freedom'). Therefore we are justified in seeing the *Prayers and Meditations* both as early soundings in the theological and spiritual themes that concerned Anselm, and as paralleling his intellectual development to maturity.

The prayers themselves are both deeply traditioned and innovative. They emerge from two monastic contexts, which Anselm developed for his own purposes: the Daily Office, the backbone of Benedictine observance; and the penning of private prayers for lay patrons, which dates back to Alcuin's devotional texts for Charlemagne in the ninth century.[4] The Office was structured around weekly recitation of the Psalms; the eight hours of Matins, Lauds, Prime, Terce, Sext, None, Vespers and Compline; and the reading of scripture and the church fathers, generally Augustine, Cassian, Gregory the Great, Jerome and Leo the Great.[5] The Office formed the structure of

---

[3]Anselm, 'Why God Became Man', in *Anselm of Canterbury: The Major Works*, ed. Brian Davies and G. R. Evans (New York: Oxford University Press, 1998), 260–356 and 'Meditation on Human Redemption', in *Prayers and Meditations*, 230–7. For a chronological overview, see Richard W. Southern, *Saint Anselm: A Portrait in a Landscape* (Cambridge: Cambridge University Press, 1990), 106–12 and Richard Sharpe, 'Anselm as Author: Publishing in the Late Eleventh Century', *Journal of Medieval Latin* 19 (2009): 1–87 (11–15).

[4]Southern, *Saint Anselm*, 96.

[5]For an overview, see Ward's introduction in *Prayers and Meditations*, 27–30 and Christopher Brooke, *The Age of the Cloister: The Story of Monastic Life in the Middle Ages* (Mahwah, NJ: HiddenSpring, 2003), 70–6.

Benedictine observance (the *ora* of *ora et labora*) and formed the life of the monk around the reading of scripture, accompanied by frequent Mass and the liturgical calendar. This structure of 'praying without ceasing' (1 Thess. 5.17) was obviously limited to the life of the enclosure; but by Anselm's times, short offices had been adapted for outside of the monastery. This is the second context for the *Prayers and Meditations*: the production of prayers and contemplative texts for lay patrons by monks, dating back to the ninth century. Again hung upon the structure of the Psalter, these prayers were generally short, emphasizing penitence and devotion, and formed an important part of the transactional relationship between the monastery and the monarch in the Middle Ages: the monarch or lord ruled over the temporal realm (notionally) with godly character; and the monks provided intercession for the ruler and the realm, forming its spiritual heartbeat, and receiving in return bequests, material donations and occasionally oblates, along with protection.

In the eleventh century this was changing. The cult of saints, already a mainstay of the liturgical calendar, was exploding, as was devotion to Mary; lay patrons, and especially aristocratic laywomen, were cultivating new forms of devotion, and forming new relationships with client or friendly monastics in the process. Anselm's development of the Daily Office, a communal monastic exercise, into a laicized affective, individual devotional regime was instrumental in all this. The backdrop is too complex to delve into here, but it is important for our purposes to recognize that Anselm, with his slim volume of prayers and meditations, was at the centre of all of it. In his hands, the reserved Carolingian prayers became florid, impassioned treatises; intercessions addressed to the saints and Mary marked theological innovations; and the patron–client relationship of aristocracy and monastery underwent a transformation that would ultimately help clear the way for the great lay saints of the thirteenth and fourteenth centuries. The effect of the *Prayers and Meditations* was wildly disproportionate to its size. It would become one of the more influential spiritual texts of the Middle Ages (especially as it expanded with pseudo-Anselmian accretions), but it also marks the first soundings in themes that would mark Anselm's later thought, and thereby, the direction of Western Christian theology.

Prayer in the *Prayers*

Prayer, as Anselm conceives of it in this text, is not simply petitionary address; instead, it is a complex rhetorical production carefully calibrated to produce emotive effects. As Thomas Bestul puts it, 'Central to Anselm's conception is the relation between private reading and the arousal of emotion.'[6] Based in the Benedictine practice of *meditatio*, the prayers are designed to stir up the torpor of the sin-sick soul, with its disordered, earthbound affections, and reorient its gaze and desire towards God. But whereas the meditative ascent Anselm would use in the *Monologion* and *Proslogion* was heavily indebted to the modified Neoplatonism of Augustine's *De Trinitate*, as I will discuss below, the *Prayers* are more reminiscent of Augustine's horror of his past sinfulness in the *Confessions*, read through the monastic technology of contrition of Gregory the Great, Cassian and Benedict.

There are generally six distinct moves or dynamics discernible in each prayer, though these are not necessarily sequential; rather, Anselm tends to follow a dialectical pattern between the praying reader (using the rhetorical first person) and the addressee of his prayer. I will use his prayer to St Peter as an example.[7]

Prologue

First is a *prologue*, which generally rehearses the themes of the prayer, particularly focusing on the merits of the addressee, often drawn from scripture or their life. Thus, the prayer to Peter begins,

Holy and most kind Peter,
faithful shepherd of the flock of God,
chief of the apostles,
prince among such mighty princes.
You are able to bind and loose as you will.[8]

Anselm acknowledges the Petrine primacy among the apostles, but the last line is the key: Peter's power to bind and loose sin (Mt. 16.19). Anselm will appeal to Peter's power to transform the subjectivity of the praying penitent, enabling the soul to rise 'from such a depth as mine to such a height as yours'.[9] The prologue is generally short, but it is essential for crafting the

---

[6]Thomas H. Bestul, '*Meditatio*/Meditation', in *The Cambridge Companion to Christian Mysticism*, ed. Amy Hollywood and Patricia Z. Beckman (Cambridge: Cambridge University Press, 2012), 159. Further on *meditatio*, see Bernard McGinn, *The Growth of Mysticism: From Gregory the Great to the Twelfth Century* (New York: Crossroad, 1994), 132–8.

[7]Anselm, 'Prayer to St Peter', in *Prayers and Meditations*, 135–40. Ward's introduction to *Prayers and Meditations* is helpful here (52–6), though I have expanded her focus on *excita mentem*, *compunctio* and *in caelis*.

[8]Anselm, 'Prayer to St Peter', l. 1–5.

[9]Anselm, 'Prayer to St Peter', l. 17.

imaginative space, usually a paratextual space formed by scripture, within which the prayer will work.

Excita mentem

The second movement is the *excita mentem*, the stirring up of the mind from sin and the lethargy of the fallen state. Anselm is thinking of more than simply laziness or cold heartedness, but recalling the *acedia* of the desert fathers, a tradition transmitted by Cassian: imperfectly translated as 'sloth', the 'noonday demon' signified the recalcitrance of the will in its resistance to God. *Acedia* was a vivid temptation to a monk trying to maintain his fervour for God in the heat of the desert afternoon or the sleepiness of the night-time prayer vigil. But it was also a sign of something deeper: human affections are distant from God, and the fallen mind is unstable, distracted – distended (*distentio*), as Augustine had put it in the *Confessions*. So for Anselm:

> Again and again I try
> to shake the lethargy from my mind,
>   to prevent the thoughts
>   from being scattered among vanities,
> but when I have gathered together all my strength
>   I am not able to break out of the shadows
>   of the torpor that holds me
>   because of the filth of my sins.
> Nor do I have the strength
>   to remain for long of the same mind.[10]

Compunction

The languor of lethargy requires a jolt to retrain one's desires. Thus the third move is one of *compunction*, the sorrow over sin, often motivated by the fear of divine judgement: 'Shatter my hardness, shine on my darkness.'[11] Compunction, frequently conveyed with the imagery of tears, is at bottom the lament of alienated selfhood, and is the posture of penitence, as is seen vividly in this passage from the prayer to John the Baptist:

> If I look within myself, I cannot bear myself;
> if I do not look within myself, I do not know myself.
> If I consider myself, what I see terrifies me;

---

[10]Anselm, 'Prayer to St Peter', l. 18–27.
[11]Anselm, 'Prayer to St Peter', l. 36.

if I do not consider myself, I fall to my damnation.
If I look at myself, it is an intolerable horror;
if I do not look at myself, death is unavoidable.[12]

The 'double bind' is a term often used to describe the dilemma of *Cur Deus Homo*, but it is woven throughout the *Prayers* as well.[13] It is the paradox of self-knowledge in Western Christian theology: to know the self is to know its distance from God, but failing to know the self is to remain mired in ignorance and alienation. The role of compunction is to mourn over this double bind and so to prepare the soul in penitence that one reaches out for the mercy of God in suitable humility. For a Benedictine monk like Anselm, forgiveness and communion with God is unthinkable without this stage, and it is not a one-time event, but a continual conversion (*conversatio morum*) throughout life. Lament of self is the cornerstone of the medieval monastic theology of selfhood – and here medievals are most distant from modern therapeutic regimes of self-care.

Elevation

The next movement is one of praise or *elevation*. This may mean praise of God, but more frequently it signifies elevation of the object of the prayer. Anselm meditates on the attributes of the addressee, often drawn from a passage of scripture, developing a motif to organize his appeal in the prayer.[14] Hence, Peter is, as the prologue announced, the 'faithful shepherd of the flock of God'. This is not simply ornamental language, but becomes the driving force of this petition: he calls on Peter to look on Anselm, 'the sickly sheep', to cure him of 'the gashes of wounds, and the bites of wolves, which he ran into when he strayed'.[15] The rhetorical heart of the prayer develops around these themes of straying, illness and wounding to characterize the sinful soul needing the care of the shepherd, Peter, who was commanded by the Lord to 'feed my sheep'.[16]

The praise of saints like Peter and particularly Mary is often extravagant and hyperbolic; this may strike the modern reader (particularly a Protestant) unaccustomed to the cult of the saints as disconcerting – for two reasons. First, Anselm is generous in assigning the addressee agency in the plan of

---

[12]Anselm, 'Prayer to St John the Baptist', in *Prayers and Meditations*, 127–34 (l. 122–7).
[13]See Eileen C. Sweeney, *Anselm of Canterbury and the Desire for the Word* (Washington, DC: Catholic University of America Press, 2012), 24.
[14]See again Sweeney, *Desire for the Word*, 18–20.
[15]Anselm, 'Prayer to St Peter', l. 43, 49.
[16]Anselm, 'Prayer to St Peter', l. 60–103.

salvation; that is certainly true with Mary, whom he describes in language reminiscent of the *Christus victor* and *admirabile commercium* themes of redemption:[17]

> The world was wrapped in darkness,
> surrounded and oppressed by demons under which it lay,
> but from you alone light was born into it,
> which broke its bonds and trampled underfoot their power. ...
> By you the elements are renewed, hell is redeemed ...
>   plenty flows from you
> to make all creatures green again.[18]

But such language is also found in the prayer to John the Evangelist ('Let me, by your prayers, be that sinner whom Jesus forgives') and Stephen ('In love and assurance I send you as my intercessor, that you may make peace between me and your powerful friend'), among others. The prayer to Paul is nearly as daring as the third prayer to Mary in addressing the apostle as both mother and father (riffing on 1 Thess. 2.7, Paul as nursemaid), before enlisting Jesus as *also* mother and father (evoking Mt. 23.37), to address both together as (co?)parents in the faith:

> Both of you are mothers. ...
> You are fathers by your effect
>   and mothers by your affection. ...
> If in quantity of affection you are unequal,
>   yet in quality you are not unalike.[19]

Second, though Anselm frequently will address God or Christ in saints' prayers, the prayers to them are far from unique in richness and theological development. The prayer to God itself is quite short and comparatively formal in emotional tone, and the prayer to Christ, while longer and among Anselm's best in literary depth, spends a good deal of time addressing the parents of Christ, and its tone of lamentation is among the starkest of his

---

[17]Anselm, 'Prayer to St Mary (3)', in *Prayers and Meditations*, 115–26. For more on this famous prayer, see Southern, *Saint Anselm*, 107–9; Travis E. Ables, *The Body of the Cross: Holy Victims and the Invention of Atonement* (New York: Fordham University Press, 2021), chapter 4.

[18]Anselm, 'Prayer to St Peter', l. 114–17, 153, 158–9.

[19]Anselm, 'Prayer to St John the Evangelist (1)', in *Prayers and Meditations*, 157–62, l. 106–7; 'Prayer to St Stephen', 174–82, l. 21–3; 'Prayer to St Paul', 141–56, l. 416, 421–2, 427–8.

prayers. He speaks of himself as an 'orphan deprived of the present of a very kind father', and mourns that he was not a witness to the passion:

> Alas for me, that I was not able to see
> the Lord of Angels humbled to converse with men. ...
> Why, O my soul, were you not there,
> to be pierced by a sword of bitter sorrow?[20]

These prayers, however, are integral to his purposes. The prayer to God functions as a prologue to the collection as a whole, focusing on the overall idea of compunction and forgiveness of sin, while the prayer to Christ features Anselm's unique contribution to early medieval prayer: the notion that, in praying to the saints (in the context of the prayer to Christ, Mary and Joseph), Anselm becomes a participant in the evangelical history itself, with the saints functioning as a kind of cloud of witnesses (Heb. 12.1) who collectively embed the reader in the biblical drama. While Anselm is a long way from Francis of Assisi, both temporally and ideologically, and the later medieval idea of the *imitatio Christi*, we can see the beginnings of such an imagination adumbrated here, in this plea to be placed at the foot of the cross and made witness to the sufferings of Christ.

Negotiation

The fifth rhetorical move of the prayers is *negotiation*.[21] Anselm is a bargainer, and is adept at bending the attributes of his addressees towards an idea that is at the heart of his work: the tension between the justice and mercy of God. To return to the prayer to Peter, in the final section Anselm sets up a paradox between the lowly sinfulness of the praying supplicant and the holy merit of Peter, to bring the reader into confrontation with this tension:

> Ah, how bitter it is to be without hope!
> That, surely, is the sentence of justice, not of mercy,
>> and who calls on justice in my cause?
>> My talk was of mercy, not of justice.
> In the wretched tribulation of my soul,
>> I beg of you, my God, the bread of mercy;
>> why do you press the stone of justice into my mouth?[22]

---

[20]Anselm, 'Prayer to Christ', in *Prayers and Meditations*, 93–9, l. 58, 73–4, 79–80.

[21]Sweeney calls this 'arguing for salvation'. See *Desire for the Word*, 30–4. I am sharpening the language somewhat with a vocabulary of negotiation and bargaining, in order to highlight Anselm's often audacious rhetoric.

[22]Anselm, 'Prayer to St Peter', l. 170–6.

This lament – startling, coming so near the end of the prayer, as it does – seems to erupt out of nowhere, but Anselm has carefully laid the groundwork, appealing to Peter as doorkeeper of heaven,[23] and beseeching him, 'Do not be difficult of access'.[24]

The implication is intriguing – and terrifying. In the *Prayers and Meditations*, God is frequently remote, sitting in judgement, more an object of fear than adoration. Recall the strikingly formal and terse prayer to God that opens the collection, or the motif of abandonment in the prayer to Christ, where Anselm is 'deprived of the presence of a very kind father'.[25] The dynamic of the prayers is not to seek union with God, or even intimacy; it is to appeal to the nature of God on the basis of the merits and compassion of the saints to negotiate forgiveness of sin. Anselm can be quite audacious in this respect; most strikingly, in his third prayer to Mary, he develops an appeal to the incarnation to justify his claim to mercy. First is a daring description of Christ's birth:

All nature is created by God and God is born of Mary.
God created all things, and Mary gave birth to God.
God who made all things made himself out of Mary,
and thus he refashioned everything he had made.[26]

The Marian flesh of Christ, or to follow Anselm's theological rhetoric, the flesh by which God made God's self out of Mary, is the basis of new creation, specifically the new creation of the sinful soul of Anselm himself. Because of this incarnational re-creation, Anselm advances an even more reckless claim: God *must* exercise mercy because of this flesh God shares with Mary through Christ.

So, most kind, do not refuse what I ask,
for though I confess I am not worthy of it,
    you cannot worthily refuse it. ...
Lord and Lady, surely it is much better for you to give grace
        to those who do not deserve it
        than for you to exact what is owing you in justice?[27]

---

[23]Anselm, 'Prayer to St Peter', l. 120, 125.
[24]Anselm, 'Prayer to St Peter', l. 58.
[25]Anselm, 'Prayer to St Peter', l. 59.
[26]Anselm, 'Prayer to St Peter', l. 184–7.
[27]Anselm, 'Prayer to St Peter', l. 309–11, 323–5; emphasis mine.

This incarnational bargain is a shrewd calculation: the birth of God through Mary means that God has irrevocably committed God's self to mercy over justice. It is in the nature of God to redeem – God 'cannot worthily refuse it'. Or, more graphically, Anselm pleads the flesh of Mary at the judgement seat of God, and looking down, finds that he bears the same flesh too.

There are two themes here that are essential in Anselm's later technical work: the fittingness of redemption (*Cur Deus Homo*) and the paradox of contrasting attributes in the simple nature of God (*Monologion* and *Proslogion*). Of course, Anselm is too skilled a theologian to hold that God's nature is in conflict with itself, mercy vying against justice in the divine counsel, and characterizing this as 'negotiation' or 'bargaining' is to speak a little loosely; Anselm would think of it as a humble pleading, but we should not miss the cunning rhetorical moves he makes to appeal to God on the basis of God's own nature and acts. His intent here is rhetorical and affective, to cast a theological tension into a dialectic within the mind and heart of the reader, in order to effect the final move of the prayer, union or *bliss*.

Bliss

The final move of the prayers, which Ward calls *in caelis* (in heaven), puts the praying reader in communion with God in final glory. Rarely does Anselm prolong this final move of the prayers – in fact, the move is so short in the prayer to Peter, as to seem almost perfunctory:

> Free me from the misery of the kingdom of sin,
> and lead me into the bliss of the kingdom of heaven,
>> where rejoicing with you
>> I may give thanks and praise God for ever. Amen.[28]

Anselm is not given to long or detailed descriptions of the *telos* of final union with God. This can be attributed to the goal of the prayers, which is to form the subjectivity of the reader in a practice of penitence and devotion that approximated the continual conversion of the Benedictine *Rule*. His contribution is the training of emotion by compunction and exciting the mind, and developing a theological method grounded in the fittingness of God in redemption. By habituating the reader in a programme of self-examination, repentance, converse with the saints and meditation on the life of Christ, Anselm helped develop a new form of spirituality: affective meditation.

---

[28]Anselm, 'Prayer to St Peter', l. 183–6.

Affective Meditation

I defined affective meditation (or devotion) earlier as the practice of prayerful devotion stressing penitence and self-formation by the imaginative portrayal of the life of Christ and emotive identification with his sufferings. Traditionally, Anselm is seen as the originator, along with John of Fécamp and Bernard of Clairvaux, of this mode of devotion, which would later be perfected by the Franciscans and exemplified in the pseudo-Bonaventurian *Meditations on the Life of Christ*.[29] This conventional narrative has recently been challenged, and in this section I want to discuss the implications of that challenge for our understanding of Anselm's contributions to Western Christian understandings of prayer.[30]

Whatever we might make of the origins of affective meditation, taken on its own merits, Anselm's *Prayers and Meditations* is a revolutionary text. Its rhetorical power, expression of a novel form of religious subjectivity, contribution to the development of mariological and christological devotion and importance for understanding Anselm's intellectual development are undeniable – all the more so for how frequently it has been ignored by theologians and historians of doctrine. This does not have to mean it was entirely new. John of Fécamp, for one, was an older contemporary and neighbour who produced a *Libellus* (Little Book, often circulated as the *Meditations* of Augustine, both in the Middle Ages and in modern times) of scripture and patristic extracts, accompanied by a set of prayers. John lacks Anselm's preoccupation with the passion, and his expression of compunction is far less extreme. Instead, John largely focuses on the bliss of heaven, even including a description of quasi-mystical union with God. Moreover, while Anselm's citational strategy echoes the lament psalms and the Gospels, John is closer to Bernard of Clairvaux in his use of spousal imagery from the Song of Solomon to portray devotion to Christ.[31] However, the two share a similar employment of emotive, imaginative imagery and prayer as a quasi-monastic device to evoke a kind of devotion and meditation in their readers. And the question of their readers is what interests us here. The *Libellus* was sent to an anonymous nun and to Empress Agnes, widow of Henry III. Anselm's *Prayers and Meditations* were sent first to Adelaide, daughter of William the Conqueror, and in a later edition, Countess Matilda of Tuscany.[32] This alone

---

[29]Now attributed to John of Caulibus. See Francis X. Taney, Anne Miller and C. Mary Stallings-Taney, ed., *Meditations on the Life of Christ* (Asheville, NC: Pegasus Press, 2000).

[30]The challenge is found in McNamer, *Affective Meditation*; a cogent summary of her argument regarding affective meditation can be found on 58–62.

[31]See McGinn, *Growth of Mysticism*, 136–7, 142–3; McNamer, *Affective Meditation*, 62–4.

[32]McNamer provides further examples of seminal texts of affective devotion written for female interlocutors; *Affective Meditation*, 60.

is striking, as it suggests a correlation of the affective mode in prayer and texts and the devotional practice of aristocratic laywomen, or women religious. Notably, Anselm seldom wrote to nuns, but frequently to laywomen.[33] This points to two important factors in understanding the rise of affective meditation and the importance of Anselm's *Prayers and Meditations*.

First is the significance of lay devotion, what we might call the 'laicization' of the Daily Office in the eleventh century. By Anselm's time the significance of the laity as a legitimate order of life, the development of lay spirituality drawing from modified monastic norms, and even the option for taking on a semi-reclusive religious lifestyle were beginning to appear, a trend Giles Constable describes 'in the interiorization of virtue, in the stress on inner responsibility and a direct relation to God, and in the consecration of the way of life of every faithful Christian'.[34] This was more characteristic of the twelfth century, but the early premonitions were present in Anselm's time, and his *Prayers and Meditations* were an essential landmark of this transformation. Devotional texts had traditionally been drawn up for royal patrons, as in the Carolingian prayers I discussed earlier; but now they became much more widely disseminated, even if their scope was largely restricted to the aristocracy – that class with the resources to devote surplus time to God. In the past the relationship between the ruling class and the monasteries had been expressed through benefices and oblates; but now the idea emerged that taking on a form of laicized disciplined spirituality was an option, particularly for women like Adelaide, recluse and daughter of William the Conqueror, who sought an education for her approximating the training for laymen at Bec.[35] Matilda, Countess of Tuscany, was one of the most powerful political rulers of the time, female or male, and Anselm's relationship with her was both politically advantageous and one of tutelage and affection.[36] Matilda underwent a series of politically motivated marriages, but McNamer argues that her solicitation and promotion of the *Prayers and Meditations* were part of a conscious programme to reimagine herself as *sponsa*, bride of Christ, and thus consolidate her rule in both devotion to God and independence from the burden of earthly marriage to yet another undesirable husband.[37]

This leads to the second point important for understanding Anselm's contribution to the practice of affective prayer: the dialogical nature of the

---

[33]Sally N. Vaughn emphasizes this point in *St Anselm and the Handmaidens of God* (Turnhout: Brepols, 2002).

[34]Giles Constable, *The Reformation of the Twelfth Century* (Cambridge: Cambridge University Press, 1996), 293.

[35]Vaughn, *St Anselm*, 100–1.

[36]See Vaughn, *St Anselm*, 241–42 .

[37]McNamer, *Affective Meditation*, 82–4.

text. Sarah McNamer has argued strongly that figures like Adelaide and Matilda deserve attention as more than simply recipients and disseminators of the *Prayers and Meditations*. It is natural to speak of Anselm as both the author and the subject of the prayers – to read as if they record his devotional practice and spiritual experience (of abandonment, lament, compunction, etc.). But his authorship was more complex than that. The first person, the 'I' of the prayers, is not simply Anselm himself but a rhetorical function, a prompt to the reader to interiorize and appropriate the subjectivity of this 'I' as their own. This helps us to comprehend why Anselm's imagery and emotion are so violent and disturbing, for the prayers function to prompt appropriate affections in his readers, without the structure of the Daily Office that habituated religious affect in a monk like Anselm. As McNamer says, 'The first-person singular is a rhetorical figure … even when the "I" seems especially sincere, personal, or impassioned.' This 'affective technology', further, functioned as an 'intimate script': a rhetorical technique conceived and authored dialogically.[38] These are not diary entries; they are scripts for devotional use, and for that use Anselm had specific women in mind. Whether or not they count in some sense as a kind of co-producer of the texts, as McNamer implies, it is certainly true that their expression and innovation of affective devotion emerges from a distinct form of eleventh-century female spirituality – '"surfacings" of affective practices among women'.[39] Later centuries would see an explosion of lay female spirituality, and Anselm's *Prayers and Meditations*, written in conversation with women like Adelaide and Matilda, was a formative text in the origins of that movement.

Anselm's Meditative Theology

Naturally, there are not two Anselms at all but one, and his authorship is in fact remarkably consistent, if slim (omitting his significant collection of letters). And although they are regularly ignored by theologians and philosophers, the *Prayers and Meditations* are illuminating not just as a record of early medieval prayer practices, but as early contemplative soundings in some of the central theological concerns that preoccupied Anselm even in his most rigorous philosophical writings. I will focus on his two most famous here, the *Proslogion* and *Cur Deus Homo*.

---

[38]McNamer, *Affective Meditation*, 68, 69–70.
[39]McNamer, *Affective Meditation*, 84; see her discussion of Hans Robert Jauss on 61 for the suggestion of shared authorship. McNamer's larger argument, that affective meditation emerges as a script for formulating legal marriage to Christ for female religious and recluses, is beyond my scope here, but worthy of careful consideration.

The *Proslogion* is almost universally known for its innovative 'ontological' argument for the existence of God, found in *Proslogion* 3–2 (often excerpted without context). But the first chapter could easily be mistaken for one of Anselm's prayers: 'Come now, insignificant man, fly for a moment from your affairs, escape for a little while from the tumult of your thoughts. Put aside now your weighty cares and leave your wearisome toils. Abandon yourself for a little to God and rest for a little in Him.'[40] It is not accidental or merely pro forma that this 'philosophical' treatise is couched as a prayer: the treatise is an exercise in contemplation, and the first chapter, interspersed with citations from the Psalms, strike the same notes of *excita mentem* ('teach my heart where and how to seek You'), lamenting compunction ('How wretched man's lot is when he has lost that for which he was made!'), and, in the final paragraph, praise ('I acknowledge, Lord, and I give thanks that You have created Your image in me, so that I may remember You, think of You, love You'). This paragraph concludes with the thesis of the treatise, and Anselm's famed slogan, 'I do not seek to understand so that I may believe; but I believe to that I may understand' (*neque enim quaero intelligere ut credam, sed credo ut intelligam*) earlier summarized as *fides quaerens intellectum*, 'faith seeking understanding'.[41]

This means that, if the *Proslogion* resembles the rhetorical pattern of the prayers, the body of the treatise itself would contain the *praise* and *negotiation* movements. And this is largely true (though we should not overemphasize the parallel). After completing his articulation of the single argument (*unum argumentum*) in *Proslogion* 2-5, Anselm turns to a series of meditations of the attributes of God, developed out of the insight of the ontological argument: God is whatever it is better to be than not to be, such that God's existence itself is logically unthinkable.[42] But this generates a series of paradoxes: How can God be omnipotent and yet limited by God's maximal goodness?[43] How can God be both merciful and just?[44] What distinguishes God's infinite and eternal essence from other disembodied spirits? How can one 'find' God in contemplation – only to realize that God is unknowable?[45] In the prayers, God's holiness continually erupts over against the praying subject's sinfulness,

---

[40]Anselm, *Pros.* 1, in *Major Works*, 84.

[41]On the literary importance of Anselm's prologues, see Sharpe, 'Anselm as Author', 60–1.

[42]Space precludes discussion of this argument itself, or a close read of the *Proslogion*. For more, see Travis E. Ables, 'The Word in Which All Things Are Spoken: Augustine, Anselm, and Bonaventure on Christology and the Metaphysics of Exemplarity', *Theological Studies* 76, no. 2 (2015): 288–92, which I echo here.

[43]Anselm, *Pros.* 7.

[44]Anselm, *Pros.* 8–9.

[45]Anselm, *Pros.* 14–16.

only to be trumped by the praying soul laying claim to God's mercy on the basis of the merits of the saints, Mary and the incarnation. In the *Proslogion*, this tension is transposed into a rigorously logical register, as the issue is now one of the nature of God itself. But the tone is still contemplative, and the basis of the *unum argumentum* remains one of prayerful paradox: the seeking of the soul for God, only for God to be found inaccessible and shrouded in mystery – even as the presence of God within drives the soul to seek in the first place.[46] God is known within the soul, to the extent that knowledge of self becomes knowledge of the God who is 'more inward than my most inward part', as Augustine put it. In later spiritual literature this paradox of self-knowledge would be portrayed as mystical union, where the two become inextricable, so that God is known in the soul and the soul is immersed or (in more radical mystical systems, like those of Marguerite Porete or Meister Eckhart) becomes annihilated in the divine. But this kind of mystical grammar was unavailable to Anselm; his vocabulary is drawn from the Psalter and the cadences of the Benedictine office. Thus, the centre of the *Proslogion* founders on a kind of aporia Anselm struggles to articulate: faith seeking understanding arrives at the heart of the divine mystery, only to find God in 'inaccessible light in which You dwell. ... My understanding is not able to attain to that light. ... It is dazzled by its splendour, overcome by its fullness, overwhelmed by its immensity, confused by its extent.'[47] Calling God 'ineffable',[48] Anselm resumes his prayerful quest, pondering the mystery of divine simplicity and infinity, before concluding with the relationship of the goodness of God to God's triunity, a goodness in which all creatures participate.[49] This finally concludes his prayer with a rapturous expression of union and 'a joy that is complete and more than complete'.[50]

The *Proslogion* is, like the *Monologion*, an exacting exercise in philosophical theology, and sets the tone for the abstract theological treatises to come in Anselm's authorship. But it is also a meditative prayer to God seeking understanding and union, and battling the barriers of finite, sinful selfhood that the praying subject brings with her. In this, it is most congruous to the *Prayers and Meditations*; too, we should not miss that its central paradox, the one that leads Anselm to express the divine ineffability, is the relationship – the tension – between justice and mercy in the divine being. Pondering their coincidence in the simple divine nature is his central quandary; had he the

---

[46]See also Sweeney, *Desire for the Word*, 120–1.
[47]Anselm, *Pros.* 16.
[48]Anselm, *Pros.* 17.
[49]Anselm, *Pros.* 23–25.
[50]Anselm, *Pros.* 26.

language of Pseudo-Dionysius at his disposal, as his later reader Bonaventure did, we might have expected him to venture into apophatic language at this point.[51] Anselm is not a negative theologian, but this core dilemma of the prayers, the juxtaposition of God's mercy and justice, reappears in this theological treatise as the great mystery of the divine essence itself. And it is the heart of his greatest work, the *Cur Deus Homo*.

This is not the place to revisit the complex question of how to interpret *Cur Deus Homo* in the history of atonement theology; however, light can be shed on the controversial treatise if we place it into the context of Anselm's theology of prayer. The treatise is not, like the *Proslogion*, couched as an exercise of prayer, nor are any of Anselm's subsequent major writings. However, his preoccupation with the relationship of mercy and justice receives its definitive statement in it: the central argument of the book concerns the 'fittingness' of redemption: whether it is fitting, and not a diminution of God's dignity, to become incarnate and enact redemption for the sake of fallen humanity. *Honour* is the term Anselm uses for this dignity, and though this term comes from a feudal background, his backdrop is more Augustinian: God's honour concerns the overall beauty and order of the created universe, in which God's sovereign purposes in creation will (and must) be fulfilled. The damnation of humanity, though just by virtue of the punishment it incurred by its disobedience, would fail to fulfill this created purpose, which Anselm calls *rectitudo*, 'uprightness'.[52] Thus, God ultimately acts in redemption by fulfilling the obedience humanity owes in the person of Jesus Christ. This is an exemplary act of *rectitudo* and satisfies God's just reward. However, Christ also dies a supererogatory death not required of him, and God shares the reward Christ earns (he doesn't need it, because he is divine) with humankind. Redemption is, therefore, the coincidence of justice and mercy insofar as both are aligned with God's created purpose towards the universe and humanity: God's justice precisely is to show mercy, by including righteous humanity in blessedness.[53]

This reading does not follow typical understandings of *Cur Deus Homo* as the invention of satisfaction atonement theory (usually interpreted as an early instance of penal substitution); instead, it is a 'theory' of redemption centred on the integrity of the nature of God, and focusing on the significance of the incarnation. In truth, the treatise is far more focused on the elect

---

[51]On Bonaventure as a reader of Anselm, see Ables, 'The Word in Which All Things Are Spoken', 293–7.
[52]Anselm, 'Why God Became Man', 1.5, 23, 288–9, 308–9.
[53]Anselm, 'Why God Became Man', 2.1, 315–16. See also Southern, *Saint Anselm*, 213–14.

angels and the rights of the devil than it is on God's 'honour', but that term, and the way Anselm ultimately ties it to the incarnation, signals that the work is an organic development of the thinking Anselm had been pursuing since the *Prayers and Meditations*. What I termed his 'incarnational bargain' was a prayerful negotiation of pardon based on God's commitment to re-creation in the merits of Mary and the birth of her Son. Because God has committed God's self to mercy over strict justice on the basis of Christ's incarnational and therefore Marian flesh, Anselm could pray boldly, even recklessly, for that mercy for himself. So, in *Cur Deus Homo*, Anselm can cogitate on the fittingness of God's act of redemption through the obedient life of that same Son, Jesus Christ. Much of this reasoning would be carried over, too, in Anselm's treatise 'On the Virgin Conception and Original Sin', which focuses on the logic of fittingness applied to Mary.[54]

So there is a thematic link between the *Prayers and Meditations* and *Cur Deus Homo*. But Anselm's concern to couch his theological speculation in the practice of meditation and prayer also recurs with *Cur Deus Homo*, for he quickly supplemented the dialectical framing of the treatise with a 'Meditation on Human Redemption'. The meditation follows the broad moves of the prayers, with a prologue summing up the theme of his redemption theology ('the strength of your salvation is the strength of Christ')[55] and sounding notes of *excita mentem* ('rouse yourself and remember you are risen').[56] However, Anselm saves his statement of compunction for the end of the piece ('I was descending into the chaos of hell'),[57] after he has presented the argument of *Cur Deus Homo* for prayerful contemplation. The core of the meditation concerns what I have called his 'negotiation', for this is the heart of *Cur Deus Homo* itself – God's commitment to redemption in Christ, and humanity's right to appeal to that redemption:

> This is the perfect and free obedience of human nature, in that Christ freely submitted his own free will to God, and perfectly used in the liberty the good will he had received. ... See, Christian soul, here is the strength of your salvation, here is the cause of your freedom. ... Chew this, bite it, suck it, let your heart swallow it, when your mouth received the body and blood of your Redeemer.[58]

---

[54]See Anselm, 'On the Virgin Conception and Original Sin', 18, in *Major Works*, 376.
[55]Anselm, 'Meditation on Human Redemption', l. 17–18.
[56]Anselm, 'Meditation on Human Redemption', l. 3.
[57]Anselm, 'Meditation on Human Redemption', l. 221–2.
[58]Anselm, 'Meditation on Human Redemption', l. 151–3, 167–9.

The eucharistic themes are obvious here, pointing to the way the incarnational flesh was mediated to a medieval reader. Finally, the conclusion of praise returns to familiar themes of obligation ('Because you have made me I owe you the whole of my love; because you have redeemed me, I owe you the whole of myself').[59] The meditation is far less focused on lamentation than the early prayers, and instead is concerned with a statement of redemption; Anselm the sinner retreats before the grandeur of God the redeemer, and his earlier affective posture develops into an eucharistic one. The core of Anselm's authorship, however, perdures from his earliest writing to his last: the lament of self and contemplation of God united in a rhetoric of prayer both bold and humble.

Lingering Questions

This chapter has stressed the continuity of Anselm's thought and its grounding in themes sounded in his early prayers – to say nothing of the consistent tone of his theological writing, which is grounded in the prayerful, meditative practice of the Benedictine Daily Office. This is not to neglect significant development or even discontinuity in his writing: the *sola ratione* (reason alone) method of *Proslogion* was a significant departure from the *florilegia* on the Psalms, which is how he presented the *Prayers and Meditations*; to say nothing of his eschewal of quotations from late antique Christian writers or scripture in the *Monologion* and *Proslogion*, which made his mentor Lanfranc so uncomfortable. And the logically stringent method of *Cur Deus Homo* and other later treatises bears little of the fervent spirituality of even *Proslogion*, though the 'Meditation on Human Redemption' shows he was still capable of it. Instead of absolute uniformity, the prayer practice of Anselm formed a kind of core to his writing, a set of themes and motifs that would guide him throughout his life. Important work has been done to show such a portrait of Anselm;[60] but thus far, too many are left with the 'two Anselms' I began this chapter with. He is a figure still needing reappraisal within the mainstream of theological writing.

Further questions arise as we zoom out and view Anselm in his wider context. He not only lived at the birth of the movement of affective devotion,

---

[59]Anselm, 'Meditation on Human Redemption', l. 245–7. For the peculiarities of Anselm's idea of freedom as a broadly Augustinian conception of liberty as the fulfilment of one's nature, see Anselm, 'On Free Will', in *Major Works*, 175–92, and Katherin A. Rogers, *Anselm on Freedom* (New York: Oxford University Press, 2008). This is a major focus of Southern, who devotes a chapter to the troubles it caused Anselm politically, *Saint Anselm*, 277–307.

[60]For example, Sweeney, *Desire for the Word*.

but was also immersed in the beginnings of Scholasticism. He was not a member of a formal school – the universities of Paris and Oxford were still decades down the road – and his textual education lacked the philosophical, especially Aristotelian, framework to build a truly rigorous system; moreover, he was not a devotee of the formal dialectical systems developed by Abelard and Lombard, which would birth the great *summas* of the thirteenth century. However, in a monastic setting such as Bec, in the devotional terms of Benedictine observance, his ventures into a form of theological style free of beholdenness to patristic and biblical authority had a marked influence on the school masters of the high Middle Ages. Their Scholastic texts are not the arid logical exercises in minutiae they are often made out to be (angels dancing on the head of a pin); Jean-Pierre Torrell, for example, has been showing Aquinas' work to be an exercise in spiritual pedagogy for decades.[61] But Anselm's ability to transition seamlessly from prayer to philosophy and back in the *Proslogion* and *Cur Deus Homo*/'Meditation on Human Redemption' is in many respects unique. He stood in a kind of historical liminal space, between two worlds, despite being in many ways a conservative thinker. His significance as a bridge between two eras is still underappreciated.

There are two further areas that are largely unexplored, and they raise significant questions for how we understand Anselm and his importance for a history of prayer. First is his relationship to his interlocutors in the context of affective devotion, especially laywomen. As I argued above, following Sarah McNamer, in a very real way Anselm's prayers are a dialogical effort, and there is much about his relationship with Adelaide, Countess Matilda and others, that is still obscure.[62] Just how he borrowed from female devotional practice, how he contributed to it, and perhaps most troublingly, how this relationship affected his use of traditionally feminine tropes of shame, embodiment, submissiveness and emotion remains unclear. Bernard of Clairvaux later developed the genre of affective meditation in terms of explicitly erotic metaphors of bridal love drawn from the Song of Solomon; but it is often left unremarked just how bizarre it was for celibate males to position themselves rhetorically as female in order to portray the Christian soul as united to God. Anselm does not go as far as Bernard or Fécamp in

---

[61] Jean-Pierre Torrell, *Saint Thomas Aquinas*, trans. Robert Royal, rev. ed., 2 vols. (Washington, DC: Catholic University of America Press, 2003, 2005).

[62] Sally Vaughn's *St Anselm and the Handmaidens of God* is essential reading in this area; however, Vaughn is a political historian and engages in very little interpretive work; McNamer's *Affective Meditation* is groundbreaking, but focuses on Fécamp over Anselm in order to (rightly) marginalize the 'great men' approach to history. She therefore leaves much to explore in Anselm within the new historical and interpretive frame she formulates.

this regard; but he does have a unique flair for the vocabulary of shame. How would Adelaide or Matilda have interpreted this?

Finally, there is a kind of violence to Anselm's prayers. The issue is not his contemplation of the passion, which is tame by the standards of later blood devotion and eucharistic mysticism.[63] Rather, it is in the frankly shocking language he draws upon to portray the sinful soul – aimed at himself, but also, given his choice of readers, functioning as a certain kind of emotional violence. There is something of the traumatic in his description of the Christian as a terrorized orphan abandoned by God. We do not have an interpretive grid to account truly for how such language might have functioned in context, and we should avoid psychologizing figures like Anselm as we grapple with their literary remains. Indeed, the gist of this chapter has been to see Anselm's traumatized orphan praying not as himself but as a rhetorical function. But in some ways this just exacerbates the question: What kind of effect was he seeking to perform in his readers?

None of this is intended to rob the power of Anselm's prayers nor their potential use in developing a contemporary theology of prayer – quite the opposite. Historical artefacts can only speak truly to our time insofar as they are allowed to be remote and alien, thereby to highlight the strangeness of our own time.[64] We must therefore allow Anselm to be a man of his times, not an extract in a philosophy of religion or theology textbook, nor a footnote in the history of emotion. He was in many respects as much at odds with his own day as he is with our own; but he is all the more fascinating because of it. And his practice of prayer is right at the heart of it all.

---

[63]See Caroline Walker Bynum, *Wonderful Blood: Theology and Practice in Late Medieval Northern Germany and Beyond* (Philadelphia, PA: University of Pennsylvania Press, 2007).

[64]'The object was to learn to what extent the effort to think one's own history can free thought from what it silently thinks, and so enable it to think differently'. See Michel Foucault, *The History of Sexuality – Volume 2: The Use of Pleasure*, trans. Robert Hurley (New York: Vintage Books, 1990), 9.

CHAPTER TWENTY

Thomas Aquinas, Scholasticism and Prayer

JACOB HOLSINGER SHERMAN

'Before all things, but especially before any theological work, it is helpful for us to begin from prayer, not because we draw to ourselves divine virtue, which is everywhere present and never closed off, but rather because through remembering and calling upon God we draw and unite ourselves to Him.'[1] Although Thomas Aquinas is justly regarded as one of the greatest teachers of Christian doctrine in church history, his reputation as a spiritual master is less replete, and his writings on prayer are too often neglected.[2] In part, this may be a legacy of the neo-scholasticism that dominated so much of the last century's understanding of who Thomas was. A certain kind of Thomism, filtered through Aquinas' sixteenth-century interpreters, and promulgated through nineteenth- and early twentieth-century papal bulls and encyclicals,

---

[1]Aquinas, *Supra De Divinibus Nominibus* III; author's translation. The Latin text is available in Thomas Aquinas, *In Librum Beati Dionysii De Divinis Nominibus Expositio*, ed. Ceslaus Pera (Taurini: Marietti, 1950). At present, the only English translation is Harry C. Marsh, 'Cosmic Structure and the Knowledge of God: Thomas Aquinas' *In Librum Beati Dionysii De Divinis Nominibus Expositio*' (Vanderbilt University, 1994), 265–549.

[2]Recent works have begun to redress this oversight. See Jean-Pierre Torrell, *Saint Thomas Aquinas: Spiritual Master*, trans. Robert Royal (Washington, DC: Catholic University of America Press, 2003); Jean-Pierre Torrell, *Christ and Spirituality in St Thomas Aquinas* (Washington, DC: Catholic University of America Press, 2011); Robert Barron, *Thomas Aquinas: Spiritual Master* (New York: Crossroad, 2008); *Albert and Thomas: Selected Writings*, ed. Simon Tugwell, CWS (New York: Paulist Press, 1988); and Denys Turner, *Thomas Aquinas: A Portrait* (New Haven, CT: Yale University Press, 2013).

cast the Angelic Doctor as primarily a source of dogmatic authority.[3] But even apart from neo-scholasticism and the much-maligned manuals of the early twentieth century, Thomas' writings might seem to have far less to teach us about prayer than about the metaphysics of material composition or the theological grammar of the Incarnation. There is very little in Aquinas of the sort of evident rapture one finds everywhere in the pages of Bernard of Clairvaux, the pathos of Julian of Norwich or the passion of Augustine, and this difference in tone issues not so much from twentieth-century developments as from medieval ones. When Thomas treats prayer, for instance, in the long Question devoted to it in the Prima Pars of the *Summa Theologiae*, he treats it in what seems to be its most ordinary and least rapturous of forms, namely prayers of petition or impetration. Those looking for devotional heat might be tempted to turn elsewhere. But that would be a mistake, for despite appearances Aquinas' teachings on prayer, and especially his mature teaching on petitionary prayer, invite his readers into an ecstatic activity of transformation, understanding and love, one that unsettles the very notion of what it is to be, to be a person and to pray.

Scholasticism and Prayer

In order to get a sense of the drama in Thomas Aquinas' teachings on prayer, it may be helpful first to situate him within the high Middle Ages. The medieval is often described as an 'age of saints and scholars', but to whom does this phrase refer? Are we to think of saints, on the one hand, and schoolmen, on the other? When it comes to figures like Anslem of Canterbury or Bonaventure, surely the answer is that they were both, but this should not be taken for granted, for the integration of great sanctity and great learning is part of what distinguishes them from many of their contemporaries. Indeed, scholasticism can be understood as the first great flowering of Christian thinking outside of a primarily liturgical and devotional context and its literature bears the marks of this institutional change. Prayer, once so bound to the vocation of the theologian, became optional to the newly dialectical task of theological learning. Hans Urs von Balthasar calls this

---

[3]The real story is far more complicated than this. Even in its neo-scholastic form, Thomism was always internally diverse, reflecting a variety of competing contexts, interpretations, and motivations. As Russell Hittinger notes, 'At times, a reactionary, legislative, and disciplinary form of Thomism was deployed, directed inward at members of the Church, chiefly about uses of philosophy in the study of sacred doctrine. At other times, Thomism was allowed to play a more constructive, synthetic, and open role, directed outward to the world, chiefly on questions of social and political order'. See Russell Hittinger, 'Two Thomisms, Two Modernities', *First Things* 184 (2008): 33.

scholastic separation of theology and sanctity one of the greatest tragedies in the history of the church.[4] How did this come about? When the high Middle Ages began, in the eleventh century, the centres of renewed scholarship were exclusively found in monasteries where the love of learning and the desire for God could be equally nourished.[5] Subsequently, this renewal of learning migrated to the Cathedral schools and the canons regular – most notably, the School of Chartres and the Abbey of Saint Victor – where the monastic element was mitigated but the commitment to learning and prayer as two sides of the same activity remained strong. Finally, in the thirteenth century, the university came into its own and the age of the schoolmen was born. As Marie-Dominique Chenu writes:

> Theology henceforward claimed to be a science, and according to the Aristotelian ideal took on a speculative and even deductive character. Like all sciences, it was disinterested; it was no longer concerned with nourishing the spiritual life, as the monastic theologians would have it do. The Scriptures were read, studied and taught with the view of the mind rather than the heart acquiring knowledge, and theological activity assumed a more purely intellectual character, less contemplative, less dependent on the atmosphere created by the liturgy. ... [T]he thirteenth century was to reap the fruit of these efforts.[6]

This institutional migration coincided with the adoption of new methods, sources, categories and norms. While Anselm is often described as the father of scholasticism because of his integration of rational argument and faith, it was Peter Lombard who gave rise to the characteristically scholastic genre: Lombard's *Sentences* sought to teach theology through a combination of Aristotelian philosophy and the collection of various theological and patristic responses (the *sententiae*) to ordered series of topics. This new genre of theology was controversial – think of Bernard of Clairvaux's polemic against Abelard's excessive rationalizing – but its intellectual appeal was powerful. As this new way of doing theology took root in the emerging universities, the scholastic study of the *Sentences* began to replace the monastic study of the Fathers and the scriptures as the beginning of learning, even perhaps

---

[4]Hans Urs von Balthasar, *Explorations in Theology – Volume 1: The Word Made Flesh*, trans. A. V. Littledale and Alexander Dru (San Francisco, CA: Ignatius Press, 1989), 181–209.
[5]Jean Leclercq, *The Love of Learning and the Desire for God: A Study of Monastic Culture*, trans. Catharine Misrahi, 3rd edn (New York: Fordham University Press, 1982).
[6]Marie-Dominique Chenu, *La Théologie Au Xiie Siècle, Études De Philosophie Médiévale*, Études De Philosophie Médiévale (Paris: Vrin, 1975). Quoted in Jordan Aumann, *Christian Spirituality in the Catholic Tradition* (San Francisco, CA: Ignatius Press, 2001), 122–3.

replacing them as authoritative sources. Concomitantly, theology and the spiritual life began to drift apart, the former proclaiming itself ever more rational, ever more secure as a science, while the latter tended increasingly towards confinement within the affections.

Along the way there were important exceptions to this general movement, and in the thirteenth century none were more important than the Dominicans and the Franciscans. Both of these new mendicant orders sought to recuperate aspects of venerable monastic rules, including the medieval practice of reciting the Divine Office, while responding in creative and vital ways to the rapid transformations of the thirteenth century, including the intellectual transformations associated with the university. Breviaries were created in order to facilitate the recitation of the divine office by individuals and small groups called to the ministry of preaching and the mobility this demanded.[7] As mendicants, the followers of both Dominic and Francis of Assisi embraced strict vows of personal poverty and ministries of preaching. But the emphases of these two orders differed according to the varying charisms of their founders: in the Friars Minor we find so much of Francis' emphasis upon simplicity, poverty, interiority and devotional abandon, while the Preachers gave themselves especially to the study of sacred scripture, *sacra doctrina*, its proclamation and the apostolic life.

Both orders found places of privilege within the new universities. The presence of the friars within the university recuperated something of the older monastic vision of theology as an integrally intellectual and spiritual pursuit. The Dominican order, especially, with its emphasis on preaching, scriptural study and the importance of sound doctrine, recognized that the university was central to the Order's calling. Indeed, the First General Chapter of the Order required that each priory be staffed with a professor. Learning was central to the Dominicans, but it was learning upheld by prayer, albeit of a rather succinct type. The modified Augustinian *Rule of Life* that the Dominicans adopted for their *vita apostolica* emphasized, among other more common religious demands, the primacy of preaching, the sedulous study of the scriptures, the importance of silence as an aid to reflection and the crisp, brief recitation of the divine office in order to give greater room for study. As the Primitive Constitutions state:

> All the hours are to be said in church briefly and succinctly lest the brethren lose devotion and their study be in any way impeded.[8]

---

[7]Andrew Louth, 'Prayer', in *Encyclopedia of Christian Theology*, ed. Jean-Yves Lacoste (London: Routledge, 2005).
[8]Aumann, *Christian Spirituality in the Catholic Tradition*, 129.

Such was the pattern of life a young Thomas Aquinas adopted when he entered the *Ordo Praedicatorum* (Order of Preachers) in 1244.[9] Although less regulated than a cloistered life, Thomas' was nevertheless structured by prayer: he rose early every morning in order to say Mass himself and then, almost immediately thereafter, to attend a second Mass in common. He passed his days reading, writing, teaching and praying alone, and finished them with compline said together in the choir.[10]

It would be wrong to think that this emphasis on brief and solitary prayer was somehow a denigration of the importance of prayer, either for the Dominicans or for Thomas. His earliest biographers closely link his intellectual life with his spiritual one. As William of Tocco recalled, 'Every time he wished to study, to undertake a disputation, to write, or dictate, he first withdrew into prayer on his own and prayed pouring out tears, in order to obtain understanding of the divine mysteries.'[11] By all accounts, Aquinas preferred others not to see this. As Denys Turner comments, 'Thomas hid his prayer as he hid his bulk. ... What Thomas does know is that some kinds of understanding will come to the theologian only within a life of faith and prayer, as a gift given to those who seek it.'[12]

Thomas' reticence to have others observe him in prayer may have come from humility, perhaps also from shyness, but he had substantive objections to making a long show of prayer, as well. He steadfastly resisted any efforts to judge the quality of prayer by its quantity. When considering the question of whether prayer ought to go on for a long time, Thomas draws a distinction between prayer considered in itself and prayer considered *secundum causam suam*, according to its cause.[13] There is a very real sense in which prayer ought to be ceaseless.

> The cause of prayer is the desire of charity, from which prayer ought to arise: and this desire ought to be in us continually, either actually or virtually, for the virtue of this desire remains in whatever we do out of charity; and we ought to 'do all things to the glory of God' (1 Cor. 10.31). From this point of view prayer ought to be continual.[14]

---

[9]For an excellent collection of primary sources reflecting early Dominican spirituality, including the Primitive Constitutions, see *Early Dominicans: Selected Writings*, ed. Simon Tugwell, CWS (New York: Paulist Press, 1982).

[10]In order to encourage their intellectual endeavours, the Dominican Canons permitted teachers like Thomas to observe the hours on their own save for Compline.

[11]Turner, *Thomas Aquinas*, 172.

[12]Turner, *Thomas Aquinas*, 173.

[13]Aquinas, *ST* II-II, q. 83, a. 14.

[14]Aquinas, *ST* II-II, q. 83, a. 14, resp.

The succinct formal observance of the hours that perforate Thomas' daily routine is intended not to exhaust his devotion but rather to suffuse all of his activities with prayer. The point of praying is to rouse devotion and to interpret our desires, to bring our desires into the intentional presence of God, and because we ought always to desire God we ought, in this sense, always to be praying. But things change if we think of prayer as a discrete activity. An activity ought to be proportioned to its purpose, and so Aquinas concludes, 'it is becoming that prayer should last long enough to arouse the fervor of the interior desire: and when it exceeds this measure, so that it cannot be continued any longer without causing weariness, it should be discontinued'.[15] His teaching here reflects not only the practice of the Dominicans but also appeals to Augustine's famous letter on the nature of prayer.[16] In his letter to the widow Proba, Augustine encourages her to emulate the Desert Fathers who employed short prayers 'shot like swift arrows' in order to prevent their devotion slackening.[17] Indeed, as Augustine continues, when it comes to prayer, words are not the main thing; rather, we ought to be concerned with

> having our hearts pulsing with prolonged and reverent fervor directed toward the One to whom we are praying. Most of the time this will consist more in sighing than in speaking, more in tears than in words. God has placed our tears in his sight, and our sighs are not hidden from him who made all things through his Word, and has no need of human words.[18]

These were lessons Thomas took to heart.

The separation of sanctity and theology that began in the thirteenth century led, in time, to the invention of new theological *topoi* under categories such as the spiritual life or mystical theology. But Aquinas himself seems never to have considered writing such a work, for his resistance to the separation of spirituality and theology was simultaneously more radical and more integral. For Thomas, the pursuit of theology was itself a kind of prayer in the wide sense mentioned above. Because theology or *sacra doctrina* involves analogical participation in God's own knowing of himself and his works,[19] its method is twofold insofar as God gives and we receive: God

---

[15]Aquinas, *ST* II-II, q. 83, a. 14, resp.

[16]Augustine, *ep*. 130; *Letters – Volume 2: 100–155*, trans. Roland J. Teske, WSA II/2 (Hyde Park, NY: New City Press, 2002), 183–99.

[17]See also Aquinas' commentary on the Lord's Prayer (Mt. 6.9-15) in Thomas Aquinas, *Commentary on the Gospel of Matthew 1–12* (Lander, WY: Aquinas Institute for the Study of Sacred Doctrine, 2013).

[18]Augustine, *ep*. 130.19.

[19]Aqunias, *ST* I, q. 1, a. 3, resp.

gives knowledge of himself in *modus revelativus*, in the mode of revelation, but we do theology in *modus orativus*, in the mode of prayer. Accordingly, at the very outset of his early *Commentary on the Sentences*, Thomas insists that rightly practised theology itself is a kind of prayer.

> The mode of any science should be sought by considering its matter, as Boethius says in *On the Trinity* 1, and the Philosopher in *Ethics* 1. The principles of this science are received through revelation, therefore the mode of receiving [*modus accipiendi*] these principles ought to be revelatory on the part of the one infusing, as in the visions of the prophets, and prayerful on the part of the recipient, as is evident in the Psalms.[20]

For Thomas, then, theology is a contemplative science, one that aims at a 'certain participation in and assimilation to divine knowledge, even while we are still on the way'.[21] As Jean-Pierre Torrell writes, 'We can easily understand why for [Aquinas] there was no need to elaborate a spirituality *alongside* his theology. His theology itself is a spiritual theology.'[22]

Prayer as the Interpreter of Desire

But how does Thomas understand prayer within the broader context of Christian life and practice? He treats prayer explicitly at a number of points throughout his extraordinary oeuvre, but his most mature thoughts are collected in Question 83 of the *Secunda Secundae* within the midst of his treatment of the cardinal virtues. Question 83, 'On Prayer', is the longest article within the *Summa Theologiae*. It is found nestled within Thomas' account of the Virtue of Religion (qq. 81-100) which itself falls within the larger context of the Treatise on Justice (qq. 57-122). Prayer, then, takes its place within Aquinas' moral psychology as an eminently human act, albeit one that aims at the supernatural virtue of charity. Indeed, for Thomas, prayer is supremely human precisely because it is directed at that which exceeds human capacities. This natural desire for the supernatural, as Henri de Lubac called it, is the shape of properly human life: we long for a kind of ecstatic fulfilment, a consummation in

---

[20]Aquinas, *I Sentences*, q. 1 a. 5, resp; Thomas Aquinas, *Selected Writings*, trans. Ralph McInerny (New York: Penguin Books, 1998), 50–84.
[21]Aquinas, *Super Boetium de Trinitate*, q. 2, a. 2, ed. Commissio Leonina, vol. 50 (Paris: Les Editions du Cerf, 1992). Quoted in Torrell, *Saint Thomas Aquinas*, 18.
[22]Torrell, *Saint Thomas Aquinas*, 18.

excess of but not in opposition to that which is either rationally calculable or autonomously attainable.[23]

Grace transforms and articulates that longing, infusing the Christian life with the theological virtue of charity, the virtue that aims at nothing less than friendship with God.[24] Of course, none of this is achieved all at once or through some sort of forensic fiat. Rather, grace works within us in so as to perfect human nature. The faculties through which this takes place are the virtues, both natural (acquired) and supernatural (infused). Charity is the summit of the virtues, their motive force and their goal. Growth in charity involves a movement through stages from the elementary desire to avoid sin, to the maturation of the virtues and finally to the consummation of love, tasted here but only enjoyed hereafter, through which our wills becomes entirely united to God's will, habitually receptive to the gift of the Spirit in a participatory union with the divine that alone fulfils the *desiderium naturale visionis dei*, the natural desire for the vision of God.[25]

Looked at from the human side of things, prayer plays a central role in all of this for prayer is the human act through which we intentionally expose ourselves and our desires to the transformations of grace. More precisely, prayer is an act of the natural virtue of religion in conjunction with other requisite virtues such as humility and faith. Through the act of prayer, then, a host of natural and supernatural virtues are brought together. As Thomas writes:

> Prayer proceeds from charity through the medium of religion, of which prayer is an act ... and with the concurrence of other virtues requisite for the goodness of prayer, namely, humility and faith. For the offering of prayer itself to God belongs to religion, while the desire for the thing that we pray to be accomplished belongs to charity. Faith is necessary in reference to God to Whom we pray; that is, we need to believe that we can obtain from Him what we seek. Humility is necessary on the part of the person praying, because he recognizes his neediness. Devotion too is necessary: but this belongs to religion, for it is its first act and a necessary condition of all its secondary acts, as stated above.[26]

---

[23]See Henri de Lubac, *Surnaturel: Études historiques* (Paris: Aubier, 1946). De Lubac later published an amended version of the *surnaturel* thesis in Henri de Lubac, *The Mystery of the Supernatural*, trans. Rosemary Sheed (New York: Crossroad, 1967). See also Henri de Lubac, *Augustinianism and Modern Theology*, trans. Lancelot Sheppard (New York: Crossroad, 2000).
[24]Aquinas, *ST* II-II, q. 23, a. 1.
[25]Aquinas, *ST* II-II, q. 24, a. 8.
[26]Aquinas, *ST* II-II, q. 83, a. 15, resp.

By prayer, *oratio*, Thomas means primarily the activity of petition or impetration: asking or requesting things, especially from God. But the semantic range of *oratio* is also wider than this and can mean simply speech, discourse, eloquence or even just the use of language. There really is no equivocation here, though, for *oratio* as prayer just is human speech oriented towards its highest end; indeed, we might even say that prayer is the hidden and highest vocation of all speech. According to Thomas, the characteristic that specifically marks us as human beings is our capacity for rational inquiry, which for social creatures like us means speech, communication and taking counsel. We do this in conversation with one another, but supremely in conversation with God.[27]

When, therefore, Aquinas treats prayer as petition, this in no way involves treating it as merely petitionary. There is nothing 'mere' about it: rather, petition rightly describes and realizes the ontological shape of the rational creature's relation to the personal Origin and End of all things. Because of this, *oratio* as prayer is able to encompass the whole range of human communicative activity, for we pray with the whole of who we are. In his early *Commentary on the Sentences* (*c.* 1252–7), Thomas defined prayer more strictly as 'petition for the good things needed in this life'.[28] But by the time he was writing of the *Secunda Secundae* (*c.* 1272), Thomas had accepted Bonaventure's contention that John of Damascus correctly defines prayer as: 'an ascent of the intellect to God', and 'asking becoming things of God'.[29] Thomas no longer sees prayer narrowly as asking God for things needed in this life, but rather recognizes that the whole movement of our return to God has this petitionary shape. Thus, in the concluding question of his article on prayer, Aquinas holds that while prayer in general involves supplications, prayers, intercessions, and thanksgivings, nevertheless prayer itself 'when distinguished from the others denotes *properly* the ascent to God'.[30]

But how, more precisely, is the mind raised to God through prayer and how is this related to impetration? Thomas describes prayer arrestingly in

---

[27]See, for instance, Aquinas' description of the Gift of Counsel as the supernatural perfection of our communicative nature: 'Now God moves everything according to the mode of the thing moved: thus He moves the corporeal creature through time and place, and the spiritual creature through time, but not through place, as Augustine declares (*Gen. ad lit.* viii, 20, 22). Again, it is proper to the rational creature to be moved through the research of reason to perform any particular action, and this research is called counsel. Hence the Holy Ghost is said to move the rational creature by way of counsel, wherefore counsel is reckoned among the gifts of the Holy Ghost.' See Aquinas, *ST* II-II, q. 52, a. 1.

[28]Aquinas, *IV Sentences*, d. 15, q. 4, a. 3; *Commentary on the Sentences, Book IV, 14–25* (Steubenville: Emmaus Academic, 2017).

[29]John Damascene, *Expositio fidei* 68 (PG 94).

[30]Aquinas, *ST* II-II, q. 83, a. 17, ad. 2.

terms of the articulation and interpretation of desire.[31] As we have seen, Aquinas takes prayer to be an act of reason; it is fundamentally discursive and not merely appetitive or intuitive. But is not prayer more essentially a matter of desire for, as the Psalmist says, 'The Lord hath heard the desire of the poor'? (Ps. 9.38). To this, Aquinas replies:

> The Lord is said to hear the desire of the poor, either because desire is the cause of their petition, since a petition is like the interpreter of a desire [*cum petitio sit quodammodo desiderii interpres*], or in order to show how speedily they are heard, since no sooner do the poor desire something than God hears them before they put up a prayer, according to the saying of Isa. 65.24, 'And it shall come to pass, that before they call, I will hear'.[32]

What is expressed in prayer is not merely desire, but desire interpreted, even articulated. While a certain popular psychoanalytic grammar today might associate intellect with the shallower reaches of human experience, Aquinas believes that the most profound aspects of the human person necessarily involve our minds. The role of the will or *voluntas* is central here. The will provides the integral direction of our lives and actions. Through the virtue of religion, which is located in the *voluntas*, the will directs the powers of the soul towards revering God. Devotion is the act of the will whereby one gives oneself or devotes oneself to the service of God.[33]

But this is not an act of mere will (*mera voluntate*), for the intellect is integrally involved in the discrimination of our ends. The *voluntas*, in Aquinas, is something much deeper and more ontological, than our word 'will' today. The will in Thomas is not simply the libertarian freedom to choose among a range of options, but rather expresses rationally ordered desire. The *voluntas* describes the person in relation to the good not as mere appetite but as the intelligible direction of one's moral life. The proper functioning of the will and the exercise of its virtues are thus bound up with the proper working of the intellect, the power of the soul nearest to the will. Accordingly, Thomas insists that 'after devotion ... prayer, which belongs to our intellectual part, is the most important act of religion, as by it religion moves our intellect toward God'.[34] Both devotion and prayer require the

---

[31]See Aquinas' commentary on 1 Timothy 2.1: 'Of all the things which are needed for the Christian life the most important is prayer, which is effective against the hazards of temptation and in making progress in good. "The persistent prayer of the righteous is very effective" (James 5.16). ... Prayer is the interpreter of our desire; in praying we ask for what we desire'. See *Albert and Thomas*, 436, 438.

[32]Aquinas, *ST* II-II, q. 83, a. 1, ad. 1.

[33]Aquinas, *ST* II-II, q. 82, a. 1.

[34]Aquinas, *ST* II-II, q. 83, a. 3, ad. 1.

use of the will and the intellect, and both are expressions of the virtue of religion, which we might speak of as the will in its adorative direction. It is the intellect that recognizes this adorative trajectory and the will that motivates us in our theotropic movement. And so it is that 'by praying we hand over our minds to God, subjecting them to him in reverence and in a way presenting them to him'.[35]

In order to understand how all of this works more concretely, it will be helpful to look at Thomas' treatment of the Lord's Prayer. Aquinas, of course, takes it as given that the Lord's Prayer is the most perfect and paradigmatic form of Christian prayer – indeed, it contains all Christian prayer in its integral fullness. What is more, according to Thomas, the Lord's Prayer 'gives shape to our whole affective life', as Simon Tugwell translates 'informativa totius nostri affectus'.[36] As Aquinas explains:

> For since prayer interprets our desires, as it were, before God, then alone is it right to ask for something in our prayers when it is right that we should desire it. Now in the Lord's Prayer not only do we ask for all that we may rightly desire, but also in the order wherein we ought to desire them, so that this prayer not only teaches us to ask, but also directs all our affections.[37]

Through prayer, we articulate our desires and bring them to God, but through this process our desires are formed and transformed, as we are brought more fully into the pattern of God's life.[38] Quoting Dionysius the Areopagite, Aquinas holds that 'when we call upon God in our prayers, we unveil our mind in His presence'.[39] Calling and unveiling coincide; both point to the intentional enactment of a posture of vulnerability, receptivity and trust. This is why the Lord's Prayer begins as it does, because 'confidence is excited in us chiefly by the consideration of His charity in our regard, whereby He wills our good – wherefore we say: "Our Father"; and of His excellence, whereby He is able to fulfil it – wherefore we say: "Who art in heaven"'.[40] Aquinas interprets the opening of the Lord's Prayer in light of

---

[35]Aquinas, *ST* II-II, q. 83, a. 3, ad. 3.
[36]Aquinas, *ST* II-II, q. 83, a. 9, resp.
[37]Aquinas, *ST* II-II, q. 83, a. 9, resp.
[38]See Aquinas, *ST* II-II, q. 83, a. 9, ad. 2: 'Since prayer is the interpreter of desire, the order of the petitions corresponds with the order, not of execution, but of desire or intention, where the end precedes the things that are directed to the end, and attainment of good precedes removal of evil.'
[39]Aquinas, *ST* II-II, q. 83, a. 1, ad. 2; citing *Divine Names* 3, in *Pseudo-Dionysius: The Complete Works*, trans. Colm Luibheid, CWS (New York: Paulist Press, 1987), 47–132.
[40]Aquinas, *ST* II-II, q. 83, a. 9, ad. 5.

1 John 4.18-19: 'There is no fear in love, but perfect love casts out fear; for fear has to do with punishment, and whoever fears has not reached perfection in love. We love because he first loved us.' Because the One to Whom we pray is Love itself, we can unveil our desire before Him, through which our desires are realigned towards their highest end: the love of God in Himself, and the love of ourselves and our neighbours in God.

Elsewhere, Aquinas writes, 'Petition serves desire, because what we ask for is what we want to have. Now in this prayer [i.e. the Lord's Prayer] all that we can desire is contained. Secondly, it is contained in the order in which we ought to desire things. Thirdly, these petitions correspond to the gifts and beatitudes.'[41] Prayer is thus the interpreter of desire in a twofold sense. We interpret our desires and bring them to articulation as we attempt to unveil ourselves before the God who loves us. But it is also the case that prayer interprets our desire to us so that in prayer we see what our desires ultimately are. As Aquinas explains:

> The primary objective of desire is the goal it is aiming at, the things which lead to that goal being secondary. ... And the ultimate goal of everything is God. So the first thing to be desired has to be God's honor.[42]

This is why we pray, 'Hallowed be thy name'. For our part as human beings, our ultimate end is beatitude or eternal life and this is why we pray, 'Thy kingdom come'. Moreover, as sojourners in this life, we rightly ask for those good but penultimate things, that is, the virtues, that serve to bring about our highest ends, and we pray for these saying 'Thy will be done'. Nor is this all. As Aquinas concludes:

> So the point of beatitude is God, and the point of the virtues is beatitude. But we need support, both temporal and spiritual, such as the church's sacraments, and this is what we ask for when we say 'our bread', meaning external bread or sacramental bread.[43]

Before we who pray ever get to the place of asking God for the good things needed in this life, we have been led through a pedagogy of desire that has begun to reshape the praying self. Nevertheless, we are instructed to ask for our daily bread. By linking prayer so intimately with the hermeneutics of desire, Thomas in no way neglects the fact that prayer often looks like human

---

[41]For the text of Aquinas' commentary on Matthew, see 'From the Lectures on St Matthew', in *Albert and Thomas*, 445-75.

[42]Aquinas, 'From the Lectures on St Matthew', 460.

[43]Aquinas, 'From the Lectures on St Matthew', 460.

beings coming to God with requests. Nor does he deny that such asking is efficacious. It is sometimes said that prayer works not because it changes things but because it changes us. This is not what Thomas believes. Of course, prayer has nothing to do with changing God, for the very nature of God's being is such that the grammar of change is unintelligible when applied to divinity. For Aquinas, God is not an item within the physical world nor a being confined to the stream of time, but is rather the cause of all that is, the simple, self-subsistent, eternal and necessary act of being itself, *esse ipsum*, both the end of all desiring and the source and creator of all finite destinies.

But, in that case, how can prayer be effective? Thomas delineates a set of ancient errors that, if true, would render the practice futile. The first he ascribes to those who do not believe that human affairs are governed by providence at all. The second involves the fatalist claim that nothing can be changed and thus there is no real use in petitioning God. The third holds that God's will can indeed be changed in response to our requests. Thomas rejects all three for each of them inclines towards a sort of practical atheism, which is another way of describing a world in which prayer is impossible. The reason for this is apparent in the first two cases, the eradication and the absolutizing of providence, respectively, but may be harder to discern in the case of the third: the open view of God's providence – indeed, some consider it to be the most sensible way to take prayer seriously.[44] As far as Aquinas is concerned, however, the theological and spiritual consequences of such a stance would be disastrous. Not only does it involve rejecting the classical view of divinity, which Aquinas believes to be both biblically and metaphysically warranted, but it also renders prayer itself strangely agonistic, even atheistic. Consider what is involved in the claim that our prayers might change God's intentions. That would mean that our prayers themselves were somehow outside of God's intentions; rather than being the elevation of the mind to God, prayer on this account would have to be the one place where God is not.[45]

---

[44]Robin Collins, 'Prayer and Open Theism: A Participatory, Co-Creator Model', in *God in an Open Universe: Science, Metaphysics, and Open Theism*, ed. William Hasker, Thomas Jay Oord and Dean W. Zimmerman (Eugene, OR: Pickwick Press, 2011), 161–86.

[45]C. S. Lewis once explained it this way: 'God and man cannot exclude one another, as man excludes man, at the point of junction, so to call it, between Creator and creature. ... You remember the two maxims Owen [Barfield] lays down in Saving the Appearances? On the one hand, the man who does not regard God as other than himself cannot be said to have a religion at all. On the other hand, if I think God other than myself in the same way in which my fellow-men, and objects in general, are other than myself, I am beginning to make Him an idol. I am daring to treat His existence as somehow parallel to my own. But He is the ground of our being. He is always both within us and over against us. Our reality is so much from His reality as He, moment by moment, projects into us. The deeper the level within ourselves from which our prayer, or any other act, wells up, the more it is His, but not at all the less ours. Rather, most ours when most His.' See C. S. Lewis, *Letters to Malcolm, Chiefly on Prayer* (New York: Harcourt, Brace and World, 1964), 68–9.

Rejecting all three of these misconceptions of divine providence, Thomas roots his account of the efficacy of prayer in a non-contrastive vision of the relation of God and creatures. Because God is not one object among others or part of the furniture of the universe, neither is God one cause among other causes. Accordingly, there is no competition between creaturely and divine agency, for everything that the creature is and all that the creature does issue from God. As Aquinas explains:

> God is the cause of everything's action inasmuch as he gives everything the power to act, and preserves it in being and applies it to action, and inasmuch as by his power every other power acts. And if we add to this that God is his own power, and that he is in all things not as part of their essence but as upholding them in their being, we shall conclude that he acts in every agent immediately.[46]

It is precisely because God transcends creatures that God can be superlatively immanent within them: 'God is in all things, and innermostly [*Deus sit in omnibus rebus, et intime*].'[47] There is, then, no competition between what God and creatures do. Here are the roots of the famous distinction between primary and secondary causation. As Thomas explains, 'God works in each agent, and in accord with that agent's manner of acting, just as the first cause operates in the operation of a secondary cause, since the secondary cause cannot become active except by the power of the first cause.'[48] Through participation in His own infinite power, God gives to finite creatures their powers to act such that 'the dignity of causality is imparted even to creatures'.[49]

This metaphysics of creation, then, provides Thomas with an explanation for how it is that prayer can be efficacious. Just as God allows us to exercise the dignity of causality in the ordinary events of life – bread is no less God's gift because we bake it, nor does it cease to come from Him when we receive it from a neighbour – so God has ordained that we exercise our agency also through praying to Him.

> Wherefore it must be that men do certain actions, not that thereby they may change the Divine disposition, but that by those actions they may

---

[46]Aquinas, *De potentia*, III.7, resp.; *Disputed Questions on the Power of God*, trans. the English Dominican Fathers (Westminster, MD: Newman Press, 1952).
[47]Aquinas, *ST* I, q. 8, a. 1, resp.
[48]Aquinas, *De veritate*, q. 24.1, a. 3; *Truth – Volume 3*, trans. Robert W. Schmidt (Chicago, IL: Henry Regnery Company, 1954), 139.
[49]Aquinas, *ST* I, q. 22, a. 33.

achieve certain effects according to the order of the Divine disposition: and the same is to be said of natural causes. And so is it with regard to prayer. For we pray not that we may change the Divine disposition, but that we may impetrate that which God has disposed to be fulfilled by our prayers, in other words that by asking, men may deserve to receive what Almighty God from eternity has disposed to give, as Gregory says.[50]

Because prayer makes visible the ontological truth that everything is gift, God has ordained that some of the goods he wishes for us should be achieved through our asking, praying and sighing. Our prayers, then, are truly a cause for what takes place through them, but a relational cause, not a mechanical one, which is to say, the answers we receive to prayer come not because of our merit, but because of God's grace.[51] Aquinas writes, 'As to its efficacy in impetrating, prayer derives this from the grace of God to Whom we pray, and Who instigates us to pray.'[52] That last line is important: it is not God who responds to our prayer, but we who respond to God in prayer. How could it be otherwise? 'For the very act of praying is "a gift of God"'.[53]

The Praying Self

Rather than directing our attention away from petition, Thomas constantly displays the theological depth and metaphysical surprise entailed by what can seem the most ordinary practice of prayer in Christian life. Bringing our desires to the Lord, articulating them and interpreting them before God turn out to involve nearly the entire drama of creation, salvation and sanctification. What seems to be *our* act, turns out not to be ours, or at least not ours alone, and this points to the transformation of the self we discover in Aquinas' teaching on prayer.

Through prayer, our desire is not only expressed but transformed, conformed to the desire that God has for us, making us fit for charity and beatitude, the friendship with God that is the end of the Christian life and the end of all prayer. Through prayer, our desires are transformed, but so too is the very shape of the praying self. Of course, we have already seen the way in which the practice of prayer unsettles any notion of competition between the one praying and the One to whom we pray. Paul had instructed the Philippians, 'Work out your own salvation with fear and trembling; for

---

[50]Aquinas, *ST* I, q. 8, a. 2, resp.
[51]Aquinas, *ST* II-II, q. 83, a. 10, ad. 1.
[52]Aquinas, *ST* II-II, q. 83, a. 15, resp.
[53]Aquinas, *ST* II-II, q. 83, a. 15, ad. 1.

it is God who is at work in you, enabling you both to will and to work for his good pleasure' (Phil. 2.12-13). Likewise, for Aquinas, it is God who is at work in us, luring us into prayer, providing us with the longings we express in prayer, empowering our prayers both for ourselves and for others.

The self in prayer learns to see God's generosity and gift constantly at work in the world and in our own depths, and in coming to see ourselves and the world as porous to God's grace, we also come to see the way in which we are linked not only to God but also to one another. The charity we learn in prayer issues not only in friendship with God, but also in friendship with one another. In his *Commentary on Matthew,* Thomas writes, 'In saying "Our Father" our feelings for our neighbors are set in order. "Is there not one Father of us all?" (Mal. 2.10). If we all have one Father, none of us ought to despise any of our neighbors on the grounds of our birth.'[54] Aquinas presses this point, asking 'Why do we not say, "My Father"?' His answer is twofold. First, because 'My Father' is appropriate only for Christ who is Son by nature rather than by adoption. But also, following Chrysostom, Aquinas recognizes that through the corporate nature of the 'Our Father', 'the Lord is teaching us not to make private prayers, but to pray generally for the whole people; this kind of prayer is more acceptable to God'.[55]

This relativizing of any notion we might harbour of our own ultimate self-possession occurs throughout Thomas' discussions of prayer. When, for example, we ask for 'our daily bread', we are again engaging the essentially communal and relational pedagogy of prayer. Following Chrysostom, Aquinas notes two aspects of this, one preventative, the other positive. First, by asking for *our* daily bread, the one who prays recognizes the obligation not to infringe upon the dignity and integrity of others. Thomas explains, 'Nobody ought to eat bread obtained by stealing; they should eat bread that comes from their own labor.'[56] But, as we have seen, the fruits of our labour are not merely ours. They come as gifts, for all things come as gifts from the triune God, maker of heaven and earth. Accordingly, Aquinas adds, 'The temporal boons which are given to us because of our need should be accepted in such a way that we share them with others'.[57] Prayer, then, by teaching us to receive all things as gifts from the divine generosity, is bound up also with our generosity and the relationships this entails. '"It is by good works", Aquinas explains, among which almsgiving is pre-eminent, that the soul is prepared for prayer. "Let us lift up our hearts, with our hands,

---

[54]Aquinas, 'From the Lectures on St Matthew', 459.
[55]Aquinas, 'From the Lectures on St Matthew', 459.
[56]Aquinas, 'From the Lectures on St Matthew', 468.
[57]Aquinas, 'From the Lectures on St Matthew', 468.

to the Lord" (Lam. 3.41), and this happens when our good works are in harmony with our prayer.'[58] We become fitted for prayer when we perform our relationality with our bodies and not just with our souls, in other words, when we refuse then fallen autarchy of merely individual concerns and give ourselves to prayerful charity.

Aquinas' communal anthropology of prayer is especially discernible in his consideration of the prayers of the saints. It is not only we that pray both for ourselves and for others, but the saints, too, pray for us. Echoing the teachings of Dionysius, Aquinas writes:

> Since prayers offered for others proceed from charity, ... the greater the charity of the saints in heaven, the more they pray for wayfarers, since the latter can be helped by prayers: and the more closely they are united to God, the more are their prayers efficacious: for the Divine order is such that lower beings receive an overflow of the excellence of the higher, even as the air receives the brightness of the sun.[59]

The picture Thomas conveys is one of glorified humanity bound in an overflow of love to those of us still on our way here below. Just as God wills to accomplish certain goods through the prayers of those on earth, so too God wills to accomplish many goods through the prayers of the saints in heaven. 'The saints impetrate whatever God wishes to take place through their prayers: and they pray for that which they deem will be granted through their prayers according to God's will.'[60] In Thomas' description, moreover, affectivity, desire and a kind of qualitative relational proximity cut across and perforate what might otherwise seem too linear a hierarchy of glory. The diagnolizing of genuine relations mediated through love both relativizes this hierarchy and ensures that it serves the end of relationship rather than distancing:

> It is God's will that inferior beings should be helped by all those that are above them, wherefore we ought to pray not only to the higher but also to the lower saints; else we should have to implore the mercy of God alone. Nevertheless it happens sometime that prayers addressed to a saint of lower degree are more efficacious, either because he is implored with greater devotion, or because God wishes to make known his sanctity.[61]

---

[58]Aquinas, 'From the Lectures on St Matthew', 446.
[59]Aquinas, *ST* II-II, q. 83, a. 11, resp.
[60]Aquinas, *ST* II-II, q. 83, a. 11, ad. 2.
[61]Aquinas, *ST* II-II, q. 83, a. 11, ad. 4.

Glorification, therefore, does not in any way remove the saints from those of us still *in via*, for in prayer and love we are bound ever more fully to one another. Indeed, the saints' knowledge of us and of our needs comes through their knowledge of God and his working in them. The saints see, as it were, in and through the Word that is at work in them; they see us in the Divine manifestation and this gives rise to their prayers on our behalf.[62]

Conclusion

In conclusion, we can return to the issue with which we began this chapter, namely Aquinas' habit of saying his prayers briefly and succinctly. When considering the propriety of this practice, Thomas provides a rare reply to his own *sed contra*, writing:

> One may pray continually, either through having a continual desire, as stated above; or through praying at certain fixed times, though interruptedly; or by reason of the effect, whether in the person who prays – because he remains more devout even after praying, or in some other person – as when by his kindness a man incites another to pray for him, even after he himself has ceased praying.[63]

Note what Aquinas is claiming here: one is able to continue one's prayer even in the activity of others. There is an implicit dismantling of the putatively natural boundaries of selfhood, a rejection of any reified individuality. For Thomas, even the most seemingly ordinary of prayers, the prayer of petition through which we lay bare our desires before God, this humble prayer radically undoes our efforts to police the boundaries of our isolated selves, for it binds us to one another in ever richer webs of impetration and to God in ever deeper interpretations of desire.

---

[62]'Whatever it is fitting the blessed should know about what happens to us, even as regards the interior movements of the heart, is made known to them in the Word: and it is most becoming to their exalted position that they should know the petitions we make to them by word or thought; and consequently the petitions which we raise to them are known to them through Divine manifestation.' See Aquinas, *ST* II-II, q. 83, a. 4, ad. 2.

[63]Aquinas, *ST* II-II, q. 83, a. 14, ad. 4.

CHAPTER TWENTY-ONE

Retrieving Luther on Prayer: Spirituality in the Production of Christian Doctrine

PAUL R. HINLICKY

My title refers to contributions of three particular theologians of recent times. From the late John Webster I draw the notion of 'retrieval' as a mode of *contemporary* theology, *not* for purposes of repristination (as the conclusion of this chapter will show).[1] I borrow the notion of theology as 'production of doctrine' from Christine Helmer.[2] And the way I will speak of prayer as the 'spirituality' of the theological subject reflects my own work: this is the one created by the Spirit of Christ to hear and respond to the Father's Word incarnate; thus, I refer to the *Holy Spirit's* 'spirituality'.[3] As we shall see, however, it was Karl Barth who actually pioneered the retrieval of Luther's

---

[1]John Webster, 'Theologies of Retrieval', in *The Oxford Handbook of Systematic Theology*, ed. John Webster, Kathryn Tanner and Iain Torrance (Oxford: Oxford University Press, 2007), 584–5. So far, however, as theology is cognitively the interpretation of human experience, the discoveries of natural science just so constrain theology as the very facts to be interpreted.

[2]Christine Helmer, *Theology and the End of Doctrine* (Louisville, KY: Westminster John Knox Press, 2014). See my review essay in *Pro Ecclesia* 25, no. 1 (2016): 105–11.

[3]Paul R. Hinlicky, *Beloved Community: Critical Dogmatics after Christendom* (Grand Rapids, MI: William B. Eerdmans, 2015), 193–293.

theology of prayer for its fecund role, as just suggested, in theologizing.[4] This 'spirituality' is the royal freedom of the Christian in her living history with the God of grace – what Luther identified as existence *coram Deo*.

Apocalyptic Prayer

The rudiments of Luther's teaching on prayer are well-known and were masterfully synthesized recently by Mary Jane Haemig in her contribution to the *Oxford Encyclopedia of Martin Luther*.[5] What I will accent in considering treatments of our topic by Haemig and other historical scholars is the *apocalyptic* setting and the *trinitarian* articulation of Luther's teaching on prayer.

Haemig's synthesis, culminating in a proposal for further reflection which she provocatively developed out of her survey, can be summarized as follows. Prayer begins in existential despair at the human capacity to reach the Creator. Without such despair of the existing self, no one learns to pray truly. While a desire to pray may in some sense characterize *homo religiosus*, such prayer under 'the light of nature' seeks only to avoid pain or to attain

---

[4]Engagement especially with the Lord's Prayer forms bookends around Karl Barth's theological life according to his biographer Eberhard Busch. His 'first theological lecture' as a student was a historical-critical examination of 'the original form of the Lord's Prayer', which would not 'call a halt even before the highest and the holiest!'. See *Karl Barth: His Life from Letters and Autobiographical Texts*, trans. John Bowden (Philadelphia, PA: Fortress Press, 1976), 37–8. It was his plan to organize Christian ethics around the petitions of the Lord's Prayer in *CD* IV/4, although declining health caused him to abandon the plan. A fulsome treatment of prayer under the rubric of creative divine command may be found in *CD* III/4, 87–115. My own interpretation of Christian ethics is likewise organized around the Lord's Prayet. See Hinlicky, *Beloved Community*, 642–90.

[5]Mary Jane Haemig, 'Prayer', in *Oxford Encyclopedia of Martin Luther*, ed. Derek R. Nelson and Paul R. Hinlicky (New York: Oxford University Press, 2017), vol. 3, 156–70. For the Luther texts usually consulted on prayer, refer to Haemig's article. Haemig states that 'Luther mentions prayer in so many places – treatises, biblical commentaries, sermons – that it is really astonishing that scholars have not given more attention to it' (personal correspondence to the author). Discussions of prayer are to be found scattered about in Luther's ecclesiological and liturgical writings, personal correspondence, biblical commentaries, especially on various psalms, the second chapter of Jonah, sermons, Jesus in the garden of Gethsemane and his cry of dereliction from the cross. Her article in the *Oxford Encyclopedia of Martin Luther* surveys samples of Luther on prayer from these and other diverse genres which the reformer employed. The essential text to be consulted is Luther's treatment of the Lord's Prayer in his *Large Catechism*. See Robert Kolb and Timothy Wengert, ed., *The Book of Concord: The Confessions of the Evangelical Lutheran Church* (Minneapolis, MN: Fortress Press, 2000), 440–67. Another essential text frequently consulted by scholars is Luther's charming instruction for his barber, 'A Simple Way to Pray', in *Luther's Devotional Writings*, trans. Carl J. Schindler, LW 43 (Minneapolis, MN: Augsburg Fortress Press, 1959), 193–211.

benefits.[6] Such prayer is not the filial communication act of a beloved child but servile bargaining with a great Unknown. On a more sophisticated level, despair at the human capacity to reach the Creator articulates as fatalism, even when glossed as prayerful resignation to the will of God. Such resignation neither asks nor expects anything other than what must be according to the inexorable laws of being, the latter tacitly regarded as the true divinity. With this analysis of the predicament of humanity before *Deus absconditus* under the mere 'light of nature', Luther teaches that genuine prayer begins where and when, as in a historically adventitious event, the God who comes pierces the fog to speak divine Law and Gospel. In this event the existing human creature comes to respond to God as convicted sinner *yet at the same time* as beloved child, an *inchoate* new creation.

Luther's celebrated triad, *oratio, meditatio, tentatio,* may thus be rightly used to summarize his teaching on the initiating place of prayer in theology, if we see that for Luther the prayer of the newborn child of God has its setting in Jesus' invitation to join him in apocalyptic battle. Prayer under the 'light of grace' is struggle through times of trial and assaults of evil, fending off terror in order to persevere in keeping the commandment to beseech the coming of God's kingdom, the hallowing of God's name and the doing of God's will on earth as in heaven. Prayer thus enables action; indeed, the Christian's prayer is *already* holy action, as Karl Barth commented, the active Christian righteousness, the very obedience of faith.[7] Thus for Luther prayer actualizes and in turn informs the renewed human vocation on the earth, the 'daily bread' responsibility for providing 'bodily goods', as Luther expansively interprets the petition arising from human need into a comprehensive political and ecological ethic. Here 'synergism' (i.e. cooperation of the renewed human creature with God) is not only permitted but enabled and expected. Here the Christian not only can but is commanded to petition God that 'our will be done'. This petition in respect to bodily need is an *ora et labora* synergism elicited by Jesus' invitation to pray and labour for all temporal needs, if only we seek first the kingdom of God and its righteousness.

For Luther the Lord's Prayer is not only the model of Christian prayer; it is this model because it is Jesus' own prayer, that is, the articulation of

---

[6]On this, see Thomas Reinhuber, *Kämpfender Glaube: Studien zu Luthers Bekenntnis am Ende von De servo arbitrio* (Berlin: De Gruyter, 2000).

[7]Barth, *CD* III/1, 264. For Luther, 'The second kind of righteousness is our proper righteousness, not because we alone work at, but because we work it with that first and alien righteousness [of Christ]'. See Harold J. Grimm and Helmut T. Lehmann, ed., 'Two Kinds of Righteousness', in *Career of the Reformer I*, trans. Lowell J. Satre, *LW* 31 (Philadelphia, PA: Fortress Press, 1957), 293–306 (299). Note the 'synergism' of the regenerate Christian with the alien righteousness of Christ in this formulation.

Jesus' own filial faith in the God of Israel as his heavenly Father. It is a faith, then, which believes contrary to present appearances and expresses a defiant hope. As such it is also Jesus' invitation to join him in his own relationship to God whose reign comes. It is not as if existential ignorance of God our heavenly Father who invites and hears prayer, however, is instantly remedied by memorizing the Lord's Prayer or reciting it woodenly. Because praying the Lord's Prayer is in the first place obedient-for-trusting participation in Jesus Christ and thus in his relation to the heavenly Father by the work of their Holy Spirit, it not only initiates with Spirit-worked despair of the existing self but ever battles against corresponding feelings of unworthiness that assail Luther's afflicted Christian, suspended in trial and stretched by tribulation. This tense battle lasts as long as life itself precisely within the regenerate Christian habituated to prayer. Thus prayer especially requires 'blunt and honest talk' about God (the Father) with God (the Son) in God (the Holy Spirit).

With Haemig's 'blunt and honest talk' about God, Luther has in mind the remarkable and perplexing correspondence between the petition in the Lord's Prayer, 'Thy will be done on earth', and Christ's surrender to his Father's will in the garden of Gethsemane. The honest talk of the Son's human feelings of terror before the trial in store for him with its accompanying perception of the heavenly Father's uncanny silence are never to be covered up but rather lifted up for us to understand what true participation in Christ the beloved Son entails: the petitioner's spiritual crucifixion with Christ. Of course that is not only what prayerful participation in Christ means. Remaining in despair is like remaining in the tomb; it robs God of his Fatherhood, just as Adam's pride in doubting the goodness of the commandment had robbed God. Holy Spirit prayer arises from despair at the existing self into newness of life in hope. Prayer *is*, as well as *expects*, change in reality.

This change in reality is a chief implication for theology which Haemig draws from her survey of Luther on prayer. In her own words,

> [Luther's] listening God, this God who hears prayer and who ... changes his intentions to respond to prayer, is very different from other conceptions of God prominent in culture or in Christianity. The Deist (clockmaker) God does not bend down to hear human petitions and change his intentions to respond to them. Another concept of God – as one who has charted out all human events in advance – also is contradicted by Luther's teaching. ... Human suffering is reframed as an opportunity for prayer, an opportunity to recognize God's goodness, and an opportunity to change reality.[8]

---

[8]Haemig, 'Prayer', 167–8.

We can corroborate Haemig's provocative claim here with a brief discussion Timothy Wengert provides in a work on Luther as a pastoral theologian.[9] He reports on Veit Dietrich's account of Luther's impassioned prayer for the healing of a colleague which healing he both expected and witnessed. Recalling the biblical parable of the persistent widow, Luther is said to have 'rubbed God's ears with his own promises'. Bold, expectant prayer is enabled because God has freely but in very truth bound himself with his promises. So God's promises are believed – often precisely against present appearances – to be omnipotent. Consequently the rationale for Christian prayer that Luther frequently gives, 'because it is commanded', does not mean that prayer is now a new legal obligation by which the Christian proves herself worthy of grace; it is not commandment in that sense of a renewed system of merit based on reward and punishment. Rather it is commandment as the creative imperative of the gracious indicative: you are promised by God, ergo, you can and should in time of need recall God to his own promises. To put it colloquially we might say that the Christian does not *have* to pray; the Christian *gets* to pray.

In addition to Wengert's insight, we can note here Robert Kolb's analysis of Luther's commentary on Jonah (to which we will return below) in that it reiterates the claim that for Luther Jonah's prayer from the belly of the sea monster (a figure of hell for Luther) caused God to change his mind.[10] Certainly such prayerful expectation of the fulfilment of God's promises – pitted against the present appearance of reality – means that prayerful hope is not a rational calculation of an outcome based upon projecting forward current conditions, but an expectation that God whose kingdom comes can and does come to alter the prevailing course of events in order to accomplish his own good and gracious will on earth as in heaven.

Prayer with Jesus in the Spirit for the Coming of the Father's Kingdom

Finally in corroboration of Haemig's chief implication for theology of Luther on prayer, we can add an accent from the penetrating discussion of our topic by Oswald Bayer. Bayer gives greater christological precision to the claim that Christian prayer is first of all participation in the prayer of

[9]Timothy J. Wengert, 'Luther on Prayer in the Large Catechism', in *The Pastoral Luther: Essays on Martin Luther's Practical Theology*, ed. Timothy J. Wengert (Grand Rapids, MI: William B. Eerdmans, 2009), 171–97.
[10]Robert Kolb, *Luther and the Stories of God: Biblical Narratives as a Foundation for Christian Living* (Grand Rapids, MI: Baker Academic, 2012), 139.

Jesus Christ. He does so by way of Luther's leading christological motif, the 'joyful exchange' of human sin for Christ's righteousness, death for life and poverty for riches.[11] Here the two natures of Christ are not conceived of as static, immobile forms somehow glued together. Rather the two natures represent the asymmetrical movement of Creator to creature and of this creature, so embraced, anew to Creator. Manifestly such an account of the incarnation *is*, as well as ever *provides for*, great change in reality; thus faith in it, too, is such a change so far as faith is nothing but a graciously embraced creature's Yes and Amen to the prayerful action of the incarnate Son of God on one's behalf. This Amen of faith to the Word of Christ, 'give me your sin and take my righteousness', is what is meant by participation in Jesus Christ, the crucified and risen Son of the Father.

Just because of this christological depth in Bayer's account of Luther on prayer, he is able to make a claim about an essential matter regarding the doctrine of God to which neither Haemig, Wengert nor Kolb adequately attended, namely, that 'Luther's understanding of prayer itself had a Trinitarian character'.[12] The dynamic movement of the 'two natures' in the person of Christ veritably requires trinitarian parsing: the Father sends the Son so that united in faith to the Son by the Spirit, renewed creatures return the glory to God alone whose kingdom comes. This trinitarian observation is important because it reveals the structural undergirding of Luther's teaching that 'prayer is constituted in the command (*praeceptum*) and the promise (*promissio*) that it will be heard, in that it comes from within a situation where there is dire need (*necessitas*), but also in that it takes place with earnestness and with passionate reliance on the promise that it will be heard (*desideratio*)'.[13]

Because Christ is the Father's Son who has joined us in our dire need, the Father's command to pray and promise to hear can be desired by the human heart as it is transformed by the faith which their Spirit works. So, commenting on Galatians 4.6, Luther writes,

> But in the midst of these terrors of the law, thunderclaps of sin, trials of death, and roarings of the devil, Paul says, the Holy Spirit begins to cry in our heart: 'Abba! Father!' And his cry vastly exceeds, and breaks through, the powerful and horrible cries of the law, sin, death, and the

---

[11]Oswald Bayer, *Martin Luther's Theology: A Contemporary Interpretation*, trans. Thomas H. Trapp (Grand Rapids, MI: William B. Eerdmans, 2007), 346. On this, see Oswald Bayer and Benjamin Gleede, ed., *Creator est creatura: Luthers Christologie als Lehre von der Idiomenkommunikation* (Berlin: De Gruyter, 2007).
[12]Bayer, *Luther's Theology*, 346.
[13]Bayer, *Luther's Theology*, 346.

devil. It penetrates the clouds in heaven, and it reaches all the way to the ears of God.[14]

Appearing on the scene here is the economic Trinity of salvation-history who comes through the gospel proclamation, bringing to naught the things that are. To be sure, the Trinity revealed as such in the gracious and creative claim upon the nothings of the present evil order therewith also claims to be – and to prove to be – the one true God who makes all things new.[15]

Death and Resurrection in the Gethsemane of Christian Prayer

Johann Anselm Steiger has studied the novel features of this christological and trinitarian positioning of prayer 'in dire need' by comparing Luther's interpretation of Jonah's prayer from the belly of the sea monster with those of antecedents, contemporaries and later followers.[16] In the antecedent history of exegesis, the church fathers generally regarded the 'whale' as a saviour sent from God to rescue the drowning Jonah,[17] but Luther, on the basis of Jonah's prayer from its belly, regards the place instead as a figure of hell; typologically, Jonah here figures Christ's descent into hell.[18] Typology is not one-for-one allegory. Luther does not exculpate Jonah, who, he avers, had sinned as gravely as Adam.[19] Insisting on Jonah's true sin bringing him under true judgement allows Luther to bring out the 'contrafacticity' of the sinner's faith in the prayer uttered from monster's belly, faith's 'nevertheless' against the presently prevailing course of events.[20] Such audacious faith can *alter God*; faith's prayer is a 'hammer' which can turn hell upside down and move God from wrath to mercy.[21]

God is also in hell, that is, in the place of absolute distance from God. Put otherwise: Even in hell, where God is not praised (Isa. 38.18), where

---

[14]Luther, *Lectures on Galatians (1953): Chapters 1–4*, ed. Jarasolav Pelikan and Walter A. Hansen, LW 26 (St Louis, MO: Concordia Publishing House, 1963), 381.

[15]The older Luther devoted attention, however, to the doctrine of the eternal or immanent Trinity. See Dennis Bielfeldt, Mickey L. Mattox and Paul R. Hinlicky, *The Substance of the Faith: Luther's Doctrinal Theology for Today* (Minneapolis, MN: Fortress Press, 2008).

[16]Johann Anselm Steiger, *Jonas Propheta: Zur Auslegungs- und Mediengeschichte des Buches Jona bei Martin Luther und im Luthertum der Barockzeit* (Stuttgart-Bad Cannstatt: Frommann-Holzboog Verlag, 2011). All translations from the German are my own.

[17]Steiger, *Jonas Propheta*, 18.

[18]Steiger, *Jonas Propheta*, 17.

[19]Steiger, *Jonas Propheta*, 24.

[20]Steiger, *Jonas Propheta*, 31.

[21]Steiger, *Jonas Propheta*, 32–7.

indeed God is not, the divine promise is and remains valid that faith has the power even here to claim the promise and through its petition (be it only a breath) to overcome hell.[22]

Steiger is careful to note: this power to alter God is for Luther not a capability inhering a pious subject,[23] but of the Word of God re-forming the existing self into a new and theological subject, conformed by the Spirit to Christ's cross and resurrection. Prayer is not human magic; but by the power of his own Word communicated by his own Spirit to form a theological subject, God lets himself be besieged and overcome. Here a dialectic of immutability and mutability in the doctrine of God is required, corresponding to the dynamic and asymmetrical interpretation of the two natures doctrine as specifying an event that takes place in a real history with humanity. God is not godly as a frozen block of immutable ice; God is no 'Stoic',[24] but manifests divine freedom to love, just as the Jonah text goes on to say in regard to Nineveh's eventual repentance. God as godly is thus properly quite able 'to repent'.[25] Calvin, according to Steiger, could still retain from Luther the motif of Jonah's sin and experience of hell,[26] but at just this point exegesis in the Reformed tradition sharply separated from Luther and his followers. God's absolute immutability demanded, according to the Reformed tradition, that such scriptural report of God's repentance be taken as 'improper language' in violation of divine simplicity, taken as metaphysically proper.[27]

Steiger's contribution to our consideration of the significance of Luther's teaching on prayer for the theological production of doctrine today points us to the abiding importance – indeed, to the abiding scandal – of Luther's passive obedience of Christ in his atoning death. Luther sees this typologically anticipated when the guilty Jonah is cast overboard to spare the innocent shipmates.[28] This very notion of substitution,[29] however, couples seamlessly with the *Christus victor* motif in Luther; it is prefigured in Jonah's 'resurrection', that is, being 'spewed forth' from the monster/tomb.[30] 'The swallowed swallows the swallower.'[31] Taking Christ's cross and resurrection

---

[22]Steiger, *Jonas Propheta*, 36.

[23]Steiger, *Jonas Propheta*, 38.

[24]Steiger, *Jonas Propheta*, 65.

[25]Steiger, *Jonas Propheta*, 207.

[26]Steiger, *Jonas Propheta*, 18.

[27]Steiger, *Jonas Propheta*, 58. See also Paul R. Hinlicky, *Divine Simplicity: Christ the Crisis of Metaphysics* (Grand Rapids, MI: Baker Academic, 2016).

[28]Steiger, *Jonas Propheta*, 116, 121.

[29]Simon Gathercole, *Defending Substitution: An Essay on Atonement in Paul* (Grand Rapids, MI: Baker Academic, 2015).

[30]Steiger, *Jonas Propheta*, 127.

[31]Steiger, *Jonas Propheta*, 133.

together as forming an integral whole, there is *action* of love in the *passion* of Christ's suffering so that the dialectic of immutability and mutability, mentioned above, here plays out christologically. Steiger relates this picture of the swallowed swallowing the swallower to the theology of baptism, even finding it engraved upon baptismal fonts from this period.[32] Christian prayer then includes a 'blunt and honest' cry of dereliction but only in the integral movement it initiates from despair of the existing self to the victory peace of the risen Christ for the redeemed sinner. God kills, as Luther frequently averred, in order to make alive.

Militant Doxology

Thus the Lord's Prayer ends in doxology. If pride robs the Father of his glory as the good Creator of all that is not God, and despair robs his self-same glory as the saviour of sinners, faith returns the glory to God by way of union with the Son in the grip of the Spirit. Not by accident the *militant* Pauline refrain, 'Let him who boasts boast in the Lord' is Latinized into the doxological battle-slogan: *soli Deo gloria*.[33] With this defiant battle cry, Luther concluded his notable christological reading of Psalm 8:

> He won the kingdom with great trouble and anguish. Now He is crowned with honor and adornment and has everything under his feet. For this we give God our praise and thanks, but especially for the fact that He has brought us to a light and knowledge that does not spring up out of human reason but out of Christ. He is our Sun, who died for us and was raised from the dead, lives and reigns, so that through him we might be saved.[34]

So also in his significant commentary on the Magnificat, Luther stressed the transformation of the human subject, exemplified by Mary. She is indeed the paradigmatic theological subject, the very one transformed in faith to become an apocalyptic warrior – precisely in depriving idols and demons of their praise by giving all glory to the God of the Gospel. This 'magnification' of God, telling 'the great works and deeds of God', is, Luther writes, 'for the strengthening of our faith, for the comforting of all those of low degree, and for the terrifying of all the mighty ones of earth'. Luther is careful to note in

---

[32]Steiger, *Jonas Propheta*, 139.
[33]Philip G. Ziegler, *Militant Grace: The Apocalyptic Turn and the Future of Christian Theology* (Grand Rapids, MI: Baker Academic, 2018).
[34]Luther, *Selected Psalms I*, trans. Jaroslav Pelikan, LW 12 (St Louis, MO: Concorida Publishing House, 1955), 136. For my full discussion of Luther's christological reading of Psalm 8, see Hinlicky, *Beloved Community*, 522–35.

passing the aforementioned dialectic of immutability and mutability: 'God is not magnified by us so far as his nature is concerned – he is unchangeable – but he is magnified in our knowledge and experience when we greatly esteem him and highly regard him, especially as to his grace and goodness.' So when Mary identifies her theological subjectivity in the statement, '*my soul* magnifies the Lord', Luther glosses that 'soul' here denotes 'my whole life and being, mind and strength'. Thus 'she is caught up as it were into him and feels herself lifted up into his good and gracious will'.[35] The ecstasy of obedient faith is no less divine gift than its object, the incarnate Word. Just so, Mary's praise of God, as it is grounded in the apocalypse of Christ such as she has experienced, is an act of spiritual warfare. The praise of God is not, then, any general instance of religious self-transcendence; it is the very specific act of ascribing all glory to the Father who loved those of low degree by joining them to the Son on whom he breathed his Spirit.

Self-transcendence is not, accordingly, for Luther a mystical ascent out of the world; it is rather this militant ecstasy of Spirit-elicited praise in the midst of adversity. 'For to praise the Lord with gladness is not a work of man; it is rather a joyful suffering and the work of God alone. It cannot be taught in words but must be learned in one's own experience.'[36] As a sword will pierce Mary's soul, so also everyone who prays in Christ in the fashion that she exemplifies experiences their own 'Gethsemane of the soul' (as I have often put it). Yet again, this spiritual Gethsemane is but a moment in the holy passage through trial with Christ to victory in Christ. Commenting on Mary's concluding peroration of praise, 'He has helped his servant Israel in remembrance of his mercy', Luther thus recalls the patriarch Jacob who wrestled with the Son of God (according to Luther's understanding) at the river Jabbok. This passage contains the

> great miracle that, by the grace of God, a man prevailed, as it were, with God, so that God does what man desires. … Through Christ she is joined to God as a bride to her bridegroom, so that the bride has a right to, and power over, her bridegroom's body and all his possessions; all this

---

[35]Luther, *Sermon on the Mount and the Magnificat*, trans. A. T. W. Steinhäuser, LW 21 (St Louis, MO: Concordia Publishing House, 1956), 306–7.

[36]Luther, *Sermon on the Mount and the Magnificat*, 302. Luther's commentary on the Magnificat is also noteworthy for the sharp correction it provides against the characteristically modern-Lutheran misunderstanding of Luther's otherwise important affirmation of the 'promeity' of gospel-elicited faith. This is Luther's pointed critique of concupiscent love of God: 'Not for the sake of the bare goodness of God, but for the sake of one's own enjoyment'. See Luther, *Sermon on the Mount and the Magnificat*, 312. The theological subject is not God captivated by human piety, but the otherwise sinful human person captivated by God's militant and transformative grace.

happens through faith. By faith man does what God wills; God in turn does what man wills. Thus Israel means a godlike, God-conquering man, who was a Lord and God, with God and through God, able to do all things. ... Israel is a strange and profound mystery.[37]

Theological Existence

We have seen that for Luther prayer is the free and joyous act of faith, elicited by the act of God which humbles the proud but exalts the humbled; we have also seen that prayer not only changes the one who prays but can also change the way things are going. And we have seen that for prayer to be such, the doctrine of God itself must allow for a dialectic of mutability and immutability.[38] Few have appreciated this difficult complex of teaching in modern theology as acutely as Karl Barth. In volume II/2 of the *Church Dogmatics*, rightly regarded as the turning point to his mature theology,[39] Barth identified the theological subject as the one 'elected to sonship'.[40] As son, not slave, as the theological subject who exists before God, this is the one who gladly wills the coming of the kingdom of God as 'consummation' – that is, the positive will of God established upon the earth.[41] Barth echoes Luther's explanation of this petition of the Lord's Prayer: 'God's good and gracious will comes about without our prayer but we ask in this prayer that it may also come about in us and among us.'[42] Barth retrieves from Luther the asymmetrical dialectic of God's immutable will to bring about his reign

---

[37]Luther, *Sermon on the Mount and the Magnificat*, 351.

[38]For the very engaging reading of the Book of Numbers, see Katherine Sonderegger, *Systematic Theology – Volume 1: The Doctrine of God* (Minneapolis, MN: Fortress Press, 2015), 271–87. She highlights the tension between Balaam's affirmation of God's immutability and Moses' intercessory prayer which presumes God's mutability. God is, in this reading of Israel's testimony, mutable Immutability – that is, faithful to his own purposes of good for creatures in a history which empowers engaged creatures to play their own parts in that history and in this defined way to affect God within the covenanted relationship. So Balaam protects Moses from turning God into a local tribal deity on the one side and on the other hand Moses protects Balaam from removing God from the necessarily local and immediate concerns of creatures. The mysterious unity of these two contrary attributions by Balaam and Moses constitutes the utter but also dynamic unicity that is God as mutable immutability, as free in his own divine nature to love such that creatures in prayer, praise and thanksgiving love God in turn. For my discussion, see *Pro Ecclesia* 27, no. 1 (2018): 56–62.

[39]Bruce L. McCormack, *Karl Barth's Critically Realistic Dialectical Theology: Its Genesis and Development 1909–1936* (Oxford: Clarendon Press, 1995), 453–68. I will accordingly confine my treatment of Barth on prayer to passages found in Barth, *CD* II/2.

[40]Barth, *CD* II/2, 125.

[41]Barth, *CD* II/2, 126.

[42]*The Book of Concord*, 357.

and the mutable will of God in response to renewed and praying creatures that they be included in, and in turn instruments of, that coming kingdom.

Accordingly, the fundamental action of the theological subject simply is prayer; the 'relative autonomy' of the theological subject is realized in the obedient action of faith which is prayer in the unique and individual circumstances of particular need.[43] This autonomy is relative to the theonomy, not tyranny, not of any god but of the God of the Gospel.[44] The theological subject freely and gladly prays, follows and obeys; its autonomy is thus not an 'independent piety' but is rather realized, revealed and as such modelled in the humanity of Jesus the Son who prays, follows and obeys his Father's will. In this relative autonomy as the personal Son vis-à-vis the personal Father, Jesus manifests a genuine individuality, exhibiting therewith the royal freedom of the Lion of Judah even as he undertakes the work of the Lamb of God bearing away the sin of the world.[45] In Jesus who prays, follows and obeys, therefore, Barth sees the true manifestation of the human image of God, not the synergism of a self-bootstrapping Pelagian to rise from its own independence to storm heaven, but the authentic cooperation of the renewed humanity with its Creator serving below on the good earth.[46]

This authentic cooperation eventuated in the humanity of Jesus was realized just because Jesus knew God as his heavenly Father; so he was the free human before the free God.[47] Because the Christian's prayer can only be her participation in the prayer of Jesus, and because this participation is the gracious union of the righteous Christ with the sinful Christian, the Christian's own action of prayer is exhibited in the 'utterly empty hands' of the publican according to Jesus' parable in Luke 18,[48] an exhibition that, for Barth, both specifies correctly and thus affirms properly Luther's teaching on justification *by faith* alone, namely, as faith in Christ alone.[49]

The compatibilism which Barth aims at in his discussion of prayer is possible not only when the genuine autonomy of the theological subject is affirmed relative to the genuine theonomy of the Gospel's God, but also when genuine theonomy is explicated in trinitarian terms. For Barth the

---

[43]Barth, *CD* II/2, 127.
[44]Barth, *CD* II/2, 177; see also *CD* II/2, 180.
[45]Barth, *CD* II/2, 178–9.
[46]Barth, *CD* II/1, 194; see also *CD* III/1, 280.
[47]Barth, *CD* II/1, 561.
[48]Barth, *CD* II/1, 751.
[49]Barth, *CD* II/1, 763. Barth further develops the proper understanding of the promeity of justifying faith as always the faith of the forgiven sinner living by faith in defiance of present appearances even of oneself to oneself in *CD* III/1, 244–5; see also *CD* III/1, 273.

humility and obedience of the Son of God are an intra-divine event, which is 'repeated' in the human freedom of the Spirit-anointed man Jesus to love God above all by loving (unworthy) neighbours as himself. The enactment of this freedom to love is the very change in reality eventuated in prayer. Barth's celebrated 'freedom to love' is his appropriation of Luther's signature Reformation manifesto, 'The Freedom of a Christian'. As this reflection on the sense of Christian prayer as reality-altering freedom to love is developed on the basis of Barth's notable revision of the Reformed doctrine of the absolute decree of arbitrary grace, it cannot but bear enormous implications for the ongoing production of Christian doctrine that would carry on the Reformation of doctrine begun in Luther and continued in Barth. This bracing conclusion may be corroborated by considering Barth's chapter on prayer in his late-in-life *Evangelical Theology*. *'Veni, Creator Spiritus!'* So Barth *prays* at the conclusion of this chapter:

> In his movements from below to above and from above to below, the one Holy Spirit achieves the opening of God for man and the opening of man for God. Theological work, therefore, lives by and in the petition for his coming. ... The certainty that this petition will be heard is consequently also the certainty in which theological work may and should be courageously started and performed.[50]

Like Luther, Barth specifies the Christian's prayer as Gethsemane of the soul: 'Without judgment and death there is no grace and no life for anybody or anything and, least of all for theology.'[51] Like Luther, Barth grounds the certainty of prayer in the speaking and hearing God who has bound himself freely by his word of grace: 'If grace is what occurs there, God can only be appealed to for it, and entreated for it, and called upon for its demonstration.'[52] 'God hears *genuine* prayer!'[53]

Thus obediently acting on this conviction of faith is the 'first and basic act' of 'courageous theological work' because in prayer:

> theological work is opened by heaven and God's work and word, but it is also open toward heaven and God's work and word. It cannot possibly be taken for granted that this work is performed in this open realm, open

---

[50]Karl Barth, *Evangelical Theology: An Introduction*, trans. Grover Foley (Grand Rapids, MI: William B. Eerdmans, 1979), 160–70.
[51]Barth, *Evangelical Theology*, 160.
[52]Barth, *Evangelical Theology*, 168–9.
[53]Barth, *Evangelical Theology*, 168–9.

toward the object of theology, its source and goal and in this way open toward its great menace and the still greater hope which is founded upon its object.[54]

In this heavenward openness, the theologian 'leaves himself and his work behind in order once again to recollect that he stands before God'.[55] Theological existence is standing before the God of the Gospel in prayer; the production of theology is thereby conscience-bound by this properly prayerful stance of 'undaunted disarmament and capitulation to its object' to God.[56] 'True and proper language concerning God will always be a response to God, which overtly or covertly, explicitly or implicitly thinks and speaks of God exclusively in the second person. And this means that theological work must really and truly take place in the form of a liturgical act, as invocation of God, and as prayer.'[57]

Whatever the theologian says about God must first be articulated to God: as I have put it, 'God is the audience of theology'.[58] So Barth:

> The object of theological work is not some *thing* but some *one*. He is not a highest or absolute something (even if this were 'the ground of Being' or the like). This object is not an 'It' but a 'He'. And He, this One, exists not as an idol and mute being for Himself, but precisely in his *work* which is also his *Word*.[59]

The polemic in the parentheses regarding God as 'the ground of Being' was not only Barth's sideway glance at the contemporaneous popularity of Paul Tillich's theology. It is, as Robert Jenson powerfully developed in his *Systematic Theology,* a profoundly substantive methodological decision in theology to give principled priority to the question of *who* God is over the question of *what* God is.[60] That does not mean, either for Barth or for Jenson, that the question about the nature of God is simply jettisoned. A 'who' without a 'what' would be a ghost.[61] Rather it means that a properly theological account of the deity of God is to be derived from and governed by the speaking and hearing God who comes and is revealed in the Gospel.

---

[54]Barth, *Evangelical Theology*, 161.
[55]Barth, *Evangelical Theology*, 162
[56]Barth, *Evangelical Theology*, 167.
[57]Barth, *Evangelical Theology*, 164.
[58]Hinlicky, *Beloved Community*, 613–31.
[59]Hinlicky, *Beloved Community*, 163.
[60]Robert W. Jenson, *Systematic Theology* (Oxford: Oxford University Press, 1997), vol. 1, 13, 51, 59. See also Hinlicky, *Beloved Community,* 123–7.
[61]Hinlicky, *Beloved Community*, 125.

As Oswald Bayer noted, this properly theological account of the deity of God is found, for Luther,[62] as for Barth and for Jenson (and even for a contemporary sympathizer with Protestant scholastic orthodoxy such as Jordan Barrett) in the doctrine of the Trinity, the Gospel's God, the One who is in motion in order to love in freedom.[63]

Divine Temporality and the Causal Joint

Does God in reality hear and respond to genuine prayer? The question of divine temporality implied by a dialectic of immutability and mutability arises here; it is a significant question in contemporary Christian theology's encounter with the natural sciences. John Polkinghorne asks, 'Does God act in the physical world?' In corroboration of our account of Luther on prayer and its implications for the production of contemporary Christian doctrine, Polkinghorne rightly notes that the

> Christian God is not just a deistic upholder of the world. If petitionary prayer, and the insights of a Providence at work in human lives and in universal history, are to carry the weight of meaning that they do in Christian tradition and experience, they must not simply be pious ways of speaking about a process from which particular divine activity is in fact absent and in which the divine presence is unexpressed, save for a general letting-be.[64]

Polkinghorne's reflection on the question so posed is theologically valuable and manifestly relevant to our present enquiry (readers should consult his chapter directly for the scientific arguments he musters on behalf of his theological proposal). In accounting for the speaking and hearing God of the Gospel, given our best-available thinking about the physics of the creation, Polkinghorne rejects Kantian or Thomistic obfuscation which declines

---

[62]On Luther's trinitarianism, see Luther, *Word and Sacrament III*, ed. Robert H. Fischer, LW 37 (Philadelphia, PA: Fortress Press, 1986), 360–72. See further, Christine Helmer, *The Trinity and Martin Luther: A Study on the Relationship between Genre, Language and the Trinity in Luther's Works (1523–1546)* (Mainz: Verlag Philipp von Zabern, 1999) and my *Luther and the Beloved Community* (Grand Rapids, MI: William B. Eerdmans, 2010), 105–38.

[63]Barth, *CD* II/1, 331. For the same conclusion with its 'revisionist' implication, see Jordan P. Barrett, *Divine Simplicity : A Biblical and Trinitarian Account* (Minneapolis, MN: Fortress Press, 2017), 171–2: 'The tension felt by many between the Trinity and simplicity is understandable … *the Trinity seems to require greater distinctions than divine simplicity will allow.*' For my review, see *International Journal of Systematic Theology* 21, no. 1 (2019): 111–15

[64]John C. Polkinghorne, *Belief in God in an Age of Science* (New Haven, CT: Yale University Press, 2003), 48–75.

to address the question of the 'causal joint' by which creator God hears and answers prayer. He also puts his finger on a deeper resistance within the Western theological tradition to pursuing the implication of divine temporality which cuts to the heart of the matter.

> The religion of the incarnation seems to imply a divine participation in the reality of the temporal, from a birth under Augustus to a death under Tiberius. The God of both the Old and the New Testaments seems to have a deep engagement with historical process, with the becomingness of the world. Allowing for all the necessary, and sometimes unsubtle, anthropomorphism's inescapable in scripture, the God of the Bible seems far from the Boethian contemplator of the complete cosmic story.[65]

This scriptural challenge to the divine contemplator of Perfect Being theology, the 'atemporal God of classical [metaphysical] theology', entails a nuanced affirmation of 'divine temporality'[66] as the 'hidden work of the Spirit, guiding and enticing the unfolding of continuous creation' by the 'continuous input of active information'.[67] Thus the ecstasy of Spirit-worked obedient faith in prayer, as we have seen from Luther, is actively, temporally and particularly produced by Polkinghorne's 'hidden work of the Spirit'. Polkinghorne regards this temporal input of information by the Spirit as the causal joint; it is a two-way corridor, however, which thus allows also for the possibility of efficacious petitionary prayer as the creature informs the Creator and in this way of petition exercises its relative causal efficacy (parallel to Barth's 'relative autonomy'). From the divine side, God's faithfulness or consistency undergirds 'the predictable aspects of natural process', while allowing also that in 'unprecedented circumstances, it is entirely conceivable that God will act in totally novel and unexpected ways (i.e. in "miracles" or "Christ's resurrection").'[68] But the decisive point is that in the open universe interpretation which contemporary cosmology allows, 'the physical universe is one of true becoming, with the future not yet formed and existing', such that even creator God does not yet know a future of creation that does not yet exist.[69] The predestination of God, we may note, may be understood, then, along the lines of Barth's interpretation from *CD* II/2 as God's self-

---

[65]Polkinghorne, 'Does God Act in the Physical World?', 48–9.
[66]Polkinghorne, 'Does God Act in the Physical World?', 70–1.
[67]Polkinghorne, 'Does God Act in the Physical World?', 72.
[68]Polkinghorne, 'Does God Act in the Physical World?', 72.
[69]Polkinghorne, 'Does God Act in the Physical World?', 72.

determination through thick and thin to be the gracious God of humanity even as that divine self-determination entails a *kenosis* of abstract divine perfections like the omniscience of the Boethian 'world contemplator'.

Polkinghorne concludes this contribution to our enquiry by laying out a weighty choice for the contemporary production of Christian doctrine. It is a choice between rival physics (roughly, between the expanding universe of the Big Bang and the steady-state theory of the cosmos) with corresponding rival theologies.[70] The latter is the Boethian God,

> composer of the whole cosmic score; the other is the Great Improviser of unsurpassed ingenuity (in Arthur Peacock's striking phrase) of cosmic performance. It is clear that the God of temporal process is the more vulnerable in relation to creation than is the atemporal God of classical theism. … In one group are atemporality, primary causality, divine impassibility, an inclination towards determinism, and an emphasis on divine control. In the other group are temporality, top-down causality, divine vulnerability, an inclination towards openness, and a recognition of creaturely self-making.[71]

The latter repudiates the 'Deistic Absentee Landlord, but it allows us to conceive of the Creator's continuing providential activity and costly loving care for creation'. It also allows us to conceive the causality of Luther's Christian prayer which changes the self even as according to God's goodwill it may change the course of natural and human historical events to anticipate the coming of the reign of God upon the earth.

We do not need process metaphysics as Polkinghorne seems to suggest, however, to embrace the deity of the God whose creative freedom is to love – even those lovelessly unworthy of love. All that is needed, as Polkinghorne in fact indicated, is the *homousios* of the Nicene Creed in which the uncreated Almighty Father, creator of heaven and earth, is identified as father to son with the creature born of Mary and crucified under Pilate. There is accordingly in the very eternal life of the triune God a dialectic of immutability and mutability ('God from God, light from light'), which many

---

[70]This is a major insight in John Hedley Brooke, *Science and Religion: Some Historical Perspectives* (Cambridge: Cambridge University Press, 1991). Historically the conflict is not between science and religion but between rival scientific theories and the cosmological or metaphysical implications attributed to them by equally rival theologies.

[71]Polkinghorne, 'Does God Act in the Physical World?', 74. See also Olli-Pekka Vainio, 'The Concept of God and the Demise of Mainline Protestantism', *Kerygma und Dogma* 64, no. 1 (2018): 68–78.

in contemporary theology are exploring, just as Luther first broke this new ground when he spoke of the 'strange and profound mystery of Israel'. Here, the creature fought the creator in the wrestling match of prayer and yet by grace prevailed. *Soli Deo gloria!*

CHAPTER TWENTY-TWO

Pour Out Your Hearts before God: John Calvin on Prayer

RANDALL C. ZACHMAN

Prayer occupies a central place in the theology of John Calvin, for Calvin sees prayer as the chief exercise of faith, and the central element in our worship of God. One might rightly say that the whole of Calvin's theology is constructed to remove every obstacle that could keep the pious from calling upon God. In order to understand the place of prayer in Calvin's theology, it is important to locate it in the context of his understanding of God, and of our redemption by Christ. According to Calvin, God is the author and fountain of every good thing, including the blessings of this life, and the good things that lead to eternal life. Humanity was given every good thing it needed for eternal life in Adam, but by his sin he lost all of those blessings both for himself and for all of his descendants, though many of the benefits of this life remain. God responded to this loss of every good thing in Adam by sending his only Son to become human, so that Christ might remove every evil thing we brought upon ourselves, especially sin, death and the curse of God, in order to restore every good thing we lack, especially righteousness, life and blessing. God offers us all of the blessings we need in the preaching of the Gospel, and when we receive the Gospel by faith through the Spirit, we are engrafted into Christ, so that every evil thing in us becomes his, and every good thing in him becomes ours. 'For in Christ he offers all happiness in place of our misery, all wealth in place of our neediness; in him he opens to us the heavenly treasures that our whole faith may contemplate his beloved Son, our whole expectation depend on him, and our whole hope cleave to and rest in him.'[1]

Prayer should be the immediate consequence of faith in Christ, for once we feel our own poverty and misery, and contemplate the fountain of every good thing that God has set forth in Christ, we are led to seek these good things in him by prayer, so that they may continually be given to us; and we are led to express our continual gratitude to God for so freely bestowing all of these good things upon us, knowing that we have done nothing to deserve them. Calvin thinks that this is why the apostle Paul links calling on God directly with faith, for only those who are certain of the goodness and mercy of God in Christ will dare to call upon God and seek to come into God's presence. 'On the other hand, we learn that the only true faith is that which brings forth prayer to God. It is impossible for a believer who has tasted the goodness of God ever to cease to aspire to that goodness in all his prayers.'[2] Thus the primary way the adoption of the children of God comes to expression is when the Spirit of adoption leads them to cry out, 'Abba! Father!' (Rom. 8.15). Hence, 'our faith can be proved only by calling upon God', since 'it is only when those who have embraced the promise of grace exercise themselves in prayers, that it is seen how serious is the faith of every believer'.[3] Calvin insists that the prayers of the pious must be bold and confident, since they are rooted in the faith that God in Christ is the author of every good thing we so desperately need. 'Thus there are three steps to be taken. First, we believe the promises of God; next, by resting in them, we conceive confidence, so that we may have a good and quiet mind. From this follows boldness, which enables us to banish fear, and to entrust ourselves courageously and steadfastly to God.'[4]

In what follows, we will first examine Calvin's criticism of the practice of prayer in the Church of Rome. We will then explore Calvin's definition of prayer as intimate conversation with God, including the role of language and gestures in prayer. We will then investigate the foundation of prayer in the personal experience of God, especially the experience of the nature of God. Finally, we will look at the way Calvin wants the faithful to respond

---

[1]Calvin, *Inst.*, 3.20.1. Citations of Calvin's biblical commentary are by book, chapter and verse. For the Psalms: *Commentary on the Book of Psalms*, trans. James Anderson, 5 vols. (Edinburgh: The Calvin Translation Society, 1844–56) – hereafter: CTS. For the New Testament: *Calvin's New Testament Commentaries*, ed. David W. Torrance and T. F. Torrance, 12 vols. (Grand Rapids, MI: William B. Eerdmans, 1959–72) – hereafter: CNTC.
[2]*Comm. Romans* 10.14; CNTC 8, 231.
[3]*Comm. Romans* 8.16; CNTC 8, 170.
[4]*Comm. Ephesians* 3.12; CNTC 11, 164.

in prayer either to abandonment by God, or to false accusations by others. The goal of the whole discussion is to show just how thoroughly Calvin attempted to remove all the obstacles that could prevent the godly from opening their hearts to God in prayer.

The Undermining of Prayer in the Roman Church

Calvin contrasts his understanding of the confidence and boldness of prayer with the teaching and practice of the Roman Church. On the one hand, the Roman Church undermines the practice of prayer by teaching that no one can be certain that God loves them. The faithful are to hope in the mercy of God, while avoiding the presumption of knowing that God loves them and the despair that God does not love them. They can only conjecture that they are in a state of grace by inferring this from the overall direction of their lives, by means of what the scholastics called 'moral conjecture', but no one can know with certainty that God loves her. This position was made the official dogma of the Roman Church at the Council of Trent, in its condemnation of 'the vain confidence of heretics'.

> For as no pious person ought to doubt the mercy of God, the merit of Christ and the virtue and efficacy of the sacraments, so each one, when he considers himself and his own weakness and indisposition, may have fear and apprehension concerning his own grace, since no one can know with the certainty of faith, which cannot be subject to error, that he has obtained the grace of God.[5]

According to Calvin, this teaching undermines the ability of the faithful to pray, for we must be certain that God loves us in Christ by the Spirit before we can ever approach God with the confidence of being heard. 'Confidence is necessary in true invocation, and thus becomes the key that opens to us the gate of the kingdom of heaven. Those who doubt and hesitate will never be heard, as James says (Jas 1.6-7). The Sophists of the Sorbonne, when they enjoin hesitation, do not know what it is to call on God.'[6]

On the other hand, the Church of Rome undermines true prayer by teaching the faithful to invoke the saints for their assistance. The intercession of the saints seems to be related to the lack of certainty regarding the love of

---

[5]*The Canons and Decrees of the Council of Trent*, trans. H. J. Schroeder (Rockford, IL: Tan Books, 1978), 35.
[6]*Comm. Ephesians* 3.16; CNTC 11, 165.

God, according to Calvin, for this uncertainty leads the members of the Roman Church to look for other forms of assistance besides God in Christ. 'But if we appeal to the consciences of all those who delight in the intercession of the saints, we shall find that this arises solely from the fact that they are burdened by anxiety, just as if Christ were insufficient or too severe.'[7] The confidence that the pious should have in God comes from their faith in Christ, in whom God reveals the fullness of God's goodness, which is made ours by the Holy Spirit. By seeking blessings and benefits from the saints, members of the Roman Church deny the fountain of every good thing that God set forth in Christ.

> Now Scripture recalls us from all to Christ alone, and our heavenly Father wills that all things be gathered together in him [Col. 1.20; Eph. 1.10]. Therefore, it was the height of stupidity, not to say madness, to be so intent on gaining access through the saints as to be led away from him, apart from whom no entry lies open to them.[8]

Since prayer is the primary way in which we worship God, to call on the saints is fundamentally to pervert the worship of God, akin to the way the Israelites called on other gods besides the Lord. 'Here is the sum total: Scripture, in the worship of God, sets the chief matter before us: how we should call upon him in prayer. Consequently, as he requires of us this duty of piety, holding all sacrifices secondary to it, to direct prayer to others involves manifest sacrilege.'[9] Given the necessary connection Calvin sees between faith and prayer, the fact that one would pray to saints instead of to God reveals that one does not in fact have faith in Christ, for Christ opens access to God for us, and intercedes for us. 'Further, it is obvious that this superstition has arisen from lack of faith. For either they were not content with Christ as pleader or they utterly deprived him of this credit.'[10]

Prayer as Intimate Conversation with God

Calvin, following the description of prayer given by Evagrius Ponticus, describes prayer as an 'intimate conversation' with God.[11] This intimacy explains why Calvin insists that we must be certain and confident that God

---

[7]*Inst.* 3.20.21.
[8]*Inst.* 3.20.21.
[9]*Inst.* 3.20.27.
[10]*Inst.* 3.20.27.
[11]*Inst.* 3.20.5. Evagrius, *De oratione* 3. The English translation of *De oratione* is taken from *Evagrius of Pontus: The Greek Ascetic Corpus*, trans. Robert E. Sinkewicz (Oxford: Oxford University Press, 2003), 183–209.

loves us and has adopted us as God's children, for otherwise we would never dare to approach God so openly and vulnerably. Engaging in this intimate conversation involves the pouring out of the mind to God, for 'true prayer ought to pour out before him the whole mind itself and whatever lies hidden within'.[12] However, the ultimate goal of this intimate conversation is to 'pour out our hearts before him [Ps. 62.8; cf. Ps. 145.19]'.[13] Hence, even though both mind and heart are engaged in this intimate conversation, Calvin states that 'prayer itself is properly an emotion of the heart within, which is poured out and laid open before God, the searcher of hearts [cf. Rom. 8.27]'.[14] Given this high degree of openness and vulnerability before God, it is no wonder that Jesus tells us to go into our bedroom so that we might pray to our Father in secret. 'For he did not mean to deny that it is fitting to pray in other places, but he shows that prayer is something secret, which is both principally lodged in the heart and requires a tranquility far from all our teeming cares.'[15] Given the secret nature of prayer, even when we pray in public, we should not seek after ostentation or recognition for our prayer, but rather make sure that 'there is present a sincere and true affection that dwells in the secret place of the heart'.[16] As a consequence, wherever we pray, we must not think that our prayers are dependent on the building or the location. 'For since we ourselves are God's true temples, if we would call on God in his holy temple, we must pray within ourselves.'[17]

Since prayer is properly an emotion of the heart within, and is therefore something secret, it is not surprising that Calvin claims that 'the best prayers are sometimes unspoken'.[18] There are times when the strength and vehemence of the emotions of the heart may break out of their secrecy, for 'it often happens in practice that, when feelings of the mind are aroused, unostentatiously the tongue breaks forth into speech, and the other members into gesture'.[19] However, the inward emotion of prayer should transcend the ability of either language or gestures to express it, for 'the mind ought to be kindled with an ardor of thought so as to surpass all that the tongue can express by speaking'.[20] Given the intensity of the emotion of the heart in prayer, Calvin acknowledges that the Spirit is needed to teach us to pray as we

---

[12]*Inst.* 3.20.44.
[13]*Inst.* 3.20.5.
[14]*Inst.* 3.20.29.
[15]*Inst.* 3.20.29.
[16]*Inst.* 3.20.30.
[17]*Inst.* 3.20.30.
[18]*Inst.* 3.20.33.
[19]*Inst.* 3.20.33.
[20]*Inst.* 3.20.33.

ought, as otherwise we would never know how to do so. Only the Spirit 'stirs up in our hearts the prayers which it is proper for us to address to God'.[21] This is not to say that prayer per se needs to be taught by the Spirit, for Calvin acknowledges that the heathen are led by 'a secret natural instinct' to call on God, especially in adversity. Indeed, he thinks that the prayers recorded in Psalm 107 all arise from this natural instinct, and that God in fact answered these prayers, even though those who called out did not thank God for answering them.[22] However, this invocation, prompted by a hidden instinct and the teaching of nature, differs considerably from the intimate conversation of the pious with God, which involves pouring out the inmost affection of the heart before God. 'Unbelievers do indeed blurt out their prayers, but they merely mock God, because there is no sincerity or seriousness in them, or correctly ordered pattern. The Spirit, therefore, must prescribe the manner of our praying.'[23] Such godly prayer would not be possible without faith in Christ, and without the Spirit opening our hearts to God. 'We are bidden to knock. But no one of his own accord could premeditate a single syllable, unless God were to knock to gain admission to our souls by the secret impulse of His Spirit, and thus open our hearts to Himself.'[24]

The Role of Language and Gestures in Prayer

Even though 'the tongue is not even necessary for private prayer', Calvin does acknowledge that both language and gestures can both express and strengthen the prayers of the faithful, by stimulating the affection of prayer more fully.[25] Calvin thinks of language as the image of the mind, and thus it should be used to express the inmost affection of our hearts. However, language can also be useful in stimulating our affections in prayer, so that we awaken a more profound longing for God in our hearts by the language we use, as well as by the language of prayer that we hear others use. 'I admit that the heart ought to move and direct the tongue in prayer, but, as it often flags or performs its duty in a slow and sluggish manner, it requires to be aided by the tongue.'[26] The same may be said even more of singing. As is well known, Calvin established the practice of singing the Psalms a cappella in

---

[21]*Comm. Romans* 8.26; CNTC 8, 178.
[22]*Comm. Psalm* 107.6; CTS 4, 249.
[23]*Comm. Romans* 8.26; CNTC 8, 178.
[24]*Comm. Romans* 8.26; CNTC 8, 178.
[25]*Inst.* 3.20.33.
[26]*Comm. Psalm* 102.1; CTS 4, 97–8.

the church. He agreed with Plato that music has the ability to stimulate the heart more than any other form of expression, and so it is especially useful in stimulating the emotions of prayer. 'And surely, if the singing be tempered to that gravity which is fitting in the sight of God and the angels, it lends dignity and grace to sacred actions and has the greatest value in kindling our hearts to a true zeal and eagerness to pray.'[27] Even though prayer as an emotion of the heart outstrips the ability of language to express it, this is not a problem, since God sees the emotion of the heart before it is ever expressed in language.[28]

Calvin also recommends the custom of kneeling when we pray, for in this way 'we rise to greater reverence for God'.[29] Moreover, when our bodies kneel, we both express and foster the humility that is a necessary part of prayer. Calvin did not think that kneeling was necessary, but he recommends it very highly. Calvin is more confident in his recommendation of lifting up our hands in prayer, since he takes it to be a symbol that is universally used in prayer, and hence of divine origin. 'Moreover, this custom has been practiced in worship in all ages, for it is natural for us to look upwards when we seek God.'[30] This gesture is very useful to stimulate our hearts to seek God in heaven, so that we let go of all carnal conceptions of God, and all earth-bound affections, so that our hearts may rise to God.[31] The combination of kneeling and lifting up our hands when we pray properly forms the affections of humility on the one hand, and confidence on the other, that are critical elements of prayer. 'But just as the lifting up of the hands is a symbol of confidence and longing, so in order to show our humility, we fall down on our knees.'[32]

Given the power of language and gesture to express and stimulate the affection of prayer, it is not surprising that Calvin advocates practising prayer both in private and in public. He claims that the one who does not pray in private and in secret does not know what it is to pray to God from the depths of the heart, whereas the one who only prays in private also does not know how to pray, for the proper use of the tongue lies in its use in the prayers of the congregation, 'by which it comes about that with one common voice, and as it were with the same mouth, we all glorify God together, worshipping him with one spirit and the same faith'.[33] However,

---

[27]*Inst.* 3.20.32.
[28]*Comm. Psalm* 139.4; CTS 5, 209.
[29]*Inst.* 3.20.33.
[30]*Comm. 1 Timothy* 2.8; CNTC 10, 214.
[31]*Comm. 1 Timothy* 2.8; CNTC 10, 214.
[32]*Comm. Acts* 20.36; CNTC 7, 190.
[33]*Inst.* 3.20.31.

as always, Calvin is deeply concerned with making sure that the language and the gestures of prayer always express the true emotions and affections of the heart, since that is the essence of prayer. 'From this, moreover, it is fully evident that unless voice and song, if interposed in prayer, spring from deep feeling of heart, neither has any value or profit in the least with God.'[34] The nature of genuine prayer means that it only arises from 'a sincere and true affection that dwells in the secret place of the heart'.[35] Calvin takes this to be the meaning of Christ's injunction to enter the inner chamber, shut the door and pray to God in secret (Mt. 6.5). Christ said this not to prohibit public prayers, but to make it clear that all prayer comes from the secret affection of the heart, and therefore to remind us that God sees the secrets of the heart even when they are not expressed in language, song or gesture. 'This is the sum of it: whether one is alone or in company at prayer the attitude to adopt is to think of God as one's witness, as though shut off in an inside room.'[36] Nor are we to think we are heard by using a multitude of words, no matter how eloquent such language may be, for 'the longings which the devout heart sends out like arrowshots are those that reach to heaven'.[37]

The Knowledge of God from Personal Experience

According to Calvin, the primary purpose of prayer is to transition from knowing of the goodness of God from the promises of God in the Gospel, to experiencing the goodness of God in our lives. 'For there is a communion of men with God by which, having entered the heavenly sanctuary, they appeal to him in person concerning his promises in order to experience, where necessity so demands, that what they believed was not in vain, although he had promised it in word alone.'[38] Calvin therefore distinguishes between the knowledge of God from the promise of God and the knowledge of God from experience. 'We must observe the distinction between the theoretical knowledge derived from the Word of God and what is called the experimental knowledge of his grace. For as God shows himself present in operation, (as they usually speak,) he must first be sought in his Word.'[39] This is what Calvin means when he says that by our prayer 'we call him to

---

[34]*Inst.* 3.20.31.
[35]*Inst.* 3.20.30.
[36]*Comm. Matthew* 6.5; CNTC 1, 203.
[37]*Comm. Matthew* 6.7; CNTC 1, 203.
[38]*Inst.* 3.20.2.
[39]*Comm. Psalm* 27.9; CTS 1, 459.

reveal himself as wholly present to us'.[40] In other words, it is not enough
for faith to trust in the word and promise of God. In order to know that
the promise is true, we must experience in our lives the blessings that God
promises in the word, so that we know that the word of God is true. 'As long
as we have only the bare promises of God, his grace and salvation are as yet
hidden in hope; but when these promises are actually performed, his grace
and salvation are clearly manifested.'[41] Calvin sees this dynamic from word
to experience in the prayers of David. David assures God that he has trusted
in God's promises of mercy, and experienced joy thereby. 'But as all our
hope would end in mere disappointment, did not God at length appear as
our deliverer, he requests the performance of that which God had promised
him. Lord, as if he had said, since thou hast graciously promised to be ready
to succor me, be pleased to make good thy word in effect.'[42] The classic
example of this movement from promise to experience is the exodus of the
descendants of Sarah and Abraham from Egypt, for God revealed by deeds
that God was the king and protector of Israel.[43]

The pious therefore seek to know God both from the word and from the
experience of God's goodness in their lives, for 'we nevertheless behold the
image of God not only in the glass of the gospel, but also in the numerous
evidences of his grace which he daily exhibits to us'.[44] These benefits include
the earthly benefits we enjoy in this life, as well as the spiritual benefits
we need to enjoy eternal life, according to the words of the apostle Paul.
'"Godliness is profitable unto all things, having promise of the life that now
is, and of that which is to come" (1 Tim. 4.8). The sum is that those who
truly serve God are not only blessed as to spiritual things, but are also blessed
by him as to their condition in the present life.'[45] The experience of the
temporal and spiritual blessings of God is directly related to prayer, for our
experience of grace gives us the confidence to come into the presence of
God in the intimate conversation of prayer. 'Again, we may hence draw
the general truth, that it is only through the goodness of God that we have
access to him; and that no man prays aright but he who, having experienced
his grace, believes and is fully persuaded that he will be merciful to him.'[46]
The Holy Spirit encourages the faithful to remember these incidents of
divine favour to strengthen their confidence in prayer. 'Nothing animates

---

[40]*Inst.* 3.20.2.
[41]*Comm. Psalm* 48.8; CTS 2, 225.
[42]*Comm. Psalm* 119.76; CTS 4, 457.
[43]*Comm. Psalm* 74.2; CTS 3, 162.
[44]*Comm. Psalm* 17.15; CTS 1, 256.
[45]*Comm. Psalm* 25.13; CTS 1, 428.
[46]*Comm. Psalm* 5.7; CTS 1, 58.

our hopes more than the recollection of the past goodness of God, and, in the midst of his prayers, we frequently find David indulging in reflections of this kind.'[47] Moreover, the experience of the goodness of God will draw our hearts more deeply to God, as God's goodness allures our hearts towards God. 'Prayer, indeed, springs from faith; but as practical proofs of the favor and mercy confirm this faith, they are means evidently fitted for dissipating languor.'[48] Moreover, our experience of the benefits of God in the past will increase our confidence that God will continue to bless us in the future, for according to Calvin God always remains like God's self.[49]

Experiencing the Nature of God

The knowledge of God from experience leads the pious to experience the nature of God for themselves. This is possible because the nature of God is revealed in the powers or perfections of God that are portrayed in God's works, such as mercy, power, goodness, righteousness and wisdom. 'To whatever subjects men apply their minds, there is none from which they will derive greater advantage than from continual meditation on his wisdom, goodness, righteousness, and mercy; and especially the knowledge of his goodness is fitted both to build up our faith, and to illustrate his praises.'[50] Our experience of these powers of God in the works that God performs in our lives gives us living and personal experience of the nature of God. Without such experience of God's nature, Calvin finds it very hard to believe that the godly could approach God in the intimate conversation of prayer, in which they open and pour out their hearts to God.

> Let us learn from the Prophet's example to acquaint ourselves with the nature of God, from the various experiences we have had of it that we may have certain evidence that he is merciful to us. And, in truth, were not his grace known to us from the daily experience we have of it, which of us would dare to approach him?[51]

One of the most important aspects of the nature of God is that it is essential to the goodness of God to hear prayer. Hence God can no more ignore our prayers than deny God's nature, and this gives us the confidence to pour out

---

[47]*Comm. Psalm* 61.3; CTS 2, 412.
[48]*Comm. Psalm* 143.6; CTS 5, 253.
[49]*Comm. Psalm* 59.10; CTS 2, 389.
[50]*Comm. Psalm* 103.8; CTS 4, 132.
[51]*Comm. Psalm* 119.132; CTS 5, 13.

our hearts before God, even when we do not seem to be heard by God. Hence, when the prophet describes God as the one who hears prayer, Calvin says:

> The title here given to God carries with it a truth of great importance, That the answer of our prayers is secured by the fact, that in rejecting them he would in a certain sense deny his own nature. The Psalmist does not say, that God has heard prayer in this or that instance, but gives him the name of the hearer of prayer, as what constitutes an abiding part of his glory, so that he might as soon deny himself as shut his ear to our petitions.[52]

The willingness of God to hear prayer is rooted in God's nature, as is the mercy of God. It is no more possible for God not to be merciful than it is for God to deny God's self. 'The goodness of God is so inseparably connected with his essence as to render it impossible for him not to be merciful'.[53] Even the promise of God's mercy in the Gospel is not founded on an arbitrary or reversible decision on God's part, but is rather an expression of the essential nature of God.

> If we imagine that God makes his promises because he is bound to do it, or because we have deserved it, doubting or mistrust will steal upon our minds, which will shut the gate against our prayers. But if we are thoroughly persuaded that the sole cause by which God is moved to promise us salvation is the mercy inherent in his own nature, we will approach him without hesitation or doubt, because he has bound himself to us of his own accord.[54]

This is why the covenant that God makes with Israel abides to this very day, as it is rooted in the goodness of God's nature, and hence cannot be annulled by any sin on the part of Israel. 'When the Jews, by their ingratitude and treachery, revolted from him, the covenant was not disannulled, because it was founded upon the perfect immutability of his nature. And still, at the present day, when our sins mount even to the heavens, the goodness of God fails not to rise above them, since it is far above the heavens.'[55] The personal experience of God's nature gives confidence to the pious to open their hearts to God, as they know that God will hear their prayer, and receive them with

---

[52]*Comm. Psalm* 65.1; CTS 2, 452.
[53]*Comm. Psalm* 77.19; CTS 3, 213.
[54]*Comm. Psalm* 119.56, CTS 5, 33.
[55]*Comm. Psalm* 89.34; CTS 3, 444.

mercy and love, because all of these qualities are rooted in the eternal and unchanging nature of God.

Calling on God when God Abandons Us

The personal experience of the nature of God is especially helpful in those times when God seems to ignore the prayers of the pious, and even seems to abandon them. If we are not familiar with the nature of God, which lies behind the promises and covenants of God, then we will think that when God abandons us, we should cease calling out to God from the depths of our hearts. But if we know the nature of God, we will learn that the best season of prayer is when we are in the depths of our affliction at the hands of God. 'In affliction, however our faith is more severely tried, and there is a propriety in specifying it as the season of prayer; the prophet pointing us to God as the only resort and means of safety in the day of our urgent necessity.'[56] This is especially difficult, because God really does appear to all intents and purposes to have abandoned the pious, either individually or corporately (as when Israel was tormented by Antiochus IV Epiphanes), and seems deaf to their cries, even those that spring from the inmost affection of the heart. The pious are often plunged into 'the deep and distressing darkness which is in the world, when God keeps silence, and hides his face. In the midst of those afflictions which he has recounted, the Psalmist might seem to be plunged in darkness from which he would never obtain deliverance.'[57] At such times even the promise of God and the past experience of the benefits of God are not enough to convince us that God has not in fact abandoned us. In fact, the remembrance of the promise and the past benefits might rather be oppressive to us, for they stand in stark contrast to our present experience of abandonment. There is no other recourse to be had, according to Calvin, than to remember the nature of God, which teaches us that God cannot really abandon us without ceasing to be God. We learn this from the voice of the prophets in the Psalms. 'This, then, is the prayer of an afflicted man, who, when apparently destitute of all help, and unable to come to any other conclusion than that he is neglected and forsaken of God, yet reflects with himself, that, for God to forsake him, was foreign to his nature and to his usual manner of procedure.'[58]

Our confidence that God's goodness and mercy are rooted in the eternal nature of God makes it possible for us to open our hearts to God, and to pour

---

[56]*Comm. Psalm* 50.15; CTS 2, 272.
[57]*Comm. Psalm* 17.15; CTS 1, 253.
[58]*Comm. Psalm* 119.132; CTS 5, 12.

out our hearts before God, to let God know of our suffering and affliction. By so doing, we hand the insufferable burden of our affliction over to God, as this is the only way we can be freed of our suffering. 'It should always be observed, that the use of praying is, that God may be the witness of all our affections; not that they would otherwise be hidden from him, but when we pour out our hearts before him, our cares are hereby greatly lightened, and our confidence of obtaining our requests increases.'[59] Prayer is all the more necessary given our innate propensity to close in on ourselves in times of affliction and grief, which leads us to ruminate on and feed on our affliction, which only increases our suffering and reinforces our despair.

> Not to insist farther upon the words, David is here to be considered as exposing that diseased but deeply-rooted principle in our nature, which leads us to hide our griefs, and ruminate upon them, instead of relieving ourselves at once by pouring out our prayers and complaints before God. The consequence is, that we are distracted more and more with our distresses, and merge into a state of hopeless despondency.[60]

Only by opening the affections of my heart to God in prayer can I free myself from this self-enclosed despair, and let go of the suffering that afflicts me. 'And as we are all too apt at such times to shut up our affliction in our own breast – a circumstance which can only aggravate the trouble and embitter the mind against God, David could not have suggested a better expedient than that of disburdening our cares to him, and thus, as it were, *pouring out our hearts before him*.'[61]

Calling on God when Wrongfully Accused by Others

Aside from being abandoned by God, Calvin thinks that one of the most painful experiences of the godly is when they are falsely accused of wrongdoing, even though they know they are innocent. Yet far from being a rare event, Calvin thinks that this kind of affliction is quite common in the lives of the pious. 'For while nothing is more painful to us than to be falsely condemned, and to endure, at one and the same time, wrongful violence and slander; yet to be ill spoken of for doing well, is an affliction which daily

---

[59]*Comm. Psalm* 10; CTS 1, 150.
[60]*Comm. Psalm* 62.7; CTS 2, 425.
[61]*Comm. Psalm* 62.7; CTS 2, 425.

befalls the saints.'[62] Calvin knows from his own experience that this is one of the most painful afflictions that a human being can experience. 'David, as is well known, encountered no heavier trial than the false and calumnious charges which were levelled against him by his enemies.'[63] Calvin agrees with the classical authors that the testimony of a good conscience is a necessary refuge when we are falsely accused, for we have the witness within ourselves that we are innocent of the charges being made against us. However, Calvin claims that the testimony of a good conscience is not enough, for the only way we can be sustained through the trial of false accusation is if we make our appeal to God in prayer. 'Although, therefore, we may have the testimony of an approving conscience, and although He may be the best witness of our innocence, yet if we are desirous of obtaining his assistance, it is necessary for us to commit our hopes and anxieties to him.'[64]

Our appeal to God in prayer, over and above the testimony of a good conscience, is necessary so that we do not succumb to the desire to retaliate against those who are falsely accusing us. This presents all the pious with a very difficult struggle, for there is no one who is free of the intense desire to retaliate against those who are falsely accusing us. Our only defence is to betake ourselves to God in prayer, so that we do not succumb to the almost overwhelming temptation to retaliate against those who are falsely accusing us. Calvin tells those being falsely accused to remain silent before their accusers, in order to direct their appeal directly to God in prayer, following the example of David.

> When the wicked directed against him their witty and scoffing remarks, as if engines of war, to overthrow his faith, the means to which he had recourse for repelling all their assaults was pouring out his heart in prayer to God. He was constrained to keep silence before men, and, being thus driven out from the world, he betook himself to God.[65]

Only by making our appeal directly to God can we be freed of the deep-seated desire to retaliate against our enemies, which Calvin describes as 'howling with the wolves'. 'The depraved desire of our fallen nature incites us to retaliate, nor do we see any way of preserving our life, unless we employ the same arts by which they assail us; and we persuade ourselves that it is lawful for us to howl among wolves.'[66]

---

[62]*Comm. Psalm* 4.1; CTS 1, 38.
[63]*Comm. Psalm* 57.4; CTS 2, 364.
[64]*Comm. Psalm* 86.2; CTS 3, 382.
[65]*Comm. Psalm* 69.13; CTS 3, 60.
[66]*Comm. Psalm* 119.110; CTS 4, 484.

Conclusion

Prayer is the only refuge of the pious, not only when God appears to be against them and no longer hears their cries, but also when other human beings falsely accuse them and seem to profit from their lies about them. In both instances, Calvin advises the godly to pour out their hearts before God, so that God can witness their affliction, in the confidence that God cannot deny God's self, and so will certainly reveal God's love and mercy once again to those who appear to be abandoned and forsaken by God.

CHAPTER TWENTY-THREE

The Spanish School of Prayer

PETER TYLER

Early sixteenth-century Spain witnessed a unique moment in the development of the Christian tradition of prayer. Spain itself, after the political and strategic union of the two crowns of Aragon and Castile under Ferdinand and Isabella and the conquest of the kingdom of Granada in 1492, was seeking at this moment to find a voice for a new unified form of Christian expression. Under the reforming Cardinal Francisco Jiménez de Cisneros, himself a Franciscan friar, the tools were found for the construction of this new language of prayer which developed several key strands of the preceding later medieval tradition previously discussed in this volume. The imposition of the ideals of reform by Cardinal Cisneros upon the Spanish hierarchy in 1494 was to lay the foundations for the great flowering of the Spanish mystical tradition in the sixteenth century. These reforming ideals, said to be attached to the 'observants', included living simple rules (often returning to 'primitive rules'), concentration on the prayer of the heart and a life of devotion and humility and were especially prevalent within the Franciscan, Dominican, Augustinian, Benedictine and Jeronomite Religious Orders.

Melquíades Andrés Martín in his monumental study of '*la mistica española*' between 1500 and 1700 stresses the continuity within the Spanish contemplative (or as he preferences it 'mystical') tradition throughout the sixteenth and seventeenth centuries placing its origins in the reform movements at the end of the fifteenth century, especially the tension between *conventualismo* and *observantismo* within the Spanish Catholic

Religious Orders.[1] These movements were often contradictory and unclear, as Andrés Martín notes:

> This reform movement oscillated between the study of theology, revivified by the Dominicans, and a certain anti-intellectualism, which would initially invoke a certain anti-verbosity, within the Franciscans and Augustinians, and much later affective prayer (*oración afectiva*) which placed more value on experience and love over study and intellect.[2]

He distinguishes several defining characteristics of this 'observant' movement such as an emphasis on biblical exegesis, a growing inclination to interiority, methodical ascetic exercises for the cultivation of virtue and the overcoming of vice, a love of manual work – in contrast to the often-cultured despising of this type of work, a tendency to talk about exceptional and revelatory acts – locutions, visions, etc., and a love of solitude and the eremetical life.[3]

Of particular importance to this nascent movement at the beginning of the sixteenth century were the reforms initiated within the Franciscan movement. To aid their reform Cardinal Cisneros permitted the publication in the vernacular of numerous late medieval books of what we would today call 'spirituality' including many of those representing the medieval tradition of *theologia mystica*.[4] These books began with the Seville edition of the *Obras de Bonaventura* of 1497 followed by the *Incendium Amoris* and *Liber meditationum* from the presses of the Abbey of Montserrat in Catalonia. Subsequently we find editions of Augustine, Bernard and Richard of St Victor rapidly being produced. This 'first wave' of outstanding spiritual literature was completed by the publication of the *Exercitatorio de la Vida Espiritual* ('Spiritual Exercises') of Abbot García Jiménez de Cisneros (cousin to the reforming cardinal) – which was to have such an impact on the young Ignatius Loyola – and the *Viae Lugent Sion* of Hugh of Balma published in Toledo in 1514 as the *Sol de Contemplativos* – later widely disseminated and quoted within the Spanish mystical tradition.

---

[1]Melquíades Andrés Martín, *Los Recogidos: Nueva Visión de la Mística Española, 1500–1700* (Madrid: Fundación Universitaria Española, 1975).

[2]Martín, *Los Recogidos*, 2.

[3]Martín, *Los Recogidos*, 22–3.

[4]For a fuller exegesis of the mediaeval *theologia mystica* and its Dionysian roots, see Peter Tyler, *The Return to the Mystical: Ludwig Wittgenstein, Teresa of Avila and the Christian Mystical Tradition* (London: Continuum, 2011).

Most scholars of the period, including most recently Bernard McGinn in his *Mysticism in the Golden Age of Spain*, stress the importance to this reform movement of a type of prayer known in Spanish as *recogimiento* which we can translate as 'recollection'.[5]

What is *recogimiento?* Although it is such a key prayer practice for the period, it is often not so easy to define. In contemporary terms, it could be compared to the current obsession with 'mindfulness' – a useful word that can mean everything or nothing depending upon who is using it and in which context.[6] McGinn defines 'recollection' in general terms as 'a spiritual way of life based on withdrawal, interiorization, and silence' and in a narrow sense as 'a method of interior mystical prayer at the center of such a way of life'.[7] However, Andrés Martín calls it 'the meditation that seeks love and knowledge of God through the will called the "affective prayer" (*oración afectiva*)'.[8] This, as we shall see, traces its origins to the late medieval traditions of affective Dionysianism which will find their way to Spain via works such as the 'Mountain of Contemplation' of Jean Gerson and the aforesaid-mentioned *Viae Lugent Sion* of Hugh of Balma. As Andrés Martín puts it, these works delineate 'an action characteristic of the will in order to know God when the action of the intellect is suspended'.[9] Such a process is cited in Mombaer's *Rosetum* of 1494 where it is called *meditación afectiva*,[10] and similar descriptions of this *meditación afectiva* are found in the works of Juan Wessel Gansfort (*Escala Meditatoria*, 1483), Gómez García (*Carro de dos Vidas*, 1500) and García de Cisneros (*Exercitatorio de la Vida Espiritual*, 1500) which would be later taken up by Alonso de Madrid (*Arte de Servir Dios*, 1521), Francisco de Osuna (*Tercer Abecedario*, 1527), Bernabé de Palma (*Via Spiritus*, 1531) and Bernardino de Laredo (*Subida de Monte Sion*, 1535). This is what is often referred to by later commentators such as Andrés Martín and McGinn as the prayer of '*recogimiento*'. However this catch-all term may not do justice to the range and varieties of understanding that lie within the practice; accordingly before we proceed it may be worthwhile dissecting the term a little more.

---

[5]Bernard McGinn, *Mysticism in the Golden Age of Spain, 1500–1650* (New York: Crossroad, 2017).

[6]For more on this perilous topic, see Peter Tyler, *Christian Mindfulness: Theology and Practice* (London: SCM Press, 2018).

[7]McGinn, *Mysticism in the Golden Age of Spain*, 24.

[8]Martín, *Los Recogidos*, 27.

[9]Martín, *Los Recogidos*, 27.

[10]Mombaer, *Rosario de Ejercicios Espirituales y de santas meditaciones.*

The Range of *Recogimiento*

For Andrés Martín the ultimate goal of *recogimiento* is 'to construe the interior person based on the essence of their centre and the simplicity of what it is to be a human being',[11] being epitomized in the last chapter of Hugh of Balma's *Sol de Contemplativos* where it is characterized as 'this act of love in the affective or superior part of our souls, without the intervention of the understanding'.[12] Or, as he sums it up later in *La Teología Española*, recollection is a 'methodical spirituality, or prayer, or art of love. It requires, then, labour and technique. It is a complete life treating of the lifting up of a person from the depths of sin to the sublimity of mysticism'.[13] In recent writing I have suggested that the term *recogimiento* needs to be refined if we are to make sense of its uses in Spain at this time. Accordingly, I would like to suggest here that the term can be seen to refer to three separate, if overlapping, phenomena.

First, we have 'recollection'/*recogimiento* as a catch-all term for a wider reform movement within religious life and Catholic Christian life in general that arises in the late medieval/early modern Iberian context. This reform movement, in common with similar reform movements in Northern Europe, seeks to revitalize the springs of faith so that the individual seeker is revivified in their faith journey. This is related to wider reform movements sweeping Europe throughout the sixteenth century.

The second aspect of recollection emphasizes a movement from a more speculative or 'head-centred' theological approach in the seeker to something connected with 'the heart', emotions and religious feeling. This is an approach that draws heavily on the affective Dionysianism of the late medieval *theologia mystica* already mentioned.

Finally, we have recollection as a distinct spiritual practice prescribed in a certain way to the seeker. These practices of 'recollection' will include, for example, withdrawal from daily life for discrete periods of prayer that will involve separation from normal activities and observation of mental processes – something, perhaps, not too distant from what is called today 'mindfulness' or 'meditation' practices.

Before we turn to the advocates of these forms of 'recollection' let us consider the key characteristics of each in turn.

---

[11] Martín, *Los Recogidos*, 15.
[12] Martín, *Los Recogidos*, 20.
[13] Andrés Martín, *La teología española en el siglo XVI*, vol. 2 (Madrid: Biblioteca de Autores Cristianos, 1976), 202.

General Recollection

In Chapter Fifteen of his *Third Spiritual Alphabet*, the Franciscan friar and writer, Francisco de Osuna, who was to have such an impact on the thought of Teresa of Avila, makes a distinction between what he calls 'special recollection' (*recogimiento especial*) and 'general recollection' (*recogimiento general*).[14] By the latter he intends to describe 'our way of going continuously alert with our hearts pacified and sealed, caring not for human things'. This, he states, will require a 'spiritual emptying whereby we realize that the heart has no other task than to approach God'. It is a '*sosegada*'[15] which even if engaged in manual work we can practise.[16] In Chapter Fifteen he gives rules for this general recollection such as keeping 'custody of the eyes', to reduce attachment to physical needs such as food,[17] to avoid perfumes and delicate fragrances and to prefer cold foods to hot.[18]

Of the three usages of *recogimiento* which we are discussing here this is the widest and most diffuse, reflecting the general concerns of the reforms of the *observantismo* at the beginning of the sixteenth century, and, as commentators such as Diarmaid MacCulloch have pointed out, also, ironically, reflecting the wider concerns of Northern European Protestant reformers.[19]

Recollection as Affective Prayer

From the publication of Francisco de Osuna's *Third Alphabet* in 1527 to the Valdés Index of 1559 the period of 1527–59 was decisive in allowing the practice and language of *recogimiento* to penetrate both the convents and the wider public of the Iberian peninsular.[20] The popularity of Osuna's

---

[14]Francisco De Osuna, *Tercer Abecedario Espiritual de Francisco de Osuna*, ed. S. López Santidrián (Madrid: Biblioteca de Autores Cristianos, 1998), 387. Throughout this chapter I have used two versions of the *Third Spiritual Alphabet*: the 1998 Spanish edition: *Tercer Abecedario Espiritual de Francisco de Osuna*, ed. S. López Santidrián (Madrid: Biblioteca de Autores Cristianos, 1998) and the 1981 English translation: *Francisco de Osuna: The Third Spiritual Alphabet*, trans. Mary A. Giles, CWS (New York: Paulist Press, 1981).

[15]Osuna, *Tercer Abecedario Espiritual*, 400. Again, another key term of the Spanish mystics, much beloved by John of the Cross and Teresa alike: 'tranquility', 'peace', 'serenity' and 'calm' could all be worthy translations. See Peter Tyler, *Teresa of Avila: Doctor of the Soul* (London: Bloomsbury, 2013).

[16]Osuna, *The Third Spiritual Alphabet*, 387.

[17]Osuna, *The Third Spiritual Alphabet*, 390, 392.

[18]Osuna, *The Third Spiritual Alphabet*, 393.

[19]Diarmaid MacCulloch, *Reformation: Europe's House Divided, 1490–1700* (London: Penguin Books, 2004).

[20]See Martín, *Los Recogidos*, 48.

Alphabet would be central to this spread which would have such an impact on later writers such as the young Teresa de Cepeda y Ahumada (Teresa of Avila). In his text Osuna is careful to relate his system to the Dionysian corpus and its interpretation, especially through the Victorines (in particular Richard of St Victor) and Jean Gerson, as well as the writings of Gregory Nazianzan, Bernard and Bonaventure. Of these he continually refers back to the Dionysian corpus:

> That you may not be able to understand Saint Dionysius does not mean he cannot be understood at all, for Gerson and many other holy theologians have comprehended him and offered advice and caution us against the wiles of the devil.[21]

The movement of *recogimiento* thus places the heart and the *oración afectiva* at the centre of its concerns – an *oración*, I have argued elsewhere, that is directly formed from the late medieval schools of affective Dionysianism.[22] Following this Dionysian programme *recogmiento* can thus, according to Andrés Martín, be seen primarily as a way of *contemplativa afectiva* centred on love *sin pensar nada* ('without thinking of anything') without any necessary prevenient or concomitant understanding.

In this respect Osuna follows Gerson in Chapter Six of the *Alphabet* (in which he introduces *recogimiento* with the phrase: '*frecuenta el recogimiento por ensayarte en su uso*') where he states that there are two types of theology: the 'speculative' and the 'mystical'.

> This [theology] has two forms: one is called 'speculative' or 'investigative', which is the same thing, the other is called 'hidden', which is treated of here and which gives the title to this Third Alphabet. I do not presume to teach it here, as no mortal can, for Christ alone reserves this teaching only for himself, in secret and in the hearts in which this hidden theology dwells as divine science and something much more excellent than the other theology of which I spoke first. ... This theology [the mystical theology] is said to be more perfect and better than the first, so says Gerson, as the first serves as an introduction leading to the second.[23]

---

[21]Osuna, *The Third Spiritual Alphabet*, 563.
[22]See Peter Tyler, 'Mystical Affinities: St Teresa and Jean Gerson', in *Teresa of Avila: Mystical Theology and Spirituality in the Carmelite Tradition*, ed. Edward Howells and Peter Tyler (London: Routledge, 2017), 36–51.
[23]Osuna, *Tercer Abecedario Espiritual*, 199–200; author's translation.

By engaging in the 'mystical theology' (that is *recogimiento*) we are thus opening ourselves up to the 'hidden teaching' which will come from Christ's love. *Recogimiento* is thus for Osuna the latest manifestation of the 'mystical theology' of Dionysius, albeit now clothed in the affective dress of sixteenth-century Spanish contemplative practice: 'Some call it [*recogimiento*] "*teología mística*", with which they mean to say "hidden", because the good master Jesus teaches it in the secret hiddeness of the heart.'[24] Central to Osuna's description of *recogimiento* in passages such as this is the importance he attaches to 'tasting' God rather than speculating about him. In his words, the 'mystical theology', and by extension *recogimiento*, is a *sabroso saber* – literally, a 'tasty knowledge'. As he puts it in Chapter Twelve of the *Alphabet*: 'Not by understanding much, but more by tasting, think to attain rest'.[25]

> Even though the understanding may discover and analyse numerous sublime matters there is good reason for you to believe that complete, fulfilling repose is not to be found through functions of the intellect (*por la operación intelectiva*) and that ultimately the least part of what we do not know exceeds everything we do know.[26]

Quoting Gregory, Bernard and Richard of St Victor, Osuna finds this 'way of love' through the 'tasting of the divine goodness':

> No-one is to think that he loves God if he does not wish to taste him, for the fruit of love is the enjoyment of what is loved, and the more it is loved, the more it is enjoyed (*porque el fruto del amor es el gusto de lo que es amado, y mientras más se ama, mejor se gusta*). Accordingly, Richard says about joyful love: 'Love is a sweetness of intimate flavour, and the more ardently one loves, the more sweetly it tastes; and love is the enjoyment of hope' ('*el amor es una dulcedumbre de sabor íntimo, y cuanto con más ardor ama, tanto más suavemente gusta, y el amor es gozo de la esperanza*').[27]

---

[24]Osuna, *Tercer Abecedario Espiritual*, 203; author's translation.

[25]Osuna, *Tercer Abecedario Espiritual*, 337; author's translation.

[26]Osuna, *The Third Spiritual Alphabet*, 316.

[27]Osuna, *The Third Spiritual Alphabet*, 329 and Osuna, *Tercer Abecedario Espiritual*, 348. As we find later in the writings of Teresa of Avila (possibly derived from her reading of Osuna) 'gusto' is a pivotal word in these passages. Variously translated as 'taste', 'enjoy' and 'console', there is a great ambiguity in its use by both authors which enables them to channel the similar ambiguity in the original Dionysian texts.

As McGinn also recognizes, Osuna's *recogimiento* 'has notes of transformation and erotic ecstasy'.[28] A note which will become a symphony in the later writings of Teresa of Avila and John of the Cross and in this respect Osuna is surely following his master, Dionysius, in restoring the *eros* at the heart of the search in prayer for mystical union with the Divine.

Special Recollection

The actual prayer practice associated with the movement is harder to describe, and, according to Andrés Martín, we cannot be sure about the exact date of the origins of it. We can say with certainty that a form of prayer entitled '*recogimiento*' was being practised by groups of Franciscans at the beginning of the sixteenth century. When Osuna talks of the prayer in 1527 in his *Third Spiritual Alphabet*, he says that he has met older folk who have been practising it 'for more than fifty years'.[29] This would mean that the prayer had been practised from at least 1475. Andrés Martín preferences the Franciscan hermitages of La Salceda (and possibly earlier in San Pedro de Arlanza), associated in particular with the reforms of Pedro de Villacreces, as the place of origin for the movement.[30] Both Cardinal Cisneros and Francisco de Quiñones (later General of the Order) would be custodians of the shrine of La Salceda, signifying its importance for the possible spread of *recogimiento*. Whatever its origins, it was in these Franciscan *conventos* and hermitages, what became known as *casas de recolección*, that it became widely practised at the turn of the fifteenth and sixteenth centuries.[31] Eventually the practitioners of *recogimiento* would 'form a circle at the heart of Spain': La Salceda, El Castañar, Cifuentes, Torrelaguna, Escalona, Alcalá, Ocaña, Toledo, Oropesa and the *Descalzas Reales* of Madrid, as well as neighbouring groups of practitioners in Andalusia, Extremadura and Catalonia/Valencia.[32]

---

[28]McGinn, *Mysticism in the Golden Age of Spain*, 45.

[29]Osuna, *Tercer Abecedario Espiritual*, 556; author's translation.

[30]See Martín, *Los Recogidos*, 44. On Salceda and its connections to the *alumbrados*, see Antonio Márquez, *Los Alumbrados: Orígenes y Filosofía* (Madrid: Taurus, 1980), 109. The *alumbrados* were practitioners of a form of prayer that we would nowadays probably call 'charismatic' or 'penetcostal'. For more on their origins and influence, see Peter Tyler, 'Alumbrados', in *The New SCM Dictionary of Christian Spirituality*, ed. Philip Sheldrake (London: SCM Press, 2005), 626–7.

[31]For more on these connections, see William J. Short, 'From Contemplation to Inquisition: The Franciscan Practice of Recollection in Sixteenth-Century Spain', in *Franciscans at Prayer*, ed. Timothy Johnson (Leiden: Brill, 2007), 449–74.

[32]Martín, *Los Recogidos*, 46.

These '*casas de recolección*' were nurtured by small groups of reforming Franciscans keen to initiate both religious and lay people alike into the practice. Osuna, in his *Third Spiritual Alphabet*, emphasizes that the book is 'to inform everyone about this exercise of recollection ... to teach all people how to approach our universal Lord who wishes to be served and loved by all'.[33] Thus in common with other proponents of the practice, Osuna is keen to establish his argument that recollection is for all, even those 'given over to carnal delights and entangled in worldly affairs'.[34] Here Osuna reflects the writings of García Jiménez de Cisneros, Abbot of Montserrat (by command of the Catholic Monarchs) from 1493 to 1510 in whose writings we find the first written definition of the 'prayer of recollection':

Recollect yourself often from low things to high, from temporal to eternal, from exterior to interior, from vain things to those that endure.[35]

Like Osuna, the good Abbot wants this form of prayer to be available to all, in many respects anticipating by several decades the later demands of the Northern Protestant reformers for a more 'democratic' approach to spirituality. As he stresses in Chapter Thirty-Two of his *Spiritual Exercises*:

Thus we have seen that just because a person is simple it doesn't mean that the contemplative life is forbidden to them; for, we have seen, and still do see by experience, devout hermits, and some women draw more profit from this contemplative life and grow to love God more deeply than many important clergy and learned religious folk (*grandes clérigos y religiosos letrados*).[36]

In this respect I do not think it is insignificant that the young knight Inigo de Loyola – the later St Ignatius of Loyola – would read this very work when he stayed in the environs of the Abbey of Montserrat after his conversion following the Battle of Pamplona in 1522. We shall discuss Ignatius' putative debt to this tradition later in the chapter.

---

[33]Osuna, *Tercer Abecedario Espiritual*, 241; author's translation.
[34]Osuna, *The Third Spiritual Alphabet*, 208.
[35]Garcià de Cisneros, *Obras Completas*, ed. Cipriano Baraut (Montserrat: Abbey Presses, 1965), 452; author's translation. I will be using the 1965 bilingual Latin/Catalan version of the *Exercises* edited by Cipriano Baraut.
[36]Cicernos, *Obras Completas*, 278. I have argued elsewhere that here, as in so much, Cisneros is heavily influenced by the work of Jean Gerson. See Peter Tyler, 'Mystical Desire: St Ignatius of Loyola and Affective Dionysianism', in *Id Quod Volo: The Dynamics of Desire in the Spiritual Exercises and Postmodernity*, ed. James Hanvey and Travis LaCouter (Leiden: Brill, forthcoming).

Like Cisneros, Osuna thus sees the special practice of recollective prayer as something not confined to 'professional religious' but available to all – clergy and lay, men and women, rich and poor alike. In Chapter Fifteen of the *Third Spiritual Alphabet* he describes how we engage in this practice by first finding a secluded place, 'be it a cell, private room, hermitage or other secret spot' to which we retire to pray.[37] 'At such times you are to consider yourself as dead to all other things, that they neither belong to you nor you to them.'[38] The place of recollection should also be 'proper, fitting, detached, healthy, devotional, suited for reverence and quiet' – that is, just like the *casas de recoleción* at Salceda and so on.[39] Once in this place:

> you are to retire into your heart and leave all created things for the length of two hours: one hour before and one hour after noon, at the most quiet time possible.[40]

If two hours are not possible, 'then at least make good use of one when you are least occupied and spend it as you see suitable'. A contemporary prayer, meditation or mindfulness manual of our own times would no doubt at this point give instructions on what we were to do once in this position – that is, breath control, use of mantra words, etc. Osuna is notable in that there are no prescribed methods of technique (here he shares common ground with his compatriots Teresa of Avila and John of the Cross, but differs from Loyola). Again this may seem odd to us, and I think we need to resist the temptation to fill the vacuum with how we think recollection was practised. This we can only speculate about – there is no written record as such.

What we do know is that these 'withdrawal' prayer techniques would, as the sixteenth century progressed, become more frowned upon within ecclesiastical circles – especially if the writer referred increasingly to 'nothingness' and 'annhiliation'. This is where the much-debated relationship between recollection, *alumbradismo* and *dejamientismo* comes into play (see McGinn for a good exposition of this).[41] Thus when Teresa of Avila founded her convent in Seville half a century after Osuna's text in

---

[37]Osuna, *The Third Spiritual Alphabet*, 254.
[38]Osuna, *The Third Spiritual Alphabet*, 388.
[39]Osuna, *The Third Spiritual Alphabet*, 397.
[40]Osuna, *The Third Spiritual Alphabet*, 388.
[41]McGinn, *Mysticism in the Golden Age of Spain*, 45–50. Both terms, *alumbradismo* and *dejamientismo*, have a long and complicated history. The former literally means 'enlightenment' and was used as a pejorative term by the Inquisition to refer to a type of prayer that was considered heretical. Likewise '*dejamiento*', literally 'abandonment', prayer was considered an equally unsafe form of prayer for Christians to practise by the middle of the sixteenth century. For more on this, see Tyler, '*Alumbrados*'.

1575, one of the problems she encountered was suspicion over nuns using suspect prayer techniques associated at this time with the *alumbrados*, such as periods of meditation after communion facing the wall in the courtyard.[42] In this later sixteenth-century context of ecclesial suspicion Osuna's words could be (mis-) interpreted by later seekers, leading eventually to them being placed on Archbishop Valdés' 1559 Index of prohibited books.

Thus we can understand this final strand of *recogimiento* as a specific, if possibly suspect, prayer practice requiring the practitioner to separate from daily activities and indeed suspend discursive thought whilst engaged in silent adoration. The timing may have varied but it seems likely that practitioners were being recommended one to two hours daily of such recollective prayer. As the sixteenth century wore on it was this aspect of the movement that would become most suspect in the eyes of church authorities and it is notable that *recogimiento* as a separate, discrete practice is less emphasized in the sixteenth-century writings of, for example, Teresa of Avila and John of the Cross.

Ignatius Loyola and the Revival of Affective Prayer

As mentioned above, it seems no coincidence that the young Inigo de Loyola, seeking his conversion following the battle of Pamplona, should find himself plunged into this controversy during his time in Catalonia in the 1520s as related in his *Reminisences*.[43] Accordingly we can identify various strands in the saint's exposition of prayer in his *Spiritual Exercises* that reflect these elements of the sixteenth-century Spanish school.[44] First there is the 'democratic' element of the *recogimiento* movement that stresses that these types of prayer are for all people in all stages of life. Like his spiritual compatriot, Teresa of Avila, Ignatius retained a love of simple and unadorned language when speaking of spiritual matters throughout his life. For him there was no need to recourse to the grand highfalutin terms of the medieval schoolmen. Indeed, many commentators have remarked on the simple and unadorned style of his writing such as found in the *Spiritual Exercises*.[45]

---

[42]Gillian Ahlgren, *Teresa of Avila and the Politics of Sanctity* (New York: NCROL, 1996), 55.

[43]Here I draw on the Spanish text of *Obras: San Ignacio de Loyola* (Madrid: Biblioteca de Autores Cristianos, 2014) and the English text of Ignatius of Loyola, *The Spiritual Exercises and Selected Works*, ed. George E. Ganss, CWS (New York: Paulist Press, 1991).

[44]For more on these connections, see Tyler, 'Mystical Desire'.

[45]Roland Barthes goes further to describe Ignatius, along with Sade and Fourier as a 'logothete' who creates a new architecture of language. See Roland Barthes, *Sade, Fourier, Loyola* (Paris: Editions du Seuil, 1971) and Joseph Munitiz and Philip Endean, ed., *Saint Ignatius of Loyola: Personal Writings* (London: Penguin Books, 1996), ix.

Brodrick goes further to suggest that as Inigo's first language was Basque he was never entirely comfortable in his adopted Castilian and he famously found the learning of Latin excruciating. Ignatius insisted, so we are told in the *Reminisences*, on addressing everyone as *vos* ('used between intimates or when speaking to inferiors, but not when speaking to superiors or persons whom it was desired to honour or placate'),[46] and Ignatius himself tells us that he explicitly used it 'because it was so that Christ and His Apostles spoke' (the Greek συ in the Gospels).[47]

The most striking manifestation of this in the *Exercises* is perhaps one of Ignatius' most important contributions to the development of the Western prayer tradition, what he calls 'the colloquy'. In *Exercises 54* he states that such a colloquy is made 'properly speaking, in the way one friend talks to another or a servant to one in authority – now begging a favour, now accusing oneself of some misdeed, now telling one's concerns and asking counsel about them'.[48] One can almost visualize here Ignatius before the governors and prelates of sixteenth-century Europe addressing them with the '*vos*' that was his trademark. In similar fashion he recommends that we turn the '*vos*' to the heavenly court of Father, Son, Holy Spirit and the Blessed Mother.

A second 'family resemblance' between the techniques of the *recogimiento* movement and the spirituality of Loyola can be found in his use of terms close to the *sabroso saber* of Osuna we mentioned earlier. Such 'tasty knowledge' is also to be found, for example, in Ignatius' *Exercises*. At the beginning of his work he instructs the giver of the *Exercises* to foster greater 'spiritual relish and spiritual fruit' (*más gusto y fruto espiritual*) in the exercitant rather than 'lengthy explanation and meaning' for 'it is not in knowing much but deep down feeling and relishing things interiorly that contents and satisfies the soul (*porque no el mucho saber harta y satisface al ánima, mas el sentir y gustar de las cosas internamente*)'.[49] When talking about the *Spiritual Exercises* in the *Reminisences* (*dar ejercicios espirituales* at Alcalá in 1526) he explicitly relates that 'many people grew in understanding and pleasure of spiritual things (*que vinieron en harta noticia y gusto de cosas espirituales*)'.[50] This savour or relish rather than

---

[46]James Brodrick, *Saint Ignatius Loyola: The Pilgrim Years 1491–1538* (San Francisco, CA: Ignatius Press, 1956), 137.

[47]Ignatius of Loyola, *The Spiritual Exercises and Selected Works*, 95.

[48]Ignatius of Loyola, *The Spiritual Exercises and Selected Works*, 138.

[49]Ignatius of Loyola, *Obras: San Ignacio de Loyola*, ed. Manuel Ruiz Jurado (Madrid: Biblioteca de Autores Cristianos, 2014), 148.

[50]Ignatius of Loyola, *Obras*, 61.

intellectual knowledge would become for Ignatius the touchstone by which the success or otherwise of the *Exercises* was held. As he says in *Exercises* 124, we should 'taste the infinite sweetness and charm of the Divinity (*oler y gustar y con el gusto la infinita suavidad y dulzura de la divinidad del anima y de sus virtudes y de todo)*'.[51]

This is explicitly described in the 'Methods of Praying' where Ignatius urges the exercitant to dwell on each phrase, word and syllable of a prayer such as the 'Hail Mary' or 'Our Father' so as 'to consider the word as long as meanings, comparisons, relish and consolations connected with it are found'.[52]

The Carmelite Reform

Again, as with Loyola, so the 'giants' of the Carmelite reform, Teresa of Avila and John of the Cross, drew upon the prevailing spirit of *recogimiento* as they developed their writing on prayer and the spiritual life. As already mentioned, Teresa was heavily influenced by Osuna and made the acquaintance of his *Third Spiritual Alphabet* at a critical period of her own spiritual development. In her first book, known to us as the *Book of the Life*, she describes this first encounter mediated by her Uncle Pedro:

> When I was on my way, the uncle of mine I have mentioned who lived along the road gave me a book. It is called *The Third Alphabet* (*Tercer Abecedario*) and treats of the teaching of the prayer of recollection (*oración de recogimiento*) and although during this first year I read good books. ... I did not know how to proceed in prayer or how to be recollected (*cómo recogerme*). And so I was delighted with this book and resolved to follow that path with all my strength. ... I began to take time out for solitude, to confess frequently, and to follow that path, taking the book for my master (*por maestro*). For during the twenty years after this period of which I am speaking, I did not find a master, I mean a confessor, who understood me, even though I looked for one.[53]

---

[51]Ignaitus of Loyola, *Obras*, 180.
[52]Ignatius of Loyola, *The Spiritual Exercises and Selected Works*, 180.
[53]Teresa of Avila, *Obras Completas de Santa Teresa de Jésus*, ed. Efrén de la Madre De Dios and Otger Steggink (Madrid: Biblioteca de Autores Cristianos, 1997), 42–3; author's translation.

The central importance of Osuna's work, and the recollection movement in general, on Teresa is apparent.[54] Thus when we turn to her own descriptions of prayer in her later mature writings, we can see how well she has learnt the lessons of *recogimiento* and made them her own. No better example of this is in the famous analogy she gives in the *Book of the Life* of the prayer journey of the seeker being like four means of watering a dried-out patch of garden. She begins by stating that the seeker has 'a plot in very infertile land (*un huerto en tierra muy infructuosa*) in which grow many weeds (*malas hierbas*)'.[55] Such a plot, she suggests, can be watered in four ways:

> By taking the water from a well, which is a lot of work; or by a water wheel and aqueducts, when the water is drawn by a windlass (I have sometimes drawn it in this way; it is less laborious than the other and gives more water); or by a stream or a brook, which waters the ground much better, for it saturates it more thoroughly and there is less need to water it often, so that the gardener has less work to do; or by heavy rain, when the Lord waters it with no labour of ours, a way incomparably better than any of those which have been described.[56]

Teresa works with a model of the spiritual life as one of decreasing effort on behalf of the seeker accompanied by a concomitant increase on God's behalf which will remain her essential spiritual anthropology for the rest of her life. Like her mentor, Osuna, she stresses firstly that God can be 'tasted' through prayer; however throughout this narrative,[57] and similar ones in the later exposition on the *Song of Songs*, she stresses that such prayer practices should not become an 'end in themselves' but, rather, the purpose of the garden is to cultivate flowers, the 'good works' she will later describe in the *Interior Castle*, that constitute the ultimate guarantor of an authentic Christian approach to prayer. As with Osuna, Christ alone can teach us how to pray and as she tells us in the later *Way of Perfection*:

> I am not asking you now to think of Him, or to form numerous conceptions of Him, or to make long and subtle meditations with your understanding. I am asking you only to look at Him. For who can prevent

---

[54]However, we can also stress the influence upon her of the writings of Jerome, Augustine and Gregory, all at this time available to her from the new folio editions being produced as a consequence of the Cisnerosian reforms.

[55]Teresa, *Obras Completas*, 71.

[56]Teresa, *Obras Completas*, 71–2.

[57]Teresa, *Obras Completas*, 73.

you from turning the eyes of your soul (just for a moment, if you can do no more) upon this Lord?[58]

Prayer, for Teresa, must not become an end in itself. If it does it has missed the point. As she puts it rather acerbically in her last work, the *Interior Castle*:

> When I see people very diligently trying to discover what kind of prayer they are experiencing and so completely wrapt up in their prayers that they seem afraid to stir, or to indulge in a moment's thought, lest they should lose the slightest degree of the tenderness and devotion which they have been feeling, I realize how little they understand of the road to the attainment of union. They think that the whole thing consists in this. No, sisters, no; what the Lord desires is works. If you see a sick woman to whom you can give some help, never be affected by the fear that your devotion will suffer, but take pity on her: if she is in pain, you should feel pain too; if necessary, fast so that she may have your food, not so much for her sake as because you know it to be your Lord's will. That is true union with His will.[59]

Teresa's homely and grounded metaphors of prayer are complemented by those of her co-worker, John of the Cross, who presents the way of prayer through a series of striking and unusual poetic images made famous in such great works as the *Dark Night of the Soul* and the *Living Flame of Love*. As with so much of the writings of the Spanish school, scholars have disputed as to the exact meaning of these metaphors. Yet, taking into account the context with which we began this chapter, it is clear that John, through his education at Salamanca University, was well versed with the Dionysian and affective traditions of prayer we discussed earlier. Accordingly, his approach to prayer can be characterized, especially in works such as the *Spiritual Canticle,* as a re-ordering of the bodily 'appetites' through the intervention of Divine grace.[60] Like Teresa with her four waters, he stresses the necessity of initial interior work at the beginning of the journey (this would correspond to Dionysius' 'path of purification') before we allow God to take the initiative and touch us with his grace. Throughout, John emphasizes the inexpressible

---

[58]Teresa, *Obras Completas,* 300–1.
[59]Teresa, *Obras Completas,* 519.
[60]John distinguishes 'natural' and 'voluntary' appetites; for more on this distinction, see Peter Tyler, *St John of the Cross* (London: Bloomsbury, 2010).

nature of this encounter (here heavily influenced by Dionysius) which may account for his extensive use of poetic metaphors to convey the message of prayer he is seeking to establish:

> One of the outstanding favours God grants briefly in this life is an understanding and experience of Himself so clear and lofty as to make one know clearly that He cannot be completely understood or experienced, for it is somewhat like that received by those in heaven, where those who understand God more, understand more distinctly the infinity which remains to be understood, whereas those who see less of Him do not realize so clearly what remains to be seen.[61]

Prayer, then, for John, exists in this precious space between our knowledge of God and God's knowledge of us filled out with the teeming symbols and metaphors of John's poetic genius.

Conclusion

We have seen in this chapter how the journey of the sixteenth-century Spanish school of prayer begins simply enough in the *casas de recolección* of the Franciscan hermitages of central Spain before eventually flowering into the great and influential works of Ignatius, Teresa and John. On the way we saw how the disputes and formulations of friars such as Osuna and monks such as Cisneros shape an attempt to formulate a spirituality that will have an enormous impact upon the 'modern age'. Beginning from the same observant roots as Teresa and John, Ignatius, in particular, concentrates less on the nature of union with the divine as with the formulation of practical steps towards leading the seeker to God through specific prayer exercises. In this respect, like Teresa, he is less concerned in his *Spiritual Exercises* with techniques of prayer, per se, as with the *good works* that arise from them. Loyola's *Spiritual Exercises*, as a practical and focused form of affective prayer, thus takes the key elements of the Spanish tradition of *recogimiento* we have explored here, but remoulds them in a way that will have an enormous impact upon Christianity for centuries to come.

---

[61]John of the Cross, *Obras Completas de San Juan de la Cruz*, ed. Lucinio Ruano de la Iglesia (Madrid: Biblioteca de Autores Cristianos, 2002), 766; author's translation.

CHAPTER TWENTY-FOUR

Prayer in Modern Philosophy

SCOTT A. KIRKLAND

Modernity is often cast as coterminous with secularization, or the slow retreat of religion from the centre of human life and thought. One of the sites at which this might be thought is through the retreat of prayer as a form of discursive subject-formation in philosophical and theological discourses. However, this would be something of a misleading story to tell. It would be misleading on two fronts. First, prayer does not disappear from philosophical modernity; indeed, it reappears at key junctures, even if in the shape of criticism. Second, it would be to locate prayer as a formally distinctive mode of address or speech. These two errors, then, correspond to both the content and the form of prayer. Any quest to understand the nature of prayer in modern philosophy needs to be attentive not only to the moments at which prayer explicitly appears in texts, but to the formal features of philosophical discourses themselves.

In this chapter, I will look to several moments at which prayer appears in the modern philosophical canon not only to the end of addressing the content of the prayer or the discourse on prayer, but to an examination of the *function* of prayer in philosophical speech ordered towards the production of subjectivities.

I would like to offer a preliminary remark on the nature of prayer that will guide this discussion. That is, prayer might be thought of as a certain practice of attention. In directing attention towards an object (even if that object is not an object, such as God),[1] prayer is an attempt to engage in a form of subject-making. Attention orders intellect, desire, will and love. As such, prayer is intimately bound to a process of intellectual (mis)apprehension. Much of what we often characterize as 'religious' enthusiasm or mysticism is a result of a process of the deracination of prayer, the dislocation from its proper discursive context. That is to say, prayer's proper context is as much the life of the mind as it is some supposed 'religious' domain of human life. In surveying these philosophical figures, then, we are looking not so much for where it is they explicitly talk about prayer – although that is important – but for the migration of prayer, the practice of attention, into other domains. This, in turn, shifts the terrain on which prayer is often positioned as a distinctively 'religious' form of discourse.

Humean Empiricism

Famously, Immanuel Kant was moved to begin his major critical projects when he read David Hume, who, Kant quips, woke him from his 'dogmatic slumbers'. One of Hume's most famous texts is Section X of *An Enquiry Concerning Human Understanding*, 'Of Miracles'. In this text Hume sets about disarming accounts of the miraculous with an argument from probability. The argument runs like this: given the miracle is by definition an event which violates the laws and regularities of nature, it is by definition impossible. This impossibility, however, militates against any possibility of verifying the miracle because, even if one did occur, it is not repeatable or able to be experienced again. Whenever we are presented with evidence of a happening, therefore, there is always a more reasonable explanation of what has taken place than the miraculous.

When considering evidence, Hume writes that the 'wise man',

> considers which side is supported by the greater number of experiments: To that side he inclines, with doubt and hesitation; and when at last he fixes his judgment, the evidence exceeds not what we properly call probability. All probability, then, supposes an opposition of experiments and observations, where the one side is found to overbalance the other, and to produce a degree of evidence, proportioned to the superiority.[2]

---

[1]This is simply to maintain a metaphysical/theological distinction between God and world such that God is never known as such, only through forms of mediation.
[2]David Hume, *An Enquiry Concerning Human Understanding and Other Writings*, ed. Stephen Buckle (Cambridge: Cambridge University Press, 2007), 80.

This empiricist procedure can be seen to work in more recent Christian philosophical and theological discourse concerning the effectiveness of prayer. Vincent Brümmer, for instance, begins by insisting that both God and human beings are not subject to causal necessity in the same way that objects are, and so the kind of evidentiary data we might seek for the efficacy of prayer would look quite different to that of a repeatable experiment.[3] Brümmer does not give up on experimentality altogether, but rather focuses precisely on the interpersonal encounter with God in prayer. The effectiveness of prayer is not to be measured by the success of invocation, lest God be reduced to an impersonal wish-granter, but in the shape of the spiritual life of the prayer. Brümmer suggests that both God and the human pray-er are subject to change in this encounter, else one or other side is relating disingenuously.[4] The important thing to note here is that this account begins by assuming a certain kind of evidentiary logic from this strand of empiricist philosophical discourses. The problem Brümmer might locate in Hume is that Hume assumes that God does not in an 'open' way engage the world, and so Hume is looking for a different *kind* of trace of divine agency. For Brümmer it is the dynamic and open relation between God and the creature that leaves open the space for prayer's efficacy to be seen.[5] We might see this as problematic to the extent that, for both Hume and Brümmer, whatever God is as a 'cause', it is both discrete and occasional. This logic is rather different to what we encounter in continental philosophical discussions.

The Kantian Problem

Kant is often read as the 'father' of modern philosophy. The Kantian revolution in thought, coinciding with the French Revolution in politics, begins with his *Critique of Pure Reason* in which he attempts to think all things beginning with the subject of enquiry, not the object. So it is that he compares his philosophical revolution to the Copernican revolution in cosmology. Often something of the subtlety of Kant's comparison of his own

---

[3]Vincent Brümmer, *What Are We Doing When We Pray? A Philosophical Inquiry* (London: Routledge, 2008), 14–17.

[4]Brümmer, *What Are We Doing When We Pray,* 71–2. Brümmer points to 'double agency', which is that both God and the creature are considered agents in prayer.

[5]This kind of argument is also made in Richard Swinburne, *Divine Providence and the Problem of Evil* (Oxford: Oxford University Press, 1998). Swinburne is similarly caught in the problem of competitive agencies relating to one another, along with Brümmer effacing the classical distinction between primary and secondary causality. For further discussion, see John C. McDowell, 'Prayer, Particularity and the Subject of Divine Personhood: Who are Brümmer and Barth Invoking When They Pray?', in *Trinitarian Theology after Barth*, ed. Myk Habets and Phillip Tolliday (Eugene, OR: Pickwick Press, 2011), 255–83.

work with that of Copernicus is lost in textbook accounts. Kant's revolution is sometimes simply narrated as being of Copernican significance. Certainly, we now know it is that, but what Kant himself thought was going on was much more strictly analogous to Copernicus' actual discovery. In 1543 Copernicus published *On the Movements of the Heavenly Spheres*. In this text he expounds a model of the solar system which challenged Ptolemy's ancient model which supposed the earth as a stationary object in the middle of the solar system around which all other bodies move. Copernicus argued that in fact it was not the earth that was the centre of the solar system, but the sun. In so arguing, Copernicus destabilized a cosmological positioning of the earth which in turn privileged human life. Kant compares his philosophy to the insight of Copernicus, stating,

> Up to now it has been assumed that all our cognition must conform to the objects; but all attempts to find out something about them a priori through concepts that would extend our cognition have, on this presupposition, come to nothing. Hence let us once try whether we do not get farther with the problems of metaphysics by assuming that the objects must conform to our cognition, which would agree better with the requested possibility of an a priori cognition of them, which is to establish something about objects before they are given to us. This would be just like the first thoughts of Copernicus, who, when he did not make good progress in the explanation of the celestial motions if he assumed that the entire celestial host revolves around the observer, tried to see if he might not have greater success if he made the observer revolve and left the stars at rest.[6]

What this highlights is that at the heart of modern philosophy is an insight that rests on a fundamental change of perspective. Just as Copernicus imagined the movement of celestial bodies from the point of view of somebody standing on the sun, so Kant is imagining that the object of our cognition or knowledge conforms to our capacities as subjects. This fundamental movement means that the subject is at the heart of philosophical enquiry, not the object. What is to be known before any-thing, and as the condition of knowing any-thing, is the subject themselves.

Let us bring this to bear on the question of prayer. Kant had been formed in a pietist tradition which had placed a premium on the formation of an inward subjective relation to God. He was catechized as a young boy and

---

[6]Immanuel Kant, *Critique of Pure Reason*, trans. and ed. Paul Guyer and Alan W. Wood (Cambridge: Cambridge University Press, 1998), 110.

brought up on a strict diet of prayer and spiritual formation which was integrated into his classroom education. Later in life he would understand this as impinging upon his freedom of thought. A correspondence from 1774 to 1775 with the Swiss theologian J. C. Lavater is instructive here. Lavater was an ardent follower of Kant, and eagerly awaiting the *Critique of Pure Reason*. In 1774 he wrote to Kant that 'until we fix our *observations* more on *human beings* all our wisdom is but folly. The reason we always fall so horribly into error is that we seek to find outside of us what is only within us'. After his efforts at flattery, largely misunderstanding the Kantian position,[7] Lavater continues by asking Kant to provide some feedback on a book of his which is concerned with prayer and faith, the 'most intimate matters of the heart'. Kant would write in response,

> You ask for my opinion of your discussion of faith and prayer. Do you realize whom you are asking? A man who believes that, in the final moment only the purest candor concerning our most hidden inner convictions can stand the test and who, like Job, takes it to be a sin to flatter God and make inner confessions, perhaps forced out by fear, that fail to agree with what we freely think.[8]

Kant's response to Lavater is revealing for several reasons. Kant believes that prayer and 'religious ritual' are extraneous superstitious attempts to gain divine favour. He will go on to describe how he believes that even the apostles abandoned the heart of Christ's teaching when they 'took the essential requirement for salvation to be not the honouring of the holy teacher's religious doctrine of conduct but rather the veneration of the teacher himself and a sort of wooing of favour by means of ingratiation and encomium – the very things against which that teacher had so explicitly and repeatedly preached'.[9] That is to say, the essence of Christian teaching, for Kant, is a religious consciousness that is manifest in moral conscience and action. The veneration of the teacher, Christ, is indicative of a distraction from this fundamental orientation of religion to moral life, the kind of life Christ lived. Prayer would be a means of ingratiating oneself in an economy of divine favour through the performance of empty ritual. This makes Kant 'like Job'

---

[7] Lavater seems to think that Kant believes the answers to everything lie in the subject. This is plainly not the case in the Kantian system, which leaves the *ding an sich*, the thing in itself, reality as it is in itself, as an aporia for thought. It is impossible, for Kant, to discover reality as such, only as it appears to us. J. C. Lavater, 'To Immanuel Kant', in Immanuel Kant, *Philosophical Correspondence*, trans. and ed. Arnulf Zweig (Cambridge: Cambridge University Press, 1999), 150.

[8] Kant, *Philosophical Correspondence*, 151–2.

[9] Kant, *Philosophical Correspondence*, 152.

who takes it as a 'sin to flatter God and make inner confessions' which are motivated by fear and disclose an inability of the subject to confront its own freedom of thought and action. Fear of God here drives the praying subject into a kind of empty ritual and distracts again from free moral action.[10]

In his 1793 *Religion within the Boundaries of Mere Reason*, Kant concludes the essay with a discussion of the relationship between nature and grace. He begins by identifying nature with whatever 'good the human being can do on his own, according to freedom', in contrast to grace, in which the creature can accomplish something only 'with supernatural help'.[11] This distinction is extended to the realm of free moral action. For Kant, we discover we are free by *nature* when we discover that we live in relation to the moral law. That I *can* obey or disobey the law is proof that I am free. The intervention of the supernatural here would degrade the freedom the subject has by nature, and so the subject would not be free in itself, but only conditionally. One of the means by which we might think of this kind of supernatural influence is by what, in Kant's view, is a problematic understanding of prayer. He writes,

> *Praying,* conceived as an *inner ritual* service of God and hence as a means of grace, is a superstitious delusion (a fetish-making); for it only is the *declaring of a wish* to a being who has no need of any declaration concerning the inner disposition of the wisher, through which nothing is thereby accomplished not is any of the duties incumbent on us as commands of God discharged; hence God is not really served.[12]

We can see that Kant here conceives of prayer as a kind of wish fulfilment, a way of invoking divine action in a subject who is otherwise naturally capable of action. Indeed, this naturally capable subject is absconding from responsibility in appealing to divine aid. In this way, supernatural agency is in *competition* with natural human agency, one agency supplementing or running-across the other.[13] This is the kind of agency that Ludwig Feuerbach would consider to be endemic to Christianity. In *The Essence of Christianity,*

---

[10]It is important to note here how for Kant this is bound up with a form of anti-Semitism when he states that 'for in those days the old miracles had to be opposed by new miracles, and Jewish dogmas by Christian dogmas'. This is to say that the 'Jewish' element in the New Testament is, for Kant, the deviation from the teachings of Christ. See Kant, *Philosophical Correspondence,* 153.

[11]Immanuel Kant, *Religion within the Boundaries of Mere Reason and Other Writings*, trans. and ed. Allen Wood and George di Giovanni (Cambridge: Cambridge University Press, 1999), 182–3 – hereafter: *Religion.*

[12]Kant, *Religion,* 186.

[13]See Christopher Insole, *Kant and the Creation of Freedom: A Theological Problem* (Oxford: Oxford University Press, 2013) for a discussion of Kant's abandonment of the mediaeval *concursus,* a non-competitive relationship between divine and creaturely agency.

Feuerbach articulates the ways in which 'God' comes to resemble a magnification of human essence, self-consciousness. Self-consciousness is the way the human addresses itself as Thou in thought. Religion is 'identical with this distinctive characteristic', God becoming the perfect subject of address, the perfect Thou and so a reflection of the I.[14]

In opposition to this, Kant suggests that we should rather think of prayer as a kind of attitude of mind, spirit: 'A sincere wish to please God in all our doings and nondoings, i.e. the disposition, accompanying all our actions, to pursue these as though they occurred in the service of God, is the *spirit of prayer,* and this can and ought to be in us "without ceasing".'[15] What emerges here is a problem that is framed in terms of the shape of freedom and moral agency, rather than an objection to prayer as such. Kant has little time for prayer as a form of pious self-indulgence. Conversely, moral attentiveness, a life that interrogates itself in relation to the moral law, Kant gives the name prayer. At once, then, Kant scolds those who pray and asks for something more substantive and integrative of the subject.

Remembering the framing question at the start of this chapter, that of the relationship between the form of prayer and the content, we might suggest here that Kant's distaste for prayer is a distaste for a form of address in which the subject comports themselves towards God through ritual practice rather than through a confrontation with that which is essential. That which is essential, for Kant, is the moral law, which is available to all through a process of rational investigation explicated in the *Critique of Practical Reason.* Religious forms – prayer, liturgy, etc. – appear here as ways of escaping what is essential content (Kant's critique, therefore, is in many ways more radical than that which will follow in this chapter).[16] This is the distinction Kant locates between the teaching of Christ and the apostles' devotion to Christ himself. Critically, however, it is in this way that Kant retains what is central to pietism, a practice in which the inward relation to God is located as absolutely fundamental. However, the mediating form of prayer and liturgy is abandoned as distracting from that purely subjective relation. In a certain

---

[14]Ludwig Feuerbach, *The Essence of Christianity*, trans. George Elliot (Mineola, NY: Dover Publications, 2008), 2.

[15]Kant, *Religion,* 186.

[16]Giorgio Agamben locates the Kantian moral ontology of duty in relation to scholastic eucharistic ontology and the development of a fifth form of causality, instrumental cause – that is, a cause in which the effectiveness of the action is not identical with the agent performing it. Hence, in sacramental action, the effect is wholly of grace. Similarly, for Kant, the 'emptiness' of ritual corresponds to the emptiness of action without effect. This maps onto the way Kant thinks about nature and grace in compelling ways. See Giorgio Agamben, *Opus Dei: An Archeology of Duty,* trans. Adam Kotsko (Stanford, CA: Stanford University Press, 2012), 89–125.

sense, Kant believes in an immediacy of moral consciousness which does away with the mediating form of prayer. His is a pietism without prayer.

Hegelian Form

Kantian philosophy structures much of what are the central concerns of modernity. The opposition between form and content repeats itself in varying ways. Much of what confuses readers of the other contender for the title of 'father' of modern philosophy, Georg Wilhelm Frederik Hegel, is his complication of the relationship between form and content in his dialectical method. For Hegel, the form of an argument is just as important as the content. This is why his *Phenomenology of Spirit* is such a difficult text for readers. It is continually *performing* a rupture that is internal to the structure of his thought in which the whole is present in every part, and therefore destroys and remakes every part.[17]

Let us open this up using one of Hegel's apparently more lucid moments, in which he identifies certain practices in modern life with prayer:

> Reading the morning newspaper is the realist's morning prayer. One orients one's attitude toward the world either by God or by what the world is. The former gives as much security as the latter, in that one knows how one stands.[18]

It is crucial to note here that it is the modern *realist* who is reading the newspaper (something not many of us do anymore; we are more likely to scroll through our social media for news). The realist, for Hegel, is someone who is interested in ensuring that their knowledge corresponds to objects in the world. Sense perception is what guides their knowing. In many ways we are familiar with this position. The realist claims: I can only know what I perceive through my senses. The realist's morning prayer, then, is reading the newspaper. This person orients themselves to the world through 'what the world is'. This gives them security because 'in that one knows how one stands'. We know this posture in our contemporary culture of 'fact checking'

---

[17]Nicholas Adams suggests that Hegel's utility for theologians rests in the concepts he provides us with. While I have some disagreement with Adams' reading of the content of those concepts, I would echo his sentiment that Hegel's utility resides not at the level of dogmatic content, but of form. See Nicholas Adams, *The Eclipse of Grace: Divine and Human Action in Hegel* (Oxford: Wiley-Blackwell, 2013).

[18]G. W. F. Hegel, *Miscellaneous Writings of G. W. F. Hegel*, ed. Jon Stewart (Evanston, IL: Northwestern University Press, 2000), 247.

and fake news. Truth and falsity correspond to the 'facts' of the matter. Prayer for the religious person performs the same function in that God *mediates* perception. However, it is through this elision of the two figures that Hegel opens up their similarity. The naive realist requires mediation just as much as the religious person. Why? Because the world is given *through* the newspaper.

Can the realist just put down the newspaper and see for themselves, then? For Hegel, even were the events described in the newspaper to take place before the realist, senses themselves require mediation in consciousness. His famous examples used to show this are the categories 'here', 'now' and 'this'. These categories are not things in themselves; they are ways of framing what is happening here, now or there. For example, what might appear to be a pure perception, 'now', even a moment after perception has ceased being 'now' and 'has become stale'. The now can then only be known in relation to what it is not. This provides access to what Hegel calls the universal. This can be demonstrated through 'here'. Hegel states, 'Here is, e.g. the tree. If I turn around, this truth has vanished and is converted into its opposite: no tree is here, but a house instead. "Here" itself does not vanish.'[19] 'Here' is what remains even in the absence of the perception; it is a universality, a backdrop against which all particulars are given. It 'abides constant in the vanishing of the house, the tree, etc.'[20] In this way, sense perceptions are always mediated by what Hegel calls *Geist*, spirit.[21]

It would be to go too far to suggest that the form of Hegel's thought is that of prayer, but it would not be entirely untrue either. To the extent that thought itself is an act of orienting attention to absolute spirit, to the universal, to the way it mediates reality, thought is a kind of prayer. We might see this in an earlier text, *Faith and Knowledge,* where Hegel identifies the shape of religious self-consciousness:

> Religion builds its temples and altars in the heart of the individual. In sighs and prayers he seeks for the God whom he denies to himself in intuition, because of the risk that the intellect will cognize what is intuited as a mere thing, reducing the sacred grove to mere timber. Of course, the

---

[19] G. W. F. Hegel, *Phenomenology of Spirit*, trans. A. V. Miller (Oxford: Oxford University Press, 1977), 98.

[20] Hegel, *Phenomenology of Spirit*, 98.

[21] This is the movement of the first part of the *Phenomenology of Spirit* concerned with sense perception. In an earlier translation of Hegel, Donald Ballie translated *Geist* as mind. Both spirit and mind have distinctive drawbacks, and translators agree now that spirit is more useful. G. W. F. Hegel, *The Phenomenology of Mind*, trans. Donald Ballie (London: Harper Colophon, 1967).

inner must be externalized; intention must become effective in action; immediate religious sentiment must be expressed in external gesture; and faith, though it flees from the objectivity of cognition, must become objective to itself in thoughts, concepts, and words.[22]

On this account religion is, in the first instance, a process of refusal. It is a denial of the intuition of God in any particular thing. This is a reference to the universality of God, where 'here' might function as a background negativity, so might God. To reduce the 'sacred grove to mere timber' would be to lose the form in the content, to lose the whole in the particular. Faith, then, appears in its becoming objective to itself in the 'sighs and prayers' finally identified as 'thoughts, concepts, and words'. What Hegel identifies here is a *dialectical process* in which faith appears to itself in words, but in appearing to itself objectively, it must be negated in order to refuse to make God a particular. Prayer makes faith objective to itself and simultaneously denies that objectivity. It is, then, formally, the shape of the dialectic itself, the ongoing formation of the subject.[23]

Nietzsche's Prayers

It may come as a surprise to many who have heard stories of Nietzsche the great atheist that his early writings are peppered with Christian prayer. For example, in his early days as a young Lutheran pietist Nietzsche writes,

I have firmly resolved within me to dedicate myself forever to His service. May the dear Lord give me strength and power to carry out my intention and protect me on life's way. Like a child I trust in His grace: He will preserve us all, that no misfortune may befall us. But His holy will be done! All He gives I will joyfully accept: happiness and unhappiness,

---

[22]G. W. F. Hegel, *Faith and Knowledge*, trans. Walter Cerf (Albany: State University of New York Press, 1977), 57. For a discussion of Hegel's mature lectures on religion, see Peter C. Hodgson, *Hegel and Christian Theology: A Reading of the Lectures on the Philosophy of Religion* (Oxford: Oxford University Press, 2007).

[23]Charles Taylor, following Karl Barth, in his study on Hegel, believes this means that the Hegelian system has no space for grace: 'The creaturely response of gratitude and praise of God takes on a radically different sense in the rarefied altitudes of the Idea. Both these responses transmute into a recognition of my identity with cosmic necessity and hence must cease to be gratitude in any meaningful sense (although something analogous to the glorifying of God remains, a sense of awe at the architecture of rational necessity)'. See Charles Taylor, *Hegel* (Cambridge: Cambridge University Press, 1975), 494. Following Karl Barth, *Protestant Theology in the Nineteenth Century: Its Background and History*, trans. Brian Cozens and John Bowden (Grand Rapids, MI: William B. Eerdmans, 2009), chapter 10.

poverty and wealth, and boldly look even death in the face, which shall one day unite us all in eternal joy and bliss. yes, dear Lord, let Thy face shine upon us forever! Amen![24]

This prayer could have been written by any number of pious Christians of the period. Nietzsche develops a famous distaste for Christianity as his career progresses, however. It becomes for him 'Platonism for the masses'. That is, it is a philosophy that directs one's attention away from the joy and pain of material existence, and towards an afterlife or towards the shadows on the wall of the cave. For Nietzsche, the philosophers had become complicit in this. In the preface to *Beyond Good and Evil,* written in 1885, he complains of previous 'dogmatic' philosophers:

> Supposing that Truth is a woman – what then? Is there not ground for suspecting that all philosophers, in so far as they have been dogmatists, have failed to understand women – that the terrible seriousness and clumsy importunity with which they have usually paid their addresses to Truth, have been unskilled and unseemly methods for winning a woman? Certainly she has never allowed herself to be won; and at present every kind of dogma stands with sad and discouraged men. *If* it stands at all! For there are scoffers who maintain that it has fallen, that all dogma lies on the ground – nay more, that it is at its last gasp.[25]

The dogmatizing philosophers he has in mind here are precisely those of the previous generations of idealists that we have already spoken about: Kant, Fichte, Schelling, Hegel, et al. For Nietzsche, the problem with these philosophers is that they are concerned with 'absolute philosophical edifices', which remain indifferent to the vicissitudes of *life*. The fundamental error with these philosophical systems can be identified with Plato's 'invention of Pure Spirit [*Geist*] and the Good in Itself'. That is, Hegel's *Geist* is seen as merely another instance of the Platonic preoccupation with directing our attention away from the material. Nietzsche, however, is here to awaken us from this 'nightmare' so that we can 'again draw breath freely'. We can do this because we realize that Platonism was 'the very inversion of truth,

---

[24]Quoted in Bruce Ellis Benson, *Pious Nietzsche: Decadence and Dionysian Faith* (Bloomington, IN: Indiana University Press, 2008), 18. Benson's thesis is that Nietzsche not only begins his career as a pietist, 'but also ends as one'. The content of the piety changes, but the form is similar in that the cult becomes the cult of Dionysius.
[25]Friedrich Nietzsche, *Beyond Good and Evil*, trans. R. J. Hollingdale (London: Penguin Books, 1990), 31; translation amended.

and the denial of the perspective – the fundamental condition – of life'.[26] In being inverted, then, the true must become not the ideal or spirit, but rather the material life. The barbs at the Hegelians and Kantians are plain for all to see, the philosophers have been recruited into the service of Christianity, which is 'Platonism for the masses'.[27] Nietzsche understands his philosophy, then, as an act of liberation. The 'struggle again the ecclesiastical oppression of millenniums of Christianity … produced in Europe a magnificent tension of soul' which is ready to aim at a new goal.[28]

Given the nature of Nietzsche's critique, we can retroactively think about what it is he might come to see as problematic in this early prayer. Central to the early prayer is a renunciation of the will of the praying subject in the face of divine grace: 'But His holy will be done! All He gives I will joyfully accept.' The divine will precedes and determines the shape of the existence of the praying person, and the benevolence of that will ensures that the subject will find fulfilment 'one day' when we are united 'in eternal joy and bliss'. This prayer defers life into the afterlife, it ensures that attention is drawn inward into the renunciation of desire rather than its realization, and it leads ultimately to a form of quietism. Prayer, then, transforms in the mature Nietzsche into a celebration of life free of Platonic shadows and Hegelian absolute spirit; it transforms into dancing to music. Famously, late in his career, Nietzsche composed a 'Hymn to Life'. Central to his work becomes the images of dancing and music: 'When one had lost the proper tension and harmony of the soul, one had to *dance* to the beat of the singer – that was the prescription of this healing art.'[29]

Returning to the question of form, as Bruce Ellis Benson has argued, Nietzsche's work in many ways begins in prayer and ends in prayer. The form of this prayer, however, has changed. It has migrated from the pious Christian devotion of his Lutheran upbringing to the raucous dancing celebration of life in his late work. Nietzsche finds in Dionysian revelry a way of confronting that which the forms of devotion he was raised within shielded him from. Hence, the definitive moment in Nietzsche's early work is his encounter with tragedy and the freedom that the tragic offered in its Dionysian revelry.[30]

---

[26]Nietzsche, *Beyond Good and Evil*, 32.
[27]Nietzsche, *Beyond Good and Evil*, 32.
[28]Nietzsche, *Beyond Good and Evil*, 32.
[29]Friedrich Nietzsche, *The Gay Science*, ed. Bernard Williams, trans. Josefine Nauckhoff and Adrian Del Caro (Cambridge: Cambridge University Press, 2001), 84.
[30]See Friedrich Nietzsche, *The Birth of Tragedy*, trans. Douglas Smith (Oxford: Oxford University Press, 2000).

Kierkegaard's Sacrifice

Søren Kierkegaard is perhaps the most explicitly Christian of the philosophers we will examine here. He helpfully intersects with the previous, however. Kierkegaard studied Hegel under Schelling in Berlin in the 1830s, and was deeply influenced by the same pietistic form of northern European Christianity that Kant, Hegel and Nietzsche were all familiar with. He, however, in many ways was on the periphery of philosophy in the nineteenth century, being located in Denmark. Nevertheless, his influence is felt significantly in the twentieth century as many theologians found solace in his criticism of Christendom, and philosophers in his existentialism.

For Kierkegaard it is in the moment of prayer that the subject finds him or herself naked before the grace of God. Kierkegaard prays, 'God in heaven, let me really feel my nothingness, not in order to despair over it, but in order to feel the more powerfully the greatness of thy goodness.'[31] All pretention to independent goodness is lost before the recognition of human inadequacy – the famed 'infinite qualitative distinction' between God and humanity.[32] This places the subject in a posture of pure receptivity.[33] The very formation and constitution of his/her subjectivity are contingent upon divine self-gift. Prayer is a moment in which the subject is both given, and given to, the divine. In this moment of disruption, the subject is made nothing. Kierkegaard understands prayer as the abandonment of self, the *kenosis* of desire. So:

the immediate person thinks and imagines that when he prays, the important thing, the thing he must concentrate upon, is that *God should hear* what *he is praying for*. And yet in the true and eternal sense it is just the reverse: the true relation in prayer is not when God hears what is prayed for, but when *the person praying* continues to pray until he is *the one who hears*, who hears what God wills. The immediate person,

---

[31]Søren Kierkegaard, *The Prayers of Kierkegaard*, ed. Perry D. LeFevre (Chicago, IL: University of Chicago Press, 1996), 5.

[32]Søren Kierkegaard, *Philosophical Fragments/Johannes Climacus*, trans. and ed. Edna H. Hong and Howard V. Hong (Princeton, NJ: Princeton University Press, 1985). See Silvia Walsh's discussion in *Kierkegaard: Thinking Christianly in an Existential Mode* (Oxford: Oxford University Press, 2008), 111–45.

[33]Joshua Cockayne, 'Prayer as God-knowledge (via Self)', *Kierkegaard Studies Yearbook 2017*, no. 1 (2017): 101–14. Cockayne argues that prayer is less about the invocation of divine agency, and more about forming the pray-er. In this way, knowledge of God is mediated by a self-knowledge.

therefore, uses many words and, therefore, makes many demands in his prayer; the true man of prayer only *attends*.[34]

The praying person does not come before God with requests for fulfilment of selfish desire. Rather, prayer is an abandonment of self in the face of the divine in order to see desire refigured by attendance to the divine voice. Not wanting to see the human and divine wills in opposition, Kierkegaard understands that the human is human insofar as the human submits to and obeys the divine will. The inevitable consequence of which is the embrace of a cruciform existence, making sense of his insistence upon the kenotic shape of desire. So, Kierkegaard notes in his *Journals*:

> There was a time – it came so naturally, it was childlike – when I believed that God's love also expressed itself by sending earthly 'good gifts', happiness, prosperity. ... Now it is otherwise. How did that happen? Quite simply, but little by little. Little by little, I noticed increasingly that all those whom God really loved, the examples, etc., had all had to suffer in this world. Furthermore, that it is the teaching of Christianity: to be loved by God and to love God is to suffer. But if that were so I dared not pray for good fortune and success because it were as though I were to beg at the same time: Will you not, O God, cease loving me and allow me to stop loving you. ... On the other hand, to pray directly for suffering appeared to me too exalted, and it also seemed to me that it might easily be presumptuous, and that God might grow angry at my perhaps wishing to defy him.[35]

Refiguring desire takes shape as ceasing to determine for oneself what is good. Kierkegaard's reticence in his consideration of petition is not due to God somehow holding back good things from the creature, but rather due to the theological reality that the creature cannot determine for herself *what is good*. So, it is 'your kingdom come, your will be done'. In this way prayer is an embrace of suffering, a crucifying of desire, of one's own determination of the good. Kierkegaard insists that it is not 'good things', as we determine them, that are signs of divine favour, but rather, all things are given by

---

[34]Søren Kierkegaard, *The Journals of Søren Kierkegaard*, ed. Alexander Dru (London: Oxford University Press, 1959), entry 56. The shape of this kenoticism is christologically given, as we shall see. David Law suggests that the entire shape of Kierkegaard's Christology follows in the train of Lutheran kenoticisms from the nineteenth century. See David Law, *Kierkegaard's Kenotic Christology* (Oxford: Oxford University Press, 2013).
[35]Søren Kierkegaard, *Journals and Papers of Screen Kierkegaard: Volume 10*, ed. Bruce H. Kirmmse, et al. (Princeton, NJ: Princeton University Press, 2018), entry 72.

God for the formation of our person. God is unchanging in his love and faithfulness, and so in that moment of suffering our person is formed by divine grace.

Kierkegaard notes again and again that to move closer to the divine is to move closer to suffering. As we saw in the quote above 'to love God is to suffer'. It is illuminating here to draw some sense of continuity between Luther and Kierkegaard. Luther's famous *theologia crucis* in many ways lies behind Kierkegaard's consideration of prayer in that there is a common theological impulse. As we have already seen, for Kierkegaard the temptation for the pray-er is always to determine for oneself good and evil. This self-determination, however, is broken on the cross, where we see how things *really* are. For both Kierkegaard and Luther, to pray is to come to comprehend the God who is displayed to us 'through suffering and the cross'.[36] In this coming to see things anew is an embrace of a different way of being. The person is formed in coming to see that Christianity costs, that the way of the Christian is the *via dolorosa* – 'the way is the truth, that is, that the truth is only in the becoming, in the process of appropriation'.[37] So, in involving herself in prayer, the Christian is opened to the special treatment of suffering: 'The Christian's good fortune is distinguished by suffering ... this is so difficult to understand that for anyone else but the elect it must be something to despair over.'[38]

Kierkegaard's consideration of the relation of God to humanity more broadly is grounded in his meditation on the incarnational embrace of flesh. It is in Christ's embrace of both sides of the covenantal relation that the new humanity is found. There is a sense in which Christ's humanity stands in our stead before the Father and so, without the incarnation, prayer will inevitably be without appropriate orientation. In considering what it means to pray in the name of Jesus, Kierkegaard writes:

> [It is] to pray in such a way that it is in conformity with the will of Jesus. I cannot pray in the name of Jesus and have my own will; the name of

---

[36]Luther, 'Heidelberg Disputation', in *Career of the Reformer I*, trans. Helmut T. Lehmann, LW 31 (Minneapolis, MN: Augsburg Fortress Press, 1959), 52–3.

[37]Søren Kierkegaard, *Concluding Unscientific Postscript to Philosophical Fragments: Volume 1*, trans. and ed. Edna H. Hong and Howard V. Hong (Princeton, NJ: Princeton University Press, 1992), 78. The question of this 'becoming' is crucial to Kierkegaard. For a discussion of Kierkegaard's inheritance of Luther via Meister Eckhart as a criticism of German idealist historicism, see David Kangas, *Kierkegaard's Instant: On Beginnings* (Bloomington, IN: Indiana University Press, 2007). For Kangas this criticism hinges upon the way temporality functions in Kierkgaard, a beginning (or origin) remaining present to the subject in 'the instant' of becoming, in contrast to forms of historicized development in figures like Hegel and Schelling.

[38]Kierkegaard, *Concluding Unscientific Postscript*, 582.

Jesus is ... the significant factor; the fact that Jesus' name comes at the beginning is not prayer in the name of Jesus; but it means to pray in such a way that I dare name Jesus in it. ... Jesus assumes the responsibility and all the consequences, he steps forward for us, steps into the place of the person praying.[39]

Surrendering self-determination in prayer is grounded in the representative humanity of Christ in whom we participate as the one who 'steps into the place of the person praying'. This is the mode of both surrender of desire and its reorientation. As we participate in that divine discourse, the prayer of Christ to the Father, we are transformed. The idolatries of our own will are relinquished as we are given to become in the face of Christ. So, Kierkegaard prays,

Lord! Make our heart Your temple in which You live. Grant that every impure thought, every earthly desire might be like the idol Dagon – each morning broken at the feet of the Ark of the Covenant. Teach us to master flesh and blood and let this mastery of ourselves be our bloody sacrifice in order that we might be able to say with the Apostle: 'I die every day'.[40]

Conclusion: Forms of Attention

This chapter has been necessarily selective with its engagements. However, I have attempted to show that there is a story to be told about prayer and philosophy in modernity that is perhaps a bit more interesting than we might think at first. It is not the case that philosophers simply become indifferent to prayer under secularized conditions. Rather, we see formal elements of prayerful discourse taken up, played with, criticized and transformed under new conditions of thinking subjectivity.

To conclude I would like to return to the question of form, attention and prayer. In *Gravity and Grace*, Simone Weil writes that 'attention, taken to its highest degree is the same as prayer. It presupposes faith and love'. For Weil, attention is an attitude of self-emptying in which one gives, attends, to the object; an 'absolutely unmixed attention is prayer'.[41] For her in this movement of attending we are given over to the good, and so lose ourselves,

---

[39]Kierkegaard, *Prayers of Kierkegaard*, 212.
[40]Kierkegaard, *Prayers of Kierkegaard*, 52.
[41]Simone Weil, 'Attention and Will', in *Simone Weil: An Anthology*, ed. Sian Miles (London: Penguin Books, 2005), 231.

as resistant to the good, in it. Elsewhere she writes that 'it is only from the light which streams constantly from heaven that a tree can derive its energy to drive its roots deep into the soil. The tree is in fact rooted in the sky.'[42] It is as we attend to grace that we are given roots deep down in the earth. So, far from opposing nature and grace like Kant, Weil roots earthly, natural, life itself in the light that shines upon all. The form the subject takes, for Weil, is bound up with the quality of its attention.

What I have tried to show throughout this chapter is that the formal elements of prayerful discourse are intended as a kind of subject-making. It is in prayer that the subject speaks in order not to wield power over a divine agent, but rather in order to have that speech become objective to itself. In hearing one's own desires spoken, one hears them relative to the shape of the divine life given in the person of Christ. For Kierkegaard, prayer is the moment at which the subject comes to crisis. Similarly, in earlier thinkers, who are not Christian in any straightforward sense, the formal feature of prayer, that it is a moment at which the subject attends to itself in another, remains.

---

[42]Simone Weil, 'Human Personality', in *Simone Weil: An Anthology*, 77. To see this developed, see Simone Kotva, *Effort and Grace: On the Spiritual Exercise of Philosophy* (London: Bloomsbury, 2020), chapter 5.

CHAPTER TWENTY-FIVE

Karl Barth's Very Theological Theology of Prayer

ASHLEY COCKSWORTH

Prayer is an underrepresented theme in the scholarship on Karl Barth's theology. You could read many an introduction to Barth without coming across the theme. After all, what we are talking about when we talk about prayer is Christian experience, a dimension of the Christian life Barth never quite knew what to do with. Likewise, you could read many an introduction to Christian theology without encountering much on prayer. However, if the emerging scholarly consensus is anything to go by, something has gone badly wrong in modern theology if prayer is no longer seen as central to the nature and task of Christian theology.[1] Yet prayer is no less periphery to Barth's thinking as it is to Christian theology itself. While there are central sections in Barth's theology where he sets his sights on explicit theorizations of prayer, in a much more fundamental sense Barth thinks his theology *through* prayer. It could be said that Barth's entire theology is a form of

---

[1] On this, see Andrew Prevot, *Thinking Prayer: Theology and Spirituality amid the Crises of Modernity* (Notre Dame, IN: University of Notre Dame Press, 2015) and Mark A. McIntosh, 'Theology and Spirituality', in *The Modern Theologians: An Introduction to Christian Theology Since 1918*, ed. David F. Ford and Rachel Muers, 3rd edn (Oxford: Wiley-Blackwell, 2005), 392–407.

prayer, an extended contemplative stretching to God undertaken in the obedience and humility of prayer.

In this chapter, I explore how prayer gets written into the logic of Barth's dogmatic thinking. From an initial consideration of the 'integrity' of dogmatics and prayer in Barth's theology,[2] my focus shifts to the doctrinal specifics of his theory of prayer, looking particularly at the Christology that sits at its heart. There I will show how Barth's Christology develops in conjunction with his theorizing of prayer – the one deepens as the other matures. The result is a very *theological* theology of prayer.[3] But first, a brief note on Barth's writings on prayer.

Barth on Prayer

I will not attempt in this chapter an overview of the full range of what Barth has to say about prayer.[4] But what follows, brief as it is, should nevertheless give an indication of the generativity of the theme. Heuristically speaking, his various engagements with prayer can be seen to intensify into two main periods: those undertaken in the late 1940s and early 1950s, and those a decade later in the 1950s and early 1960s. The first period comprises his treatments of prayer in the doctrine of providence (*CD* III/3) begun in the summer of 1948 and finished a year later; the ethics of creation (*CD* III/4) completed in 1951; and in the seminars on the Lord's Prayer delivered in Neuchâtel in 1947 and 1949.[5] A decade or so later, Barth circled back, with yet more intensity and verve, to the theme of prayer in two main textual contexts. First, in the lectures that would have become the ethical

---

[2]The use of the term 'integrity' is borrowed from Mark A. McIntosh, *Mystical Theology: The Integrity of Spirituality and Theology* (Oxford: Blackwell, 1998).

[3]This is a gesture to John Webster's use of the term 'theological theology', which develops in dialogue with fundamental movements in Barth's theology. In various publications, Webster, often mediating Eberhard Jüngel, has been a crucial voice in the reception of the moral and ethical dimensions of Barth's theology of prayer. See John Webster *Barth's Ethics of Reconciliation* (Cambridge: Cambridge University Press, 1995) and *Barth's Moral Theology: Human Action in Barth's Thought* (Edinburgh: T&T Clark, 1998).

[4]For better coverage, see my *Karl Barth on Prayer* (London: T&T Clark, 2015), especially 1–24. For other engagements with Barth on prayer, see John C. McDowell, '"Openness to the World": Karl Barth's Evangelical Theology of Christ as the Pray-er', *Modern Theology* 25, no. 2 (2009): 253–83; Matthew Myer Boulton, '"We Pray by His Mouth": Karl Barth, Erving Goffman, and a Theology of Invocation', *Modern Theology* 17, no. 1 (2001): 67–83; and JinHyok Kim, *The Spirit of God and the Christian Life: Reconstructing Karl Barth's Pneumatology* (Minneapolis, MN: Fortress Press, 2014).

[5]Barth, *CD* III/3, 265–88; Barth, *CD* III/4, 87–115; and Karl Barth, *Prayer*, trans. Sara F. Terrien, ed. Don E. Saliers (Louisville, KY: Westminster John Knox Press, 2002) – hereafter: *Prayer*.

part-volume to the doctrine of reconciliation.[6] These lectures, published posthumously as *The Christian Life* and left unfinished at the time of his death, are structured around the controlling theme of the invocation of God and organized around the petitions of the Lord's Prayer. The significance of the *Church Dogmatics*, the sum of Barth's life and work, finding its end in a sustained meditation on prayer, should not be missed – on this, more later. The ethics of prayer developed in the doctrinal context of reconciliation is complemented by a second treatment of prayer in roughly the same period in which Barth offers his most articulated reflection on the relation between prayer and the task of theology. The material was first given as the lectures he delivered on the occasion of his retirement from the University of Basel in the winter semester of 1961–2 and then later published as *Evangelical Theology: An Introduction.*[7]

The mature engagements with prayer are not direct repetitions of the earlier material so much as improvisations.[8] The later material recapitulates the doctrinal moves enunciated in the late 1940s both extensively (extending into new territory, not least breaking new ground in terms of pneumatology and the politics of prayer) and intensively (what was earlier treated as one aspect of a broader package of practices is now positioned front and centre as the single structuring motif around which the entire part-volume and thus Barth's mature account of Christian existence spin). As such, Barth's theological thinking about prayer, like his prayer-life, is constantly *in via* – it is on the move,[9] shifting and changing as it plays catch-up with the twists and turns of his dogmatic theology. What difference would a hermeneutical lens such as prayer make to the way Barth's dogmatics is read?

---

[6]Karl Barth, *The Christian Life: Church Dogmatics IV/4 – Lecture Fragments* (Edinburgh: T&T Clark, 1981) – hereafter: *ChrL*. For scholarly comment, see Eberhard Jüngel, 'Invocation of God as the Ethical Ground of Christian Action: Introductory Remarks on the Posthumous Fragments of Karl Barth's Ethics of the Doctrine of Reconciliation', in *Theological Essays I*, trans. John Webster (Edinburgh: T&T Clark, 1989), 154–72.

[7]Karl Barth, *Evangelical Theology: An Introduction* (London: Collins, 1965), 159–70 – hereafter: *ET*. Other treatments on prayer include an early paper on the Lord's Prayer: Karl Barth, 'Die ursprüngliche Gestalt des Unser Vaters, 1906', in *Vorträge und kleinere Arbeiten 1905–1909*, Gesamtausgabe III.21, ed. Hans–Anton Drewes and Hinrich Stoevesandt (Zürich: Theologischer Verlag, 1992), 126–47; a section on prayer in the Münster Lectures of the 1920s translated as Karl Barth, *Ethics* (Edinburgh: T&T Clark, 1981), 472–88; and his lecture delivered in October 1929 on the Christian life published as: Karl Barth, *The Holy Spirit and the Christian Life: The Theological Basis of Ethics* (Louisville, KY: Westminster John Knox Press, 1993).

[8]There is significant overlap, however – not least in the way these mature deliberations reassert the Christology of prayer first developed in *CD* III/3 and the centrality of the theme of petition and the Lord's Prayer.

[9]This is the conclusion Jonathan D. Teubner also reaches of Augustine in his chapter in this volume.

Dogmatics and/as Prayer

On the opening pages of the first part-volume of the *Church Dogmatics*, Barth sets the doxological tone for everything that follows.[10] 'Prayer' is 'the attitude without which there can be no dogmatic work', he writes.[11] Although these words, published in 1932, were a fitting way to begin his systematics, the move to prayer first occurred outside the literary context of the *Church Dogmatics*. It was in his engagement with Anselm a few years earlier, from whom he learnt so much, that he settled on a theological methodology that would not only initiate the starting over of his dogmatic project but begin a life-long commitment to the integration of theology and prayer.[12] Like Anselm, who received his argument for the existence of God (which is more prayer than proof) in the liturgical context of Matins and would offer those insights in the context and form of prayer, Barth's theology would unfold as an exercise in prayer seeking understanding.[13] Although unlike Anselm, Barth does not write in the register of prayer, it remains very much the case that the context, if not the language, of prayer is what makes theological language *theological*, situating as it does knowledge of God in the story of fall (penitence) and redemption (praise), of impossibility and possibility.

While Barth assumes the integrity of prayer and dogmatics early in his theology, it is not until much later that he begins to unpack the assumption. In his 1953 'The Gift of Freedom' lecture delivered at the meeting of the *Gesellschaft für evangelische Theologie* in the German city of Bielefeld, Barth offers this ringing endorsement of the *lex orandi*: 'Far from being a pious statement, [*lex orandi, lex credendi*] is one of the most profound descriptions of the theological method.'[14] Three years later in his 'The Humanity of God' lecture, which is famous for providing a rare moment of autobiography and self-reflection, Barth would go one step further in not only endorsing a theological methodology that has the 'character of prayer', but strikingly

---

[10]In the subtitle to this section, I am alluding to and adapting the 'of/as' dynamic Travis LaCouter helpfully articulates in his chapter in this volume in respect of Balthasar's handling of prayer.
[11]Barth, *CD* I/1, 23.
[12]Karl Barth, *Anselm: Fides Quaerens Intellectum* (London: SCM Press, 1960).
[13]As others have noticed, Barth's theory of knowing is driven by doxological rather than strictly epistemological (in the modern sense of that term) matters. For example, see Alan J. Torrance, *Persons in Communion: An Essay on Trinitarian Description and Human Participation* (Edinburgh: T&T Clark, 1996). Although reading Barth as a spiritual writer is not customary, there are exceptions, such as Mark A. McIntosh, 'Humanity in God: On Reading Karl Barth in Relation to Mystical Theology', *Heythrop Journal* 34, no. 1 (1993): 22–40.
[14]Karl Barth, 'The Gift of Freedom', in *The Humanity of God* (Louisville, KY: Westminster John Knox Press, 2002), 69–96 (90).

claiming that the 'fundamental form of theology is ... prayer'.[15] His dogmatics is a sort of prayer, even if it does not necessarily take the form of prayer.

However, as mentioned above, it is in the lectures that would formally end Barth's academic career that the most compelling reflections on the theology-prayer relation occur. Here Barth returns full circle to the theological methodology of Anselm of Canterbury, retelling for his readers the contemplative circumstances of Anselm's philosophical inspiration.

> Gazing upon himself, Anselm prayed: ... Reveal me from myself to thee! Grant that I may understand!) And gazing upon God: ... Restore thyself to me! Give thyself to me, my God! In the performance of theological work the realization of this double act of God (together with this double entreaty) is necessary throughout, since God's act in both respects can occur only as his free act of grace and wondrousness.[16]

It is worth noting that when given the opportunity to use these lectures to pick up where his lecturing on the *Church Dogmatics* left off (i.e. with the third petition of the Lord's Prayer in the ethics of reconciliation), Barth decided instead to offer an introduction to Christian theology. At the end of his life, he returned to fundamentals. And in his introductory exploration of the building blocks of theological work, which includes study, love and solitude, the 'keynote' to all this, Barth says, is prayer.

> The first and basic act of theological work is *prayer*. ... But theological work does not merely begin with prayer and is not merely accompanied by it; in its totality it is peculiar and characteristic of theology that it can be performed only in the act of prayer.[17]

Prayer does not make theological work any easier, Barth is clear. It does not permit the theologian to shy away from 'crack[ing] the hard nuts' , or passing over into some uncritical piety.[18] Contrary to the modern assumption that prayer risks diluting the intellectual credibility of the theological task with an uncritical piety, a theology undertaken in the context of prayer 'is work; in fact, very hard work'.[19] Arguably, a theology that embraces the cognitive and the affective via the praying body in the way that a contemplative theology

---

[15]Karl Barth, 'The Humanity of God', in *The Humanity of God*, 37–65 (57).
[16]Barth, *ET*, 169.
[17]Barth, *ET*, 160.
[18]Barth, *ET*, 167.
[19]Barth, *ET*, 160.

should is more not less conceptually demanding than one that trades on the notion of propositional assent alone.[20] Prayer is a complex domain – full of tensions, paradoxes and contradictions. Hence, in Barth's theorization of prayer, God is not simply present or absent but complexly both; God is not simply immutable or mutable but complexly both; and agency is not simply divvied up as a work of human making or an activity of grace but complexly both – divinely propelled but no less human because of it. Although conceptually inelegant, these tensions are part and parcel of the lived reality of prayer. Indeed, written into the practice of prayer is an inherent paradox. It is something we cannot do as we ought, but is nonetheless to be undertaken unceasingly. On these terms, could it be that the dialectics for which Barth's theology is famed are the products of the very dialectics he felt in prayer? Could it be that prayer supplies him with the conceptual dexterity to think dialectically and then the confidence to proceed without the urge to tidy things up into something more conceptually straightforward?

At this point, a sideward comparison can be made to Barth's Basel colleague, Hans Urs von Balthasar. Often Balthasar is read in the shadow of Barth. Balthasar, twenty years Barth's younger, was clearly influenced by several of Barth's emphases – christocentrism, the themes of beauty and glory, a critical stance towards modernity, a positive reclamation of the theological tradition and much else.[21] In fact, Balthasar freely acknowledges that he is most Barthian at the time of writing his classic book on prayer, *Das betrachtende Gebet* (1955), with its strong Christology of (contemplative) prayer.[22] However, when it comes to the reclaiming of the lost unity of prayer and theology, it is tempting to see Barth borrowing more from Balthasar than the other way around.[23] If there is one name in twentieth-century European theology associated with a theology undertaken on its knees, that name is Balthasar. Nevertheless, although Barth and Balthasar might

---

[20]See Sarah Coakley, *God, Sexuality, and the Self: An Essay 'On the Trinity'* (Cambridge: Cambridge University Press, 2012), 16. When it comes to Barth scholarship, the affections remain a neglected theme. While more work is required to understand the positive place of experience in Barth's theology, it is suggestive that there is something of an affective turn in these swansong lectures which we encounter Barth speaking more comfortably than ever of the emotions he feels as he goes about his theological work: gratitude, wonder, concern, doubt. See Joseph L. Mangina, *Karl Barth on the Christian Life: The Practical Knowledge of God* (New York: Peter Lang, 2001).

[21]Hans Urs von Balthasar, *The Theology of Karl Barth: Exposition and Interpretation* (San Francisco, CA: Ignatius Press, 1992).

[22]See Balthasar, *The Theology of Karl Barth*, 400. For the prayer book, see Hans Urs von Balthasar, *Prayer* (San Francisco, CA: Ignatius Press, 1986).

[23]For example, see Hans Urs von Balthasar, 'Theology and Sanctity', in *Explorations in Theology – Volume I: The Word Made Flesh* (San Francisco, CA: Ignatius Press, 1989), 181–210.

agree on the principle of *lex orandi*, the law of prayer comes to behave quite differently in their respective theologies.

While working as a student chaplain at the University of Basel, Balthasar met Adrienne von Speyr, whom he received into the Roman Catholic Church in 1940, and soon after came under the influence of her extraordinary visions and mystical experiences, of which Balthasar acted as a kind of scribe.[24] They say Speyr lived simultaneously on earth and in heaven and had on this basis access to the prayer lives of the canonized dead. As well as transcribing these visions, Balthasar sought to incorporate them directly into his theology. This is part of what gives Balthasar's theology such a distinctive style. However, for a critic such as Karen Kilby, Balthasar's *kniende Theologie* is not unproblematic. 'It can give rise to a theology which too often goes too far, which knows and asserts too much, which argues too little, which has a persistent tendency to exceed all bounds – a theology, indeed, that does not seem to hold itself accountable to scripture, tradition, or its readers, but somehow soars about them all.'[25] His authorial voice often assumes a 'divine perspective' in ways Sarah Coakley's contemplative theology could appear to give privileged access to the otherwise inaccessible realm of divine things (though Coakley's is persistently checked by an 'appropriately apophatic sensibility' that grounds knowledge of God in the priority of unknowing).[26] This becomes especially problematic for Kilby if Balthasar's theology relies on the experience of Speyr to whom we have almost no access except through Balthasar. While Balthasar seems to integrate the experience of prayer with his theology to assume knowledge that might not otherwise be known (on matters trinitarian, on sin and suffering, and even on the status of our salvation), Kilby finds no such temptation in Barth's theology. 'Barth very clearly understands himself as *one* Christian voice in disagreement with others: he stands *opposed* to, rather than above, other theological positions.'[27] An example to illustrate the point can be found in Barth's account of petitionary prayer.

One of the defining marks of Barth's theology of prayer is its strong prioritization of petitionary prayer. In *CD* III/3 and *CD* III/4, he expends a great deal of energy defending the distinctiveness and centrality of prayer as

---

[24]I am drawing on Karen Kilby's reading of the Balthasar–Speyr relationship in *Balthasar: A (Very) Critical Introduction* (Grand Rapids, MI: William B. Eerdmans, 2012), 26–31. For critical engagement with Kilby's Balthasar, see Travis LaCouter's chapter in this volume.

[25]Kilby, *Balthasar*, 40.

[26]Coakley, *God, Sexuality, and the Self*, 45. I explore this line of critique in 'On Prayer in Anglican Systematic Theology', *International Journal of Systematic Theology* 22, no. 3 (2020): 383–411.

[27]Kilby, *Balthasar*, 164.

petition. In fact, these sections are largely dominated by lengthy and repetitive apologias, biblical and otherwise, for selecting petition as 'the constitutive element in what takes place in prayer'.[28] Part of the reason for such a strong defence of the petitionary is contextual. In the theological context in which Barth was writing, petitionary prayer, and the thorny theological issues it throws up, was increasingly unfashionable.[29] Barth sees himself deliberately departing from some of the theories of prayer that de-prioritize petition and retrieving instead especially from the Reformation tradition what was sometimes seen as an almost childlike practice the pray-er would otherwise leave behind as they matured in faith. The foil here, as can be expected, is really Schleiermacher whom Barth later charges with switching petition for 'self-help', thereby reducing the dialogue of prayer to a mere monologue – a conversational incurvature.[30]

However, for all Barth has to say about petitionary prayer and the anthropology it implies he appears almost entirely uninterested in spelling out the mechanics of how these petitions get answered. This is partly because his concern is as much with the ethical as the theological (prayer does something to the pray-er as much as it does something to God in a version of Thomas' account of petitionary prayer as the transformation of desire) and partly because of his ever strong Christology of prayer. God answers prayer because it is God who prays, in the voice of the praying Son and in whom we find our own praying voice. But Barth's ambivalence towards over-explaining the given of the divine answering of prayer is also in part because he knows that knowledge reaches a limit when it approaches, as prayer does, the 'innermost centre' of the covenant of grace.[31] In one of the few instances when Barth pauses to reflect on the mysteries of the divine answering of the petitions we pray, he has this to say:

[Prayer] is a genuine and actual share in the universal lordship of God. The will of God is not to preserve and accompany and rule the world and the course of the world as world-occurrence in such a way that He is not affected and moved by it, that He does not allow Himself to converse with it, that He does not listen to what it says, that as He conditions all things He does not allow Himself to be determined by them. God is not free and immutable in the sense that He is the prisoner of His own

---

[28]Barth, CD III/3, 267.

[29]Albeit covering a different context, Rick Ostrander's study is instructive, *The Life of Prayer in a World of Science: Protestants, Prayer, and American Culture, 1870–1930* (New York: Oxford University Press, 2000).

[30]Barth, *ChrL*, 103.

[31]Barth, CD III/4, 93.

resolve and will and action, that He must always be alone as the Lord of all things and of all occurrence. He is not alone in His trinitarian being, and He is not alone in relation to creatures. He is free and immutable as the living God, as the God who wills to converse with the creature, and to allow Himself to be determined by it in this relationship. His sovereignty is so great that it embraces both the possibility, and, as it is exercised, the actuality, that the creature can actively be present and co-operate in His overruling. There is no creaturely freedom which can limit or compete with the sole sovereignty and efficacy of God. But permitted by God, and indeed willed and created by Him, there is the freedom of the friends of God concerning whom He has determined that without abandoning the helm for one moment He will still allow Himself to be determined by them.[32]

I am quoting at length show that Barth makes no attempt to resolve these paradoxes. It is wrong to think God does not answer prayer; and it is equally wrong to suppose that God answers prayer in a way that compromises either God's sovereignty or human freedom. But Barth does not, as Kilby notices in respect of his treatment of evil, present a third option that resolves the paradox of God's changeable immutability.[33] In the absence of a neat resolution, he simply affirms the paradox, invites 'humble astonishment' of it and offers its mystery as a gift to be received rather than a problem to be solved.[34]

Knowing where to draw the line on things unknown is a sign of a theological honesty and learning to be comfortable in this space of unknowing is a product of prayer. It is curious that around the time modern theology was pulling away from a theology that depended on prayer, the dialectical notion of God's 'changeable immutability' (a version of the patristic dialectics of God's 'immutable suffering') was no longer reputable. Now God either has to suffer or cannot suffer in a similar way to how human agency has to be either wholly free or wholly determined by God.[35] In other words, by pulling away from the mysterious dynamics of prayer, modern theology began to lose something of the conceptual dexterity to think dialectically and the willingness to allow those tensions to remain unresolved. Unlike Balthasar's desire to go further than you can go, Barth's theology does not proceed with such confidence. It knows when to hold back. Put differently,

---

[32]Barth, *CD* III/3, 285.
[33]Kilby, *Balthasar*, 165–6.
[34]Barth, *CD* III/3, 266.
[35]See Paul L. Gavrilyuk, *The Suffering of the Impassible God: The Dialectics of Patristic Thought* (Oxford: Oxford University Press, 2004).

Barth's getting on his knees to pray is less about accessing that which is otherwise unavailable and more about confession. There is no ascent of the mind into the realm of the divine to say what otherwise cannot be said, but a penitential grounding in the humility of the theological task. Barth is brought to his knees in the confession that the words the theologian speaks are fragile and fallen, in the supplication that God may take these words and make them holy, and in the thanksgiving that despite all this 'theological work may and should be courageously started and performed'.[36]

While the circumstances of life forced the *Church Dogmatics* to remain incomplete at the time of Barth's death, there is something of theological, even spiritual, significance in the unfinished character of his theology. Unlike Balthasar's, Barth's *magnum opus* remains unfinished – partial and imperfect. Despite saying so much, Barth is not the sort of writer who wants to have the last word. For all those many millions of words, he could not get to the end of speaking about the God experienced in prayer and revealed in Jesus Christ. Part of the sensibility of a theology undertaken on the knees is its critical awareness of its own vulnerability, its finitude, its resistance to 'total perspective'.[37] Indeed, there is something doubly significant about the ending of the *Church Dogmatics* – not only that it remains unfinished, but that it ends where it does. If Anna Williams is right in understanding Aquinas' *Summa* as both contemplation and an exhortation to pray,[38] then something similar could be going on in the *Church Dogmatics* in the sense that part of the project of the *Church Dogmatics* is to lead the reader to their knees and back into prayer. This is literally the case given where the *Church Dogmatics* ends: with that lengthy and incomplete petition-by-petition examination of the Lord's Prayer.

If finished, Barth's final treatment of the Lord's Prayer would have been unrivalled in terms of size and scope. Unravelling an entire and extended Christian ethics around the petitions of the Lord's Prayer was always an ambitious if exhilarating plan, and it is not surprising that it proved too much even for the ambition of a figure such as Barth. He made no plans to finish his treatment of the Lord's Prayer. He left no sketch of where he might end up. He gave no indication of where his thinking on prayer would lead him in the way he hints at how his unwritten doctrine of the Lord's Supper might be constructed from his doctrine of baptism. There is something about

---

[36]Barth, *ET*, 170.
[37]The phrase is Rowan Williams', used in the context of talking about a prayerful, 'honest' theology in *On Christian Theology* (Oxford: Blackwell, 2000), 8.
[38]A. N. Williams, 'Mystical Theology Redux: The Pattern of Aquinas' Summa Theologiae', *Modern Theology* 13, no. 1 (1997): 53–74.

prayer that outstrips even Barth's commanding mind. His theology, like his prayer life,[39] is always *in via* and never 'arrived'. It is developmental, constantly evolving, never fully stable – confidently insecure.

In the next section, I turn from considering the prayerful character of Barth's dogmatics to the dogmatic character of his theory of prayer, paying particular attention to the way his Christology develops in dialogue with his writings on prayer.

Christology and Prayer

Barth was not in the business of producing a practical 'guide' to praying. If anything, he thinks instead that 'prayer begins where this kind of exercise leaves off'.[40] The closest he comes to giving concrete advice is the criteria for 'true prayer' delivered as part of his ethics of creation. While these criteria have practical implications (e.g. whereas individual prayer can be silent, he instructs prayers in church to be vocal; extemporary prayer should be avoided, but set times of prayer can be helpful; morning and evening prayer have 'a solid basis'; and grace at meals 'is also well founded as a serious expression of human need'), the overriding concern in *CD* III/4 remains, as elsewhere, with the articulation of the theological shape of prayer.[41] There are systematic reasons for Barth's very theological description of prayer.

For Barth, it is no more possible to produce a spirituality independent from the dogmatic task than it is to produce an independent Christian ethics.[42] As a consequence, Barth's writings on prayer, somewhat uncustomarily for a modern theologian, become complexly embedded into his dogmatic project. His very theological approach to prayer could mean that in order to get a handle on his theory of prayer you need first a sense of the broader doctrines that sit behind and drive his doxological thinking. These would include, for example, his doctrines of grace, God's mutable immutability, the *concursus Dei*, ecclesiology, pneumatology, Christology, election and so on. While Barth draws down, as it were, doctrinal priorities enunciated elsewhere to help him theorize prayer, that dogmatics *is* spirituality means that the

---

[39]I am thinking of how the harshness of Barth's critique of Catholic spiritual practice mellowed towards the end of his life, embracing even the *Ave Maria* during one spell in hospital, as reported in Eberhard Busch, *Karl Barth: His Life from Letters and Autobiographical Texts* (London: SCM Press, 1976), 471.

[40]Barth, *CD* III/4, 98.

[41]Barth, *CD* III/4, 113.

[42]On this, see *Karl Barth: Spiritual Writings*, ed. Ashley Cocksworth and W. Travis McMaken, CWS (New York: Paulist Press, 2022).

hermeneutical lens also points in the other direction. What I mean by this is that Barth's writings on prayer themselves reveal new aspects of his doctrinal thinking, nuancing and giving texture to his doctrinal thought. Approaching doctrinal matters through what a theologian has to say about prayer leads to unexpected results. Barth himself speaks of how he gets caught out when Luther starts unexpectedly sounding much more like Calvin and Calvin like Luther when he approaches them through their writings on prayer rather than more familiar doctrinal routes.[43] And, in turn, Barth's own settling on prayer as the chief practice through which the reconciled Christian life is concretely expressed catches out some of Barth's commentators. As Colin Gunton remarks: 'So, really, surprisingly he likes all this stuff about invocation – who would have guessed it?'[44]

To gain a full measure of what a theologian thinks doctrinally means attending, then, to what they have to say on prayer as well as what might come from their more doctrinally explicit writings. This is certainly the case for a figure such as Barth. Take his doctrine of the Holy Spirit, a doctrine that has frequently come to disappoint his commentators.[45] When accessed via his writings on prayer (which take textual cues from Romans 8) rather than his more doctrinal teaching, his pneumatology ends up looking a good deal livelier than the standard critiques suggest. The Holy Spirit, far from having much to do, is the transformative agent who catches the human pray-er up into the life of the divine. Likewise, approaching his doctrine of human agency via his writings on prayer makes the rather tired jibe that Barth's concept of creaturely freedom is more apparent than real difficult to sustain.[46] In prayer, Barth says, again, far from not having anything to do, we 'find ourselves at the very seat of government, at the very heart of the mystery and purpose of all occurrence'.[47] As we have seen, Barth goes all out to affirm the full human reality of prayer. He not only builds prayer into his ethics of creation as the paradigmatic embodiment of human freedom before God, but singularly arranges his most mature account of the Christian life around the theme of invocation and the actual petitions of the Lord's Prayer.

---

[43]Barth, *Prayer*, 4.

[44]Colin E. Gunton, *The Barth Lectures*, ed. Paul H. Brazier (London: T&T Clark, 2007), 232.

[45]For example, Robert W. Jenson, 'You Wonder Where the Spirit Went', *Pro Ecclesia* 2 (1993): 296–304.

[46]Critics of Barth on freedom would include: John Macken, *The Autonomy Theme in the Church Dogmatics: Karl Barth and His Critics* (Cambridge: Cambridge University Press, 1990) and Nigel Biggar, *The Hastening that Waits: Karl Barth's Ethics* (Oxford: Oxford University Press, 1993). For a defence of Barth's doctrine of freedom which makes constructive use of his theology of invocation, see Robert Leigh, *Freedom and Flourishing: Being, Act, and Knowledge in Karl Barth's Church Dogmatics* (Eugene, OR: Cascade Books, 2017), 207–12.

[47]Barth, *CD* III/3, 288.

My argument, then, is that the sections on prayer in Barth's theology can be understood as doctrinally disclosive. They do not only depend on the doctrinal work undertaken elsewhere in the *Church Dogmatics*, but are themselves sites of doctrinal significance. This is the case for the pneumatology that emerges from his writings on prayer and for his understanding of human freedom too. Likewise, his non-conflictual account of the divine–human relation developed elsewhere remains in the abstract until it gains concrete expression in his treatment of prayer.[48]

In what follows, I am going to test the argument for the doctrinally disclosive nature of prayer against the most Barthian of Barth's doctrines: his Christology. If Christology is an exercise in clarifying speech about God, it is also (or should be) an exercise that clarifies what we are theologically up to when we speak *to* God in prayer. And if these two – speaking about and speaking to God – are connected in the way Barth suggests they are, these should be mutually illuminating of each other: a clarification of one illuminates the other. Barth's Christology thus clarifies and complexifies his theology of prayer and, in turn, his theology of prayer clarifies and complexifies his Christology. The two develop in 'complexifying' conjunction with each other.[49]

Barth's theology of prayer is stamped by his Christology. I will come to the strengths of his christological take on prayer in a moment, but not before identifying one vulnerability. There is least a suggestion that Barth overplays his hand when it comes to the Christology of prayer. He unfairly and too swiftly rejects entire swathes of the tradition of Christian prayer for emphasizing too strongly the subjective dimensions of Christian prayer – both Quakerism and the Ignatian traditions are named targets, but others are implied.[50] The subjective dimensions need to be cleared to make way for a fully 'objective', he says, and by that he means a fully *christological* account of prayer.

> We can never rate too highly the objective significance of the Christian attitude, even if we are thinking only of the individual Christian as such. Nor can we reject too strongly those theories which seek to restrict the significance of prayer to the subjective sphere alone.[51]

It is not only these traditions Barth has little time for, but the canonical figures they represent. There is little by way of substantive interaction in

---

[48]As articulated through the *concursus Dei* in Barth, CD III/3, 90–154.
[49]For further theorization of the 'complexifing' dynamic of prayer, see my 'Theorizing the (Anglican) *lex orandi*: A Theological Account', *Modern Theology* 36, no. 2 (2020), 298–316.
[50]Barth, CD III/4, 97–8, 112.
[51]Barth, CD III/3, 288.

his lengthy treatments of prayer or elsewhere for that matter with the likes of Meister Eckhart, the author of The Cloud of Unknowing, Thérèse de Lisieux, Thomas à Kempis, John of the Cross, and Teresa of Avila or Ignatius of Loyola. It would appear that Barth needs to look no further than Jesus Christ for matters pertaining to the spiritual life of prayer. There is more to Barth's anxiety than meets the eye here. When rejecting these traditions of prayer as too subjectivistic, it is Schleiermacher (and all that that name comes to represent) in the cross hairs.[52] On Barth's terms, an unchecked over-privileging of the experiential in prayer is just another production of the self-absorbed subject that seeks self-mastery and self-discovery. That is not to say Barth is entirely unwilling to plumb the inner depths of prayer, but he would want to insist that whatever is excavated requires testing in the corporate context of the praying community (hence the overriding emphasis across the iterations of his theory of prayer on the 'we', the 'our' of the Lord's Prayer) and then qualifying, and decisively so, via Christology. This is ultimately why Barth prioritizes petitionary prayer. We call upon God in prayers of petition becasue Jesus teaches us to pray 'like this' (cf. Matt. 6.9). What is lost by sidelining so much of the history of Christian praying? What would his theory of prayer look like had it been worked out in actual dialogue with some of the great theorizers of prayer the Christian tradition has to offer?

It is undeniably the case that whatever Barth has to say about prayer is shaped christologically, but it is equally, though less obviously, the case that Barth's Christology is shaped by prayer. For example, the work undertaken in the first of the two periods of his intensive thinking on prayer generates some complex christological resources that invites in-depth doctrinal unpacking further down the line in the *Church Dogmatics*. Threaded through Barth's writings on prayer of the early 1950s is an embryonic version of his (soon to be extensively developed and rejigged) doctrine of the threefold office of Christ.[53] What is referred to *in nuce* in his writings on prayer comes to

---

[52]On closer inspection, Schleiermacher's theology of prayer is much more christological – orientated as it is around the 'name of Jesus' – than Barth lets on. See Friedrich Schleiermacher, *The Christian Faith* (Edinburgh: T&T Clark, 1999), 668–75. It would seem that it is all that Schleiermacher comes to represent in Barth's theology that Barth is targeting, rather than specifically his writings on prayer.

[53]For comment on the use of the offices in Barth's thinking on prayer, see Christopher C. Green, *Doxological Theology: Karl Barth on Divine Providence, Evil and the Angels* (London: T&T Clark, 2011), 140 and Hans Theodor Goebel, 'Struktur und Aussageabsicht der Vorsehungslehre K. Barths Historische und dogmatische Analyse von KD III/3', *Zeitschrift für dialektische Theologie* 10, no. 2 (1994): 135–57. Tom Greggs also thinks with Barth to organize his Christology of prayer in this volume around the offices of Christ; and John C. McDowell in respect of Torrance, also in this volume.

occupy entire part-volumes in the doctrine of reconciliation in which the offices of Christ would be tackled separately and then put back together in the ethics of reconciliation via the integrative logic of prayer. Moreover, as well as generating the dogmatic raw material for more extensive doctrinal investigation, his writings on prayer complexify his Christology. As John Webster notices, when approached via his writings on prayer, 'Barth's Christology ... is considerably more diverse than is often assumed'.[54]

For Barth, 'something has happened in Jesus Christ' that 'enables' the Christian to pray.[55] The 'something' Barth has in mind is not a single christological insistence, but is more complicated, more multi-dimensional than any one thing. To be more specific, his theory of prayer oscillates between and sometimes conflates altogether at least three christological affirmations: the exemplary, the vicarious and the incorporative. First, the exemplary. This aspect of Barth's Christology of prayer concerns the emphasis he places on Christ's human existence as providing the pattern for human action. Jesus Christ is the example pray-er *par excellence*. Paul's injunction that 'we do not know how to pray as we ought' (Rom. 8.26) suggests that in order to pray we need first to be taught how to pray. For Barth, Jesus taught by example. 'This man prayed', he writes.[56] Jesus Christ prayed at the transfiguration; he prayed in the Garden of Gethsemane before his arrest; he prayed at the crucifixion; he prayed during his ascension; and he continues to pray at the right hand of the Father. And most significantly for Barth when the disciples ask him how to pray, Jesus instructed by praying: 'pray, then, in this way' (Matt. 6.9) and prayed a 'string of petitions'.[57] Barth's prioritization of petitionary prayer is driven by his Christology because to petition means to follow Jesus' exemplary prayer practice as set out in the prayer that takes his name: the Lord's Prayer. 'It was Jesus Christ who led His disciples in prayer and therefore taught them and the whole Church to pray.'[58] In this sense, the petition I pray is 'a repetition of His petition, that it is enclosed in His asking'.[59] At this point we find Barth slipping from the exemplary ('repeating' the prior example of Christ) into the incorporative and vicarious (our prayer being '*enclosed*' in 'His asking').[60]

---

[54]Webster, *Barth's Ethics of Reconciliation*, 185.
[55]Barth, *CD* III/3, 269.
[56]Barth, *CD* III/3, 276.
[57]Barth, *CD* III/3, 268.
[58]Barth, *CD* III/4, 94.
[59]Barth, *CD* III/3, 277.
[60]Webster, *Barth's Ethics of Reconciliation*, 185.

To follow Paul's logic, we cannot pray as we ought because prayer is not, primarily at least, something we 'do'. By this, Barth does not mean there is a gap in our knowledge that Christ's exemplary action and teaching on prayer needs to fill, providing us with all the information we need to go about our praying. Instead, prayer is inherently something we cannot 'do' because prayer is first and foremost the action of the one who lives and acts in our stead. In Barth's consciously 'objective' theory of prayer, 'the first and proper suppliant is none other than Jesus Christ Himself'.[61] This christological 'fact is of decisive practical importance for the meaning and character of Christian prayer', not least because it introduces the second christological affirmation: the vicarious.[62]

Second, Jesus Christ acts on behalf of humanity, standing in our stead, representing us before God in his priestly office as mediator, doing for us what we cannot do for ourselves. Christ, in 'His intercession as that of the great High-priest', takes our place.[63] The judge judged in our place, to use Barth's idiom, becomes the pray-er who prays in our place and both are aspects of his priestly ministry. As Jesus Christ stands in for us (as 'Substitute'), he acts for us (as 'Representative'). 'This means that He, Jesus Christ, is properly and really the One who prays.'[64] Prayer is not so much that which we 'do' (what Barth denigrates with suggested scathe as 'human achievement') but is a more complex participation in a prior divine movement of prayer.[65] Our prayer is divinely enabled, propelled by grace – a responsive calling out (invocation) to a prior calling (vocation) to partake in the doxological flow of glory that moves eternally in the divine life of God. Remember that the first full construct of his account of prayer takes place in the third volume of the *Church Dogmatics*, the doctrine of creation, which is positioned against the doctrinal confession that creation (and all that can be counted as 'creaturely occurrence') is the work of God. The protagonist in prayer, as in the creating of creation, is God, and the pray-er, Barth says, stands under the universal lordship of the God who proceeds, accompanies and rules over all things created.[66]

Nowhere does Barth suggest these two christological movements are to be understood sequentially (as if first the exemplary *then* the vicarious). These are instead part of a singularly complex christological moment. As Christ prays for us, we are given an example of how to pray for ourselves. And as

---

[61]Barth, *CD* III/3, 274.
[62]Barth, *CD* III/3, 274.
[63]Barth, *CD* III/3, 277.
[64]Barth, *CD* III/4, 94.
[65]Barth, *CD* III/3, 277.
[66]Barth, *CD* III/3, 284.

the vicarious moves back into the exemplary, petition becomes intercession. 'For this reason its asking [that is, the church's asking], too, is at the deepest level intercession. As it asks for its own existence, it asks for the world from which it is separated and into which it is sent.'[67] Just as Christ prays for us, the church prays for others – standing in their stead, representing others when they cannot pray themselves, doing for others what Christ does for all. Again, Barth could not conceive a situation where there are two prayers: the prayer of the church 'down here' and the prayer of the interceding Son 'up there'. There is one prayer, the prayer of the praying Christ, into which our prayers are 'enfolded'.

The boldest feature of Barth's Christology of prayer is this third, interlocking insistence that Jesus Christ is not only the one who teaches us to pray and not only the one who himself prays, but is the life of prayer itself in which the pray-er participates. At different points, Barth utilizes different terminology – 'participation', being 'enclosed', 'corresponding' – to make the same claim that Jesus Christ is the pray-er and the very embodiment of what prayer 'is'. True prayer 'is participation in Jesus Christ',[68] or more dynamically, prayer is incorporation into a trinitarian 'movement in the cycle which goes out from God and returns to God'.[69] This is what it means, he says, to pray 'in the name' of Jesus. As we pray in the name of Jesus we are 'lifted up', Barth says, to the place of God.[70] This is Barth's equivalent of the eucharistic *sursum corda* he would not get to write.[71] When the theme of participation eventually gets articulated through the ever-resourceful motif of 'correspondence' (*Entsprechung*) in the ethics of reconciliation, creaturely participation in the prayer of Christ is complemented with a movement in the other direction and thus with a strong affirmation of 'the promise of his [as in *God's*] corresponding action' in our prayer.[72] It is worth dwelling on this third, incorporative movement in Barth's Christology of prayer in which the exemplary and vicarious are fused together in a bit more detail.

Barth's wish to 'depart' from the over-prioritization of the subjective dimensions he encountered and rejected in many theories of prayer instigates a departure from some of the most significant strands of the traditions of Christian prayer. However, his 'objective' theory of prayer is not exactly

---

[67]Barth, *CD* III/3, 278.
[68]Barth, *CD* III/3, 282.
[69]Barth, *CD* III/4, 101.
[70]Barth, *CD* III/3, 287.
[71]Jüngel, 'Invocation of God', 160.
[72]Barth, *ChrL*, 104. For more on Barth's use of the correspondence motif, see my *Karl Barth on Prayer*, 107–16.

a case of Barth going at it alone. Instead, it locates himself a long tradition of Christian spirituality, and one that finds its fullest articulation in Calvin. Barth gets much of his theology of prayer from Calvin,[73] enthusiastically citing and more than once the Reformer's notion that we 'pray, as it were, by His mouth'.[74] This is a term Barth lifts from the Geneva Catechism in its answer to a question which also refers to Romans 8 and which Barth utilizes to tackle the ontologically weighty question of what prayer 'is'.

Praying by 'the mouth of Christ' is useful imagery in the sense that it affirms, simultaneously, the full reality of human prayer (this is the prayer 'we pray'), the embodied nature of prayer (there can be no prayer without the body) and a strong sense of incorporation in the *corpus Christi*, the body of Christ (it is by 'His mouth' that we pray). Whereas Barth sees precedence in Calvin, the source material from which Calvin himself is drawing is thoroughly Augustinian. Neither Barth nor Calvin acknowledges Augustine directly, but on this doxological matter the intellectual borrowings are clear. Augustine, like Calvin and like Barth, articulates his experience of prayer in dialogue with Pauline literature (this time Galatians) as 'putting on' (*induere*) or being 'clothed by' Christ.[75] As Augustine 'puts on' Christ in prayer, he can speak back, as it were, to God 'with Christ's voice'.[76] In his sermon on Psalm 85, he speaks of how 'we must recognize our voices in him, and his accents in ourselves'.[77] And again, 'we pray, then, to him, through him and in him; we speak with him and he speaks with us. We utter in him, and he utters in us'.[78] Although Augustine's christological notion of *induere* takes on certain modifications under Barth's theorization, there is a similarly incorporative logic to be found. By putting on Christ we are adopted into the life of Christ and become children of God. And as with Augustine so too with Barth, it is by being incorporated into the humanity of Christ that we are 'clothed with His divine glory'.[79]

Praying by the mouth of Christ implies and requires a logic of sanctification. Christ takes what is unholy and cleanses it, making it holy. This is why Barth is relatively unconcerned about getting prayer 'right'. He is more concerned *that* we pray than what we pray for or how we pray. 'The whole of human

---

[73]As Gunton notes, this includes the theme of the invocation of God, the textual stress on Romans 8 and the Christology of prayer. See Gunton, *The Barth Lectures*, 232.

[74]Barth, *Prayer*, 14; Barth, *CD* III/4, 94, 108; and Barth, *ChrL*, 105.

[75]I am indebted here to the fascinating analysis of *induere* by Jonathan D. Teubner in *Prayer after Augustine: A Study in the Development of the Latin Tradition* (Oxford: Oxford University Press, 2018), 66–84.

[76]Augustine, 'Psalm 85', in *Expositions of the Psalms – Volume 4: 73–98*, trans. Maria Boulding, WSA III/18 (Hyde Park, NY: New City Press, 2000), 220–45 (220).

[77]Augustine, 'Psalm 85', 220; cited in Teubner, *Prayer after Augustine*, 79.

[78]Augustine, 'Psalm 85', 221.

[79]Barth, *CD* III/4, 105.

egoism, the whole of human anxiety, cupidity, desire and passion, or at least the whole of human short-sightedness, unreasonableness and stupidity, might flow into prayer.'[80] But that does not concern Barth because Christ takes our petitions and makes them 'holy petitions'.[81] Again, taking textures cues from Romans 8, Barth offers the following explanation:

> It is not a twofold but a single fact that both Jesus Christ with His prayer and also the Holy Spirit with 'unutterable groanings' is our Mediator and Intercessor. This can and must be said both of Jesus Christ and of the Holy Spirit, and in both cases it concerns the one event of laying a foundation for prayer, i.e. for the cry, Abba, Father. It is He – Jesus Christ through the Spirit, the Spirit as the Spirit of Jesus Christ – who makes good that which we of ourselves cannot make good, who brings our prayer before God and therefore makes it possible as prayer, and who in so doing makes it necessary for us.[82]

He continues:

> And this means that although what we do is in itself very unholy, even when we pray, it will not fail to be sanctified. ... God Himself, accepting it as it stands, gives to it the pure and holy form, the ordered and cleansed meaning, which it did not have in our hearts and mouths. For He understands us better than we do ourselves, and on this side, too, what we do badly is made good by His grace.[83]

Contained within this curious christological movement is the enabling of prayer in the first place and the 'guarantee', Barth says, of being heard. 'Now if the Son asks Him, how can the Father possibly fail to hear Him?'[84]

In the ethics of reconciliation, Barth reverses the already complex dialectic of praying by the mouth of Christ to position the pray-er as the mouth that proclaims Christ to the world – in thought and word and deed – and the eyes that are poised to see the signs of God's grace and discern the forces that work against God's grace (the 'lordless powers'). Indeed, more so than anywhere else, in the ethics of reconciliation it is apparent that simply speaking the petitions of the Lord's Prayer does not go far enough in participating in the ongoing ministry of Jesus Christ. Through the language of correspondence,

---

[80]Barth, *CD* III/4, 100.
[81]Barth, *CD* III/3, 280.
[82]Barth, *CD* III/4, 94.
[83]Barth, *CD* III/4, 101.
[84]Barth, *CD* III/4, 108.

to pray truly means to speak with God the divine project of reconciliation, and thus to speak against the injustices of the world. To 'put on' Christ, then, means to participate in Christ's prophetic revolt against the disorder of the world.

Just as Barth insists on the integration of dogmatics and prayer, Barth also saw prayer and ethics as inherently connected. The *lex agendi* as much as the *lex credendi* is discovered in the *lex orandi*. For all he has to say about the relation between prayer and theology, most of his reflections on prayer take place in ethical sections. And because prayer is ethical so too is it political. There are hints of the politics of prayer in Barth's mid-career work (in the late 1940s and early 1950s) and indeed in his own prayer practice. A contributing factor of his expulsion from his professorial position in Bonn was his refusal to begin his lectures with the oath of loyalty to Hitler, as was required of him. He began instead the final lecture before his suspension with this prayer of praise:

O may this bounteous God
Through all our life be near us
With ever joyful hearts
And blessed peace to cheer us.
And keep us in his grace
And guide us when perplexed
And free us from all ills
In this world and the next.[85]

Barth preached regularly on the Lord's Prayer during his time ministering in Safenwil,[86] as if to say, though not saying it outright, that the petitions of the Lord's Prayer articulate hope in light of despair. The politicization of prayer, or better, the consolidation of what has always been there, was given sustained and concrete expression, however, at the end of Barth's life in the unfinished ethics of reconciliation. There Barth comes to see prayer as not only leading to political action, but itself as a political act. Prayer is *inherently* political. Here he is channelling the broadly Augustinian thesis that through prayer our desires are interrogated, transformed and reordered towards the good – towards God. The more we pray the more our disordered desires are conformed to the likeness of Christ. The result is like dropping a pebble in water. There is a rippling effect, moving outwards from the centre that is

---

[85] Busch, *Karl Barth*, 256.
[86] Busch, *Karl Barth*, 61.

prayer and reordering the world as it flows outwards. The disorder of the world is reordered from the inside out, as it were.

There is an externally facing side to Barth's politics of prayer that complements this internal dynamic of the reordering of the pray-er's desire. The word Barth uses to describe the political shape of prayer is *Aufstand*, literally 'stand-up' (which happens to reflect the most ancient posture for prayer: the *orans*) but is translated as 'revolt' and indicates an ethic of protesting and speaking out against the structures of injustice. 'Christians are summoned', Barth says, 'by God's command not only to zeal for God's honor but also to a simultaneous and related revolt, and therefore to entry into a conflict'.[87] Prayer, if it is to count as Christian, must be accompanied with action against the lordlessness of injustice, oppression and falsehood.

Conclusion

Barth's theology of prayer is made all the richer and more engaging because of its consciously theological shape. In this chapter, I have shown how Barth's dogmatic thinking hinges on prayer. I have also explored the way Barth constructs for his reader and through his theology of prayer a way of seeing the world as permeated by God's grace and thus a way of relating to the world that is both responsive to the divine calling, dependent on that calling, and participative in God's redemptive hallowing of the divine name in the world.

---

[87]Barth, *ChrL*, 206.

CHAPTER TWENTY-SIX

The Scope and Status of Prayer in Balthasar's Theology

TRAVIS LaCOUTER

That Hans Urs von Balthasar was a theologian for whom the inseparability of theology and spirituality was an issue of paramount importance is today so well-known as to seem a truism. His celebrated essay 'Theologie und Heiligkeit' (first published in 1948) is one of his better-known pieces of writing outside of his famous trilogy and has attracted a fair amount of attention among English-language commentators.[1] In that essay, Balthasar is concerned to give an account of how theology and sanctity came apart – of how it came to be, as Balthasar pointedly notes, that, 'since the great period of Scholasticism, there have been few theologians who were saints'.[2] In pursuit of an answer, Balthasar engages in a typically ambitious historical, theological

---

[1]For a representative example, see Antonio Sicari, 'Hans Urs von Balthasar: Theology and Holiness', in *Hans Urs von Balthasar: His Life and Work*, ed. David L. Schindler (San Francisco, CA: Ignatius Press, 1991), 121–32. Other studies substantively concerned with the question of holiness include Matthew Rothaus Moser, *Love Itself Is Understanding: Hans Urs von Balthasar's Theology of the Saints* (Minneapolis, MN: Fortress Press, 2016); Victoria Harrison, *The Apologetic Value of Human Holiness: Von Balthasar's Christocentric Philosophical Anthropology* (London: Kluwer, 2000); and Pauline Dimech, *The Authority of the Saints: Drawing on the Theology of Hans Urs von Balthasar* (Eugene, OR: Wipf and Stock, 2017).
[2]Hans Urs von Balthasar, 'Theology and Sanctity', in *Explorations in Theology – Volume 1: The Word Made Flesh*, trans. A. V. Littledale and Alexander Dru (San Francisco, CA: Ignatius Press, 1989), 181–209 (181).

and doctrinal survey during which he sets his sights on a number of *bêtes noires* that any regular reader of his theology will have come to expect: 'theological rationalism'; the vain philosophical tendency towards introspection; and an 'unctuous [and] platitudinous piety' that grew increasingly untethered from any solid doctrinal basis.[3] This spiritual 'impoverishment' of theology reached a nadir, for Balthasar, in the manualist tradition, which, whatever use it may have had in the context of seminary classrooms, offered precious little 'nourishment' for those seeking to encounter a 'living' theology – one that had the power to proclaim and embody the Good News in any convincing way.[4] A theology divorced from prayer, in other words, lacks what Rowan Williams calls 'integrity' since it 'displace[s] its real subject matter' – in this case the living God – and 'foreclose[s] the possibility of a genuine response'.[5]

As I say, this much of Balthasar's theology is familiar enough even to casual readers. What is more often overlooked, however, is that Balthasar's vision of a reintegrated theology consists in no facile return to a time before the 'divorce' in question. 'There is no question of turning back the wheel of history', Balthasar writes, nor is there any point in denying the obvious 'progress wrought by Scholasticism'.[6] Neither does it consist in an equally facile (re-)combination of 'theology and sanctity', as if these actually were independent realities that simply needed to be held together by the perspicacious theologian. It must be said that commentators otherwise sympathetic to Balthasar's project have not always been as clear as one would hope on this latter point. For instance, in his recent handbook of fundamental theology Gerald O'Collins distinguishes between three 'styles' of theology which he names as the academic, the practical and the contemplative styles, with Balthasar cited as a standout example of a Western theologian from the third category.[7] O'Collins' three 'styles' are meant to complement one another and so account for certain weaknesses apparently characteristic of each (in the case of the 'contemplative style' the weaknesses are said to be a lack of rigour and a weak social consciousness). Despite O'Collins' admirable commitment to irenicism, however, this is not an exceedingly helpful way of understanding Balthasar's approach, either in the 'Theology and Sanctity' essay or elsewhere. The point of a 'kneeling theology' for Balthasar is not that it is just *one more way* of doing theology.[8] It is, rather,

---

[3]Balthasar, 'Theology and Sanctity', 189, 196, 208.
[4]Balthasar, 'Theology and Sanctity', 192–3.
[5]Rowan Williams, *On Christian Theology* (Oxford: Blackwell, 2000), 3–4.
[6]Balthasar, 'Theology and Sanctity', 208.
[7]Gerald O'Collins, *Rethinking Fundamental Theology: Toward a New Fundamental Theology* (Oxford: Oxford University Press, 2011), 323–5.
[8]For the idea of 'kneeling theology', see Balthasar, 'The Place of Theology', in *Explorations in Theology*, vol. 1, 147–60.

that the contemplative style (if we want to retain this terminology) is the 'form of theology that is indispensable for all succeeding forms'.[9] Theology and sanctity implicate one another and stand in a unity of purpose – they are in this sense coterminous.[10] Put differently, prayer 'is not just a piece of material that can be easily incorporated into the existing structure [of theology], or else a sort of stylistic quality to be reproduced anew', but the very ground and premise of theological reflection.[11]

All this is to say that the relationship between theology and prayer in Balthasar has often been thought of far too schematically. Ultimately, no theological system of whatever sophistication can reveal more of God than God reveals willingly in prayer. And, furthermore, in prayer God demonstrates that which the theologian is always endeavouring to show: that God is a God with us (*Immanuel*). 'The Christian stands and falls with prayer', Balthasar writes, and there can be no escape into 'mere action or simply the liturgy' as substitutes for this essential relationship that God desires to have with each and every one of us, for it is in the context of this relationship that the praying person comes to understand 'simply that God has loved him [*sic*] and all [persons]'.[12] In other words, it is in prayer that the theologian has a vignette of the history of grace in microcosm. A coherent theology of prayer is in this sense the practical and 'realistic' option for the theologian who wants to understand better the mysterious depths of divine love at work.[13] Put more strongly, a theology undergirded and animated by prayer is, for Balthasar, the only way to ensure theological 'integrity' (in Williams' sense again), since it ensures that the theologian remains focused on their actual subject matter (i.e. God and all things in relation to God). Not only does this mitigate against the imposition of siloed schemas such as O'Collins' (which Balthasar might have considered another example of the

---

[9]Hans Urs von Balthasar, *The Von Balthasar Reader*, ed. Medard Kehl and Werner Löser (New York: Crossroad, 1985), 357. Indeed, Balthasar's call for kneeling theology first arises in a discussion of scriptural interpretation – a task which O'Collins reserves to the 'academic theologian' but that Balthasar claims cannot be done adequately without the 'conviction that the written word has within it the spirit and power to bring about, in faith, contact with the infinity of the Word'. See Balthasar, 'The Place of Theology', 150.

[10]Graham Ward, *How the Light Gets In: Ethical Life I* (Oxford: Oxford University Press, 2016), 26.

[11]See Hans Urs von Balthasar, 'Spirituality', in *Explorations in Theology – Volume 2: Spouse of the Word*, trans. A. V. Littledale and Alexander Dru (San Francisco, CA: Ignatius Press, 1991), 211–26 (214).

[12]Hans Urs von Balthasar, 'Unmodern Prayer', in *Elucidations*, trans. John Riches (San Francisco, CA: Ignatius Press, 1998), 173–80 (173).

[13]Balthasar, 'Theology and Sanctity', 206. A clarification: by a 'theology of prayer' I mean less a guide to prayer than an objective account (as much as this is possible) of prayer's proper theological shape and purpose. It is such an account that Balthasar presents across his vast body of work and that I aim to reproduce certain essential dimensions of here.

'strange anatomical dissection' often perpetrated by theologians),[14] but it suggests moreover that such a contemplative theology need not necessarily suffer from the weaknesses O'Collins mentions. Indeed, I aim to indicate in this chapter some ways in which Balthasar's theology of prayer contains, on its own terms, a coherent vision of the eschatological future that amounts to a constructive social dimension.

To see how any of these claims gain purchase in Balthasar's theology, however, a much more focused approach is required. I will sketch an account of prayer's overall shape and scope as Balthasar understood it, paying special attention (for reasons of space but also priority) to prayer's trinitarian foundations and eschatological ends. These two dimensions together show the integral and integrating function of prayer in Balthasar's theology: prayer is rooted in God, and thus our participation in it is an eschatologically significant grace with ramifications that go far beyond individual spiritual 'development'. I will end by returning to some of the methodological questions with which I have opened this chapter and suggest how reading Balthasar in this way resolves some of the challenges that have been raised against his way of doing theology. Despite Balthasar's often magisterial tone and some of his more idiosyncratic tendencies, it is by understanding Balthasar's theology of/as prayer that we see more clearly how his is a theology that does in fact allow for the possibility of a genuine response.

Prayer's Foundation

For Balthasar, prayer is emphatically not a form of human introspection, meditation or therapeutic self-discovery. 'Christian prayer is always addressed to the living God. It is never the search for one's own "self" or for the transcendental ego.'[15] Prayer is a 'dialogue', as Balthasar puts it at

---

[14]Balthasar, 'Theology and Sanctity', 193.

[15]Hans Urs von Balthasar, *Love Alone is Credible*, trans. David L. Schindler (San Francisco, CA: Ignatius Press, 2004), 267. See also Hans Urs von Balthasar, *Prayer*, trans. Graham Harrison (San Francisco, CA: Ignatius Press, 1986), 56. See Kant's disparaging view of prayer as introspection at *Religion within the Boundaries of Mere Reason and Other Writings*, trans. and ed. Allen Wood and George di Giovanni (Cambridge: Cambridge University Press, 1998), 188. Contrast this with the altogether more positive view of Sandra Schneiders, who views prayer as 'the experience of consciously striving to integrate one's life in terms not of isolation and self-absorption but of self-transcendence toward the ultimate value one perceives'. See Sandra Schneiders, 'Spirituality in the Academy', *Theological Studies* 50, no. 4 (1989): 676–97 (684). As Bernard McGinn notes, however, Schneiders' anthropological notion of prayer 'leaves open the possibility for forms of non-religious or secular spirituality'. See Bernard McGinn, 'The Letter and the Spirit: Spirituality as an Academic Discipline', in *Minding the Spirit: The Study of Christian Spirituality*, ed. Elizabeth A. Dreyer and Mark S. Burrows (Baltimore, MD: Johns Hopkins University Press, 2005), 25–51 (32). These 'secular spiritualities', whatever else they are, cannot be considered properly theological in the sense Balthasar intends.

the start of his one book on prayer *Das Betrachtende Gebet*, a 'conversation' in which 'we try not to be tedious, not to say and think the same thing day after day'.[16] And yet it is just this obligation not to be 'tedious' that we often find most difficult in prayer, especially at first. The dialogue is stilted, at the very least, and it frequently seems as if it is being carried out in a foreign tongue, so that we find ourselves 'wanting to say something but unable to do so'.[17] Reading the traditional devotional literature rarely helps, Balthasar admits, since this is like being hungry and being forced to 'observe someone else eating'.[18] Balthasar's theology has often been accused of idealism and of existing 'up in the clouds',[19] but such accusations seem to me implausible when one considers the eminently practical (indeed pastoral) way in which he begins his treatment of the central topic of prayer.

Prayer's difficulty has to do with its trinitarian foundations. It is a dialogue that *precedes* the praying person, one into which we are invited by the God who wants to know us as unique individuals possessed of our own 'imagination and reason'.[20] In one representative formulation, Balthasar says, 'Prayer [is] not only ... something that ascends from man to God, but, more profoundly, what descends from God to man.'[21] There is something in prayer that derives from, and thus reveals, the very heart of God. For Balthasar, this 'something' is captured in the free mutual exchange that the Trinity is: word and response, *kenosis* and *pleroma*, love and trust.[22] These are the rhythms of divine love that prayer forms us in and ultimately conforms us to. This is what I meant a moment ago by referring to prayer as an eschatologically

---

[16]Hans Urs von Balthasar, *Prayer*, trans. A. V. Littledale (London: Geoffrey Chapman, 1961), 111–12; a similar sentiment is expressed at Balthasar, *Prayer*, 246. There are two English translations of *Das Betrachtende Gebet* (Einsiedeln: Johannes, 1955), one by A. V. Littledale published by Geoffrey Chapman and the other by Graham Harrison published by Ignatius Press. Of these, the Littledale translation more often captures the lyrical and meditative rhythms of Balthasar's German. I quote from both in this chapter, although more frequently from Harrison's due to its wider availability to readers. *Prayer* is obviously a key text for understanding the theology of prayer that I am seeking to explore here, although it is very much part of my argument that the emphasis on prayer is constant, if often implicit, aspect of Balthasar's theology. Thus I will cite liberally from various texts in the Balthasarian corpus.

[17]Balthasar, *Prayer* (Harrison trans.), 14.

[18]Balthasar, *Prayer* (Harrison trans.), 7.

[19]Gerard O'Hanlon, 'The Jesuits and Modern Theology: Rahner, von Balthasar and Liberation Theology', *Irish Theological Quarterly* 58, no. 1 (1992): 25–45 (34).

[20]Balthasar, *Prayer* (Littledale trans.), 112.

[21]Hans Urs von Balthasar, *Test Everything: Hold Fast to What is Good: An Interview with Hans Urs von Balthasar by Angelo Scola*, trans. Maria Shrady (San Francisco, CA: Ignatius Press, 1989), 89.

[22]On the characterizations of trinitarian prayer, see Lucy Gardner, 'Hans Urs von Balthasar: The Trinity and Prayer', in *A Transforming Vision: Knowing and Loving the Triune God*, ed. George Westhaver (London: SCM Press, 2018), 193–205.

significant grace. Perhaps unsurprisingly, strictly philosophical accounts of prayer often neglect this trinitarian dimension entirely, conceiving of prayer as originating in a 'subject' (the praying person) and being directed towards an 'object' (the thing prayed for).[23] On that approach, a whole cluster of questions to do with petition, epistemology and intercession tend to arise which for Balthasar prove to be non-starters: there is no negotiating one's way through prayer nor any sure way to anticipate its precise rhythms ahead of time. As something grounded in the trinitarian life, prayer is pure freedom. Whatever precepts or structures one wants to introduce into prayer (such as guidance about posture, breathing, setting and verbal formulae), however provisionally helpful they may be, must ultimately give way to the dramatic interaction of finite and infinite freedom.[24] Thus Balthasar erects a bulwark against anthropocentric notions of prayer which would reduce its scope to merely one more form of human ritual.

The grounding of prayer 'in' the Trinity is one of many theological insights that Balthasar gleaned from the work of his long-time collaborator Adrienne von Speyr. Speyr's 1951 monograph on prayer *Die Welt des Gebetes* opens with a particularly dense section on 'Prayer in the Trinity' in which she introduces several themes which re-emerge in Balthasar's work not just in *Prayer* but elsewhere.[25] Central to Speyr's approach is the idea that prayer is a form of 'participation in the center of [God's] being', and as such it 'has no beginning' (i.e. it does not begin with the praying person).[26] She also establishes creaturely petition as an analogy of the Son's eternal eucharistic adoration of the Father (we will see Balthasar develop this theme in a moment). And most importantly Speyr stresses that this eternal trinitarian dialogue is oriented towards action. 'It is no meaningless conversation, no superfluous disclosure of what is already fixed and settled [rather] every word spoken is both adoration *and commitment.*'[27] All these features are present in Balthasar's account, and we should find no reason

---

[23]See Scott A. Davison, *Petitionary Prayer: A Philosophical Investigation* (Oxford: Oxford University Press, 2017), 24.

[24]This formulation draws on the definition of prayer put forward by Andrew Prevot, *Thinking Prayer: Theology and Spirituality amid the Crises of Modernity* (Notre Dame, IN: University of Notre Dame Press, 2015), 1–3.

[25]See Adrienne von Speyr, *The World of Prayer*, trans. Graham Harrison (San Francisco, CA: Ignatius Press, 1985), 11. See Hans Urs von Balthasar, *Theo-Drama: Theological Dramatic Theory – Volume 5: The Last Act*, trans. Graham Harrison (San Francisco, CA: Ignatius Press, 1998), which draws heavily on *The World of Prayer* (especially 50–1, 87–8, 273–94) and *Theo-Logic – Volume 2: Truth of God*, trans. Adrian J. Walker (San Francisco, CA: Ignatius Press, 2004), 288–9.

[26]Speyr, *The World of Prayer*, 13, 28.

[27]Speyr, *The World of Prayer*, 28.

to disagree with Balthasar's own assessment that Speyr's rich volume was the 'impetus' to his work in *Prayer*.[28] As is well known, nearly all Speyr's published work was compiled, edited and published by Balthasar himself, so it is significant that, as he explains in the Foreword to Speyr's book, it was his decision to foreground the trinitarian section despite its relative difficulty compared to the rest of that work.[29] Evidently he believed these to be insights worth highlighting. Nor is it unreasonable to presume that Balthasar and Speyr were responding in tandem to Karl Barth's 1949 book on the Lord's Prayer, *La Prière*. Notwithstanding Barth's obvious influence on Balthasar, especially during the 1950s (Balthasar would later admit that he was decidedly 'Barthian' when writing *Prayer*), *La Prière* does not develop the trinitarian dimensions of prayer at any great length.[30] It was thus for the dual purposes of consolidating Speyr's insights and responding to his Basel rival's latest work that Balthasar insists upon prayer's trinitarian basis in his account.

But what are we to make of this immediate turn to the Trinity? How does it help the praying person approach the vast mystery of prayer? The first thing to note here is that the trinitarian dimensions of prayer are not so much imposed by Balthasar himself (or Speyr) as they are indicated already by Christology.[31] Christ is a person of prayer, constantly in dialogue with the Father through the Spirit. The Gospels record significant moments of prayer at the beginning (e.g. Mt. 4.1-11), the middle (e.g. Lk. 9.18, Mk 8.6) and the end (e.g. Jn 17) of his public ministry. This is an especially strong theme in Luke (e.g. Lk. 3.21; 9.18, 28; 11.1; 22.42; 23.34).[32] So Christ is Christ *at* prayer. But he is also Christ *as* prayer, inasmuch as prayer serves as the realm in which Christ's

---

[28]See Balthasar's Foreword to *The World of Prayer*, 11.

[29]See Balthasar's Foreword to *The World of Prayer*, 10. For insight into Balthasar and Speyr's working relationship, see Maximilian Greiner's illuminating interview with two founding members of the Johannesgemeinschaft in *Hans Urs von Balthasar: His Life and Work*, ed. David L. Schindler (San Francisco, CA: Ignatius Press, 1991), 87–101.

[30]See Karl Barth, *Prayer: 50th Anniversary Edition*, trans. Sara F. Terrien (London: Westminster John Knox Press, 2002) and especially Daniel L. Migliore's critical essay in that volume, 'Freedom to Pray: Karl Barth's Theology of Prayer', 95–113. As Ashley Cocksworth argues, the Neuchâtel material on which *Prayer* is based is clearly an important indicator of Barth's developing thought on prayer, but the most mature treatments do not appear until *CD* IV/2, *CD* IV/3 and the *ChrL* by which time the concerns about prayer's trinitarian neglect are addressed in part. See Ashley Cocksworth, *Karl Barth on Prayer* (London: Bloomsbury, 2015).

[31]Balthasar insists more than once that the economic Trinity is the authoritative 'interpretation' of the immanent Trinity. See Hans Urs von Balthasar, *Theo-Drama: Theological Dramatic Theory – Volume 3: Dramatis Personae: Persons in Christ*, trans. Graham Harrison (San Francisco, CA: Ignatius Press, 1992), 508 and *A Theology of History* (San Francisco, CA: Ignatius Press, 1963), 56.

[32]See Balthasar's discussion in *The Glory of the Lord: A Theological Aesthetics – Volume 7: Theology: The New Covenant*, trans. Brian McNeil (San Francisco, CA: Ignatius Press, 1989), 244–50.

Sonship plays out.[33] When I say that Christ is Christ as prayer, I mean that, for Balthasar, Christ is a person of prayer not merely as a concession to his human nature but as an expression of his divine one. He is 'the language of God' in human form, and as such he is the creature's indispensable entry point to the trinitarian dialogue.[34] In scenes such as the agony at Gethsemane, we can see that prayers are 'the integral part' of Christ's mission,[35] holding together and harmonizing his divine will and his divinized human will.[36] Christ never addresses the Father, whether in thanksgiving or for intercession, without acknowledging his mission as the one who has been sent (Mt. 11.25 and Mt. 11.27). Even the High Priestly Prayer of John 17 must be understood as a prayer of mission ('Glorify your Son, *so that your Son may glorify you*').[37] The Son's openness to the Father's will while in mission – expressed in a special and demonstrable way in prayer – is so constant as to be the 'pedal note, sounding beneath all the intricacies of the fugue of his [earthly] actions'.[38] In this way prayer connects Christ's identity and his mission. Many commentators have discussed the fact that in Balthasar's Christology the unity of mission and identity is of paramount importance; what is less often noted is how prayer serves as the connective tissue between these two.

It is through the Son, then, that our inarticulate and uncertain words in prayer can start to acquire something like a fluency capable of being understood. But how can this be? Surely, it is not just a matter of slavishly imitating Christ's prayer life: this would violate the overarching rule of freedom in prayer – and besides, how would one imitate Christ's many private prayers in the wilderness for instance? It must be that Christ, as prayer, expands the trinitarian conversation to include us. 'Father, I want those you have given me to be with me where I am' (Jn 17.24). The Spirit is

---

[33]As Mark Yenson notes, 'prayer and action do not exist in juxtaposition in Jesus' life but mutually inhere'. See Mark Yenson, *Existence as Prayer: The Consciousness of Christ in the Theology of Hans Urs von Balthasar* (New York: Peter Lang 2014), 132.

[34]Hans Urs von Balthasar, *Man in History: A Theological Study*, trans. W. Glen-Doepel (London: Sheed and Ward, 1968), 275.

[35]Balthasar, *Theo-Drama*, vol. 3, 110.

[36]Especially in his reading of the Agony in the Garden, Balthasar is influenced by Maximus the Confessor's Christology, in which, according to Doucet, there is an 'alterity' of wills but 'no contrariety in the object shared respectively by each will' – namely mission proper to Sonship. Marcel Doucet, 'Est-ce que le monothélisme a fait autant d'illustrés victimes? Réflexions sur un ouvrage de F.-M. Léthel', *Science et esprit* 35 (1983): 53–83 (55). See also Paul Blowers, *Maximus the Confessor: Jesus Christ and the Transfiguration of the World* (Oxford: Oxford University Press, 2016). See Hans Urs von Balthasar, *Cosmic Liturgy: The Universe According to Maximus the Confessor*, trans. Brian Daley (San Francisco, CA: Ignatius Press, 2003).

[37]See Balthasar's discussion at *Theo-Drama*, vol. 3, 170.

[38]Hans Urs von Balthasar, *Engagement with God: The Drama of Christian Discipleship*, trans. R. John Halliburton (San Francisco, CA: Ignatius Press, 2008), 50.

implicated in a special way at this point, since it is under the guardianship of the Spirit that the Son's prayers can be said to express in an economic form the same stance of eternal eucharistic openness that seeks to give everything it has and is to the Father.[39] By 'breathing forth the Spirit' (Jn 20.22) at the end of his earthly mission, Christ makes it possible for his followers to enter into the same stance of eucharistic openness of the Son vis-à-vis the Father under the same guardianship of the Spirit in the form of prayer (which, again, is Sonship expressed economically). It is in this sense that Balthasar understands the Pauline teaching that it is the Spirit who prays in us (cf. Rom. 8.26). In light of what was just said about the Son's role in prayer, we might say that it is the Son who makes creaturely prayer possible and the Spirit who makes it effective.

The Spirit does this work in many and various ways. Of particular importance, to be sure, are the visible structures of the church such as 'sacraments, scripture, liturgy, and preaching'.[40] But likewise does the Spirit work through invisible means such as the 'sighs too deep for words' (Rom. 8.26) which guide us through the depths of prayer. Pinning down the Spirit is, of course, an impossible task, and despite the decisive role of the Spirit in Balthasar's theology, he shows a healthy reticence to systematizing the pneumatological dimensions of prayer.[41] Yet by whatever means the Spirit in its freedom chooses to act upon us, the final test is always the same: prayer's issuance in charity or love, understood as service and communion. By inference we can thus say that inasmuch as the Spirit retains guardianship of our prayers, it (therefore) retains guardianship over our ongoing awareness of mission-consciousness, as well. In the end, this mission-consciousness is the only true test of genuine Christian prayer. This is no esoteric Gnosticism, but a simple affirmation of the fact that each praying person is historically situated in a particular web of relations, obligations and potentialities to which they are

---

[39]This is Balthasar's doctrine of the so-called trinitarian inversion, in which the Spirit acts as the 'architect of the Son's return to the Father'. See Balthasar, *Prayer* (Harrison trans.), 74. Balthasar develops this theme explicitly at *Theo-Drama*, vol. 3, 183–91 and 515–23, although it is already present in the section on 'The Spirit's Role' in *Prayer*. For more on the 'inversion', see John O'Donnell, 'In Him and Over Him: The Holy Spirit in the Life of Jesus', *Gregorianum* 70, no. 1 (1989): 25–45 and Matthew Sutton, 'A Compelling Trinitarian Taxonomy: Hans Urs von Balthasar's Theology of the Trinitarian Inversion and Reversion', *International Journal of Systematic Theology* 14, no. 2 (2012): 161–76.

[40]Balthasar, *Prayer* (Harrison trans.), 74.

[41]See Balthasar's disclaimers about the Spirit's 'invisibility', *Glory of the Lord*, vol. 7, 389 and *Theo-Logic: Theological Logical Theory – Volume 3: The Spirit of Truth*, trans. Graham Harrison (San Francisco, CA: Ignatius Press, 2005), 13. For a thorough study of Balthasar's pneumatology (such as it is), see Kossi Tossou, *Streben nach Vollendung: Zur Pneumatologie im Werk H. U. v Balthasars* (Freiburg: Herder, 1983).

called to apply their 'imagination and reason' in service of mission. Balthasar goes as far as to say that unless contemplation gives rise to this missionary 'outfolding', it is to be considered 'spurious and demonic'.[42] Nothing, for Balthasar, not even prayer, is ever 'self-sufficient and purposeful' outside of its capacity to instantiate love in the world.[43] Thus the Spirit acts as a check on unfettered 'experience' in prayer and at the same time guarantees the praying person's personality is 'affirmed', not annihilated, since love is by its nature always a personal act and missions are always concrete in their historicity.[44]

But now we have broached prayer's relationship to mission and activity, and in this sense must turn to consider its specifically eschatological dimensions. If the dialogue into which we have been invited by God is to be a source of healing, it must be oriented towards the collective eschatological future. Indeed, this is the *point* of God's involving us in the dialogue, since God does not wish to be God without us.[45] It is through prayer that God does the work of transforming us into collaborators in God's plan for the future of the world. By now it should be clear, however, that prayer is no ancillary concern for Balthasar's theology but the very heart and summit of the Christian life. Nor is it to be regarded as merely a desirable add-on to theological work, but rather the ever-flowing fountain to which such work must continually return.

Prayer's Ends

'God's Kingdom is God himself', Balthasar writes in a pithy form of his whole eschatology.[46] Thus if prayer is a realm of engagement with the trinitarian God, then it is by definition also an eschatological realm in which action and decision are implicated. By eschatological action I mean action that is

---

[42]Balthasar, *Prayer* (Harrison trans.), 74. See also Grace M. Jantzen, 'Eros and the Abyss: Reading Medieval Mystics in Postmodernity', *Literature and Theology* 17, no. 3 (2003): 244–64.

[43]Hans Urs von Balthasar, *The Christian State of Life*, trans. Mary Frances McCarthy (San Francisco, CA: Ignatius Press, 2002), 82.

[44]See Balthasar's ambivalence towards 'experience' as a theological category in 'Experience God?', in *New Elucidations*, trans. Mary Thereslide Skerry (San Francisco, CA: Ignatius Press, 1986), 20–45 and 'Understanding Christian Mysticism', in *Explorations in Theology – Volume 4: Spirit and Institution*, trans. Edward T. Oakes (San Francisco, CA: Ignatius Press, 1995), 309–35. On the Spirit's affirmative method, see *Prayer* (Harrison trans.), 77.

[45]See James Hanvey, 'Tradition as Subversion', *International Journal of Systematic Theology* 6, no. 1 (2004): 50–87 (61).

[46]Hans Urs von Balthasar, *Who is a Christian?*, trans. John Cumming (London: Burns and Oates, 1968), 63. On a 'theocentric' eschatology specifically, see *Theo-Drama*, vol. 5, 57 and 'Some Points of Eschatology', in *Explorations in Theology*, vol. 1, 255–77 (260). See also Nicholas Healy, *The Eschatology of Hans Urs von Balthasar: Eschatology as Communion* (Oxford: Oxford University Press, 2005).

oriented to the *eschaton*. Simply put, the 'dialogue' with God is meant to *go somewhere* (this is the point of claiming above that even prayer on its own is not 'self-sufficient' outside of its capacity to instantiate love in history). Balthasar was hardly the only Catholic theologian contributing to a general renewal of eschatology in the latter half of the twentieth century, with prominent figures like Edward Schillebeeckx and Joseph Ratzinger producing major works on the theme.[47] However, it is useful to see Balthasar's retrieval of eschatology as a function of his prior account of prayer.

Balthasar's theology of prayer has several significant eschatological dimensions. First, if prayer is the dialogue with God in which the praying person has an obligation to 'not be tedious', this implies the corollary obligation to remain *attentive*, which Balthasar describes in terms of 'watching', so much so that he appears to elide the dual injunctions of Luke 21.36 ('Watch ye therefore and pray always') such that 'prayer apart from watching ... is not Christian prayer at all'.[48] At one point Balthasar invokes Augustine's formula on the essence of eternity to describe what prayer is: *videntem videre* ('to look at him who is looking at you').[49] Yet here again this obligation to be attentive signals a difficulty in prayer. When asked to 'watch and pray' with Jesus in the Garden of Gethsemane, the disciples let the dialogue fall silent by succumbing to sleep (Mt. 26.40). This failure of attention, or simply distraction, is the essence of sin, a fact that becomes explicit in the context of the prayer-relationship and so can be thematized and addressed – never once and for all but over time and with conscious effort. As a school of attention, then, where distraction is turned into 'decision', prayer can have soteriological (and thus eschatological) effects on the praying person, even if it cannot ever act as a perfect prophylactic against sin.[50]

The second major eschatological dimension to prayer is christological, since it is to Christ that we 'look' in prayer. This looking 'back' (to Christ) is not merely regressive, since in looking back to the Son we enter into his prayer perspective, which was a future-oriented one of expectation and trust in the Father through the Spirit. As one enters further into this Christoform perspective, one will see more clearly the tragic gap between the world

---

[47]See Joseph Ratzinger, *Eschatology: Death and Eternal Life*, trans. Michael Waldstein (Washington, DC: Catholic University of America Press, 1988) and Edward Schillebeeckx and Boniface Willems, ed., *The Problem of Eschatology* (New York: Paulist Press, 1969). See also the illuminating study by Steven Rodenborn, *Hope in Action: Subversive Eschatology in the Theology of Edward Schillebeeckx and Johann Baptist Metz* (Minneapolis, MN: Fortress Press, 2014).
[48]Balthasar, *Prayer* (Littledale trans.), 119–20.
[49]See Hans Urs von Balthasar, *The Grain of Wheat: Aphorisms*, trans. Erasmo Leiva-Merikakis (San Francisco, CA: Ignatius Press, 1995), 4.
[50]Balthasar, *Prayer* (Harrison trans.), 148.

as it is and the world as God wills it to be ('Thy Kingdom come'). Thus, prayer becomes an impetus to mission and the source of eschatologically meaningful activity in history.[51] Christian prayer understood as this form of active 'watching' inaugurates a meaningful sense of futurity not despite but as a result of its basis in the concrete person of Christ. And so prayer also serves to introduce a definite shape onto the praying person's experience of history, thus making the very concept of an eschatological future coherent in the context of a given life.

And third, if prayer is the form of attention in which one contextualizes one's life vis-à-vis the eschatological future, it is thereby also a form of socialization, since that eschatological future towards which prayer is aimed, when it comes, will not belong to any one person individually nor in isolation. The community of prayer is a community constituted by mutual support and what Balthasar calls at one point a 'complete communism in all goods and graces'.[52] This can be seen with particular clarity in the case of intercessory prayer, in which the living and the dead draw upon one another's 'portion' of love in order to sustain each other in mission.[53] In such moments, Balthasar says, the walls between heaven and earth seem to come tumbling down: there is but one community, constituted and sustained by love and actualized in prayer.[54] Indeed, it is among the chief eschatological functions of prayer, for Balthasar, to overcome any ego-centric notion of salvation, so that the praying person's 'I' is seen more and more to consist in the universal 'we' (here again prayer's trinitarian foundations are implicated).[55] Prayer serves as a primary means of this 'stretching', thereby substantiating ecclesial solidarity and establishing a bridge between the earthly and heavenly church.[56] It is from this admittedly 'realized' perspective that we can see what eschatological work God is doing in prayer: 'gathering together' all beloved children of God (cf. Mt. 23.37) in an action that is at once both a gift and a call.

---

[51]See Balthasar, *Prayer* (Harrison trans.), 142–3.

[52]Hans Urs von Balthasar, *Two Sisters in the Spirit: Therese of Lisieux and Elizabeth of the Trinity*, trans. Donald Nichols and Ann Englund Nash (San Francisco, CA: Ignatius Press, 1992), 205.

[53]A prayer for a 'double portion' was a common theme of Thérèse of Lisieux. See Balthasar, *Two Sisters in the Spirit*, 204–7.

[54]Balthasar remarks that in prayer there is 'in principle no need for any special way or effort in order to rise from nature to supernature'. See Balthasar, *Prayer* (Harrison trans.), 45.

[55]Balthasar, *Prayer* (Harrison trans.), 89–90. See also Michele Schumacher, 'Ecclesial Existence: Person and Community in the Trinitarian Anthropology of Adrienne von Speyr', *Modern Theology* 24, no. 3 (2008): 359–85. In this sense, Balthasar anticipates the profound insight of the Second Vatican Council that 'God … does not make [human beings] holy and save them merely as individuals, [but] rather has it pleased Him to bring [them] together as one people, a people which acknowledges Him in truth and serves Him in holiness', *Gaudium et Spes*, 9.

[56]Balthasar, *Prayer* (Harrison trans.), 142.

Such are some of the eschatological dimensions of prayer according to Balthasar. When seen alongside what was said above about prayer's basis in God's trinitarian life, a picture of prayer emerges as a holistic and transforming grace with which God brings about the eschatological future. Prayer describes to a very considerable degree the type of communion with humanity that God seeks to achieve, one in which 'asking and receiving flow into one another, and the fact of having [already] received does not exclude asking'.[57]

To sum up the various considerations which have been raised so far, and to indicate some of the further avenues down which this account of prayer leads us, I believe it is useful at this point to invoke a feature of Balthasar's account far too infrequently noted within the relevant literature: *parrhesia*. A watchword in the Johannine and Pauline texts with roots in ancient Greek conceptions of political and philosophical freedom, *parrhesia* (literally the right to 'say anything' although also 'bold speech'), is for Balthasar a characteristic fruit of genuine Christian prayer.[58] In prayer, God demonstrates *parrhesia* first, speaking the free Word that makes the human response possible.[59] The Son represents this *parrhesia* in the flesh, exercises *parrhesia* in mission and, crucially, initiates his followers into it by the sending of the Spirit who in turn inaugurates bold 'new tongues' (Mt. 16.17, cf. Acts 2.4). It is in learning to respond to God's *parrhesia* that the creature comes to find a voice, one that can speak honestly with and need not hold anything back from the God who is already *interior intimo meo*. This unconcealedness of the creature before God is the essence of what it means to be 'co-heirs with Christ' (Rom. 8.17), since likewise Christ holds nothing back from the Father. For Balthasar, the 'most important' aspect of Christian prayer is that it produces individuals who can:

> come to [God] with their head held high, as those who have an innate right to be there and to speak. We may look into the Father's face without fear; we do not have to approach him as if he were an aloof monarch, with downcast eyes and obsequious gestures, within the confines of strict

---

[57]Balthasar, *Glory of the Lord*, vol. 7, 410.

[58]For illuminating surveys of the biblical usage, see William Klassen, 'παρρησία in the Johannine Corpus' and David Fredrickson, 'παρρησία in the Pauline Epistles', both in *Friendship, Flattery, and Frankness of Speech: Studies on Friendship in the New Testament World*, ed. John Fitzgerald (Leiden: Brill, 1996), 227–54 and 163–83, respectively. In the twentieth century, Michel Foucault did much to return the term to prominence with a series of lectures, especially at the University of Berkeley the year before his untimely death. See Foucault, *Discourse and Truth and Parrēsia*, ed. Henri-Paul Fruchaud and Daniele Lorenzini (Chicago, IL: University of Chicago Press, 2019), although Foucault's treatment remains idiosyncratic and largely allusive.

[59]On God's prior *parrhesia*, see *Prayer* (Harrison trans.), 43–5.

ceremonial and a prescribed form of address. The door stands open, [and] the door … is Christ [cf. Jn 14.6].[60]

Notice that this turn to *parrhesia* neatly illustrates nearly the entire scope and status of prayer in Balthasar's theology: it is in prayer that God's *parrhesia* becomes real for us (thus prayer as revelation of trinitarian life); it is in prayer that Christ's *parrhesia* becomes our own (thus prayer as a realm of reparative encounter with God in Christ); and it is through exercising *parrhesia* in prayer that we demonstrate the hope that is in us, namely that we are heard by the Father (thus prayer as an eschatological act guided by the Spirit).

Here perhaps more clearly than anywhere else we can also see what I earlier suggested was Balthasar's practical/pastoral purpose in rendering a theology of prayer. By interpreting '*parrhesia* [as] one with prayer' Balthasar seeks to overcome that chief obstacle to prayer, namely, getting started.[61] We *already have* the voice with which to address God (not out of merit but as a result of grace), and there is no need for 'lengthy psychological adjustments' or a complex process of purification, such as one finds in some mystic schemas.[62] Balthasar poses Christian *parrhesia* specifically against those forms of mysticism which emphasize self-annihilation or perfect stillness.[63] Nor is silence a terminal position in prayer, although Balthasar does emphasize that every word of prayer should first be leavened by contemplative silence lest it devolve into mindless 'chatter'.[64] *Parrhesia* helps ensure, however, that our silences do not become barren – that they instead always give way to those words of mission with which we signal our attentiveness to the dialogue with God, and our willingness to ratify

---

[60]Balthasar, *Prayer* (Harrison trans.), 46. See also *Glory of the Lord*, vol. 7, 409.

[61]Balthasar, *Prayer* (Harrison trans.), 48.

[62]Hans Urs von Balthasar, *Christian Meditation*, trans. Mary T. Skerry (San Francisco, CA: Ignatius Press, 1989), 19.

[63]In particular, Balthasar seems to have in mind Eastern concepts like *nirvana* in Buddhism or *advaita* in Vedantic Hinduism. See Balthasar, *New Elucidations*, 150; *Prayer* (Harrison trans.), 54; and Hans Urs von Balthasar, *You Crown the Year with Your Goodness: Radio Sermons*, trans. Graham Harrison (San Francisco, CA: Ignatius Press, 1989), 27–8. Balthasar's understanding of the East is arguably too simplistic, but it at least reveals significant features of what he takes to be distinctive about Christianity (i.e. Christian prayer's dialogical nature and the positive obligation for a word of response).

[64]See Balthasar, *Theo-Logic*, vol. 2, 277. In this understanding of word and silence Balthasar largely follows Max Picard, for whom 'silence indwells the word'. See Balthasar, *Theo-Logic*, vol. 2, 113 and Max Picard, *Die Welt des Schweigens* (Zurich: Rentsch, 1948), 23.

our participation in the dialogue with an offering of ourselves in service: '*Ecce ancilla Domini*'. Indeed, it was with such positive words of mission that Mary, the creaturely parrhesiastes *par excellence*, kept up her part in the dialogue. It is the overarching purpose of Balthasar's theology of prayer to get us to see how each of us, in our own way, is likewise capable of a similarly positive response.

Concluding Methodological Remarks

My earlier claims about the scope and status of prayer in Balthasar's theology can now hopefully be seen to rest on firmer ground. We have seen how, for him, 'spirituality' (if we understand this as the discourse of and about prayer) is in no way a component part of an otherwise freestanding theological system but is coextensive with the theological task on a deeper and prior level. The theologian interested in trinitarian theology or Christology or even ecclesiology cannot afford to ignore what prayer has to teach us about these topics. By this, I do not mean to suggest straightforwardly that prayer is some kind of noetic privilege with which the theologian can easily overcome whatever difficulties they may face in their efforts to speak of God and all things in relation to God. There is always the danger of 'platitudinous piety', with which Balthasar showed so little patience. In order that the turn to prayer not be seen as a pious escape, prayer's integral relationship to theology must be understood less as a normative claim than a descriptive one: in prayer God does what God does continually and repeatedly, namely, 'crosses over' the distance that separates us from God and reclaims us as God's own.[65] This is the objective shape of prayer for Balthasar – it is the framework within which we must contextualize our own experience of prayer and, subsequently, any supposed insights that flow from it.

But does this conception of theology really allow for the 'possibility of a genuine response', which Williams identified as a key aspect of theological integrity? To be sure, some prominent critics of Balthasar have answered this question in the negative. Karen Kilby, for instance, insists that Balthasar is ultimately an 'unfettered' theologian operating from a position seemingly 'above his readers' and '[doing] his theology in part on the basis of information not available to the rest of us'.[66] Presumably, much of what I

---

[65]Hans Urs von Balthasar, *Tragedy under Grace: Reinhold Schneider on the Experience of the West*, trans. Brian McNeil (San Francisco, CA: Ignatius Press, 1991), 204, 200; and *Prayer* (Harrison trans.), 112.

[66]Karen Kilby, *Balthasar: A (Very) Critical Introduction* (Grand Rapids, MI: William B. Eerdmans, 2012), 38, 13, 99. See the concurrent opinion by George Pattison in *Reviews in Religion and Theology* 24, no. 1 (2017): 147–50.

have said about Balthasar's conception of the relationship between theology and prayer risks inviting just this sort of critique. While this is not the place to respond exhaustively to such charges, I do want to bring this chapter to a close by indicating some ways in which Balthasar's theology of prayer mitigates, rather than exacerbates, concerns such as Kilby's.

First, approaching Balthasar's theology through the route of prayer expands the traditional repertoire to include important texts often left out of critical discussions. I mean here not just mystical writings and popular practices, but also various texts within Balthasar's own oeuvre. Balthasar's theology must be read with a sensitivity to the variances of style, voice and genre which mark his work. I generally find it helpful to think of Balthasar's major works as falling into one of three broad categories: first, the systematics (i.e. the numerous volumes of *Glory of the Lord*, *Theo-Drama* and *Theo-Logic*); second, the polemical and programmatic works like *Razing the Bastions* (1952), *The Moment of Christian Witness* (1966) and *Love Alone is Credible* (1968); and in a third category are what we might call devotional or pastoral works such as *Prayer,* the sermons, personal prayers and perhaps most importantly the semi-mystical prayer-poem *Heart of the World* (1954). These 'categories' are not, of course, hard and fast nor mutually exclusive: there are times in the systematics where Balthasar speaks with a depth of feeling that is almost existentialist (the meditations on death in the fourth volume of *Theo-Drama*, for instance) just as, in the sermons, he is prone to slip into a decidedly professorial tone.[67] The point of these proposed categories is thus not to introduce rigid distinctions, much less oppositions, but merely to help indicate where we might find what type of material. This bears upon the concerns about authorial voice since it is the third category which is most often neglected by critics of Balthasar's theological style – Moser notes that Kilby does not cite *Heart of the World* once in her critique, for instance.[68] The general neglect of the third category is unfortunate, since it is often in these books, rather than the systematics, that Balthasar shows the beating heart of his theology.[69] It is in this material that Balthasar invites us in to his prayer, therefore giving us another point of access to his theology

---

[67]Indeed, as Stephan van Erp notes, the 'systematics' are perhaps mislabelled, inasmuch as their method is often eclectic and, at times, self-contradictory. See Stephan van Erp, *The Art of Theology: Hans Urs von Balthasar's Theological Aesthetics and the Foundations of Faith* (Leuven: Peeters, 2004), 84.

[68]Moser, *Love Itself Is Understanding*, 276.

[69]For Andrew Louth's argument for the importance of *Heart of the World* within Balthasar's oeuvre, see 'The Place of *Heart of the World* in the Theology of Hans Urs von Balthasar', in *Analogy of Beauty: The Theology of Hans Urs von Balthasar*, ed. John Riches (Edinburgh: T&T Clark, 1986), 147–63.

and making certain presuppositions and commitments apparent – which is precisely what Kilby claims he does not do. Naturally, one is still not obliged to find Balthasar's theology any more compelling for these reasons, but the very presence of this material does seem to me to go some way towards blunting the charge that Balthasar is operating in bad faith.

Second, it is simply not the case that Balthasar's incorporation of prayer into his theology serves to make his theology any less transparent or any less 'fettered' to traditional sources. On the contrary, I have already shown how Balthasar poses the pneumatological-ecclesial dimensions of prayer as an explicit check on unfettered experience or mystic escapism. As long as prayer remains something private and separable from mission (which is by its nature social), it remains, for Balthasar, something potentially 'demonic'. In addition, the extent to which Balthasar's theology of prayer derives its shape from Christ as and at prayer suggests its overall basis in scripture, thus another 'fetter' on his account. And rather than abstracting from history, Balthasar understands prayer as essentially a method for making the Christian responsible for history, insofar as prayer yields mission and 'mission implies responsibility'.[70] So the turn to prayer, *pace* O'Collins and O'Hanlon, does not leave Balthasar's theology open to charges of abstraction but rather constitutes his particular form of attention to history and tradition. And *pace* Kilby, this turn to prayer shows that far from 'standing above' his sources and his readers, Balthasar again and again situates his theological project in its proper ecclesial, and thus communal, context.

Third and most important, however, is the notion of *parrhesia*. Kilby sums up her argument by declaring that Balthasar 'asserts too much [and] argues too little' and thus 'the one thing ... one ought *not* to learn from [Balthasar] is how to be a theologian'.[71] In a sense, Kilby is taking issue with what we could call Balthasar's parrhesiastic tendencies – that is, not just the status *parrhesia* plays in his account but his own enactment of *parrhesia* in his theology (exemplified for instance in his daring speculative leaps, his ambitious historical scope, the intermixing of personal experience and polemic, and his often forceful, even biting, tone). These are, of course, precisely some of the features of Balthasar's writing that attract some of his most ardent followers, and on one level it is simply a matter of attending to those stylistic differences which are always at play in expert theological

---

[70]Balthasar, *Theo-Drama*, vol. 5, 179.
[71]Kilby, *Balthasar*, 167. Though altogether more sympathetic to Balthasar's project, Junius Johnson concurs in part, noting that it is often when precision is most called for that Balthasar resorts to stylistic flourishes and speculation. See Junius Johnson, *Christ and Analogy: The Christocentric Metaphysics of Hans Urs von Balthasar* (Minneapolis, MN: Fortress Press, 2013), 18.

writing. But nor should Kilby's concerns be dismissed so easily: for Balthasar *does* present a challenge to the reader. More to the point, Balthasar's way of doing theology is not simply self-sufficient (its systematic pretensions notwithstanding). He acknowledges this fact explicitly in the first pages of the *Theo-Drama*, describing his work as an 'apparatus' that has been erected so that future 'gymnasts may eventually exercise upon it'.[72] He makes a similar claim at the start of *Prayer*, which he intends primarily in order to provide 'stimuli [for] contemplation'.[73] At these (and other) points in Balthasar's theology, we see the bold impulses emphasized by Kilby tempered by an awareness of the limits of his own approach. Moreover, we see Balthasar consciously inviting his readers into a dialogue that calls forth their own imagination and reason. Thus we might wish to say that Kilby has identified as a defect that aspect of Balthasar's theology which is one of its chief virtues: the fact that it provokes a response.

It is in these respects that Balthasar most clearly models the integrity of theology and prayer. *Parrhesia*, whether in prayer or theology, is always dependent on an audience for being heard and desirous of a response. The reasons for staying silent are many, but ultimately God desires that we find a voice – *our* voice – to say what we can. It is only then that we can become part of the chorus which never wearies. In both theology and prayer, Balthasar reminds us, true solidarity is best expressed by 'the one who for the benefit of all contributes what he has'.[74] If Balthasar's theology does nothing but lead us to this threshold of speech, it has done the essential thing. The reintegration of 'theology and sanctity' that he envisioned consists in just this movement, inasmuch as these two endeavours name aspects of the single indispensable word of the creature towards God: *Amen*.

After all, we do not stand silent before God, but are 'called by name' (Jn 10.3), and in prayer the ability to respond to this call becomes an obligation to do so. It would be a shame indeed if we were to decline the dialogue.

---

[72]Balthasar, *Theo-Drama*, vol. 1, 9.
[73]Balthasar, *Prayer* (Harrison trans.), 8.
[74]Balthasar, 'Unmodern Prayer', 180.

CHAPTER TWENTY-SEVEN

Thomas F. Torrance on Christ, the Mediator of Christian Prayer

JOHN C. McDOWELL

Kathryn Tanner claims that 'not everything that Christians are prone to say, feel or do is properly Christian and therefore to be included in one's sense of the whole'.[1] What would count as a mistake, as improperly Christian, with regard to practices of prayer? Thomas Forsyth Torrance's theology of prayer can be understood to function as something of an articulation of a particular type of answer to that question. It offers an understanding of what Torrance regards as appropriately the speakable theological ground and grammar of prayer as Christian practice and as 'a rational account of knowledge [of prayer] beyond the limits of mere this-worldly experience'.[2] If it is to operate with integrity, a theology of prayer is required to take its shape in, with and under the conditions whereby God subjects God's self to communicative action that engages the creature through making communion with God's communicative self. 'It cannot be otherwise in a disciplined theology.'[3] Torrance's dogmatic framing of practices of prayer,

---

[1]Kathryn Tanner, *Jesus, Humanity and the Trinity: A Brief Systematic Theology* (Edinburgh: T&T Clark, 2001), xv.

[2]Thomas F. Torrance, *Space, Time and Incarnation* (Oxford: Oxford University Press, 1969), 20.

[3]Torrance, *Space, Time and Incarnation*, 20.

then, would indicate that creaturely life takes its place decisively as God's gift, and it has its beginning and end in creatures' worship/service of God in Christ as it is figured in the communicative action of Christ as representative creaturely subject. It is only here, in union with the ongoing history of the life-act of Jesus the High Priest, that human beings are formed as pray-ers, those who pray.

Theological Science as an Appropriate Following

While Torrance only addresses the matter of prayer with any intensity on a relative handful of occasions, overwhelmingly displaced by the inordinate amount of attention devoted to methodological matters under the heading 'theological science', his theological framing of it remains eminently consistent over the span of his writing. With regard to the mounting of his theological account within 'theological science', a few observations will suffice. In an introduction to a collection on *Incarnation*, he announces:

> Far from imposing an alien meaning upon the evangelical witness, theological language of this [theologically appropriate] kind is adapted under the impact of divine revelation to convey the message of the Gospel, so that in spite of the inadequacy of human language in itself it is made to indicate divine realities beyond its natural capacity and is to be understood in their light.[4]

It is from this perspective that Torrance contests the notion that theology is grounded in a form of phenomenological reasoning from the perceived structures of natural order, or at least where those structures are not understood *in the light* of their divine ground. This entails that Torrance's challenge is to an inappropriate form of natural theology that takes shape 'as an *independent* conceptual system', a system that is '*antecedent* to actual or empirical knowledge of God upon which it is then imposed, quite unscientifically, as a set of necessary epistemological presuppositions'.[5] Resisting this 'false start', Torrance instead proclaims that theology operates as a form of knowing that is appropriate to the nature of that which is known, in the mode of knowledge that is concretely proper to it. Dogmatics,

---

[4]Thomas F. Torrance, 'Introduction', in *The Incarnation: Ecumenical Studies in the Nicene-Constantinopolitan Creed*, ed. Thomas F. Torrance (Edinburgh: The Handsel Press, 1981), xi–xxii (xii).
[5]Thomas F. Torrance, *Space, Time and Resurrection* (Edinburgh: T&T Clark, 1976), 1.

properly ordered as scientific theological thinking, 'is not "free thinking", but *thinking bound to its chosen object* ... appropriate to the nature of that object'.[6] Theology, then, occurs as a moment of noetic conformity, a following after that to which it is adapted, and the discipline of theological thinking involves, accordingly, an interrogation of theology's own claims so as to emancipate it 'from the *Zeitgeist* which always threatens the thinking and teaching of the Church'.[7]

Such a positive theology involves something of a decentring and a recentring since 'in a genuine theology we do not think out of a centre in ourselves but out of a centre in God and his activity of grace toward us. ... Thus there can be no question of trying to understand man out of himself, or from his relation to the world'.[8] The crucial step in Torrance's theonoetic logic that indicates where the provision of theology's very ground and grammar occurs is a *christological* one. The substantial 'centre', consequently, 'is the place where heaven and earth meet, the place of reconciliation within our historical existence in flesh and blood. Jesus Christ is himself among us God's mercy-seat, God's place in the world where he is really present to us in our place'.[9] So Torrance proclaims in rather homiletic terms that 'in the very act of our knowing Christ he is the master, we are the mastered'.[10]

The *Homoousion*

Rather than the geometric image of a 'centre', Tanner uses the image of Christ as the key to articulate the role a well-ordered Christology plays in dogmatic considerations. 'Key' is a metaphor that works well only as a way of indicating the generativeness of Christology, the shaping and reshaping of doctrine and practice from an appropriately christological perspective, or the formation of 'one's ideas ... from the way God works in Christ'.[11] To return to Torrance, Christology provides a formal and material condition for theological speech, and one of the images he uses is of 'the christological pattern'.[12] Accordingly, he claims, as the very pattern of God, 'Jesus Christ is

---

[6]Thomas F. Torrance, *Incarnation: The Person and Life of Christ*, ed. Robert T. Walker (Downers Grove, IL: InterVarsity Press, 2008), 5.

[7]Thomas F. Torrance, 'The Place of Christology in Biblical and Dogmatic Theology', in *Essays in Christology for Karl Barth*, ed. T. H. L. Parker (London: Butterworth Press, 1956), 13–37 (34).

[8]Thomas F. Torrance, *Theology in Reconstruction* (London: SCM Press, 1965), 9, 102.

[9]Torrance, *Space, Time and Resurrection*, 129.

[10]Torrance, *Incarnation*, 2.

[11]Kathryn Tanner, *Christ the Key* (Cambridge: Cambridge University Press, 2010), 275.

[12]Torrance, 'The Place of Christology', 13.

himself the manifestation, the setting forth (*prothesis*), of the eternal purpose (*prothesis*) of God.'[13]

Theologically this claim emerges as the fruit of a set of ontological arguments concerning the *homoousion* that are themselves grounded in the ecclesial confession of Jesus as the manifestly intensive incarnate performance of God's own self-communicative act. The assertion made by the Nicene Creed, highly controversially in its time of course, necessarily 'took on the role of an interpretive frame through which general understanding of the evangelical and apostolic witness was given more exact guidance throughout the Church'.[14] It involves an irreducibly pronounced indication of the place of Christology in knowledge of God and of the presence of God's own self in Christ. 'This is God's unique act, his reality-in-the-act, and apart from this act there is no God at all.'[15] So, refusing any notion of a *deus absconditus*, Torrance declares that 'what the Father is and does Jesus is and does, and what Jesus is and does the Father is and does. There is in fact no God behind the back of Jesus, no act of God other than the act of Jesus, no God but the God we see and meet in him'.[16] That means, of course, that 'God is inherently and antecedently in himself, and will be to all eternity, what he has revealed himself to be in Jesus Christ. God is not one thing in Christ and another thing in himself. He has not shown us one face in Jesus Christ but kept his real face hidden from us behind the inscrutability of his ultimate unknowableness.'[17] As the comment 'will be to all eternity' here entails, this is not a 'transient' mode 'of God's self-communication to us'.[18] Torrance's concern is with 'any kind of damaging dualist framework of thought' which generates a disjunction between God and Christ, between 'the divine Gift and the divine Giver'.[19] 'A damaged understanding of God to the world affects our understanding of the *self*-giving of God to us in Jesus Christ, for it refracts the inherent oneness of the Giver and the Gift, and so alters the way in which we conceive of the real presence.'[20] By way of presenting that to whom the Gift is given by the Giver, Torrance emphasizes that 'the relationship we have with Jesus is therefore identical to relationship with God. ... The deity of Christ is thus the guarantee that the actions of Christ

---

[13]Torrance, *Incarnation*, 165.

[14]Torrance, 'Introduction', xii.

[15]Torrance, *Incarnation*, 107.

[16]Torrance, 'Introduction', xvii.

[17]Torrance, 'Introduction', xvii–xviii.

[18]Torrance, 'Introduction', xx.

[19]Citations from Torrance, 'Introduction', xviii; *The Mediation of Christ*, rev. edn (Edinburgh: T&T Clark, 1992), 125.

[20]Thomas F. Torrance, *Theology in Reconciliation: Essays towards Evangelical and Catholic Unity in East and West* (London: Chapman, 1975), 131.

are not in time only, not just temporary or temporal actions, but the eternal action of God, eternally real in the Godhead'.[21]

If 'in Christ, what God communicates to man is not something, but his very self', that which is communicated is so from a communicative ground within God and God alone, and thereby cannot be claimed as anything other than sheer grace or love.[22] 'Through the *homoousion* ... we are able to understand that what God is toward us in the condescension of his love and grace in Jesus Christ he is in his very own Being.'[23]

Christic *Telos*

Torrance's worry over 'dichotomous ways of thinking' manifests his commitment to the creedal *homoousion*, and therefore to the expression *pro nobis* of the very unique and transcendent antecedence of God *in se* so that between God's act and God's being as God's self there is no separation.[24] In the incarnation 'God became man, ... yet without ceasing to be God'.[25] Consequently, 'Jesus Christ *is* the Revelation of God'.[26] However, it belongs to a second commitment as well, and this element itself has two components. The first of these is the commitment of God to the creature, to 'a reality wholly distinct from himself', that is given in and from the sheer graciousness of God that is unconstrained by anything other than the relational givingness of God's own inner life that *needs* nothing outside of itself, but provides 'an eternal election of love, an everlasting covenant'.[27] Under the conditions of the subsequent sinfulness of human beings, Torrance announces that 'God binds himself in Jesus to sinful men and women and graciously accepts them'.[28]

The flip side of this is the renewal of the creature to be the actualization of the reality of God's covenanted creature. That has to do, then, with the *creaturely response* to the sheer gracious 'act of pure condescension of God' that takes its form in the intelligibility that divine self-accommodation or

---

[21]Torrance, *Incarnation*, 187.

[22]Torrance, *Incarnation*, 107.

[23]Torrance, 'Introduction', xx.

[24]Citation from Thomas F. Torrance, *The Mediation of Christ* (Exeter: Paternoster Press, 1983), 11.

[25]Thomas F. Torrance, 'The Goodness and Dignity of Man in the Christian Tradition', in *Christ in Our Place: The Humanity of God in Christ for the Reconciliation of the World-Essays Presented to James Torrance*, ed. Trevor Hart and Daniel Thimell (Exeter: Paternoster Press, 1989), 369–87, 385.

[26]Torrance, *The Mediation of Christ*, 33.

[27]Torrance, *Incarnation*, 107, 109.

[28]Torrance, *Incarnation*, 110.

revelatory adaptation provides.[29] Consequently, 'it is as such [as the choosing man and as the choosing God] that he binds humanity to himself for ever'.[30] Accordingly, Torrance cites with approval the noetic doubleness in John Calvin's account of divine and human knowing that 'there can be no true knowledge of man except within our knowledge of God' and vice versa.[31] The decisive factor is again christological. Christ 'is the eternal Word of God by whom and for whom all things were created and in whom they all hold together'.[32] Such a statement entails that 'the humanity of every man, whether he knows it or not, whether he believes it or not, is ontologically bound up with the humanity of Jesus, and determined by it', having its image of God in Jesus as 'the unique image-constituting Image of God'.[33] Consequently, it is in and through his humanity alone that 'access to God the Father is freely open for all the peoples of mankind'.[34] In addition, humanity exists in Christ pre-eminently as a gift whose ground cannot be lost, even if the image on the human side can be, and is, distorted by sinfulness so that God's 'original intention remains, no matter what happens'.[35] Finally, it entails that communion-making communicative action of God for humanity is the *telos* of God's creative agency. 'God does not wish to exist alone, and has freely brought into being alongside of himself and yet in utter distinction from himself another upon whom he may pour out his love, with whom he may share his divine Life in covenant-partnership.'[36] The theological ground of this may be the *ex nihilo* of pure grace, but it is rooted in the grace of the perichoretic *triune personal relations* of love that constitute God's inner eternal life. What does God's grace give, then, but God's own self *anhypostatically* incarnate? This amounts to an irreducibly engraced human life in which God is bodied forth or imaged.

While falling foul of his own concerns about container imagery or 'the receptacle notion of space', having had 'a fateful necessity in the history of Lutheran theology' of the *kenosis* of God in Christ and the Eucharist as well Newtonian mechanics, Torrance explains the simultaneous double movement involved.[37] 'Jesus Christ ... [is] the place where God has made room for Himself in the midst of our human existence and as the place

---

[29]Torrance, *Space, Time and Incarnation*, 3.
[30]Torrance, *Incarnation*, 113.
[31]Torrance, *Theology in Reconstruction*, 99.
[32]Torrance, 'The Goodness and Dignity of Man in the Christian Tradition', 376.
[33]Torrance, 'The Goodness and Dignity of Man in the Christian Tradition', 380.
[34]Torrance, *The Mediation of Christ*, 19.
[35]Torrance, *Theology in Reconstruction*, 105.
[36]Torrance, 'The Goodness and Dignity of Man in the Christian Tradition', 375.
[37]Citations from Torrance, *Space, Time and Incarnation*, 35, 34.

where man on earth and in history may meet and have communion with the heavenly Father.'[38] Through a geometric image, Torrance argues that:

the world, then, is made open to God through its intersection in the axis of Creation-Incarnation. … [This is] the place where the vertical and horizontal dimensionalities intersect, the place where human being is opened out to a transcendent ground in God where the infinite Being of God penetrates into our existence and creates room for Himself within the horizontal dimensions of finite being in space and time.[39]

At its best, Torrance's claim here focuses theological attention irreducibly in and through the concrete particularity of Jesus Christ as the One in whom God and creature are identifiable as having their form. Accordingly, he warns, dichotomous ways of thinking have had the effect of disastrously detaching 'Jesus from Israel, and … Christianity from Christ himself', abstracting 'Jesus Christ from the matrix of natural or inherent relations in which he is found, and then … [abstracting] the external appearance of Christ from the objective frame of event and significance with which he is bound up in the Gospel'.[40] This desire to account for the concreteness of God's revelatory act is intensified by Torrance's refusal to de-mediate grace. The point here usually emphasizes the form of discontinuity that is the result of sin, so that God has to break into the sinful performance, or to 'invade and destroy the barrier of death and all that separates men and women from God'.[41] Torrance does occasionally indicate the *moral* setting of the distance that requires God's action to overcome it.[42] For instance, 'the ascension of Jesus *from* Peter, James and John' involved the opening up of God's time for the church as the body through which the saving witness to Christ is to be embodied for the sake of God's world. This time is the time of God's patience 'in order to allow the world time for repentance'.[43]

The problem, however, is that without appropriately careful handling, the rhetoric presses towards something more ontological. The space–time discourse can all too easily slip into exhibiting a form of exclusion that has to be negotiated through what Rowan Williams calls 'a bridge concept'.[44]

---

[38]Torrance, *Space, Time and Incarnation*, 24.
[39]Torrance, *Space, Time and Incarnation*, 74–5.
[40]Torrance, *The Mediation of Christ*, 11, 12.
[41]Torrance, 'Introduction', xvii.
[42]Thomas F. Torrance, *Doctrine of Jesus Christ* (Eugene, OR: Wipf and Stock, 2002), 159.
[43]Thomas F. Torrance, *Royal Priesthood: A Theology of Ordained Ministry* (London: Bloomsbury, 1993), 61, 60.
[44]Rowan Williams, *On Christian Theology* (Oxford: Blackwell, 2000), 110.

The concerning way Torrance handles the material here is accentuated when he appeals to language of divine interventionist immediacy, for example, 'in eschatological suspension of the liturgy'.[45] Torrance, then, utilizes a range of images that unwittingly pressure creaturely mediation and forms of agency. In this regard, it is notable that Torrance liberally utilizes imagery of divine inbreaking, invasion, penetration and so on, when adapting language of the 'transparent mode' of perception into, or 'transparency' of, the media through which 'the reality God's ways and works' may be discerned.[46] This displays an implied competitiveness, here a spatially described one, between God and creature. Yet, as Tanner argues, 'the glorification of God does not come at the expense of creatures'.[47] The implication of this for a theology of prayer will become clearer in the discussion later. For now, it is important to recognize Tanner's warning against such ontologically dualistic conceptions in its construal of the relation between divine and human agencies. 'If human life is what it is (for all the corrupting influence of sin) because of God's working and not in independent self-sufficiency from God, there is no reason to think that God is working more the less we are.'[48]

Jesus' Praying Humanly without Ceasing

In Torrance's hands, the *homoousion* grounds the actualization of God's incarnate presence and the realization of God's creative *telos* in creatures' obedient response. The implication of such claims for Torrance's theology of prayer is that Jesus Christ is regarded as the One through whom the pray-er has her shape, as much as the One who himself prayed in the Spirit through to the Father. As the obedient One in our place, then, in terms of Herbert McCabe, 'he is not first of all an individual person who then prays to the Father, his prayer to the Father is what constitutes him as who he is. He is not just one who prays, not even one who prays best, he is sheer prayer'.[49]

Picking up Jungmann's contested thesis, Torrance laments a liturgical shift in the role of Christ in prayer towards a 'liturgical monophytism ... based upon an assimilation of the Mediatorship of Christ to his Lordship, and a Priesthood interpreted in terms of his mediating divine holiness to man, not in offering holiness from the side of man to God'.[50] Early liturgies

---

[45]Torrance, *Atonement*, 65.
[46]Torrance, *Space, Time and Resurrection*, 141.
[47]Tanner, *Jesus, Humanity and the Trinity*, 2.
[48]Tanner, *Christ the Key*, 280.
[49]Herbert McCabe, *God Matters* (London: Continuum, 2005), 220.
[50]Torrance, *Theology in Reconciliation*, 115.

offered eucharistic prayers through Christ to the Father, whereas later ones moved to offer prayers directly to Christ. In this shift comes a displacement of Christ's humanity, and the effects of this are substantive. For one thing, Torrance argues, this has 'meant the subordination of revelation to the natural forms of man's rationality and piety' among Catholics, 'and in Protestant theology has meant the transmutation of revelation into the subjectivity of the religious consciousness or Christian experience or faith'.[51]

Secondly, there emerges an 'instrumentalist notion of sacramental grace' so that, under an Aristotelianized form of Augustinianism, 'a causal connection [is introduced] into the relation between the grace of God and the liturgical event in the Eucharist'.[52] From this is 'forced upon the Latin Church a physicalist reinterpretation of the old patristic consecratory "conversion" of the elements of bread and wine on the basis of an Aristotelian doctrine of substance and accidents, i.e. in terms of *transubstantiation*'.[53] Consequently, 'the effect of this new doctrine of transubstantiation became evident in the increasing tendency to restrict the real presence of Christ to the real presence in the Eucharist of his body and blood defined in this phenomenalist, physico-causal way'.[54] This account explains why prayer often comes to be associated with ways of gaining power or control over divine action, with the asking even for what McCabe calls requests from out of 'shabby infantile desires'.[55] Such accounts of this gifting God struggle to resist Ludwig Feuerbach's criticism that 'God is the Love that satisfied our wishes, our emotional wants. ... God is the nature of human feeling, unlimited, pure feeling, made objective. ... Thus what is prayer but the wish of the heart expressed with confidence in its fulfilment?'[56]

Torrance's repair is to refer to Christ's humanity. 'The humanity of Jesus, as Calvin used to say, is not merely the instrument of God's salvation, but the "material cause" of it.'[57]

The Kingdom of God as God's will for man has been realized for us intensively in the humanity of Jesus, and what has been realized intensively for us *in Christ* must be worked out extensively *in us* in the world, by the

---

[51]Torrance, 'The Place of Christology', 20.
[52]Torrance, *Theology in Reconciliation*, 123.
[53]Torrance, *Theology in Reconciliation*, 123.
[54]Torrance, *Theology in Reconciliation*, 123.
[55]McCabe, *God Matters*, 224.
[56]Ludwig Feuerbach, *The Essence of Christianity*, trans. George Eliot (London: Harper and Row, 1957), 121–2.
[57]Thomas F. Torrance, 'The Priesthood of Jesus: A Study in the Doctrine of the Atonement', in *Essays in Christology for Karl Barth*, ed. T. H. L. Parker (London: Lutterworth Press, 1956), 155–73 (160).

Holy Spirit, through the mission of the Church. Through the preaching of the Gospel we are called to become now in ourselves what we already are in Christ.[58]

The humanity of Jesus is the realization of God's creative making of communicative creatures. With a further significant theological step, Torrance suggests that prayer is more than an episodic act. Developing a familiar *exitus-reditus*, *katabasis-anabasis*, scheme, he speaks of Jesus' very life before the Father 'as answering word in perfect fulfilment of his will'.[59] The entirety of Jesus' life is prayer, his living in obedience. Even though Christ was himself a worshipper 'among us worshippers', and was in turn 'worshipped', his very life is itself worship, and this is the nature of 'his life in the form of a servant'.[60] Drawing on 1 Thessalonians 5.17 to depict this scope of what is meant by prayer within the service of Christ's true human life, Torrance maintains that 'it was a prayer without ceasing, lived prayer'.[61] Prayer is prayer only as it expresses the prayerful life, and it does that by being disciplined by its being offered in and through, and therefore being shaped by, the substitutionary or vicarious humanity of God and human being in Jesus Christ, our 'Mediator, Advocate and High Priest'.[62] Alexander Schmemann is helpful here when he explains that the liturgy cannot properly be reduced to '"cultic" categories, its definition as a sacred act of worship, different as such not only from the "profane" area of life, but even from all other activities of the Church itself'.[63] 'This', he explains, 'is not the original meaning of the Greek word *leitourgia*. It meant an action by which a group of people become something corporately which they had not been as a mere collection of individuals'.[64] That means, Schmemann continues, that 'the Church itself is a *leitourgia*, a ministry, a calling to act in this world after the fashion of Christ, to bear testimony to him and his kingdom'.[65] Within this account, prayer becomes less a discrete set of practices than a mode of being in the world, the shaping of life as imaging forth the creatively

---

[58]Torrance, 'The Priesthood of Jesus', 165–6.

[59]Torrance, *Atonement*, 277.

[60]Torrance, *Theology in Reconciliation*, 113.

[61]Torrance, *Incarnation*, 118. See James B. Torrance, 'The Vicarious Humanity of Christ', in *The Incarnation: Ecumenical Studies in the Nicene-Constantinopolitan Creed*, ed. Thomas F. Torrance (Edinburgh: The Handsel Press, 1981), 127–47 (130).

[62]Torrance, *Theology in Reconciliation*, 113–14.

[63]Alexander Schmemann, *The World as Sacrament* (London: Darton, Longman and Todd, 1966), 28.

[64]Schmemann, *The World as Sacrament*, 28.

[65]Alexander Schmemann, *For the Life of the World: Sacraments and Orthodoxy* (Crestwood, NY: St Vladimir's Seminary Press, 1973), 25.

communicative work of God in Christ by the Spirit. When Paul enjoins praying without ceasing (1 Thess. 5.17), according to Lochman, he has in view 'here a whole dimension of human existence before God. ... In this sense all thoughts and actions that respect God and his creation are acts of prayer. ... No sphere of human life, and especially no urgent human need, lies outside prayer's terms of reference'.[66]

This argument takes its shape in and through a parallel with Torrance's account of the liturgical practices of the sacraments. He makes it clear that there is one primordial sacrament, the humanity of Jesus Christ as 'the primary *mysterium* or *sacramentum*', the 'all-inclusive Sacrament of the Word made flesh'.[67] The sacramental signs of baptism (the sacrament of justification or incorporation, administered once and for all) and the Eucharist (the sacrament of sanctification or renewal in that incorporation, administered continually) are sacramentalized by the Spirit, or given as 'two "moments" of the one Mystery' as effective signs or witnesses to it that in the Spirit 'so that we in our mortal bodies may bear about the dying of the Lord Jesus Christ that His life also may be made manifest in our mortal flesh'.[68] They have their *raison d'être* 'beyond all religious and ethical acts, indispensable as they may be, upon the *inner relations* of the incarnate Son of God'.[69] Through them 'the Spirit begets the Church as Body in sacramental union with Christ'.[70] Here Torrance resists an interpretation that would reduce the sacramental signs to phenomenal expressions of the believer's pious inwardness or the acts of the church in memory of Christ. In contrast, they are effective signs of 'both the act of Christ and the act of the Church in his name', in which Christ gives and the church 'is one which serves the act of Christ and directs us away from itself to Christ'.[71] In other words, they are effective signs of the gift of God and the *telos* of communicative incorporation of creatures which involves, Torrance argues with respect to the Eucharist, 'the healing of our disorder'.[72] Specifically drawing together the Eucharist and prayer, Torrance argues that 'the Eucharist ... must be understood as act of prayer, thanksgiving and worship, ... as act in which through the Spirit we are given to share in the vicarious life, faith, prayer,

---

[66]Jan Milič Lochman, *The Lord's Prayer*, trans. Geoffrey Bromiley (Grand Rapids, MI: William B. Eerdmans, 1990), 6.

[67]Torrance, *Theology in Reconciliation*, 82; Torrance, *Royal Priesthood*, 75.

[68]Torrance, *Royal Priesthood*, 75.

[69]Torrance, *Theology in Reconciliation*, 108.

[70]Torrance, *Royal Priesthood*, 75.

[71]Torrance, *Theology in Reconciliation*, 107.

[72]Torrance, *Royal Priesthood*, 105.

worship, thanksgiving and self-offering of Jesus to the Father, for in the final resort it is Jesus Christ himself who is our true worship'.[73]

Incorporation into Jesus' High Priesthood: Prayer through Christ

Prayer, then, involves incorporation into the life of prayer or the praying-without-ceasing that is grounded in the vicarious performance of the humanity of Jesus. This is a corresponding movement of responsiveness to God's movement of self-givingness, a corresponding and participatory 'movement of our repentance and faith and vision of God' 'to the descent and ascent of the Word in his movement of revelation'.[74] Torrance unpacks the notion of participation in the Mediator's prayer to the Father by conceptualizing the vicarious and mediatorial humanity of Jesus in and through imagery of the High Priesthood of Jesus. This adapts the notion of the *triplex munus* so that for Torrance Christ's High Priesthood becomes a *Royal Priesthood*. Torrance explains the High Priesthood in the context of the raising up of Jesus that 'begins ..., paradoxically, with his crucifixion, and his ascension [which] begins, paradoxically, with his lifting up on the cross'.[75] Jesus, as Representative man, the One in whom all things come to be and are, ascends to the right hand of the Father so that in him 'all humanity is gathered up and made participant in his self-offering, so that in his ascension Christ is installed as the head of the new humanity, the prince of the new creation, the king of the kingdom which he has won and established through his incarnate life and passion'.[76]

Jesus' High Priestliness is of 'quite a different order', then, to that of the Aaronic priesthood since what he does transcends the liturgical cult that bears witness to something other than itself, and that has its appointment by 'legal ordinance'.[77] This entails that 'it is not only the prayer of the victim but of the priest made on our behalf'.[78] Jesus is himself, as God in 'incarnational solidarity with sinners', that very One to whom his priesthood bears witness.[79] This means, among other things, that 'God is not acted upon by means of priestly sacrifice. ... It is actually God Himself who performs

---

[73]Torrance, *Theology in Reconciliation*, 109.
[74]Torrance, *Incarnation*, 77–8.
[75]Thomas F. Torrance, *Atonement: The Person and Work of Christ*, ed. Robert T. Walker (Milton Keynes: Paternoster Press, 2009), 269.
[76]Torrance, *Atonement*, 270–1.
[77]Citation from Torrance, *Atonement*, 272.
[78]Torrance, *Incarnation*, 120.
[79]Citation from Torrance, *Atonement*, 272.

the act of forgiveness and atonement, but the priestly cultus is designed to answer to His act and bear witness to His cleansing of the sinner'.[80] If being the Royal Priest has primarily to do with his divine appointment to be offering and offeror, it also has to do with his ongoing mediation as advocate, 'as himself the *leitourgos* [Heb. 8.2], the leader of the heavenly worship'.[81] Here 'Christ is the eternal leader of our prayer and intercession, in which he makes himself the true content and sole reality of the worship and prayer of mankind'.[82] He *is* the eternal content of the prayer he puts into our mouths, the prayerful life of obedience to God, the Son who can pray the 'Our Father', the hallowing of God's Name and the coming of God's kingdom. 'He makes himself the true content and sole reality of the worship and prayer of man.'[83] Jesus, then, becomes the primary eucharistic worshipper and pray-er. Torrance explains this through the category of Jesus not merely as Representative creature/human being, representing *our* prayers to the Father, but also as vicarious *Substitute* so that 'he acts in our place and offers worship and prayer which we could not offer' in a way that identifies and makes his prayer our own in the indwelling Spirit.[84] This, then, is fulfilled in the echo of Christ's worship among creatures and the filling of 'all things with his presence' and the bestowal of the 'gifts of the Spirit upon men and women'.[85] Accordingly,

> while it is we who pray, we pray not in our own name but in the name of Christ, and yet it is not we but He who prays in us, so that the prayer which we pray in the flesh we pray in the faith of the Son of God who loved us and gave Himself for us (Gal. 2.20).[86]

To return to the relation of God and creature, it is apparent that Torrance does not construe them as competitively related, or at least not consciously in any straightforward sense. What results from accounts that construe the Creator–creature relation in inverse proportion is both a sense in which God is an agent on the same ontologically causal plane as creaturely agents (what McCabe understands to be idolatry),[87] so that what is worshipped is part

---

[80]Torrance, *Royal Priesthood*, 3.
[81]Torrance, *Atonement*, 273.
[82]Torrance, *Atonement*, 275.
[83]Torrance, *Space, Time and Resurrection*, 116.
[84]Torrance, *Atonement*, 275.
[85]Torrance, *Atonement*, 276.
[86]Torrance, *Theology in Reconciliation*, 209.
[87]'God is not a kind of thing among other kinds of things', Tanner, *Jesus, Humanity and the Trinity*, 4.

of the universe, and ways of construing human action as free from divine involvement other than in specifically discrete divine interruptive episodes. As Torrance warns, when critiquing the Lutheran receptacle construal of space–time with its 'radical disjunction between the divine and the human in which there was no interaction between them',[88] 'when we say that God exists, we mean that God exists as God, in accordance with the nature of God. Hence divine existence is of an utterly unique and transcendent kind'.[89] From this refusal to imagine God and creature as competitive categories, univocally imagined, Torrance is able to 'think together the relation of God to space and time and the relation of man to space and time'.[90] In other words, Torrance's efforts are to think from out of what God gives, 'by the nature of God himself', rather than from out of what the creature projects.[91] This enables the claim that God's transcendence from and over space and time is not to be construed competitively, but rather so as to allow a proper articulation of how God remains unboundedly 'everywhere'.[92] For Tanner, and it is evident for Torrance too, 'the perfection of created life, the perfection of the creature in its difference from God, increases with the perfection of relationship with God: the closer the better'.[93] Prayer, then, emerges from a situation of plenitude, from the gift of sharing 'in the communion of knowing within God himself',[94] so that, in the words of McCabe, 'the notion of the needy creature simply appealing to his creator is not merely an inadequate account of prayer; it is not prayer at all'.[95] It is heard by the Father in and through the filiality of relation.[96]

The implications for a theology of prayer are pronounced. For instance, the relay-race-type construal of prayer (the pray-er offers prayer to the listening God, and then awaits God's response) is subverted. The competitive model results in human inactivity beyond the act of praying so that prayer has become a substitute action. In contrast, 'the creature's receiving from God does not then require its passivity in the world: God's activity as the giver of ourselves need not come at the expense of our own activity. Instead, the creature receives from God its very activity as a good'.[97] Commenting

---

[88]Torrance, *Space, Time and Resurrection*, 125.
[89]Torrance, *Space, Time and Resurrection*, 126–7.
[90]Torrance, *Space, Time and Resurrection*, 127.
[91]Citation from Torrance, *Space, Time and Resurrection*, 128.
[92]Torrance, *Space, Time and Resurrection*, 128.
[93]Tanner, *Jesus, Humanity and the Trinity*, 3.
[94]Torrance, *The Mediation of Christ*, rev. edn, 116.
[95]Herbert McCabe, *God Still Matters* (London: Continuum, 2002), 71.
[96]See Torrance, *Incarnation*, 117.
[97]Tanner, *Jesus, Humanity and the Trinity*, 4.

on the petition of the Lord's Prayer 'Your will be done on earth as it is in heaven', Jan Milič Lochman declares:

> the petition does not drug the devout. It does not make them ready to accept without question anything that might come. It is not a spiritual anesthetic or opiate to reconcile them a priori to circumstances. On the contrary, it encourages them constantly to orient themselves to the true will of God, which means ... to confront circumstances with promises.[98]

Torrance, then, has little time for unmediated accounts of prayer as 'spiritual', whereby that term is understood as a practice that bypasses the integrity of the Spirit's uniting pray-ers in the prayerful humanity of God in Christ. Such a 'spirituality' would, in fact, undermine the very identifiability of the processes through which talk of God, God's action and prayer are Christianly intelligible, and succumb to Feuerbach's criticism that 'in prayer ... man excludes from his mind the world, and with it all thoughts of intermediateness and dependence'.[99] After all, Torrance argues, 'to be a spiritual body is not to be less body but more truly and completely body, for by the Spirit physical existence is redeemed from all that corrupts and undermines it, and from all or any privation of being'.[100] Furthermore, it is equally a dislocation from the givingness of God's self-humanization in Christ, and it is this that for Torrance underlies certain kinds of institutional attempts to control divine grace. To articulate a theology of prayer in and through the form of God's Spirit-ual agency humanly expressed and constitutively imaged in Jesus Christ subverts the ways in which grace can be channelled by creaturely control.

In addition, the spirituality of the performance of prayer in and through the humanity of Christ resists an evasion of the conditions of creatureliness. One thing that the eucharistic elements direct us to in Torrance's reflections is the irreducibility of the *bodily* existence of the gift of creatureliness, even of the eschatological renewal of creaturehood. Communion with God through participative union with Christ does not make human beings anything other than what they are: humans being loved and engraced by God in Christ who 'share in the life of God while remaining what we were made to be, human beings and not gods'.[101] Torrance, therefore, maintains the integrity of the *'contingent* nature of creaturely being'.[102] In the ascended life of the

---

[98]Lochman, *The Lord's Prayer*, 71.
[99]Feuerbach, *The Essence of Christianity*, 123.
[100]Torrance, *Space, Time and Resurrection*, 141.
[101]Torrance, *Atonement*, 295.
[102]Torrance, 'The Goodness and Dignity of Man in the Christian Tradition', 370.

resurrected Lord 'creaturely space and time, far from being dissolved, are confirmed in their reality before God'.[103] In fact, the resurrected Christ himself ascends to the right hand of the Father 'without ceasing to be man or without any diminishment of his physical, historical existence'.[104] It is this that makes him 'the First-fruits of the new *creation* and the First-born of every *creature*'.[105] Creatures are reordered, healed and restored through the materiality of Christ's saving being-in-act.

A further implication of this approach has to do with understanding the relation of the pray-er's prayer and the world. Human dignity *qua* creatureliness does not involve being created in and for the ontological solitariness of individuality. Human being is made to 'live out of the transcendence of God in and through Jesus alone'.[106] And what does this shape human being for? Fellowship with God that is eminently related to the renewing of the fellowship with all creatures. Humanity, Torrance argues, 'must be regarded as an essentially relational being', related to 'all things' that have been made by the Word 'in whom they hold together'.[107] That means that for Torrance, 'a truly Christocentric approach ... must surely keep in view the place that man *in Christ* must have within the whole created order of visible and invisible realities'.[108] Does this mean that the world can be depicted *sacramentally*? That would, however, require considerable theological care. For Torrance there is but one sacrament, Jesus Christ. It is in him that the practices of sacramental signification take their shape, participate and provide a witness or signs. All things have their being in Christ, the communicative selfhood of God in whom all creatures are bound up and represented for communion with God, to be eschatologically fulfilled. Yet it is precisely from here that a short step can be taken to proclaiming the sacramental-quality of all things as they participate in the communion of God through Christ and in the Spirit.[109] Moreover, this too presses towards an inclusive universalization. Eschatological fulfilment involves the redemption of the world already perfected in Christ and not the making of a new or 'other' world.

The Church

According to Schmemann, 'the Church is not a society for escape – corporately or individually – from this world to taste of the mystical bliss of eternity. ...

---

[103]Torrance, *Space, Time and Resurrection*, 127.
[104]Torrance, *Space, Time and Resurrection*, 129.
[105]Torrance, *Space, Time and Resurrection*, 142.
[106]Torrance, *Space, Time and Resurrection*, 136.
[107]Torrance, 'The Goodness and Dignity of Man in the Christian Tradition', 371, 369.
[108]Torrance, 'The Goodness and Dignity of Man in the Christian Tradition', 369.
[109]See Schmemann, *For the Life of the World*, 122.

It is the very communion with the Holy Spirit that enables us to love the world with the love of Christ'.[110] So, if the church is not 'a society for escape' what is it for? According to Karl Barth, the covenant is the internal basis of creation, the *telos* of God's creating, and Torrance makes the case with an explicit appeal to prayer. 'That covenant prayer belongs to the inner purpose and ground of creation.'[111] Torrance's claim that God's ecclesial people are drawn into the priestly work of the ascended Christ, among other things, 'means that the church is constantly summoned to look beyond its historical forms to the fullness and perfection that will be disclosed at the *parousia*'.[112] The christic shape that this eschatological framing of God's ways with the world takes requires that the church 'must never identify the structures it acquires and must acquire in the *nomistic* forms of this-worldly historical existence with the essential forms of its new being in Christ himself'.[113] That means that 'the Church does not exist by and for itself, and therefore cannot be known and interpreted out of itself'.[114] Such a move would displace the *telos* of God's creative and redemptive action for creatures, and the church's service 'of the well-being of all' in its 'humanizing task ... of humanizing the world'.[115]

The 'royal priesthood' of the church, its 'participating in the one priesthood of the ascended king through its *service* of him', entails that its task is crucially to be 'only a reflection of the one indivisible priesthood of Christ'.[116] This is its *raison d'être*, its true nature, its service. Led by the Spirit of Christ, the church has its matter as 'the empirical correlate of the *Parousia* of the Spirit in our midst'.[117] Torrance, however, would hesitate to make Schillebeeckx's claim: 'The Church therefore is not merely a means of salvation. It is Christ's salvation itself, ... the earthly prolongation or, better, visibility of, Christ's high priesthood in heaven.'[118] This language, if pressed too hard, can unwittingly make the church a substitute for the now absent Christ rather than the instrument of God in Christ's ongoing pneumatic presence to the world, displacing Christ's own 'work in this

---

[110]Schmemann, *The World as Sacrament*, 53.

[111]Torrance, *Incarnation*, 117.

[112]Torrance, *Atonement*, 313.

[113]Torrance, *Atonement*, 313.

[114]Torrance, *Theology in Reconstruction*, 192.

[115]Edward Schillebeeckx, *God the Future of Man*, trans. N. D. Smith (London: Sheed and Ward, 1969), 128, 124.

[116]Torrance, *Atonement*, 277.

[117]Thomas F. Torrance, *The Trinitarian Faith: The Evangelical Theology of the Ancient Catholic Church* (London: Continuum, 2003), 252.

[118]Edward Schillebeeckx, *Christ the Sacrament of the Encounter with God* (London: Sheed and Ward, 1963), 48, 159.

continuing ministry [of the church] ... making the preaching of the gospel effectual as word and power of God'.[119] Moreover, this imagery can deflect from the ongoing *healing* that the church herself requires so that 'it is Christ himself who confers forgiveness, builds up his church on earth, renews it in the power of the resurrection and resents it as his own body to the Father'.[120] Such a healing involves participating in, and following of, Christ's 'utter self-humiliation in κένωσις, in ταπείνωσις'.[121] Schillebeeckx, for his part, is profoundly attentive to that, and he warns against triumphalistic claims of God's eschatologically renewing ways in the world in and through the church since 'the Church on the way is not yet the kingdom of God'.[122] Torrance himself emphasizes that while the church's sacramental actions 'are signs of the new order which has once and for all broken into our world in Jesus Christ and which we have constant participation through the Spirit', with 'the eschatological pause in the one *parousia* of Christ' that is the ascension, 'that new order is veiled from our sight'.[123] While the church, then, is grounded in, and sustained by, 'our union with Christ', nonetheless, 'there is an eschatological reserve ..., an eschatological lag waiting for the last Word or the final Act of God'.[124] In other words, the church and its actions are *not* clear signs of God's new life of communion in Christ. As the Christ-formed action of living responsibly in service to God, 'prayer becomes essentially *redemptive activity*'.[125] In this regard, Torrance proclaims, 'the prayer of mediation or intercession occupies an essential place in the fulfilling of the saving covenant, in the offering of obedient sacrifice as well as in the prayer for divine succor and help'.[126]

This works itself out in several ways, reflecting the 'political and corporate sense' of the work of the *ergon* and *laos* in the 'profane Greek' of *leitourgein* and *leitourgia*.[127] The first is reparative. According to Torrance, the church's 'witness [occurs] in the face of resistance and even persecution'.[128] Under these conditions, grace has a reparative function. In social terms, grace is conflictual in that it participates in the redemptive work of God that mortifies a sinful world.

---

[119]Torrance, *Atonement*, 280.
[120]Torrance, *Atonement*, 281.
[121]Torrance, *Royal Priesthood*, 87.
[122]Schillebeeckx, *God the Future of Man*, 125.
[123]Torrance, *Atonement*, 306, 304, 306.
[124]Torrance, *Royal Priesthood*, 45.
[125]Torrance, *Incarnation*, 117.
[126]Torrance, *Incarnation*, 117.
[127]Torrance, *Royal Priesthood*, 15.
[128]Torrance, 'Service in Christ', 15.

It is because Christ crucified and risen again dwells in the Church and makes it the earthly form of His Body that He leads it into the unavoidable conflict between the mercy of God and the inhumanity of man and between the holiness of God and the sin of mankind. The Church cannot withdraw from the affliction and suffering which this conflict brings without contracting out of its witness and betraying its Lord.[129]

With regard to prayer, then, 'it is in our place that Jesus prays, standing where we stand in our rebellion and alienation. ... Jesus prays against the whole trend of our existence and against all the self-willed movement of our life'.[130]

The second involves the witness to God's restorative or vivifying work so that 'the church's engagement in prayer is already a participation in the final victory of the kingdom of Christ'.[131] Here Torrance develops the image of human being as 'called to be a kind of midwife to creation' by 'assisting nature out of its divinely given abundance constantly to give birth to new forms of life and richer patterns of order'.[132] In contradistinction to our sinful rebellion, Christ offers 'a prayer of obedience' as 'his very mode of life as the Son of the Father on earth'.[133] This is the 'not my will but yours be done' offered in Gethsemane in which Christ expresses what it means to life in prayerfully 'without ceasing', or in 'utterly unbroken life of fellowship ... and unrelenting prayer'.[134] 'Jesus', then, 'resorted to prayer and unswervingly held fast to God the Father throughout it all'.[135] In this faithful life-act 'in worship and adoration', Jesus 'perfected the positive self offering of man to God'.[136] What results is the Father's answer of Jesus' prayer through the forging of 'a new covenant relation of prayer between God and his creation, into which Jesus leads all who believe in him and share in his vicarious obedience to the Father ... in the teeth of all evil'.[137] Torrance proceeds by unpacking the form that that answer takes: the 'answer in life and deed in the raising up of his beloved Son from death'.[138] By offering himself as

---

[129]Thomas F. Torrance, 'Service in Christ', in *Service in Christ: Essays Presented to Karl Barth on His Eightieth Birthday*, ed. James I. McCord and T. H. L. Parker (London: Epworth Press, 1966), 1–16 (15).

[130]Torrance, *Incarnation*, 117.

[131]Torrance, *Atonement*, 297.

[132]Torrance, 'The Goodness and Dignity of Man in the Christian Tradition', 387.

[133]Torrance, *Incarnation*, 118.

[134]Torrance, *Incarnation*, 118, 119.

[135]Torrance, *Incarnation*, 119.

[136]Torrance, *Incarnation*, 119.

[137]Torrance, *Incarnation*, 118.

[138]Torrance, *Incarnation*, 118.

our Mediator, Intercessor, Advocate, the ascended Christ forever offers us up in his humanity-in-our-place for the renewal of our humanity. In fact, herein 'all creation is turned and brought back to God the creator and Father almighty'.[139] As our humanity echoes his, our prayer participates in (we pray his prayer given to our mouths) and echoes 'his prayer in life and death and eternal intercession'.[140] Prayer, then, is the basic service of the church's ministry. As, Lochman maintains, 'prayer can be the most faithful act of living for others'.[141]

Conclusion

Our time, Torrance argues, 'is to be understood as *time for* something'.[142] What we mean by prayer, the time for lived prayer, is constituted by a series of claims about God, the ground and *telos* of all things, and the shape of relatedness of those things.[143] Depending on the form that those claims take conditions whether we are actually talking about prayer at all, at least in a Christian sense. It is here that Torrance's refusal to segregate divine self-communication and prayer as the actualization of human response has its ground, and its critical attentiveness to a range of pressures to reconfigure the relation and therein the very nature of prayer. Our prayer-acts are always our acts, without the divine displacement of our agency. 'They differ from other acts not in the cessation of human activity but in their extrospective shape, their attention to what is being done by God for us.'[144] Among other things, that entails that, as Torrance observes, ethics, or 'Christian discipleship', is 'the disciplined habit of thinking and acting *in Christ*'.[145] 'Christ', Tanner maintains, 'forms us but what is so formed is our action'.[146]

If prayer as Christ-formed practice is the performance of creatures' flourishing in communicative participation in the resplendent self-communicative life of God, in Jesus Christ and by the Spirit, then it has its intelligibility in a social and eschatological understanding of human good or flourishing, and can hope for nothing less.

---

[139]Torrance, *Incarnation*, 119.
[140]Torrance, *Incarnation*, 121.
[141]Lochman, *The Lord's Prayer*, 9.
[142]Torrance, *Space, Time and Resurrection*, 130.
[143]Torrance, *Incarnation*, 118.
[144]Tanner, *Jesus, Humanity and the Trinity*, 73.
[145]Torrance, *Atonement*, 376.
[146]Tanner, *Jesus, Humanity and the Trinity*, 72.

The intercessory prayer of the Church is direct engagement in the mighty apocalyptic battle between the Kingdom of Christ and the kingdoms of this world and the triumphant reign of the Enthroned Lamb over all the forces of evil and darkness in history. The Church's greatest need is to *believe again* in the intercession of Christ and to find through prayer the sole source of power in its mission.[147]

When that is said and done, the question remains, however, whether Torrance's account can adequately engage in contextual interrogation that takes seriously the irreducible humanness of the praying agent and her cultural concreteness. Even to ask what taking that seriously might look like suggests that one wonders where pray-ers went.

---

[147]Torrance, 'Service in Christ', 15.

PART FOUR

Contemporary Perspectives

CHAPTER TWENTY-EIGHT

Prayer and Natural Science: Brains, Bodies and Effects

ANDREW DAVISON

At first glance, we may not expect science to feature in a discussion of prayer and yet the sort of empirical questions asked by scientists bear upon the study of prayer at several points. In what follows, we will consider a range of topics, including the efficacy of prayer, not least on the one who prays, and the need to think about prayer as a bodily practice.

Science and the Efficacy of Prayer

Although questions about the efficacy of prayer have featured prominently in recent work on the relation between theology and science, theologians have been thinking about the difference that prayer might make in the world long before that.

Questions about the efficacy of prayer in discussions of theology and science have typically taken two paths. One is empirical: it asks *whether* scientific investigations uncover evidence for, or against, answered prayer. The second is theoretical: it asks *how* prayer could be effective, if we approach that question from within some scientific perspective or other. Often, though problematically, the assumption is that a certain construal of science – taken to be correct, obvious and determinative – curtails the possibility for answered prayer or of divine action in the world more generally.

Does prayer work?

Scientific studies on whether prayer is effective have involved comparing the outcomes, often health-related, for two groups of people: one prayed for, the other not. Theologians may have reasons to be wary about studies of this sort, perhaps recalling the injunction in Deuteronomy not to put God to the test (Deut. 6.16; Mt. 4.7; Lk. 4.12), and finding something impious in subjecting God to statistical scrutiny. Hiddenness has been listed among divine attributes (Isa. 45.15). We might therefore doubt that God can be caught out by experiments and statistics, and flushed into the open.

Although these concerns are real, the Christian tradition provides at least one case where empirical investigation of the effect of prayer is part of official church practice, namely the investigation of miracles by the Roman Catholic Church as part of its discernment of whom to recognize as a saint. The scientific element of this process includes the work of a 'board of medical experts', reporting to the Congregation for the Causes of Saints.[1]

Scientific investigation of the effects of prayer was proposed in an anonymous letter to the *Contemporary Review* in 1972, suggesting that prayers be offered for some patients at a London hospital, but not others, and the results compared.[2] Around the same time, Francis Galton compared life expectancies for different groups of people, to the same end. While his assumptions about 'praying' and 'non-praying classes' may be problematic, his finding that monarchs did not live longer than contemporary 'lawyers, gentry or military officers' was creative, given that the *Book of Common Prayer* stipulated prayer for the monarch and royal family twice each day.[3]

The first empirical study of the effects of prayer is usually credited to Randolph Byrd, involving patients in the coronary care unit of the San Francisco General Hospital in 1988.[4] He claimed to discern some positive

---

[1]John Paul II, *Divinus Perfectionis Magister*, II.12, in *Acta Apostolicae Sedis*, 75.1 (Vatican: Typis Polyglottis Vaticanis, 1983), 349–55.

[2]For an account of the public debate this provoked, see Stephen G. Brush, 'The Prayer Test: The Proposal of a "Scientific" Experiment to Determine the Power of Prayer Kindled a Raging Debate between Victorian Men of Science and Theologians', *American Scientist* 62, no. 5 (1974): 561–3, cited by David Wilkinson, *When I Pray, What Does God Do?* (Oxford: Monarch, 2015), 68. The unfortunate notion of a 'the centuries-old warfare between science and religion' (Brush, 'The Prayer Test', 561) has been significantly disproved by more recent historians. For documents relating to the controversy, see John O. Means, ed., *The Prayer-Gauge Debate* (Boston, MA: Congregational Publishing Society, 1876).

[3]Brush, 'The Prayer Test', 562.

[4]R. C. Byrd, 'Positive Therapeutic Effects of Intercessory Prayer in a Coronary Care Unit Population', *Southern Medical Journal* 81, no. 7 (1988): 826–9.

effects. A sober assessment, however, taking in all the available studies on this question is that no clear 'effects', positive or negative, have been discovered. A survey in the *Cochrane Database of Systematic Reviews* (2007) concluded that the results were equivocal: only one showed an improved outcome, but the study was small. A revised edition two years later reported that 'although some of the results of individual studies suggest a positive effect of intercessory prayer, the majority do not, and the evidence does not support a recommendation either in favour or against the use of intercessory prayer'.[5]

Of the various problems that might afflict studies of this kind, perhaps the most problematic concerns whether a true scientific 'control' is ever possible: can we arrange for benchmark cases where *nothing* is done, to contrast with cases where prayers are offered? What of countless people around the world praying for everyone in distress? What of members of religious orders keeping perpetual vigils of prayer for those in need? What of the intercession of Christ or, as most of the world's Christians would see it, of saints and angels? A 'control' situation, of someone for whom no prayers are offered at all, seems impossible to arrange.

Finally, the theologian might point to serious problems with the idea that these experiments are being conducted 'blind', given that the chief 'agent' under investigation, if we can put it that way, is God: all-knowing and outside of time. Given the omniscience of God, we can ask whether such experiments would really be investigating whether God heals the sick when asked or – to put it bluntly – whether they would be testing whether God chooses to reveal himself in scientific trails.

Can prayer work?

Prayer, and its efficacy, has often been seen as a provocation for thinking about how God acts in the world ('divine action'). We therefore move from scientific investigations of whether prayer 'works' to scientific angles on the 'method' by which prayers might be answered.

Divine action became a problem in modernity for several reasons. One concerns *order*, picking up an existing theological commitment to a pattern

---

[5]Leanne Roberts, Irshad Ahmed and Steve Hall, 'Intercessory Prayer for the Alleviation of Ill Health', *Cochrane Database of Systematic Reviews*, 2000, CD000368, with later versions in 2007 (CD000368.pub2) and 2009 (CD000368.pub3) under the authorship of Leanne Roberts, Irshad Ahmed and Andrew Davison. The first version considered only four studies and concluded that 'data in this review are too inconclusive to guide those wishing to uphold or refute the effect of intercessory prayer on healthcare outcomes'. The second version, which like the third considered ten cases, concluded that the body of experimental findings in the area could not 'sensibly' be interpreted 'with great confidence'.

within nature, and asking why and how God would go beyond it. Another follows from the sense, growing from the seventeenth century, that the order within matter and space is mechanistic, and *predetermined* in every detail. We can chart a course here from René Descartes, for whom mind was immaterial and matter (including animals) deterministic,[6] to Isaac Newton, and his laws of motion that see the world operating like billiard balls colliding on a felt table, and on to the deterministic French mathematician Pierre-Simon Laplace, who wrote that 'we ought then to consider the present state of the universe as the effect of its previous state and as the cause of that which is to follow', all unfolding along a determined and unchangeable trajectory.[7]

Thirdly, and finally, there is a mindset – perhaps as much an unchallenged background assumption as an articulated position – that sees God as an agent comparable to the created world, such that God has to 'intervene' in order to effect a change. Much is smuggled into the discussion of divine action simply by an unquestioned adoption of this word, *intervention*.

The concern about *determinism* is undermined from the side of science, by the revolution in thinking that we call quantum mechanics (at least according to its most widely accepted interpretation). Instead of determinism, it sees nature as unfolding according to chance and contingency. The cosmos is ordered but, especially at the smallest level, that shapes the probabilities of things happening, rather than supporting the necessity imagined by Laplace.

Theologically speaking, the concern about *intervention* betrays an impoverished view of the doctrine of creation. God and the world do not sit alongside one another, as two sorts of 'being': as the cause of all beings, God is not another being among beings; as the cause of there being creaturely causes, God is not one more cause among them.[8] As Herbert McCabe put it, 'it is not possible that God and the universe should add up to make two'.[9] God is absolute, unbounded and uncreated; the universe is contingent, and it depends upon God at every moment for all that it is. God, in other words, is transcendent, and there is an 'absolute ontological distinction' between creator and creatures, whether earthworm or archangel. The language of 'intervention' does not take this difference seriously enough. It is mistaken

---

[6] René Descartes, 'Letter to Henry Moore', in *Oeuvres de Descartes*, ed. Charles Adam and Paul Tannery (Paris: J. Vrin, 1956), v, 277.

[7] Pierre-Simon Laplace, *Philosophical Essay on Probabilities*, trans. and ed. Andrew I. Dale (New York: Springer-Verlag, 1995), 2.

[8] See Andrew Davison, *Participation in God: A Study in Christian Doctrine and Metaphysics* (Cambridge: Cambridge University Press, 2019), 13–41, 217–38.

[9] Herbert McCabe, *God Matters* (London: Chapman, 1987), 6.

in a somewhat comparable way to saying that a novelist 'intervenes' in the novel she is writing.

One time-honoured way to speak about the relation of God as cause to creaturely causes is with the distinction between primary and secondary causes.[10] Everything that happens in the usual course of things has a natural, secondary cause (which, at the quantum level, may unfold according to probability). These secondary causes are what science studies, with human agency as one of them. The primary cause of all things – including secondary causes – is God; God is the reason there are causes at all. God's causation and that of a creature do not compete. They operate on different levels, and the former is the reason for the second. Writing in this vein, Thomas Aquinas commented that God's will, as primary cause, is achieved as God wishes: God can dispose secondary causes as he wishes, including even the free exercise of causation by conscious beings.[11] That is what it means for their causative powers to be 'secondary'. To suppose that God has to 'intervene' in creation is to mistake God as one more secondary cause, rather than as the primary cause of all causation.

The concern about *order* most likely remains the longest, since it has long occupied theological minds. Theologians will disagree about where to draw lines there. Some will subordinate the maintenance of order in creation to the sovereignty of God: God might cause things to proceed in one, ordered, way, or to proceed differently; the choice rests with the creator. Others will say that God's actions are free but also shaped by divine goodness and wisdom. That shaping does not prevent God from operating outside the usual order of things, but it does help us to understand what is happening when God does. Colin Gunton set this out in trinitarian terms. From the Son, or Word, comes the order of nature, which is good and God-given. Most of the time, things proceed that way. Nonetheless, like the wind, the Spirit 'blows where it chooses' (Jn 3.8). Such 'blowing', however, is not aimless. Rather, the work of the Spirit – not least in the miraculous, or in answering prayer – serves to draw creation back to a good order (for instance, in healing) and, even more foundationally, to the ultimate order of our relationship to God. Consequently, as Gunton had it, a 'miracle

---

[10]For instance, in Thomas Aquinas, *Commentary on the Book of Causes*, trans., Vincent A. Guagliardo, Charles R. Hess, and Richard C. Taylor (Washington, DC: Catholic University of America Press, 1996), prop. 1. The language of 'primary' and 'secondary' causes was developed by later scholastic philosophers. For a discussion, see Armand Maurer, 'Darwin, Thomists, and Secondary Causality', *Review of Metaphysics* 57, no. 3 (2004): 491–514.

[11]Thomas Aquinas, *Summa contra Gentiles* (Notre Dame, IN: University of Notre Dame Press, 1975), III.70.8, 94.11; *ST* I, q. 105, a. 5; and *De veritate*, q. 23.1 – translated as *Truth – Volume 3*, trans. Robert W. Schmidt (Chicago, IL: Henry Regnery Company, 1954).

is, to be sure, a kind of divine compelling, but it takes place in order to overcome creation's bondage, not to force normal reality out of place ... the miraculous is a violation only of the rule of evil', rather than of the nature of things.[12] This helpful analysis suggests that while God is free to operate outside the usual order, not least in the fulfilment of prayers, that does not take the form of some random deflection, but brings things back to Christ, as the Way, and to God's good intention for creation.

The effect of prayer on those who pray

Before moving on from empirical evaluations of the effect of prayer, it will be worth noting a further avenue for consideration. Alongside an investigation of whether prayer 'works', and of how to conceive of that within a particular scientific and philosophical outlook, there is the additional empirical question of the effect of praying *on those who pray*.

Although interpretation of work in this area is complex, and further research is called for, the evidence clearly favours a positive correlation between religious practice and physical and mental health.[13] In broad summary, a positive relation between religious practice and health has been found for heart disease, cerebrovascular disease, dementia, immune function, endocrine function, cancer and length of life.[14]

Ongoing work attempts to discern whether such associations remain after other factors are taken into account. It would seem that these correlations do persist, even correcting for 'baseline health, social support, and health behaviors'.[15]

A useful body of work to consider in assessing the role of prayer in health is the burgeoning field of studies on the effect of meditation. Although not identical to Christian prayer – as we will consider below – meditation bears comparison, not least with aspects of contemplative prayer. A wide range

---

[12]Colin Gunton, *The Christian Faith: An Introduction to Christian Doctrine* (Oxford: Wiley-Blackwell, 2001), 35.

[13]A wide range of this research is summarized by Harold G. Koenig and his associates in the *Handbook of Religion and Health*. The first edition covers research to 2000, edited by Michael E. McCullough, David B. Larson and Harold G. Koenig (Oxford: Oxford University Press, 2001); the second picks up research from 2000, edited by Dana E. King, Verna Benner Carson and Harold G. Koenig (Oxford: Oxford University Press, 2012).

[14]King, Carson and Koenig, *Handbook of Religion and Health*, 585–7. An accessible summary of the area can be found in Crystal L. Park and Jeanne M. Slattery, 'Spirituality, Emotions, and Physical Health', in *The Oxford Handbook of Psychology and Spirituality*, ed. Lisa J. Miller (Oxford: Oxford University Press, 2012), 379–87.

[15]Doug Oman, et al., 'Religious Attendance and Cause of Death over 31 Years', *International Journal of Psychiatry in Medicine* 32, no. 1 (2002): 69–89, cited by Park and Slattery, 'Spirituality, Emotions, and Physical Health', 380.

of positive effects of meditation upon health have been reported, even, for instance, in relation to recovery from cancer.[16]

In thinking about beneficial effects from prayer and other religious practices we should recall that they can also be harmful or abusive. 'Negative effects' have been reported as sometimes arising from meditation, although these seem to be less prevalent when it is carried out within the context of a religious tradition.[17] Careful attention to what is meant by 'negative' is called for here, however. While experiences in prayer or meditation can be negative in some destructive sense, they can also be 'negative' in the constructive sense of being part of a difficult process of spiritual or moral development. This, as with progress in mental or physical health, can involve much that is 'unpleasant' or challenging.

One striking empirical effect of meditation is observable changes to the structure of the brain. Certain parts of the brain were found typically to be denser in those who meditate, compared to those who do not. Subsequent studies showed that this change could be induced in a relatively short space of time among those new to meditative practice. Later, the effect was seen in a clinical setting, among patients with Parkinson's disease.[18]

Studies of the Praying Brain

In recent decades, as we have seen, the praying (and meditating) person has been of considerable interest to scientists of the brain. The headline finding from neurological studies is that our brains are deeply involved in the act of praying, and of meditation. On the face of it, this observation – that we pray with our brains – might not come as a surprise. Nonetheless, investigation of the praying brain, and commentary upon it, has become something of an industry. What are we to make of that?

---

[16]Linda E. Carlson, et al., 'Randomized Controlled Trial of Mindfulness-Based Cancer Recovery Versus Supportive Expressive Group Therapy for Distressed Survivors of Breast Cancer (MINDSET)', *Journal of Clinical Oncology* 31, no. 25 (2013): 3119–26; Caroline J. Hoffman, et al., 'Effectiveness of Mindfulness-Based Stress Reduction in Mood, Breast- and Endocrine-Related Quality of Life, and Well-Being in Stage 0 to III Breast Cancer: A Randomized, Controlled Trial', *Journal of Clinical Oncology* 30, no. 12 (2012): 1335–42.

[17]Marco Schlosser, et al., 'Unpleasant Meditation-Related Experiences in Regular Meditators: Prevalence, Predictors, and Conceptual Considerations', *PLoS ONE* 14, no. 5 (2019): e0216643.

[18]Omar Singleton, et al., 'Change in Brainstem Gray Matter Concentration Following a Mindfulness-Based Intervention is Correlated with Improvement in Psychological Well-Being', *Frontiers in Human Neuroscience* 8:33 (eCollection 2014); Britta K. Hölzel, et al., 'Mindfulness Practice Leads to Increases in Regional Brain Gray Matter Density', *Psychiatry Research: Neuroimaging* 191, no. 1 (2011): 36–43; B. A. Pickut, et al., 'Mindfulness in Parkinson's Disease Leads to Increases in Gray Matter Density', *Journal of the Neurological Sciences* 333, no. 1 (2013): e111.

First, we should acknowledge that these findings will be startling news to religious thinkers if they hold a position of extreme dualism, supposing that the human being is fundamentally a soul or spirit, only tangentially related to the body or flesh. They would still pose a challenge if one thought, a little less drastically, that the human being is composed of a body and a soul (or of body, soul and spirit), with a sharp division of labour between them.

To such comments, however, at least two responses should be made. First, on such a view, finding that prayer shows up in a brain scan would not be the end of the matter. Finding that the brain is involved with solving a problem in geometry, or composing a shopping list, ought to be equally problematic, since they are also mental, soulish activities. Secondly, contrary to what is often supposed by those who comment on such matters from the outside, extreme dualism of this sort is not the default option among the major philosophical positions found within Christianity (or many other religions, for that matter).[19] Precision is called for: to say, for instance, as many Christians will, that the human form, or soul, can survive between death and the general resurrection does not commit someone to a dualistic sense that the person is fundamentally the soul or that the body is not integral to full human function. The pattern of personhood might be able to survive without the body, but that would not be a natural state. Even those who propose that certain mental functions go beyond the capacities of the body (as is characteristic, for instance, of Roman Catholic theology of a traditional form), such as reasoning about universals on the basis of our experience of particulars, are likely perfectly aware of the role of the body, and indeed the brain, as a support for those processes.[20] No mediaeval Dominican, for instance, would be surprised to hear that the brain is involved in praying. It belongs to the brain, he or she would say, to remember, for instance, which is integral to an act of prayer.[21]

The scientific study of prayer and the question of the boundaries of religion

We also encounter a danger, in studies of the brain in relation to spirituality or religion, of taking a restricted view of what that means or looks like. Interest in these matters from neuroscientists has not typically been in prayer in a broad sense, but often in something more specific, namely on *meditation* and, even more specifically, on meditation as a cause of religious *experiences*.

---

[19]Stephen Yates offers a perceptive analysis that Christianity has been committed to a *duality* to the human being, not a *dualism*. See Stephen Yates, *Between Death and Resurrection: A Critical Response to Recent Catholic Debate Concerning the Intermediate State* (London: Bloomsbury, 2017).
[20]Here, following Aquinas, *ST* I, q. 75, a. 2.
[21]See Aquinas, *ST* I, q. 84, a. 7.

We could call this the tendency to focus on the religious experiences of meditating nuns.[22]

A pair of essays by leading researchers in the field illustrate this. Both Andrew Newberg and Mario Beauregard place religious experience at the heart of what they think it means to investigate religion and spirituality. Beauregard, for instance, sets out his survey as addressing work on 'the neuroscience of spirituality [using] neuroscience methods'. Immediately after, however, he reduces that to – or equates it with – the study of 'religious, spiritual, and mystical experiences.'[23]

Focusing on meditation, the neuroscience literature has little to say about correlations of brain states with praise or adoration, for instance, or with the confession of sins, thanksgiving or intercession. We can also note a widespread tendency – to which we will return below – to treat prayer as something private, inward and sedate: which it can be, but often is not. These are studies of people sealed off in laboratories, not praying together; these are people rendered more or less immobile in brain scanning equipment, not standing and kneeling, or raising their hands, or prostrating themselves.

Studies of prayer by brain scientists, then, have tended to be narrow. This aligns with the distinctly modern tendency to conceive of religion in a restricted fashion. As a now well-established argument runs, the notion of a sacred or religious domain to life, defined in contradistinction to a profane or secular domain, was not prominent across much of Christian history, and it would sit uneasily even today with many Christians and members of other religions. The birth and propagation of a sharp demarcation between the sacred and the secular served the interests of those who wished to see religion relegated to a subordinate and, crucially, private domain.[24] Something of this

---

[22]Andrew B. Newberg, et al., 'The Measurement of Regional Cerebral Blood Flow during Glossolalia: A Preliminary SPECT Study', *Psychiatry Research* 148, no. 1 (2006): 67–71; Andrew B. Newberg, et al., 'Cerebral Blood Flow during Meditative Prayer: Preliminary Findings and Methodological Issues', *Perceptual and Motor Skills* 97, no. 2 (2003): 625–30; Mario Beauregard and Vincent Paquette, 'Neural Correlates of a Mystical Experience in Carmelite Nuns', *Neuroscience Letters* 405, no. 3 (2006): 186–90.

[23]Mario Beauregard, 'Neuroimaging and Spiritual Practice', in *The Oxford Handbook of Psychology and Spirituality*, ed. Lisa J. Miller (Oxford: Oxford University Press, 2012), 500; Andrew Newberg, 'Transformation of Brain Structure and Spiritual Experience', in *The Oxford Handbook of Psychology and Spirituality*, ed. Lisa J. Miller (Oxford: Oxford University Press, 2012), 489–99.

[24]See, for instance, William T. Cavanaugh, *Theopolitical Imagination: Christian Practices of Space and Time* (London: T&T Clark, 2003) and *The Myth of Religious Violence Secular Ideology and the Roots of Modern Conflict* (Oxford: Oxford University Press, 2009); Nicholas Lash, *The Beginning and the End of 'Religion'* (Cambridge: Cambridge University Press, 1996); and John Milbank, 'The End of Dialogue', in *Christian Uniqueness Reconsidered: The Myth of a Pluralistic Theology of Religions*, ed. Gavin D'Costa, John Hick and Paul F. Knitter (Maryknoll, NY: Orbis Books, 1990), 174–91.

seems reflected in the sense in the neuroscientific literature that one can study prayer and religious practice in isolated, immobile, inwardly focused people.

We should also question the sense that religious experience – to the fore in these studies – can in any easy way be set apart from other forms of experience. Boundaries between sacred and secular, and between 'religious' and 'non-religious' experience, ought to be problematic to police. Contemplation of the beauty of a divine attribute is not necessarily a different endeavour, or 'experience', from contemplation of the beauty of nature, or from contemplation of the grace of ballet, or football, or a good deed. Meditation on God's mercy is not necessarily entirely different from wonder at human mercy, not least if we see it as a channel for God's own mercy, or an imitation.

The 'secular' is spiritual and of religious significance. Conversely, we have no reason to worry that the 'religious' can make natural sense, whatever else we might want to say in addition. The theologian need not be perturbed that prayer, and religious practice, has benefits that are open to the investigation of scientists, coming, for instance, from the sociality of communal worship, practices of memorization or the value of ritual.[25] That aligns with the attention recently given to the value of aspects of religious practice by atheist authors, who have sought to translate it into an atheist context.[26]

Religion is no less what it is for being human or for aligning with nature. Religion and its practices of prayer are cohesive wholes; they are not what is somehow left when a putatively 'merely natural' element is removed. The value of starting the day with prayerful contemplation of what it is likely to hold, or of closing it with Compline or the Ignatian Examen, is not diminished on the grounds that this makes good psychological sense. There is a parallel here to saying that the sacramental use of matter does not make it any less material, or that the incarnation of the Son does not make his human nature any less human.

---

[25]C. Neil Macrae, et al., 'A Case of Hand Waving: Action Synchrony and Person Perception', *Cognition* 109, no. 1 (2008): 152–6; Michael Hove and Jane Risen, 'It's All in the Timing: Interpersonal Synchrony Increases Affiliation', *Social Cognition* 27, no. 6 (2009): 949–60; Tanya Vacharkulksemsuk and Barbara L. Fredrickson, 'Strangers in Sync: Achieving Embodied Rapport through Shared Movements', *Journal of Experimental Social Psychology* 48, no. 1 (2012): 399–402; Michael I. Norton and Francesca Gino, 'Rituals Alleviate Grieving for Loved Ones, Lovers, and Lotteries', *Journal of Experimental Psychology: General* 143, no. 1 (2014): 266–72.
[26]Alain de Botton, *Religion for Atheists: A Non-Believer's Guide to the Uses of Religion* (London: Penguin Books, 2012) and Sam Harris, *Waking Up: A Guide to Spirituality without Religion* (London: Bantam Press, 2014).

Charismatic prayer and worship

A particularly arresting example of what it means for prayer to be natural and human, whatever else it might also be, offering striking possibilities for scientific exploration, comes with Pentecostal or charismatic traditions of prayer and worship, not least in investigation of the brain states involved in glossolalia or 'speaking in tongues'.

From the perspective of the psychological sciences, the practice of speaking in tongues does not seem to be associated with psychopathology.[27] Direct study of the brain during glossolalia is still in its infancy, although Andrew Newberg – already cited for his work on meditation – offers a beginning. Centrally, he found that when his subjects manifested glossolalia, the part of the brain involved in intentional mental control (the prefrontal cortices) showed a decrease in activity.[28] This, as Newberg commented, is 'consistent with the subjects' description of a lack of intentional control over the performance of glossolalia'.[29] In contrast with his work on meditating subjects, he found no decrease in the activity of the part of the brain associated with one's sense of self (the superior parietal lobe). This aligns with Newberg's finding that while those engaged in meditation (in previous experiments) typically reported an altered sense of self, glossolaliacs did not.[30]

None of this needs to be taken as offering a reductive explanation of what is going on when someone is speaking in tongues, as scientists are often at pains to point out, unless one supposed that in 'authentic' glossolalia nothing of the human person could be involved at all. More challenging, perhaps, for the charismatic is the observation that something like glossolalia is found across other religious traditions, and indeed in certain musical settings, such as 'scatt' singing in Jazz. Useful future work might consider how Christian glossolalia compares, neurologically, with those phenomena.[31]

---

[27]Virginia Hine, 'The Pentecostal Glossolalia: Toward a Functional Interpretation', *Journal for the Scientific Study of Religion* 8, no. 2 (1969): 211–26; James T. Richardson, 'Psychological Interpretations of Glossolalia: A Reexamination of Research', *Journal for the Scientific Study of Religion* 12, no. 2 (1973): 199–207; Leslie Francis and Mandy Robbins, 'Personality and Glossolalia: A Study among Male Evangelical Clergy', *Pastoral Psychology* 51, no. 5 (2003): 391–6; Stephen Louden and Leslie Francis, 'Are Catholic Priests in England and Wales Attracted to the Charismatic Movement Emotionally Less Stable?', *British Journal of Theological Education* 11, no. 2 (2001): 65–76. References from Newberg, et al., 'Blood Flow during Glossolalia', 69–70.
[28]Newberg, et al., 'Blood Flow during Glossolalia', 70.
[29]Newberg, et al., 'Blood Flow during Glossolalia', 70.
[30]Newberg, et al., 'Blood Flow during Glossolalia', 68.
[31]May L. Carlyle. 'A Survey of Glossolalia and Related Phenomena in Non-Christian Religions', *American Anthropologist* 58, no. 1 (1956): 75–96; Stephen J. Casmier and Donald H. Matthews, 'Why Scatting is Like Speaking in Tongues: Postmodern Reflections on Jazz, Pentecostalism and "Africosmysticism"', *Literature and Theology* 13, no. 2 (1999): 166–76.

Prayer and Embodied Cognition

Several times already, we have seen that scientific investigation of prayer ought to attend to it as a material and bodily practice. We might suppose that it falls to the scientist here – being interested in materiality and the body – to direct the attention of the religious person. Just as much, however, we could reply that the very fact that prayer has been carried out in such bodily ways down the centuries equally suggests that religious traditions already know a good deal about corporeality. Indeed, we could go further and suggest that the interest of scientists in the *brain* at prayer may, in fact, betray only a partial awareness of prayer's bodiliness. 'Nun in a brain scanner' experiments, as we have seen, are apt to exclude a wide range of aspects of bodily life, not least movement, posture, vocalisation and inter-subjectivity. They probe a valid aspect of prayer, but stand a good way off from many real world practices (sometime called the question of 'ecological validity').[32] To be provocative, then, we may say that studies that focus on the brains of static subjects espouse a tacit dualism of their own: not a mind–body dualism, but a brain–body dualism.

Happily, however, trends in biological, philosophical and psychological study of cognition are now placing the whole of the body freshly in view. In thinking about how an appreciation of contemporary science might enrich our understanding of prayer, we will turn to some of these, first setting out the approach that has come to be known as an 'embodied' understanding of cognition (or 'embodied cognition').

Approaches to the embodiment of cognition

A good way to begin to appreciate the integral role of the body in cognition is to consider the vocabulary used in linguistic thought. This, it turns out, is strongly grounded in embodied experience and action. Pioneering work here came from George Lakoff and Mark Johnson in *Metaphors We Live*

---

[32]Work on the bodiliness of prayer has attracted the attention of both Catholic and Protestant writers. See Simon Chan, *Liturgical Theology: The Church as Worshiping Community* (Downers Grove, IL: IVP Academic, 2006); Warren S. Brown and Brad D. Strawn, *The Physical Nature of Christian Life: Neuroscience, Psychology, and the Church* (Cambridge: Cambridge University Press, 2012); Sarah Coakley, 'Beyond "Belief": Liturgy and the Cognitive Apprehension of God', in *Vocation of Theology Today: A Festschrift for David Ford*, ed. Tom Greggs, Rachel Muers and Simeon Zahl (Eugene, OR: Cascade Books, 2013), 130–45; James K. A. Smith, *Imagining the Kingdom: How Worship Works* (Grand Rapids, MI: Baker Academic, 2013); Nicholas Wolterstorff, *The God We Worship: An Exploration of Liturgical Theology* (Grand Rapids, MI: William B. Eerdmans, 2015); David Grumett, *Material Eucharist* (Oxford: Oxford University Press, 2016); and Terence Cuneo, *Ritualized Faith: Essays on the Philosophy of Liturgy* (Oxford: Oxford University Press, 2016).

By and *Philosophy in the Flesh*.[33] Metaphor, they argued, is not a minor backwater in our use of language, the preserve of poets. Rather, the way we generally speak is woven out of metaphors, through and through. Examples of that proposal, from what I have written so far in this paragraph, come in my use of 'grounded', 'backwater' and 'woven'. This is not odd; it is how we speak and write. Furthermore, Lakoff and Johnson argued, 'orientational metaphors', derived from our active ('sensorimotor'), spatial engagement with the world around us, are particularly central. We associate strength and well-being with 'up', for instance, with phrases such as 'I have power over him' and 'She is at the peak of health', and think of the future as ahead of us ('What lies ahead'), and the past behind ('I put it behind me'). Our language and allied ways of thinking spring from our experience of bodily involvement in the world.[34] Even just in as much as prayer is linguistic – and it is often that, although often also more – it is already directly connected to our embodiedness.

A crucial aspect of this (often known as the *conceptualization hypothesis*) is the argument we have just encountered, that our concepts remain 'grounded' in our bodily experience of the world. To understand this, it is helpful to contrast it with a view of the brain as functioning basically like a computer: a perspective associated with 'cognitivism'. On a cognitivist view, the body might provide 'inputs', and execute 'outputs', but the workings of thought would be abstracted from all of that. The idea of 'dance', for instance, and the idea of 'sleep', would be just that, ideas, and neither of them – being ideas – would be any more kinetic than the other, just as there is nothing soft (on this view) about the idea of a frog or hard about the idea of a stone. That perspective is sometimes described as 'amodal', meaning abstracted-from-mode: while mental representations of things might initially be informed by our distinct ways ('modes') of interacting with the world (such as the senses), all of that – all that is particular about

---

[33]George Lakoff and Mark Johnson, *Metaphors We Live By* (Chicago, IL: University of Chicago Press, 1980); George Lakoff and Mark Johnson, *Philosophy in the Flesh: The Embodied Mind and Its Challenge to Western Thought* (Chicago, IL: University of Chicago Press, 1999).

[34]For discussion of these insights from a theological perspective, see John Sanders, *Theology in the Flesh: How Embodiment and Culture Shape the Way We Think about Truth, Morality, and God* (Minneapolis, MN: Fortress Press, 2017); Robert Masson, *Without Metaphor, No Saving God: Theology after Cognitive Linguistics* (Leuven: Peeters, 2014); and, especially, Tobias Tanton's monograph *Corporeal Theology* (forthcoming). I offer a worked example in my sermon on the Ascension in *The God We Proclaim: Sermons on the Apostles' Creed*, ed. John Hughes and Andrew Davison (Eugene, OR: Cascade Books, 2017). I acknowledge my debt, throughout this chapter, to conversations with Dr Tanton, and the opportunity to read a draft of the manuscript of this book.

any of those modes of engagement – would be stripped out of the concepts or symbols with which we think.[35]

Thinking of cognition as embodied stands in contrast to cognitivism, and typically views thought as deeply 'modal', which is to say deeply embedded in particular bodily means of knowing and responding. Those various modes of interacting with the world (such as sight, touch, or pushing and feeling the world push-back) would not simply hand information on to some abstract computing centre in the brain, and then sign off. Rather, the 'modality' of sense and interaction with the world remains integral. This is borne out by the observation that we use many of the same parts of our brains to *think about* something as we would use to *interact with* that thing in the world.[36]

The exploration of the embodiment of cognition, however, has gone even further, and shown that we undertake at least some of our thinking interaction with the world – some of our processing of goals, situation and environment – *with* our bodies, *in* our interaction with the world. Part of this is the non-trivial sense in which we think by manipulating objects around us: a perspective often called 'extended cognition'. We think with material objects: with an abacus, paper and pen or social media app.[37] We can recognize parallels with prayer. In various ways, people pray with objects, such as prayer beads or lists. We also pray within the context of our environment, travelling to church, for instance, or to a retreat house, and people adapt their environments for that purpose, whether that involves a prayer corner or niche at home, or cultivating a garden as a place for reflection. The importance of place and environment for prayer might be as simple, but significant, as saying that if I want to be a prayerful person, I will increase the likelihood of spending time in prayer if I take myself, in a bodily fashion, to that church, or retreat house.

Alongside this attention to material culture and environment, suggested by extended cognition, a now classic baseball-derived example of how cognition, or problem solving, can be deeply bodily is provided in the so-called 'out-fielder' example. Again, this offers something very different from the idea that the body enters into cognition only as a source of inputs and as an executor of outputs (as imagined by the 'cognitivism' described above).

---

[35]'Representations are autonomous from perceptual systems, bodily action, and their operational details'. See Robert A. Wilson and Lucia Foglia, 'Embodied Cognition', *The Stanford Encyclopedia of Philosophy* (Spring 2017).

[36]'Our thoughts about things 'are modal because they are represented in the same systems as the perceptual states that produced them'. See Lawrence W. Barsalou, 'Perceptual Symbol Systems', *Behavioral and Brain Sciences* 22, no. 4 (1999): 577–660 (578). Celebrated examples involve mirror and canonical neurons.

[37]See Autumn Hostetter and Martha Alibali, 'Visible Embodiment: Gestures as Simulated Action', *Psychonomic Bulletin and Review* 15, no. 3 (2008): 495–514 (497).

The problem in question addresses how a fielder in a ball game goes about catching the ball. Having seen the ball hit by a bat, the fielder has to work out where to catch it. Were the person to function like a computer, with the body only involved with inputs and outputs, we might imagine a process like this: the fielder collects data from the senses about the trajectory of the ball; on that basis, he calculates its trajectory; finally, with that information, he moves to the position where the ball will land. This, however, does not prove to be the way a human being actually operates in this situation for two good reasons. First, the amount of information provided by the movement of the ball in the sky is likely not sufficient for this calculation, especially at the beginning of its flight. Secondly, if that computational approach were the way we worked, a fielder would be expected to run in a straight line to the position where the ball would land as the most efficient course. In fact, however, a fielder typically sweeps out a curve, which is consistent with a different, highly embodied way of working out where to put oneself: if you move your position in such a way that the ball seems to be moving in a linear fashion, you will be guided to the place where it will land (the 'linear optical trajectory' method). That is deeply non-cognitivist (and thoroughly 'modal') way of working something out, since there is no need to represent the trajectory of the ball mentally at all. We would 'perform' the necessary computation simply by engaging with the world by moving one's body.[38]

The praying person might well recognize something in the outfielder example. We do not necessarily go about prayer in a calculating way, as if it were an exercise in abstract thought, worked through by means of concepts. Rather, prayer can be a way of negotiating, or responding to, the world, to our situation, our sense of need, our desire to reach out to God. Imagine that a friend is sick. I will not necessarily respond, as a person inclined to pray, by thinking analytic thoughts. I might close my eyes, bow my head and ask for God's mercy. I may reach for a prayer book and recite some prayers from it. I might say some decades of the Rosary. I might walk to a nearby church and kneel, kneeling being a prayer of its own.

The practice of pilgrimage also serves as a useful example. Down history, when people have felt a strong need to work something through – for instance, a fundamental question of vocation, or a compelling need to reorient one's life, or sense of being in a particularly profound situation of need or gratitude – the practice of going on a pilgrimage has been of central importance. By pilgrimage, one does not sort things out, or even express them before God, in some abstract and linguistically ordered way.

---

[38]Andrew D. Wilson and Sabrina Golonka, 'Embodied Cognition is Not What you Think it is', *Frontiers in Psychology* 4, no. 58 (2013): 1–13 (5–6).

Rather, the quest for direction, or the need – be it of lack or of gratitude – is expressed physically by travelling.[39]

The out-fielder example does not suggest that all thinking works that way. There is obviously something deeply computational about working out a problem in geometry or logic, although we might also note that the further we get into abstraction, the more likely we are to turn to aspects of extended cognition, and bring in something bodily and material in the form of a pen and paper, or a computer. All the same, awareness of the embodied dimension of human thought can help to guard against placing exclusive attention, not least in thinking about prayer, on the sort of cognition (which we might call 'ratiocination') that most involves or resembles language, mathematics or procedures of logic. There are other ways of thinking; there are other ways of navigating the world as a rational agent. They are deeply bodily in their own way and they, too, bear upon praying.

The meditating nun might serve the purposes of the neuroscientist, not least because we can more easily take measurements from someone in a state of stillness, but that is only one aspect of the repertoire of bodily forms prayer involves. For centuries in the West, to pray was to kneel, even if that is less common today. For Coptic Christians, prostration is a significant practice, just as prostrations (*sajadāt*) are integral to the prescribed pattern of daily prayer for Muslims. Although we might think that the sort of bodiliness, and formal practices, that I have been highlighting belong mainly to liturgical, 'high church' forms of prayer, involving ritual, evangelical or 'low church' traditions are also bodily, in their own way.

Prayer, Habit and Posture

In thinking about the body in prayer, habit is also a useful category: the way we come to have a 'knack' for doing something, such that it comes naturally, without needing to reason out the steps. There is a habit to riding a bicycle, or driving a car, to playing a guitar or a sport, to dicing a potato, or typing at a keyboard. This sort of ingrained bodily competence is often called 'muscle memory'; more technically, it is known as 'procedural' or 'motor' memory. As Richard Shusterman has put it, habit means that we can 'act skilfully and intelligently without having to think about what we are doing with our limbs'.[40] By means of acquired habits, our bodies come to have a 'purposive

---

[39]Relatively little scientific work has been devoted to pilgrimage. An isolated example would be P. A. Morris, 'The Effect of Pilgrimage on Anxiety, Depression and Religious Attitude', *Psychological Medicine* 12, no. 2 (1982): 291–4, which found an immediate, and sustained, reduction in anxiety and depression after pilgrimage, in this case to Lourdes.
[40]Richard Shusterman, *Thinking through the Body: Essays in Somaesthetics* (Cambridge: Cambridge University Press, 2012), 333.

yet unthinking spontaneous performance in perception, speech, art, and other forms of actions'. Just because this is spontaneous, rather than reasoned out, does not make it 'uneducated'.[41] Rather, habit illustrates an important *bodily* angle on what education means, relevant to our understanding of prayer, or of religious formation.[42] Christian theologians, from across traditions, have recently drawn attention to the place of liturgy as a 'site' for religious and ethical formation, for instance, often with a strong bodily dimension.[43] Again, Shusterman is helpful here, pointing out that our habits go a long way to define who we are. They set us each up with what he calls a distinctive 'somatic style' (from the Greek word *soma*, meaning body).[44] For those who pray, prayer will be part of that somatic style.

Recognizing the link to religious practice, Shusterman turns to Confucianism, and its sense that 'one's character' cannot be divided from one's 'somatic comportment'. Confucius, he writes, insists 'on the importance of countenance or demeanour in the practice of ethical virtues',[45] not least in terms of ritual practice. 'Ritual, by stylizing our bodily actions and gestures, also shapes and harmonizes our character, both in terms of self-unity and in coordination with others in the social context.' This means, for instance, that 'a teacher can teach without words, but instead by his embodied example of behaviour'.[46] Within the Christian tradition, Aquinas picked up a similar connection between moral character and bodily comportment, drawing on Aristotle. He thought it characteristic, for instance, of 'a magnanimous man that his gait is slow, his voice deep, and his utterance calm'.[47] Earlier in the Judeo-Christian tradition, the idea is found in the deuterocanonical book Ecclesiasticus:

> A person is known by his appearance, and a sensible person is known when first met face to face. A person's attire and hearty laughter, and the way he walks, show what he is.
>
> (Ecclus. 19.29-30)

---

[41]Shusterman, *Thinking through the Body*, 92.
[42]See, for instance, Alison Milbank and Andrew Davison, *For the Parish: A Critique of Fresh Expressions* (London: SCM Press, 2010), 100.
[43]Samuel Wells, 'How Common Worship Forms Local Character', *Studies in Christian Ethics* 15, no. 1 (2002): 66–74; Timothy Jenkins, 'An Ethical Account of Ritual: An Anthropological Description of the Anglican Daily Offices', *Studies in Christian Ethics* 15, no. 1 (2002): 1–10; Warren S. Brown and Kevin S. Reimer, 'Embodied Cognition, Character Formation, and Virtue', *Zygon* 48, no. 3 (2013): 832–45.
[44]Shusterman, *Thinking through the Body*, 333.
[45]Shusterman, *Thinking through the Body*, 319, 320.
[46]Shusterman, *Thinking through the Body*, 319.
[47]*Nicomachean Ethics*, IV.3. It is a limitation to Aristotle's thought here that he has men, and not women, in view. Aquinas comments on these observations in *ST* II-II, q. 129, a. 3, ad. 3.

When the early Dominicans wanted to record what they had learnt from Dominic about prayer, in the document known as *The Nine Ways of Prayer of St Dominic*, the emphasis rested on what he had exemplified in terms of posture and bodily practice.[48] His 'nine ways' were (1) to bow his head before the altar; (2) to prostrate himself upon the ground; (3) to beat his back with a chain; (4) to gaze upon a crucifix, sometimes standing upright, sometimes bending his knee in genuflection; (5) to stand sometimes with hands facing upward ('in the manner of an open book'), sometimes joined, sometimes raised to shoulder height (the '*orans*' position); (6) in moments of greatest seriousness, to hold his arms out in the shape of the cross; (7) to raise his hands above his head, holding them apart, as one would do if expecting to receive something; (8) to read not simply in stillness, but also with various bodily movements, and to venerate the book, especially the book of the Gospels; and (9) to mediate while walking.[49] To appreciate this list we should not simply read it; we should imagine ourselves in these postures, even work through them physically (minus the chain), trying them on for size.

Today's scientific insights about the role of the body in thought, consciousness and awareness help us to recognize the wisdom in the profound bodiless of prayer for Dominic and early Dominicans (even if we find beating oneself with a chain disturbing). In the practice of kneeling, for instance, we can recognize a complexion of things: we could say that kneeling comes after a disposition of submission to God, as its expression, or that it goes before that disposition, as conducive to it, or that the act of kneeling *is* the act or disposition of submission. Tobias Tanton has pointed to the poverty of supposing that a posture such as kneeling only has a symbolic meaning, at least if by 'symbolic' we mean that it stands in arbitrary relation to what it symbolizes. That would mean that, as he puts it, 'presumably a handstand would be an equally apt prayer posture.'[50] Rather, there is something intrinsic to the posture of kneeling that accords with an attitude of prayer. Scientific work suggests that posture bears upon both capacity for memory recall and feelings of what the authors called a reduced self-esteem or empowerment but which, in this context, might also be seen as

---

[48]Work on posture as an aspect of cognition as embodied has focused on two forms of perception: 'proprioception' (one's sensation of the disposition of one's body in space) and 'kinesthetic' (awareness of changes to that disposition).

[49]For another list of postures in prayer, see Origen, *On Prayer* 20; *An Exhortation to Martyrdom, Prayer and Select Works*, trans. Rowan E. Greer, CWS (New York: Paulist Press, 1979). I am grateful to Tobias Tanton for this reference.

[50]Tanton, *Corporeal Theology* (forthcoming).

humility before God.[51] Tanton offers a parallel analysis of the raising of hands during prayer, as a gesture intrinsically bound up with 'approach (rather than avoidance)', again at once representing, conducing and being itself an act of openness.[52]

Thinking, and being a conscious, rational animal, involves bodily skills and habits. There will be an element of that to prayer. We may seem a long way from the nun in the brain scanner – problematically far, if that is taken to be representative of prayer more generally – but, even there, a 'skill' at prayer will be in evidence, involving habits of bodily stillness and calm, and likely of breathing. She may once have been taught that explicitly, maybe not; even if she was, it will have become habit, second nature, no longer followed as a programme or formula.

At the other end of the scale of experience, for the person only just beginning to explore prayer, or religious practice and belief, we might recall the words of Blaise Pascal, who wrote – wisely if hyperbolically – that if people want to enter into faith, they ought to begin by taking up the bodily practices and habits of faith: 'by behaving just as if they believed, taking holy water, having masses said, etc. That will make you believe quite naturally.'[53]

Towards the end of life, it seems that the bodily, habitual dimension of prayer becomes particularly significant – tragically so, yet also sometimes poignantly, and as invested with hope – in the religious practice of people with dementia. As John Swinton has commented – and as many who have prayed with those suffering from dementia will testify – ritual and the bodily aspects of prayer (alongside repeated and remembered prayers, words and phrases) remain when much else has passed away. Swinton has commented on ritual gesture and ritually engrained words, that they:

> represent the habits of a lifetime inscribed by Jesus on the bodies of those who love and, in an odd way, remember Jesus 'in the now' in ways that do

---

[51]John Riskind and Carolyn Gotay, 'Physical Posture: Could It Have Regulatory or Feedback Effects on Motivation and Emotion?', *Motivation and Emotion* 6, no. 3 (1982): 273–98; Katinka Dijkstra, Michael P. Kaschak and Rolf A. Zwaan, 'Body Posture Facilitates Retrieval of Autobiographical Memories', *Cognition* 102, no. 1 (2007): 139–49; Johannes Michalak, Judith Mischnat and Tobias Teismann, 'Sitting Posture Makes a Difference-Embodiment Effects on Depressive Memory Bias: Embodiment Effects on Depressive Memory Bias', *Clinical Psychology & Psychotherapy* 21, no. 6 (2014): 519–24.

[52]Tanton, *Corporeal Theology* (forthcoming). Tanton cites Sabine Stepper and Fritz Strack, 'Proprioceptive Determinants of Emotional and Nonemotional Feelings', *Journal of Personality and Social Psychology* 64, no. 2 (1993): 211–20; Riskind and Gotay, 'Physical Posture'; John T. Cacioppo, Joseph R. Priester and Gary G. Berntson, 'Rudimentary Determinants of Attitudes. II: Arm Flexion and Extension Have Differential Effects on Attitudes', *Journal of Personality and Social Psychology* 65, no. 1 (1993): 5–17.

[53]Blaise Pascal, *Pensées and Other Writings*, ed. Honor Levi (Oxford: Oxford University Press, 1999), 156. Differing numbering systems give this as section 6-233, 343 and 680.

not require recall or cognition. They know and remember Jesus in their bodies. Unless we choose to yield to the apparently inevitable thrust of dualism here, we can do nothing other than recognise that *the memory of the body is a real and profound conduit that leads people into the presence of Jesus*.[54]

The relation of the body, posture and movement to prayer

I will close by returning to the idea that bodily practice in prayer relates to belief, disposition and intention as at simultaneously expressive, conducive and embodying. We may be used to thinking that bodily practices in prayer, such as kneeling or bowing one's head, are useful as a bridge, as a way of entering into a state that is conducive to prayer, yet still suppose that prayer itself is distinctly 'mental', even perhaps more distant from the body than everyday life and experience. Scientific studies, however, complicate the idea that our consciousness, mood or experience are best seen as simply internal, or separate enough from the body that the emotion (for instance) would come first, and its 'display' in the body second.

The relation between physiological states, and emotions or states of mind is familiar: in situations of embarrassment, we blush; in situations of anxiety, the heart beats faster. We may assume that the emotion or mental transition came first, with the bodily change as a later correlate. However, we do not simply smile because we are happy, or frown because we are apprehensive: smiling can induce happiness, and frowning can induce apprehension.[55] The paper that brought this to particular attention involved surreptitiously inducing a smile or a frown by asking people to hold a pencil in the mouth in a particular way, and gauging the effect on mood. More recently, we might consider work which suggests that Botox injections can inhibit emotional life, *because* they inhibit the ability of the face to express those emotions.[56] Other studies found that brain injuries that hinder the facial expression of an emotion affect the ability of those concerned to register the emotion at all, even though the brain lesions involved are in parts of the brain associated

---

[54]John Swinton, 'What the Body Remembers: Theological Reflections on Dementia', 26 June 2013, www.abc.net.au/religion/what-the-body-remembers-theological-reflections-on-dementia/10099780 (accessed: 2 September 2020); emphasis original.

[55]Some of the studies that underlie this consensus have proved difficult to replicate, but the overall point is not contentious.

[56]Joshua Ian Davis, et al., 'The Effects of BOTOX Injections on Emotional Experience', *Emotion* 10, no. 3 (2010): 433–40; David A. Havas, et al., 'Cosmetic Use of Botulinum Toxin-A Affects Processing of Emotional Language', *Psychological Science* 21, no. 7 (2010): 895–900.

with the control of the face, rather than in parts of the brain not previously connected with the emotions themselves.[57]

We ought, then, perhaps not to say so much that the disposition of the body mirrors or expresses, or even conduces, certain inner states – or not only that – and suggest a much closer relation. This accords with a scriptural theme. Abraham was commended for his faith, for instance, but not as a matter of pristinely inward consent to an idea. The faith that was 'reckoned to him as righteousness' involved journeying into a strange land; it involved taking his son up Mount Moriah (Gen. 12, 15, 22; Rom. 4.9). The Parable of the Two Sons (Mt. 21.28-32) is also instructive: what pleases the father is not inward disposition, but action.

The act of the body and the act of faith are often intimately connected. Writing in the second century, amid martyrdom, Tertullian did not say that the Christian first responds to God mentally, followed by physical manifestation: the response to God, he thought, was in the fasting, in the sexual restraint, in the giving of one's body to death.[58]

Fasting offers another useful example. It accompanies prayer across major religious traditions, and across Christian traditions. Both a Roman Catholic and a Pentecostal might place significant emphasis on fasting and abstinence as part of what it means to live a prayerful life. That language of 'accompaniment' may not be adequate, however. Fasting may not simply go alongside prayer; it can *be* prayer. One may, certainly, fast in order to remind oneself of the need for penitence, or to remind oneself of the need to prioritize God above bodily comfort. On the other hand, we need not see prayer as so resolutely inward, such that the bodily discipline functions simply as a pointer or reminder. Ask someone who fasts during Lent, or on Fridays, and she may say that the fasting is not simply a reminder to be penitent, but that it *is* penitence, that the fasting *is* a prioritization of God, not simply a reminder.

Conclusion

As the human work of corporeal creatures, prayer is bound to raise scientific questions. The same could be said of the sense, among those who pray, that their prayers have consequences in time and space, among matter and

---

[57]Antonio R. Damasio, *Descartes' Error: Emotion, Reason and the Human Brain* (London: Vintage, 2006), 148.

[58]Tertullian, *On the Resurrection of the Flesh* 8; *Latin Christianity: Its Founder, Tertullian*, ed. Alexander Roberts and James Donaldson, ANF 3 (Grand Rapids, MI: William B. Eerdmans, 1985), 545–94.

organisms. Although we may first suppose that the chief scientific question, when it comes to prayer, is the rather limited matter of 'whether prayer works', it may be that the livelier areas for further discussion are the promise this interchange with science offers for richer understanding of what prayer means for those who pray, and for understanding prayer as a bodily practice, with habit, posture and movement.

Both theology and the sciences are commendably broad in their attention – each in their own way – to what it means to be human. 'I am human, and nothing human is alien to me', speaks a character in a play by Terence (c. 195–159 BCE).[59] Both theology and the sciences can, should and do say the same.

---

[59]*Homo sum, humani nihil a me alienum puto* (*The Self-Tormentor*, Act 1, Scene 1); author's translation.

CHAPTER TWENTY-NINE

Prayer in Analytic Theology

JAMES M. ARCADI

Analytic theology is a recently named approach to theological enquiry that operates on the borderlands between systematic theology and philosophy of religion. Practitioners of analytic theology deploy the tools, methods and sensibilities of contemporary analytic philosophy in the service of constructive theological exploration. Although the cluster of theological topics initially addressed by analytic theologians was relatively narrow, prayer has been one such area of investigation since almost the inception of analytic theology. Largely, analytics have tended to focus their research within this theological locus on puzzles relating to the nature of petitionary prayer, yet not exclusively.[1] In this chapter, I offer a brief history of analytic theology and describe some of the main contours of this theological methodology. Then, in the bulk of the chapter, I trace some of the analytic theological conversations with respect to petitionary prayer. This survey also shows the manner in which the analytic discussion of petitionary prayer intersects with

---

[1] Those in the analytic stream have tended to focus on theological beliefs over theological practice; yet, there is a growing body of literature on the latter, most notably in the area of the investigation of liturgical practices. See Nicholas Wolterstorff, *Acting Liturgically: Philosophical Reflections on Religious Practice* (Oxford: Oxford University Press, 2018); Terence Cuneo, *Ritualized Faith: Essays on the Philosophy of Liturgy* (Oxford: Oxford University Press, 2016); and, for an overview of the recent literature, Joshua Cockayne, 'Philosophy and Liturgy Part 1: Liturgy and Philosophy of Action' and 'Philosophy and Liturgy Part 2: Liturgy and Epistemology', *Philosophy Compass* 13, no. 10 (2018).

discussion of such divine attributes as God's foreknowledge, omniscience, (im)mutability, (im)passibility and (a)temporality. I then offer an example of how speech act theory – as an instance of analytic theology – might aid in the task of understanding some interpretive options with respect to petitionary prayer. Finally, I suggest some ways in which one might think of analytic theology as helpful for the practice of prayer.

Analytic Theology: History and Method

The term 'analytic theology' comes from the 2009 Oxford University Press publication *Analytic Theology: New Essays in the Philosophy of Theology* edited by Oliver D. Crisp and Michael C. Rea.[2] However, analytic theology is simply a contemporary instantiation of the enduring relationship between theology and philosophy. Not only does this relationship go back millennia, but the relationship between theology and analytic philosophy – the origin of the 'analytic' in analytic theology – predates the publication of the volume with this movement's name in the title. Here I sketch some of the history of analytic theology, finding it as but another version of a long-standing methodological approach. This will be followed by a portrayal of analytic theology as an intellectual culture where certain sensibilities, tools and characteristics are borrowed from analytic philosophy for properly theological ends.

An ancient handmaiden

Within the study of religion – and religious beliefs in particular – it is often not easy to demarcate clearly the boundary line between philosophy and theology. We must not forget that an Athenian jury convicted none other than the quintessential philosopher Socrates on the very theological charge of impiety towards the gods. When one reads such medieval thinkers as the Christian Thomas Aquinas, the Muslim Avicenna or the Jewish Maimonides, one sees that this boundary line is frequently artificial. Within the Christian tradition, one can point to the second-century church father Clement of Alexandria as the scholar who first characterized the relationship between philosophy and theology as one of a handmaiden – philosophy as the aid and

---

[2]Oliver D. Crisp and Michael C. Rea, ed., *Analytic Theology: New Essays in the Philosophy of Theology* (Oxford: Oxford University Press, 2009). For further introductory material, see Thomas H. McCall, *An Invitation to Analytic Christian Theology* (Downers Grove, IL: IVP Academic, 2015) and the *T&T Clark Handbook of Analytic Theology*, ed. James M. Arcadi and James T. Turner, Jr. (London: Bloomsbury, 2021).

assistant to the theological task.[3] This aiding and assisting role of philosophy pervades the Christian theological project throughout the centuries, even as the particular philosophical school serving as handmaiden may change. Hence, whether the philosophical school was Neoplatonism with Clement or Augustine, Aristotelianism with Thomas Aquinas or Peter Martyr Vermigli, or phenomenology with Schillebeeckx or Marion, theology has always been done in some kind of conversation with philosophy. Analytic theology is no different in this overall methodological approach to philosophy. Its difference lies simply in that the philosophical dialogue partner is analytic philosophy – a dialogue partner often found absent from the major theological conversations of the twentieth century.[4]

The strands of St Basil and St Alvin

William Abraham has demarcated the development of analytic theology as emerging independently along two main strands, with two key players.[5] From the middle of the twentieth century onwards, Basil Mitchell and Alvin Plantinga serve as paradigm examples of analytic philosophy being pressed into the service of theology. Mitchell represents an Oxbridge approach to philosophy of religion that renewed Christian theism as a viable component of philosophical enquiry. In North America, the strand of St Alvin centres on Alvin Plantinga, the philosophy department of the University of Notre Dame and the Center for Philosophy of Religion that resides therein. Like Mitchell, Plantinga's work created space within analytic philosophy for theism to be taken seriously. I might be inclined to place Richard Swinburne within the strand of St Basil, for he succeeded Mitchell as the Nolloth Chair at Oriel College. However, his work proceeded so independently of other Basilians (but not Bayesians) that he perhaps ought to be considered a strand in himself.

These three philosophers, along with Thomas V. Morris, Nicholas Wolterstorff, William Alston, Norman Kretzmann, Eleonore Stump and Marilyn McCord Adams, might all be considered the first generation of – anachronistically named – analytic theologians. These initial practitioners of what would come to be called analytic theology were mostly analytic

---

[3]See Clement of Alexandria, *Stomata*, in *Hermas, Tatian, Athenagoras, Theophilus, Clement of Alexandria*, ed. Alexander Roberts and James Donaldson, ANF 2 (Grand Rapids, MI: William B. Eerdmans, 1979), 305.

[4]For another historical antecedent of analytic theology, fourteenth-century scholasticism, see James M. Arcadi, 'Analytic Theology as Declarative Theology', *TheoLogica* 1, no. 1 (2017): 37–52.

[5]William J. Abraham, 'Turning Philosophical Water into Theological Wine', *Journal of Analytic Theology* 1, no. 1 (2013): 1–16.

philosophers attempting to address topics typically considered theological. This still takes place. However, in the second and third generations of analytic theologians, we see more and more scholars with theology and divinity training building the bridge between theology and philosophy from the theological side. Here is where the work of seminary and divinity school professors such as Alan Torrance, Sarah Coakley, Oliver Crisp, Thomas McCall, Kevin Hector and Adonis Vidu comes to the fore. McCord Adams is perhaps a paradigm example of an analytic theologian, one with specialized training in both philosophy and theology, and having taught in appointments in both philosophy and theology departments, most notably as the Regius Professor of Divinity at Oxford.

Analytic theological methodology

Rather than seeing analytic theology as bound by hard and strict guidelines, I follow Oliver Crisp in holding analytic theology to be most akin to a MacIntyrian intellectual culture. Crisp defines this as 'a rough grouping within a particular intellectual discipline … that identifies itself as having a distinctive approach to its subject matter'.[6] As an intellectual culture and not a rigid methodology, it is at times difficult to outline analytic theology definitively.[7] Nevertheless, following William Wood, I hold that this intellectual culture can be marked by formal and substantive characteristics.[8]

Formally, analytic theology tends to follow the, almost canonical, prescriptions laid down by Michael Rea in the original *Analytic Theology* volume. These prescriptions (not restrictions) include:

P1. Write as if philosophical positions and conclusions can be adequately formulated in sentences that can be formalized and logically manipulated.
P2. Prioritize precision, clarity and logical coherence.

---

[6] Oliver D. Crisp, 'Analytic Theology as Systematic Theology', *Open Theology* 3 (2017): 156–66 (163).
[7] Ironic, I know, for a movement that is often concerned with definitional clarity. This state of affairs is not due to lack of trying. See, for example: the aforementioned Abraham, 'Turning Philosophical Water into Theological Wine'; Marc Cortez, 'As Much As Possible: Essentially Contested Concepts and Analytic Theology: A Response to William J. Abraham', *Journal of Analytic Theology* 1, no 1. (2013): 17–24; William Wood, 'Trajectories, Traditions, and Tools in Analytic Theology', *Journal of Analytic Theology* 4 (2016): 254–66; Max Baker-Hytch, 'Analytic Theology and Philosophy of Religion: What's the Difference', *Journal of Analytic Theology* 4 (2016): 347–61; the special issue of *Open Theology* 3 (2017): 'Analytic Perspectives on Method and Authority in Theology'; and James M. Arcadi, Oliver D. Crisp and Jordan Wessling, *The Nature and Promise of Analytic Theology* (Leiden: Brill, 2019).
[8] See Wood, 'Trajectories, Traditions, and Tools'.

P3. Avoid substantive (non-decorative) use of metaphor and other tropes whose semantic content outstrips their propositional content.
P4. Work as much as possible with well-understood primitive concepts and concepts that can be analysed in terms of those.
P5. Treat conceptual analysis (insofar as it is possible) as a source of evidence.[9]

These prescriptions are largely drawn from the ambitions and style of analytic philosophy and have been discussed extensively in the literature – I will not repeat those discussions here. I simply offer these as a brief description of the formal shape of the analytic theological intellectual culture. Formally, there is nothing about analytic theology that limits it to any one substantive theological tradition. The Tillichian, Torrencian or Thomist might all follow Rea's prescriptions, and hence could do analytic theology in this formal sense.[10]

However, in addition to these formal characteristics, there have been some key substantive components to this theological intellectual culture as well. The substantive theological commitments of the analytic theological research programme tend to include commitment to (a) some form of theological realism, (b) the truth-apt and truth-aimed nature of theological inquiry and (c) the importance of providing theological arguments for substantive doctrinal positions. This has brought about the tendency among analytic theologians to discuss and defend largely traditional positions within the history of Christian theological reflection including trinitarianism, Chalcedonian Christology and Classical Theism.

The latter, as we begin the pivot towards prayer in this chapter, requires some further expounding. As noted, there is nothing formally about analytic theology that prevents one from holding such diametrically opposed substantive positions on the doctrine of God as Thomist *actus purus* or Hartshornian process theism. Thus there are analytic open theists, analytic theistic personalists, analytic Calvinists, analytic Thomists, etc. There is simply no one substantive doctrine of God that is *the* analytic conception of God. What there is, however, in conjunction with the formal commitments outlined, is the tendency to have a desire to find a harmony between the conception of God described within the pages of Holy Writ and the conception of God arrived at by way of the deliverances of perfect being theology. Drawing from the title to one of the chapters of first-generation analytic theologian Thomas Morris' early works, the analytic conception

---

[9]Rea, 'Introduction', in *Analytic Theology*, ed. Rea and Crisp, 4–5.
[10]In fact, although discussion of which is outside the bounds of this volume, formally analytic theology is not the purview of only Christian theology and there are instances of Jewish and Muslim analytic theology as well.

of God is often aptly characterized as 'the God of Abraham, Isaac, and Anselm'.[11] On this score, most analytics are going to agree that the Bible and philosophy teach that God possesses the attribute of, say, omniscience. Where they might disagree, however, is on just what this term means, what knowledge is and what it means for God to possess it. Hence, the analytic Thomist and the analytic open theist will tend to agree that God is omniscient. But *contra* the Thomist, the open theists will hold that God does not know the future, for the open theist will aver that the future is not something that can be known. Consequently, as we now make the pivot complete, an analytic theologian's understanding of the nature of petitionary prayer will be intimately connected with that theologian's understanding of a plethora of substantive positions on divine attributes that fall within the wider bounds of analytic theology formally and substantively.

Some Puzzles of Petitionary Prayer

Analytic theologians are not the only thinkers to raise puzzles regarding the compatibility between the practice of petitionary prayer and the classical conception of God, but perhaps their philosophical acumen have made them especially sensitive to the issues in the neighbourhood of this theological locus. The genesis of the analytic theological discussion of petitionary prayer can arguably be traced to a 1979 article by Eleonore Stump, wherein she states the overarching puzzle of petitionary prayer 'is belief in the efficacy and usefulness of petitionary prayer consistent with a belief in an omniscient, omnipotent, perfectly good God?'[12] From my vantage point, there are a variety of puzzles related to the practice of petitionary prayer within this overarching puzzle.[13] There seems to me at least two ways of carving up the kinds of petitionary prayer puzzles discussed in the analytic literature: (a) puzzles pertaining to *why* God would enjoin prayers of petition and (b) puzzles pertaining to *how* God could be said to respond to prayers of petition.

Yet both of these families of puzzles rest on a conception of the effectiveness of the petitionary prayer. For a definition, Scott Davison writes,

---

[11]Thomas V. Morris, *Anselmian Explorations: Essays in Philosophical Theology* (Notre Dame, IN: University of Notre Dame Press, 1989). However, as Morris himself is an example of, Anselmianism as a methodology does not necessarily deliver the God of Classical Theism. For a merger of biblical theism and perfect being theology that is an instance of analytic classical theism, see Eleonore Stump, *The God of the Bible and the God of the Philosophers* (Milwaukee, WI: Marquette University Press, 2016).

[12]Eleonore Stump, 'Petitionary Prayer', *American Philosophical Quarterly* 16, no. 2 (1979): 81–91 (81).

[13]Following others, I include intercessory prayer and prayers for oneself in the category of petitionary prayer.

'a prayer is effective if and only if God brings about the thing requested because of the prayer, so that had the prayer not been offered, the thing in question would not have occurred'.[14] What is key in this conception is the relationship between the petition and the bringing about of the target of the petition – this is the 'because of' clause in the definition. A component such as this is an attempt to head off Gettier-style 'answers' to prayer where God would have brought about the desired effect whether anyone prayed for it or not. Rather, effective prayer is understood in the literature to be prayer that plays a contributing role in the bringing about of the effect. Still, the puzzles remain of *why* God would do this and *how* prayers could be said to elicit responses from God, given certain conceptions of God. I turn now to the first category of puzzles.

The 'why' of prayer

Nicholas Smith and Andrew Yip put the 'why' question this way, 'Why would God make us ask for some good He might supply, and why would it be right for God to withhold that good unless and until we asked for it?'[15] They also offer an answer to this question, but first I return to Stump's article for a first go at addressing the 'why' puzzle. Stump's basic response to the 'why' question is 'friendship'; petitionary prayer creates a relational dynamic between the human and God that fosters the friendship between the human and God.[16] Stump points out that it might seem a great challenge for there to be a genuine friendship between a 'fallible, finite, imperfect' human and the God of Classical Theism – the challenge being on the order of the challenge of a friendship between a 'slum child' and a very rich child.[17] God could

---

[14]Scott A. Davison, 'Petitionary Prayer', *The Stanford Encyclopedia of Philosophy* (Summer 2017). Davison is likewise to be consulted for his *Petitionary Prayer: A Philosophical Investigation* (Oxford: Oxford University Press, 2017). See the response from Caleb Cohoe, 'How could Prayer Make a Difference? Discussion of Scott A. Davison', *Petitionary Prayer: A Philosophical Investigation'*, *European Journal for Philosophy of Religion* 10, no. 2 (2018): 171–85; and Davison's rejoinder, 'Requests and Responses: Reply to Cohoe', *European Journal for Philosophy of Religion* 10, no. 2 (2018): 187–94. Cohoe's earlier work is also to be consulted, 'God, Causality, and Petitionary Prayer', *Faith and Philosophy* 31, no. 1 (2014): 24–45.
[15]Nicholas Smith and Andrew Yip, 'Partnership with God: A Partial Solution to the Problem of Petitionary Prayer', *Religious Studies* 46, no. 3 (2010): 395–410. See also Smith's 'Philosophical Reflection on Petitionary Prayer', *Philosophy Compass* 8, no. 3 (2013): 309–17.
[16]Incidentally, this is a recurring theme of Stump's constructive work. See especially, Eleonore Stump, *Wandering in Darkness: Narrative and the Problem of Suffering* (Oxford: Oxford University Press, 2012).
[17]Stump, 'Petitionary Prayer', 87. Further discussion can be found in Joshua Hoffman, 'On Petitionary Prayer', *Faith and Philosophy* 2, no. 1 (1985): 21–9, with a response in Eleonore Stump, 'Hoffman on Petitionary Prayer', *Faith and Philosophy* 2, no. 1 (1985): 30–7, and a rejoinder by Hoffman, 'Reply to Eleonore Stump', *Faith and Philosophy* 2, no. 1 (1985): 38–42.

bestow upon the human whatever is good for the human without the human ever asking for it. But were this to happen, so Stump describes, the result could be an 'overwhelming' of the human by God in two kinds: oppression or spoiling. Rather, petitionary prayer 'acts as a kind of buffer' between the human and God to protect against these kinds of overwhelmings.[18]

A similar relational response to the 'why' question is offered by Smith and Yip. They suggest that partnership with God 'is central to the value of petitionary prayer'.[19] In this manner, the value or dignity of the human is retained as the human participates with God in bringing about what God wishes to bring about. They state 'by obeying God the petitioner acts in concord with God, which increases and grows the good will of the petitioner in future actions. By loving God and one's fellow human beings, the petitioner gains motivation in willing and doing good to others.'[20] Another related line of approach comes from Michael Murray and Kurt Meyers who argue that, among other things, petitionary prayer helps to avoid idolatry and self-sufficiency in the one who prays.[21] On the former, Murray and Meyers pick up a thread of thought from Thomas Morris who observed that the avoidance of perils often drove people towards idolatry – attempting to manipulate capricious and unpredictable causes. On the latter, modern life might lead humans to think that they really need nothing else in the cosmos but themselves. Petitionary prayer serves to personalize the source of all things. 'In this way, the creature remains humble in the face of the recognition that God is the ultimate source of all goods and thankful for this sustained provision.'[22] Hence, 'why' would God enjoin petitionary prayer? Because it brings about a relational good between the one praying and God.

In addition to relational lines of response to the 'why' question, some have argued that the God who creates the best (or a better) possible world

---

[18]Stump, 'Petitionary Prayer', 90.

[19]Smith and Yip, 'Partnership with God', 404. A somewhat similar 'collaborative' approach is in Gianluca di Muzio, 'A Collaborative Model of Petitionary Prayer', *Religious Studies* 54, no. 1 (2018): 37–54.

[20]Smith and Yip, 'Partnership with God', 404.

[21]Together, see Michael J. Murray and Kurt Meyers, 'Ask and It Will Be Given to You', *Religious Studies* 30, no. 3 (1994): 311–30 and Michael J. Murray, 'God Responds to Prayer', in *Contemporary Debates in Philosophy of Religion*, ed. Michael L. Peterson and Raymond J. VanArragon (Oxford: Blackwell, 2004), 242–55, 264–5. The latter includes helpful discussion by David Basinger, 'God Does Not Necessarily Respond to Prayer', in *Contemporary Debates in Philosophy of Religion*, ed. Peterson and VanArragon, 255–64. Basinger should also be consulted in 'Why Petition an Omnipotent, Omniscient, Wholly Good God?', *Religious Studies* 19, no. 1 (1983): 25–41 and 'Petitionary Prayer: A Response to Murray and Meyers', *Religious Studies* 31, no. 4 (1995): 475–84.

[22]Murray and Meyers, 'Ask', 314.

will include responses to prayer as an added value to the goodness of this world. A 'possible world' is simply a way of thinking about how things could be in the world. There is a possible world in which it rains on the last Thursday of May in my location, there is a possible world in which it does not rain on the last Thursday of May in my location, and there are even possible worlds in which there are no Thursdays. Some hold that possible worlds have values and that God – being perfect – brings about the best possible world. Perhaps a world with rain on the last Thursday of May in my location is better than one without, and so God would bring about the former and not the latter.

Consequently, a 'goodness of a possible world' answer to the 'why' question is available. Suppose there are two possible worlds, world 1 where God does A and world 2 where God does A but in addition in world 2 person P prays for A to come about. Hence, in this instance, world 2 would have the benefit of God being able to respond to P's prayer for A. Thus, world 2 has more value. Similarly, Charles Taliaferro introduces the concept of a 'mediatory good' as a possible good that could be added to a positive world.[23] Suppose A is some good thing for a certain person S. Suppose also that God is going to bring about A for S. But suppose also that some other person, P, intercedes for S for God to bring about A for S. This world includes a mediatory good that is not a component of a world where God brings about A for S without the prayer of P. Hence, then, the world which includes the mediatory good is a better possible world. Similarly, Daniel and Frances Howard-Snyder have argued that a world in which God allows humans the ability to influence the direction of the world by their prayers is a better world than one in which God does not allow this freedom.[24] Moreover, Smith and Yip likewise go so far as to argue that a possible world in which genuine partnership exists between humans and God by means of petitionary prayer is a better possible world in which no such partnership is instantiated.[25] So 'why' God enjoins prayer is to add value to the worlds in which he brings about the targets of prayer.[26]

[23]Charles Taliaferro, 'Prayer', in *The Routledge Companion to Philosophy of Religion*, ed. Charles Meister and Paul Copan (London: Routledge, 2007), 621.
[24]Daniel Howard-Snyder and Frances Howard-Snyder, 'The Puzzle of Petitionary Prayer', *European Journal for Philosophy of Religion* 2, no. 2 (2010): 43–68. See also Scott A. Davison, 'On the Puzzle of Petitionary Prayer: Response to Daniel and Frances Howard-Snyder', *European Journal for Philosophy of Religion* 3, no. 1 (2011): 227–37.
[25]Smith and Yip, 'Partnership with God', 408.
[26]Further on the possible worlds motif, see Ryan Parker and Bradley Rettler, 'A Possible-Worlds Solution to the Puzzle of Petitionary Prayer', *European Journal for Philosophy of Religion* 9, no. 1 (2017): 179–86.

The 'how' of prayer

Even if we take it that God has good reasons for enjoining God's followers to petition God, we still might run into puzzles regarding just how it is we are to conceive of God's responding to our petitions. This is a two-way street. Perhaps one's view of God is such that as simple, immutable, impassible and existing completely *a se*, humans are in no way able to influence God. In this case, one needs to revise one's conception of 'petitions' when they apply to God in a manner different from when one petitions a human agent. On the other hand, perhaps one's understanding of the scriptural material or one's own religious practice concerning petitionary prayer will cause one to hold a conception of God that allows for the kind of responsiveness one desires.

(Im)mutability and/or (im)possibility

One particular puzzle that touches directly on one's doctrine of God comes to the fore when one reflects on the attributes of God's purported immutability or impassibility. If God is simply unchanging and unchangeable then there is clearly no point to human effort to change God. Rather, human petitions only seem effective when it just so happens that one requests what God was going to do anyway. But then this would be an instance of a Gettier-style answer, and would not be efficacious on the present definition of efficacy. The theological determinist, of which there are multiple varieties – Augustinian, Thomist, Reformed, Lutheran, Leibnitzian, etc. – could hold with Aquinas that not only does God determine states of affairs to come about, God also determines the means by which they come about.[27] In this regard, petitioning God is not so much about how God responds to prayers, as how the various responses to the why question come back to the fore.

Of course, one could just hold that God is neither immutable nor impassible and that our prayers do in fact change God.[28] Perhaps our petitions change God's mind, God's intentions, God's plans of action. A kind of process theism would be especially amenable to this conception and I take it that a dynamic relationality between the creation and God is one of process theism's main selling points. However, even the defender of

---

[27]For an analytic approach to petitionary prayer in the Reformed tradition, see Christopher Woznicki's trilogy, 'Is Prayer Redundant? Calvin and the Early Reformers on the Problem of Petitionary Prayer', *Journal of the Evangelical Theological Society* 60, no. 2 (2017): 333–48; 'What Are We Doing When We Pray?: Rekindling a Reformation Theology of Petitionary Prayer', *Calvin Theological Journal* 53, no. 2 (2018): 319–43; and 'Peter Martyr Vermigli's Account of Petitionary Prayer: A Reformation Alternative to Contemporary Two-Way Contingency Accounts', *Philosophia Christi* 20, no. 1 (2018): 119–37.

[28]For views on divine immutability, see Brian Leftow, 'Immutability', *The Stanford Encyclopedia of Philosophy* (Winter 2016).

God's mutability still has a puzzle to address regarding why some prayers are efficacious and some are not. In this regard, it might seem as though one has traded a solution to the 'why' for a solution to the 'how'.

Omniscience

I place issues of the relationship between divine foreknowledge and human freedom under the divine attribute heading of omniscience. The issue with respect to petitionary prayer can be put as this: if God knows what will come about at some point in the future, how can my petition for some state of affairs at all factor into God's bringing this about? Suppose I have some tomato plants that are looking rather droopy,[29] and so I petition God to bring some rain to water my plants. But God, given one's view of God's knowledge, may or may not already know what the precipitation patterns will be at my location in the near future. How God interacts with this bit of knowledge – my expressed desire for rain for my tomato plants – depends on one's commitment to certain views of God's knowledge.

The classical view of God's knowledge is that God stands outside of time and space and is hence able to 'see' and know all things in one moment, in God's eternal specious present. On this view, in God's one moment of knowledge God knows everything about the situation with my tomato plants: for example, that they are droopy, that I wish they were not, that rain will or will not come at my location soon, that I request of God rain for my tomato plants, etc. Like the defender of theological determinism, the proponent of this classical view of God's knowledge will need to hold that even though God knows the rain will come, this does not remove the 'because of' aspect of my prayer for it.

The proponent of God's middle knowledge holds that God knows the totality of the counterfactuals of creaturely freedom. Thomas Flint provides one of the more thorough discussions of this view.[30] In the logical 'moment' between God's determination to create and his actualizing a particular world, God knows what every agent would freely do in any given situation (freedom understood here in a purportedly libertarian sense). Suppose God knows that I will freely pray for rain if my tomato plants are looking rather droopy on the last Thursday of May and God wants to answer this petition affirmatively. God then chooses to actualize the world wherein both I do so

---

[29]Suppose also that I do not have a hose or a well or a stream in my backyard!

[30]See Thomas Flint, *Divine Providence: The Molinist Account* (Ithaca, NY: Cornell University Press, 1998). See also William Lane Craig, *The Only Wise God: The Compatibility of Divine Foreknowledge and Human Freedom* (Grand Rapids, MI: Baker Books, 1987). A related, but explicitly non-middle knowledge approach is found in Peter Forrest, 'Answers to Prayer and Conditional Situations', *Faith and Philosophy* 15, no. 1 (1998): 41–51.

pray and rain comes on the last Friday of May. The Molinist holds that the free potential act of my praying on Thursday played a causal role in God's bringing it about that it rained on my location on Friday, and hence the prayer was efficacious. Yet, this view of God's knowledge is not without challenges, for it is not clear that one can maintain both that a counterfactual of creaturely freedom is genuinely free in a libertarian sense and that God can be said to actually know this.

Finally, an analytic proponent of the Open view of God's knowledge has the easiest time saving the phenomenon of a genuine request.[31] On this view, God does not know the future for the future is not something that can be known. God can have very sophisticated estimations of weather patterns, but as there is no truth to be had about the yet non-existent rain, it cannot be known even by the omniscient God whether my tomato plants will acquire the moisture they desire. Hence, when I pray for rain for my tomato plants, God comes to know this fact and can take it into consideration as he deliberates what weather he might aid in bringing about at my location in the near future.[32]

Speech act theory as an example of analytic theology

If analytic theology utilizes the tools of analytic philosophy, what then are those tools and how might they be used? In what follows in this section, I deploy one such tool from the analytic philosophical tradition, speech act theory, to help get clear on some of the conceptual contours of the nature of petitionary prayer. Since prayer, especially petitionary prayer, is a kind of speech, this tool in the analytic toolbox will, I hope, serve both as an aid towards understanding petitionary prayer and as an example of the kind of utility that analytic philosophy might have for the theological task. I here utilize the speech act theoretic framework of first-generation 'analytic theologian' William Alston, specifically from his *Illocutionary Acts and Sentence Meaning*.[33]

Alston divides speech acts into three acts – in a typical instance of speech, all three will be present. These are (a) the sentential act, the specific

---

[31]See, for instance, William Hasker, *God, Time and Knowledge* (Ithaca, NY: Cornell University Press, 1989).

[32]An area left unexplored here, but one Davison addresses in his work, is the compatibility of petitionary prayer with the divine attribute of goodness. For discussion, see Jonathan Reibsamen, 'Divine Goodness and the Efficacy of Petitionary Prayer', *Religious Studies* 55, no. 1 (2019): 131–44.

[33]William Alston, *Illocutionary Acts and Sentence Meaning* (Ithaca, NY: Cornell University Press, 2000). Incidentally, Alston has waded into the prayer discussion as well in, 'Divine-Human Dialogue and the Nature of God', *Faith and Philosophy* 2, no. 1 (1985): 5–20.

phrase or sentence uttered; (b) the illocutionary act, the specific action that a speaker performs by way of her sentence; and (c) the perlocutionary act, the response of a hearer or audience to the illocutionary act. In instances of prayer, the hearer is clearly God and the desired perlocutionary response is the desired effect of the one praying. The illocutionary act is the locus of meaning in Alston's system and it is on this level that we understand what speakers are doing or purportedly doing with their prayers. Alston delineates five illocutionary act types: assertives, directives, commissives, exercitives and expressives. Petitionary prayers, so I think, fall into the directive category of illocutionary act types. This class of illocutionary acts 'are typically intended to "direct", or "influence", the behavior of the addressee'.[34] When one petitions God for, say, rain to water tomato plants, one is allegedly attempting to direct or influence God's activity in the world. Alston provides conditions under which an illocutionary act is a directive illocutionary act.[35]

U D'd in uttering S if and only if in uttering S, U R'd that:

1. Conceptually necessary conditions for the existence of the obligation are satisfied. (These include such things as that it is possible for H to do D, that D has not already been done, etc.)

2. Circumstances of the utterance of S are appropriate for the production of the obligation in question. (This includes the appropriate authority for orders, the right kind of interpersonal relationship for request, etc.)

3. By uttering S, U lays on H a (stronger or weaker) obligation to do D.

4. U utters S in order to get H to do D.

There are many variables in Alston's schema, but I can illustrate an instance of a petitionary prayer by filling in the variables with terms from a paradigmatic prayer of request. For instance, we can use the prayer for rain from the classic Anglican prayer book:

O GOD, heavenly Father, who by thy Son Jesus Christ hast promised to all them that seek thy kingdom, and the righteousness thereof, all things necessary to their bodily sustenance: Send us, we beseech thee, in this our

---

[34]Alston, *Illocutionary Acts*, 97.
[35]Alston, *Illocutionary Acts*, 102–3. In typical analytic fashion, the standalone letters here are stand-ins for variable terms: U – an utterer or speaker, S – some sentence, H – a hearer or audience, R – taking responsibility for and D – a term for some directive illocutionary act type (such as requesting or ordering or entreating), a purporting to be producing a certain kind of obligation on H to do D.

necessity, such moderate rain and showers, that we may receive the fruits of the earth to our comfort, and to thy honour; through Jesus Christ our Lord. Amen.[36]

Here, amidst other phrases, is the specific request to *send rain*; yet, I will take the reciting of the entirety of the prayer to be performing the illocutionary act of requesting rain. We can plug this instance of a petitionary prayer into the Alstonian schema for a directive illocutionary act. Because this is a long sentence, I will just use '*The prayer for rain*' to stand in for the entire prayer. Thus:

James *requested rain* in uttering *The prayer for rain* if and only if in uttering *The prayer for rain*, James took responsibility that:

1. Conceptually necessary conditions for the existence of the obligation are satisfied. (Which might include the following ...)

   a. It is possible for God to send rain.

   b. God has not already sent rain.

2. Circumstances of the utterance of *The prayer for rain* are appropriate for the production of the obligation in question. (Which might include the following ...)

   a. The relationship that exists between God and myself provides a context in which requesting rain is not out of the ordinary.

3. By uttering *The prayer for rain*, James lays on God a (stronger or weaker) obligation to send rain.

   a. Again, requests are weaker than demands or commands. But regardless of the strength of the directive it would seem that most would have a perception of God such that God is not required to acquiesce to every request made of God.

4. James utters *The prayer for rain* in order to get God to send rain.

   a. This is to show that my sentential act was intended to be an illocutionary act of this kind and that there is a connection between the content of the sentential and the perlocutionary effect or act I hope to produce in God.

Utilizing a schema such as this helps to home in on just where the tension might be in one's understanding of the relationship between human prayer and God's purported response, which of course impinges upon one's understanding of the doctrine of God.

---

[36]'Prayers and Thanksgivings', *Common Worship*.

For instance, suppose one were a deist. On this understanding of God, God has created the cosmos and then has simply allowed the cosmos to continue along according to natural law. Since God does not causally engage with the cosmos, there is no perlocutionary act available for which a human who prays could hope. The illocutionary act here fails to be a directive, due to its failure to satisfy conditions 1a and 4. It is not possible, on deism, for God to send rain. Neither, then, can the proponent of deism utter *The prayer for rain* as a directive illocutionary act. The deist must utter that sentence for some other purpose, for instance, as an expressive illocutionary act.

Plausibly, the open theist who is also a strong interventionist with respect to special divine action could easily maintain this prayer as a directive-type illocutionary act. On this understanding, the future is undetermined and so completely open, and God proceeds along the timeline of the universe with humans, perhaps anticipating what will come next. God can take into consideration a person's prayer at time t1 in God's engagement with bringing about some state of affairs at t2. This allows the open theist to hold to real perlocutionary effects in God, and to maintain that responses God makes to human illocutionary acts (including directive-type illocutionary acts) are properly perlocutionary acts.

What of the Classical position? There seem to be two routes to go here. One, the Classical Theist will wish to maintain God's immutability, strong omniscience and asiety, but also the directive nature of petitionary prayer. At which point the Classical Theist will need to hold that God has ordained the prayer as a means to bring about what God could bring about without the directive. Or, secondly, the Classical Theist could, perhaps like the deist, translate *The prayer for rain* from what seems like a directive to what is really an expressive illocutionary act. In his discussion of the Lord's Prayer in the context of other instances of liturgical prayer, Nicholas Wolterstorff is representative of this tradition:

> Given that this is the paradigmatic prayer ... the conclusion, surely, is that our prayers in general are not to consist of, and are not to be understood as consisting of, asking God for things in addition to the coming of God's kingdom. They are not to consist of, and are not to be understood as consisting of, asking God to intervene in the causal order so as to bring about various things that we very much want to happen in addition to God's kingdom. They are instead to be understood as the church's concrete expression of her longing for the full manifestation of God's kingdom.[37]

---

[37]Wolterstorff, *The God We Worship*, 111.

Requests must become expressions of psychological states. For Wolterstorff, the Lord's Prayer is the expression of one's longing for God's kingdom. On these families of views, it does not really make sense to speak of perlocutionary effects. God is not affected, nor does God act in response to illocutionary acts directed to God. A request for rain must be understood to be the expression of some psychological state in the utterer, and not an effort to produce a perlocutionary effect.

Finally, as noted, the Molinist attempts to preserve the directive phenomenon of a genuine petition, while maintaining God's knowledge and control of the events related to the prayer. The routes open for explanation on this view, it seems to me, are the same as on the Classical view. Regardless of where one comes down on views of God's knowledge or divine action in the world, the speech act motif, and hence a tool from analytic philosophy, proves helpful in clarifying where the conceptual challenges really lie.

Analytic Theology as Prayer

I do not intend the following comments to indict or accuse other theological methodologies of the vice to which the virtues potentially inherent in analytic theology are opposed. I simply offer a way of thinking about one feature of analytic theology that might be particularly harmonious with a commendable posture in Christian prayer and might even be considered a kind of prayer itself. It is rather ironic that at times one hears – whispered, not published – a complaint that the analytic concern for logical rigour and clarity of argumentation is due to spiritual pride, intellectual hubris or undue optimism regarding human rational capabilities. I certainly admit that analytics are as liable to these vices as are any. However, I see the desire for clarity, in fact, in the service of the pursuit of intellectual humility.[38]

When one is clear, one is vulnerable. When one is open regarding one's ideas and the rationale for those ideas, one is liable to being shown that one's ideas are wrong or incoherent. The practitioner of analytic theology attempts to avoid hiding behind rhetorical flourishes or decorative use of metaphor in a humble act of embracing the possibility of being found wrong. One's argument cannot be found in error if one's interlocutors cannot understand the argument sufficiently to attempt a refutation. This is where the truth-aimed nature of the substantive analytic intellectual culture comes to the fore. When one aims at truth, one can miss the mark. Like the archer with

---

[38] The seed of this notion was first planted in my mind by way of a conversation with Trent Dougherty in the Fall of 2015.

her bow, by logical rigour and clarity of expression, the analytic attempts to chart the course of her argumentative arrow as accurately as possible. It is as if she says, 'I think I have hit the bull's eye but if not, please show me where in the aiming, in the tension of the string, in the composition of the arrow, in the estimation of the distance to the target, have I gone awry and I will happily make corrections.'

Moreover, one aspect of the Christian approach to prayer – petitionary or non-petitionary – is the act of laying oneself bare before God. Christians openly and honestly express to God what is within them: desires, laments, sins, praises, requests. Those enculturated in the intellectual culture of analytic theology will regularly inhabit a space wherein it is encouraged to open one's thinking up in humility and vulnerability. These virtues can then be transferred to the venue of prayer as well. Yet even further, analytic theological reflection on prayer is itself a laying bare and open one's thoughts about prayer. These thoughts are laid bare not just to other theologians, but to God as well. The analytic can view her work as an expression to God of her thoughts about God in the hopes and expectation that God will correct the course of thoughts whose trajectory will not result in hitting the mark. In this regard, the analytic follows once again in the footsteps of St Anselm whose rigorous theological and philosophical argumentation were often expressed as prayers directed specifically to God.

Conclusion

Analytic theology utilizes some of the tools, methods and sensibilities of contemporary analytic philosophy for the purpose of the exploration and explication of standard Christian theological topics. Given many of the puzzles that arise out of the conjunction of the human practice of prayer and the conception of God derived from Abraham, Isaac and Anselm, it is understandable that scholars with interests in problem-solving and argument analysis would engage in addressing these puzzles. This theological locus will likely continue to serve as a fertile area of analytic theology.[39]

---

[39] I am grateful to my research assistants Wesley Aaron Pendergrass and Eric Anthony for procuring bibliographic materials.

CHAPTER THIRTY

Inter-Religious Dialogue: A Provocation to Pray

CATRIONA LAING

Prelude

It's a quarter past one on a Friday afternoon at the church where I serve in downtown Washington, DC. I've just finished the Eucharist, where we had our usual Friday gathering of about ten people. It's a loyal group who work or spend their days downtown and join us at midday on Fridays for a short service of Holy Communion. Church of the Epiphany is situated two blocks from the White House in the heart of Washington; we are flanked by government buildings, international institutions and the large number of banks and law firms that jostle for space in this busy part of the city. Our congregants hail from all of these offices as well as from the streets and shelters of downtown DC.

As I clear away the elements and tidy up after the service a new cross-section of people start to come into the church. From a cupboard in the corner of the Church they take out a pile of Muslim prayer mats, which will in a few minutes cover the entire floor of the sanctuary. It's time for ADAMS, the All Dulles Area Muslim Society, otherwise known as the Muslim community of the greater Washington area, to hold their weekly Jumma prayers in our church.[1]

---

[1] In February 2019, Church of the Epiphany was photographed and featured in an article in the Economist about Muslim integration in Europe and North America. See Nicolas Pelham, 'The 30m Muslims Living in Europe and America Are Gradually Becoming Integrated', www.economist.com/special-report/2019/02/14/the-30m-muslims-living-in-europe-and-america-are-gradually-becoming-integrated (accessed: 10 September 2019).

For the past fifteen years or so ADAMS have been meeting at the Church of the Epiphany to pray the daily lunchtime prayer. Today, I decide to stay and sit at the back of the church to listen to the prayers and the weekly sermon.

More and more people enter the church. Having made their ablutions they remove their shoes and find a space on the mats. A small number of women gather to one side in the left transept, whilst men of every age, colour and socio-economic background occupy the main space. The imam begins the call to prayer while people make their way into our church. By the time the sermon starts, I'm looking at the backs of around 250 men and women. I'm struck again by how close together Muslims pray, shoulder to shoulder. It reminds me of scenes in some of the Muslim capitals of the world where I grew up. At lunchtime on Fridays you would hear the call to prayer ringing out from the mosques and everything would stop whilst people hurried to find a space to pray, ideally but not necessarily in a mosque.

The call to prayer is followed by the sermon, but what hits me today are the prayers. The imam, who is Indian by birth, offers prayers in Arabic on behalf of the gathered community. He then proceeds to chant the prayers for the midday order of prayer. The chant has a sacred tone to it as the words waft around the sanctuary. It is beautiful. As I sit and listen to the invocations to God my eyes are drawn to the east-end window above the Imam's head. It's an image of Christ, flanked by the Virgin Mary and John the Baptist. It could not be more overtly Christian, but it doesn't seem to distract those gathered in prayer from their devotions.

I feel caught up in a holy moment. I notice that I recognize something of the Divine, something familiar in what I'm experiencing, and yet I'm acutely aware that these are not my prayers. It's as if someone else has moved into my house, but I haven't really moved out. There are pieces of furniture that I recognize as my own; as I look around the space, memories are triggered of other moments celebrated here, but at this precise moment it doesn't quite feel like my place.

I leave the sanctuary at the end of the service and retreat to my office where I light a candle; I feel a strong urge to pray. Forty-five minutes in the presence of the praying other has encouraged me to go and offer my own praises and petitions to God.

*****

This chapter argues that the worlds of inter-religious dialogue and prayer occupy a complex, but potentially enriching shared space. The premise of this chapter is that prayer does not lend itself as an interfaith practice per se. However, drawing on an historical example, the chapter demonstrates the power of prayer to open the individual's mind to a religion different from her own, in a way that fosters new understanding of the other whilst taking her deeper into the particularity of her own faith. This argument is grounded in the work of Constance Padwick, the early twentieth-century Anglican missionary, who spent most of her career working amongst Muslims in the Middle East. Drawing on Padwick's experience, my focus is primarily on Muslim and Christian prayer, but the arguments offered apply to the wider question of inter-religious prayer.

I first examine approaches to inter-religious dialogue and prayer, which resonate with the way in which I am exploring the question. Secondly, I offer a brief critique of some contemporary practices of interfaith prayer. And finally, in the third section, I turn to the historical example that frames the argument.

Some Instructive Approaches to Inter-Religious Dialogue and Prayer

In an increasingly inter-connected and pluralized world the need for inter-religious dialogue has become urgent. People of different religious and cultural traditions live side by side and are confronted with one another's differences on a daily basis (and even where physical contact is less common, the internet makes it hard to ignore the presence of the religious other in our lives). It is also undeniable that the violence and conflict that we experience are often influenced by exclusivist religious extremism.

My approach to inter-religious dialogue is informed by practical and theoretical approaches. On the practical level Scriptural Reasoning exemplifies a model of inter-religious dialogue that seeks to take the religious believer deeper into her own tradition. People of different religious traditions gather to read and study their sacred texts.[2] The Scriptural Reasoning website describes the practice: 'Unlike some forms of inter-faith engagement, it is not about seeking agreement but rather exploring the texts and their possible interpretations across faith boundaries, and learning to "disagree better". The result is often a deeper understanding of others' and one's own scriptures, as well as the development of strong bonds across faith communities.'[3]

Scriptural Reasoning endorses an approach to inter-religious dialogue that shies away from establishing a series of points of 'common ground', which in an effort to focus on our similarities can end up neutralizing the particularities of each religion. Rather, it celebrates difference and examines what those differences might teach members of different religions about their

---

[2]For an introduction to Scriptural Reasoning, see David F. Ford and Chad Pecknold, ed., *The Promise of Scriptural Reasoning* (Oxford: Blackwell, 2006).
[3]www.scripturalreasoning.org (accessed: 10 September 2020).

respective beliefs. The goal of Scriptural Reasoning is to build friendship rather than consensus. At the end of a session participants find that study of the scriptures of another religion has encouraged them to engage more deeply with their own religious tradition.[4]

In a similar vein, but with a more theoretical approach, David Burrell makes the case for the importance of friendship and community for the individual's journey towards a deeper relationship with God – friendship both within and across religious traditions. Burrell writes of the ways in which friends 'open our hearts and minds to interfaith dialogue, moving it beyond the specter of "relativism" to a fruitful stage of "mutual illumination"'.[5] He is particularly interested in what study of the other can teach us about ourselves. Burrell observes: 'Our location in a world where diverse traditions become aware of their mutual presence to one another invites us precisely "on a voyage of discovery stripped of colonising pretensions: an invitation to explore the other on the way to discovering ourselves."'[6]

Examples of how friendship can lead to 'mutual illumination' are described in Sarah Coakley and Frances Ward's edited collection *Fear and Friendship: Anglicans Engaging with Islam*, which offers several accounts of engagement across religious traditions in which the writers find themselves inspired to ask more questions of their own religions and explore their own faith more deeply as a result of the encounter.[7]

A further example of this mode of inter-religious dialogue, which begins from within the specific parameters of one's own religion, can be found in the Church of England's statements about Anglican engagement with the religious other. In 2008 the Anglican Communion Network for Inter Faith Concerns published *Generous Love: The Truth of the Gospel and the Call to Dialogue*.[8] The publication sought to establish an Anglican approach to inter-religious dialogue. A theological approach emerged that is rooted in the Trinity and the church. Richard Sudworth has dubbed it the 'ecclesial-turn' in Anglican theology of interfaith relations.[9] Sudworth observes a shift from an

---

[4]For a description of this experience, see Ben Quash, 'Deep Calls to Deep: The Practice of Scriptural Reasoning', www.themathesontrust.org/papers/comparativereligion/Quash-DeepCallstoDeep.pdf (accessed: 10 September 2020).

[5]David Burrell, *Friendship and Ways to Truth* (Notre Dame, IN: University of Notre Dame Press, 2000), 6.

[6]Burrell, *Friendship and Ways to Truth*, 6.

[7]Frances Ward and Sarah Coakley, ed., *Fear and Friendship: Anglicans Engaging with Islam* (London: Continuum, 2012).

[8]Anglican Communion Network for Inter Faith Concerns, *Generous Love: The Truth of the Gospel and the Call to Dialogue* (London: Anglican Consultative Council, 2008).

[9]Richard J. Sudworth, 'Anglicanism and Islam: The Ecclesial-Turn in Interfaith Relations', in *Living Stones Yearbook 2012* (London: Melisende, 2012), 65–105.

'external discourse' *about* religion to a vision of inter-religious dialogue that 'begins with God' and the consequent nature of the church within the life of God.[10] Much like Scriptural Reasoning and the approaches that influence the subject of this chapter, the focus is on the implications of inter-religious dialogue for the deepening and growth of faith within a particular tradition.

In *Faith, Hope and Love: Interfaith Engagement as Practical Theology* Ray Gaston echoes the same argument.[11] As the title suggests, Gaston's work focuses on a practical theology developed from his work with theological students and ordinands as well as his experiences of parish ministry in Leeds where engagement with the local Muslim community was a significant part of his ministry. Gaston seeks to move the Christian theological discourse on engagement with other religions from a focus on theologies of religions or missiology in a practical theological direction. He writes:

> In readjusting our interpretive lenses ... we turn the focus away from 'analysing' the other, either in relation to their salvific efficacy or as targets for apologetic or evangelistic engagement, and instead focus on how encounter with other faith traditions has an impact on Christian self-understanding. The subject of exploration becomes ourselves and our relationship with others and with God ... how do other faith traditions enable us to enter into a deeper relationship with Christ?[12]

The idea of engaging in inter-religious prayer from an established commitment to one specific tradition is at the heart of the argument for engaging in Christian-Muslim prayer presented by the Benedictine Abbot and theologian Timothy Wright.[13] In his account of how Muslims and Christians have and should come together to pray, Wright presents a practice of inter-religious prayer as a dialogue of spirituality that is grounded in scripture.

Wright starts from the premise that Muslims and Christians share a commitment to the Word of God. For Christians the scriptures are the revealed Word of God, for Muslims the Qur'an is God speaking to humanity:

> If we accept that God speaks through the Word, whether the Hebrew scriptures, the Christian New Testament, or the Muslim Qu'ran, we can look for echoes from the other that inspire us. The purpose of the

---

[10]Sudworth, 'Anglicanism and Islam', 85.

[11]Ray Gaston, *Faith, Hope and Love: Interfaith Engagement as Practical Theology* (London: SCM Press, 2017).

[12]Gaston, *Faith, Hope and Love*, 23.

[13]Timothy Wright, *No Peace without Prayer: Encouraging Muslims and Christians to Pray Together – A Benedictine Approach* (Collegeville, MN: Liturgical Press, 2013).

dialogue is not simply clarifying what is obscure but recognizing the value of positive echoes of the 'other' which will enhance one's own faith.[14]

Wright illustrates this form of spiritual dialogue through the work of the Trappist monk, Thomas Merton, whose friendship and correspondence with the Pakistani Sufi Abdul Aziz led him not only to use Sufi spirituality for his own Christian devotion, but to teach it to the novices.[15] The final section of Wright's book offers examples of monastic communities who have achieved something akin to what he is endorsing – a deepening of one's faith through engagement with a religious other. The goal of prayer is not dissimilar.

Prayer for the Christian is about God's work in us. It is about how we get to know God, but it is also about how we get to know ourselves as God's creation. In a description of Christian prayer offered to a group of Muslim and Christian scholars Rowan Williams quoted George Herbert, who described prayer as 'God's breath in man returning to its birth'. 'We pray', Williams writes, 'because God breathes into us a capacity to be related to him, to serve and love him, to be united, as far as any creature can be, with his will, his purpose, his life'.[16] It is with prayer as God's action in me that I explore how the believer's witness of the prayers of another religion might be a form of God's action in her and whether inter-religious engagement can therefore include prayer.

These approaches to inter-religious dialogue and prayer share a common goal: to inspire the believer to travel further on her own religious journey, whilst along the way offering insights to a different religion. In what follows, a critique of some contemporary approaches to prayer as an interfaith practise will be explored. This will frame the ensuing argument that whilst interfaith prayer is not an interfaith practice per se, it can play a valuable role in provoking the believer to engage more deeply both across and within religious traditions.

A Survey of Contemporary Practices of Interfaith Prayer

In 1986 Pope John Paul II invited representatives of the major world religions to an international day of prayer for peace in Assisi, Italy. The Pope called the meeting because he claimed that the world religions share a belief that

---

[14]Wright, *No Peace without Prayer*, 45.
[15]Wright, *No Peace without Prayer*, 143.
[16]Rowan Williams, 'Preface', in *Prayer: Christian and Muslim Perspectives*, ed. David Marshall and Lucinda Mosher (Washington, DC: Georgetown University Press, 2013), xvii.

lasting peace cannot be achieved by human efforts alone. In his address to the Assisi gathering the Pope declared:

> For the first time in history, we have come together from everywhere, Christian Churches and Ecclesial Communities, and World Religions, in this sacred place dedicated to Saint Francis, to witness before the world, each according to his own conviction, about the transcendent quality of peace.[17]

The Assisi gathering was a moment when members of different world religions were invited to pray *together*. Religious leaders started to claim that the physical proximity of members of different religious traditions in an increasingly globalized world and the presence of religious extremism has meant that the adherents to the world religions had a responsibility to use their faith as a conduit for peace. A statement published in 1998 following a consultation on inter-religious prayer arranged jointly by the Office on Interreligious Relations of the World Council of Churches and the Vatican Pontifical Council for Interreligious Dialogue reflects the same sense of obligation to pray *with* the religious other:

> Participation in inter-religious prayer is not an optional activity restricted to an elite group, but an urgent call for a growing number of Christians today, and should be a matter of concern for all Christians.[18]

In *Interreligious Prayer: A Christian Guide*, Thomas Ryan outlines different theological rationales for inter-religious prayer.[19] The first point is that prayer is a form of covenant. In God's covenant with every living creature, God calls all people to prayer.

The second explanation is that prayer is communion. Recalling the Second Vatican Council's statement, which recognized the work of the Holy Spirit outside of the church, Ryan suggests that in a manner known only to God, the Holy Spirit becomes a vehicle for including everyone in an act of prayer which will lead ultimately to union with the Divine. Prayer is no longer restricted along religious boundaries.

---

[17]Address of John Paul II to the Representatives of the Christian Church and Ecclesial Communities and of the World Religions.

[18]Findings of an Exploratory Consultation on Interreligious Prayer, 'Final Statement (Bangalore, India, 1996)', *Pro Dialogo* 98, no. 2 (1998): 231–6.

[19]Thomas Ryan, *Interreligious Prayer: A Christian Guide* (New York: Paulist Press, 2008).

Furthermore, Ryan argues that if Christianity recognizes the presence of the Holy Spirit in other religions and cultures (a theme that appears in the writing of John Paul II), the prayers of people in other religions may also be gifts of the Holy Spirit. Ryan observes: 'interreligious prayer, then, may well express our being united in the Holy Spirit, a coming into the presence of God *together* even if this *together* is in a limited way in our understanding'.

Having established a Christian rationale for prayer as an interfaith practice, Ryan lists the different forms that inter-religious prayer can take. They are first, 'just being there', where the believer is present for the prayers of the other. A second approach consists of the multi-faith services where representatives of different religions pray in full fidelity to their own faith – 'we come together to pray, rather than we come to pray together' – and offers a step towards more integrated inter-religious prayer. Finally, there is integrative religious prayer, where the intention is not simply to come together to pray, but actually to pray together.

Ryan's arguments resonate with the many gatherings that now take place where members of different religious traditions gather, usually to mark a significant event or in the wake of tragedy. This stems from a need, articulated by Pope John Paul II, which is felt by people of different faiths to unite around a shared desire for peace and to support one another in affirming that the majority of faithful believers do not recognize the extremist forms of their religion which can be so violent.

Practitioners of contemplative prayer and meditation have also begun to explore how prayer can serve as a tool for interfaith relations. Parts of the Christian Wisdom tradition are drawn to the idea of shared prayer. Perennial Wisdom is one such example, which has the Christian theologians Richard Rohr and Cynthia Bourgeault among its better-known advocates, and presents a rediscovery of *philosophia perennis*. An early nineteenth-century phrase, it pointed to an idea of a shared universal truth. Rohr describes how 'hearing the same thing in a different language and images helps us see the same reality more clearly'.[20] The perennialists maintain that the different wisdom traditions of the world religions each offer a different interpretation of the same reality. They would concur with the depiction, made famous by John Hick, of a number of different people holding on to different parts of the same elephant only later realizing that they are simply seeing the same animal from a different angle.[21]

---

[20]Richard Rohr, 'Perennial Tradition', 30 July 2018, www.cac.org/perennial-wisdom-2018-07-30 (accessed: 10 September 2020).

[21]John Hick, *A Christian Theology of Religion* (Louisville, KY: Westminster John Knox Press, 1995).

The essence of perennial wisdom is that there are some constant themes, truths and recurrences in all of the world religions. They maintain that there is a divine reality underneath and inherent in the world of things, that in the human soul there is a natural capacity, similarity and longing for the Divine Reality and that the final goal of existence is union with this Divine Reality. Cynthia Bourgeault writes: 'It's remarkable how, no matter which spiritual path you pursue, the nuts and bolts of transformation wind up looking pretty much the same: surrender, detachment, compassion, forgiveness. Whether you're a Christian, a Buddhist, a Jew, a Sufi or a *sannyasin* you will still go through the same eye of the needle to get to where your true heart lies.'[22] For the perennialists the stage is set for members of different religions to gather together in meditation. Because at the heart of it, their quest is the same: union with the divine. The fact that they get there by different means is secondary.

This approach is unsatisfactory because whilst the shared experience of silence in meditation *may* enhance inter-religious dialogue, the perennialists achieve this shared silence by focusing on a lowest common denominator where believers can occupy a shared space because they have abandoned the understanding of prayer particular to their religion. They do not subscribe to the idea that contemplative practice is always rooted in a specific worldview, community, context and tradition. Rather than a path to discovering depth of religious commitment it requires a watering down of difference.

In addition to the work of the perennialists the rapidly expanding field of contemplative studies is emerging with some propositions for overlap between inter-religious relations and prayer, which seem more promising. In his extensive introduction to contemplative studies *Contemplative Literature*, Louis Komjathy emphasizes particularity amongst the contemplative traditions as he identifies twenty-four major types of contemplative practice with global distribution and which span the religious and secular.[23] Komjathy's approach chimes with the overall premise of this chapter, namely that a study of prayer, contemplative or other, can be instrumental in developing greater understanding and empathy for the religious other. But greater understanding is contingent, Komjathy argues, on an appreciation of the standpoint from which that study takes place. Hence, while a case can be made for the experience of inter-religious prayer described by Paul

---

[22]Cynthia Bourgeault, *The Wisdom Way of Knowing: Reclaiming an Ancient Tradition* to Awaken the Heart (Oxford: Wiley-Blackwell, 2003), xvii.
[23]Louis Komjathy, *Contemplative Literature: A Comparative Sourcebook on Meditation and Contemplative Prayer* (New York: State University of New York Press, 2016), 6–8.

Ryan as 'just being there' the practitioner must first have identified her own assumptions and ingrained opinions.[24]

Let me now turn to the historical examples, which help to tease out how prayer can contribute to a deeper engagement within and across religious traditions along the lines articulated by Wright and Komjathy. Examining the work of an early twentieth-century Anglican missionary to the Muslim world, I suggest that her experience might prove more fruitful for fostering understanding for the religious other, whilst provoking a deepening of one's own faith.

Prayer Inspired by Inter-Religious Encounter

Constance Evelyn Padwick was an Anglican missionary who spent most of her career working as a literature missionary for the Church Missionary Society in Egypt and Palestine. Prior to her move to Cairo with the CMS, Padwick studied at the School for Oriental Studies in London, through which she was able to travel to Egypt to conduct research into Egyptian folklore traditions among the rural population of lower Egypt. This experience kindled in Padwick a desire that would remain with her throughout her missionary career – namely to study the traditions and practices of 'ordinary' people from religions and cultures different from her own in order to understand them better.

In 1923 Padwick joined the CMS mission to Cairo where she was responsible for CMS' contribution to the translation, editing and publication of Christian missionary literature for the Muslim world. Whilst she was there, Padwick began a life-long exercise of collecting and studying the devotional prayer books of Islam. This eventually issued in 1961 in the publication of an introduction to Islam entitled *Muslim Devotions: A Study of Prayer Manuals in Common Use.*

In an article discussing her work on Islamic prayer, Padwick recalled the events that had led her to study Muslim devotional prayer books:

> The writer, believing that in a most practical sense *lex orandi* is *lex credendi*, has for some years used her leisure for a study of the small manuals for Muslim devotion which she found to be on sale in our day in the cities of Cairo, Damascus, Jerusalem, Amman, Tunis and Algiers, together with others kindly sent by friends from the Muslim bookshops of North India,

---

[24]Komjathy, *Contemplative Literature*, 39.

Obdurman and other centres. … With these Muslim manuals the writer's first aim has not been the disentangling of their history, fascinating as that might be, but an effort to grasp the devotional thought and attitude of those who use the words today.[25]

By collecting and studying Muslim prayers, Padwick embarked on exploring her own form of *lex orandi, lex credendi*, whereby the prayers of Islam became the vehicle through which she sought to understand the religion of 'those who use the words today'. It is important to stress that Padwick was a missionary. Her explicit aim was to provide a more effective approach to the evangelization of Muslims. Padwick's missiological focus notwithstanding, her work presents an example of how one person's engagement with the prayers of another religion not only informed her understanding of Islam, it also inspired her own Christian devotion.

The prayer manuals in Padwick's collection date from between the eighth and twentieth centuries, and come from across the Muslim world. They contain prayers and devotions written by saints and scholars compiled to enrich the worship of the Muslim believer. These include a combination of traditional prayers of the Prophet, Qur'an verses, blessings of the Prophet, forgiveness-seekings, refuge-seekings and cries of praise. A contemporary translation describes their purpose as 'the sanctification of daily life – the perception of the Divine in all that we experience, and in all that we do'.[26]

Padwick's study of Muslim devotional prayer influenced her understanding of the religious other and her own practice of prayer in three significant ways. First, the prayers became a vehicle through which Padwick developed greater understanding of Islam and was inspired to present 'corrections' to Western misunderstandings of the religion. Second, she began to identify what she described as 'kinships' in the prayers of her Muslim brothers and sisters (akin to the familiarity I sensed when sitting and silently witnessing Muslims at prayer in my church, or the 'echoes' to which Wright refers). Third, Padwick's study of the devotional lives of Muslims directed her to Roman Catholic theologians whose work in Muslim-Christian engagement had a significant influence on her spiritual life.

Arguing that her mode of encounter with Islam offered 'a truer way to some knowledge of the working beliefs of religious folk than one based on more formal theological treatises',[27] Padwick sought to deepen her missionary

---

[25]Constance Padwick, 'I Take Refuge with God', *The Muslim World* 28, no. 4 (1938): 372–85.
[26]T. Al Azem *Prayers of Occasions: A Handbook of Muslim Salah* (Oxford: Oxford Traditional Knowledge Foundation, 2010), 1.
[27]Constance Padwick, *Muslim Devotions: A Study of Prayer-Manuals in Common Use* (London: SPCK, 1961), xxix.

colleagues' understanding of Islam by using the prayers to correct what she perceived to be some common Western misunderstandings of the religion.

One example found in *Muslim Devotions* is an extended discussion of the Muslim understanding of sin. Exhorting the Christian reader to 'look deeper', a call she made throughout the book, Padwick challenged the European notion that 'any sense of personal sinfulness is rare amongst the people of Islam'.[28] She translated excerpts of the prayers that convey a form of worship of penitence that is not dissimilar to the Christian worshipper's sense of herself set in a world of temptation and testing. Critiquing the canon of Christian scholarship of Islam, which claimed that Islam has a purely external conception of sin and salvation, Padwick used the prayers to demonstrate that the popular piety of the manuals alluded to a strong sense of the all-seeing eye of God and an intense interior awareness of human sinfulness.[29] This is just one example of many whereby Padwick's engagement with Muslim prayer equipped her to present a different perspective on the faith of the religious other.

As her study of the Islamic prayers progressed, Padwick began to identify what she described as 'kinships' between Christianity and Islam. These emerge in the headings ascribed to the sections of *Muslim Devotions*. Each chapter contains a careful translation and detailed interpretation of the meanings of the Muslim prayers. However, the sections have titles that are highly suggestive of Christian themes: 'the broken and contrite heart', 'the forgiveness of sins' and 'answers to prayer' are three such examples. Through her chapter headings Padwick sought to challenge the notion widely held by Christian students of Islam that Muslim prayer was first and foremost a series of set prayers learnt by heart and recited corporately. Padwick used the prayer books to expose the world of private devotional Muslim prayer, which highlighted the extent to which the Muslim faithful grappled with the same issues in their relationship with the Divine as the Christian. What was the role of intercessory prayer? How did God forgive sins? How does the believer make herself right with God?

Padwick also used language to highlight these areas of kinship. She showed how the same Arabic phrases were used to express praise and worship in Christianity as in Islam. She selected prayers of praise, *tasbih* to illustrate the relationship. The prayer entitled *Tasbih Subhana 'llah,* meaning 'I proclaim the glory of God', lies at the heart of the Muslim praise of God. Padwick observed that Arabic Christians use the same word to praise God.

---

[28]Padwick, *Muslim Devotions*, 174.
[29]Padwick, *Muslim Devotions,* 174.

The same is true for the words used to describe God's holiness *taqdīs*. It is related in both religions to *Tasbīh*, praise, and is the name given in the Arabic translation of the trisagion of the Greek Orthodox Liturgy. The Christian form of the *taqdīs* is 'Holy God, Holy Strong One, Holy Immortal One' and echoes the Muslim equivalent Padwick found in the manuals: *Subbuh, quddūs, rabb, 'l-mala'likati wa 'r-ruhī-r*. Most glorious, most transcendent, Lord of the Angels and the Spirit'.[30]

Padwick's study of Muslim prayer not only developed her understanding of Islam, it also had implications for her own Christian prayer. Here, Padwick was influenced in part by two French Roman Catholic theologians and scholars of Islam: Louis Massignon, who in turn directed her to the contemplative priest and writer, Charles de Foucauld.

Padwick and Massignon were contemporaries who met through their shared interest in the Middle East. Their paths crossed a number of times in Cairo and in Paris. They first met when Padwick visited Massignon in Paris to elicit his assistance in translating the works of the thirteenth-century Spanish Franciscan Raymond Lull. Padwick and Massignon became regular correspondents sharing their experiences of working in the Middle East.

Massignon modelled the idea that engagement with another religious tradition could inspire an awakening of one's own faith. He attributed his own re-conversion to Roman Catholicism to the prayers of Muslims. Massignon believed that his studies of Islam had shown him something of the Transcendent, which through the intercession of Muslims had been made immanent and real for him in Jesus Christ.[31] Building on this experience, Massignon argued that prayer and devotion could be an important channel for Christian engagement with Islam. He reasoned that the faith of the church could be strengthened through its interaction with Islam. Rather than suggesting that people of different religious faiths should pray together, Massignon was interested in how the prayers of one might inspire and deepen the spiritual life of the other.

This work led to Massignon's establishment of the Christian sodality the *Badaliya* in 1934. The group's name was taken from *badal*, meaning 'acceptance of the suffering of another'. Members of the *Badaliya* believed in the power of one person's mystical substitution for the sinfulness of another. They justified this approach by drawing on biblical models of this exemplified in Moses, the Suffering Servant of Isaiah and the Incarnate Word. The *Badaliya* took it upon themselves to pray, fast and perform acts of charity on behalf

---

[30]Padwick, *Muslim Devotions*, 66.
[31]For more on Louis Massignon, see Anthony O'Mahony, 'Louis Massignon, the Melkite Church and Islam', *ARAM* 20 (2008): 269–97.

of Muslims. The justification was subtle; this was not in anticipation of an 'external conversion' from Islam to Christianity, where Muslims would ask to be baptized and turn to the church for religious instruction. Massignon's understanding of these prayers encapsulated the idea that salvation does not automatically entail conversion; he emphasized that the group in no way aimed at the external conversion of their non-Christian friends. Rather, it asked them to deepen their current denominational position through an internal conversion. The subtleties of the justification notwithstanding, it did have evangelistic connotations: it stemmed from a belief that the prayers of the members of the *Badaliya* could elicit a deeper move by Muslims to faith in God and eventually lead, internally, to a turning to Christ.[32]

Massignon described Islam as the 'provocateur' of Christianity, because he believed that Islam could serve as the summons and conscience of Christianity. He described Islam as *'le signe Marial'*: 'like the lance of an angel piercing the side of Christianity'.[33] Massignon argued that if Islam served to hold Christianity to account, by encouraging Christians to pray, a case could be made for a bolder Christian presence amidst Islam, because it would benefit Christianity spiritually (as Christians were encouraged to pray more) as well as Islam (as Muslims benefitted from the substitutionary prayers of Christians). Christianity in the Muslim world would become a praying, spiritual presence rather than an explicitly evangelistic presence.

Massignon's description of the way in which he believed the prayers of the religious other could 'provoke' the believer to greater holiness directed Padwick to the work of Charles de Foucauld. Charles de Foucauld has been described as the 'contemplative apostle'. Through his missionary practice he exemplified the idea of prayer and the Eucharist as forms of Christian witness. Similar to Massignon, de Foucauld ascribed his return to Roman Catholicism to his engagement with Muslim prayer. Describing how 'Islam produced in me a profound "over-turning (*boulversement*)"', de Foucauld recalled how the sight of Muslims at prayer, in adoration of the Divine Transcendent, had a profound effect on him.[34]

Charles de Foucauld thus developed a mission of presence whereby humanity was represented before God in prayer. The duty of Christian witness, de Foucauld argued, was complete surrender to Jesus in order to

[32]Anthony O'Mahony, 'Our Common Fidelity to Abraham is What Divides', in *Catholics in Interreligious Dialogue*, ed. Anthony O'Mahony and Peter Bowe (Leominster: Gracewing, 2006), 151–90.

[33]An interview with Louis Massignon, 'Le Signe marial', *Rythmes du monde* 3 (1948–9): 7–16.

[34]Charles de Foucauld, *Lettres à Henri de Castries: Présentées avec une introduction par Jacques de Dampierre*, ed. Jacques de Dampierre (Paris: Grasset, 1938).

make him present: 'My work is first and foremost to make Jesus present amongst them, Jesus who is present in the Holy Sacrament, who descends among us every day in the holy sacrifice.'[35]

Inspired by her engagement with de Foucauld and with Massignon, Padwick developed a missionary approach that proposed strengthening, supporting and endorsing the presence of indigenous Christian communities already present in the Muslim world, whilst encouraging missionaries to become what she called 'Presence bearers'. In an article written in 1938 she articulated this new approach:

> The present writer longs to see praying Orders established alongside of and in union with active mission work in all Muslim lands, their aim to pray in unison with the prayer of the Priest upon his Throne above, to win the battle against the principalities and powers of the invisible world, to create the atmosphere in which the message can be given and received.[36]

Padwick proposed that the Christian missionary move from preaching the Word to 'being' the word by establishing a praying Christian presence in the Muslim world. Like Massignon, she suggested that Christians were called to bear Christ to Muslims until the time Christ might become real for them. Echoing de Foucauld she called for a 'preparation of prayer' an exhortation to Christian missionaries to work, not at instructing Muslims in the Christian faith, but rather to prepare for it through an exemplary life of prayer.

Through her changing ideas about the priorities for mission, brought about by her study of Islam and of the work of other scholars of Islam, Padwick experienced a call to more Christian prayer. Her writing in later life testifies to this 'conversion' in her own spiritual life as she found herself moving away from the Protestant Evangelical tradition of the Church Mission Society towards the contemplative tradition of Roman Catholic spirituality.

Padwick's engagement with Muslim prayer was conducted in the specific context of the work of an Anglican missionary to Islam in the early twentieth century. As far as is known, Padwick never prayed *with* Muslims, but what is certain is that through her engagement with the prayers of a different religion Padwick experienced 'provocation', both in her understanding of that religion and in the deepening and development of her prayer life, which inspired a 'conversion' in her own Christian spiritual life.

---

[35]Charles de Foucauld, *Écrits Spirituels* (Paris: J. de Gigord, 1923), 254.
[36]Constance Padwick, 'North African Reverie', *The International Review of Missions* 27, no. 3 (1938): 341–54 (352).

Conclusion

The idea of 'bouleversement', the re-igniting of a dormant faith or 'conversion' due to a spiritual encounter with the religious other (whether directly or indirectly) links the experiences of de Foucauld, Massignon and Padwick. Each of them had a sense that their Christian life had been enriched by their encounter with Islam.

This experience and Padwick's call to Christian presence are represented more recently in the example of the French Trappist monk Christian de Chergé and the community he led in the late 1990s in Tibhirine, a village an hour and half inland from Algiers. Like Padwick, de Chergé was inspired by de Foucauld's approach. From 1972 to 1996 Christian de Chergé was the prior of this small monastery in rural Algeria. For decades the monks enjoyed a close relationship with the local Muslim community by developing a strong sense of mutual affection based on their commitment to God, mutual help and hospitality. The life of the community came to a brutal end on 27 March 1996, when seven of the monks were kidnapped and murdered during the Algerian Civil War.[37] However, their legacy lives on as an example of the kind of community which Timothy Wright believes is critical to future peace – a community engaged in a dialogue of spirituality through the experience of witnessing one another's prayers and daily living.

In an account of the life and work of Christian de Chergé Christian Salenson writes: 'Both the Muslim and the Christian are called to prayer, whether by muezzin or bell. When the sound is heard, de Chergé recognises he cannot remain indifferent: "On the contrary they provoke me to engage in prayer" ... for de Chergé "the calls to prayer establish between us [Muslims and Christians] a healthy reciprocal emulation."'[38]

****

Sitting in the sanctuary of Epiphany listening to the bells peal and the Muslim call to prayer reminds me of de Chergé's experience. I see 200 Muslims on their knees in prayer in my church and my response is one of being 'provoked' not to join in their prayers, but to take a step further on my own journey of prayer and discovery of myself in relation to God and the other.

This is the goal of prayer in the context of inter-religious dialogue: that the believer finds herself provoked to pray and to a deeper understanding

---

[37]The life and brutal end of this Trappist Community has been vividly portrayed in the film *Of Gods and Men.*
[38]Christian Salenson, *Christian de Cherge: A Theology of Hope,* trans. Nada Conic (Collegeville, MN: Liturgical Press, 2012), 182.

of the religious other.[39] The echoes or 'kinships' perceived through this engagement will not only open her eyes to the religion of the other but also elicit a deeper commitment to her own prayers and devotions. As a result of witnessing and studying prayers that are not her own, the believer is inspired to go and pray her own prayers.

---

[39]This was the theme that pervaded the 2013 gathering of the Building Bridges Seminar, an annual three-day gathering of Muslim and Christian scholars from across the world. They met to discuss Christian and Muslim perspectives on prayer. Joint Christian-Muslim prayer was not organized, but there were opportunities for Christians to attend Muslim devotions and vice versa. The resulting publication offers a series of rich accounts from Muslims and Christians about how they understand prayer, how they practise prayer, how they go deeper in prayer and how prayer shapes them. For an account of the 2013 Building Bridges Seminar, see *Prayer: Christian and Muslim Perspectives*.

CHAPTER THIRTY-ONE

Prayer: An Orthodox Perspective

ANDREW LOUTH

Any Christian understanding of prayer must begin with the prayer of Christ, meaning by that both the prayer of Jesus as we see it in the Gospels and the way in which the prayer of the Christian church, as well as the prayer of the individual Christian, is fundamentally to be regarded as Christ's own prayer.

Throughout the Gospels, Jesus is shown as a man of prayer. He rises early and prays (Mk 1.35); on one striking occasion, we are told that the Lord went up into a mountain to pray at night, while his disciples crossed the Lake of Galilee and got caught in a storm; just before dawn the Lord appeared to his disciples on the water and dismissed the storm (Mt. 14.23-33; Mk 4.35-41; Jn 6.15-21). These were not occasional events. The impression given is that this was his way of life. Luke, in particular, mentions the Lord as praying at the time of his baptism (Lk. 3.21) and at the Transfiguration (Lk. 9.28). Jesus teaches his disciples to pray, and gives them the Lord's Prayer, the 'Our Father' (Mt. 6.7-13; Lk. 11.1-4). Finally, before his passion, the Lord prays in the Garden of Gethsemane (Mt. 26.36-46; Mk 14.32-42; Lk. 22.40-46). In drawing attention to the prayer of Christ, the Evangelists are drawing attention to his humanity, for prayer is how human beings relate to God. The human-ness of Christ is perhaps especially manifest in the prayer of the agony in Gethsemane: 'Abba, Father, all things are possible to you. Let this cup pass from me. Nevertheless, not what I will, but what you will' (Mk 14.36). It is interesting to note, in passing, how close a parallel Luke sees between the prayer of the agony and the Lord's Prayer: addressing God as simply 'Father', as in the Lucan version of the Lord's Prayer, twice exhorting the disciples to prayer against entering temptation (the closing petition of Luke's 'Our Father') and the echo of 'Your will be done' (a strongly attested reading in Luke's version) in the Lord's prayer in the Garden. But even in the Gospel accounts, Jesus is manifest as not simply human: not in the sense of being super-human, but as one to whom we are to relate *as God*. The most obvious places are the occasion in Matthew's Gospel, where Jesus turns from prayer to his Father, and turns to – well, it is not exactly clear whom, and that may be the point – saying, 'Come to me all who labour and are burdened, and I will give you rest. Take my yoke on you and learn of me, because I am gentle and humble of heart, and you will find rest for your souls; for my yoke is easy and my burden is light' (Mt. 11.28-30), and the account of the Transfiguration, where the Lord appears transfigured in glory (Mt. 17.1-8; Mk 9.2-8; Lk. 9.28-36). The account of the Transfiguration – like the account of the Baptism of Christ, 'where the worship of the Trinity was made manifest' (as one of the liturgical verses for the Theophany puts it) – reveals the Lord declared to be the 'Son' of the Father. Here we find adumbrated the idea that Jesus unites in himself sonship in two ways – as 'Son of man', understood by the Fathers to mean 'one among human sons', and 'Son of God', begotten by the Father. It is further developed in the fourth Gospel: there the Lord is the Son of the Father, sent into the world. Here in the world, we can enfold our prayer in his, but at the same time, he is one who manifests the Father (Jn 14.9), and to whom the disciples and first of all his own mother (Jn 2.5) turn in prayer, finally and openly in the Apostle Thomas' exclamation, 'My Lord and my God' (Jn 20.28). Furthermore, John makes it explicit – especially in the great high priestly prayer of John 17 – that, both as Son among human children and as Son of the Father, this sonship is manifest in prayer. Jesus is then presented as the one to whom we pray – as God the Son, within the life of the Trinity, as well as one in whose prayers ours can be enfolded – as man.

Such reflection on the Gospels has taken us a long way: to the notion of Jesus' prayer as expressing his relationship as Son to the Father, as well as expressing the way in which our own attempts at praying are reflections of Jesus' own prayer, so that as we pray, our own prayer, in some mysterious way, leads us into the life of the triune God. In some parts of the New Testament this trinitarian dimension is made quite explicit. In the 'last discourses' of John's Gospel, for instance, in which Jesus speaks of the Spirit, the Paraclete – 'the Paraclete whom I will send you from the Father, the spirit of truth who proceeds from the Father' (Jn 15.26) – whose coming will draw the disciples in the mutual abiding expressed in Jesus' prayer to the Father. The trinitarian dimension of Christian prayer is also clear in the

Apostle Paul's letters, when, for instance, he speaks of receiving 'the Spirit of adoption in which we cry, "Abba, Father", as the Spirit bears witness together with our spirit that we are children of God' (Rom. 8.15-16).

Another line we might pursue in seeking to understand the nature of Christian prayer involves reflecting on who Jesus was, who he thought himself to be. There are plenty of ways of thinking of him that are to hand in the scriptures: teacher, preacher, philosopher, prophet, priest, sacrifice. But there are two ways Jesus gave his disciples by which he wanted to be remembered: when the disciples asked him how to pray, he gave them the Lord's Prayer, the 'Our Father'; and on the night before he suffered, he asked his disciples to remember him by gathering together to break bread and share wine, receiving them as his body and blood. Had Jesus presented himself as a philosopher, we would naturally have looked to him for teaching on the nature of God and his relationship to the world, the nature of divine providence and so on. Had Jesus presented himself primarily as a moral teacher, we would not be surprised if his notion of God turned on how God is a source of moral values, moral commandments and so on. But the ways Jesus wanted his disciples to remember him seem to point to a different understanding of God, not as some philosophical principle, metaphysical or moral, but rather as mystery approached in prayer. The Lord's Prayer first and foremost teaches us that God is the One to whom we pray; we call him 'Father'; we are his children, his sons and daughters.

The Lord's Prayer is said or sung at all the services of the Orthodox Church. It has its place at the very heart of the Divine Liturgy: leading into the receiving of Holy Communion in the Body and Blood of Christ, and itself following the Eucharistic Prayer, the Anaphora ('Offering'), in which we celebrate the mysterious reality of God, give thanks to him for all that he has given us 'known and unknown, manifest and hidden', call upon the Holy Spirit to come upon us and the gifts of bread and wine and transform them into the Holy Body and Blood of Christ, and then, in Christ's very presence, beseech him for the church and the world. It is the church's prayer *par excellence*. If God is the one to whom we pray, it is a natural question to ask: How do we speak about God in the central prayer of the Divine Liturgy? The Eucharistic Prayer used most frequently in the Orthodox Liturgy, the Anaphora of St John Chrysostom, begins thus:

> It is right and fitting to hymn you, to bless you, to praise you, to give you thanks, to worship you in every place of your dominion; for you are God, ineffable, incomprehensible, invisible, inconceivable, ever existing, eternally the same, you and your only-begotten Son and your Holy Spirit; You brought us out of non-existence into being, and when we had fallen

you raised us up again, and left nothing undone until you have brought us up to heaven and granted us your Kingdom that is to come.

For all these things we give thanks to you, and to your only-begotten Son and your Holy Spirit; for all the benefits that we have received, known and unknown, manifest and hidden.

We thank you also for this liturgy which you have been pleased to accept from our hands, though there stand around you thousands of archangels and tens of thousands of angels, the cherubim and the seraphim, six-winged and many-eyed, soaring aloft upon their wings, singing, crying, shouting the triumphal hymn, and saying:

Holy, holy, holy, Lord of Sabaoth; heaven and earth are full of your glory. Hosanna in the highest. Blessed is he who comes in the name of the Lord. Hosanna in the highest.

We stand before God and worship him, addressing him as Trinity: the Father manifest through the Son and in the Holy Spirit. The prayer continues, evoking Isaiah's vision in the Temple (Isa. 6) of the worship of God by the angelic powers of heaven. After joining our song with the song of the celestial power in the *Sanctus*, the prayer continues:

With these blessed Powers, Master, Lover of mankind, we also cry aloud and say: Holy are you and all-holy, you and your only-begotten Son and your Holy Spirit, and magnificent is your glory. This is how you loved your world: you gave your only-begotten Son, so that whoever believes in him might not perish, but have eternal life.[1]

What this prayer teaches and exemplifies is that we stand before God, taking from his own revelation the words and phrases with which we address him. We address him as he has revealed himself – in mystery and majesty, beyond any human conception – and also as Father, Son and Holy Spirit, again expressed in words and phrases drawn from the scriptures themselves. What the scriptures have given us is a way of addressing God, a way that matches something of the glory of his nature, but not a way of defining him.

It is something like this that St Maximos the Confessor develops in his short treatise on the *Our Father*. The petitions of the Lord's Prayer constitute a theology, but it is theology of a special kind. As Maximos puts it:

For hidden within a limited compass this prayer contains the whole purpose and aim of which we have just spoken [namely, the divine counsel

---

[1] *The Divine Liturgy of St John Chrysostom* (Oxford: Oxford University Press, 1995).

whose purpose is the deification of our nature]. ... The prayer includes petitions for everything that the divine Word effected through His self-emptying in the Incarnation, and it teaches us to strive for those blessings of which the true provider is God the Father alone through the natural mediation of the Son in the Holy Spirit.[2]

Maximos goes on to discuss the seven mysteries contained in the prayer: 'theology, adoption of sons by grace, equality with the angels, participation in eternal life, the restoration of human nature ..., the abolition of the law of sin, and the destruction of the tyranny ... of the evil one'.[3] These are not just mysteries to ponder, still less to solve; they are mysteries that draw us into communion with God. They reveal the mystery of the Trinity (which is what Maximos, following normal patristic use, means by 'theology', θεολογία) and that this opens up to us the possibility of adoption as sons and daughters in the Son, Christ. This state of adoption grants us equality with the angels ('on earth, as in heaven'). We participate in the divine life through making Christ himself our food, pre-eminently in the Holy Eucharist. Human nature is restored to itself; for humanity has been fragmented by the Fall, we are separated from one another, opposed to each other – restoration takes place through forgiveness ('forgive us our debts, as we forgive our debtors'). But life on earth remains a constant struggle against evil; we recognize this as we pray for deliverance from temptation. And we seek deliverance from the power of the evil one. Because these mysteries are about our transformation into God, deification, they are presented to us in the Lord's Prayer as petitions, expressions of our desire, or perhaps better, to use a phrase of Thomas Aquinas which defines prayer (*petitio*) as interpreting our desire: *desiderii interpres*.[4] Maximos sees this desire as a response to God's love for us, in particular, God's love for us manifest in the incarnation and self-emptying of the Son of God, and a response that demands of us a similar self-emptying. 'Moreover, by emptying themselves of the passions they lay hold of the divine to the same degree as that to which, deliberately emptying Himself of his own sublime glory, the Word of God truly became man.'[5]

Both these approaches – looking at what we know about the prayer of Christ himself and looking at the ways in which Jesus enjoined his disciples

---

[2]Maximos the Confessor, *Expositio orationis dominicanae* (CCSG 23); *The Philokalia: The Complete Text – Volume 2*, trans. G. E. H. Palmer, Philip Sherrard and Kallistos Ware (London: Farrar, Straus and Giroux, 1981) – hereafter: *On the Lord's Prayer*.
[3]The passage summarized from Maximos' commentary on the Lord's Prayer can be found *The Philokalia*, 286–90.
[4]Aquinas, *ST* II-II, q. 83. a. 1, ad. 1.
[5]Maximos, *On the Lord's Prayer*, 287.

to remember him – lead in the same direction: towards an understanding, not just of prayer, but of the pre-eminence of prayer, for it is in prayer that we begin to grasp something of the mystery of God as the one to whom we pray.[6] This might seem a somewhat roundabout way of trying to express something of the understanding of prayer in the Orthodox tradition, but I have taken it because we shall understand nothing about the Orthodox attitude to prayer, if we have not grasped the essential entailment of this approach, namely, that God is no object of thought, no concept, nothing that we can deploy in our human attempts to make sense of the world and our lives, but rather one to whom we pray: the mystery that evokes an aboriginal perception that at the heart of being human is a sense that there is one whom we can beseech, and 'this we call God', to adopt the conclusion of each of Aquinas' five ways.[7]

So, to be human is to pray, and what does that mean? To beseech God: for what? Ultimately to beseech God to draw us into union with him: something we have already encountered in our brief discussion of St Maximos the Confessor's treatise on the *Our Father*. To pray is to open ourselves to a relationship in which we shall be transformed. Pondering on this leads us in several directions.

First of all, the Lord's Prayer begins '*Our* Father'. We address God as Christians together with other Christians; we do not say 'my Father', though, in Christ, he is uniquely the Father of each one of us. St Maria of Paris (Mother Maria Skobtsova) comments on this:

> Thus what is most personal, what is most intimate in an Orthodox person's life, is thoroughly pervaded by this sense of being united with everyone, the sense of the principle of *sobornost'*, characteristic of the Orthodox Church. This is a fact of great significance; this forces us to reflect.[8]

Sobornost' – a noun coined in Slavophil circles in the nineteenth century from *soborny*, the word used to translate καθολικός in the Slavonic version of the creed, meaning something like an integral togetherness – neither individualism nor an imposed uniformity – that characterizes what it is to be Christian in Orthodox understanding, so that there are no 'individual' Christians, cut off from one another, but only Christians as forming the

---

[6]My treatment so far re-works material from my book, *Introducing Eastern Orthodox Theology* (London: SPCK, 2013), chapters 4 and 2, especially 55–7, 16–21.

[7]Aquinas, *ST* I, q. 2, a. 3, resp.

[8]Mother Maria Skobtsova, 'The Second Gospel Commandment', in *Mother Maria Skobtsova: Essential Writings*, trans. Richard Pevear and Larissa Volokhonsky (Maryknoll, NY: Orbis Books, 2003), 45–60 (47).

church, bound up with one another and bound up with one another through mutual prayer. As Alexei Khomiakov, who created the concept, if not the word, *sobornost'*, says:

> we know that when any one of us falls, he falls alone; but no one is saved alone. He who is saved is saved in the Church, as a member of her, and in unity with all her other members. If anyone believes, he is in the communion of faith; if he loves, he is in the communion of love; if he prays, he is the communion of prayer. Wherefore no one can rest his hope on his own prayers, and everyone who prays asks the whole Church for intercession, not as if he had any doubts about the intercession of Christ, the one Advocate, but in the assurance that the whole Church ever prays for all her members.[9]

This sense of the church as a community in which all her members find their identity is reaffirmed in the Eucharist: the other way in which Jesus wished to be remembered. The Eucharist (or the Divine Liturgy, as the Orthodox call it) is essentially a service of the whole church; unlike the West, there has never developed the idea of a 'private mass', celebrated by a priest alone (or with just a server) – the Divine Liturgy is a service in which all participate. In what is still a fundamentally important work on the liturgy, *The Shape of the Liturgy*, Gregory Dix had this to say:

> The unity (rather than 'union') of the church's eucharist with the sacrifice of Christ by Himself is one consequence of the general pre-Nicene insistence on the unity of Christ with the church, of the Head with the members, in one indivisible organism. ... The church corporately, through the individual offertory by each member for himself or herself personally, offers itself to God at the offertory under the forms of bread and wine, as Christ offered Himself, a pledged Victim to the Father at the last supper. The Body of Christ, the church, offers itself to *become* the sacrificed Body of Christ, the sacrament, in order that thereby the church itself may become within time what in eternal reality it is before God – the 'fulness' or 'fulfilment' of Christ; and each of the redeemed may 'become' what he has been made by baptism and confirmation, a living member of Christ's Body. ... As Augustine was never tired of repeating to his African parishioners in his sermons, 'So the Lord willed to impart His Body, and

---

[9]Aleksei Stepanovich Khomiakov, *The Church is One* (London: Fellowship of St Alban and St Sergius, 1968), 38–9.

His Blood which He shed for the remission of sins. If you have received well, you *are* that which you have received'. 'Your mystery is laid on the table of the Lord, your mystery you receive. To that which you are you answer "Amen", and in answering you assent. For you hear the words "the Body of Christ" and you answer "Amen". Be a member of the Body of Christ that the Amen may be true.'[10]

There are several points made by Dix that need underlining. First, this paragraph opens a section called 'The Eucharist in Action', for it is an important point, frequently made by Dix, that the Eucharist is not primarily a set of words, a text, but rather an *action*. So far as we know, in the early centuries there was no 'text' of the Eucharistic Prayer. The bishop (or priest) prayed extempore; insofar as anything was settled, it was the *action* of the Eucharist, the action that Dix sought to elucidate (perhaps in an over-prescriptive manner) in the book he significantly called *The Shape of the Liturgy*. This, secondly, leads on to the question: Whose action? Who is it who acts in the Liturgy? The quotation from Dix makes it clear that it is Christ himself; the church and its members share in this action insofar as they are caught up by Christ in his action. *Corpus Christi*, the body of Christ, means both the body of Jesus that was sacrificed on the cross and rose from the dead *and* the church as the body of Christ, of which Christ is the head. Dix remarks, 'The unity of Christ and the church is not something achieved (though it is intensified) in communion; it underlies the whole action from start to finish.'[11] There is an interplay, amounting almost to identity, between the two meanings of the Body of Christ: 'As the *anamnesis* of the passion, the eucharist is perpetually *creative* of the church, which is the fruit of the passion.'[12]

The liturgical mystery is, then, an action: an action performed by *Christ*. This is stated quite explicitly in the Divine Liturgy, when the priest says in the prayer before the Great Entrance (the prayer of the Cherubic Hymn):

Do not turn away your face from me, nor reject me from among your children, but count me, your sinful and unworthy servant, worthy to offer these gifts to you. *For you are the one who offers and is offered, who receives and is distributed, Christ our God.*[13]

---

[10]Gregory Dix, *The Shape of the Liturgy* (London: Dacre Press, 1945), 247.

[11]Dix, *The Shape of the Liturgy*, 247.

[12]Dix, *The Shape of the Liturgy*, 248.

[13]*The Divine Liturgy of St John Chrysostom*, 23; emphasis mine.

The whole action of the Eucharist is performed by Christ: he offers, and is what is offered, he receives the offering and is distributed to the faithful as the Holy Gifts. The consequence of this is that the community that forms the church is not a gathering together of like-minded souls; the community of the church, its *sobornost'*, is created by Christ, and this is reflected in the Eucharist as Christ's action – every aspect of it – and in the entailment of this that our prayer is always the prayer of the community of the church, or, more precisely, the prayer of Christ, together with those who belong to him.

There is a further consequence of such a way of understanding the *sobornost'* of the church. One of the earliest – and for the Orthodox East, without doubt one of the most influential – accounts of the Divine Liturgy is that found Dionysios the Areopagite's *Ecclesiastical Hierarchy*. He begins his account by describing the censing of the church at the beginning of the Liturgy:

> For the thearchic blessedness, which transcends all, if it proceeds in divine goodness to communion with the sacred ones who participate in it, yet it never goes outside its essentially unmoved state and foundation, and gives radiance to everyone deiform, each in their measure [ἀναλόγως], being always secure in itself, in no way departing from its proper identity. So too the divine rite of the *synaxis*, although having a unique, simple, and enfolded beginning [or principle: ἀρχή], out of love for human kind is multiplied into a sacred manifold of symbols, reaching out through the whole range of hierarchic depiction of images, but from these gathering them together in a unifying way into its own unity [μονάδα], making those whom it has sacredly raised up to itself one.[14]

For Dionysios, the Eucharist is almost solely an action, in this case the circular motion of censing the church in a way that evokes God's love reaching out from unity into the manifold that is the world, being multiplied into symbols, so that that love can reach throughout the whole cosmos and draw it all back into union with God. Dionysios has very little to say about the words of the prayers made by the hierarch or the songs sung by all present – not that they are not important – but their importance is found in the context of the action of the Divine Liturgy.

Dionysios is famous, too, for his seeing the goal of God's love, manifest in the incarnation (to which he gives the neo-Platonic term *theurgy*, divine action), and celebrated in the Divine Liturgy, as union with God, deification,

---

[14]Dionysius, *De Ecclesiastica Hierarchia* (PTS 36.82.17-83.3), 3.3.3.

θέωσις, and unfolding this process in terms of purification, illumination and perfection. For Dionysios this threefold process is something primarily received by participation in the sacramental mystery of the church, but it was soon (or really: already) applied to the process by which, in prayer, we come closer to God, indeed are assimilated to God, deified.

This does not detract from the emphasis we have found on the primary togetherness of the church, but adds another dimension, that of the life of prayer pursued by each Christian: something that picks up that other aspect of the prayer of Christ, as we find it depicted in the Gospels – his seeking out solitude, especially at night, in order to be with the Father. The corporate prayer of the church needs to be complemented by the personal life of prayer and ascetic struggle undertaken by each Christian. Even in this, the individual is not cut off from the community of the church. The daily prayers each Orthodox Christian is expected to observe are all drawn from the cycle of prayer in the offices performed within the community of the church: the major hours of Vespers and Mattins, and the shorter services performed at the first, third, sixth and ninth hours, together with a short service, after the evening meal and before going to bed, corresponding what is known in the West as compline (*completorium*, the 'completion' of the day's cycle of prayer; in the East: *apodeipnon*, 'after supper'). In the daily office of the Orthodox Church, the day begins with Vespers, in the evening, following the Jewish practice of beginning the day in the evening (see, Genesis 1, where each day is called 'evening and morning', in that order). Each evening we look forward to the coming rising of the sun; vespers begins with Psalm 103/104, which is in praise of creation – as we praise the created order we look forward to the recreation of the cosmos through the resurrection. This eschatological sense is enhanced on Saturday evening, when with vespers we begin the celebration of Sunday, the first, and also the eighth, day of the week: the dawning of the day that looks forward to 'the day without evening of your Kingdom' (ἡ ἀνέσπερος ἡμέρα τῆς βασιλείας σου). This eschatological dimension of prayer is underlined in another way: in the sense in which all prayer takes place in the invocation of the Holy Spirit. It is well known that in the Divine Liturgy the presence of Christ is brought about, not by the priest standing in Christ's place and uttering his words, but by invocation (ἐπίκλησις) of the Holy Spirit, 'whom the Father will send in my name, [for] he will teach you all things and bring all that I have said to you to your remembrance' (Jn 14.26), bringing about Christ's presence. It is through invocation of the Spirit that the church is constituted through the presence of Christ. This – what one might call 'epikletic ecclesiology' – pervades the life and prayer of the church. All services of the church, not least the Divine Liturgy, begin with a prayer to the Holy Spirit. 'Heavenly King, Comforter, Spirit of Truth, present everywhere and filling all things, Treasury of good things and Giver of life, come and abide in us, cleanse us from every stain and, O Good One, save our souls.' This prayer begins the morning and evening prayers of the Orthodox faithful, as well as being a prayer said before any significant activity.

Personal prayer is not easy: the mind is easily distracted; it is only too easy to spend one's prayer time in a state of constant distraction. The first thing it is necessary to learn is something quite obvious: that the person who stands before God is the same as the person who goes about his daily life; there is no other. And the cares and concerns of our daily life invade the time when we seek to bring ourselves before God.

The answer to this is to ensure, as far as possible, that the way we live our lives is consonant with the one we want to be when we stand before God. If we are envious and arrogant, constantly seeking our own way, or empty-minded and easily distracted, then all this will invade our attempts at prayer. If we are to pray, then we need to tackle the way in which we live. Over the centuries, a whole body of wisdom has grown up in the church on which we can draw in our attempts to pray: ways in which we can come to recognize our faults and seek God's grace and mercy to overcome them. But we need not only advice, but some kind of spiritual companionship, which can take many forms. There has continued in the Orthodox Church a tradition of spiritual fatherhood (and, less recognized, spiritual motherhood); through such spiritual fathers (and mothers) one can find, not just the generalized help that spiritual literature inevitably gives, but personal support – guidance and, most important, prayer. Spiritual fathers are often monks, but there are others, married priests and lay people, who can fulfil this role.

There are other ways in which the practice of prayer is enabled within Orthodox practice. Some of these are ancient Christian practices that seem to have fallen into desuetude in the West. In the early church, as we learn, mostly, from surviving treatises on the Lord's Prayer, Christians stood to pray, and faced east, looking towards 'our ancient fatherland', as St Basil the Great put it, looking in the direction from which the Lord's second coming would take place. This underlines two aspects of Christian prayer. First, its eschatological dimension; and secondly, that prayer is performed by the whole person, body and soul – it is not just a 'spiritual' activity (something already manifest in seeing the Eucharist as an action, rather than a gathering together for spiritual comfort).[15]

---

[15]On this dimension of prayer, see Gabriel Bunge, *Earthen Vessels: The Practice of Personal Prayer According to the Patristic Tradition* (San Francisco, CA: Ignatius Press, 2002).

There are two other aspects of personal prayer in the Orthodox tradition that need to be mentioned: icons and the Jesus Prayer, both regarded as distinctively Orthodox, though both increasingly familiar within Western traditions of prayer. It is normal in an Orthodox household for there to be what the Russians call a 'beautiful corner', either facing east (as it should be) though sometimes in the right-hand corner of a room, as one enters it. In the *krasny ugol*, there will be icons, and often a desk bearing the Gospel book and crucifix; also, in one way or another, there will be lamps or candles burning, maybe even incense. It appears to be, and is intended to be, a kind of miniature church, or an evocation of a church building. It helps one to compose oneself for prayer: going and standing before the icons, and making the sign of the cross, one joins with other Christians in praying – such personal prayer is in touch with the prayer of the whole church, not just an individual praying on his or her own. How do the icons 'work'? it might be asked. There are various answers: first and foremost, they 'work' by reminding us that when we pray we are turning towards, even entering, the heavenly courts and finding ourselves in the presence of the saints. Icons, as it were, embody forth the presence of those – Christ, the Mother of God, the Saints – depicted; they recall something that is true, that, in praying, we enter into the company of the saints. This helps us to realize what is simply true: that we are not on our own, but surrounded by a 'cloud of witnesses' (Heb. 12.1), from whom we can draw support and encouragement.

Nevertheless, we are engaged in a spiritual struggle in seeking to follow Christ and come to union with God. The struggle is essential, for our fallen humanity is estranged from God. Although we are created in the image of God, that image has been disfigured and is often barely perceptible. If we are to follow Christ and come to the restoration of the image of God in which we were created, then this will entail change, and change is always painful; it is something that we embark on with reluctance. And again and again – each Lent, Sunday by Sunday, we sing at Mattins this verse: 'Open to me, Giver of Life, the gates of repentance; my spirit rises early in the morning towards your holy temple, bearing the temple of the body, wholly defiled; but, as you are compassionate, cleanse me by your tender mercy.' Again and again, we need to repent, to turn our minds back to Christ; it is a constant struggle. There is, then, for each Christian an ascetic struggle, and this struggle is tested, and furthered, in prayer. The aim of prayer is to stand before God in penitence and attention. One way in which this is spoken of in the Orthodox tradition is to think in terms of prayer of the heart: that is, prayer from the very centre of our being, a centre that, indeed, we need to rediscover, for pulled this way and that in this fallen world, we live, as it were, ec-centrically, not from our true centre, the heart, the place of the image of God, but from an imagined centre of our being, a mask that we have adopted, that we have come to identify ourselves with – a mask that we have thought up, in order to cope with the world of daily living. St Theophan the Recluse, one of the great spiritual Fathers in nineteenth-century Russia, said that 'the principal thing [in prayer] is to stand with the mind in the heart before God, and to go on standing before Him unceasingly day and night, until the end of life'.[16] Over the centuries, the practice of the Jesus Prayer has developed as a way of attaining such prayer of the heart, a prayer rising from our heart, from the centre of our true being. The prayer usually takes this form: 'Lord Jesus Christ, Son of God, have mercy on me, a sinner' (or other similar forms). The origins of the prayer are not entirely clear,[17] but it has come to prominence in the last century or so, largely because of the popularity of a Russian book, generally known in English as, *The Way of a Pilgrim*.[18] As a result of its popularity, the Jesus Prayer, once essentially confined to Orthodox monasticism, is now practised more widely than ever and even among those who are not Orthodox. Normally, the Jesus Prayer is repeated, slowly and attentively, for a good period of time (half-an-hour, upwards), often 'counting' them with a prayer rope (Greek: *komvoschini*, Russian: *chotki*), more as a way of avoiding the distraction of trying to time oneself, often in a sitting position (sometimes kneeling or standing). This quiet and persistent repetition has the intention of driving away distraction, and helping one to focus on God, on Christ. There are several points that need to be made about the Jesus Prayer. First, it is a prayer, addressed to Jesus, seeking his mercy. It is not a mantra; its primary purpose is petition, seeking from Jesus his mercy. The aim of the prayer is to draw our hearts closer to God, to kindle the love of Jesus, of God, in our hearts. It expresses both worship – the exclamation 'Lord Jesus Christ, Son of God' is a cry of love and worship – and repentance, the desire to turn one's life around and follow Christ – 'have mercy on me, a sinner'. This is repeated, because it bears repetition: the simple truth of the prayer can be affirmed again and again. As a prayer

---

[16]Quoted in (then) Timothy Ware, *The Art of Prayer: An Orthodox Anthology* (London: Faber and Faber, 1966), 17.

[17]For a short and accurate account of the history of the Jesus Prayer, see Kallistos Ware, *The Power of the Name: Jesus Prayer in Orthodox Spirituality*, Fairacres Publication 43 (Oxford: SLG Press, 1974).

[18]See the recent translation: *The Way of a Pilgrim: Candid Tales of a Wanderer to His Spiritual Father*, trans. Anna Zaranko (London: Penguin Books, 2017).

to Jesus Christ, it unites us to him, and through him to the whole body of Christians. As Porphyrios put it:

> Pray for others more than for yourself. Say, 'Lord Jesus Christ, have mercy on me', and you will always have others in your mind. We are all children of the same Father; we are all one. And so, when we pray for others, we say, 'Lord Jesus Christ, have mercy on me', and not, 'have mercy on them'. In this way we make them one with ourselves.[19]

---

[19]Porphyrios, *Wounded by Love: The Life and Wisdom of Elder Porphyrios* (Limni of Evia: Denise Harvey, 2005), 132.

CHAPTER THIRTY-TWO

Silence, Breath, Body, Cry: Poetry and Prayer

ELIZABETH S. DODD

The connection between poetry and prayer goes back to the oral roots of the earliest written literature. Ancient epic poems were introduced by an invocation to the gods for inspiration, while prayers have been couched in poetic form from the Hindu Vedas of the fifteenth century BCE, through the Hebrew scriptures to the Greek and Latin hymns of Gregory of Nazianzus and Ambrose, medieval Christian lyrics, Sufi mystical poetry and beyond. The 'songs' of Moses, Miriam, Deborah and Hannah, the Psalms and Lamentations, along with New Testament prayers such as the Magnificat, the Songs of Simeon and Zechariah, and possibly the Lord's Prayer, are testament to the significance of poetic forms of prayer and praise in foundational texts for Christian theology.[1]

---

[1]Modern Christian interpretations of Hebrew poetry remain founded on the work of Robert Lowth, *Lectures on the Sacred Poetry of the Hebrews*, trans. G. Gregory (London: J. Johnson, 1787). See *Lectures* 25–27 on the Hebrew Ode or Psalms and *Lecture* 28 on the Song of Deborah. The status of these texts as poetry has been questioned by James Kügel, *The Idea of Biblical Poetry: Parallelism and Its History* (New Haven, CT: Yale University Press, 1981). On the prayer-poetry of the Dead Sea Scrolls, see Cecilia Wassen, Jeremy Penner and Ken M. Penner, ed., *Prayer and Poetry in the Dead Sea Scrolls and Related Literature* (Leiden: Brill, 2012) and Esther G. Chazon, Ruth Clements and Avital Pinnick, ed., *Liturgical Perspectives: Prayer and Poetry in Light of the Dead Sea Scrolls* (Leiden: Brill, 2003). On the lack of consensus surrounding the poetic forms of the New Testament, see Michael Peppard, '"Poetry", "Hymns" and "Traditional Material" in New Testament Epistles or How to Do Things with Indentations', *Journal of the Study of the New Testament* 30, no. 3 (2008): 319–42 (321). On suggestions for the poetic form of the Lord's Prayer, see Floyd V. Filson, 'How Much of the New Testament Is Poetry?', *Journal of Biblical Literature* 67, no. 2 (1948): 125–34 (128).

Despite this long-standing association, the relationship between poetry and prayer has also been problematic. Passages such as Ezekiel 33.32 and the admonition of Matthew 6.7-8 are suggestive for the ambivalence of Christian reflection on the poetics of prayer, but such tensions have taken a particularly acute form in the modern era. In the 1770s Samuel Johnson charted a fault line between secular and religious language by warning against poetic pretensions to raise the heart in prayer. 'The intercourse between God and the human soul, cannot be poetical. Man, admitted to implore the mercy of his Creator, and plead the merits of his Redeemer, is already in a higher state than poetry can confer.'[2] Johnson's attempt to preserve a veil between poetry and prayer reflected a desire to defend the distinctive sacrality of religious language. A century later, Matthew Arnold's vision of poetry's high calling portended, by contrast, the aestheticizing replacement of prayer by poetry. The attempted revival of religious emotion through prayer-poems such as 'Desire' reflected the predictions of his famous 'Study of Poetry' that 'most of what now passes with us for religion and philosophy will be replaced by poetry'.[3] These trends presaged a competitive jostling for position between theologian and literary critic in the increasingly secular context of the early twentieth-century academy, where poetry and prayer became almost a cipher for the relationship between literature and religion.[4]

In the second half of the twentieth century, trends in modern theology combined with the rise of the field of theology and literature left the door open to a renewed consideration of the kinship between poetry and prayer.[5]

---

[2]Samuel Johnson, 'Life of Waller', in *The Lives of the English Poets* (Frankfurt am Main: Outlook, 2018), 31.

[3]Matthew Arnold, 'Desire' (1849/1855), in *The Poems of Matthew Arnold, 1840–1867*, ed. Arthur Quiller Couch (Oxford: Oxford University Press, 1909), 75–76; Matthew Arnold, 'The Study of Poetry', in T. H. Ward, *The English Poets* (London: Macmillan, 1880–1918), xvii–xlvii (xviii).

[4]Consider, for example, Henri Brémond's influential *Prayer and Poetry: A Contribution to Poetical Theory*, trans. Algar Thorold (London: Burns, Oates and Washbourne, 1927), 187–9, which, in competition with emerging trends in literary criticism, defends the pre-eminence of prayer over poetry, arguing that 'poetic activity [is] a profane, natural sort of preliminary sketch of mystical activity. The poet in the last resort is but an evanescent mystic whose mysticism breaks down'. For a summary of twentieth-century scholarship on poetry and prayer, see Francesca Bugliani Knox, 'Introduction' and David Lonsdale, 'Poetry and Prayer: A Survey of Some Twentieth-Century Studies', in *Poetry and Prayer: The Power of the Word II*, ed. Francesca Bugliani Knox and J. F. Took (Farnham: Ashgate, 2015), 1–16 and 17–39.

[5]See Nathan A. Scott, Jr., 'Poetry and Prayer', *Thought* 14, no. 1 (1966): 61–80. From a literary critical perspective, Jahan Ramazani's study of twentieth-century English language poetry explains this revival of 'the age-old congress between poetry and prayer'. See Jahan Ramazani, *Poetry and Its Others: News, Prayer, Song, and the Dialogue of Genres* (Chicago, IL: Chicago University Press, 2013), 126, 128, 171. For other recent forays into the subject consider, for example, three essays from *CrossCurrents* 62, no. 1 (2012): Eric Caplan, 'Kaplan's Approach to Prayer Appreciated and Challenged'; Rachel Barenblat, 'On Poetry and Prayer'; and Edward Feld, 'Poetry and Prayer'. See also Vittorio Montemaggi, 'Forgiveness, Prayer and the Meaning of Poetry', *Literature Compass* 11, no. 2 (2014): 138–47 and Paul Murray, 'Aquinas on Poetry and Theology', *Logos* 16, no. 2 (2013): 63–72.

Alongside the revival of an Anselmian theology rooted in prayer and a growing interest in the contribution of poetic language to the grammar of God-talk, there has also been an increased literary critical acknowledgement of the religious and spiritual contexts of poetic expression.[6] Such developments make the relationship between poetry and prayer a subject of more than passing interest for contemporary theology. After an overview of key questions, this chapter suggests four ways in which the interrelationship of poetry and prayer might be considered theologically against the background of a representative selection of modern theologians and a reading of Romans 8.14-16 and 26-28. The discussion addresses petitionary practices of prayer as dialogue with God alongside contemplative traditions of prayer as communion or ascent. Consistent with Karl Barth's view of prayer as 'at once word, thought, and life', it takes an interest not just in matters of form, but in connections between poetry and prayer that go beyond words.[7]

'Teach Us to Pray': Poets and Prayer

Can poets teach us to pray?[8] Is prayer a gift of the Spirit alone or is it also an art, craft or discipline?[9] Can poems indeed be prayers?[10] If so, can only 'devotional' or 'religious' poetry be prayerful?[11] At what point does poetry end and prayer begin?[12] These are all questions posed by scholarly discussions of poetry and prayer, which have implications for theological reflection on the subject. Responses may vary in part according to whether what is addressed is the source or end of poetry/prayer, their processes or their verbal form.

---

[6]The theological turn to prayer is also reflected in the work of Karl Barth, Hans Urs von Balthasar, Karl Rahner and, more recently, Mark A. McIntosh and Sarah Coakley among others. The field of theology and literature might be represented by trends emerging out of the 1960s and 1970s such as the work of Amos Wilder and Nathan A. Scott, Jr. in North America and David Jasper, Stephen Prickett and Heather Walton in the UK. The 'sacred turn' in literary studies might be represented by Terry Eagleton, Mark Knight and the Literature and Religion Centre at Lancaster University.

[7]Karl Barth, *Prayer: 50th Anniversary Edition*, trans. Sara F. Terrien (London: Westminster John Knox Press, 2002), 7, x.

[8]Edward Shillito answers in the affirmative in *Poetry and Prayer* (London: SCM Press, 1931).

[9]Ramazani treats prayer as a literary form that is open to appropriation, adaptation, secularization and subversion by the poet. See Ramazani, *Poetry and Its Others*, 126, 128, 171.

[10]On this question, see Roger Nash, *The Poetry of Prayer* (Harleston: Edgeways, 2004), 20; Francis X. McAloon, *The Language of Poetry as a Form of Prayer: The Theo-Poetic Aesthetics of Gerard Manley Hopkins* (Lewiston: Edwin Mellen, 2008), 1–46.

[11]For a defence of the 'religious' poem in a secular age and the similarities between poetry and prayer, see Helen White, *Prayer and Poetry* (Latrobe: Archabbey Press, 1960), 3–24.

[12]See Antonio Spadaro, 'Poetry at the Threshold of Prayer', in *Poetry and Prayer: The Power of the Word II*, ed. Francesca Bugliani Knox and J. F. Took (Farnham: Ashgate, 2015), 57–66.

The idea of a single source for poetry and prayer takes modern theological form in the work of Karl Rahner, for whom their common root is the divine Word that emerges out of silence. This is a theology of poetry founded on Christology, where the connection between the human 'poetic word' and the divine *Logos* both makes prayer possible and makes receptiveness to the poetic a preparatory to faith.[13] An understanding of both prayer and poetry as human words with a divine origin as well as a divine object relates to theological debates about the nature of revelation and its mediation through language. It also has pneumatological implications that resonate with themes in classical poetics. For example, it is easy to see how a Platonist poetics might lead one to connect the in-spiration of the Spirit in prayer with poetic inspiration, making the creative act itself a form of prayer. In his dialogue on Homeric poetry, Plato's Socrates describes the poet as divinely inspired, composing and reciting in a state of spiritual rapture.[14] Flying free from reason, this spiritual state may be equated not only with godliness but also with ecstasy, disorder and even madness. The divine source of prayer and poetry may therefore be connected not only with revelation, but also with a Dionysian power to disrupt and transform.

A focus on the *telos* or purpose of poetry and prayer is more likely to lead to an emphasis on what divides them than what unites them. For example, poetry might be considered as designed for entertainment and set prayers for edification, or poetry might be considered as focused on self-reflection, prayer on dialogue with a divine other.[15] Reflecting Jacques Maritain's distinction between knowledge-seeking religion and creativity-seeking poetry, Jesuit and literary scholar William T. Noon sought to preserve the supernatural object of prayer and resist the absorption of religion by literature by contrasting the faithful commitment characteristic of prayer with the artistic freedom of poetry.[16] Any attempt to establish a strict demarcation between the two may however come up against the layered nature of experience and the testimony of poets regarding their vocation.[17]

---

[13]Karl Rahner, 'Poetry and the Christian', in *Theological Investigations – Volume 4*, trans. Kevin Smyth (London: Darton, Longman and Todd, 1966), 357–67 (364).

[14]'A poet is a light and winged and sacred thing, and is unable ever to indite [compose or recite] until he has been inspired and put out of his senses.' Plato, *Ion* 534b, in *Plato in Twelve Volumes – Volume 9*, trans. W. R. M. Lamb (London: William Heinemann, 1925).

[15]Ramazani characterizes the key differences between poetry and prayer as: 'originality' versus 'convention', 'fictionality' versus 'performativity', 'Self-reflexivity' versus 'self-immolation' and the extent to which the medium is the message, or language is a vehicle for divine encounter. See Ramazani, *Poetry and Its Others*, 130–4, 141.

[16]William T. Noon, *Poetry and Prayer* (New Brunswick, NJ: Rutgers University Press, 1967), 5, 53–4.

[17]Consider, for example, Mary Falk, 'Prayer as Poetry: Poetry as Prayer, a Liturgist's Exploration', in *Feminist Theologies: Legacy and Prospect*, ed. Rosemary Radford Ruether (Minneapolis, MN: Fortress Press, 2007), 139–54.

For example, mystical poets and poet-mystics might highlight the similarities between practices of poetic composition and disciplines of prayer. Mystic and poet Evelyn Underhill saw it as natural that the two vocations should overlap in the figure of 'the articulate mystic' who seeks words to express, however imperfectly, inexpressible experience.[18] Mystical philosopher Simone Weil made an influential contribution to this field through the category of attention, reflecting in *Gravity and Grace* that 'absolutely unmixed attention is prayer. ... The poet produces the beautiful by fixing his attention on something real.'[19] Underhill's discussion of verbal articulation might draw a more straightforward connection between poetic and prayerful practice, but Weil's account of poetic production through a receptive attitude opens up a potentially more fundamental connection between the two.

It might be argued that what matters for the status of a text is less authorial intention or practice than reader response. This is the view of literary critic Käte Hamburger, who concludes that Novalis' *Sacred Songs* number 5 could be heard as poem or prayer depending on the context of performance.[20] For Hamburger the text might be *either* a poem *or* a prayer but not both, but once again the testimony of experience suggests a less dualistic phenomenology. Simone Weil charted the transition of George Herbert's poem 'Love (III)' from an aesthetic to a performative function through the ritual process of recitation, by which it became 'without my knowing it ... a prayer'.[21] A similarly nondualist approach to poetic and sacred texts, albeit much less well articulated, is reflected in the range of popular devotional literature where poems, set prayers and liturgical texts sit alongside each other as an aid or guide to prayer.[22] The ambiguities surrounding reception of texts that

---

[18]Evelyn Underhill, *Mysticism* (London: Methuen, 1911), 83. Consider Underhill's poem 'Invocation' in *Theophanies* (London: J. M. Dent, 1916), 117, as an example of the mystical prayer-poem. On the relationship between poetry and mystical prayer, see Alfred Allen Brockington, *Mysticism and Poetry on a Basis of Experience* (London: Chapman and Hall, 1934), 129–36.

[19]Simone Weil, *Gravity and Grace*, trans. Emma Crawford and Mario von der Ruhr (London: Routledge, 2002), 117–19. This sentiment was echoed by W. H. Auden, *The Complete Works, Prose – Volume 6: 1969–1973*, ed. Edward Mendelson (Princeton, NJ: Princeton University Press, 2015), 235. For a contemporary poet inspired by Weil, see Ed Block, 'Poetry, Attentiveness and Prayer: One Poet's Lesson', *New Blackfriars* 89, no. 1020 (2008): 162–76.

[20]Käte Hamburger, *The Logic of Literature*, 2nd edn (Bloomington, IN: Indiana University Press, 1993), 239–40.

[21]Simone Weil, *Waiting for God*, trans. Emma Craufurd (New York: HarperCollins, 1973), 68–9.

[22]For examples of popular collections of poems and prayers, see John Davey, *The Paradise Tree: Personal Prayer through Poetry* (Durham: Sacristy Press, 2018); Richard Griffiths, *Poetry and Prayer* (London: Continuum, 2005); Nash, *The Poetry of Prayer*; Patricia Thomas, *Poetry and Prayer* (Broadstone: Poppet, 1998); and Robert G. Waldron, *Poetry as Prayer: Thomas Merton* (Boston, MA: Pauline Books and Media, 2000).

may be considered as mystical poetry, secular prayer poetry, a subversive poetic appropriation or even a parody or rejection of prayer are reflected in the criticism that surrounds poems such as Rainer Maria Rilke's *Prayers of a Young Poet* or Paul Celan's 'Radix, Matrix'.[23] Poems may not be all things to all people, but the very latitude of interpretation facilitated by the polyvalent language of poetry complexifies any discussion of its reception as prayer.

A concern not with substance or practice but with verbal form leads to an entirely different conversation. If poetry is considered an aid to prayer, it might be thought the poet's particular purview to find, in S. T. Coleridge's words, 'the *best* words in the best order'.[24] The structures and conventions of invocation, adoration, confession or petition may be considered as outward rhetorical forms that can be employed by the faithful or exploited by the poet.[25] However, the issues raised by form are not reducible to questions of aesthetics alone, nor of liturgical propriety. Debates over the form of prayer often reflect deeper ecclesial and theological principles, as reflected in the disputes between advocates of the prayerbook and extemporary prayer in post-Reformation Britain.[26] Isaac Watts' preference for Hebrew idioms in prayer not only reflects 'the beauty and glory of [the scriptures'] style', but also reveals a particular commitment to scripture as a source of theology. His advocation of moderation in the style of prayer could be considered along the lines of good poetic taste, but also reflects a belief in the power of words not only to express devotion but also to shape it, 'to awaken the holy passions of the soul' and 'to form and perfect the ideas and inclinations

---

[23]On the debate over Rilke's status as poet or mystic, see Rainer Maria Rilke, *Prayers of a Young Poet*, trans. Mark S. Burrows (Brewster, WA: Paraclete Press, 2016), 2. See also the interpretation of Eudo C. Mason in Rilke, *The Book of Hours*, trans. A. L. Peck (London: Hogarth, 1961), 28–9. In his study of Paul Celan, Philippe Lacoue-Labarthe argues that 'every poem is a prayer' in the sense of addressing a (possibly divine) other. Identified in a post onto-theological world as 'no-one', this other who is addressed may also signal both the death of God and the end of prayer. See Philippe Lacoue-Labarthe, *Poetry as Experience*, trans. Andrea Tarnowski (Stanford, CA: Stanford University Press, 1999), 71–86 (84).

[24]S. T. Coleridge, *Table Talk*, ed. J. P. Briscoe (London: Gay and Bird, 1899), 46.

[25]Louis Martz, *The Poetry of Meditation*, rev. edn (New Haven, CT: Yale University Press, 1962), notes the strong influence of structures of prayer and meditation on early-modern metaphysical poetry. Ramazani comprehensively summarizes the formal features of prayer as including: apostrophe, 'intimate address, intercession, adoration, awed colloquy, ritual incantation, solemn petition, anthropomorphism, musical repetition, the language of the Bible'. See Ramazani, *Poetry and Its Others*, 126, 171.

[26]Ramie Targoff's influential study of the development of common prayer in Britain after the Reformation seeks to explore the relationship between authorized forms and extemporary expressivity, arguing that public and private need not be divided and that 'a first-person and subjective poetics emerged out of public devotional practice'. See Ramie Targoff, 'The Poetics of Common Prayer: George Herbert and the Seventeenth-Century Devotional Lyric', *English Literary Renaissance* 29, no. 3 (1999): 468–90 (471).

of our minds'.[27] The long tradition of poetic translations of the Psalms has implications for theological reflection on the beauty of truth and the sacramentality of words. It also illustrates how catechetical teaching, private devotion, public worship and theological reflection can all coincide in poetic forms of prayer.[28] John Donne praised the Psalms as 'the highest matter in the noblest form', implying not only the proper congruence of the two but also their distinction. The Psalms are sung in a 'cloven tongue' and so the relationship between form and substance, between poetry and prayer remains a complex yet fruitful area for exploration.[29]

Difficulty and Desire: 'We Do Not Know How to Pray'

The complex and often problematic interrelationship between poetry and prayer may be interpreted as a reflection of the problem of prayer in general, that is, the tension between the desire for prayer and its difficulty or, in the words of William Cowper:

> What various hindrances we meet
> In coming to a mercy-seat!
> Yet who that knows the worth of pray'r,
> But wishes to be often there?[30]

Karl Barth expressed this paradox in his lectures on the subject, which began with 'the problem of prayer'. Prayer, he argues, is a natural response to God. It is made possible by the presence of God and so is tantamount to a requirement. However, obedience to this command is impossible for sinful

---

[27]Isaac Watts, 'Expression in Prayer', in *A Guide to Prayer*, 10th edn (London, 1753), 71–89.

[28]See Walter Brueggemann and William H. Bellinger, Jr., *Psalms* (Cambridge: Cambridge University Press, 2014), 3–4. For Robert Alter, the Psalms exemplify the crossover between public and private prayer, between cultic ritual and the language of the heart, the conventional language of the former being no barrier to the latter. See Robert Alter, *The Art of Biblical Poetry*, rev. edn (New York: Basic Books, 2011), 139–70. On poetic translations of the Psalms, see the following essays in *The Oxford Handbook of the Psalms*, ed. William P. Brown (Oxford: Oxford University Press, 2014): F. W. Dobbs-Alsopp, 'Poetry of the Psalms', 79–98; Peter S. Hawkins, 'The Psalms in Poetry', 99–113; and Michael Morgan, 'Singing the Psalms', 596–607.

[29]John Donne, 'Upon the Translation of the Psalms by Sir Philip Sidney, and the Countess of Pembroke, His Sister', in *Poems – Volume 1*, ed. E. K. Chambers (London: Lawrence and Bullen, 1896), 188–90.

[30]William Cowper, 'Exhortation to Prayer', *Olney Hymns* (1779), in *Poetical Works*, ed. William Benham (New York: Macmillan, 1893), 2.2.4/29. See also R. L. Stevenson: 'Heed not, I pray Thee, Lord, my breast, / But hear my prayer', 'Prayer', *New Poems* (London: Chatto and Windus, 1918), 1.

humanity without faith, which is only possible through God's grace. This makes prayer both obligatory and entirely dependent upon gift, a paradox expressed in the tension between the exhortation of 1 Thessalonians 5.17 to 'pray without ceasing' and the assertion in Romans 8.26 that we 'do not know how to pray as we ought'.[31]

In *The Poet, The Warrior, The Prophet*, Brazilian liberation theologian and theo-poet Rubem Alves takes this paradox to heart. He reflects on the difficulty of prayer in what he calls a '*Theopoetic*' style, which is itself a poetic and prayerful form that emerges out of and speaks into silence: 'empty word-cages with open doors, with the purpose of creating the void for the Word which cannot be said, but only heard'.[32] Alves' reflections on prayer emerge at the end of a chapter on silence. Through a poetic *reversement* of John 1, Alves writes of the silence out of which the poetic Word is birthed. Human knowledge is a paradoxical forgetting of this silence, a 'state of oblivion'. Describing this fallen state, the passage concludes: '"We do not even know how to pray"'. The quotation marks imbue this phrase with the authority of the scriptural source (Rom. 8.26), but Alves' addition of the word 'even' makes it more emphatic. Not only do we 'not know how to pray as we ought', but we do not know how to pray at all. There is a sense of pathos and incredulity that this most natural of creaturely activities should have been rendered so opaque.[33]

Alves returns to his meditation on prayer in the chapter on 'Words and Flesh'. In the following fragment, he adopts conventions of lineation, rhythm and repetition in a form that is both poetic and semi-liturgical. The use of the first-person plural 'we' and the singular 'Our body' with its ecclesial resonances indicates that this is not a private meditation but something closer to a corporate prayer.

> We dwell in oblivion.
> We don't know how to pray.
> We have forgotten the name of our deepest desire.
> Our sighs are too deep for words.
> Our body speaks in tongues.[34]

Resonating with Romans 8.14-16, which refers to the sharing of the Spirit in the cry, 'Abba Father', prayer for Alves consists not in words alone but

---

[31]For Barth's lectures on the 'problem of prayer', see Barth, *Prayer*, 9–12. See also Ashley Cocksworth, *Karl Barth on Prayer* (London: T&T Clark, 2015), 132.

[32]Rubem Alves, *The Poet, The Warrior, The Prophet* (London: SCM Press, 1990), 99, 17–18.

[33]Alves, *The Poet, The Warrior, The Prophet*, 34.

[34]Alves, *The Poet, The Warrior, The Prophet*, 56.

in the cry of the heart. If prayer articulates 'the name of our deepest desire', then we do not know how to pray because we do not know what we want, what we should pray *for*. We name our deepest desires not through words but through cries: of joy, fear, lament, hope or longing. The forgetting of desire is a forgetting of the wordless cry of infancy. This is a paradox because as we grow in the articulation of speech we become mute in the language of the cry.[35]

The phrase 'Our sighs are too deep for words' is another obvious echo of Romans 8.26. Back in chapter two, Alves misquotes this reference: 'We have forgotten how to speak: signs which are too deep for words, inarticulate groans.'[36] The spoonerism between 'sighs' and 'signs' emphasizes the struggle to find the right words in prayer, but this misquotation also exploits the poetic resonances of the word 'sign'. Referring the reader to the relationship between sign and signified or the way that words point beyond themselves, the sacramentality of language is hereby extended beyond words to wordless sighs and 'inarticulate groans', the noises of breath that point to the presence of the Spirit.

Where words fail the body speaks, and in so doing the body prays. Alves' image of the body as a tongue has a tinge of the ridiculous, but the metaphor of glossolalia here also implies a form of language that goes beyond linguistic understanding.[37] He may be a poet, but Alves is not concerned with the craft of language or the charm of the 'web of words'. He advocates instead a process of 'unlearning' through which humanity learns again to hear the silence, and to speak in the language of breath, body and cry, and so learns again to pray.[38] The following sections explore these deep structures of prayer further through an analysis of silence, breath, body and cry in poetic and theological reflections on prayer.

Silence and Breath: 'Sighs Too Deep for Words'

The poetic relationship between words and silence has clear significance for understandings of contemplative prayer. Poetry and prayer can both be considered, in the words of Thomas Merton, 'raids on the unspeakable', words that reach into the divine silence that stretches beyond them.[39]

---

[35]On the wisdom of cries, see David F. Ford, *Christian Wisdom: Desiring God and Learning in Love* (Cambridge: Cambridge University Press, 2007), 14–51.

[36]Alves, *The Poet, The Warrior, The Prophet*, 34.

[37]For literary critical perspectives on glossolalia, see Harris Feinsod, 'Glossolalia', in *The Princeton Encyclopedia of Poetry and Poetics: Fourth Edition*, ed. Stephen Cushman, Clare Cavanagh, Jahan Ramazani and Paul Rouzer (Princeton, NJ: Princeton University Press, 2012), 572–3.

[38]Alves, *The Poet, The Warrior, The Prophet*, 4, 18.

[39]Thomas Merton, 'Message to Poets', in *Raids on the Unspeakable* (London: Burns and Oates, 1977), 118–24.

Rowan Williams has developed this theme in relation to the contribution of the poetic to theological language. For Williams, the gaps on 'the edge of words' are both the silence into which the poet moves with their world of words and the space at the edge of the page that 'makes form happen'.[40] Silence gives words shape or meaning by providing them with a boundary or frame. Poetry and prayer need not thereby be considered as an aspiration towards divine silence alone, but as words sanctified and empowered by their participation in silence.

In his discussion of this theme, Williams is primarily concerned with the hinterland of speech and writing in silence and the 'white margin'. However, in the oral recitation of poetry it is not the blank white page nor the gap between words that structure a piece, but the movement of breath, guided by punctuation. Williams hints at this possibility when he writes: 'The stillness between words and acts … is what actually keeps speech and thought moving. When we stop thinking/speaking/imaging, there is not so much a void as a plenitude.'[41] In this passage, the spatial landscape of the page intertwines with the phenomenal metaphor of breath. The paradoxical conjunction of void and plenitude, stillness and movement that results opens up a world suggested by Heideggerian poetics, where the void of silence becomes the plenitude of the fertile chaos out of which creation is birthed.[42]

Resonant with the sound of breath, poetic silence is not just the apophatic absence that paradoxically says the unsayable. The gaps on the page, marked by punctuation, express a participation in the Spirit that breathes through humanity as the foundation of speech and the substance of prayer.[43] The regular breathing of silent meditation connects the natural rhythms of the body with the world that surrounds it or, in Wendell Berry's terms, brings one to the place 'where / breathing is prayer'.[44] The poet's creative licence goes beyond nature, exploring the presence of the Spirit in prayer through a playing with breath. For example, Elizabeth Jennings' excessive use of commas in 'A Chorus' is a visual (on the page) and aural (in recitation) cue of the prominence of spiration in both poetic recitation and the practice of prayer:

This spirit, this power, this holder together of space
Is about, is aware, is working in your breathing.[45]

---

[40]Rowan Williams, *The Edge of Words: God and the Habits of Language* (London: Bloomsbury, 2014), 131–5.
[41]Williams, *The Edge of Words*, 167.
[42]Luce Irigaray, *The Forgetting of Air in Martin Heidegger* (London: Athlone, 1999).
[43]See Williams, *The Edge of Words*, 156–85.
[44]Wendell Berry, 'Sabbaths 2001: VI', *Poetry* (2002), 7.
[45]Elizabeth Jennings, 'A Chorus', in *Collected Poems, 1953–1985* (Manchester: Carcanet, 1987), 176.

Through poetry the wind of spiration that is central to prayer is connected with the active presence of the Spirit of in-spiration that indwells human creativity.[46]

A theology of the Spirit as, in Francis de Sales' words, the infinite 'spiration of love' breathed out from Father and Son and in-spired by the human soul also conduces to an understanding of prayer as an ex-piration back to God.[47] English metaphysical poet and Anglican priest Thomas Traherne described praise as a returning of the breath that has been given: 'Praises are the breathings of interior love ... overflowing gratitude, returning benefits, an oblation of the soul.'[48] The poetry of George Herbert provides a good example of this sacrifice of praise because of the way it brings together traditions of set, public liturgical prayer with more expressive practices of personal piety.[49] 'Prayer (I)' is a description of and meditation on prayer. It proceeds through what initially feels like a jumbled series of images, metaphors, conceits and imaginings of what prayer might be, not as a form of words but as an act or a state of being:

The soul in paraphrase, heart in pilgrimage,
The Christian plummet sounding heav'n and earth,

The poem is not ostensibly concerned with verbal prayer but does describe prayer as an exhalation, the sound of breath:

Prayer the Churches banquet, Angels age,
Gods breath in man returning to his birth,

---

[46]Consider the designation of the Spirit as *ruach*, *pneuma* or *spiritus* in the Judaeo-Christian scriptures: words that signify breath, air or wind as well as spirit.

[47]Francis de Sales, *Treatise of the Love of God*, trans. Henry Benedict Mackey (London: Burns and Oates, 1884), chapter 13. See also Aquinas, *ST* I, q. 32, a. 1, for the spiration of the Spirit as the 'procession of love' from the Father which humanity returns in worship.

[48]Thomas Traherne, *Centuries of Meditations*, ed. H. M. Margoliouth (Oxford: Oxford University Press, 1958), III.82; for a contemporary example of poetry described as an exhalation of the soul, compare Hester Pulter (1607–78), 'Poems Breathed Forth' and 'Sighs of a Sad Soul', *Poems, Emblems, and The Unfortunate Florinda*, ed. Alice Eardley (Toronto: Centre for Reformation and Renaissance Studies, 2014).

[49]On the violence and ambiguity of Herbert's poetics of prayer in its combination of courtly, social and devotional discourse, see Michael Schoenfeldt, *Prayer and Power: George Herbert and Renaissance Courtship* (Chicago, IL: University of Chicago Press, 1991), 154–95.

This line expresses a sense of gift, ease and homecoming – of prayer as a giving back to God in praise of the breath that is given. The theme comes again later, but in an altogether different tone:

Engine against th'Almightie, sinners towre,
Reversed thunder, Christ-side-piercing spear,

'Reversed thunder' is the roar of wrath, pain or fear that sends back the lightning bolts of suffering or distress that have been rained down from heaven, straight into the body of God. This sonic shockwave is not however unlike the sigh at the beginning of the poem, an exhalation directed heavenward, a response to the creator from whom comes all life and breath.

The regular breath rhythms in this poem echo those of public forms of poetic prayer, where the shared rhythm of breath sets the pace. The custom when reciting the Psalms of taking a shared breath at the end of each line or pair of lines is echoed in the rhythm of Herbert's 'Prayer (I)', which is a single sentence sonnet. It progresses through the natural speech rhythms of iambic pentameter, with a comma at the end of each line and frequently a caesura in the middle.[50] This creates a regular rhythm interspersed by breath, giving the sense of a poem infused by the breath of the Spirit.[51] Breath is the raw material of poetic recitation, without which no sound would be heard. Every utterance is preceded by a breath, a gasp that brings words to birth, the rushing of the tide that signals the wave. Breath gives poetry shape, structure, rhythm and energy. It also provides space for contemplation and the emergence of conceptual understanding. Breath is an echo of the divine name. In this way, the in-spiration and ex-piration of poetic recitation can become an echo of the Spirit's 'sighs too deep for words'.

Body: Speaking in Gestures[52]

In the first volume of her systematic theology, Sarah Coakley advocates a theology 'purified in the crucible of prayer'.[53] She adopts a trinitarian theology of prayer that begins with pneumatology and takes seriously the erotic aspect of spiritual desire.[54] Following contemplative traditions,

---

[50]Apart from the end of line 8, which is a semi-colon. See George Herbert, 'Prayer (I)', *The Temple: Sacred Poems and Private Ejaculations* (Cambridge: Cambridge University Press, 1633), 43.

[51]'A Wreath' adopts a similar rhythm to depict Herbert's prayer-poetry as 'a crown of praise'. See Herbert, 'A Wreath', *The Temple*, 179.

[52]See Denise Levertov, 'The Prayer Plant (or Maranta Leuconeura)', in *Sands of the Well* (New York: New Directions, 1994), 119, line 4.

[53]Sarah Coakley, *God, Sexuality, and the Self: An Essay 'On the Trinity'* (Cambridge: Cambridge University Press, 2013), 2.

[54]Coakley, *God, Sexuality, and the Self*, 6, 13–14, 16.

Coakley defines prayer as 'commitment to the discipline of *particular* graced bodily practices which, over the long haul, afford certain distinctive ways of knowing'.[55] Interestingly Coakley does not mention poetry in this volume, but the passionate desire expressed by contemplative poets such as Teresa of Avila and John of the Cross is of undoubted influence on her work.

The Anglo-American Roman Catholic Denise Levertov's poetic meditation on desire and the body, 'The Prayer Plant (or Maranta Leuconeura)', provides a case study in the poetic implications of Coakley's contemplative theology of prayer. The prayer plant is a common houseplant native to Brazil, so called because when night falls its flat oval leaves lift up and close as if like hands raised in prayer. John Damascene defined prayer as the raising of mind or heart to God, a movement imaged by the raising of the leaves.[56] Often prayer plant leaves do not touch completely, raised in an open gesture of adoration as in charismatic worship or in the *orans* posture of Eastern Orthodox tradition, but Levertov uses the word 'fold' to describe it, implying the closed hands of Western piety. The act of folding knees and raising hands is a regular contemplative discipline, just as the prayer plant raises its leaves every evening, following its body clock. As an analogy for the believer's desire to pray, this is an image that connects prayer with physical movement, the natural world and the natural cycles of day and night. In seeking poetic expression for this experience, there is a sense that the poet desires to move beyond words into a different kind of knowing, to speak in gestures expressed through the body's glossolalia.

Levertov speaks of the plant 'longing' for the dark as prayer happens at night, the time of lovers. This nocturnal imagery connects the 'palm to palm' of praying hands with Romeo's blasphemous seduction of Juliet, that styles kissing as an act of devotion: 'palm to palm is holy palmers' kiss'.[57] The coming together of hands is an act of consummation and communion, akin to the coming together of lips. Prayer is the expression of that desire for union, and so prayer is itself something immensely to be desired, as reflected in the 'relief' of the 'shy believer' as they come to kneel in prayer. Bodily prayer is an act that speaks in gestures, but also an act that hears, which 'afford[s] … distinctive ways of knowing'. Raising hands and folding knees express desire, but are also a preparation for listening. As the final word of

---

[55]Coakley, *God, Sexuality, and the Self*, 19.
[56]John Damascene, 'Exposition of the Orthodox Faith', in *Hilary of Poitiers, John of Damascus*, trans. S. D. F. Salmond, NPNF-2 9 (Edinburgh: T&T Clark, 1898), III.24.
[57]William Shakespeare, *Romeo and Juliet* (1623), Act I, Scene 5.

the poem, 'You', introduces the second person for the first time, the speaker recognizes themselves at the end as in relationship to the one before whom they kneel, turning this poem finally from a reflection into itself a prayer.

Coakley's and Levertov's theological and poetic reflections on the bodiliness of prayer have relevance for a consideration of prayer and poetic form. Poets consider words not only as conceptual communicators but as embodiments of meaning. A concern with rhythm, rhyme, assonance and alliteration, syntax and diction, whose magnetic force draws words together or pulls them apart, is a concern with the bodies of words.[58] David Jones, the Roman Catholic convert and First World War poet, applied his knowledge of craft (particularly the making of woodcuts) to the practice of poetry. Just as the builder works with stone and the carpenter with wood, so the poet works with words. Jones viewed poetry as the craft of words, but also viewed words as inherently sacramental.[59] If the meaning of a poem is embedded not just in its denotative sense but in its connotative shape and sound, and if the sound of a word is sacramental, then it follows that the most ordinary poetic phrase might be heard as a prayer.

Jones' epic poem on his experiences in the First World War is entitled *In Parenthesis*. Its overall conceit imagines that a period of time such as the war, or a reflection on that time, or the span of human life, might be considered as held between the curved arms of two brackets, out of time or on the edge of time, a short interruption in the story of eternity. In chapter three, the company march at night towards the trenches and the front line for the first time. The men call out warnings to each other about the path ahead, which Jones records as follows:

> The repeated passing back of aidful messages assumes a cadency.
> Mind the hole
> mind the hole
> mind the hole to left
> hole right
> step over
> keep left, left.[60]

---

[58]The relationship between sound and sense is complex, and it is debatable to what extent a reader or critic can accurately interpret the meaning embodied in particular sounds, but that does not render them semantically unimportant. On this subject, consider George Steiner, *On Difficulty and Other Essays* (Oxford: Oxford University Press, 1972), 160.

[59]See David Jones, 'Art and Sacrament (1955)', in *Epoch and Artist: Selected Writings*, ed. Harman Grisewood (London: Faber and Faber, 1959), 143–79.

[60]David Jones, *In Parenthesis* (London: Faber and Faber, 1937), 36.

The rhythm and the words of these lines are those of the march – 'left, left, left right left!' – but the musical cadence of the repeated phrases also has the character of a litany or repeated prayer of supplication. These lines are a call to keep on the right path, a petition for preservation. Each boot-step echoes the prayer: 'save us', 'have mercy on us', as each man descends into the mouth of hell. In this passage, the bodies of words speak in tongues of the desires of the men's hearts for comfort and safety. Words have form, and so they have bodies. Poets grace these bodies with beauty: sometimes using the natural features of language, sometimes through sophisticated techniques and ornamentation. The function of the poem is not thereby merely to entertain or persuade, but to explore new ways of knowing. Thus through the glossolalia of the body of words in poetry, the mind may come to hear the wordless cry of prayer.

Cry: 'O Living Flame of Love'

The genre of poetry that ostensibly fits most closely the verbal language of petitionary prayer is the love lyric, whose intimate second-person address suggests a dialogue with a beloved other. The devotional lyric of the early-modern metaphysical poets that addressed God as lover emerged out of the secular sonnets of the sixteenth century, represented by John Donne, George Herbert and Henry Vaughan. The sacred love lyric is also exemplified by the mystical poetry of such as John of the Cross, in its echo of the poetry of the *Song of Songs*:

> O living flame of love
> That tenderly wounds my soul
> In its deepest center![61]

In his popular book on contemplative prayer, Hans Urs von Balthasar called prayer a 'dialogue, not man's monologue before God' but a reciprocal relationship between 'an I and a Thou'.[62] Even if only one voice is heard, prayer can never be mere monologue, soliloquy or private meditation

---

[61]John of the Cross, 'The Living Flame of Love', in *Collected Works*, rev. edn, trans. Kieran Kavanaugh and Otilio Rodriguez (Washington, DC: Institute of Carmelite Studies, 1991).

[62]Hans Urs von Balthasar, *Prayer* (San Francisco, CA: Ignatius Press, 1986), 14. Jane Hirschfield also defines 'poetry of spiritual dialogue' as 'the one-sided conversation we call prayer', or as an imaginary dialogue where 'the writer … inhabits both sides, yet by entering into the language of interchange reaches for a knowledge undiscoverable in any other way'. See Jane Hirschfield, *Nine Gates: Entering the Mind of Poetry* (New York: HarperCollins, 1998), Gate 8.

because God precedes, transcends and is at the centre of the human 'I', so in this conversation God has always spoken first.[63]

According to contemporary lyric theory there are not two but three participants in this conversation. Lyric is characterized by 'triangulated' or indirect address, through which device the poet speaks to the reader by way of speaking, or appearing to speak, to another.[64] This form of address is most evident in the use of apostrophe, when the poem's speaker addresses an absent, inanimate or silent other such as a lover, the wind or God. The cry, 'Oh', is a common signal of lyric apostrophe, as in 'O living flame of love' or in Shelley's 'O wild West Wind, thou breath of Autumn's being'.[65] In the act of overhearing this address, the audience is not eavesdropping on a private conversation or listening in to the poet's thoughts, because they are always the intended hearer.[66] Applied to the devotional lyric of John of the Cross, one could say that although God is the addressee, *we* are the intended hearers, and so this poem is more than a prayer, being also an exercise in teaching or guiding others to pray. Triangulated address in this case allows the poet to teach us to pray while avoiding the didacticism of an imperative or indicative mood of 'you should pray like this' or 'this is how to pray'.

The vocative 'O' of triangulated address is an exclamation of heightened emotion, a nonverbal cry. It is also a liturgical invocation, a call to be heard and a call for the hearer to respond, as in the call 'O come, in any way you want' that opens Kevin Hart's poem 'Prayer'.[67] In both senses, as heartfelt cry and ritual invocation, the vocative indicates that the poem is more than a reflection or meditation on God but a poetic or performative event that expresses, enacts or constructs relationship.[68] The hyperbolic tone and liturgical overtones of this language may be a cause of embarrassment for secular modernist poetics, but even secular lyrics may share in the prayerful voice of invocation through triangulated address.[69] Carol Ann Duffy's famous poem 'Prayer', for example, might be considered a secular prayer-poem. She writes as a lapsed Catholic and agnostic for whom literature has

---

[63]Balthasar, *Prayer*, 23.
[64]See Jonathan Culler, *The Pursuit of Signs* (Ithaca, NY: Cornell University Press, 1981), chapter 7.
[65]Percy Bysshe Shelley, 'Ode to the West Wind', in *Prometheus Unbound: A Lyrical Drama* (London: C. and J. Ollier, 1820).
[66]On the lyric poem as an overheard prayer, see Northrop Frye, 'Theory of Genres' (1957) in Virginia Jackson and Yopie Prins, ed., *The Lyric Theory Reader: A Critical Anthology* (Baltimore, MD: Johns Hopkins University Press, 2014), 32.
[67]Kevin Hart, 'Prayer', in *Flame Tree: Selected Poems* (Tarset: Bloodaxe, 2002), 205.
[68]On theological performativity, see Nicholas Lash, *Theology on the Way to Emmaus* (London: SCM Press, 1986), 43.
[69]On the embarrassment of lyric, see Culler, *The Pursuit of Signs*, chapter 7.

replaced religion, emphasizing the ritual aspect of public prayer with no notion of dialogue with a divine other: 'Poetry and prayer are very similar, I write quite a lot of sonnets and I think of them almost as prayers: short and memorable, something you can recite.'[70] However, if the principle of triangulated address is applied then dialogue may be impossible to avoid. This sonnet is addressed not to God but to us through the collective first person 'we'. Following the principle of triangulated address, are we really the intended hearers, or is this secular meditation in spite of itself also a dialogue with something other? There are moments where the vocative tone of invocation comes through directly, such as the brief point of apostrophe: 'Pray for us now' which carries the implicit 'O' of 'O pray for us'. This is a ritual phrase drawn from the Hail Mary but it sounds like a cry from the heart. The invocation seems to turn the ordinary objects of the world from the 'It' of the tree, the train or the piano to the 'Thou' of a Marian figure through whom prayer can be uttered. The desire for prayer expressed through these lines seems to be answered at the end, through 'the radio's prayer' which chants the words of the shipping forecast.[71] The petition is answered as the sounds of the world pray for those who cannot. The prayer of this poem is not in the literal, denotative or verbal meaning, but in the vocative tone of address and the nonverbal sound of the cry.

Conclusion

The relationship between poetry and prayer is complex, ambiguous and frequently problematic, reflecting the sometimes fractious relationship between theology and literature and the difficulty of prayer itself. However, this relationship is also deeply rooted and holds significant potential for theological reflection. In the words of Mark Twain's Huckleberry Finn, 'You can't pray a lie'. Les Murray added, 'You can't poe one either'.[72] Where poetry and prayer share a response to, articulation of or seeking after the real, they will be kindred human activities. The connections between poetry and prayer go beyond words but are also rooted in the form and substance of words and in the relationship between words and the Word. Such connections are to be found in the mystery of silence, the movement

---

[70]Hephzibah Anderson, 'Christmas Carol', Interview with Carol Ann Duffy, *The Guardian*, 4 December 2005.

[71]Carol Ann Duffy, 'Prayer', *Mean Time* (London: Picador, 2013), 48.

[72]Les Murray, 'Poetry and Religion', *Collected Poems* (Melbourne: Schwartz Publishing, 2006), 265.

of breath, the shape of the body and the emotion of the cry. In all of these aspects, poetry illustrates the nature of prayer not as internal monologue nor as a purely rhetorical or ritual practice but as an expression of relationship undertaken, in the words of the Anglican bidding prayer, 'in the power of the Spirit and in union with Christ'.

CHAPTER THIRTY-THREE

Reconciliation: The Place of Prayer in Conflict and Peace-Making

SIOBHÁN GARRIGAN

There are as many ways of praying as there are people who pray, from across all faiths and none. For this chapter, I am going to focus on corporate prayer in Christian traditions. Mostly, this delineation of focus is due to the availability of such prayers to the scholar: it is not straightforward to account for what is going on for any individual prayer practitioner other than (and perhaps including) oneself during religious ritual in a place of worship, but it is nearly impossible to do so in the many other locations in which the Christian prays, from the bed and its side to the pub, car, shop and so many others, due to the limits of privacy. I am also going to focus on conflict and post-conflict contexts in general, and the British–Irish relationship in particular, because that is my own area of study, while acknowledging that reconciliation is a far broader phenomenon than this delineation, and prayer has a concomitantly varied effect and role in reconciling with oneself and one's close relatives, broader family members and friends, society and its historic offences and prejudices, neighbours, colleagues, political affiliates, non-human animals and the earth.

Reconciliation is typically encountered by its agents as deliberate effort and as ongoing process, its perceptibility as actual achievement usually being confined to the rear-view mirror. Like any praxis, it first has to be chosen and then wrought; it requires significant attentiveness, commitment, mental agility, flexibility, repetition and patience. Such effort, when undertaken by a Christian, is intimately related to one's identity, character and commitment as a Christian. The first thing to remark, therefore, is the need for a baseline understanding of the work of reconciliation as somehow also spiritual. The work of negotiating ceasefires, reforming a police force, altering unjust public housing policies, releasing prisoners, decommissioning weapons, creating new governmental structures and so on, is tedious, difficult and fraught. These tasks are typically undertaken over lengthy periods of time and require an acute determination to achieve a particular vision despite inevitable setbacks, opposition and personnel changes.

To name these tasks as politics while naming prayer as the recitation of, say, the Our Father is both to neglect the somatic similarities between them as tasks undertaken over time in corporate settings and to misunderstand the relationship between emancipative endeavour and Christian spirituality. As Latin American liberation theologies insist from the 1970s onwards, the material is spiritual.

> The historical reality of the poor is something that not only ought to be analysed and responded to in accordance with its materiality, but ought to be the object of a spiritual experience, a reality that can 'implode' into our lives and so become a mediation of the experience of God. On the other hand, the spiritual experience of encountering God, or of being encountered by God, includes, in virtue of its own dynamic, and not only as heterogeneous conclusion of a process of ratiocination, the act of going forth to meet historical poverty and applying a remedy.[1]

And if the latent Marxism of such a view of materiality is a distraction, then consider its fundamentally Aquinan roots and its further confirmation in recent eco-theological turns. Roberto Dell'Oro, for example, renders a comparable claim for the spirituality of the material via bio-ethics, arguing for the urgent need to think in unitive ways that undo false assumptions of separation and ingrained dualistic conceptual habits. His articulation of what it is to be enfleshed, a body, is:

> The body is not the separated substance existing next to, or behind, some mysterious personal presence (the soul), but the very incarnation

---

[1] Jon Sobrino, *Spirituality of Liberation: Toward Political Holiness* (Maryknoll, NY: Orbis Books, 1988), 67. Sobrino is here discussing the implicit theorization of the relationship between the spiritual and the material (and the theological) in the work of Gustavo Gutiérrez.

of that presence in the 'communication of properties' (*communicatio idiomatum*) that defines the fleshed embodiment of the self: in the person, the material is the spiritual, the spiritual is the material.[2]

If this is the case, then it is *all* the body's activities, its entire participation in history, that constitute the spiritual.

Thus, while the case has been well made elsewhere that prayer is political,[3] it has yet to be adequately explored whether or to what extent it is appropriate to conceive of the political as prayer. It seems an important lacuna in an investigation of their relationship, especially one that demarcates prayer as what individuals do in and learn from corporate worship. However, there is perhaps a distinction between 'prayer' and 'the spiritual' that is in need of articulation, particularly when it comes to entering or furthering the work of reconciliation. To this end, Andrew Prevot holds up political, liberation and Black theologies as 'examples of *spirituality*', a categorization designed

> to bring out their most striking achievement: connecting prayerful thought and doxological contemplation unmistakably with a real, historical, and active affirmation of life – as demonstrated particularly by their compassionate attention to the lives of the most vulnerable and forsaken. ... There is a marked intensification of the prayerful affirmation of life (i.e. of spirituality) that comes only through overt struggles against particular structures of violence and only through intimate, cooperative relationships with those whose lives are regularly impeded and destroyed by such structures.[4]

This definition can helpfully be deployed for reconciliation scenarios as well, at least in the British–Irish context, because it captures both what one is up against (the sheer extent of the intersectionality of political, structural, historic, racialized, religious and ideological realities) and the positive, transforming difference that happens when 'thinking prayer' meets 'overt struggles'.

---

[2]Roberto Dell'Oro, 'Embodiment as Saturated Phenomenon: Medicine, Theology, and Some Metaphysical Premises of Modernity', *International Journal of Philosophy and Theology* 2, no. 4 (2014): 69–84 (83).

[3]See, for example, the final chapter of Ashley Cocksworth, *Prayer: A Guide for the Perplexed* (London: Bloomsbury, 2018), 193: 'May's and Ward's theories of the political saturating the praying body and therefore the body of Christ support this chapter's overall claim that prayer is not simply political but as an embodied practice is *inherently* political – unavoidably receptive of the political. The praying body ... is both receptive of the political and also actively political.'

[4]Andrew Prevot, *Thinking Prayer: Theology and Spirituality amid the Crises of Modernity* (Notre Dame, IN: University of Notre Dame Press, 2015), 168.

By contrast with the integrative, global, character of spirituality, prayer can then be distinguished (but not isolated) as an activity that is at once both disciplined and disciplining. It is the central technique of Christian discipleship (the etymology being remarkable in passing), and as such one might add that the nature of it often involves 'going against yourself'. It is a going against yourself not in any way to harm yourself, but in the sense of altering one's awareness so as to see(k) Christ, take on Christ and thus become part of the body of Christ, not in a transcendental way, but through inhabiting the extended ministry of Christ in the midst of the creaturely community. This is undertaken via constant political engagement as turns of mind and body (*metanoia*), self-denial, and acts of mercy and care. Prayer is to spirituality what cooking is to sharing a meal: a technique, but one that is essential to the realization of the ultimate phenomenon. You cannot have spirituality without prayer.

So, while the category of reconciliation cannot be collapsed as a phenomenon into that of prayer, it is important to honour the ways in which for Christians those actual practices are spiritual. But while recognizing that the gritty, unpleasant, tenacious work of reconciliation can itself be understood *as* spiritual, it is also necessary to ask whether there is anything particular to praying within the specific context of a conflict or immediate post-conflict situation. Can one pray the same here as elsewhere? Are there specific or unique conditions that have to be met in order for prayer to take effect? Is something more, or new, or different required of the prayer itself? How does prayer work in a situation in need of reconciliation?

I would like to suggest that there are at least three problems that distinguish 'reconciliation' situations from ones in which there is merely disagreement. First, given that reconciliation means 'to bring back together',[5] then the existential character of the ground for its necessity is *separation*. Separation presents two peculiar difficulties (that sporadic disagreement, for example, does not). First, separation is typically the earliest trauma that each human being experiences and later experience of other separation can retain the feeling of trauma in many adults, resulting in pain, resistance and/or denial when attempts are made to address it. Second, separated people are, by definition, notoriously difficult to get into the same space, such that reconciliation work could commence; as a result, efforts to bring-back-together the separated often fail at a very early stage due to the seeming normalcy to each camp of separate spheres of operation. The alternative (a coming together) can seem exceedingly threatening, if it can even be imagined.

---

[5]'Reconciliation' is a modern derivative of the late Middle English 'reconcile', which came, via Old French (*reconcilier*), from the Latin *re* (back) and *conciliare* (bring together).

Third, in these situations, unlike with disagreements, there is no automatic appeal to discourse when seeking relief or resolution; words are extremely limited as agents of reconciliation. This is particularly significant when considering the relationship of prayer and reconciliation. Words are the currency of most Christian prayer practices in the modern West, and this is truly problematic in conflict situations, especially ones with a religious inflection (which is nearly all of them) because the same words can mean different things to different people. Obvious examples include Eucharistic Prayers ('This is my body'), over which wars have been fought, but also more recent issues with gender in prayer language, to which I will return.

In the remainder of this chapter, I will offer some preliminary responses to these three problems by exploring one specific approach to prayer in conflict and post-conflict situations (praying *with*) and suggesting another (praying *for*).

Praying With

'For where two or three are gathered in my name, I am there among them' (Mt. 18.20). This verse appears in a relatively lengthy discussion of sin and forgiveness, prompted by the question of how to deal with transgressions by members of the early church, but it also has long been understood as relevant to other gatherings, especially to the basic act of assembly for the purpose of prayer which is at the root of Christian worship and Christian identity.[6] In particular, to gather 'in my name' implies a requirement to invoke the name, and an altered context once this has occurred. As a result, most verbal Christian prayer traditions begin and/or end 'in the name of'. Furthermore, to gather in the name of Jesus is to engage our bodies in their most fundamental prayer: gathering, coming together, to compose and become the body of Christ. It is itself a mini-reconciliation, bringing together the temporarily separated parts of that body so that, by the power of the Holy Spirit, it can act.

However, when thinking of conflict or post-conflict situations (as opposed to those in which people are merely temporarily apart), this passage is of particular value, because it both encourages and offers a technique for coming-together that the first problem outlined above is habitually restricting. It does this by positioning Christ (and not any other mediating agency) as the fundamental reconciling agent in the cosmos. Worldly divisions are relativized, and thereby minimized, because in Christ, so much more than

---

[6]The word 'church' is itself derived from the Greek word *ecclesia*, which was an assembly, a gathering of those called.

our own temporal conflict is already reconciled. In Christ, humanity and divinity are reconciled. In Christ, all God's people are gathered into One (Jn 17.11, 21, 22). In Christ, 'there is no longer Jew or Greek, there is no longer slave or free, there is no longer male and female; for all of you are one in Christ Jesus' (Gal. 3.28). For those habituated to the pain of separation and the threat posed by reconnecting, to recall this central aspect of Christian belief is to recontextualize one's own locus: Christ has already won for the world ultimate reconciliation of its divisions and hostilities; the work is therefore not all ours alone to do. Furthermore, being able to take a step out of separation by invoking Christ's name provides a relatively simple first step.

Moreover, having affirmed the value of gathering in Christ's name (18.20), Matthew's Gospel proceeds to share the teaching to forgive not seven but seventy-seven times, situating the (terribly difficult, necessarily repetitive) work of forgiveness full square within the category of reconciliation. Others have explored whether or to what extent forgiveness is needed in the work of reconciliation.[7] What I wish to accentuate here, rather, is the sense that to gather in Jesus' name with others, repeatedly, is the blueprint for prayer's role in reconciliation. What it suggests to or demands of Christians is, fundamentally, that they gather together and pray with one another. For most people at an intra-denominational, local church level, this is self-evident. But in contexts in which there is centuries-old antipathy, misunderstanding or just rueful separation between Christian communities, it is very challenging indeed. It is also, as will be seen, a very powerful contributor to the work of reconciliation, if it can happen.

Of course, 'reconciliation' refers not only, or not least, to what is yet required to mend civic and political processes of reform, but also to what is needed in the church itself. It would be a mistake to think of reconciliation contexts as essentially profane or secular (racism, war zones) and prayer as a sacred, healing, reconciling schema. Some of the most desperate situations in need of reconciliation are essentially religious, for example, between and within churches themselves. I refer to not only contexts, such as my own, where faith positions have been co-created alongside the oppressions and resistances of colonization, poverty and misogyny, but also throughout the world's separated denominations of Christianity. A long history of excluding one another from worship, declaring one another not sufficiently Christian

---

[7]For example, see Ani Kalayjian and Raymond F. Paloutzian, *Forgiveness and Reconciliation: Psychological Pathways to Conflict Transformation and Peace-Building* (New York: Springer, 2009) and Solomon Schimmel, *Wounds Not Healed by Time: The Power of Repentance and Forgiveness* (New York: Oxford University Press, 2002).

and asserting one's own true faith, or just peddling pernicious snobberies, persists in church life without need for militia or UN Councils to qualify them as 'conflict' zones.

The World Council of Churches has done much to attempt to address the structural and doctrinal roots of these divisions (as have national-level Councils of Churches) but without the membership of the Roman Catholic Church and most Pentecostal communities, it has its work cut out for it. Such work is invaluable, but slow and painstaking, with declarations and accords coming at irregular intervals and involving only a fraction of the worldwide church's adherents. Common prayer has been accredited with playing an important role in these formal, official ecclesial processes.[8] It both gives a more immediate experience of commonality than verbal/textual negotiations and contributes indirectly to the progress of those dialogues. Designing prayer for such gatherings is difficult, and participating in such prayer can be too. Designing prayer for or participating in *any* ecumenical gathering is difficult, because beyond gathering in the name of Christ, there is much that one cannot do if the event is to register as authentic worship with the congregation.

But at grassroots levels at least, praying with one another, across the boundaries of difference, can have more immediate positive effects than attempting dialogue alone, and may significantly aid dialogue in eventually achieving greater mutual understanding. This is partly because the vast majority of human communication is non-verbal; humans understand one another through non-verbal languages far more than they do through verbal dialogue or written text.[9] It is also partly because in the development of Christian identity and emic theology, worship/prayer is generally prior to doctrinal formation. And it is also partly because the body of Christ is embodied, and so to gather together in Christ's name, to pray with one another, gives the participants an experience of the presence of God with and even through the presence of one another and this is a potentially powerful counter-point to the wounds that caused the separation between them.

And so the Christian is called to pray-with by means of sharing a meal, listening to stories and telling them, reading and listening to poems, taking and sharing photographs, making and sharing all manner of visual arts and

---

[8]For example, see Eden Grace, 'Worship in the World Council of Churches: The Tradition of "Ecumenical Worship" in Light of Recent Orthodox Critique', *Ecumenical Review* 54, no. 1 (2002): 3–27.

[9]A figure of 93 per cent is often put on non-verbal and 7 per cent verbal in human communication; while the actual figures are contended, it is widely agreed that non-verbal is the far greater technique. For example, www.psychologytoday.com/ie/blog/beyond-words/201109/is-nonverbal-communication-numbers-game (accessed: 5 January 2020).

architecture, symbolizing in every possible way and to value it at least as highly as 'dialogue' because it works (i.e. it fosters, forges, wreaks reconciliation) where dialogue may stall.[10] Early results of recent research suggest this is true at interfaith as well as inter-denomination level. Christians are under no instruction to gather in the name of Christ to use only verbal prayers; the earliest Christians ate together, gathered alms for distribution, told stories, read scripture, created art throughout their gathering space, sang psalms and much more.

Perhaps the most accessible such symbolization to the modern Westerner, and perhaps the most effective first step in reconciliation, is the act of singing together – and not only in church. 'When my family comes over', said the Country music legend Linda Ronstad recently, 'we would all sing together. That way we don't have to talk about politics. It makes for harmonious – I don't mean the pun – relations.'[11] Not talking about politics, but instead doing something creative together, is prayer when done in the context of gathering in Christ's name. Much of liturgical theology focuses on table fellowship as the prime ecumenical activity, and eating and drinking together is indeed famously corrosive of supposedly impenetrable boundaries in all sorts of anthropological scenarios. But sharing a meal with those from whom one is separated is often not possible as a first step in reconciliation work because it is too emotionally raw, or unsafe or, in some ecclesial contexts, too theologically difficult. Luckily, there are many activities that are typically experienced as easier for Christians to do as praying-with each other, and singing is one of them. For over half a century now, thanks to the Churches Together movement (and others), Christians in many parts of this archipelago have gathered together to sing psalms in Lent, to sing as part of civil rights (and other) protests, to conduct ecumenical carol services before Christmas and to sing while carrying together a large chunk of wood symbolizing the cross of Christ, like one great name, on Good Friday.

These gatherings have been extremely important in breaking down the generational hardness of heart, and the matrix of misunderstandings that each community has about the other, as identified in the second problem above. Typically, this leads to two things: a recognition of the other as different to what was expected and an outlet for pent-up grief (in some cases generationally received). Singing can allow for the expression of grief better than mere words alone because the musical elements (such as the melody, the chords, the key, the tempo) can evoke and emit the grief at a

---

[10]See, for example, Siobhán Garrigan, 'A New Model for Ecumenical Worship', *Studia Liturgica* 43, no. 1 (2013): 32–53.
[11]Linda Ronstadt, interviewed by Michael Schulman in *The New Yorker*, 1 September 2019.

deep, bodily level. Additionally, some of these instances of praying-with by singing together explicitly build into the ritual of gathering some time, space and expressive outlet for grief. For example, in one community I studied in the west of Northern Ireland on Good Friday, a Protestant pastor framed the morning's ecumenical service as the start of a whole day and night of mourning and, later that day, prior to singing the Reproaches in a Roman Catholic church, the congregation was given a period of reflection and asked to bring to mind all the personal, local and national unresolved griefs of the previous year, including carryovers from previous years and 'sing them to the foot of the cross'.

And so in response to our third problem, while recognizing what ritual studies have shown for a century across human activity, and what liturgical theology has shown for half that century in Christian contexts (i.e. the primacy in religious understanding of bodily, symbolic actions rather than formulas of words), words nonetheless matter in reconciliation contexts. Indeed, the world church at an international level experienced significant progress in this regard during the latter part of the twentieth century. The reforms to the liturgy that Vatican II instigated transformed not only the experience of prayer for Roman Catholics but also the sense of possibilities for ecumenical relations. In the subsequent decades, all of the major Protestant denominations revised their Books of Worship and Prayer in ways that consciously sought common ground, where possible, across denominational practices, often by reviewing translations of earlier, common texts and by reviving earlier, common ritual practices.

The work that went into such reforms should not be overlooked or underestimated *as* the work of reconciliation. It was extensive, difficult and controversial and required enormous skill, imagination and courage on the part of those involved because it concerned verbal language, which is ferociously difficult to agree upon once disagreement has occurred. However, these efforts and the greater ecumenical understanding they generated were dealt a severe blow by the new translations of the Mass that have issued from the Vatican's *Liturgiam authenticam* in 2001.[12] Praying-with has been made a good deal less possible by its determination to 'avoid a wording or style that the Catholic faithful would confuse with the manner of speech of non-Catholic ecclesial communities or of other religions'.[13] Reconciliation is not linear and, in the church as in secular contexts, progress towards it can be undone.

---

[12]See Maxwell Johnson, 'The Loss of a Common Language: The End of Ecumenical-Liturgical Convergence?', *Studia Liturgica* 3, no. 1 (2007): 55–72.
[13]*Liturgiam autenticam*, article 40.

Praying-with has been recognized to be such a potentially effective technique in overcoming both separation and repressed grief that some groups and communities have emerged specifically around praying with one another with a view to enacting reconciliation. The Corrymeela community is known for its reconciliation work and its contribution to peace-making both during the Troubles and in this post-conflict period. It has won accolades for its work with education (bringing school children from different backgrounds together), the survivors of sectarian violence, and community and political leaders. But at the heart of its programming, people are invited several times a day to a small building (literally called the *Croí* – heart in Irish) to pray with one another. Often this takes the form of silence, trusting that one's bodies alone, doing nothing other than gather in Christ's name, are a form of prayer. Although the Corrymeela community started in 1965, it was not until 1979 that The *Croí* was opened. The community only learnt the peculiar value of praying-with through realizing that putting it at the centre rather than the edges of its work let prayer function as a reconciliation technique unlike all others.

Another Northern Irish example of praying-with where the actual praying-with leads the venture rather than merely supplementing it is the IKON community. It meets in community venues such as pubs rather than churches, including a monthly meeting at The Menagerie pub in Belfast, deliberately to claim a space in which the boundaries causing such tension and separation can be rethought by being re-enacted, re-created. As its founder, Peter Rollins, writes, not only does this offer 'a range of people spanning the liberal/conservative, Protestant/Catholic and theist/atheist divides' an opportunity to encounter one another through 'a cocktail of live art, poetry, prose, ritual, liturgy and music so as to immerse the individual in a sensually rich environment that is designed to draw out an openness to the incoming of God',[14] but it also alters people's understandings of one another and the griefs that divide them. As Rollins' reflections demonstrate, praying with one another leads people to 'rethink the structures of religious community in a contemporary environment' in ways that inter-religious dialogue alone cannot.[15]

The reconciling work of these two communities evolved on the edges of the institutional churches in Northern Ireland, but praying-with as a technique in the work of reconciliation has happened within those churches too. One outstanding example is the relationship between the congregations at Fitzroy Presbyterian Church and the Clonard Redemptorist Monastery in

---

[14]Peter Rollins, *How (Not) to Speak of God: Marks of the Emerging Church* (Brewster, NY: Paraclete Press, 2008), xiv.

[15]Rollins, *How (Not) To Speak of God*, xiv.

Belfast from 1991 to 2015. This was built on a range of ways of cultivating friendship between the actual members of the churches, including attending one another's worship services where possible.[16] But such fellowship was, and remains, remarkably rare in the British–Irish context. Many people here will not, cannot, gather in the name of Christ with others because while to the wider world they are perceived as members of the same faith, to each other they are of different faiths.[17]

Because the British–Irish conflict is laminated with Protestant–Catholic accounts of identity, my examples so far have mostly been drawn from inter-denominational contexts, but intra-denominational contexts can equally be sites in need of reconciliation activities, as can intra-congregational contexts, and they suffer from the same three problems identified above. Examples in intra-denominational contexts are often caused by ethical teachings, racism and disagreements over church polity and, in intra-congregational contexts, by interpersonal issues (often to do with leadership) and aesthetic issues (usually to do with worship style). Prayer's place in any attempt to reconcile these matters is complex, not least because quite often the form or style of prayer itself is contributing to the source or object of the conflict. The 'worship wars' of the late twentieth and early twenty-first centuries were not accidentally named.[18]

Of particular significance in this respect is the question of 'inclusive' language. The work of secular, civic institutions in English-speaking countries no longer to refer to all human beings as men (replacing words such as 'man', 'mankind' and a normative 'him') with gender-neutral or gender-inclusive words has been difficult enough, but in ecclesial contexts, even more so. This is because, as Janet Walton notes, when it comes to the language of prayer, it is not merely a case of making sure women are equally represented; it is also a matter of accuracy. 'Precision in naming speeds a process of truth telling and faithful relationships. It is an act of justice.'[19] Such accuracy is necessary in all matters, but particularly regarding God. If God is consistently named only in masculine words, and rarely in feminine or transgendered or non-gendered words, then one's apprehension of God may be radically restricted or even distorted.

---

[16]The Fitzroy/Clonard Fellowship was given the Pax Christi International Peace Award in 1999 in recognition of the power of grassroots fellowship in the work of reconciliation.

[17]Perceptions which have been formed by the specific history of the region. For example, see Joseph Ruane and Jennifer Todd, *The Dynamics of Conflict in Northern Ireland: Power, Conflict and Emancipation* (Cambridge: Cambridge University Press, 1996).

[18]See Marva Dawn, *How Shall We Worship: Biblical Guidelines for the Worship Wars* (Eugene, OR: Wipf and Stock, 2015).

[19]Janet Walton, *Feminist Liturgy: A Matter of Justice* (Collegeville, MN: Liturgical Press, 2000), 34.

And it's not just about God; naming the greatest power only or largely in masculine terms distorts human understanding of itself, one another and how power works in human relations. As Mary Daly put it, 'if God is male then the male is God'.[20] In response, some churches have made transformations to their language of prayer and praise, others concessions, and others have changed only the bare minimum. While many worshipping Christians have assented to using these altered words in prayer, there are others to whom this issue matters too acutely, on both sides of the debate, who cannot now pray-with one another, because they cannot gather with them in the name of Christ. One side finds it impossible to gather in the name of the Father, over and over, with plentiful additional Lords, Kings, Hims and Hises restricting their faith to a misogynistic, patriarchal norm they wish to dismantle/ emancipate. And the other side finds it impossible to gather in the name of Christ if Christ is to be conceived as anything other than binarily masculine or if traditions of specific vocabulary for prayer are to be altered for reason, as they see it, of fad or political correctness.

In exploring the ways in which Western society's endemic violence against women is related to Christian theology, Marjorie Procter-Smith draws explicit attention to prayer's potential role as an agent of harm and schism rather than as an agent of reconciliation.[21] Even where agreement or compromise is reached on the words to be spoken in ritual repetition, Procter-Smith notes the potential destructiveness of those non-verbal aspects of praying that are so much a part of the practice of prayer – bodily gestures, movements and dispositions. The somatic experience of prayer can be perceived as consonant with and reinforcing of traits of misogyny in society at large. She suggests that, for many women, kneeling directly in front of a man who is standing above you, or being instructed to close one's eyes, or to bow one's head, is to mimic postures of submission and habits of control that have been among the techniques of domestic abuse.

Praying For

And so, from women who cannot kneel before a man in prayer to Christians in Northern Ireland who cannot enter one another's church buildings, praying-with has its limits or may simply not be possible. Blueprints cannot always be followed.

---

[20]Mary Daly, *Beyond God the Father: Toward a Philosophy of Women's Liberation* (Boston, MA: Beacon Press, 1973), 19.
[21]Marjorie Procter-Smith, *Praying with Our Eyes Open: Engendering Feminist Liturgical Prayer* (Nashville, TN: Abingdon Press, 1995).

The particular challenge this presents to Christians arises from the very core of Jesus' teaching: the demand to 'love your enemies' (Mt. 5.44). Asked to identify the prime commandment, Jesus replied: '"You shall love the Lord your God with all your heart, and with all your soul, and with all your mind, and with all your strength." The second is this, "You shall love your neighbour as yourself." There is no other commandment greater than these' (Mk 12.30-31). Thus, while the option of gathering in prayer with those with whom one needs reconciliation may sometimes not be available, the option of not being (in some meaningful sense) reconciled with the other does not exist because the option of not loving them does not exist. But often, those who are profoundly hurt by and separated from one another, or prone to despising one other, do not acknowledge their enmity, do not name their enemy as such and so seemingly escape the command to love them.

In his essay on theological responses to torture and terrorism (after the 9/11 and 7/7 attacks), Alistair McFadyen remarks how Christians have shied away from facing enmity in general and enmity for terrorists in particular. He suggests that this lack of attention to enmity 'is rooted in the assumption that Christians should not have enemies or practise enmity'.[22] But Jesus did not say: 'do not have enemies'; he said, 'love your enemies'. And so the challenge for the Christian is to develop *ways* of loving the enemies that they (inevitably) have. McFadyen explores this via various contexts, including that of policing in Britain, and points to practices such as restraint in the use of force with prisoners and treating prisoners with dignity as possible illustrations of the difference that a Christian theological perspective can make. '"(S)olidarity", "love" and "justice" might be read together as indicating an alternative *way* of having enemies without attendant demonization or dehumanisation, rather than as an alternative to *having* enemies.'[23]

To return, then, to the question of whether prayer has any particular role or shape in the work of reconciliation, it is to be remarked that Jesus did not only say, 'love your enemies'; he also said, 'love your enemies and pray for those who persecute you' (Mt. 5.44). How the 'and' functions in this verse can be interpreted in various ways. It might indicate a sort of a list: love your enemies and (also) pray for those who persecute you. Or it might indicate a distinction: love your enemies, who may be different to those who persecute you and, for the latter, pray. But the interpretation I favour is that it offers a

---

[22]Alistair McFadyen, 'On Having Enemies: Terror, Torture, Theology … Policing', www.academia.edu/1819337/On_having_enemies_Terror_Torture_Theology_Policing (accessed: 12 December 2019).
[23]McFadyen, 'On Having Enemies', 17.

method, with the second clause offering guidance as to how to carry out the first: love your enemies by praying for them.

How do you pray for those who persecute you? There are remarkably few resources available to the Christian who sets out to research prayers for enemies, perhaps because the problem identified by McFadyen (denial of *having* enemies) has become quietly normative for Christians in the modern West. Or perhaps because praying for one's enemies is a terribly difficult thing to do. Or because Christians do not know what to pray *for*. Indeed, an internet search will quickly reveal all sorts of prayers that ask God to cause the suffering or demise of one's enemies, which is almost certainly not what Jesus had in mind.

There are prayers in various Christian traditions 'for separated brethren', but usually without any acknowledgement of enmity nor specificity about what is prayed *for* these brothers (and, one assumes, sisters and others). There are prayers for peace, but to pray for peace is not the same as to pray for one's enemies; indeed, it could be argued that prayers for peace are prayers primarily for oneself. And of course there is the prayer Jesus taught us, in which Christians pray to be able to forgive those who trespass against them; but that, too, is a prayer for one's own well-being and development rather than *for* those who have done the wronging.

I would like to suggest an analogy with McFadyen's analysis: praying for one's enemies is a *way* of *having* enemies (and neither denying that they are enemies or denying that they are fully, equally human), and that it is, in itself, a way of loving them. How might this be developed? Christians could perhaps follow the example of their Quaker siblings and 'hold in the light' those for whom they feel enmity. Or they could hold open an imaginative space, one in which their enemy is beloved by God and thriving in that love, and this could be prayed through song, imagery, poetry, meditation or even verbal prayer. Indeed, one can easily imagine a deliberate insertion of a prayer for one's enemies into all acts of corporate worship, although uttering it would no doubt be far from easy at first. Such a prayer would have to be specific enough to note (and not gloss over or deny) the harm done and the cause of the enmity, and also to state what is prayed *for* the enemies. Such a practice might cultivate in Christians the ability to name more openly their enemies, and thereby to engage in the work of loving them.

Conclusion

In conclusion then, where conflict is concerned, Christians in need of reconciliation can rely upon two particular gospel texts for guidance: pray *with* where you possibly can, and, whether you can or you cannot, pray *for*. Praying *with* has been proven to aid, or exceed, the efficacy of dialogue in the grassroots work of reconciliation. And praying *for*, while largely unexplored in the corporate worship of the Western church, has been given to Christians as the *way* to go.

CHAPTER THIRTY-FOUR

The Lord's Prayer in the Life and Liturgy of the Church

MEDI ANN VOLPE

Many volumes have been written on various aspects of the Lord's Prayer as it has been employed by Christians through the centuries. The topics addressed therein range from the forms of the Lord's Prayer from the New Testament onwards, the place of the Lord's Prayer in Christian liturgies, the meaning of the Lord's Prayer and its relation to the rest of the Gospel, just to name a few. The Lord's Prayer has been the subject of sermons and commentaries in the thousands. In this chapter, I offer a broad overview of the ways the Lord's Prayer has been used by Christians, with some close-ups of particularly illuminating moments in the history of its use.

Because the early church set the plumb line for future interpretations and uses of the Lord's Prayer, I rely heavily on sources from that period and have allowed it to set the framework for the chapter. Robert Taft, whose essay on the Lord's Prayer in the liturgy of the early church is considered authoritative, explains:

> The Our Father was an integral part of the initiatory catechesis and rites … [because] for the Fathers, the Lord's Prayer was a 'summary of the whole Gospel' … and they pair it with the creed as part of the *arcanum*, to be 'handed over' to the neophytes as the summary of their heritage.

So the *Pater* is not only a privilege and a prayer. It is also a continual
catechesis, a mirror of Christian life given to us in baptism, and a constant
reminder of the commitment made at that time.[1]

The dimensions suggested by Taft's description provide the structure for this
survey: privilege, prayer, catechesis, a mirror of discipleship and a reminder
of the commitment made (by us or on our behalf) at our baptism. I take
them in a slightly different order, however, and start with the Lord's Prayer
as *prayer*. As 'prayer', the Lord's Prayer forms the basis for all Christian
prayer. In the first section of the chapter, we will look at how and why that
is the case, and also why praying the Lord's Prayer is a privilege. I consider
the other dimensions in the second section of the chapter, and suggest that
the Lord's Prayer teaches us to forgive and forms us as people of forgiveness.

Before I begin in earnest, a few of items of housekeeping are in order.
First, I write from within the Christian faith, and at various points I refer
to Christians as 'we' because continuing to describe Christian practice in the
third person would be awkward. I do not assume that every reader of this
chapter will share my faith. Second, I hope that readers will not be frightened
off by references to the *Catechism of the Catholic Church* (CCC). Its final
section (roughly a quarter of the volume) is devoted to Christian prayer; half
of that examines the Lord's Prayer and relates it to the liturgy and life of the
body of Christ (CCC 2759-2865), offering an overview and synthesis of the
interpretations and uses of the prayer. So it is a useful resource for Christians
across the church universal. Third, a note about language. My ancient (and
some not so ancient) interlocutors name the unmarked individual human
being 'man'; I have not changed their wording but have referred to the one
praying the Lord's Prayer throughout using female pronouns to subvert this
language.

Praying the Lord's Prayer

Although early Christian commentators on the Lord's Prayer attend carefully
to its place in the young church's rites, the first mention of the Lord's Prayer
refers not to weekly gatherings but to daily prayer. The *Didache*, a first-
century text that describes Christian practices, exhorts readers to say the
Lord's Prayer at the three times set for daily prayer. The sacramental setting
of the Lord's Prayer emerged alongside such practices of piety. I consider the

---

[1]Robert F. Taft, 'The Lord's Prayer in the Eucharistic Liturgy: When and Why?', *Ecclesia Orans*
14, no. 2 (1997): 137–55 (150).

Lord's Prayer as prayed by individuals and communities and then turn to the place of the prayer in the sacraments of baptism and the Eucharist.

From the *Didache* onwards, the Lord's Prayer has occupied an important place in the spiritual life of believers. In the Sermon on the Mount, the Lord's Prayer follows Jesus' advice to pray in secret, and not to 'heap up empty words' (Mt. 6.5-13). Luke's version of the prayer records it as a response to his disciples' request, 'Lord, teach us to pray' (Lk. 11.1-4). As a prayer, then, the first setting of the Lord's Prayer is personal.

The instructions in the *Didache*, however, hint at the communal dimension of the prayer. Christians ought to say the prayer *at the times set* (see, for example, Acts 3.1 and 10.30). So although a Christian might have been on her own while praying, she would be praying in unison with the rest of the community. The first-person plural points to familial bonds between those who pray the 'Our Father': saying the Lord's Prayer in private at once unites a Christian to the rest of the community and binds her to the family of God.

Within a few centuries, Christians had formed communities specifically devoted to prayer, often housed in monasteries. The best-known guide for monastic life is probably *The Rule of St Benedict*. In the early fifth century, Benedict gave instructions for those wishing to live a monastic life, including set times and orders for prayer: seven times a day, with a set number of psalms at each office. The structure he laid out continues to regulate the prayer of monastic communities in the present. 'Of course', he wrote in chapter 13, 'Matins [morning prayer] and Vespers [evening prayer] should not ever go by without the Lord's Prayer being said by the abbot at the end, with all listening.' (Later guides to prayer for communities, such as the Anglican *Book of Common Prayer*, likewise include the Lord's Prayer at morning and evening prayer.) The practice of attending to the fifth petition, 'forgive us, just as we forgive', Benedict reasoned, would guard against the 'thorns of dissension which are accustomed to sprout' amongst people living in community.[2] Benedict's *Rule* reflects a long history of practice: praying the Lord's Prayer as a prayer for forgiveness. For example, Cyprian noted that the Christian was 'commanded to make prayer daily on account of his sins'.[3] Benedict must have believed that the monastic community needed to be reminded at least *twice* a day of their need for forgiveness.

Not everyone could (or wanted to) become a monk or a nun, but all Christians learnt the Lord's Prayer. The earliest treatises on the Lord's Prayer

---

[2] *Regula Benedicti* 13; *The Rule of St Benedict*, trans. Bruce L. Venarde (Cambridge, MA: Harvard University Press), 73.
[3] Cyprian, *De dominica oratione* 22; Tertullian, Cyprian and Origen, *On the Lord's Prayer*, trans. Alistair Stewart-Sykes (Crestwood, NY: St Vladimir's Seminary Press, 2004), 81.

emerged out of the catechetical instruction given to baptismal candidates, who would have learnt the prayer in the week prior to their baptism. Robert Taft, whom I have quoted above, draws the description of the Lord's Prayer as the 'summary of the whole gospel' from a treatise by a contemporary of Cyprian: Tertullian. His treatise *On Prayer* opens with exposition of, and commentary on, 'this rule of prayer'.[4] That is, he takes the Lord's Prayer as a guide to the form and content of all Christian prayer. Following his short discussions of each of the petitions, Tertullian gives a précis. 'We honor God in "Father", witness to the faith in "name", offer obedience in "will", remember our hope in "Kingdom", seek life in "bread", confess our debts in "pardon", and show concern for temptation in the request for safekeeping.'[5] The Lord's Prayer gave Christians a pattern for praying well, and praying without omission. Tertullian was the first to write in this fashion on the Lord's Prayer, but not the last. Sermons and commentaries on the Lord's Prayer abound throughout Christian history, and we will consider that tradition below.

The Lord's Prayer, for the theologians of the early church, is prayer *par excellence*. They would heartily approve of the use of the Lord's Prayer at moments when prayer is required, but one does not know what to say. In fact, they might argue that to pray the Lord's Prayer would be *better* than offering the first words that come to mind. After all, 'God alone could teach us the manner in which he would have us pray', Tertullian wrote.[6] It makes sense that Christians continue to follow this divine teaching, alone and in community.

The Lord's Prayer and the sacraments: Baptism and Eucharist

From the early treatises on the Lord's Prayer, we know that it was taught to catechumens just before their baptism. We who are used to thinking about the Lord's Prayer as (almost) a cultural commonplace might be surprised to learn that in the early church catechumens were presented the Lord's Prayer together with the creed, only when they were nearing the end of the catechumenate – and they did not pray the Our Father until after their baptism. Only the baptized could properly address God as 'Our Father', a sign of their adoption by God into Christ Jesus, his son, and also a sign of their inclusion into the body of Christ. Indeed, baptism continues to set the tone for the Lord's Prayer, as the *Catechism* indicates. 'When the Church prays the

---

[4]Tertullian, *De oratione* 1; *On the Lord's Prayer*, 42.
[5]Tertullian, *De oratione* 9; *On the Lord's Prayer*, 49.
[6]Tertullian, *De oratione* 9; *On the Lord's Prayer*, 49.

Lord's Prayer, it is always the people made up of the "new-born" who pray and obtain mercy' (CCC 2769). Baptized Christians would have been (and perhaps still ought to be) expected to say the Lord's Prayer daily, and would also have encountered the prayer in the celebration of the Eucharist – at least since the late fourth century. Although there has been some lively discussion amongst scholars about when and where the Lord's Prayer was first used in the Eucharist, the widespread use of the Lord's Prayer in eucharistic liturgies seems to date from the second half of the fourth century. Theologians writing around the same time mention it, and two liturgies attributed to theologian-bishops of the late fourth/early fifth centuries both include it: the liturgies of Basil and John Chrysostom. Unfortunately, the earliest manuscripts of these liturgies date from the eighth century, as does the earliest surviving text of the Roman canon – the Eucharistic Prayer used for centuries in the Roman Catholic Church.

Although we cannot be certain when the Lord's Prayer first appeared in eucharistic liturgies, we know that it has a long history of use in that context, and that the inclusion of the Lord's Prayer in the celebration of the Eucharist survived the Reformation. For example, the Lord's Prayer is found in John Knox's order of worship (1556) and the *Scottish Prayer Book* (1637) – to name just two. The manner and the place in which the Lord's Prayer has been included vary, however. Readers might be surprised to discover that both Martin Luther and John Calvin used paraphrases of the Lord's Prayer and that the *Scottish Prayer Book* indicates that the Lord's Prayer is to be said by a presbyter (elder) rather than the congregation. At the time of the Reformation congregations did not recite the Lord's Prayer in unison, as is common today. For example, in his order for the Mass (1523), Luther dictated that the pastor would recite the Lord's Prayer. The practice of praying the Lord's Prayer together in celebrations of the Eucharist grew slowly over time across Christian communities; in the Roman Catholic Church the Lord's Prayer was said, in Latin, by the altar boy on behalf of the people until after the second Vatican Council.

In the Roman rite, the Lord's Prayer appears between the doxology (which concludes the part of the Eucharistic Prayer that recalls the institution of the Eucharist at the last supper) and the kiss of peace, and is closely followed by communion. The instructions for the celebration of Mass drawn up after Vatican II preserve this order, which is also found in the Anglican *Book of Common Prayer* and the *Lutheran Book of Worship*. At this point, the people pray together for the fulfilment of all the petitions of the Lord's Prayer in the coming of God's kingdom, which is anticipated in the Eucharist: 'The Lord's Prayer sums up on the one hand all the petitions and intercessions expressed in the movement of the epiclesis [priestly gesture of blessing and invocation of the Holy Spirit] and, on the other, knocks at the door of the Banquet of the kingdom which sacramental communion anticipates' (CCC 2770).

This description of the place of the Lord's Prayer also says something about why the Lord's Prayer shows up in eucharistic liturgies: the sacramental and eschatological trajectory of the petitions. Maximus the Confessor offers this meditation: 'The Holy Spirit has made them adopted sons, as shown by the prayer where they have been found worthy to call God, "Our Father". And then they are assimilated to His unity by participation.'[7] Maximus points to the next aspect of the Lord's Prayer we will consider: the privilege of calling God Father.[8]

The privilege of praying 'Our Father'

We are used to seeing texts like the Lord's Prayer as in the public domain, freely accessible to any and all. But in the early church the Lord's Prayer was the prayer of the baptized. It is the privilege of the baptized because it is through Christ's sonship that Christians become children of God. So, as I will show, it is a *shared* privilege. Moreover, the baptized share not only in the privilege of calling God Father but the responsibility of carrying on the Son's mission to the world. We should also note here, as commentators from Tertullian to Martin Luther insisted, that Christians exercise the privilege of calling God Father in obedience to a command.

Because the Lord's Prayer is so universally prayed, the prize of being allowed to call God 'Father' might not seem particularly exciting to modern Christians. The idea that doing so is a privilege only for the baptized sounds strange to us. Yet the commentators on the Lord's Prayer from Tertullian to Maximus the Confessor all considered it the prayer of the members of Christ's body. For example, Cyril of Jerusalem, in his fourth-century catechetical lectures, included a short commentary on the Lord's Prayer nestled in his explanation of the eucharistic liturgy. The setting of the commentary corresponds to the practice of reserving the Our Father to the baptized: Cyril's five lectures are called 'mystagogy' – instruction to the newly baptized.

For the early church, claiming God as Father, which praying the Lord's Prayer implied, depended on being joined to Jesus Christ the Son. The

---

[7]Maximus the Confessor, *Mystagogia* 13; *Maximus the Confessor: Selected Writings*, trans. George Charles Berthold, CWS (New York: Paulist Press, 1985), 200.

[8]Readers who have difficulty with this form of address may wish to read Roberta Bondi, 'Praying the Lord's Prayer: Truthfulness, Intercessory Prayer, and Formation in Love', in *Liturgy and the Moral Self: Humanity at Full Stretch before God*, ed. E. Byron Anderson and Bruce T. Morrill (Collegeville, MN: Liturgical Press, 1998).

theological reasons for this are christological and ecclesiological as well as soteriological. When Jesus addresses God as Father throughout the Gospels, he does so without precedent. Although God may liken himself to a Father or Mother, and describes himself as acting in the role of a parent (as in Hos. 11.3, for example: 'was it not I who taught Ephraim to walk?') the people of Israel are not taught to call God Father. Cyprian, one early commentator on the Lord's Prayer, argues for the novelty of calling God Father in the New Testament on the grounds that the name God reveals to Moses is not *Father*. Writing centuries later, liberation theologian Leonardo Boff similarly observed that the experience of having God as Father begins with Jesus. Christians imitate Jesus' novel way of addressing God.[9]

Early Christian theologians offered a more robust accounts of the unity of the baptized, however: Christians are allowed this form of address because in baptism they have been joined to the Son, whose filial privilege they share. For example, Gregory of Nyssa declares that the Lord's Prayer is the prayer of those who have become partakers of the divine nature. In so doing, he states a theological commonplace, an idea often found in the earliest commentaries on the Lord's Prayer. Tertullian cites John 1.12 in his argument that the Lord's Prayer is the prayer of those who have been newly born, begotten of God. Fellow third-century commentators Origen and Cyprian both cite the same passage from John's Gospel, and Cyprian goes on to explain that 'anybody who is renewed, reborn, and restored to his God by grace', he writes, 'first of all says "Father", because he is now become a son'.[10] In addition to the Prologue, patristic theologians look to the third chapter of John's Gospel, in which Jesus explains to Nicodemus that in order to see the kingdom of God, one must be 'born anew ... of the Spirit' (Jn 3.3-8). Because of passages like these, the Gospel of John figures prominently in patristic discussions of Christians' adoption as children of God.

For early Christians, believers were saved by their union with the triune God, effected at baptism. The church, as the community of the baptized, was the body of Christ. It is a short step from this understanding of Christian salvation, especially as regards the unity of those who are being saved, to the realization that this is not an individual privilege. Christians pray the Our Father always in the first-person plural, not just in the opening address but also in the latter four petitions: *give us*, *forgive us*, *lead us*, *deliver us*. Thus, in praying the Lord's Prayer each Christian prays always as a member of Christ's body.

---

[9]Leonardo Boff, *The Lord's Prayer: The Prayer of Integral Liberation* (Maryknoll, NY: Orbis Books, 1983).

[10]Cyprian, *De dominica oratione* 9; *On the Lord's Prayer*, 70.

Baptism does not only afford Christians a privilege, however, but lays on them a charge. As Gregory of Nyssa writes, 'it is dangerous to use this prayer and call God one's Father before one's life has been purified', because addressing God as Father claims kinship and assumes participation in the divine life. Gregory urges the faithful to circumspection: 'Before we approach God we should first examine our life, if we have something worthy of the Divine kinship in ourselves and so we may make bold to use such a word.'[11] We will return to the way of life appropriate for the adopted children of God below.

The Lord's Prayer suggests that the children of God do not merely enjoy a privilege and try to behave nicely, however: those who have been joined to the Son offer themselves for God's kingdom and submit to God's will. Jesus teaches his followers to pray in this way; he also sends them out into the world, as the Father sent him (Jn 20.21). Moreover, union with Christ means sharing Christ's mission. Jean Daniélou takes this to indicate the mission of the church as a whole, and locates the Lord's Prayer in this context. The Lord's Prayer, he writes in *Prayer: The Mission of the Church*, 'is a missionary prayer: from one end to the other, the Our Father includes the presence of those who do not yet know Christ, who are in the midst of spiritual suffering'.[12] The privilege of the baptized is not 'private', not for the baptized alone: the prayer is for the whole world. Although the Lord's Prayer is the prayer of the baptized, the kingdom of God is universal. As Jesus came as the sign of God's love for the world and the means of the world's salvation, so also those who are baptized into him are called to bear that love and spend themselves in pursuit of God's kingdom.

Gregory of Nyssa further suggests that the privilege of calling God Father suggests a commensurate way of life. 'If therefore the Lord teaches us in His prayer to call God Father, it seems to me that He is doing nothing else but to set the most sublime life before us as our law.'[13] Even if all Christians no longer conceptualize the church and salvation as the early theologians did, Gregory's homilies on the Lord's Prayer fill out for us what it means to live out the privilege of calling God Father. The 'sublime life' of the children of God involves unstinting forgiveness and self-giving, as we shall see below.

---

[11]Gregory of Nyssa, *Sermon* 2; *The Lord's Prayer, The Beatitudes*, trans. Hilda C. Graef, ACW 18 (New York: Paulist Press, 1954), 43–4.

[12]Jean Daniélou, *Prayer: The Mission of the Church* (Grand Rapids, MI: William B. Eerdmans, 1996), 26.

[13]Gregory of Nyssa, *Sermon* 2; *The Lord's Prayer*, 39.

Living the Lord's Prayer

In the passage I quoted at the beginning of this chapter, Taft describes the Lord's Prayer as 'continual catechesis, a mirror of Christian life given to us in baptism and a constant reminder of the commitment made at that time'. I take the first two descriptions together, as naming the dimensions of the Lord's Prayer that teach and form Christian disciples. Forgiveness here emerges as a key theme, which I will explore in some detail. I conclude the chapter with the final aspect, the commitment implied in the Lord's Prayer.

The Lord's Prayer: Teaching and formation

The catechetical dimension of the Lord's Prayer should remind us – especially Christian leaders and teachers – of the church's duty to teach, to form her members in the way of the Gospel. We should note two things at the outset. First, Taft's 'continual' means that the Lord's Prayer is neither the beginning of catechesis nor is it sufficient on its own. The catechesis within which the Lord's Prayer is embedded, and which it continues, began prior to initiation into the church. Second, discipleship is the indispensable companion to catechesis, especially with regard to the Lord's Prayer – which is why I have taken these two dimensions together. Every Christian thinker we have consulted so far believed that the Lord's Prayer ought to be prayed with understanding and put into practice by the faithful. The Lord's Prayer not only teaches Christians about God, or about a way of life, but also inculcates that way of life in us and spurs us to live it out.

In the next several paragraphs, I tease out some threads from the history of the Lord's Prayer in the formation of Christian imagination and practice. The first of these threads is the assumption that the Lord's Prayer continues to teach us as scripture. The second is that the Lord's Prayer shapes Christian lives as part of a process of formation in conjunction with other key texts. Third, the Lord's Prayer takes us in directions that we might not have guessed, leading Christians into the struggle for justice and forming us as a people of forgiveness.

I begin with an early Christian theologian whose work is particularly associated with the interpretation of scripture, whom we have already met: Origen. His commentary on the opening address of the Lord's Prayer combines the two injunctions 'Pray like this ...' (Mt. 6.9) and 'Pray without ceasing ...' (1 Thess. 5.17, but implied in the Gospels: see Mk 13.32-37 and Mt. 26.40-41). He wrote:

We should not imagine that we are being taught to say these words at a certain fixed time for prayer. Rather, if we have understood what was said above concerning ceaseless prayer, may our entire life pray unceasingly by saying 'Our Father, who are in heaven'. For our citizenship is in no way upon earth but is in every way in the heavens (Phil. 3.20) which are the thrones of God, in that the Kingdom of God is established in all those who bear the image of the heavenly one (1 Cor. 15.49) and have so themselves become heavenly.[14]

In these few lines from Origen's commentary we glimpse the tone of early Christian writing on the Lord's Prayer and indeed on scripture more generally. The Lord's Prayer may be an iconic passage of scripture, particularly susceptible to moral interpretation. Origen did not devise a new method of interpretation to get at its deeper meaning, however: he read it as a part of the whole of scripture. His commentary on the opening address makes clear the identity between the words prayed and the life lived. A Christian prays constantly by living as the image of God, reflecting the Father to whom she prays. The Lord's Prayer draws her into this way of life.

Commentaries

Origen's third-century commentary, along with those of Tertullian and Cyprian, began a tradition that included – just to name a few – Gregory of Nyssa, Augustine, Maximus the Confessor and Thomas Aquinas in the pre-Reformation period, and scores more in the centuries since. Commentaries tend to follow the order of the petitions, especially in the pre-modern church, explaining the meaning of each one and describing the implications for Christian faith and practice. The tone of the commentaries is exhortative (like Origen's, tending towards a moral interpretation), and late ancient commentaries often took the form of sermons. Most commentators regard the Lord's Prayer as the form and content of all Christian prayer, referring to the dominical injunction: 'Pray like this' (Mt. 6.9). So the Lord's Prayer teaches Christians in two registers, which we might consider 'faith' (the theological content of the Lord's Prayer; the implied beliefs of one who prays the Lord's Prayer) and 'practice' (a technical guide to how and for what we ought to pray). This is something of a caricature; yet, the Lord's Prayer has been used to teach Christians in these ways from Tertullian's day to the present.

The last several decades have seen commentaries on the Lord's Prayer that recall the older ways of interpreting scripture, drawing attention to the moral sense. For example, Leonardo Boff highlighted the implications of the Lord's

---

[14]Origen, *On Prayer* 22.5; *An Exhortation to Martyrdom, Prayer and Select Works*, trans. Rowan E. Greer, CWS (New York: Paulist Press, 1979), 81–170 (125).

Prayer for the work of social justice in his 1983 study, *The Lord's Prayer: The Prayer of Integral Liberation*.[15] His commentary shares the structure set by the early church, meditating deeply on each of the petitions in turn. His tone is hortatory, like that of the early Christian theologians. Those who pray earnestly, 'hallowed be thy name', ought to bear in mind, Boff urges, that Christians 'sanctify the name of God when by our own life, by our own actions of solidarity, we help to build more pacific and more just human relationships, cutting off access to violence and one person's exploitation of another'.[16] For Boff, as for commentators throughout history, praying the Lord's Prayer implies a form of life commensurate with its petitions.

Gregory of Nyssa on the Lord's Prayer

Here I wish to delve more deeply into Gregory of Nyssa's commentary on the Lord's Prayer. The first sermon urges his hearers to pray, leaving the opening address for the second. His commentary on 'Our Father, who art in heaven' describes starkly what is required of one who calls God Father. She must set aside sin and base desires when she approaches God in prayer. Otherwise, she does not show herself to be the child of God, who is pure, holy and perfect. Tempering this seemingly impossible demand, Gregory reminds readers that praying the Lord's Prayer puts Christians in the place of the prodigal son. He writes:

> the words [our Father in heaven] seem to me to indicate a deeper meaning, for they remind us of the fatherland from which we have fallen and of the noble birthright which we have lost. Thus in the story of the young man who left his father's home and went away to live after the manner of swine the Word shows the misery of men in the form of a parable which tells of his departure and dissolute life; and He does not bring him back to his former happiness until he has become sensibly aware of his present plight and entered into himself, rehearsing words of repentance. Now these words agree as it were with the words of the prayer, for he said, *Father, I have sinned against Heaven and before thee.* He would not have added to his confession the sin against Heaven, if he had not been convinced that the country he had left when he sinned was Heaven. Therefore this confession gave him easy access to the father who ran towards him and embraced and kissed him.[17]

---

[15]Boff, *The Lord's Prayer*.
[16]Boff, *The Lord's Prayer*, 49.
[17]Gregory of Nyssa, *Sermon* 2; *The Lord's Prayer*, 41.

For Gregory, the simple address reminds Christians who God is and our relation to God: the prodigal children who, turning to God in prayer, implicitly acknowledge our fallenness and receive the Father's welcoming embrace. This passage sets the bearing for what follows. Gregory insists throughout that Christians are at once children of God and citizens of heaven and, at the same time, wayward 'sons' who have fallen short of the virtue that is our birthright. When we call God Father we admit that we have fallen short and prepare to receive God's forgiveness (on which more to follow).

In Gregory's sermons on the Lord's Prayer, the privilege of the baptized morphs into the responsibility to live into the image of the One to whom we were thereby joined. Shouldering that burden might seem impossible, but the prayer itself helps the Christian to live according to her privilege: in teaching his disciples the Our Father, Jesus 'gives them not only the vision of, but a share in, the Divine power, bringing them as it were to kinship with the Divine Nature'.[18] I consider two aspects of this responsibility, relating to the third and fifth petitions of the Lord's Prayer.

In commenting on the third petition, Gregory emphasizes the humility of asking merely for bread, and not for any delicacies. He connects our satisfaction with plain bread, and only the minimum we need, to care for the poor. 'You are the master of your prayer', he writes, 'if abundance does not come from another's property and is not the result of another's tears; if no one is hungry or distressed because you are fully satisfied. For the bread of God is above all the fruit of justice, the ear of the corn of peace, pure and without any admixture of the seed of tares'.[19]

Gregory's association of the Lord's Prayer, particularly the third petition, with social justice is hardly unique to his commentary, even in the early church. His reading – perhaps surprisingly – anticipates a reading like that of Boff, who argued that 'in the Lord's Prayer we encounter in a practical way the correct relationship between God and humankind, between heaven and earth, between the religious and the political, while maintaining unity throughout'.[20]

The Lord's Prayer does not bear the burden of shaping disciples alone, however. Early Christians used both the creed and the Lord's Prayer in catechesis, and theologians wrote careful guides for those instructing new believers, before and after their baptism. Later, especially after the Reformation, the Lord's Prayer took its place alongside the Ten

[18]Gregory of Nyssa, *Sermon* 2; *The Lord's Prayer*, 35.
[19]Gregory of Nyssa, *Sermon* 4; *The Lord's Prayer*, 67.
[20]Boff, *The Lord's Prayer*, 4.

Commandments and the creed. Luther used the three texts in this way, as did other Reformed and Anabaptist communities.

Among the practices of Christian discipleship towards which the Lord's Prayer leads us, forgiveness stands out. The Lord's Prayer itself draws our attention to it: although Luke's Gospel records a considerably shorter iteration of the Lord's Prayer, his rendering of the fifth petition is just as long as Matthew's. The prayer for forgiveness merits further consideration here for two reasons. First, the fifth petition, unlike the others, includes a reference to the action of the petitioner. Moreover, the 'petition is so important that it is the only one to which the Lord returns and which he develops explicitly in the Sermon on the Mount' (CCC 2841). If Jesus so marked out the prayer for forgiveness, we ought to pay attention to it. Secondly, because this is so, the fifth petition has engendered a good deal of discussion throughout the history of the church. Over the course of that history, this little phrase has perplexed commentators. It is tempting to read it as a *quid pro quo*: God forgives, because we have forgiven. If we don't do our bit, then God won't do his. But we misunderstand the prayer and its place in the life and liturgy of the church if we read the fifth petition in that way. A handful of early Christian theologians steer us towards a reading that brings it into a different light: since God only can forgive sins, those who forgive show most clearly that they belong to the Father.

Gregory of Nyssa is one such theologian. Forgiveness, he reasons, marks out Christians as those who are like the Father, for forgiveness is a thing reserved to God. His reading of the fifth petition is worth discussing in detail, as it is archetypical and striking.

> One [who] would approach God ... is almost no longer shown in terms of human nature, but, through virtue, is likened to God himself, so that he seems to be another god, in that he does those things that God alone can do. For the forgiving of debts is the special prerogative of God, since it is said, *No man can forgive sins but God alone.* If therefore a man imitates in his own life the characteristics of the Divine Nature, he becomes somehow that which he visibly imitates. What therefore does the prayer teach? First that we should be conscious of our likeness to God through the liberty of our life, then to be bold to call God our Father, and to ask that our sins should no more be remembered.[21]

In this passage Gregory does not imply that forgiveness is due to the petitioner because she has done her part by forgiving others. He hints rather that the

---

[21]Gregory of Nyssa, *Sermon* 5; *The Lord's Prayer*, 71.

petitioner has provided, in her small way, an example of what she wishes the Lord to do for her. Gregory maintains that we are made like God through forgiving, and that this is the very peak of virtue, yet allows that even the one who has achieved such moral stature needs to ask for forgiveness. This paradox may be one reason why commentators opt for the *quid pro quo* reading. But Gregory highlights (here as elsewhere) the tension in Christian life, which the Lord's Prayer captures perfectly. The one who prays 'Our Father' does so, as we have seen, by participation in the Son who is without sin. She also claims, in the fifth petition, to have done that which only God can do. She asserts – or so it seems – moral perfection. She asks for God's forgiveness in imitation of what she has already done. And yet she asks for forgiveness of sins. This is the paradox of Christian discipleship, and the Lord's Prayer does not resolve it for us but invites us to hold it in tension.

Perhaps the difficulty in Gregory's reading of the fifth petition (which is anticipated by Origen and developed further by Maximus) lies in the difficulty of imagining ourselves as 'exemplars' for *God*. Jesus provides the example, the one true image of the invisible God. Christians falter in our imitation of Christ and we know it. But we should not allow the brute fact of our fallibility to obscure the reality that the opening address of the Lord's Prayer indicates. *Our Father* receives us as his children, by the Holy Spirit incorporates us into Christ himself and transforms us into his image. For Gregory and like-minded interpreters, the clause 'as we forgive ...' brings to light this image within us and goes a step further: Christians who forgive reflect God and thereby become examples for God. Perhaps we should pray the fifth petition in the sure knowledge that 'as we forgive those who trespass against us' becomes the reality as we pray it. Gregory's reading of the Lord's Prayer makes possible a new way of thinking about the fifth petition: Christians can go out and forgive others because, in a sense, in Christ we have already done it.

Conclusion

The Lord's Prayer does not simply teach Christians what to believe, but how to live what we believe. The teaching it contains is to be appropriated and *lived out*. That is the commitment made at baptism: to live as a son or daughter in God's family, to seek God's will and God's kingdom, to pray and work so that all may receive daily bread and to forgive all those who have wronged us, as befits the children of the most merciful Father. The Lord's Prayer serves as a reminder, as often as we pray it, of the way of discipleship. It serves in the life and liturgy of the church as a guidepost and comfort for all who follow Christ.

CHAPTER THIRTY-FIVE

Prayer and Pastoral Ministry

STEPHEN BURNS

To begin with the obvious, ministry is about 'service', translating the New Testament term *diakonia*. It is applied to what later became designated different orders of ministry, and to both ordained and lay persons. The term 'pastoral' pertains to keeping sheep or cattle, and related imagery is employed in Old and New Testaments in depictions towards God and Christ. Biblical images of a divine shepherd (e.g. Ps. 23; Ez. 34) and of Christ as great or good shepherd (e.g. Jn 10; 1 Pet. 2) provide a crucial wider context whenever certain persons in Christian community are appointed and termed 'shepherds', 'pastors'.[1] This biblical material provides a transcendent horizon and superlative referent for the pastor's ministry and so correctives to over-reached ideas of pastors themselves – for their meaning is dependent on God and is skewed apart from that dependence.[2]

In Christian traditions with diaconal and presbyteral orders in either two- or threefold patterns, contemporary diaconal rites have tended to accent service (and sometimes ambassadorship) while rites for presbyters – in

---

[1] Gail Ramshaw, *Treasures Old and New: Images in the Lectionary* (Minneapolis, MN: Fortress Press, 2002), 363–70. Throughout this chapter, I write with the conviction (i) that though prayer is wider than liturgy, liturgy is prayer and (ii) though theology is wider than liturgy, liturgy is theology.

[2] Throughout I use plural pronouns to avoid the gender binary 'he or she' (likewise 'her or his') and to acknowledge the presence – at least sometimes, and in principle – of transpersons.

some traditions, 'priests', in others, 'ministers of the word' or 'ministers of word and sacrament' – typically bring forward imagery of shepherding, albeit carefully distinguishing those ordained from Christ Jesus as supreme shepherd. To take as an example the wording of the highly influential rites of the Church of South India, formed in 1946, the ordination of presbyters reads in part, 'make them watchful and loving guardians over thy flock; as followers of the Good Shepherd who gave his life for the sheep'.[3] Use of servant and shepherding imagery can be tracked back to patristic materials, with a stress on service appearing in Ignatius of Antioch's writing on deacons, and shepherding associated with presbyters in *The Apostolic Tradition*.[4]

The 'Clerical Paradigm'

At the present time the weight of two important shifts should be felt in any consideration of pastoral ministry. The first is a challenge to what Bonnie Miller-McLemore has depicted as the 'clerical paradigm' of much pastoral theology and pastoral work.[5] In contest to this clerical model, the term 'pastoral' is now applied widely to lay ministers in very many settings – hospitals, prisons, schools, sporting clubs, shopping centres and so on. This is to say that the term 'pastoral ministry' now commonly encircles much more than the work of the clergy in settings like parishes. Yet it should also be noted that, for better or worse, however wide ranging pastoral ministry may now oftentimes be considered to be, a certain reticence can still be spotted in rites of commissioning for such (lay) pastors where biblical images of shepherding can be either avoided or downplayed, that is, liturgical traditions tend to continue to cluster shepherding images around presbyters in particular.[6]

---

[3]For the text, see Paul F. Bradshaw, *Rites of Ordination: Their History and Theology* (Collegeville, MN: Liturgical Press, 2014), 193. Of course, liturgy is more than text: an event, with words breathed from bodies in ceremonial scenes, ritual pictures in communal space, to say the least.
[4]Paul F. Bradshaw, *Ordination Rites of the Ancient Churches of East and West* (Collegeville, MN: Liturgical Press, 1990), 63, 73.
[5]A string of Bonnie J. Miller-McLemore's essays have this focus. For example, 'The "Clerical Paradigm": A Fallacy of Misplaced Concreteness', *International Journal of Practical Theology* 11, no. 1 (2007): 19–36 and *Christian Theology in Practice: Discovering a Discipline* (Grand Rapids, MI: William B. Eerdmans, 2012).
[6]A salient example: the British Methodist Church's *Methodist Worship Book* (Peterborough: Methodist Publishing House, 1999) includes a section on 'Admission, Commissioning and Welcome Services', 329–68. Services of welcome to presbyters and deacons employ imagery of shepherding and services, as do the ordination services to which they correspond; other services are more reticent of shepherding imagery, with just one reference to Christ as 'Shepherd and Saviour' without any corresponding association suggested of 'pastoral visitors'. See *Methodist Worship Book*, 308, 309, 321, 323, 325, 346, 358, 360.

The Baptismal Covenant

The second shift involves more movement in the liturgies of a range of traditions. Both baptism and ordination oftentimes now insist that 'ministry' is a baptismal category, that is, it is not to be reserved to the ordained. This conviction is in fact a kind of prerequisite for the widening of pastoral ministry to lay persons. As just one of many possible examples to which reference might be made, part of the baptism service of the Uniting Church in Australia's *Uniting in Worship 2* reads: 'Claimed by God, we are given the gift of the Holy Spirit that we may live as witnesses to Jesus Christ, share his ministry in the world and grow to maturity.'[7] This conviction is echoed in many places through that church's liturgical resources, including those for ordination where a stress on the ministry of the baptized is emphatic at the beginning of the rite for setting apart some to orders.

Of particular importance ecumenically is a text emerging in the past fifty or so years, known in the place where it was first printed (the US-based Episcopal Church's *Book of Common Prayer 1979*) as 'the Baptismal Covenant'.[8] In variants and adaptations this text has migrated around and beyond the Anglican Communion, sometimes renamed as an Affirmation of Commitment, Commitment to Christian Service or Commitment to Mission,[9] but under whatever heading giving some descriptive contour to the ministry of the Christian people. First highlighting the ecclesial practices of Acts 2.38 – continuing in the community of faith, the apostles' teaching, the breaking of bread and the prayers – it then turns to spotlight witness to Christ in 'word and deed', striving for justice and peace and 'recognizing the dignity of every human being'.[10] When convictions appear like Gabe Huck's, that ministry 'is basically the way Christians are, the way they behave',[11] something like the Baptismal Covenant is in play, whether or not that particular liturgical form is known. Likewise, when *A New Zealand Prayer Book* – that country's much-lauded Anglican book – includes (as well as a version of the Baptismal Covenant) in its catechism the uncompromising

---

[7]The Uniting Church in Australia, *Uniting in Worship 2* (Sydney: Uniting Church Press, 2005), 74.
[8]The Episcopal Church, *Book of Common Prayer* (New York: Church Hymnal Incorporation, 1979), 306.
[9]As in the Church of England, Anglican Church of Aotearoa New Zealand and Polynesia, and the Uniting Church in Australia, respectively.
[10]The background to the wording is detailed in Ruth Meyers, *Continuing the Reformation: Re-visioning Baptism in the Episcopal Church* (New York: Church Publishing, 1997).
[11]Gabe Huck, *Liturgy with Style and Grace*, rev. edn (Chicago, IL: Liturgy Training Publications, 1984), 42.

response to the question 'Who are the ministers of the Church?' 'They are the lay persons, deacons, priests and bishops; all the baptised'.[12]

This second shift to see – so catechize and ritualize – ministry as a baptismal category means that in traditions which ordain persons to certain kinds of ministry, identifying the focus of ministry to which such persons are ordained is crucially important. However, identifying that focus has not always been straightforward,[13] though the view that presbyters are ordained as something closely akin to 'pastor, priest, and teacher' prevails in many traditions, with the particular focus of their ministry being said to be word and sacrament: preaching with scripture, and presiding at font and table central to their ministry, perhaps inaugurated by ordination rites that involve the giving of a Bible (to deacons and presbyters) as well as sometimes (to presbyters) paten (plate) and chalice for communion. Around such symbolic actions *A New Zealand Prayer Book,* for example, then affirms deacons as follows: 'to search and to serve is the priceless contribution God calls you to make'. And with respect to priests, it says to them: 'You are marked as a person who proclaims that among the truly blessed are the poor, the troubled, the powerless, the persecuted. You must be prepared to be what you proclaim.'[14] While some traditions make vocational (i.e. lifelong) deacons, other transitional ones (i.e. people are made deacon prior to priesting), and other traditions again have both vocational and transitional deacons, where transitional practices are enacted, presbyters do not cease to be deacons but are understood to build a presbyteral ministry upon the basis of service central to the ministry of the diaconate.

Both movement away from a clerical paradigm and emphasis on a 'baptismal ecclesiology' suggest ways of beginning to critique inherited theologies,[15] still scripted into many liturgies, which propose Christ as

---

[12]Anglican Church in Aotearoa New Zealand and Polynesia, *A New Zealand Prayer Book* (Auckland: Collins, 1989), 931.

[13]See contrasting and contested documents of the Uniting Church in Australia collected into *Theology for Pilgrims: Selected Theological Documents of the Uniting Church in Australia*, ed. Rob Bos and Geoff Thompson (Sydney: Uniting Church Press, 2008), 230–399, for example. For discussion of this tension, see Stephen Burns, 'Ministry', in *An Informed Faith: The Uniting Church at the Beginning of the Twenty-First Century*, ed. William W. Emilsen (Melbourne: Morning Star, 2014), 37–68.

[14]*A New Zealand Prayer Book*, 895, 901, 902, 907.

[15]For an exposition of this in the (US-based Anglican) Episcopal tradition, see Louis Weil, *A Theology of Worship* (Cambridge, MA: Cowley Publications, 2000). For a Roman Catholic understanding, see Paul J. Philibert, *The Priesthood of the Faithful: Key to a Living Church* (Collegeville, MN: Liturgical Press, 2005) with its intriguing chapters like, 'An Intentional Symbolic Life', on the *laity*.

shepherd as a 'pattern' for those in presbyteral orders.[16] Although as Frank Wright points out shepherding imagery may have some merits:

> Our readiness in our pastoral work to be known as a person without any façade ('they know my voice'); our readiness to be available, and fully committed ('I lay down my life for the sheep').

This imagery also rightly attracts some reserve. In Wright's own words it 'barely conceals notions completely unworthy of lay people, and sorely tempting to the ingrained authoritarian temper of clergy'.[17] It is not unproblematic. But nor, as Gordon Lathrop notes, are numerous common names for ministers, which like 'pastor' are also at best 'broken symbols'. So rector means 'ruler', reverend suggests a special holiness, vicar is entangled in vicariousness and so on – and all are in some respects ill-fit to ministry in ways that Lathrop illumines against biblical correctives. Yet Lathrop also sagely counsels that ditching these titles in place of a personal name is by no means a simple solution to the problems that titles present:

> 'Pastor Sue', 'Father Jim', 'Reverend Mike', or even just 'Sue' or 'Jim' or 'Mike' ... may be used by some people who think that they are thereby avoiding the use of any symbols. ... Probably, however, the symbol resides in the very familiarity of the names. This symbolic use points towards a longing for intimacy.[18]

That is, when referred to a pastor, a personal name is also symbolic, likewise broken, 'made up of the unexpected, the ordinary, the failed, the equivocal rather than the absolute'. Like the broken titles, a focus on the personal is mediated, and as such in its fragility perhaps yet also able sometimes to be 'powerful in [its] reference, in the hope [it] evoke[s]'.[19] The *mediated* nature of pastoral ministry is common to such ministry whether it is exercised by

---

[16]For example, Anglican Church of Australia, *A Prayer Book for Australia* (Alexandria: Broughton Books, 1995), 793. Johannine Gospel memory presents additional questions given Anthony Dyson's important challenge as to 'the question of the historical Jesus and of the extent to which He (sic) may be regarded as the historical and/or theological norm for pastoral theology and practice'. See Anthony Dyson, 'Pastoral Theology: Towards a New Discipline', in *Faith or Fear? A Reader in Pastoral Care and Counselling*, ed. Michael Jacobs (London: Darton, Longman and Todd, 1987), 150.

[17]Frank Wright, *Pastoral Care Revisited* (London: SCM Press, 1996), 5–6. For shepherding imagery within a very wide range of alternative imagery, see Robert Dykstra, ed., *Images of Pastoral Care: Classic Readings* (St Louis, MO: Chalice Press, 2004).

[18]Gordon W. Lathrop, *The Pastor: A Spirituality* (Minneapolis, MN: Fortress Press, 2006), 12.

[19]Lathrop, *The Pastor*, 5.

ordained or lay persons; it has ecclesial, representative and public dimensions entangled up in it, and it relates to prayer.

Ecclesial, Representative, Public Ministry

Ordained pastors are made not only by the giving of a Bible and perhaps also plate and cup, and not even by words addressed to pastors in a charge, but by *epikleptic* prayer: ordination involves the laying on of hands with prayer as its central action.[20] Authorized lay ministry also involves commissioning of some kind in the context of prayer for the person so authorized, with a liturgy likely at least in some respects to be derivative of rites for the ordained even as such rites perhaps avoid a shepherding motif. Moreover, pastors are ordained (and lay persons, commissioned and/or appointed) by the church; in many cases this is at least in part in order to lead rites of the church.[21] Public worship makes pastors prominent, with the descriptor 'pastor, priest, and teacher' used in numerous ordination charges suggesting that priests and teachers, presiders and preachers, are called to these ministries *because* they are first of all pastors.[22] While many traditions reserve eucharistic and other sacramental presidency to the ordained, this is not true of all ecclesial groups. But pastors lead prayer, sacramental or otherwise, in Sunday assembly and/ or at other times. Ordination rites typically ask the candidate to be faithful in prayer. Roman Catholic rites, for instance, directly echo 1 Thessalonians 5 to charge ordained pastors to 'pray without ceasing', while other traditions sometimes recast a similar stress in creative ways: so *A New Zealand Prayer Book* involves the striking affirmation made by those about to be ordained, 'You are my God. I can neither add to your glory nor take away from your power. Yet will I wait upon you daily in prayer and praise.'[23]

When pastors pray, they pray not only as a member of a Christian assembly at prayer but they sometimes also voice prayer on behalf of others in the assembly. In some traditions, ritual/prayer books may prescribe or in other

---

[20]See Bradshaw, *Ordination Rites* and Bradshaw, *Rites of Ordination*.

[21]In many traditions, this is more a focus for presbyters, less so deacons, though unlikely to be absent in either order in any ecclesial stream. Note, for example, how the Uniting Church in Australia's ordination services use the same wording for deacons and ministers of the word, bar only the former's single use of 'servant', the latter's single use of 'shepherd', but otherwise exactly the same sentences charging those ordained to different orders of ministry, except only that they are presented in a different order, so as to suggest their particular orientation: presbyters to the church gathered, deacons to the church dispersed.

[22]On Anglican tradition, see Stephen Pickard's most informative account of theologies of ordination in his *Theological Foundations for Collaborative Ministry* (Aldershot: Ashgate, 2009).

[23]*A New Zealand Prayer Book*, 896, 906, 919.

ways direct words for their prayer,[24] but a pastor presiding in the assembly may, to adopt a phrase used repeatedly by Don E. Saliers, serve as a 'sign of living prayer' with a distinctive focal as well as vocal role.[25] Notwithstanding that the *orans* posture (palms up, hands out) is now commonplace in at least many Pentecostal/charismatic assemblies, it may long have been the gesture of the entire assembly at eucharistic prayer,[26] and whether a congregational gesture or not is often a key presidential one across a wide range of traditions. This posture may be perceived to set the tone for the participation of others, inviting either physical adoption of like-kind shapes by others or proposing an appropriate interior posture by the celebrating assembly. The pastor may also have a distinctive ministry to word prayer that involves either or both representation and extemporization.[27] This is to say that within Christian liturgy, of whatever style, a pastor has some distinctive roles in liturgical celebration which distinguishes their participation from that of others, at a practical and embodied level if not also at a theological one (so one may jettison an ontology of ordination, for example, but still contend with inherited disciplines of presiding).

Everyday and other orders ('daily prayer', 'liturgy of the hours' and all kinds of devotions) may then relate not only scripture but modes and moods of prayer[28] from Sunday assembly across the rest of the week – notably thanks and praise (practices, according to Daniel Hardy and David F. Ford, of 'completing the completed' and 'perfecting perfection')[29] and intercession (a practice that involves, in Saliers' evocative depiction, 'look[ing] where God's love is already looking').[30] In the to-and-fro between Sunday and

---

[24]In traditions with prayer books, prescribed texts often sit alongside other texts governed by permissive rubrics allowing for 'these or other suitable words' or like-kind directions, while other traditions' liturgical resources are intended to enable something like 'ordered liberty' in which the book's text may serve as a standard and norm, not least for doctrine which with locally composed alternatives should be congruent. For the latter approach, see, for example, *Uniting in Worship 2*.

[25]Repeated with much significance in Don E. Saliers, *Worship and Spirituality* (Akron, OH: OSL Publications, 1996), 18, 20, etc.

[26]See Nathan Mitchell and John Leonard, *The Postures of the Assembly during the Eucharistic Prayer* (Chicago, IL: Liturgy Training Publications, 1994).

[27]Representation may involve using the texts prescribed in a prayer book, or composing or employing alternatives that cohere with the norms of a denominationally produced resources; extemporization may refer not only to spontaneous 'ad-lib' prayer but to specially prepared local composition, with coherence with denominational doctrinal norms in a book or otherwise also part of this pastoral responsibility.

[28]For discussion of praise, thanksgiving, intercession and confession, see Stephen Burns, ed., *Liturgical Spirituality: Anglican Reflections on the Church's Prayer* (New York: Seabury Press, 2013).

[29]Daniel W. Hardy and David F. Ford, *Jubilate: Theology in Praise* (London: Darton, Longman and Todd, 1984), 6–7.

[30]Saliers, *Worship and Spirituality*, 74.

everyday prayer, pastors may find themselves 'formed by the liturgy'.[31] That is, pastors not only practise in other settings the central things in which they lead others in Sunday celebrations, but may at best (like others who join them in these prayerful practices) imbibe them as a way of life. As Carol Doran's hymn 'As a Chalice Cast of Gold' has it, when dancing or chanting praise, singing psalms or hymns, preaching the loving ways of the divine, 'let [the] heart add its Amen', such that the 'outward rite' reflects the 'inward light' of the divine.[32]

Yet just as tension emerges around difference in the ordination of some (deacons, presbyters) and commissioning of others (lay persons) for forms of ministry – with shepherding imagery being more readily used of the ordained – so tension may run throughout other rites. Particular liturgical seasons bring images of servanthood to the fore: Holy Week with its Holy/ Maundy Thursday foot-washing, for instance, rubrics for which sometimes curiously retain the act of foot-washing itself to the ordained.[33] At the Eucharist on that day and many other occasions, if the *Agnus Dei* ('Lamb of God') is used shepherd themes are alluded to while the pastor is likely to be visibly prominent, and at every eucharistic celebration the presider will likely recite the so-called institution narrative that recalls the Last Supper, either as a biblical warrant for a eucharistic prayer (also called 'prayer of great thanksgiving') that follows (or precedes) it or else as part of eucharistic prayer itself. In recalling the assembly to this gospel memory, the presider is placed in an especially powerful association with Jesus, which in some traditions is amplified by understandings of a priest acting *in persona Christi* as well as in a mode more readily acceptable to a wider range of traditions, *in persona ecclesiae*.[34] Not only at the eucharistic table, a presider's 'liturgical direction' gestures the presider in prayer sometimes to face the same way as others as their representative, and at other times towards others, perhaps

---

[31]Goffredo Boselli, *The Spiritual Meaning of the Liturgy: School of Prayer, Source of Life* (Collegeville, MN: Liturgical Press, 2014), where 'Presbyters Formed by the Liturgy' is a chapter title. See also Stephen Burns, 'Yearning without Saying a Word: Unembarrassed Presiding in Liturgy', *Worship* 85, no. 1 (2012): 1–16.

[32]Carol Doran, 'As a Chalice Cast of Gold', in *Together in Song: An Australian Hymn Book II* (Sydney: HarperCollins, 1999), no. 476.

[33]'The president may wash the feet of some members of the congregation.' See *Common Worship: Times and Seasons* (London: Church House Publishing, 2006), 298; though for other possibilities, see Bryan Cones, '"How Beautiful the Feet": Discerning the Assembly's Path on Holy Thursday', in *Liturgy with a Difference: Beyond Inclusion in the Liturgical Assembly*, ed. Bryan Cones and Stephen Burns (London: SCM Press, 2019), 3–18.

[34]See Louis Weil, *Liturgical Sense: The Logic of Rite* (New York: Seabury Press, 2013) and especially Bryan Cones, 'On Not Playing Jesus: The Gendered Liturgical Theology of Presiding', *Pacifica* 30, no. 2 (2017): 128–45.

as representative of Christ or God.[35] These dynamics are a most potent dimension of prayer in pastoral ministry. One of most sensitive articulations of them is in the Uniting Church in Australia's 1994 document on 'Ordination and Ministry':

> The minister presiding at the Eucharist represents not only the local congregation (both those present and those absent) who together celebrate the sacrament, but the universal church at all times and places which joins us 'with choirs of angels and the whole creation in the eternal hymn.' In another liturgical sense, the minister may represent Christ, although all Christians share that responsibility.[36]

Yet even when the *in persona Christi* tradition's vulnerability to 'playing Jesus' is kept in check, liturgical celebration still requires someone to announce blessing, proclaim forgiveness, preach the gospel word of Jesus and so on.[37]

On any given occasion, eucharistic presidency may or may not involve preaching at the same eucharistic celebration, but both preaching and presidency at table are central to many pastors' ministry. The pastor not only reads scripture privately, but likely at least sometimes also in public,[38] and they also proclaim/expound those scriptures in preaching and 'contemporary witness'.[39] Whether such portions have been discerned by the pastor or may have come via a lectionary used by an ecclesial tradition (with the latter at least sometimes allowing for local construction of lectionary patterns), in order to preach, the pastor must have paid attention in prayer to the

---

[35]Graham Hughes, *Worship as Meaning: A Liturgical Theology for Late Modernity* (Cambridge: Cambridge University Press, 2004), 160–4.

[36]Bos and Thompson, ed., *Theology for Pilgrims*, 363.

[37]Though proposals for the communalization of these actions are also to be found, not least in feminist liturgical literature. See Stephen Burns, 'Four in a Vestment? Feminist Gesture for Christian Assembly', in *Presiding Like a Woman*, ed. Nicola Slee and Stephen Burns (London: SPCK, 2010), 9–19.

[38]In many traditions, scripture reading is one of several tasks rubrics typically deemed to be 'appropriate' to laypersons, according to notes concerning the celebration and rubrics of many liturgy. Some traditions, however, curiously reserve the gospel announcement to clergy, most often deacons – a practice perhaps not congruent with a shift just noted to ministry as a baptismal category?

[39]A term used for preaching in *Uniting in Worship* 2, see Service of the Lord's Day 3 and 4. The Uniting Church, like various others, has wide-ranging definitions of the sermon, akin to this from the Church of England: 'The term "sermon" includes less formal exposition, the use of drama, interviews, discussion, audio-visuals and the insertion of hymns or other sections of the service between parts of the sermon. The sermon may come after one of the readings, or before or after the prayers.' See *New Patterns for Worship* (London: Church House Publishing, 2008), 14.

scripture proclaimed.[40] And whatever preparation goes on for preaching, daily lectionaries used in everyday prayer provide a whole ecology of scriptural – and sometimes other – reading which leads to and from Sunday.[41] Some traditions charge pastors to uphold (and open up to others) shared forms of common prayer on a daily basis. Yet while an Office of Readings is central to Roman Catholic and some other traditions' mandated engagement with scripture by its pastors, the forms of daily prayer made available to pastors and other members of their churches now range very widely indeed,[42] far beyond their long-standing centre around lectionary and the Lucan canticles – of Zechariah, Mary and Simeon (all Lk. 1–2) – themselves among the most durable prayers of the Christian tradition.

Furthermore, where lectionaries are used, either Sunday by Sunday or each day of the week, they relate an assembly, and a pastor's, reading to other churches using the same sequence of readings. Certain lectionary patterns, notably the Revised Common Lectionary, are now in very wide use across many Christian traditions (and are sometimes being enthusiastically taken up by churches with previously thin traditions of using centralized lectionaries). As such their use may be an important part of how some pastors express their sense of connection to and sign-value of the universal church, catholicity – another thing they symbolize.

Dynamics of representation may also be more diffuse. In a moving essay, Stephen Cherry writes of multiple aspects of representation in ordained ministry. These map onto and stretch those noted in the Uniting Church document already cited: the representation of the wider church to the local church (and vice versa), the representation of the local church to the wider community and the representation of the wider community itself.[43] His signal example of the latter is of felt-expectation and explicit invitation to speak for a local community, well beyond the worshipping community, at the time of a tragic and brutal death of a child in the town where he was an Anglican minister. Cherry's essay gives a striking account of the cost of his own prayer and of attempts to open opportunity for prayer for those so moved across wider community.

---

[40]At least, various churches' 'Code of Ethics' and such-like presume this. For a worthwhile account of practical preparation to preach, see Lathrop, *The Pastor*, 55–8.

[41]*Revised Common Lectionary: Daily Readings* (Minneapolis, MN: Fortress Press, 2005), which for Monday through Wednesday has readings which follow from Sunday, and those for Thursday through Saturday move towards Sunday.

[42]On richness in just the Anglican tradition, see Stephen Burns, '"Learning Again and Again to Pray": Anglican Forms of Daily Prayer, 1979–2014', *Journal of Anglican Studies* 15, no. 1 (2017): 9–36.

[43]Stephen Cherry, 'Representation', in *Praying for England: Priestly Prayer and Contemporary Culture*, ed. Sarah Coakley and Samuel Wells (London: Continuum, 2008), 20–40.

This public dimension of pastoral ministry may depend on a pastor's visibility beyond the rounds of congregational life. Clerical haberdashery (collars, robes and so on) has been and in some places may sometimes remain an invitation to such ministry, and not least to prayer as part of it, as the moniker 'say one for me' invoked of clergy has at least sometimes in the past suggested, notwithstanding the vicarious problems of the request.[44] Less happenchance interaction with the wider community may find a focus in provision of pastoral services (sometimes 'occasional offices') still sometimes called upon by members of the wider community beyond regular worshippers. Alan Billings' work on what he calls the 'sacred hearts' of 'secular lives' provides much insight into the prayer which pastoral ministers may be invited to share at such times, often quite beyond the orthodoxies of official liturgical forms.[45] Billings insists that un-churched persons, though not embracing the church's teaching, nevertheless often make valuable meaning of Christian rites; for example, baptism of children may be an epiphany, a 'showing' of a child to others at least in this respect akin to the biblical story of the magi bringing gifts to little Jesus. While pastoral services constitute one kind of 'outreach', the dynamics of current preoccupation in some places with 'Fresh Expressions' of church also invite engagement with related dynamics. Fresh Expressions seek new ways of inviting persons to Christian community, including eventually to the central things of word and sacrament – though not in liturgies currently to be found in 'inherited' expressions of church.[46] It can be helpful here to remember James White's observations about a so-called 'hierarchy in liturgical studies'. Much liturgical study may put the Eucharist at the top of its attention, with other services lower in the 'hierarchy', but as White reminds 'millions of alumni and alumnae of the churches' have as their only link with public worship rites of passage/occasional offices/pastoral services and 'in terms of evangelization' these may be more important than the Eucharist.[47] To these, the un-churched whom Fresh Expressions of church now seek to welcome can be allied.

The pastoral processes around occasional offices oftentimes at least involve visiting – which Protestant traditions may have emphasized to counter losses

---

[44]Wesley Carr, *Say One for Me: The Church of England in the Next Decade* (London: SPCK, 1992).

[45]Alan Billings, *Secular Lives, Sacred Hearts: The Role of the Church in a Time of No Religion* (London: SPCK, 2004).

[46]See discussion of Billings alongside Fresh Expressions of Church in Stephen Burns, 'Pastoral Ministry Today', in *A Pastoral Handbook for Anglicans*, ed. Bradley Billings (Alexandria: Broughton Books, 2018), 25–52.

[47]James White, *Christian Worship in North America: A Retrospective, 1955–1995* (Collegeville, MN: Liturgical Press, 1997), 312–13.

felt in their abolition of sacramental confession – even when visiting has fallen away at other times and for other reasons.[48] The biography of the renowned writer on prayer Alan Ecclestone notes that he sometimes 'felt incredibly awkward' visiting, but 'the reason for this daily torture was plain enough: one had to get to know people, to get acquainted with their daily life.' 'The awareness of the multiplicity of human nature, the eccentricities, the disasters, heroisms, follies, and a faint discernment of the person behind the outworks was what it taught him', as, in his twenty-seven years as Anglican minister in a parish in Sheffield, northern England, he visited each of the 5,600 homes in the parish – not only those of congregation members – three times, in all that time being turned away only once.[49] Visiting is nevertheless one occasion amongst others in which it might be important for pastors to ask self-critically 'for whose benefit?' prayer is offered.[50] Yet in visiting, a pastor may also often aptly draw on a 'treasury of prayer' 'for various occasions' provided in many denominational liturgical resources,[51] some of which a pastor may possibly know by heart, or else be able to extemporize in ways shaped by the denominational norms. While perhaps also having a role in indicating ecclesial identity and the representative ministry of the pastor, a most valuable aspect of such collected prayer is that it can suggest what might wisely be said in difficult circumstances,[52] providing a repository of pastoral wisdom and beginning to word a theology of divine action, salvation, healing and presence.

---

[48]Prayer books often involve prayers in the home before or after funerals, for example. The Church of Scotland's *Common Order* (Edinburgh: St Andrew's Press, 1994) includes a schema of biblical reading for visiting across a whole range of occasions.

[49]Tim Gorringe, *Alan Ecclestone: Priest as Revolutionary* (Sheffield: Cairns Publications, 1994), 50, 88. The main works of Ecclestone himself were *Yes to God* (London: Darton, Longman and Todd, 1975), *A Staircase for Silence* (London: Darton, Longman and Todd, 1977), *The Night Sky of the Lord* (London: Darton, Longman and Todd, 1980), and *Scaffolding of Spirit* (London: Darton, Longman and Todd, 1987), with a collection of his papers edited by Jim Cotter, *Firing the Clay: Occasional Writings of Alan Ecclestone* (Sheffield: Cairns Publications, 1999).

[50]See Michael Jacobs, *Still Small Voice: An Introduction to Pastoral Care and Counselling*, 2nd edn (London: SPCK, 1993), 66.

[51]Various prayer books include a section on 'prayers for various occasions'. The Uniting Church in Australia's *Uniting in Worship 2* evocatively recasts these as 'a treasury of prayer' amplifying a classic tradition that can also be seen in the selections made in, for example, 'Prayer During the Day' in the Church of England's *Common Worship: Daily Prayer* (London: Church House Publishing, 2006).

[52]Note, for example, the Church of England's intentionally ambiguous wording at funerals: 'all who have died in the love of Christ'. See *Common Worship: Pastoral Services* (London: Church House Publishing, 2005), 262, 278 341.

Personal Prayer

Aside from the prayer in which a pastor engages in the course of their ministry, the forms a pastor's prayer takes may be manifold. The New Testament's hints at apostolic requests for 'parchments' alongside 'scrolls' (1 Tim. 4) may be suggestive of the importance of personal jottings, margin notes as it were to more authorized materials. 'Classic' insights into pastors' prayer lives, their responses to their role, might be found in the like of *The Priest to the Temple/A Country Parson* by George Herbert with, for instance, 'Aaron' (1633) indicative of a prayer when preparing to lead Christian assembly. Contemporary poets continue this tradition of reflection on pastoral ministry, the less-known Manon Ceridwen James,[53] for example, or the better-known Rowan Williams and, perhaps above all, R. S. Thomas – all three, as it happens, priests of the Church of Wales. The latter's 'The Priest' (1974) depicts the pastor 'limping through life on his prayers', at least as he is seen in the eyes of others seemingly 'sitting at table / contented, though the broken body/ and the shed blood are not on the menu'.[54] Jim Cotter's attractive compilation of some of Thomas' work, *Etched by Silence*, notes the large number of questions that pervade Thomas' poetry, which Cotter sets alongside multiple 'questions from the gospels', there placed on the lips of Jesus.[55]

Across the Irish Sea, the Irish priest-poet Pádraig J. Daly's words capture the depths and humdrum of his pastoral ministry. The wrenching 'Vita Brevis', on the death of children, speaks of a little one who lived for just one day, and whom Daly as priest 'blessed with water' and named. 'Crucifixes' catches something of the perhaps more trivial arena for religion in his parish, Christ's 'emaciated limbs' forgotten, and instead 'cast in gold', with 'floating drapery' around the top of his legs and 'jolly cherubs' at his shins – 'beautiful enough/ to grace the bedroom/ of any strumpet queen' – though this may of course not have been so trivial for the girl who kept the devotional ornament at her home. Turning to the liturgy, he notes in lauds, 'minds no longer linking with the words', 'mouthing …

---

[53]www.manonceridwen.wordpress.com/author/manonceridwen (accessed: 29 April 2019); also discussed in Mark Pryce, *Poetry, Practical Theology and Reflective Practice* (London: Routledge, 2019).

[54]Set in fascinating context of discussion of 'Failure and Pastoral Care' by Stephen Pattison, *A Critique of Pastoral Care* (London: SCM Press, 1993), 145–68 (152).

[55]Jim Cotter, ed., *Etched by Silence: A Pilgrimage through the Poetry of R. S. Thomas* (Norwich: Canterbury Press, 2013), 109–39.

blankly'.[56] Daly also wrote some 'small psalms', with biblical precedent ranging through many emotions and reactions to a sense of divine presence or absence.[57]

Over the Atlantic Ocean, in Massachusetts, USA, the poet Franz Wright suggests in 'Kyrie': '*Lord, I had such a good time and I don't regret anything*', and then asks: 'What happened to the prayer that goes like that?'[58] And whether or not he saw it as ministry, after his conversion to Roman Catholic Christianity – a conversion apparent in his later collections like *God's Silence*, written in the years when he was himself dying – he volunteered as a visitor to dying children in a Boston hospital. Among the searing texts in *God's Silence* he describes 'following / in the blue stained-glass footsteps of a doctor who works with doomed children', 'the last day of somebody's childhood'.[59] Amidst reflection on this experience, he speaks movingly of his own looming death, imagining a time when angels sing that time and tears are ceased, giving way to a new earth and sky, prompting his thought about what he will have to say. Wright's answer, he imagines, is to ask 'what end?' And adding that his life allowed witness to a world 'sufficiently miraculous for me'.[60]

Another lay pastor – in her case by virtue of being the first woman to teach the clergy of the Church of England and by leading many others in retreat (and necessarily a lay person on account of her gender in the time and context in which she lived) – the sometime reluctant Anglican laywoman Evelyn Underhill produced a personal prayer book, collecting hundreds of prayer-texts from a range of Christian traditions that reflect the breadth of her survey *Worship* (1936) and even to a small extent draw on prayer beyond Christian traditions. Only recently discovered and published by Robyn Wrigley-Carr,[61] Underhill's prayer book indicates some possibilities for prayer in a kind of pastoral ministry, reflecting the life she found once 'compelled to experience Christ', as she put it. One of her own compositions, perhaps in some ways indicative of the 'unselfconscious absorption in God' she looked for in pastors when they lead worship,[62] is as follows:

O God! Give Yourself to us! restore Yourself to us! We love you! If it be too little, let us love You with more might. ... O God supreme!

---

[56]Pádraig J. Daly, *God in Winter* (Dublin: Dedalus Press, 2015), 54, 77, 79.

[57]Pádraig J. Daly, 'Small Psalter', *Image Journal* 95 (2017).

[58]Franz Wright, *Wheeling Motel* (New York: Alfred A. Knopf, 2009), 7.

[59]Franz Wright, *God's Silence* (New York: Alfred A. Knopf, 2007), 37, 38.

[60]Wright, *God's Silence*, 62.

[61]Robyn Wrigley-Carr, ed., *Evelyn Underhill's Prayer Book* (London: SPCK, 2018).

[62]Brenda Blanch and Stuart Blanch, ed., *Heaven a Dance: An Evelyn Underhill Anthology* (London: Triangle, 1991), 80.

Most secret and most present, most beautiful and strong. Constant yet incomprehensible, changeless yet changing all. What can I say, my God, my life, my holy joy, and what can anyone say when they speak of You?[63]

Juanita Colon, a Latina Cistercian Sister, spent the last seventeen years of her life in her own particular kind of ministry making a personal prayer book, in her case not like Underhill's in compiling others' prayers and mixing them with her own but closely focused on the biblical psalms, indeed 'writing the psalms in her own words … not withholding from God any of her humanity'.[64] The night prayer of her community would, like that of other religious orders, have included Psalm 4, which reads in part in her own translation: 'Think. Think hard as you lie on your beds in the still of the night, and then come – admit defeat and join the worshiping crowd. Cast your lot with the Lord!' – lines which reflect her own choices.[65] Colon's psalter became known to others only when she asked other nuns in her community to read it aloud to her as she was dying, but it was until then a treasured secret, a personal discipline of intimacy with God.

Not including psalms, and neither only composed of prayers, but a much more eclectic – and fascinating – collection suggests something of Alan Ecclestone's prayer life. He spent his ministry as a presbyter in the Church of England in northern England, not only in urban Sheffield but also in rural West Cumbria, where he then retired and from which he compiled his 'book of days', *Gather the Fragments* (1993). Made up of very diverse extracts, one for each day of the year, his anthology includes selections from a range of literature mainly from his English heritage: portions of contemporary novels, writings on science and politics (he was a Communist), and history; hence, it is like his own spirituality 'profoundly rooted in secular sources'.[66] Nor is the book organized around the liturgical calendar, but rather in relation to more personal reasons. For example, material he and wife used to recollect their marriage service just before his wife died is used on the anniversary of her death: Kathleen Raine's 'Parting'—'Darling…, this is goodbye', and an extract from Thomas Hardy's *The Woodlanders* which Ecclestone inscribed in his diary on the day his adult son, Giles, died: 'I can never forget

---

[63]Wrigley-Carr, *Evelyn Underhill's Prayer Book*, 68.
[64]Juanita Colon, *The Manhattan Psalter: The Lectio Divina of Sister Juanita Colon* (Collegeville, MN: Liturgical Press, 2002), 9.
[65]Colon, *The Manhattan Psalter*, 16.
[66]Gorringe, *Alan Ecclestone*, 136; see also 33.

'ee: for you was a good man, and did good things.'[67] A rare choice from beyond Ecclestone's Western bent is from Chinese bishop and theologian Ting Kuang-Hsun.[68] Each extract in his book of days is followed by brief comment, sometimes quite quirky (so that for 12 April begins: 'Augustine. I detest him! ...'),[69] and in an insightful Foreword, Alan Webster identifies Ecclestone as – we might note, like R. S. Thomas according to Cotter – 'a questioner. He was part of that crucial "apostolic succession", those who ask God's questions in the world today' – which is what, presumably, the book of days attempts to do.[70]

Other arts make their own efforts to suggest pastors in prayer, with BBC television characters *Rev.* and even *The Vicar of Dibley* being among the most popular contemporary examples (and with both key characters apparently shaped by clergy advisors). Their soliloquy-like prayer-scenes are sometimes akin to Paul J. Philibert's imagining of 'a typical presbyter named Sam', 'follow[ing] him through a day of his life as a priest'.[71] On the way to his morning shower, for example, Roman Catholic pastor Sam prays 'a prayer he wrote himself a few years ago': 'Source of all Being, loving God, I offer you my life this day ...'. After his shower and coffee Sam then gives himself to the Jesus Prayer: 'He tries to listen, to allow his breathing, his physical presence, and his love to be both the prayer he says and the prayer the Holy Spirit prays within him.' Again, later, bike-riding with a friend, Sam extols God: 'Thank you for this refreshing interlude. ... Be praised.'[72] Philibert's 'typical presbyter' is perhaps less questioning than at least some of the other examples just cited. Yet insights into pastors at prayer, from many other sources, across all sorts of genres, might be multiplied, reflecting as they would diverse appreciation for what Dorothy L. Sayers called 'the manifestation of the Divine glory in whatsoever beloved thing becomes to every man his own particular sacramental experience'.[73] Yet however broad a pastor's prayer may be, it also needs some focus. Tim Gorringe notably

---

[67]Gorringe, *Alan Ecclestone*, 159, 161; Alan Ecclestone, ed., *Gather the Fragments: A Book of Days* (Sheffield: Cairns Publications, 1993), 218–19, 272–3.

[68]Ecclestone, ed., *Gather the Fragments*, 111; see also 86. Ting visited Ecclestone in Sheffield, and a banner of Ting's words hung in the church building there, see Gorringe, *Alan Ecclestone*, 80, 137.

[69]Gorringe, *Alan Ecclestone*, 151. Ecclestone, ed., *Gather the Fragments*, 75.

[70]Alan Webster, 'Foreword', in *Gather the Fragments: A Book of Days*, ed. Alan Ecclestone (Sheffield: Cairns Publications, 1993), xiii.

[71]Paul J. Philibert, *Stewards of God's Mysteries: Priestly Spirituality in a Changing Church* (Collegeville, MN: Liturgical Press, 2004), 63.

[72]Philibert, *Stewards*, 65, 66–7.

[73]Dorothy L. Sayers, *Further Papers on Dante* (London: Methuen, 1957), 192–3.

remarks that at the sixtieth anniversary of Alan Ecclestone's ordination, at a celebration at Carlisle Cathedral, Eccelstone's voice 'broke in tears at one point only – when he mentioned Jesus Christ'.[74]

Writing from the vantage point of his oversight of the North American Association of Theological Schools, Dan Aleshire writes in his 'hopeful reflections on the work and future' of those schools, *Earthen Vessels*:

> People tend to assess the work of ministers and priests in terms of three broad questions: Do they truly love God? Do they relate with care and integrity to human beings? Do they have the knowledge and skills that the job requires? ... Not only do people tend to ask them, they tend to ask them in this order. If the answer to the first question is 'no', people don't even proceed to the second and third questions.[75]

We may suppose – or hope – that in their ecclesial, representative, public and personal prayer, pastoral ministers renew this love, or seek to, and so at least sometimes come to suggest to others something of what the World Council of Churches' document, *Baptism, Eucharist and Ministry* (1981, the 'Lima Document'), suggests that the ordained are 'for': 'publicly and continually' to point to the church's 'fundamental dependence' on Christ Jesus.[76]

---

[74]Gorringe, *Alan Ecclestone*, xiv.
[75]Daniel O. Aleshire, *Earthen Vessels: Hopeful Reflections on the Work and Future of Theological Schools* (Grand Rapids, MI: William B. Eerdmans, 2008), 31.
[76]World Council of Churches, *Baptism, Eucharist and Ministry*, M8 (Geneva: World Council of Churches, 1981), 11.

CHAPTER THIRTY-SIX

Prayer, Gender and the Body

NICOLA SLEE

The earliest Christians, as faithful Jews, prayed in ways learnt in the synagogue, adopting the *orans* posture – a posture practised more widely throughout the ancient world, and frequently found in the art of the catacombs.[1] Whilst women may not have frequented the synagogue often or at all, it seems likely that women and men prayed aloud in the semi-public forum of house-churches, as well as prophesying and speaking in tongues.[2] It is clear that particular gendered attire (head covering for women, for example, and none for men) was adopted, if only not to cause offence in the wider culture (1 Cor. 11.1-16). Thus, from the beginning, the practice of Christian prayer was embodied and gendered in specific, culturally shaped ways.

Whilst this is obvious, it has only become the subject of explicit attention in recent decades, through the lens of feminist and other gendered, queer and postcolonial theologies. In what follows, without ignoring other

---

[1] For brief notes on the *orans* posture (standing with outstretched arms), see Jeremy Haselock, 'Gestures' and 'Posture', in *The New SCM Dictionary of Liturgy and Worship*, ed. Paul F. Bradshaw (London: SCM Press, 2002), 227–30, 377–9. The *orans* posture, replaced by kneeling in much of Christian tradition, is being increasingly reclaimed in both practice and theology. See, for example, Stephen Burns, *SCM Studyguide: Liturgy*, 2nd edn (London: SCM Press, 2018), 67–8 and Ashley Cocksworth, *Prayer: A Guide for the Perplexed* (London: Bloomsbury Clark, 2018), chapter 6.

[2] New Testament scholars debate the few instructions for women to 'keep silent' in church, but such injunctions would not have been necessary if women had been totally silent!

sources, I shall draw mostly upon feminist liturgical scholarship and practice to critique prayer practices that are still all too prevalent in many churches, to unearth the far richer and more nuanced traditions of prayer that remain unknown to many ordinary believers, and to suggest ways of praying that reflect the diversity of gendered and embodied experience in our world.

Three preliminary points may be in order. First, whilst there is an extensive literature on feminist liturgy (much of which I will draw on), there is much less on feminist prayer per se.[3] This is striking, since there has always been a strong sense in feminist theology that, as Marjorie Procter-Smith has put it, prayer is both primary and urgent,[4] a crucible of theological critique, deconstruction and renewed language for and to God. Those who pray cannot wait on the theologians to sort out their concepts and language for God; they need and mint words out of the urgent compulsion to pray. Thus an examination of feminist prayer will bring us close to the heart of the central concerns of feminist theology: the nature and names of God; the nature of the divine–human relation, especially the divine–woman relation but also including the God–world relation; the most appropriate ways to understand and articulate the person and work of Jesus Christ and of the Spirit of God; and so on.

Second, since there is a paucity of literature on feminist prayer per se, this chapter draws widely on the literature of feminist liturgy and slips somewhat between the terms 'liturgy' and 'prayer'. Liturgy, of course, simply means 'the work of the people' and refers to the public worship of the church (whether or not it is based around a set text) and therefore provides the larger context within which individual or personal prayer is rooted. Prayer and liturgy are mutually interdependent, with each nourishing and informing the other and it is hardly possible to consider one without considering the other. Nevertheless, some of those who pray will relate more readily to the use of liturgy, and even to the word itself, than others. When I use the word 'liturgy', I intend the widest possible sense to refer to any and all traditions of common or public prayer/worship, whether or not those traditions would describe what they do as 'liturgy'.

---

[3]Two notable British theologians make the exception: Sarah Coakley, in several publications and most notably in *God, Sexuality, and the Self: An Essay 'On the Trinity'* (Cambridge: Cambridge University Press, 2013) and Tina Beattie, *Woman: New Century Theology* (London: Continuum, 2003), chapter 9 and *New Catholic Feminism: Theology and Theory* (London: Routledge, 2006), chapter 4. Both Coakley and Beattie seek to reclaim contemplative, kenotic prayer as liberating feminist practice.

[4]Marjorie Procter-Smith, *In Her Own Rite: Constructing Feminist Liturgical Tradition* (Nashville, TN: Abingdon Press, 1990), 88.

Third, it is important to note that much discussion of prayer, including its relationship to gender, tends to be dominated by linguistic considerations. Yet liturgy (and, by association, private prayer) is not only concerned with words, still less with texts. As Procter-Smith has argued, liturgy employs a range of different discourses, of which verbal discourse is only one. To this she adds visual and physical discourse,[5] and we might also add spatial and aural (including but not limited to musical) discourse. Without ignoring words and texts, I want to give proper attention to the other discourses of prayer: to the ways in which the body may pray, with or without words; to the comportment of physical space and the placement of bodies in space and time; and to the engagement of the senses in prayer: the sights, sounds, aromas and tastes that may accompany or embody prayer. Much, perhaps even most, prayer is articulated through 'sighs too deep for words' (Rom. 8.26), in tongues, in movement and dance, in hands held aloft or stretched out, or in contemplative silence.

Even where prayer follows written texts (and in many traditions it does not), to focus only on texts is to miss the many performative features of lived ritual and the ways in which they interact in complex, subtle ways. Words may be underlined or undone by the visual clues and dominant spatial arrangements in the liturgy, for example. In some settings, words may be of limited interest to those who pray: to young children or adults with profound learning needs, for example, but also to many adults for whom the cognitive function of words may be far less important than their affective or aural functions. None of this implies that words do not matter – only that they are not the whole story.

Feminist Critique and Reclamation of Prayer

We must pray with eyes wide open, refusing to see nothing of what is hidden, secret – blatant lies.

We must pray with heads held high, refusing to bow in obsequiousness to prelate, priest or pope.

We must pray with tongues loosened, ready to cry out our anger, rage, pain and desire, refusing any longer to be silent.

We must pray with bodies known, bared: touching our own knowledge, knowing our instinctual wisdom, refusing to be violated or shamed.

---

[5]Procter-Smith, *In Her Own Rite*, chapter 3.

We must denounce false ways of praying, false names for God, false myths and images and stories.[6]

Many of the ways in which the church has taught individuals and the corporate body to pray are unhealthy, hierarchical and dualistic, forming Christians in ways which run counter to the liberating praxis of Jesus. According to Marjorie Procter-Smith, 'traditional Christian public prayer (and, by extension, private and personal prayer) is based on problematic assumptions about the nature of God, about the nature of human life and need, about the necessary rituals which surround the act of prayer'.[7]

In contrast to the view that the purpose of prayer is obedience to God and conformity with the life of discipleship as modelled by the saints, liberationists tend to speak in different tones and accents, foregrounding values of advocacy, liberation and empowerment of the oppressed. Thus, Procter-Smith advocates that 'the goal of feminist [liturgical] prayer is resistance and transformation. Resistance to patterns of domination, not only domination of women by men, but also domination of women by women'.[8] Janet Walton suggests: 'Feminist liturgy seeks to engage imagination, resist discrimination, summon wonder, receive blessing and strengthen hope. It intends to enact redeemed, free and empowered relationships.'[9] In other words, prayer is a political act, whether this is recognized or not. It can never be a merely 'private' affair, even where one person prays alone. Neither Christian doctrine of the body nor feminist insistence that the personal is political will permit such privatization. If prayer is not to serve to 'reinforce and spiritualize multiple forms of oppression',[10] it must consciously challenge all forms of intersectional oppression, paying attention to race, class, gender, sexuality, culture, bodily as well as mental health and ability, age and every other factor that shapes human experience.

The Discourse of Space

Prayer takes place in the body, both corporate and individual, and this means that it always takes place in time and space: in particular spaces and places, at particular times and seasons. Feminists have much to say about the

---

[6]Nicola Slee, 'Praying Like a Woman', in *Praying Like a Woman* (London: SPCK, 2004), 1.
[7]Marjorie Procter-Smith, *Praying with Our Eyes Open: Engendering Feminist Liturgical Prayer* (Nashville, TN: Abingdon Press, 1995), 9.
[8]Procter-Smith, *Praying with Our Eyes Open*, 14.
[9]Janet R. Walton, *Feminist Liturgy: A Matter of Justice* (Collegeville, MN: Liturgical Press, 2000), 31.
[10]Procter-Smith, *Praying with Our Eyes Open*, 10.

ways in which prayer is embodied in space and time. I will focus first on the question of space before going on to consider time.

Feminists protest against male ownership of religious space and the exclusion of women from significant presence and active ministry within that space. Enormous buildings that dominate towns and cityscapes, costing millions to build and upkeep, with high towers thrusting up into the skyline, are hardly subtle symbols of patriarchal and colonial potency, pride and will to control. Inside these vast edifices, architectural space both reflects and shapes theology. The placing of altar and pulpit are only two of the most obvious of spatial symbols that encode gendered and hierarchical social relations, elevating the actions and words of some, while excluding or marginalizing those of others. Other clues are given by noting who moves about the building freely and who does not: in some churches laity are limited to the main body of the church and may only move out of their pews at certain, defined points in the liturgy, whilst clergy, vergers and robed officers move about as they wish, commanding the space. Equally significant is whose voices are permitted to fill the space: who speaks – preaches, leads prayers, offers notices and so on – as well as who sings (a fierce battle to allow girls and women to join Anglican cathedral choirs is one indication of this) and who does not.[11] 'We shape our buildings', as Winston Churchill said; 'thereafter they shape us'.[12]

Feminists have employed a range of strategies to protest patriarchal ownership of space. Some have walked out and called others to come with them, perhaps most famously Mary Daly in her Exodus from Harvard Memorial Church in 1971, when invited as the first women preacher in Harvard's 366-year history.[13] Some have invaded male space: a powerful example of this is Pussy Riot's performance in the sanctuary of the Russian Orthodox Cathedral of Christ the Saviour in Moscow, in February 2012, as a means of protesting the Orthodox Church's support of Putin's policies.[14] Others have created their own alternative spaces in neglected, marginal or uncelebrated sites; when the St Hilda Community was evicted by the Bishop of London from St Benet's chapel, they celebrated the Eucharist in the

---

[11]June Boyce-Tillman has worked tirelessly for the inclusion of female voices and wisdom in the Anglican choral tradition. See June Boyce-Tillman, *In Tune with Heaven or Not: Women in Christian Liturgical Music* (Leuven: Peter Lang, 2014).

[12]In a speech in the House of Commons, 28 October 1944.

[13]See the account in Mary Daly, *Outercourse: The Be-Dazzling Voyage* (London: Women's Press, 1993), 137–40.

[14]For fuller discussion and analysis, see the special issue of *Religion and Gender* 4, no. 2 (2014) on Pussy Riot's Punk Prayer.

carpark, thus dramatizing their eviction into a liminal wilderness on the edges
of the church that would not welcome them.[15]

Feminists have reclaimed liturgical space in at least three ways. First,
women's homes are affirmed as a vital centre of ritual and prayer, as they
have been for millennia; much feminist liturgy takes place there, and
the ancient tradition of women's home altars continues.[16] Jan Berry's
ethnographic study of the rituals created by British women to mark
significant transitions in their lives notes that the majority of women
favoured domestic space as the setting for their rituals. They offered a
range of reasons for this, from the practical (ease of access, low or no cost)
to the social and psychological (the safety of the space and its integral
connection to the women's identity, a strong desire to practice hospitality
and inclusion) and the theological (the holiness and intimacy of the home
as a space of divine encounter).[17]

Recognizing that the home is a primary site of domestic violence, home-
based liturgies may also be rites of lament and mourning, healing and
exorcism.[18] Looking beyond the home, a second form of feminist liturgical
space is a borrowed or owned public space. Whilst many feminist liturgical
communities continue to meet in borrowed public spaces – churches,
synagogues, schools or halls – some have been able to resource their own,
purpose-built, feminist-inspired gathering spaces.[19] Other feminist liturgical
communities have bought or rented property which, while not purpose-
built, nevertheless embodies the 'space of our own' to which women
aspire. Inspired by the novel of the same name, the Red Tent movement,[20]
widespread across North America and Europe, locates women's rituals in
the red, womb-like space of a tent – an economically more viable option
for many groups than a building. Alongside the creation of physical space,
the internet and social media platforms offer alternative *virtual* spaces for

---

[15]For a brief history of the community, see Monica Furlong, 'Introduction: A "Non-Sexist"
Community', *Women Included: A Book of Prayers and Services* (London: SPCK, 1991), 5–15.

[16]For a popular account, see Kay Turner, *Beautiful Necessity: The Art and Meaning of Women's
Altars* (London: Thames and Hudson, 1999).

[17]Jan Berry, *Ritual Making Women: Shaping Rites for Changing Lives* (London: Equinox, 2009),
105–10.

[18]See Rosemary Radford Ruether, *Women-Church: Theology and Practice* (San Francisco, CA:
Harper and Row, 1985), chapter 8, for example, and Procter-Smith, *Praying with Our Eyes Open*,
chapter 2 for a broader discussion of the importance of 'the prayer of refusal' in feminist liturgy.

[19]See, for example, the Sophia Community Centre in Adelaide: www.sophia.org.au (accessed:
2 September 2020).

[20]Anita Diamont, *The Red Tent* (London: Allen and Unwin, 1997). For a scholarly account, see
Chia Longman, 'Women's Circles and the Rise of the New Feminine: Reclaiming Sisterhood,
Spirituality and Wellbeing', *Religions* 9, no. 9 (2018).

feminist discussion, theologizing and ritual making and this is likely to become more, rather than less, significant with time.[21]

Third, feminist liturgies affirm and honour the seasons, the elements and the vital connections between human well-being and the care and preservation of the cosmos. Eco-feminism explores the close connection between women's oppression and the ravaging of the earth, and looks for the healing of both through political action as well as through rituals that reverence the environment.[22] Such liturgies lament and mourn the destruction of habitats and species and the breakdown of human awareness of our dependence upon, and connection with, other living creatures. Symbols from the natural world abound in feminist liturgies. Berger notes the 'intense predilection for symbols' in feminist liturgies and lists many drawn from nature, as well as women's domestic lives: 'rose-scented water, freshly baked bread, milk and honey, fragrant oil, burning incense, flowers, candles, branches, ashes, earth, grain, bulbs, straw, wine, fruit – yes, even apples'.[23]

An outdoor setting is thus frequently favoured for feminist liturgies, whether open spaces (commons, moorlands, fields), or in woods, by rivers or wells (which are, of course, frequently ancient sites of pilgrimage and ritual). Neo-pagan, Goddess, wiccan, Celtic and other influences mix with feminist strands to create many variations on this theme. From Starhawk to Tess Ward,[24] feminists create outdoor rituals, not only at threshold times, such as solstices and equinox, but in every season. Participants may be encouraged to stand barefoot; to feel their connection to the earth; to breathe deeply of the fresh air; to listen to natural sounds of wind, birdsong and animal movements; to smell the aromas of earth, plants, herbs and flowers – all as manifestations of the divine. Some specific sites may be regarded as symbolic of female morphology and therefore as peculiarly appropriate for feminist liturgy. Stone circles, mounds and burial chambers, caves and wells may be regarded as symbolic of women's dark, internal spaces running with life-giving water: nurturing, circular and womb-like, inviting descent into the depths, in contrast with church buildings which are totemic and phallic in shape and design.

---

[21]See, for example, Gina Messina-Dysert and Rosemary Radford Ruether, ed., *Feminism and Religion in the 21st Century: Technology, Dialogue, and Expanding Borders* (New York: Routledge, 2015).

[22]For examples of ecofeminist rituals, see Diann L. Neu, *Return Blessings: Ecofeminist Liturgies Renewing the Earth* (Glasgow: Wild Goose, 2004) and Tess Ward, *The Celtic Wheel of the Year: Celtic and Christian Seasonal Prayers* (Winchester, CA: O Books, 2007).

[23]Teresa Berger, *Women's Ways of Worship: Gender Analysis and Liturgical History* (Collegeville, MN: Liturgical Press, 1999), 126.

[24]Starhawk, *The Spiral Dance: A Rebirth of the Ancient Religion of the Great Goddess* (New York: HarperRow, 1999) and Ward, *The Celtic Wheel*.

Wherever feminist liturgies take place, they employ space in particular ways that enshrine core feminist values. On the whole, feminist liturgies tend to take place *in the round*, *on the level* and in *face-to-face* configurations. Circles are the norm in feminist liturgical writing and practice, symbolizing mutuality and reciprocity, the dynamic flow of energy around and between persons who make up the circle. There is space for everyone – a circle can expand or contract as required – and, at the same time, there is always space within a circle, symbolizing the hospitable space of God and the church. 'Circle principles' are now widely used in many gatherings, organizations and communities inspired by egalitarianism, consensus-based decision-making and feminist visions of mutual ministry and empowerment.[25]

Another feature of the circle is that all are on the same level. The horizontal plane takes precedence over the vertical. No one is elevated above another, no one looks down on another and no one is diminished within the circle. In the circle, all are listened to with equal respect and all are heard into speech. All are empowered to talk back to the tradition, to 'level with' all that they experience as discriminatory or patronizing, to challenge and critique taken-for-granted assumptions about ministry, leadership and power. Inclusion does not imply sameness but respect for difference and an attentiveness to the lived experience and wisdom of each. Within the conversation circle and around the kitchen table, diversity within equality is the norm.

Theologically, the primacy of the horizontal over the vertical axis suggests a strong emphasis on divine immanence rather than transcendence. The divine manifests within, rather than above or beyond, the gathered community, in solidarity with human community rather than standing in judgement or opposition to it. While some have strongly condemned this feature of architectural modernism,[26] it concurs with feminist theologies which prefer to speak of God in mutual, relational terms (Friend, Companion, Lover, Beloved) rather than hierarchical ones (Lord, Father, King, Judge). This raises the question about the place of transcendence within feminist liturgical expression and whether (as I believe) it is possible for immanence and transcendence to co-exist. One clue to this may lie in architectural spaces which, whilst in the round, nevertheless still manage to gesture towards divine transcendence through use of vertical space. For example, the large modern cement chapel at Malling Abbey which is home to a community of enclosed Benedictine nuns, and where I have gone on retreat for many years, is a huge ark-like space in which the nuns sing the daily office and celebrate

---

[25]See Ruether's design for a Women-church building enshrines the circle principle in *Women-Church*, 146–8.
[26]See, for example, Moyra Doorly, *No Place for God: The Denial of the Transcendent in Modern Church Architecture* (San Francisco, CA: Ignatius Press, 2007).

the Eucharist in the round, yet with a vast, empty roof space in which the play of light and echoes of rain, wind and weather evoke a sense of transcendence within the immanence of the community's life. Multiple similar examples in post-Vatican ll Roman Catholic architecture come to mind.

Being in the round and on the level implies being face-to-face, with the priority of the personal over the institutional. This is a theology in which the human gaze and touch are emblematic of the divine–human encounter. In a circle, all are joined, sometimes by touch but more frequently by sight and bodily proximity. Unlike the traditional cross-shaped church, in which laity are separated from each other in rows and have their gaze fixed on the actions of clergy in front of them, feminist liturgies insist on the fully embodied, face-to-face gaze and encounter. Sarah Coakley's advocacy of east-facing presidency as a model of reformed gender relations is hardly in line with most feminist liturgical trajectories.[27]

Whilst face-to-face relation implies mutuality of engagement within a non-hierarchical circle of ministry, it does not necessitate symmetry or sameness. It is possible to engage 'in the round', 'on the level' and 'face-to-face', with those who are utterly unlike me and who may possess greater or lesser degrees of power. It is precisely in encountering the other in all their strangeness, challenge and difference as a brother or sister with whom I am intimately joined, that I may meet the divine Other.

The Discourse of Time

Human beings live in time as well as space, and prayer is shaped by patterns and seasons of time, as well as by spatial arrangements. In the church, prayer is shaped by different units of time: across the lifespan, by the liturgical year and by the liturgical week. Rites of passage mark significant moments in the life cycle: baptism at the birth of a child, confirmation traditionally marking the passage to adolescence, marriage ritualizing a change in familial status and funerals signifying the end of life. The liturgical year, or calendar, offers two main cycles of prayer focused around the incarnation (Advent, Christmas and Epiphany) and passion of Christ (Lent, Passiontide, Easter and Ascension), as well as a long season of 'ordinary time', within which the scriptures are read systematically and thematically, according to agreed lectionaries. The year is also marked by a multitude of local and universal feast days, celebrating a variety of saints. The liturgical week is shaped around Sunday as the first day of the week, marking Christ's resurrection, when the assembly normally gathers for its main eucharistic celebration.

---

[27]Sarah Coakley, 'The Woman at the Altar: Cosmological Disturbance or Gender Subversion?', *Anglican Theological Review* 86, no. 1 (2004): 75–93.

Other days are traditionally associated with other aspects of the Christian narrative: Friday as the day of Christ's passion, for example.[28]

Feminists have critiqued all the major ways in which time is demarcated and ritualized in Christian tradition, showing how Christian prayer has largely enshrined male experience, meanings and rites of passage. A range of alternative resources – lectionaries, rites and feastdays, for example – are on offer to provide a richer, more expansive repertoire of prayer in time.

Thus, the rites of passage marked by the church have assumed the male heterosexual lifecycle as the norm. Significant events and cycles within the lives of women and girls, such as the onset of menstruation and menopause, healing and recovery from assault or rape, and coming out as a lesbian are entirely absent from prayerbooks.[29] From Ruether's *Woman-Church* onwards, feminist, LGBT and queer prayerbooks have provided new rites of passage for such events in the lives of women, queers and others for whom the church has made only negative provision.[30]

Similarly, the liturgical year marginalizes or ignores the presence of women, in a multitude of ways. A recent article in the *Church Times*, Rosalind Brown notes how 'the lectionary silences women's experiences', giving numerous examples of the omission of women's stories from the systematic reading of scripture, with no good or obvious reason.[31] Indeed, since women feature much less frequently in scripture than men, one might think there was more rather than less reason for the lectionary to include them. The two main

---

[28]In some prayerbooks, such as the recent SSF Daily Office, Monday is associated with Pentecost and the Spirit, Tuesday with the Advent season and waiting, Wednesday with creation, Thursday with Epiphany, Friday with Lent and passiontide and Saturday both with the Jewish Sabbath and Christ's resting in the tomb.

[29]The rite of churching of women is an interesting exception, although ambivalent in its functions and meanings. See Joanne M. Pierce, 'Churching of Women', in *The New SCM Dictionary of Liturgy and Worship*, ed. Paul F. Bradshaw (London: SCM Press, 2002), 117–19.

[30]To choose a few titles at random, Hannah Ward and Jennifer Wild, ed., *Human Rites: Worship Resources for an Age of Change* (London: Mowbray, 1995); Elizabeth Stuart, *Daring to Speak Love's Name: A Gay and Lesbian Prayer Book* (London: Hamish Hamilton, 1992); Teresa Berger, ed., *Dissident Daughters: Feminist Liturgies in Global Context* (Louisville, KY: Westminer John Knox Press, 2001); Geoffrey Duncan, ed., *Courage to Love: An Anthology of Inclusive Worship Material* (London: Darton, Longman and Todd, 2002); Jan Berry, *Naming God* (London: Granary/URC, 2011) and Tess Ward, *Alternative Pastoral Prayers: Liturgies and Blessings for Health and Healing, Beginnings and Endings* (Norwich: Canterbury Press, 2012).

[31]*Church Times*, 25 October 2019, 16. For a longer consideration of the evidence of omission of women from the lectionary, see Ruth Fox, 'Women in the Bible and Lectionary', www.futurechurch.org/women-in-church-leadership/women-and-word/women-in-bible-and-lectionary (accessed: 2 September 2020). There have been various attempts to create alternative feminist lectionaries, for example, Barbara Bowe, Kathleen Hughes, Sharon Karam and Carolyn Osiek, *Silent Voices, Sacred Lives: Women's Readings for the Liturgical Year* (New York: Paulist Press, 1992). See also Gail Ramshaw, *Treasures Old and New: Images in the Lectionary* (Minneapolis, MN: Fortress Press, 2002).

cycles that shape the liturgical year – the incarnation and passion of Christ – tend to focus on the actions and characters of leading men in the story of Jesus; this is reflected both in the choice and arrangement of lectionary readings and in the liturgical celebrations associated with each cycle. There is necessarily some focus on Mary at Advent, Christmas and Epiphany, but very little on the actions of the women disciples in the rites and readings associated with Lent, Passiontide and Holy Week, for example. The title of Elisabeth Schüssler Fiorenza's, *In Memory of Her*,[32] highlights the anonymity of the woman who anointed Jesus in Mark's Gospel, about whom Jesus declared: 'Wherever the good news is proclaimed in the whole world, what she has done will be told in remembrance of her' (Mk 14.9). Not only is her name missing in the biblical account, but her story is accorded little ritual significance in Holy Week liturgies, passed over in favour of acts of betrayal and denial by the male disciples. This is only one instance of a more general invisibility of women in the liturgical year, not least in the calendar of saints' days which, until recently, has eclipsed women's lives and stories and tended only to honour celibate women, naming them 'Holy virgins' or 'mystics' rather than, say, 'teachers' or even 'Doctors of the Church'.[33] New liturgical resources have been needed to offer a reading of the liturgical year in which women's lives might be central, rather than peripheral.[34]

Feminist critique of the shaping of the liturgical week has tended to focus particular attention on the ways in which the church has celebrated the Eucharist, not only excluding women from presiding at the table (and even, in some traditions, from being physically present in the sanctuary, particularly when menstruating) but, more insidiously, offering theologies of eucharistic sacrifice which marginalize women and are problematic in their valorization of suffering, violence and self-sacrifice.[35] Feminist readings of

---

[32]Elisabeth Schüssler Fiorenza, *In Memory of Her: A Feminist Theological Reconstruction of Christian Origins* (London: SCM Press, 1983).

[33]For an overview of women's absence in the liturgical calendar, see Michael D. Whalen, 'In the Company of Women? The Politics of Memory in the Liturgical Commemoration of Saints – Male and Female', *Worship* 73, no. 6 (1999): 482–504.

[34]For example, Miriam Therese Winter's series of feminist lectionaries and psalters in *WomanWisdom: Women of the Hebrew Scriptures – Part 1* (New York: Crossroad, 1991), *WomanWitness: Women of the Hebrew Scriptures – Part 2* (New York: Crossroad, 1997) and *WomanWord: Women of the New Testament* (New York: Crossroad, 1992); Elizabeth A. Johnson, *Friends of God and Prophets: A Feminist Theological Reading of the Communion of the Saints* (London: SCM Press, 1998); Teresa Berger, *Fragments of Real Presence: Liturgical Traditions in the Hands of Women* (New York: Crossroads, 2005).

[35]See Procter-Smith, *Praying with Our Eyes Open*, chapter 6. For feminist reclamation, as well as critique, of eucharistic theologies and practice, see Susan A. Ross, *Extravagant Affections: A Feminist Sacramental Theology* (New York: Continuum, 2001) and Anne Elvey, Carol Hogan, Kim Power and Claire Renkin, ed., *Reinterpreting the Eucharist: Explorations in Feminist Theology and Ethics* (Sheffield: Equinox, 2003).

the Eucharist which affirm the role of Mary as a type of embodied priesthood and which emphasize incarnation rather than passion, nurturing and feeding imagery rather than violent death sacrifice, have an important role to play in shaping more biophilic, woman-affirming eucharistic practice.[36] New feminist eucharistic liturgies enact what such theological accounts suggest.[37]

The Discourse of Embodiment

The body, situated in space and time, prays, not merely the mind or the tongue.

Recent decades have seen a chorus of voices and texts calling for the reclamation of the sexed, gendered, culturally inscribed, wounded and hugely varied bodies of believers in both theology and practice. Feminists have joined others to insist on the centrality of the body, the senses, the emotions, the passions and the erotic in spirituality and prayer. This is prayer in which 'all desires [are] known', the title of Janet Morley's collection of prayers and poems,[38] which take the classic Anglican prayer form of the collect and infuse it with female desire and bodily experience. Women have reclaimed the words of Jesus repeated at every Eucharist, 'This is my body, this is my blood', to hold up their own bodily experience as holy and worthy of blessing.[39]

Within a wider reclamation of the body, the physical gestures and postures of prayer have been scrutinized and reworked by feminists in various ways. Praying with eyes closed is critiqued in favour of a world-embracing spirituality which regards creation as the sacrament of divine presence and therefore invites eyes to be wide open. Feminists also warn that, in a patriarchal church where power is still largely assumed by men and frequently used to harm women, children and non-dominant men, it is simply not safe to close one's eyes in the public assembly of the church. Women need to pray with eyes wide open, alert to what is going on around them and on the look-out for danger. Similarly, bowing, kneeling and prostration in prayer are largely rejected by those who have been on the

---

[36]See Elvey, et al., *Reinterpreting the Eucharist*. Karen O'Donnell, *Broken Bodies: The Eucharist, Mary, and the Body in Trauma Theology* (London: SCM Press, 2019) is a recent example of such a reading, which builds on the work of earlier scholars.

[37]For example, Procter-Smith, *Praying with Our Eyes Open*, chapter 6. John Henson, *Other Communions of Jesus* (Winchester, CA: O Books, 2006), is an interesting attempt to develop eucharistic rites based on a wide range of Jesus' meals, not only the Last Supper.

[38]Janet Morley, *All Desires Known*, 3rd edn (London: SPCK, 2005).

[39]My own reworking of a eucharistic prayer, 'This Woman's Body', in *Praying Like a Woman*, 90–2, written to prepare for a hysterectomy, is one example of many.

underside of history. Kneeling may 'remind us of reverence for God and one another, but when women kneel to receive Communion or a blessing from men, rather than promoting an experience of reverence, it can be a reminder of sexual violation or subservience. Since women are frequently victims of violence at the hands of men, we practice standing and sitting rather than kneeling.'[40] Postcolonial theologians such as Cláudio Carvalhaes and Nancy Pereira Cardoso have also pointed to the ways in which kneeling prayer was used as a form of control by the colonizers.[41]

The iconography of Christian tradition is rife with examples of kneeling theology in which biblical narratives are represented in ways which reinforce visually the dominance of white males. Representations of women interacting with Jesus (who is almost always white) generally represent him in an elevated position with the women on their knees or on the ground, holding up hands in gestures of pleading and supplication. This tends to be the case, whether or not there is any biblical evidence for a prostrate posture. To take one example, artistic representations of the meeting between Mary Magdalene and the risen Christ, based on John 20, regularly depict Mary on the ground at a distance from Christ who is standing upright. She reaches out towards him imploringly; he withdraws from her reach. The focus is on Christ's rejection of Mary's desire to be reunited with him and emphasizes the disparity of power between them. Such images reinforce the myth of the Magdalene as the repentant prostitute who, in other images, is represented in eroticized, sexualized terms. It is rare to find images of the encounter between the Magdalene and the risen Christ that focus on her commission to 'go and tell the disciples' the news of Christ's resurrection and that embody her authority as the 'apostle to the apostles'.[42] The impact of such iconography upon centuries of Christian worshippers is not difficult to deduce: they learn that it is given to men to lord it over women whose place is always beneath them, and act accordingly.[43]

---

[40]Walton, *Feminist Liturgy*, 38.

[41]As discussed in Cocksworth, *Prayer*, 196–9. Cláudio Carvalhaes, '"Gimme de Kneebone Bent": Liturgies, Dance, Resistance and a Hermeneutics of the Knees', *Studies in World Christianity* 14, no. 1 (2008): 1–18; Nancy Pereira Cardoso, 'De-Evangelization of the Knees: Epistemology, Osteoporosis, and Affliction', in *Liturgy in Postcolonial Perspectives: Only One Is Holy*, ed. Cláudio Carvalhaes (New York: Palgrave, 2015), 119–23.

[42]For an exception, see the St Alban's Psalter: www.abdn.ac.uk/stalbanspsalter/english/index.shtml (accessed: 28 November 2019).

[43]See Lauren F. Winner, 'Interceding: Standing, Kneeling, and Gender', in *The Blackwell Companion to Christian Ethics*, ed. Stanley Hauerwas and Samuel Wells, 2nd edn (Oxford: Blackwell, 2011), 264–76, for a similar critique of the representation of the 'kneeling slave' in Western art.

The Discourse of Words

And so we come, finally, to words. The language of Christian prayer has also been gendered from the beginning, although in more complex and nuanced ways than is sometimes taken for granted. Drawing on the Hebrew scriptures and, in particular, the Song of Songs, theologians from earliest times conceived of the relation between the human soul and God in terms likened to the erotic relation between the male lover and his beloved, the bride and the groom, with the soul envisaged as the passive female recipient of the active male God who woos and wins the beloved. Male and female medieval mystics, in particular, developed this erotic tradition with a striking freedom and in many diverse and complex forms.[44] The erotic conception of the divine–human relation provided the model for private prayer, but was also applied to the relation between Christ and the church, and has therefore had a profound impact on the shaping and conduct of public worship. Christ, envisaged as the male Head or Groom, expends his sacrificial love upon the Body of the church, or the Bride. While some New Testament passages hint at a degree of mutuality in this relationship, the dominant note is one of subservient relation. Nevertheless, as commentators have noticed, some of this imagery is distinctly queer, pulling against a literal or hegemonic reading. If Christ is the (male) head of a (female) body, there can be no straightforward, linear gendered relationship between the church and Christ; the relationship is already queered.[45]

At the same time, the dominant traditions of male, patriarchal language for God, which feminist, womanist and queer theologians have been deconstructing for decades, were never as unilateral as the language of public Christian worship has tended to reflect. Whilst God is certainly modelled on the ruling power of dominant male elites, and named accordingly as King, Judge, Lord, Master, Father and so on, this is by no means the only lexicon of Jewish and Christian prayer. The scriptures contain multiple names and images for God, not only from the realm of gendered human relations, but also from the animal kingdom and from so-called inanimate nature. The Psalms and prophetic literature are rich with imagery of God as rock, refuge, mother

---

[44]The literature on gender, sexuality and mysticism is vast. For contemporary feminist approaches (in contrast to historical studies), see Beverly J. Lanzetta, *Radical Wisdom: A Feminist Mystical Theology* (Minneapolis, MN: Fortress Press, 2005) and Jennie S. Knight, *Feminist Mysticism and Images of God: A Practical Theology* (St Louis, MO: Chalice Press, 2011).

[45]See Elizabeth Stuart, 'Camping around the Canon: Humour as a Hermeneutical Tool in Queer Readings of Biblical Texts', in *Take Back the Word: A Queer Reading of the Bible*, ed. Robert E. Goss and Mona West (Cleveland, OH: Pilgrim Press, 2000), 23–34 for a queer reading of Ephesians 5.21-33.

bird and bear, water, fire and much, much more. Anyone who takes seriously the richness of biblical language for, and address to, God will question the dominance of male-gendered God-language in Christian worship. Biblical literalists, above all, should be 'bringing many names' to their prayer,[46] if they want to reflect the letter and the spirit of scripture, which constantly pushes against idolization of any one name or model for God. Even if we accept that Jesus' preferred address to God was 'Abba, Father', it by no means follows that 'Father' must be *our* dominant form of address for God today. If, as Sallie McFague has argued, Jesus' understanding of, and relation to, his Father provides a radical critique of the Roman paterfamilias, contemporary Christian prayer may require alternative terms to adequately mirror Jesus' subversive and liberating intention.[47] Due to the ways in which patriarchy has enacted paternity (i.e. as a coercive, hierarchical and possessive relation of power-over others), paradoxically, naming God as 'Father' may be the *least* helpful way of modelling Jesus' prayer practice, unless language of divine paternity is qualified and expanded in radical ways.

Feminist prayer challenges and refuses words and texts that inscribe unjust power relations and seeks to create liberating and expansive language and imagery for prayer. It suggests that to name God 'Lord', 'King' or 'Master' (unless done with irony or via paradoxical tension) is to ascribe to hierarchical and implicitly coercive relationships, not only in relating to the divine but also in the human realm and in relation to other orders of creation. To call God 'Father' (if this is not balanced and critiqued by other images) risks placing ourselves in infantile relationship and reinforcing patriarchal power and patriarchal social structures.

Feminist prayer pays attention not only to *what* is said in prayer, but also to the register and range of *ways* in which prayer is offered. In company with Jewish, Black, postcolonial, queer and other discourses, feminist prayer engages anger, lament, protest and critique as well as celebration, praise and contemplation. It is prayer which refuses to be polite or decorous, conforming to the stereotype of the feminine as charming, placating, quiet and softly-spoken. On the contrary, feminist prayer is not well-behaved, seeking to disrupt patterns of relationship which have kept half the human race in infantile relation. It wrestles with what has been passed down in order to wrest a blessing from what seems intractable and unsustaining, seeking to turn stones to bread and wilderness to garden.

---

[46]This is the title of a chapter in Brian Wrenhymn, *What Language Shall I Borrow? God-Talk in Worship: A Male Response to Feminist Theology* (London: SCM Press, 1989), 137–8.
[47]See Sallie McFague, *Metaphorical Theology: Models of God in Religious Language* (London: SCM Press, 1982), chapter 5.

In any consideration of the language of prayer, hymnody and chant are powerfully significant. In most Christian traditions, music is a major carrier of meaning and it is widely recognized that words learnt in hymns or songs are far more deeply embedded in the somatic memory than words alone. At the same time, music is much more than a carrier for words; music is an aural discourse of extraordinary range and depth, which makes a physical and emotional as well as cognitive, impact upon the community. Music in prayer and worship can soothe, heal, calm, aid meditation and contemplation; conversely, it can rouse, motivate, activate and become an outlet for heightened emotions such as grief, anger and protest. Whether calming or rousing, music has the capacity to fuse and weld worshippers gathered together. Feminist hymn-writers and composers have begun to create new forms of hymnody, song and chant in order to create a rich, many-textured repertoire of aural discourse that can contribute towards the liberating imperative of feminist liturgy. June Boyce-Tillman, Janet Wootton, Kathy Galloway, Jan Aldredge Clanton, Shirley Erena Murray and Brian Wren are only some of the better-known musicians who have helped to create new, more inclusive and expansive forms of music for worship in recent decades.[48]

The sung and spoken words of prayer, then, are by no means insignificant, and we should recall that, in public prayer at least – and in much private prayer too – words are primarily *spoken, chanted* or *sung* and are thus embodied, not to be disassociated from the other forms of discourse of which I have written above.

And Yet: An Addendum

In rejecting patriarchal prayer and replacing it with feminist alternatives, there is a danger of inscribing a new orthodoxy which does not admit of critique, nuance or variation. It would be counter-feminist to coerce particular ways of prayer, however authentic they are, and to outlaw cherished forms of prayer which many Christians continue to value. Moreover, to insist that certain prayer practices, postures and symbols only have one, circumscribed meaning

---

[48]See, for instance, June Boyce-Tillman, *A Rainbow to Heaven: Hymns, Songs and Chants* (London: Stainer and Bell, 2006); Janet Wootton, *Eagles' Wings and Lesser Things: Hymns, Prayers, Drama and Other Resources for Worship* (London: Stainer and Bell, 2007); Jann Aldredge-Clanton, *Praying with Christ-Sophia: Services for Healing and Renewal* (New London, CT: Twenty-Third Publications, 1996); Shirley Erena Murray, *Faith Makes the Song: New Hymns Written between 1997 and 2002* (Carol Stream, IL: Hope Publishing, 2003) and *Touch the Earth Lightly: New Hymns Written between 2003 and 2008* (Carol Stream, IL: Hope Publishing, 2008).

would be to espouse an essentialism which reads reality in flat, monovalent terms and is little more liberating than the literalism of patriarchy.

In the experience of praying as a feminist, reality is always more complex, multilayered and paradoxical than any one account of it can admit. In my own prayer, I generally do not kneel to receive communion from a priest (particularly a man) because I regard this as enacting an unhealthy power relation which reinforces clericalism. However, I will happily kneel to pray with the brothers and other guests at the local monastery which I visit, as we gather in the antechapel before the reserved sacrament, since we are all kneeling together and there is a profound mutuality in our shared prayer. And I often choose to sit these days, rather than to stand, due to the complaints of an ageing body. Similarly, I open and close my eyes in different settings, according to how safe, powerful, exposed or engaged I perceive myself to be. I rage, lament, wrestle and protest against a patriarchal church, but it is simply too exhausting continually to adopt the posture of the angry critic; sometimes I must rest in the quietness, acceptance and unknowing of divine darkness and of self-compassion, coming 'under the brooding breast'.[49] I generally seek to create a circle for shared prayer, but I understand when someone wants to place themselves outside the circle, as I sometimes also choose to do. Being in a circle can be too exposing for those who are hurting or are unsure of their ground; they may need to hide or place themselves at a tangent to the circle.

Perhaps there is a way of allowing prayer, like the circle, to be fluid, constantly shifting and changing, forming and reforming to allow individuals to arrive and leave, to come to the centre or to be at the edges. The circle can be as wide and spacious as it needs to be, with plenty of room for manoeuvre within and around it. There are no rigid rules but rather an evolving series of experimental practices, a prayerful poesis which unfolds as it is risked, constantly, anew. 'Following no blueprint, copying no precursor, we'll craft a journey unpredictable, cast a pattern asymmetrical and intricate, as delicate as it is unrepeatable, tender and indestructible, made of colours vivid, tenacious, wild.'[50]

---

[49]The title of chapter 4 of my *Praying Like a Woman*.
[50]Slee, *Praying Like a Woman*, 4.

CHAPTER THIRTY-SEVEN

Christian Prayer in Black and Blue

ANDREW PREVOT

The story of Christian prayer in modernity cannot be told without remembering the lives and deaths of those millions of God's darkly coloured children whose existence was torn from West Africa and 'remade' through resistance against the body- and soul-crushing instruments of the slave ship, the auction block, the plantation field, the lynching tree, the segregated church, the impoverished ghetto, the underfunded school and the prison cell. This refashioned existence may be called 'black', and in the same breath it may be called 'blue'. These colours express deep wounds from centuries of horrific mistreatment and a human beauty difficult to describe, consisting of rich hues, textures, rhythms, strengths, loves, sorrows, victories and untold possibilities. They define a sense of peoplehood without necessarily implying any racial essence or narrow black nationalism. These colours are not meant to be accurate representations of any human body, however dark it may be. Rather, they are symbols of a phenotypically diverse people united by a particular set of traumas, strivings and modes of creative endurance. Louis Armstrong gives voice to the spirit of this people when he croons, 'My only sin is in my skin. / What did I do to be so black and blue?'[1]

For many of these black and blue children of God, survival (even today) depends on carving out spaces of refuge within, or apart from, dominant

---

[1] Louis Armstrong, 'Black and Blue', *The Essential Louis Armstrong*, BMG Music/Sony, 2004.

structures of racialized terror. Black people seek safe havens for love and sadness, for music and food, for the healing presence of family and friends, and for that most intimate experience of all: dialogue with God. Such dialogue, such prayer, means knowing that whatever hateful things the world says about you and does to you because of your supposed racial identity, God has created and redeemed you, God loves you and will vindicate you. A living communal memory of African ancestors preserves some traces of their (often) non-Christian spiritualties and habits of devotion even in the midst of explicitly Christian forms of worship. The shouts, songs, silences and ecstasies of the ancestors live on in their 'New World' Christian descendants. Embodied connections with both such indigenous roots and the mysteries of Jesus and his Spirit bring solace and power. In countless life-giving ways, Africa prays in the Americas.[2]

This prayer of the black and blue becomes recognizably Christian in those cases where it addresses itself to the triune God of Christian faith attested in scripture. Some have lamented this Christianization of Afrodiasporic prayer because it seems to draw it uncomfortably close to the deadly prayer of so-called-Christian white supremacists who for centuries have treated darkly coloured peoples like animals, commodities or worse, with a Bible in one hand and a whip or rope or gun in the other. Despite this unsettling connection, the concrete political, psychological, moral and theological significance of these two traditions of (at least ostensibly) Christian prayer could hardly be more dissimilar. If modern Christians were asked to decide which of these two traditions best represents the essential meaning and promise of Christian prayer in the present age, the correct choice would be obvious. A study of Christian prayer in black and blue allows one to glimpse the healing and liberating power that Christian prayer should, but sometimes tragically does not, bring into this violent world. From the prayer remembered in slave spirituals and narratives, to the prayer of the black freedom struggle, to the prayer of the victims and survivors of the 2015 massacre at Charleston's Mother Emanuel, this black and blue tradition is revelatory of what Christian prayer must remain and become if it is to render true worship to the living God of infinite justice and mercy revealed in Christ and the Holy Spirit.

---

[2]Albert J. Raboteau, *Slave Religion: The 'Invisible Institution' in the Antebellum South* (New York: Oxford University Press, 2004); M. Shawn Copeland, *Knowing Christ Crucified: The Witness of African American Religious Experience* (Maryknoll, NY: Orbis Books, 2018), 37–58; and Dwight N. Hopkins, *Down, Up, and Over: Slave Religion and Black Theology* (Minneapolis, MN: Fortress Press, 2000), 107–54.

Christian Prayer in Slave Spirituals and Narratives

Slaveholders prayed and did so while supposing themselves to be good Christians. This is a disturbing fact we must not forget. We cannot even say (as if to reassure ourselves) that their prayers generally took the tearful, self-interrogating and somewhat empathic form that Willie James Jennings finds in the records of Gomes Eanes de Azurara ('Zurara'), the chronicler who told the story of the arrival of 235 African slaves in Portugal on 8 August 1444. Such morally conflicted prayer seems to have been a rarity. This is how Zurara prayed that day:

> O, Thou heavenly Father – who with thy powerful hand, without alteration of thy divine essence, governest all the infinite company of thy Holy City, and controllest all the revolutions of higher worlds, divided into nine spheres, making the duration of ages long or short according as it pleaseth Thee – I pray Thee that my tears may not wrong my conscience; for it is not their religion but their humanity that maketh mine to weep in pity for their sufferings. And if the brute animals, with their bestial feelings, by a natural instinct understand the suffering of their own kind, what wouldst Thou have my human nature to do on seeing before my eyes that miserable company, and remembering that they too are of the generation of the sons of Adam?[3]

Zurara's praise of God is followed quickly by his confession that he recognizes the humanity of the Africans being imported as slaves. Their suffering causes him to 'weep in pity'. His request of God is not for their liberation, however, but rather that his weeping 'not wrong [his] conscience'. Why would it? He indicates the reason when he notes that it is not 'their religion' that moves him to cry but rather 'their humanity'. His Christian judgement against their non-Christian religion provides such a strong rationale in his mind for their enslaved condition that he is pressed to find an acceptable justification, not for their slavery, but for his emotional response. He feels the need to defend his tears before God. He does so by appealing to the common humanity he shares with the slaves, and certainly this aspect of his prayer is commendable as far as it goes, but strictly speaking the aim of his prayer is only that God understand his reasons for weeping. Although Zurara's prayer displays some surprising empathy (surprising because he is an agent of a slaveholding state),

---

[3]Quoted in Willie James Jennings, *The Christian Imagination: Theology and the Origins of Race* (New Haven, CT: Yale University Press, 2010), 17.

this empathy inspires no meaningful resistance on his part to the violence being perpetrated against the hundreds of Africans before him.

Other examples of Christian prayer among slaveholders prove more callous still. Consider the case of the Episcopalian priest, 'Rev. Mr. Pike', described in Harriet Jacobs' 1861 *Incidents in the Life of a Slave Girl*. Jacobs, writing under the pseudonym 'Linda Brent', recounts the following episode:

> After the alarm caused by Nat Turner's insurrection had subsided, the slaveholders came to the conclusion that it would be well to give the slaves enough of religious instruction to keep them from murdering their masters. ... When the Rev. Mr. Pike came, there were some twenty persons present. The reverend gentleman knelt in prayer, then seated himself, and requested all present, who could read, to open their books, while he gave out the portions he wished them to repeat or respond to. His text was, 'Servants be obedient to them that are your masters according to the flesh, with fear and trembling, in singleness of your heart, as unto Christ.'[4]

Perhaps Pike's kneeling in prayer was supposed to symbolize the sort of submission to earthly masters that he instructed his enslaved congregants to practise, 'as unto Christ'. If so, he may have experienced only the highest coherence in his sermon about obedience and his own practice of Christian prayer, unable (or unwilling) to perceive any grave moral contradiction between them. But the contradiction was real and terrible. Pike was in effect asking his Christian brothers and sisters to give themselves over to cruel, life-destroying powers whose interests he represented. Compared to Zurara's prayer, Pike's is more hardened and orchestrated. There is not the slightest trace of cognitive dissonance in it and thus, evidently, a more thorough forgetting of shared humanity. Pike's is the more typical example of Christian prayer among slaveholders: untroubled, self-righteous and coldly indifferent to the misery that surrounds it.

Slavery was hell. It was rape, torture and murder. It was physical, psychological, sexual and every other kind of abuse. One slaveholder 'shot a woman through the head, who had run away and been brought back to him. No one called him to account for it. If a slave resisted being whipped, the bloodhounds were unpacked, and set upon him, to tear his flesh from his bones'. Jacobs clarifies that 'the master who did these things was highly educated, and styled a perfect gentleman. He also boasted the

---

[4]Harriet Jacobs/Linda Brent, 'Incidents in the Life of a Slave Girl', in *The Classic Slave Narratives*, ed. Henry Louis Gates, Jr. (New York: Penguin Books, 2002), 437–665 (516–17).

name and standing of a Christian, though Satan never had a truer follower'.[5] In her 1831 autobiography, the formerly enslaved Mary Prince recalls the mercilessness of her master 'Mr. D—': 'Nothing could touch his hard heart – neither sighs, nor tears, nor prayers, nor streaming blood; he was deaf to our cries, and careless of our sufferings. ... Yet there was nothing very remarkable in this; for it might serve as a sample of the common usage of slaves.'[6] If Christian prayer is a tool of the oppressor, an exercise meant to train the slave's body and soul to submit to such horrors, and indeed the very silencing of their cries for help and mercy, then it is an evil which ought to be abolished together with the white supremacist regimes of violence that it serves.

However, this is not what Christian prayer meant for the enslaved Afrodescendant peoples that embraced it and practised it in secret. Jacobs recalls a Methodist prayer meeting in which she sat next to a 'poor, bereaved mother' who exclaimed:

'My Lord and Master, help me! My load is more than I can bear. God has hid himself from me, and I am left in darkness and misery.' Then, striking her breast, she continued, 'I can't tell you what is in here! They've got all my children. Last week, they took the last one. God only knows where they've sold her. They let me have her sixteen years, and then – O! O! Pray for her, brothers and sisters! I've got nothing to live for now. God make my time short!'[7]

This lament is reminiscent of Job's, of those in the Psalms and of Jesus' on the cross. It is a prayer to God from the Godforsaken. It is also a request *for* prayer from a community: 'Pray for her, brothers and sisters!' It is an act of speech which barely expresses the ocean of grief within: 'I can't tell you what is in here!' Who would dare deprive this woman of her prayerful voice on the hasty assumption that Christian prayer is only ever an instrument of oppression? Can modern scholars hear and understand this woman's cry?

To be able to speak one's pain in prayer and be heard by a community of brothers and sisters may provide a modicum of comfort, even if one remains in a pit of anguish too deep for words. Although the grief remains, one may

---

[5]Jacobs/Brent, 'Incidents in the Life of a Slave Girl', 495.
[6]Mary Prince, 'The History of Mary Prince', in *The Classic Slave Narratives*, ed. Henry Louis Gates, Jr. (New York: Penguin Books, 2002), 249–321 (268).
[7]Jacobs/Brent, 'Incidents in the Life of a Slave Girl', 519.

find more consolation and empowerment still in the embodied experience of joining together in song. After this woman spoke her heart:

> The congregation struck up a hymn, and sung as though they were as free as the birds that warbled around us:

> Ole Satan thought he had a mighty aim;
> He missed my soul, and caught my sins.
> Cry Amen, cry Amen, cry Amen to God!

> He took my sins upon his back;
> Went muttering and grumbling down to hell.
> Cry Amen, cry Amen, cry Amen to God!

> Ole Satan's church is here below.
> Up to God's free church I hope to go.
> Cry Amen, cry Amen, cry Amen to God!

Jacobs concludes: 'Precious are such moments to the poor slaves. If you were to hear them at such times, you might think they were happy.' *Happy*. To guard against complacency, she adds, 'But can that hour of singing and shouting sustain them through the dreary week, toiling without wages, under constant dread of the lash?'[8] Jacobs offers an important reminder that it is not enough merely to pray, because the unjust system of slavery must be actively dismantled. But it is also striking just how valuable prayer is to the wounded people she describes. Christian prayer practised as lament over the evils of slavery and communal celebration of God's tender mercies and promises of redemption is a lifeline for those in bondage. The God who through Christ endures the scourge of the Roman crucifiers also becomes present in the crucifying, hellacious circumstances of slavery and offers its sufferers the sustaining hope of freedom.

W. E. B. Du Bois expresses the quality of this black and blue prayer tradition well when he says, 'Through all the sorrow of the Sorrow Songs there breathes a hope – a faith in the ultimate justice of things.'[9] To some extent, this hope in ultimate justice refers to a heavenly end where, as Howard Thurman puts it while reflecting on the slave spirituals during the Jim Crow era, 'there will be no proscription, no segregation, no separateness,

---

[8]Jacobs/Brent, 'Incidents in the Life of a Slave Girl', 519–20.
[9]W. E. B. Du Bois, *The Souls of Black Folk* (New York: Simon and Schuster, 2005), 251.

no sorrow, but complete freedom of movement – the most psychologically dramatic of all manifestations of freedom'.[10] Although many slave songs make such final expectations explicit, they have also inspired a struggle for liberation in history. This is especially clear with the hymn, 'Oh Freedom':

Oh Freedom! Oh Freedom!
Oh Freedom! I love Thee!
And before I'll be a slave,
I'll be buried in my grave,
And go home to my Lord and be free.

The singer would rather die than be enslaved. The implication is that he or she would fight for freedom even if this meant risking his or her life. Interpreted in this light, the eschatology in the prayer of the slaves does not so much suppress as enkindle a rebellious spirit. It is, therefore, unsurprising to see songs such as 'Oh, Freedom' cited frequently in James Cone's black liberation theology. Cone helpfully explains that the slaves sang about a freedom 'that *included* but *did not depend upon* historical possibilities' because, although they obviously wanted their concrete oppressive circumstances to change, they did not often have the political power to effect such changes immediately.[11] Whatever historical transformations were or were not imaginable, spirituals such as 'Oh, Freedom' empowered enslaved communities to connect with the God who created them to be free in both this life and the next.

This was the God who raised Jesus from the dead. The God encountered in the movements of the Spirit. The God about whom the ex-slave abolitionist Sojourner Truth exclaimed, 'Oh God, I did not know you were so big!'[12] This was a divine mystery greater than any devilish designs of slaveholders. Those who participated bodily and communally in the singing of such spirituals desired membership in 'God's free church' and experienced this through their prayer. Slavery was hell, but prayer was a hidden opening through which heaven might appear and bring comfort and strength to the afflicted. On the lips of slaveholders, prayer was death, but in the feet and hearts and lungs of the enslaved it was new and abundant life.

---

[10]Howard Thurman, 'The Negro Spiritual Speaks of Life and Death (1947)', in *A Strange Freedom: The Best of Howard Thurman on Religious Experience and Public Life*, ed. Walter Earl Fluker and Catherine Tumber (Boston, MA: Beacon Press, 1998), 76.

[11]James H. Cone, *The Spirituals and the Blues: An Interpretation* (Maryknoll, NY: Orbis Books, 1991), 82.

[12]Sojourner Truth, *The Narrative of Sojourner Truth*, ed. Nell Irvin Painter (New York: Penguin Books, 1998), 45.

Christian Prayer in the Black Freedom Struggle

After the abolition of slavery in the United States, the domination of God's precious black and blue children continued by other means: discrimination, segregation, political disenfranchisement, economic deprivation, false criminalization, lynchings and massacres, and other forms of violence. The struggle for freedom was not over. In many ways, it was just beginning. Christian prayer played a crucial role in this struggle by vocalizing suffering and hopes, providing much-needed comfort and strength, and engendering acts of nonviolent resistance.

With unparalleled clarity, Martin Luther King, Jr. reveals the significance of prayer for collective, antiracist struggle. He does this in one way through his public practice of prayer. This practice could be seen not only at any given Sunday morning church service where King would lead the congregation in song and supplication, building them up after the latest experience of white supremacist terror, but also in the streets, in a well-organized act of protest, indeed *as* this very act of protest. Lewis Baldwin gives the example of the 1965 struggle for voting rights: 'As the demonstrators prepared for the great march from Selma to Montgomery, the media captured King and other ministers in a circle on their knees, with Ralph Abernathy, King's closest associate, praying that blacks and whites would learn to live together in peace.'[13] To kneel in prayer before policemen wielding clubs and angry mobs spewing hate is, for King and his companions, a courageous form of direct action. Although we have every reason to believe that this prayer is genuine – that those on their knees are really opening their hearts to God in desperate longing for a better world – it is also a carefully crafted performance designed to move and teach those who witnessed it. The lesson is simple: these are humble children of God, precious human beings who do not deserve the abuse that is regularly heaped upon them. Such prayer in the light of day and in the glaring light of television cameras is meant to provoke a change of hearts, minds and recalcitrant institutions.

No less important to the black freedom struggle are private acts of prayer, such as the justly famous episode in which King, distressed by death threats received prior to the 1956 Montgomery bus boycott, feels helpless and frightened – in a word, blue. He descends to the kitchen. The hour is late and the house is still. In his solitude he begins to pray. This is how he describes his experience:

> The words I spoke to God that midnight are still vivid in my memory. 'I am here taking a stand for what I believe is right. But now I am afraid.

---

[13]Lewis V. Baldwin, *Never to Leave Us Alone: The Prayer Life of Martin Luther King, Jr.* (Minneapolis, MN: Fortress Press, 2010), 80.

The people are looking to me for leadership, and if I stand before them without strength and courage, they too will falter. I am at the end of my powers. I have nothing left. I've come to the point where I can't face it alone.' At that moment I experienced the presence of the Divine as I had never experienced Him before. It seemed as though I could hear the quiet assurance of an inner voice saying: 'Stand up for righteousness, stand up for truth; and God will be at your side forever.' Almost at once my fears began to go. My uncertainty disappeared. I was ready to face anything.[14]

Such private acts of prayer are vital to the struggle for freedom insofar as they cast out fear and give one the strength to endure. Without laying his soul bare in this honest manner and receiving 'the presence of the Divine' through 'the quiet assurance of an inner voice', would King have found the courage needed to persist in the face of credible death threats? Would the civil rights victories he helped win have ever come to pass? Even when it takes place in moments of isolation and apparent inaction, prayer can facilitate social transformation by steadying and grounding its vulnerable human agents. King is part of the oft-overlooked contemplative strand in African American Christian prayer.[15] In addition to the sermons, songs and shouts which give bold expression to black religion, there is also the quiet reception of everyday grace without which meaningful freedom, whether personal or collective, would never fully take hold.[16]

Before King, there is Ida B. Wells (later Wells-Barnett). She similarly models the radical unity of a life of prayer and antiracist struggle.[17] Cornel West characterizes her as 'the most courageous Black organic intellectual in the history of the country', noting that 'you have to wait to get Martin King to get another courageous intellectual like that'. He describes her as the leader of an 'anti-terrorist movement', which 'was going to call into question the bestiality and barbarity and brutality of Jim Crow and American terrorism and lynching, but would do it in the name of something that provided a higher moral ground and higher spiritual ground given her Christian faith'.[18]

---

[14]Martin Luther King, Jr., *Stride toward Freedom: The Montgomery Story* (Boston, MA: Beacon Press, 1958), 125.

[15]Barbara A. Holmes, *Joy Unspeakable: Contemplative Practices of the Black Church*, 2nd edn (Minneapolis, MN: Fortress Press, 2017), 112.

[16]Kevin Quashie, *The Sovereignty of Quiet: Beyond Resistance in Black Culture* (New Brunswick, NJ: Rutgers University Press, 2012), 80 and Katie G. Cannon, *Black Womanist Ethics* (Atlanta, GA: Scholars Press, 1988), 127–43.

[17]Emilie M. Townes, *Womanist Justice, Womanist Hope* (Atlanta, GA: Scholars Press, 1993), 69–106.

[18]Cornel West with Christa Buschendorf, *Black Prophetic Fire* (Boston, MA: Beacon Press, 2014), 141.

Wells-Barnett fights against lynching and other injustices in a nonviolent way simply by reporting the truth about them. Like King, she faces constant death threats. And like King, she finds courage in the presence of God.

One story from her life particularly illuminates how she thinks about the purpose of prayer in the midst of struggle. Black sharecroppers in Elaine, Arkansas, had begun to organize in order to push for fairer pay and more just working conditions. They met in a church on the evening of 30 September 1919. A group of white men opened fire on the church, and a gunfight broke out. One white man was killed. In response, a large number of armed white men from Arkansas and surrounding states, including 500 troops sent by the governor, began slaughtering black men, women and children. When the massacre ended, more than 200 black people and exactly five white people had been killed. The only arrests made were of black people, and twelve black men in particular ('the Elaine Twelve') were tried for murder and sentenced to death. At the time, Wells-Barnett was living in Chicago, exiled from the South, but she made her way to Arkansas in secret, to visit these twelve men in prison and to advocate for them. Hiding amongst their wives and loved ones, so as not to be detected by the guards, she witnessed the incarcerated ones raise their voices in prayer:

> I listened to those men sing and pray and give testimony from their overburdened hearts, and sometimes the women would take up the refrain. They shed tears and they got 'happy', and the burden of their talk and prayers was of the hereafter. Finally, I got up and walked close to the bars and said to them in a low tone, 'I have been listening to you for nearly two hours. You have talked and sung and prayed about dying, and forgiving your enemies, and feeling sure that you are going to be received in the New Jerusalem because your God knows that you are innocent of the offence for which you expect to be electrocuted. But why don't you pray to live and ask to be freed? The God you serve is the God of Paul and Silas who opened their prison gates, and if you have all the faith you say you have, you ought to believe that he will open your prison doors too. If you do believe that, let all of your songs and prayers hereafter be songs of faith and hope that God will set you free; that the judges who have to pass on your cases will be given the wisdom and courage to decide in your behalf.'[19]

---

[19]Ida B. Wells, *Crusade for Justice: The Autobiography of Ida B. Wells*, ed. Alfreda M. Duster (Chicago, IL: University of Chicago Press, 1970), 402–3.

Although Wells-Barnett, like Jacobs before her, appreciates the 'happiness' that comes from prayer even in the midst of sorrow (the heavenly hopes that momentarily comfort the oppressed), she resists the notion that the purpose of prayer is only eschatological or palliative. She calls to mind the biblical witness of Paul and Silas, and on this basis argues that the Elaine Twelve ought to pray for God to act directly in history. She points towards a potential effectiveness of prayer which does not rest on the moral suasion that may result from its public performance or on the personal fortitude that its private practice may impart but on God's ability to hear the cries of the poor and actively respond.

Such beliefs in divine agency may seem naïve, or even hurtful, given the grim state of the world. Certainly, they raise questions of theodicy. If God could respond to our prayers by overcoming whatever afflicts us, especially if this affliction is undeserved, then why is no such response usually forthcoming? How can God be almighty and just if God lets the innocent suffer? With good reason, unanswered petitions often give way to cries of lament. For some black intellectuals, such as William R. Jones and Anthony Pinn, this line of thinking culminates in a form of protest atheism or agnosticism, where the prayer of complaint finally morphs into a decision against the existence of God.[20] However, this is not the path that Wells-Barnett takes. Although her circumstances are incredibly daunting, she remains undeterred in both her activism and her prayer. She writes *The Arkansas Race Riot* to raise awareness about the massacre and the unjust court proceedings following it.[21] Thanks to the legal action of the NAACP, of which she was a founding member, and other social justice organizations the case eventually makes its way to the Supreme Court, which rules in favour of the falsely accused on the grounds that they were denied due process (*Moore vs Dempsey*). One of the twelve later visits Wells-Barnett in Chicago and attributes his freedom to the kind of historically focused prayer that she exhorted them to practise: 'We never talked about dying anymore, but did as she told us, and now every last one of us is out and enjoying his freedom.'[22] Is this man's liberty the result of divinely answered prayers or direct human efforts (such as honest reporting and sound legal strategy)? Wells-Barnett would suggest *both*. She refuses to choose.

---

[20]William R. Jones, *Is God a White Racist? A Preamble to Black Theology* (Garden City, NY: Anchor Books, 1973) and Anthony B. Pinn, *Why, Lord? Suffering and Evil in Black Theology* (New York: Continuum, 1995).
[21]Ida B. Wells-Barnett, *The Arkansas Race Riot* (Createspace Independent Publishing, 2013).
[22]Wells, *Crusade for Justice*, 404.

Just as unanswered prayers rightly give way to lament, so too answered ones rightly occasion gratitude and rejoicing. Recall the stirring final lines of King's 'I Have a Dream' speech:

> When we allow freedom to ring – when we let it ring from every village and every hamlet, from every state and every city, we will be able to speed up that day when all of God's children, black men and white men, Jews and Gentiles, Protestants and Catholics, will be able to join hands and sing in the words of the old Negro spiritual, 'Free at last, free at last, thank God Almighty, we are free at last.'[23]

This Christian prayer of thanksgiving belongs to the indefinite time of the already and the not yet. King quotes a hymn from his spiritual forebears in order to anticipate a future that he only dreamt of and that we must still await. The examples of King and Wells-Barnett challenge Christians today to be grateful for God's liberative presence in the struggle to abolish slavery and to achieve equal rights for all human beings and grateful too for the many courageous actors in this struggle, including those remembered and forgotten. At the same time, these holy examples demand that Christians remain expectant and unyielding in the fight for a more grace-filled world, drawing on all their resources of prayer and protest to engage the fight, because the lives of God's black and blue children are continuing to be destroyed well into the twenty-first century. The hour is too soon for gratitude alone.

Christian Prayer at Mother Emanuel

It had seemed an ordinary, peaceful Wednesday evening at Mother Emanuel, a historic African Methodist Episcopal (AME) church in Charleston, South Carolina. Several people, young and old, were gathered for the weekly Bible study. Then a cataclysmic eruption of violence.

> Felicia's Bible fell to the floor. A bullet pierced it.
> Beneath the table next to her, she spotted her old friend Polly Sheppard cowering, as yet unhit. The killer's heavy boots marched toward her.
> Felicia prayed silently, Polly prayed out loud.

---

[23]Martin Luther King, 'I Have a Dream', in *A Testament of Hope: The Essential Writings and Speeches*, ed. James M. Washington (New York: HarperCollins, 1986), 217–20 (220).

The gunman stopped shooting when he reached Polly, dead eyes looking down at her, his heavy black pistol pointed at her feet.

'Shut up!' he snapped.[24]

Members of the church were praying together before the shooting started. The prayer continued during the carnage, and it continued afterwards. This prayer at Mother Emanuel demonstrates the vitality and the importance of the long, ongoing tradition of Christian prayer in black and blue. The resurgent culture of anti-black, white supremacist violence that the world is presently witnessing wants to put a stop to such prayer. It yells, 'Shut up!' It murders, it burns down,[25] and it desecrates. But it cannot stifle the Holy Spirit that moves in the hearts and bodies of this resilient people.

17 June 2015 was not the first time that Mother Emanuel fell victim to white supremacist attack. In the early months of 1822, after years of racist harassment and persecution, Denmark Vesey, an ex-slave and a leader of the church's Bible study, began organizing free and enslaved members of the church for a slave revolt and an Exodus experience. Like the Hebrews of old, they planned to flee Egypt (i.e. the United States) and make their way to the promised land (in this case, Haiti, which after the Haitian Revolution of 1791–1804 was the only black-led country in the 'New World'). Their plans were exposed before they could be enacted, and thirty-five people including Vesey were executed. The church was burnt to the ground, and the surviving members were scattered, forced to go elsewhere or meet in secret until the end of the Civil War.[26] During the freedom struggle of the 1950s and 1960s, Mother Emanuel was a site of activism. Both Martin Luther King, Jr. (1962) and Coretta Scott King (1969) spoke there, and many members participated in local boycotts and peaceful demonstrations.[27] That the killer decided to target this particular church was no accident.

The biblical text being studied that evening was the parable of the sower. This was Myra Thompson's first time leading the Bible study. 'She described a world of sin in which hatred and worldly desires had hardened hearts, leaving too many people unable to nourish the seeds of God's grace within themselves.' Dylann Roof's heart was already too hardened

---

[24]Jennifer Berry Hawes, *Grace Will Lead Us Home: The Charleston Church Massacre and the Hard, Inspiring Journey to Forgiveness* (New York: St Martin's Press, 2019), 17.

[25]Richard Fausset, '3 Black Churches Have Burned in 10 Days in a Single Louisiana Parish', *New York Times*, 5 April 2019.

[26]Herb Frazier, Bernard Edward Powers, Jr. and Marjory Wentworth, *We Are Charleston: Tragedy and Triumph at Mother Emanuel* (Nashville, TN: W Publishing Group, 2016), 68–70.

[27]Frazier, et al., *We Are Charleston*, 123–39.

to appreciate just how aptly this parable described his own situation. In his case, the seeds of grace had fallen on the inhospitable ground of white supremacy. Though he was a stranger, the twelve black Christians in the church welcomed him, gave him a Bible, let him join their intimate prayer meeting, let him sit next to the pastor, Reverend Clementa Pinckney. As a child, Dylann had played with a biracial, black friend. He had attended Sunday school at a Lutheran church. None of these seeds of grace was a match for the toxic soil of white supremacist web content in which he found his malignant sense of purpose. Reports indicate that he immersed himself in a slew of hateful websites after watching news coverage of the murder of the unarmed, black, seventeen-year-old Trayvon Martin on 26 February 2012 and Googling 'black on white crime' (already a telling search term).[28]

While at prayer, Myra and Clementa were shot to death. So too were Cynthia Hurd, Susie Jackson, Ethel Lance, DePayne Middleton-Doctor, Tywanza Sanders, Daniel L. Simmons, Sr., and Sharonda Coleman-Singleton. These are the 'Emmanuel Nine', each a precious child of God gone too soon. Polly, Felicia Sanders (Tywanza's mother) and Felicia's granddaughter were present at the Bible study but did not get hit. Clementa's wife, Jennifer, and their daughter Malana, who huddled together in an adjacent church office, also survived. After the shooting, these five shaken survivors, other church members, family and friends, press and government officials congregated in a nearby hotel. 'Some cried, some prayed, some paced.' Receiving the news on her cell phone that her mother Ethel was one of those killed, Nadine Collier screamed aloud in her car. While everyone awaited the coroner's report, the Reverend Norvel Goff Sr asked people to gather and hold hands. For those too overcome to stand, people knelt to wrap themselves in arms of comfort. Goff's voice rose in prayer, then in song. He began the first lines of an old Christian hymn, and the group joined him.

> My hope is built on nothing less
> than Jesus' blood and righteousness
> I dare not trust the sweetest frame,
> but wholly lean on Jesus' name.

The people sang together, hundreds of human voices converging in a sombre river of shock and grief.[29]

---

[28]Hawes, *Grace Will Lead Us Home*, 14, 182, 185 and 248.
[29]Hawes, *Grace Will Lead Us Home*, 35, 44 and 50.

Such prayers of mourning and togetherness continued almost unceasingly in the coming days. There were prayer vigils of solidarity in churches throughout Charleston and many other US towns and cities. Twenty-five thousand people joined together for a march dubbed 'the Bridge to Peace', in which 'there were nine minutes of silence, spontaneous singing, and prayers – always prayers'.[30] President Barack Obama gave a eulogy at Rev. Pinckney's funeral and sang 'Amazing Grace'.[31]

These prayers in the immediate aftermath of the massacre were significant in countless ways known only to those who voiced them or held them in their hearts, and perhaps their meaning remained partly hidden even for such persons. What were these prayers doing? In response to such violence, many agreed it was not enough merely to offer 'thoughts and prayers', as the rote expression goes. There was a need for action of other sorts, such as removing the Confederate flag from the capitol building, seeking greater gun control measures and continuing to struggle for an end to white supremacy in all its forms. Yet these prayers after the shooting were doing something very real and irreplaceable that is not easy to categorize. One can see this clearly by considering what happened when the prayers began to subside. After the news cycle had shifted, and most people had moved on with their busy lives, the survivors still ached. Felicia felt neglected by the leaders of her church, who had stopped visiting. 'She desperately needed a person of the cloth to say, "God didn't leave you. He's still with you." That was all she wanted, an assurance that God would pull her through this.' Praying together was a way to feel connected with God's abiding love and presence in times of agony, and without it there was bitter isolation. She eventually found some spiritual support by speaking and praying with a minister at a nearby Presbyterian church. 'At one point [in this meeting] she cried, "I don't know what my purpose is!"' Prayer is a way to express questions borne of grief and confusion, a time to be oneself without pretence or polish, a chance to let everything go and let everything out. It is a space for wounded bodies and souls to be heard and to heal.[32]

For many survivors of violence, prayer may also eventually be a context in which to explore the possibilities of forgiveness and to find the power to forgive. The only conditional petition in the Lord's Prayer is 'Forgive us our trespasses as we forgive those who trespass against us.' Such forgiveness is a lofty expectation when one is faced with a coldblooded, racially motivated

---

[30]Frazier, et al., *We Are Charleston*, 8–9.
[31]Hawes, *Grace Will Lead Us Home*, 287–94.
[32]Hawes, *Grace Will Lead Us Home*, 142, 143.

killer such as Roof, who has not shown even an inkling of remorse. On the contrary, he has said, 'I would like to make it crystal clear. I do not regret what I did. I am not sorry. I have not shed a tear for the innocent people I killed.' Moreover, his hardened heart is only one individual inflection of what seems to be an increasingly hard-hearted culture that stubbornly refuses to repair the harms done by five centuries of institutionalized racism and, in fact, seems intent on exacerbating them.

Nevertheless, some of the survivors and family members of the deceased stunned the world by publicly offering forgiveness to Roof at his bond hearing. Nadine spoke the words first. Looking at him, she said,

> I just want everybody to know, to you, I forgive you! You took something very precious from me. I will never talk to her ever again. I will never be able to hold her again. But I forgive you! And have mercy on your soul. You. Hurt. Me! You hurt a lot of people. But God forgives you. And I forgive you.

Myra's husband, Reverend Anthony Thompson, made a similar statement:

> I forgive you. And my family forgives you. But we would like you to take this opportunity to repent. Repent. Confess. Give your life to the one who matters most – Christ – so that he can change it, can change your ways no matter what happens to you.

Felicia added her voice too:

> We welcomed you Wednesday night in our Bible study with open arms. You have killed some of the most beautiful people that I know. Every fiber in my body hurts! And I'll never be the same. Tywanza Sanders is my son, but Tywanza was my hero. Tywanza was my hero! But as we say in the Bible study: We enjoyed you, but may God have mercy on you.[33]

What should observers make of such statements of forgiveness, which call on the names of God and Christ, which convey unspeakable grief, and yet which express kindness and request divine mercy for an unrepentant white supremacist murderer?

One important point to remember is that not everyone touched by the massacre responded in this manner or found it appropriate to do so. For

---

[33]Hawes, *Grace Will Lead Us Home*, 74–5, 272.

example, 'DePayne Middleton-Doctor's cousin, Waltrina Middleton, [was] upset about the way the statements of forgiveness were immediately used to interpret the larger meaning of what happened at Emanuel Church: it "took away our narrative to be rightfully hurt. I can't turn off my pain."'[34] Similarly, Nadine's sister Sharon was angry about such a quick offer of forgiveness: 'Before Sharon could think about forgiving in any honest way, she needed to know more. She needed to be angry and cry and know exactly what happened.' Yet for Sharon it was a question of time. After the trial ended, she felt God move her heart in a new way: 'She could forgive Roof, at least for now. Forever? Time would tell.' Everyone's path is different on such questions, and for some deeply prayerful Christian people forgiveness may never come in this life because the hurt is just too great and the injustice too persistent. At the sentencing, 'some screamed at Roof, calling him evil. Several hoped he burned in hell for eternity. They called him a coward. Satan. An animal. A monster.' Given the severity and remorselessness of the crime, my own view is that no one who remains in a state of righteous anger ought to be judged for this. Their outrage is warranted and may itself become the occasion for honest and meaningful prayer. It is also crucial to acknowledge that those who do forgive do not thereby tolerate the murderous behaviour or advocate any unwarranted slackening of the black freedom struggle. Many who spoke forgiving words were relieved to hear that Roof was given a maximum sentence (even if they had misgivings about the death penalty in general) and many have gone on to agitate for social reform in various areas.[35]

Although there is a range of perspectives on the matter which must be respected, I do believe as a Christian that it is a good and astonishing thing that the practice of prayer at Mother Emanuel has brought some of those most deeply hurt by this most recent massacre to a place where they feel empowered to forgive. Arguably this is much more than one can reasonably expect from anyone, but it is what the extraordinary tradition of Christian prayer in black and blue has made possible. This tradition has been a refuge for the racially oppressed, a site specifically set apart. But it has also been a place of welcome, strength and healing that has grace to offer all of God's children, if they can only learn to receive it. The God worshipped in this tradition is one who seeks the lost and who accomplishes wondrous deeds in history. This God heals and liberates, reserving the tenderest mercies for the most afflicted, while empowering them for renewed action. This God

---

[34]Frazier, et al., *We Are Charleston*, 172.
[35]Hawes, *Grace Will Lead Us Home*, 78, 279, 281, 283.

CHAPTER THIRTY-EIGHT

Praying with the Unwanted People at the End of the World

CLÁUDIO CARVALHAES

We are all feeling in one way or another that the world is moving towards a rather difficult place and that we are all moving towards an impeding collective death. Inequality soars with the vast majority of people around the earth poor and very few individuals having more money than entire countries together. Middle classes everywhere are disappearing amid the growth of poverty. The anthropocene or capitolocene as the new designation of our time has been marked by an indisputable notion that we, known as the exclusive form of humanity, are extracting more from the earth than its own limit. Global warming, ice caps melting, uneven seasons, draughts, devastations and death are showing up everywhere with immigrants and refugees moving due to climate change and civil wars, searching for solace. Democracies are collapsing, violence growing under alternative powers, state-nations dissolving into dictatorships with fascist leaders, states of exception becoming normalized and the consequences of a neoliberal unrestrained economy throwing us towards a place of no return.

What prayers are we called to pray during these times? How are we to pray as we are confronted by this situation? It seems that the condition of our world begs for different prayers and different forms of prayer. As we hear the pain of the poor, the collapsing of the world we know, the disasters we are watching right in front of our eyes, there is no prayer, again, it seems, that can respond to it. From where should our prayers come from? What prayer can we Christians offer to the world?

If we are to pray today, we have to learn a new grammar for our faith. And if prayer is the grammar of our faith, we have to learn a new grammar for a new faith. We will have to look at tradition differently, we will have to retire or use our current prayer books differently, we will have to delve into other resources, engage with the earth more fully, to be more open to other religions, and to be church differently, since the grammar of the prayer we Christians current have is not enough to sustain us or the world in our present times. God's voice in the world is also in our prayers and through prayers we are called to be radically converted.

> Painting toenails in the place
> Of death
> At least twenty bottles
> Of nail polish on the floor
> She sits with her friend
> Even as her mother
> Shows me where the bullets
> Come through her broken wall
>
> Hope in the place of death
> Colour where colour has drained away
> Painting beauty where there has
> Been so much ugliness
>
> God help us always to
> Walk with the
> Hope of this
> Toenail painting
> Resurrection.[1]

Only a prayer that has its ear attached to the earth, its eye upon those who suffer and hands stretched in solidarity can make us realize our distance from God and a world of pain and demand of us repentance and conversion. If prayer is about listening to the whispers and cries of the suffering, if it is

---

[1] All of the prayers in this chapter can be found in Cláudio Carvalhaes, ed., *Liturgies from Below: Praying with People at the End of the World* (Nashville, TN: Abingdon Press, 2020). I am grateful for Ken Sawyer for editing and offering his wisdom to this chapter. These prayers emerged out of a global project called *Re-Imagining Worship as Acts of Defiance and Alternatives in the Context of Empire* undertaken in four different countries with poor communities and churches.

about leaning towards those who are alone, holding close those who are falling, connecting our hearts towards somebody else's heart, then we are able to listen to God's voice. If prayer is about loving God, then prayer is about building a house for the abandoned, becoming a wall against the vulnerable and giving our life away to those who are at the brink of disappearance. Prayer then becomes breathing the breath of God in the world.[2]

Prayers must be expressions of a radical commitment with the poor. But we have been away from the poor. Protestantism is often a church for middle- and upper-class people. From there we try to survive and deal with what we usually call secularism and a society in flight away from God. However, if we pay attention, there is a Christian renewal going around the fringes of the empire amidst the poor and this renewal has been done through the ritual of Christian worship and prayers. While our grammar has been enough for our survival, the Christian neo-pentecostalism exploding everywhere has given people another grammar to give sense and mission and purpose to lives often exposed to social threats and loss.[3] In these churches near the poor, we learn a grammar that gives people tools to move on with their lives, to battle their depression, to fight economic hardships, to find happiness. Perhaps this is not with the best theology, not with the ways of self-affirmation we would imagine, but they are offering something that, while we can rationalize it well, we can't even fathom to think how to engage it. It seems that our 'first world' white middle-class theology serves as impediment to getting closer to those 'racialized' and those who live in lower classes. However, while many of these churches are exploiting many without mercy, they are very close to the ones giving shape to the souls of the unwanted around the world.

Why in our suffering, you, O Lord, are you so far away?
Why don't we hear your voice?
Why don't we feel your presence?
You say to love our neighbors as much as we love ourselves.
But Lord, all we see is hatred, envy, and violence everyday.
You promised to protect, provide, and preserve
But we are defenseless against greed, deceit, and death.
Have you covered your face?
Have you turned away your eyes and blocked your ears?

---

[2]Cláudio Carvalhaes, 'Praying with the World at Heart', *Dialog: A Journal of Theology* 52, no. 4 (2013): 313–20.
[3]Jung Mo Sung, *Reclaiming Liberation Theology: Desire, Market, Religion* (London: SCM Press, 2012).

This chapter is based on an insistence that we need to get closer to the poorest and abandoned in the world. Thus, the main question here is: how are we to pray with the unwanted in the world? Do we have prayers that suffice? Can our prayers respond to the disasters of our times? Once in a worship class, I had an invited guest who told my students that we need to pray the prayers of the church for at least twenty years before they could say their own prayers. Does this still apply? I don't think so. Not abandoning the prayers of the church, we also must learn to pray differently so we can be faithful to Jesus in these disastrous times. And the way to pray is to pray with and for those unwanted, those who are the 'undercommons', which includes the earth and the animals. For their conditions of living and their very existence is also the life and conditions of existence of all of us. Fred Moten makes us see that the condition of oppression and death and disaster of our world is not only bad for the poor. The situation we are living in is death for all of us. The difference is that it kills the refugees faster than the documented citizens of the world. The undercommons are those who are under the line of full citizenship, of full humanity. From what Motten says, we could include also the earth and all living creatures. He says:

> If you want to know what the undercommons wants, black people, indigenous peoples, queers and poor people want, what we (the 'we' who cohabit in the space of the undercommons) want, it is this – we cannot be satisfied with the recognition and acknowledgement generated by the very system that denies a) that anything was ever broken and b) that we deserved to be the broken part; so we refuse to ask for recognition and instead we want to take apart, dismantle, tear down the structure that, right now, limits our ability to find each other, to see beyond it and to access the places that we know lie outside its walls. We cannot say what new structures will replace the ones we live with yet, because once we have torn shit down, we will inevitably see more and see differently and feel a new sense of wanting and being and becoming. What we want after 'the break' will be different from what we think we want before the break and both are necessarily different from the desire that issues from being in the break.[4]

Our prayer must help us all go through the new breaks that are happening and will continue to happen in our world. We can birth a new world with our

---

[4]Stefano Harney and Fred Moten, *The Undercommons: Fugitive Planning and Black Study* (Durham, NC: Duke University Press, 2013), 6.

prayers through *ora et labora*, if they are a true expression of the movements of desire and work.

> A lost voice. Squatting in my little street corner this very dark night. It is cold and the and the darkness is scary. Who can hold me – the hand of God. Is there a God out there? God if you are there – if you can hear me, hold me through the night. I really want to sleep but my belly is rumbling. Please don't let them find me here, stop them from taking and hurting me. God–if you are there – hear my voice!

Lex orandi, credendi, vivendi **and** *natura*

How do we connect our faith, the *polis* and the *oikos* of God? We have received from the tradition of the church the expansive notion of the *leges* (plural of *lex*, 'law' in Latin) of the church: *lex orandi, lex credendi, lex agendi/vivendi*.

According to Prosper of Aquitaine, 'the law of supplicating may constitute the law of believing', which can be interpreted as prayer shaping beliefs which also means that we are under the grace of God.[5] This process is sometimes understood as God's full agency which mostly cancels the way of seeing human agency.[6] Every agency is to be deemed wrong since we depend on God's agency and initiation. Within and beyond this battle between God and human agency, what is at stake is the nature and sources of our prayers. How do we relate prayer, belief and ways of living? What does it mean to utter a prayer when bombs are flying over our heads? Where do we even start to pray when people's lands are going to be subsumed under water because of global warming? How does praying shape our beliefs when the violence and power dominance of empires are breathing death and destruction over us? Using the laws, we can ask: How does the *law of prayer* challenge the empire? How does the *law of our beliefs* defy the self-enclosed sense of self that is not correlated to the earth and its suffering? How does the *lex vivendi*, the way of life, our ethical mode, based on a just way of living, help to transform the logic and practice of our prayer-beliefs within a sordid economic system?

---

[5]'Prosper of Aquitaine, disciple of Augustine and Gallican monk at Louvain, makes to the liturgy is one made precisely in defense of the necessity of divine grace, on "reemphasizing the divine agency and initiative" in salvation and every act, a role that would seem quite consistent with a Protestant theological stance and method.' See Maxwell E. Johnson, *Praying and Believing in Early Christianity: The Interplay between Christian Worship and Doctrine* (Collegeville, MN: Liturgical Press, 2013), 1.

[6]Michael Aune, 'Liturgy and Theology: Rethinking the Relationship, Part 2 – A Different Starting Place', *Worship* 81, no. 2 (2017): 141–69.

Often the relationship of the *leges* happens within a theological inner-circle that protects the boundary contradictions of the faith by analysing liturgy with liturgy. In spite of all of the dialogue liturgy has done with other areas of knowledge, the praying and the believing of liturgy seem to be encircled within a tradition that looks mostly, if not totally, upon itself.[7] So we tend to juxtapose liturgical things with liturgical things: gathering to word, baptism to eucharist, word to sending and so on. However, we need to expand the notions of the *leges* and put prayer into a greater risk, so to speak, through perhaps frightening 'external' juxtapositions, placing prayer with wars, praise with all forms of violence, confession with poverty and patriarchy, word with ecological destruction, sending forth with refugees and immigrants, and so on. That is what I am proposing, the relation of the *leges* with the 'outside' of church worship.

If we think about these juxtapositions, we can easily realize how much the church has kept its worship sacred by avoiding such 'worldly' issues. The naming of some of these issues is always tangental and goes beyond the very constitution of the ritual sacred parts. One fundamental issue we have avoided is the central presence of the earth. If, on the one hand, we have been able to expand the relation between liturgy and culture through the very timid relation with the inculturation of the liturgy, on the other, we have failed mightily in our prayer relation with the earth.

Since global warming is increasingly a deadly disaster to the earth and ourselves, we need to add a new *lex* for our time, namely *lex natura*.[8] Due to the rampant reports we read and the actual disasters already in place all over the globe, the *lex natura* must be a pre-condition for the law of prayer, belief and way of life to exist. For our common survival, the *lex natura* must be our guiding principle in praying. Through *lex natura*, we gain an orienting ground from which we can learn how to pray, to believe and to act. Thus, to pray will be an orientation towards Gaia, the earth, in this time of the anthropocene. *Lex natura* can help us pay attention to the cries of the earth, the burning of God's *oikos*, the desolation of peoples across the globe and the extinction of so many species. All of us, especially the poor, are dying right in front of our eyes. Thus, we are called to *ora et labora* with the earth and those who live at the ends of the earth.

---

[7]On liturgical juxtaposition, see the work of Gordon W. Lathrop, *Holy Things: A Liturgical Theology* (Minneapolis, MN: Fortress Press, 1993); *Holy People: A Liturgical Ecclesiology* (Minneapolis, MN: Fortress Press, 1999); and *Holy Ground: A Liturgical Cosmology* (Minneapolis, MN: Fortress Press, 2003).

[8]Cláudio Carvalhaes, 'Lex Natura – A New Way into a Liturgical Political Theology', in *T&T Clark Handbook to Political Theology*, ed. Rubem Rosário-Rodriguez (London: Bloomsbury, 2019), 449–66.

Praying with those Unwanted around the World

Arise in us
As the voice of justice, truth, liberation, and transformation
Give power to our voice speaking with the oppressed
Give strength to our fight when we stand for justice
Make us fathers to the fatherless
Make us mothers to the motherless
Make us advocates to the poor and outcast
Make us passionate friends and caretakers of creation
So that together we can build a community
Where love's power overcomes all violence against your creation.

I say this with a hint from what I have learnt being in very poor communities around the world. Through the generosity of the Council of World Mission, a prayer project from the ground developed between 2018 and 2019. The project's name is *Re-Imagining Worship as Acts of Defiance and Alternatives in the Context of Empire* and it happened in Manila, Philippines, Johannesburg, South Africa, Kingston, Jamaica and Sicily, Italy. The idea was to gather twenty-five to thirty scholars, pastors, students, artists and activists from four continents and visit one country in that area, live with poor communities for a few days and then create liturgical resources, expressions of those communities.

In Manila, we talked about a Jeepney liturgy based on the daily transportation of Pilipino people using old jeeps left from the Second World War. The past of colonization, of wars and the current abandonment of the government to its people can be seen in the daily transportation of the people in these Jeepneys.[9] Seventy percent of the Pilipino people use the Jeepney and they are the poor of the country. Daily life happens in those Jeepneys, conversations, sharing, lament; the life of the Pilipino people happens in those Jeepneys. As Revelation Velunta taught our group:

Jeepney hermeneutics acknowledges the depth and the breadth of meanings represented by the Filipino Jeepney as symbolic of a people's capacity to beat swords into ploughshares. In simple terms, this book is

---

[9]Several theologians and Bible scholars are calling their work 'Jeepney hermeneutics'. For example: www.jeepney.blogspot.com (accessed: 10 September 2020).

about bringing Jesus' parables out of a US military jeep and bringing them into a Filipino jeepney.[10]

Our task there was to figure out what a Jeepney liturgy would be like, engaging the oppressive past and the brutal present of the Philippines.

In South Africa we focused on the African notion of Ubuntu and the multiple struggles of apartheid and post-apartheid in South Africa. One of the most precious gifts South Africa has given us is Ubuntu. Desmond Tutu, describes Ubuntu like this:

> Ubuntu is very difficult to render into a Western language. It speaks of the very essence of being human. When we want to give high praise to someone we say, 'Yu, u nobunto'; 'Hey so-and-so has ubuntu'. Then you are generous, you are hospitable, you are friendly and caring and compassionate. You share what you have. It is to say, 'My humanity is inextricably bound up in yours'. We belong in a bundle of life.[11]

What does it mean to engage Ubuntu in a place of apartheid and the pillage of Africa? How do people hold on to Ubuntu in its proposal and its radical possibility and recover what has been erased and establish it as a prophetic way of being in the world? How can prayers help with that? How can prayer be that?

In Kingston Jamaica, we talked about the wounds of colonization starting with the arrival of Christopher Columbus in 1494 and the consequent possession of Jamaica by Spain and the British Empire who traded sugar and brought Africans as slaves from Jamaica to the world. We talked about forms of resistance and deliverance and Jamaican history that carries with them movements of transformation and revolution, and we named Nanny of the Marrons, Paul Bogle,[12] Marcus Garvey,[13] and Bob Marley. Bob Marley was key to help us understand the ways of resistance. Marley carries the whole history of his country in his songs and especially in his 'Redemption Song'. Based on these redemption songs we struggled to find ways to listen to people

---

[10]Revelation Velunta, *Reading the Parables of Jesus Inside a Jeepney* (Philippines: Union Theological Seminary, 2017), 231–5.

[11]Desmond Tutu, *No Future without Forgiveness* (New York: Image Books, 2000), 31.

[12]For example, Fred W. Kennedy, *Daddy Sharpe: A Narrative of the Life of Samuel Sharpe, A West Indian Slave Written by Himself, 1832* (Kingston: Ian Randle Publishers, 2008).

[13]David van Leeuwen, 'Marcus Garvey and the Universal Negro Improvement Association', *National Humanities Center*, www.nationalhumanitiescenter.org/tserve/twenty/tkeyinfo/garvey. html (accessed: 10 September 2020) and 'Declaration of Rights of the Negro Peoples of the World'.

and their forms of resistance and redemption. Then in Italy, as theologians, pastors and liturgists, we responded to the challenge of immigration and the plight of the refugees. How can we use our liturgical resources to move the church to have a radical commitment to the immigrants, the foreigners, the asylum seekers, the refugees and the outsiders?

When we gathered in Sicily, we were also called to face the empire of death who has lived with resources from all over the earth and made its fortune on the riches of the land and the exploitation of the people of Africa, Latin America and Asia. We were called to pay close attention to the situation of immigrants/migrants and the refugees, knowing that the issues around these precious people are vast and complex. Our task there was not to attempt a full study of those matters but rather listen to the people and pray with them and from their precarious conditions. However, in order to pray with them in ways that can foster transformation and solidarity, we needed to engage with the political, social, racial, gender and economic ways we are living in the present times so we might imagine theological and liturgical responses to these situations. The immigrant and the refugee are the stamp of the new neoliberal citizens of our time. Displacement, precariousness and loss are the predicaments of their condition. Thus, when we talk about immigrants and refugees we must talk about abjection wretchedness, defacement and public secrecy, dispossession and displacement, violence and fear. Surely, we don't have time to engage it all in this chapter but let us engage in four concepts that mark our empire today as it relates to migrants and refugees so we can start our conversation:

- Citizenship and Borders versus Dispossession and Displacement;
- Permanency and Belonging versus Abject Wretchedness;
- Land or Occupation versus Violence and Fear;
- Futurability or Existence versus Defacement and Public Secrecy.

How do we engage in hospitality in such a complex situation? What do the sacraments call us and demand us to do?[14] Nowhere else does the ancient and ecumenical symbol of the church as a boat make more sense than at the Mediterranean Sea. A boat of around sixty precious people died while we were there praying and writing prayers together. What is the concrete meaning of the boat for our times from Europe? What are the redemption

---

[14]Cláudio Carvalhaes, *Eucharist and Globalization: Redrawing the Borders of Eucharistic Hospitality* (Eugene, OR: Pickwick Press, 2013); Michael L. Budde, *The Borders of Baptism: Identities, Allegiances, and the Church* (Eugene, OR: Cascade Books, 2011); Trinh T. Minh-ha, *Elsewhere, Within Here: Immigration, Refugeeism and the Boundary Event* (London: Routledge, 2010).

songs we heard in Jamaica that we can sing? What are the cries of Africa we need to raise every day? What are the forms of solidarity we must offer to the indigenous in Asia? How can prayer help create and sustain Ubuntu for all peoples?

What we realized was that our prayers were not for the poor, but for ourselves, as we were challenged by the situations we saw. The change was on us. We couldn't just pray for them and walk away. We had the hard task to pray and be transformed by the prayers we were challenged to say. It was based on our experiences with them that we tried to change our grammar, pray differently, trying to get closer to their cries. All we tried to do was to figure out ways to engage in solidarity. Our hope is that the book of prayers that came out of this experience will help churches to develop a language to name violence, racism, poverty, women and children's abuse, economic exploitation, carelessness with the earth and so on.[15] How do we engage prayer as a subjective matter in relation to an objective reality of suffering and pain? Throughout, we must be aware of what we are attending. We cannot cling to a speech that does not work in the reality of the poor, but because analytical mediations need renewal, these prayers can be the language we must pursue now.

The Christian liturgy began as a movement of people who believed in sharing bread, in solidarity among people because of Jesus Christ. However, this logic is not accepted anymore and we are fighting against an empire whose logic is profit, abuse of the earth and people's sources for benefits, comfort and way of living that has no bounds. Even this radical sharing of the bread and living as equals is denied by main churches. Our work remains ever the same: returning to Jesus and his solidarity with the poor as 'our tradition'. This seems to be a forgotten but important old path to return.

In each place, we witnessed to pain and hurt. We saw the cognitive dissonance between the language of our faith and the conditions of violence we witnessed. Thus, we must repeat, the *Re-Imagining Worship* project was about us hopefully being transformed by the Holy Spirit by being with the certain kind of Jesus that we, as a church, don't get to be so close to. This was a life-changing experience, a denunciation of our detached liturgical resources, a call into a life of connections and fullness that can be sparked by prayers that resound the pain and joy of those unwanted. In this way, many of us could not see liturgy and prayer being done the same way anymore.

We witnessed how the empire can make us feel so frail. At the same time, we saw how prayers can become a powerful way of discovering a God much more vivid than our thoughts; how prayers can be a way of finding ourselves

---

[15]See Carvalhaes, ed., *Liturgies from Below*.

in the midst of others, a way to breathe in the wonder of God and create conditions of resistance; and how prayers can help us 'organize' forms of consciousness that give us a sense of agency, grounded in the power and love of God. It may seem that prayers are almost nothing to fight empire. And yet, it can crack the walls of empire with its sound and persistence. As we read in Ezekiel 22.30, we must 'stand in the breach', between the empire and the unwanted, the powerful and the least of these, the centre and the periphery, listening to the local stories of the margins, learning their wisdom and knowledge, and help provide spaces for sustenance and expansion. Prayers carry an immense possibility to break the structures of evil and violence.

The most fascinating thing that happened in these places of violence and suffering is that praying with a new grammar changed us. Testimonies of the participants pointed out to their life transformations. Most of them never thought that church could be so important and could mean so much to the people. Through the *Re-Imagining Worship* project, we saw that it is possible for Christians to decolonize patterns of words/actions and create liturgies that open fissures within the walls of empire as it brings and receives light and voice from the people who live under the shadows. We realized that by creating liturgies from the places where vulnerable people live, we ourselves gain a more radical voice, one closer to where Jesus lived, along with those Jesus offered his life.

With this project, we were able to receive a light into our own way of living the Christian faith that offer forms of transformation, with praying being a form of *liturgical solidarity*.

Desolation
Expansive plains littered with lost lives, tin and bricks scattered, stranded
Homes shaped of what was tossed away by others, human and object indiscernible
Weathered faces with cracks and crinkles, splotches of colours and scars
Arrogant, bombastic banners and buildings boom: imposed by slave drivers in blood covered suits
Rumbles of empty stomachs reverberate raucously in skeletal frames
And yet, a flicker
Light
Jubilant eruptions with holey-grins as children gallivant through rubble and debris
Uncontainable contentment in the peace of a grandmother watching over them
All consuming passion filling defiant daughters abandoned by disinterested dear-ones

How is it possible?

Hope? Here?

Humanity

Rich resource of life and abundance trapped in bias and prejudice

False perceptions, fake love and forbidden interaction forcing it away

Foolish ones! Fear not! Face yourself!

The hope you seek is buried under the lies of those who seek to keep you under

The hope you seek has been formed under the crushing weight you set on other people

The hope you seek is in them, it is in you: God ingrained, God inspired, God breathed

Open your arms! Release your greed! Fill yourself anew!

Hope burns when your brother is embraced, your sister supported, your elders upheld.

Reclaim your people! Reclaim them: your home, your hope.

Decolonial Liturgies and Unruly Juxtapositions

The prayers that flowed from the *Re-Imagining Worship* project and were gathered in the *Liturgies from Below* book are an attempt to stay closer to decolonial religious knowledges, an anti-colonial look into the gaze of coloniality. Illuminated by Fanon, we can read and pray these prayers as ways to learn about our inferiorization and work on the internalization of our colonial proclivities. Since prayer is a subjective work, these prayers can help us excavate ourselves to see what are we made of and why we speak with the voices that we speak. Bodies to words to practices, practices to words to bodies, we are constructing the possibilities of resistance and for new worlds to appear. As Raúl Zibechi reminds us so powerfully, 'we are facing collective thoughts that are born putting body to the system and its repressions'.[16] Zibechi gives us the signs of these correlations:

> First, it's impossible to separate ideas from practices. The massive and constant actions of the peoples are the fuel of critical thinking. ... Second, it's the imprint of the women from below. The third thing is that we are facing collective, communitarian thoughts, which make it almost impossible to determine who coined this or that concept. ... Ideas that are germinating outside the institutions, although they always try to

---

[16]Raúl Zibechi, *Gramsci, Fanon y después*, 21 June 2019, www.jornada.com.mx/2019/06/21/opinion/016a2pol (accessed: 10 September 2020).

co-opt them. ... Finally, the new developments are only valid if they show some usefulness for strengthening collective emancipations; and, above all, for constructing the new. Because what it's about, besides putting limits on the projects from above, is constructing and creating life where the system, the right and the left, only produce death.[17]

These prayers, hopefully, entangled with other prayers and people enunciating other prayers, will create a liturgical solidarity that will be a small part of a 'collective emancipation ... constructing the new ... and putting limits to projects from above'.[18] Hopefully, these prayers will gather a group of people around helping to build the people's movements.

We do here the work of juxtaposition. However, this is not to juxtapose what is allowed to what is acceptable but to juxtapose the forbidden, the forgotten, the unwelcomed. Traditioning entails the necessary perspective of heresy and betrayal so we can continue with tradition enriched by its opposition and otherwise perspectives. To juxtapose the voice of the poor with the voice of tradition is to show how the Christian project has never been a pure and pristine project, how it has never been only European or only captive to the empire. Christianities have been spurred from within and beyond the canon shaping the many identities of Christianity. The tradition that runs on the streets carries along with the proper, the disavowal of people's practices, other concerns and struggles, other interests and commitments.

Thus, juxtaposition does not intend to get the prayers exactly right, at the right time in the tradition so the liturgy can be under control and do the trick of God's presence. The idea here is praying *with* those who are living at the end of the world without much to sustain themselves. They must be at the centre of any Christian tradition. Praying with the unwanted people shifting of our attention, our consciousness, our concerns, our commitments and allegiances to them was what made us realize we need a new grammar. This prayer, these prayers, shows the juxtaposition of what is with what should be, paying attention to the needed and unattended desires of the people, not aiming to capture the proper rationality of white Christianity or phantom its dreams, control its desires or adjudicate its proper righteousness.

What we have to learn is to undo this knowledge and embrace different forms of knowledges that come out of the people. We have to open ways to learn from what we don't know and don't feel comfortable with and are left out insecure. Thus, to engage with this bricolage of knowledges, we

---

[17]Raúl Zibechi, *Gramsci, Fanon and After*, www.chiapas-support.org/2019/07/09/gramsci-fanon-and-after (accessed: 10 September 2020).
[18]Raúl Zibechi, *Gramsci, Fanon and After*.

try to move away from fossilized forms of the unhinged universality of the Christian liturgical project in all its traditional and also alternative ways of being. Considering the Christian modern gaze, *Liturgies from Below* is a blurry guide to practical theology, an anti-colonial and colonial gaze from within and away from the structures of the Christian faith.

The bricolage of knowledges, the juxtaposition of symbols, and the scandal of including words and resources that these prayers/stories hint highlight people's theories and practices through prayer. It shows the resistance of indigenous people, the street strikes of workers without any right, the anger of mothers who lost their sons to the drug war in the Philippines, the living of faith in churches locked by several locks during the worship and the daily struggles of black people in the townships in Johannesburg, the screaming of market workers being displaced by gentrification and power of the real state and the mighty stubbornness of being alive amidst landfills in Jamaica, or the impossible hope of people becoming refugees by trying to reach Europe. What we perceived as we prayed in these four continents is that globalization has globalized the causes and the pain and suffering of the poor. The globalization of pain and suffering comes from the same neoliberal structures of neo-colonization, plunder, fascism, death and destruction.[19] This destruction can be seen in all the communities we visited. That is one of the reasons we decided not to mention the place of each prayer. They can be felt and lived in various places. A demonstration that these local prayers are markers of the universalization of pain brought up by coloniality.

> Land, land, land our treasure
> God gave us land to till
> God gave us seeds to sow in the land
> Whose land is it anyway?
> Land, land, land our treasure
> Land, land, land our treasure
> Some call it the land of our ancestors
> Some call it the land of the Great Spirits
> The Empire has taken the land for itself
> But the land is our land, our treasure
>
> God has created the earth and all its fullness
> Land, land, land: this treasure belongs to God
> We all belong to God as land belongs to God
> Come share with him, her, me this treasure

---

[19]Wendy Brown, *Undoing the Demos: Neoliberalism's Stealth Revolution* (New York: Zone Books, 2017).

Land, land, land our treasure
Economy depends on our land
Our future as Africa depends on this treasure
Our fears concerning our economy and future are real – why steal our land, our treasure?

Why sell and privatise our land, our treasure?
God, bless our land, your land, our treasure
God, quench the fires of human greed that inspire the privatising of land
God grant us strength and wisdom to be good stewards of the land
Land, land, land our treasure.

Bricolage

These prayers are mostly a bricolage of knowledges that go along with the tradition, not as the historical account of the liturgical proper but taking liturgy as that which must be in service of the poor.[20] Instead of tradition that never pays attention to the voices of the ones excluded from societal structures, our engagement with tradition was a way of offering an attentive listening to the ways of the poor and with the poor, to the ways they are living and surviving. This traditional engagement follows what Orlando Espin calls *traditioning*. Here is one of the ways Espin describes traditioning:

> To conceive of traditioning as the unfailing transmission of a set of doctrinal contents (a pre-established depositum) is to cheapen traditioning's importance as well as to ignore the cultural, historical, and contextual facts. ... How can Christians tradition their hope without adulterating its subversive challenge? A hope that subverts all that humans regard as definitive has been one of the crucial forces driving the complex of traditioning processes that created and have sustained the religion we call Christianity.[21]

This traditioning goes beyond the Roman Catholic sphere from which Espin speaks and enters into a broader sense of faith, including the possible spectrum of knowledges that we might grasp and engage. Its horizon is the ground of existence where excluded people live. This locus and horizon demand a certain reading of reality, one that is closer to the poor, where

[20]Eduardo Viveiros de Castro, 'Contra-antropologia, contra o Estado: uma entrevista com Eduardo Viveiros de Castro', *Revista Habitus* 12, no. 2 (2004): 146–63.
[21]Orlando E. Espin, *Idol and Grace: Traditioning and Subversive Hope* (New York: Orbis Books, 2014), 171.

our allegiances happen. It has to be open to a multifaceted, multivalent and pluriformative and multiple form of knowledge creating a composition of several sources, as a true bricolage.

Vincent Wimbush explains bricolage for African American people:

> Survival for Africans meant learning to assemble cultural pieces from radically and involuntary shattered social-cultural experiences, from rupture, disconnection. It meant developing facility for taking what is left of shattered experiences and 'making do', learning what it takes to survive on what is at hand and forge and identity for themselves – a 'new name – in strange settings and under most difficult circumstances.[22]

These prayers are a bricolage of resources from the colonizers, sources taken away, sources kept through fractured realities dismantled by coloniality. Anything that is at hand, whatever moves through pain, resistance, salvation and its various shades of sacredness, can be useful in bricolage. It is a way to insist in the ways poor people find their own ways of writing their names in whatever they can find sustenance; a form of a dream, even if perhaps forever deferred. This insistence continues the work feminist theologian Ivone Gebara taught us when she was living amidst poor women in the northeast of Brazil. She says:

> The dream is a form of escape, even when it does not come true. The dream helps the body bear suffering. salvation for young women is a good table, a home, a family, medical care, respect for their rights, a tender and courteous place, buying a new dress, receiving a radio as a gift. Salvation is above all a concrete issue, immediate, tied to some actual lack, a suffering that is evident every day and tied to some evil that seems to be multiplying in history at this very moment. This is resurrection today.[23]

These prayers do not aim at complete redemption. Formed in official Western Christianity, for a long while I wrestled with a notion of redemption as a unified, universalized act. Following the notion of redemption by the Christian empire I imagined that unless redemption is a full blast of complete transformation, redemption would never exist. Since redemption wasn't a real thing, I started to get used to live in a world without redemption. It was with Ivone Gebara and Bob Marley that I learnt about redemption.

---

[22]Vincent Wimbush, *African Americans and the Bible: Sacred Texts and Social Structures* (New York: Continuum, 2001), 13.

[23]Ivone Gebara, *Out of the Depths: Women's Experience of Evil and Salvation* (Minneapolis, MN: Fortress Press, 2002), 127.

Gebara describes redemption not as a totalizing event but a frail one, always precarious, 'only temporary, a light in the dark systems of institutionalized violence'.[24]

This is what our prayers can do: offer to the world, if only temporary, an alternative to the systems of institutionalized violence.

Somewhere there is a home
A place of return
Of reunion
Safety and security
Of peace
A communion of friends, equals
No only in God's eyes
But ours too

Believing in that home
Gives us hope and strength

I will work to make that home
A house for you, for we
For us
I want to live there
With you
My children and yours
My parents and yours
My ancestors and yours

I will work to make that home
Today, tomorrow
And in the days to come
Join me when you can

Conclusion

We have retrieved prayer into a subjective event, something you do in your heart. So much so that we have a rhetoric that says we have to move from prayer to action, or prayers are not enough. We must instead see prayer as a continuous movement between subjectivity and objectivity. In Latin

---

[24]Gebara, *Out of the Depths,* 127.

America we learn to do our work thinking-feeling and our work is an endless tuning between feeling and thinking. Thus, prayer must also be a think-feel, meditate, be, do. Contemplate-act. *Ora et labora*.

In this process, there must happen a conversion of the knees,[25] followed by a conversion of the heart. Our colonized knees need to stand before those who continue to crush us down. We cannot pray the way we use to pray, believe the way we use to believe, or think the way we used to think. We need a new way of moving our knees, since our knees can offer new hermeneutics for our *ora et labora*. We start by moving into those places of hurt and disasters. There, with those who are suffering, we bend our knees in solidarity. We hold each other up in strength. We offer what we have, call on God's name together so God's name will not be in vain. We cry out loud together. *Ora pro nobis*. Against all of the neo-colonizers of our times – empires, states, agribusiness, banks, financial market, churches, institutions and people who continue 'to steal and kill and destroy' – we will stand on our knees and pray in the name of the 'life, life abundant' promised by Jesus and continue the struggle.

The prayers are a movement of our hearts shifting the movements of the world. This collective praying-thinking-feeling-acting-contemplating-listening-speaking in the *Re-Imagining Worship* project was only possible because we were together, *with* each other. In many ways, there was no individual prayer because we were all together. In solidarity. As theologian Anne Joh says of solidarity in a rather brunt way:

> You don't just pull solidarity out of your ass. Solidarity/solidarities is an act now or for hopeful futures. It's un/learning ways of cultivating relations w others, it's learning to hear, embrace, to speak and to even fight differently. Solidarity is a labor of love, repentance and choosing to risk oneself in being with another whose life and living, whose histories and politics may not even resonate or be in direct opposition from what may be familiar to oneself. Solidarity is being w another in acts of dissensus that most likely will be the target of systemic and social wrath. Stand up. Speak/shout up, act up![26]

This is what prayer needs to be and do! Create, perform, enact solidarity. Benedict's *ora et labora* is fundamental here; praying as a labour of love, moving, risky, challenging, always transformational by the lives and the

---

[25]See Cláudio Carvalhaes, '"Gimme the Kneebone Bent": Liturgics, Dance, Resistance and a Hermeneutical of the Knees', *Studies in World Christianity* 14, no. 1 (2008): 1–18.
[26]Anne Joh (19 July 2019), in a Facebook post.

living ways of somebody else and the earth. It is the synergy of each other together that makes possible for us to feel, compose and utter these prayers as a body, a body that encompasses all of the animals, the living creatures of the earth, the leaves, the rocks, the skies, the stars. Then, if prayer is solidarity, we might be able to learn what Ubuntu is all about, when no one is forgotten in a community of singularities, dissensus and difference. That is how we all might survive, together, with interbeing solidarity! Life in fullness intertwined with the earth; in awe, respect, honour, expressing hope, frustration, anger, pain, love and endurance, inviting each one to participate in Ubuntu by bearing witness and presence to each other's experiences within the struggles and possibilities of each community. That is how we pray, by becoming alive. But in order to do that we must move to the ends of the world where the unwanted are suffering and breathe the breath of their lives. Then, by being with them we learn a new grammar, thus a new faith, and denounce what is wrong. This is a prayerful revolution! Rabbi Abraham Joshua Heschel highlights the revolution that prayer creates:

> Prayer is meaningless unless it is subversive, unless it seeks to overthrow and to ruin the pyramids of callousness, hatred, opportunism, falsehoods. The liturgical movement must become a revolutionary movement, seeking to overthrow the forces that continue to destroy the promise, the hope, the vision.[27]

To pray is to undo ourselves by the presence of the another, losing our bearings and dismantling forms of power by hearing voices from the margins, lingering a little longer at the end of the world, especially with those unwanted! In this way we can hope to overthrow the forces of death. To pray is to *be with,* breathing under the breath of coloniality, of empire, of trauma and destruction breathing as we resist, all along, singing redemption songs, for this is all we ever had. I finish with two prayers:

> Open house that shares bread
> For the long road
> Open house that gives
> Water of life and peace to drink
> Open house that receives,
> Accompanies and resists

---

[27]Abraham Joshua Heschel, 'On Prayer', in *Moral Grandeur and Spiritual Audacity: Essays by Abraham Joshua Heschel*, ed. Susannah Heschel (New York: Farrar, Straus and Giroux, 1997), 262.

CHAPTER THIRTY-NINE

Psalm 139: A Prologue to Prayer

TINA BEATTIE

In this chapter I seek to show how a prayerful approach to the theological study of scripture, informed by postmodern methods of reading and analysis, can break open familiar texts to new interpretative possibilities. Focusing on Psalm 139, I draw on my personal experience of prayer as a Catholic woman theologian, as well as on Christian and rabbinic biblical studies, psychoanalysis and gender theory. My intention is to suggest ways in which scholarship and prayer together enable ancient texts to speak anew to those whose faith means wrestling with God amidst the tumultuous babel of postmodernity with its competing and conflicting narratives of identity, believing and belonging. The Psalms were written over a time span of several centuries about 3,000 years ago, but they continue to speak to the human condition as few other writings do. Scholars disagree about their origins and authors, but my concern is to read Psalm 139 as part of a living tradition which includes both Jewish and Christian influences.

This psalm is an introspective meditation on the omniscience and omnipresence of God. It is usually interpreted as a reassuring reflection on God's all-pervasive, loving presence, and I have used it that way myself in workshops and lectures. I have also tried to use it to express a sense of closeness to and dependence upon God in prayer, but I found myself resisting the image it evoked of a divine panopticon. It made me feel imprisoned by the all-seeing, all-knowing judge of human affairs. At first I thought this was a sign of spiritual weakness, but I began to ask if perhaps I was being drawn in to a deeper and more challenging reflection on the psalmist's own struggle to draw near to God in prayer. I share that process of exploration here.

Praying the scriptures is a risk and an adventure which involves setting aside our preconceived ideas about the self in relation to God, and about how the Bible should be read. It calls for an act of surrender, a willingness not just to read but to be read. Before this can happen there is an arduous psychological struggle to break through layers of conditioning and concealment in order to be transformed and reborn through grace.

Approaching Psalm 139 from this perspective, I have concluded that many Christian interpretations domesticate the text. Its jagged edges have been smoothed away and its capacity to stir up deeply unsettling emotions has been glossed over in translations which skirt round potentially disturbing images and metaphors. I seek to unleash the psalm's capacity to probe the most hidden aspects of what it means to come before God naked in prayer.

Postmodernity eschews the pretence of the disembodied and objective scholar by recognizing that all readers are positioned by their gendered, psychosomatic engagement with texts, the cultural linguistic lenses through which they read, and the many other texts which influence their interpretation of the text in hand. It is a way of reading which, to quote Jacques Derrida, 'proceeds like a wandering thought on the possibility of itinerary and of method. It is affected by nonknowledge as by its future and it *ventures out* deliberately'.[1] In venturing out upon the text of the psalm I also follow Derrida's widely quoted insight that 'we must begin wherever we are … in a text where we already believe ourselves to be'.[2] I use an imaginative narrative hermeneutic inspired by and faithful to the text, but not constrained by the kind of limits that might be imposed if this claimed to be a work of critical biblical exegesis. My reading is a work of 'bricolage', a 'making do' which, in the words of Michel de Certeau, entails users of language making 'innumerable and infinitesimal transformations of and within the dominant cultural economy in order to adapt it to their own interests and their own rules'.[3] This means recognizing, with Derrida, that 'every discourse is bricoleur'.[4]

---

[1]Jacques Derrida, *Of Grammatology*, trans. Gayatri Chakravorty Spivak (London: Johns Hopkins University Press, 1976), 162.
[2]Derrida, *Of Grammatology*, 162.
[3]Michel de Certeau, *The Practice of Everyday Life*, trans. Steven F. Rendall (Berkeley, CA: University of California Press, 2011), xiv.
[4]Jacques Derrida, 'Structure, Sign and Play in the Discourse of the Human Sciences', in *A Postmodern Reader*, ed. Joseph Natoli and Linda Hutcheon (New York: State University of New York Press, 1993), 223–42, 232.

My engagement with the work of Jewish scholars is eclectic and filtered through my own Christian theological lens, but it is also a dialogue in which I discover new possibilities of interpretation in rabbinic sources. This intertextual approach has midrashic resonances. Explaining the relationship between intertextuality and midrash, Daniel Boyarin writes:

> Every text is constrained by the literary system of which it is a part and … every text is ultimately dialogical in that it cannot but record the traces of its contentions and doubling of earlier discourses. … Reality is always represented through texts that refer to other texts, through language that is a construction of the historical, ideological, and social system of a people.[5]

Scriptural texts collide with one another. They rupture one another's coherence and destabilize established meanings. This is how revelation functions, for only by these iconoclastic struggles can they break open the finite human mind to the divine mystery. As Rowan Williams observes, 'So long as language remains possible, so does contradiction. There is nothing sayable that cannot be answered or continued or qualified in some way or another. … Thus there is no end to writing.'[6] This dialogical, open-ended approach to language is of the essence of prayer. To quote Ashley Cocksworth, 'offered as prayer, language is ventured in humble recognition of its fractured self'.[7] This means, according to Cocksworth, 'prayer is not so much a polite back-and-forth between the human pray-er and God as a messy "polyphony" of voices intersecting each other in ways that break the mould of what would ordinarily count as conversation'.[8]

I read Psalm 139 as this kind of polyphonic tussle between the psalmist, God and the pray-er. I call it a prologue to prayer, for it is the clearing away of the believer's 'baggage', a cathartic expression of anxiety, desire, alienation and rage, which only at the end enables the one who prays to come before God in a face-to-face encounter. Such an approach constitutes 'the iconoclastic reordering, reforming and redirecting of the desires of our hearts towards that which God intends: the love of God' by way of a process through which 'the Holy Spirit stirs up desire and progressively purifies human desire into the likeness of divine desire'.[9]

---

[5]Daniel Boyarin, *Intertextuality and the Reading of Midrash* (Bloomington, IN: Indiana University Press, 1994), 14.

[6]Rowan Williams, *Dostoevsky: Language, Faith and Fiction* (London: Continuum, 2008), 45.

[7]Ashley Cocksworth, *Prayer: A Guide for the Perplexed* (London: Bloomsbury, 2018), 66.

[8]Cocksworth, *Prayer*, 36, referencing Carol Harrison, *The Art of Listening in the Early Church* (Oxford: Oxford University Press, 2013), 183–228.

[9]Cocksworth, *Prayer*, 70.

As Lytta Basset demonstrates in her study of anger in the Bible, this is a process which entails facing up to our suffering and acknowledging that the rage we feel against others is ultimately rage against God at the injustices of life. According to Basset, we are called to 'be angry with God, rather than bow our heads beneath the blows of fortune as if they were the result of God's anger'.[10] Basset write:

> to assume our suffering fully ultimately leads us to stand up straight and come face to face with the OTHER that has knocked us down. Without this growing awareness of our own capacities, without this confirmation of our own power through confronting the OTHER, we will never shake off the doubt in our own ability to face up to the tragic in our lives.[11]

Basset's study has helped me to track the psalmist's and my own journey through the various stages of prayer – from platitudinous praise through terror, desire and rage, until finally one can meet God face-to-face. I do not claim to have arrived at that ultimate encounter, but my studies over the years have led me to reflect on how one might get there.

There is, however, a paradox in my title for in one sense there is no prologue to prayer, if that would suggest a distinction between thoughts and imaginings about God which are not prayer, and some acquired ability to pray 'properly'. Psalm 139 is a prayer from beginning to end, but by tracing its polyphonic struggle through different stages of fear and desire, we can I believe begin to understand what is entailed if we seek to go beyond the domesticated platitudes of prayer by rote, to arrive at that point of silence wherein 'deep calls to deep' (Ps. 42.7) in the abyss of the surrendered self.

Imagined Authors

The Psalms are attributed to David, though there is widespread agreement that they are the works of multiple authors over a long period of time. However, I imagine that 'David' authored Psalm 139, because the story of the beautiful young shepherd chosen by God to become the King of Israel (1 Sam. 16.11-13) offers a potent insight into the psychological conflicts that haunt humanity and unravel our most noble intentions and dreams. Our family histories may not all be as colourful as David's, but his biography can

---

[10]Lytta Basset, *Holy Anger: Jacob, Job, Jesus*, trans. Bruce Henry and Monica Sandor (London: Continuum, 2007), 13.
[11]Basset, *Holy Anger,* 13.

be read as a meditation upon the formative influences of desire, fear, faith and defiance on the human condition.

After being anointed as the future King of Israel, David serves a turbulent apprenticeship under King Saul (1 Sam. 16.14ff.) His affair with Bathsheba and her subsequent pregnancy lead him to arrange for her husband Uriah to be killed (2 Sam. 11), and he then interprets the death of the infant he has fathered with her as God's punishment for adultery and murder (2 Sam. 12.15-23). Later, his beloved son Absalom rises up in battle against him, and when Absalom is killed David is devastated by grief: 'O my son Absalom, my son, my son Absalom! Would I had died instead of you, O Absalom, my son, my son!' (2 Sam. 18.33). The 'David' to whom Psalm 139 is attributed has experienced the extremes of love and betrayal, desire and mourning, terror and shame, and these are the roiling emotions that rise to the surface when he comes before God in prayer. So let us call the author David as the signifier we give to the body that bears the burdens and hopes of the human condition.

There are comparisons between the Book of Job and Psalm 139.[12] Both Job and David reflect on the cosmic mystery, the otherness and omniscience of God. Yet Job believes himself to be the victim of a terrible injustice and he wants to call God to account. He is self-righteous in his grief, angry with God in his suffering and his loss. He has done nothing to deserve his this: 'O that I had one to hear me! … Let the Almighty answer me!' (Job 31.35). Going against more popular interpretations, I suggest that David comes before God stricken with guilt and shame, seeking to hide from the judgement of God because he cannot bear to be exposed. Unlike Job, David has brought his suffering upon himself. He has nobody to blame but himself. Uriah's death haunts him, as we are all haunted by our worst acts of failure, violence or betrayal. Every torment that befalls us can feel like one more punishment for the wrong we have done.

Another imagined author in midrashic exegesis is the first human of creation in Genesis.[13] Here, the reference to the 'unformed substance' of the psalmist in verse 16 is taken in some sources to refer to the *golem,* the lifeless mass which filled the earth. Alexandra Wright refers to legends 'about Adam's stature … in which Adam was a gigantic monster without any intelligence and moved about by creeping'.[14] I shall come back to that,

---

[12]See Will Kynes, *My Psalm Has Turned into Weeping: Job's Dialogue with the Psalms* (Berlin: De Gruyter, 2012).

[13]See Alexandra Wright, 'An Analysis of the Relationship between *mSanhedrin* 4:5, Four Traditions about Adam Attributed to Rav in *bSanhedrin* 38A-B and Psalm 139', *European Judaism* 40, no. 1 (2007): 100–14.

[14]Wright, 'An Analysis', 103.

but for now I want to hold in tension this polyphony of imagined voices speaking through the text.

The God Who Knows

Psalm 139 forms a chiastic structure comprising four stanzas of six verses, with the second half of the psalm echoing the language and imagery of the first half in reverse order. In verses 1–6, the psalmist praises the all-knowing and all-seeing Lord. There is, I suggest, a sense of ambivalence and even resentment in these verses, which intensifies in verses 7–12, when reflection on God's omniscience causes David to take flight and try to hide. In verses 13–16, the maternal body becomes a refuge where he appears to rest for a while, no longer fleeing from God but meditating on the wonder of his own embryonic existence. In verses 17–18 he emerges from this blissful pre-oedipal reverie and in verses 19–22 he rages against the enemies of God, only to lapse into quietude and trust at the end in verses 23–24. Here, I suggest, he has at last arrived at a psychological state of integration in which prayer as an encounter with God becomes possible. With that preliminary summary in mind, let me turn to a closer analysis of the psalm.

> O Lord, you have searched me and known me.
> You know when I sit down and when I rise up;
>   you discern my thoughts from far away.
>
> (Ps. 139.1-2)

The chiastic structure means that the psalm returns to this theme at the end:

> Search me, O God, and know my heart;
>   test me and know my thoughts.
> See if there is any wicked way in me,
>   and lead me in the way everlasting.
>
> (Ps. 139.23-24)

The change in meaning between the first and last verses is so subtle that it might escape notice, but it is important because the psalmist does not end where he began. Between the perfect tense of the Hebrew at the beginning of the psalm and the imperative of the translation at the end, David has wrestled with God as Jacob and Job did. The meaning in the first verse implies a completed action. God's searching of David is a past event, and therefore it suggests total knowledge of David's complex personal history, including his failures and transgressions.

By the end of the psalm, David has been on a searing journey into the depths of his bodily self. All his secret fears and desires, his yearnings and rages, his regrets and failures have been exposed and he is at last able to invite God into his heart. God's searching is no longer focused on David's past. It is a continuous activity, ongoing throughout David's life, and able to accommodate not only David's pieties but also his 'wickedness'. In Psalm 139, we can follow David's maturing relationship with God from the guilt-stricken, traumatized penitent and mourner to the one who, secure in the knowledge of God's guidance and love, becomes the revered King of Israel and, for Christians, the ancestor and prototype of Jesus. So how can Psalm 139 guide us through the stages and struggles of prayer until we too stop running away and turn to face God with nothing left to hide?

'The Hound of God'

You search out my path and my lying down,
　　and are acquainted with all my ways.

(Ps. 139.3)

Most translations of verse 3 gloss over the unsettling imagery of the Hebrew text, so that they elide the sense of danger and fear that David begins to experience when he comes before the Lord who knows everything he has ever done. Robert Alter translates this verse as follows:

My path and my lair You winnow,
And with all my ways are familiar.[15]

Alter's translation makes clear how odd the third verse is for those accustomed to more idiomatic translations. He observes that the unusual use of the Hebrew *rov a* 'generally indicates the place where an animal lies down'.[16] The agricultural word translated as 'winnow' can, suggests Alter, be used as it is in English to mean 'to analyse and critically assess'.[17] Yet if we resist this interpretation, the more immediate image of a lair being winnowed evokes an image of God as the hunter intent on flushing out his

---

[15]Robert Alter, *The Book of Psalms: A Translation with Commentary* (London: W. W. Norton, 2009), 479.

[16]Alter, *The Psalms*, 479.

[17]Alter, *The Psalms*, 479.

prey. This sense of fear and alienation becomes particularly intense in the Targum, which Edward Cook translates as, 'Now when I walk in the road or when I recline to study the Torah, you have become a stranger; and you have made all my ways dangerous'.[18]

The psalmist is beginning to feel like a hunted animal. In verse 2 of the Targum, David says that the Lord searches him out and knows him 'when I sit down to study the Torah, and when I rise up to go to war'. No matter what he does, even when he attempts to study God's Word, the Lord has become a threatening stranger to him. David's claim to be known through and through by the Lord cannot hide the pain and shame of adultery, betrayal, murder and bereavement which he has experienced in his journey of faith. He knows what it is to be hunted and to flee for his life (1 Sam. 19.8ff.), but now it is God and not King Saul who is pursuing him.

How often do we harbour deeply negative ideas about God beneath our flowery words of humility and praise? The Christian doctrine of salvation can create in us a fearful image of a god who takes pleasure in the torture and death of his Son, demanding the suffering of the innocent as the price that must be paid in order to avert his wrath from sinful humanity. In his book *God of Surprises*, Gerard Hughes reflects on how the image we have of God influences our ability to pray. He creates a caricature, 'an identikit image', of an idea of God that he calls 'Good Old Uncle George' – the ostensibly much-loved uncle who punishes family members who do not visit him often enough by throwing them into a blazing furnace.[19] Hughes writes, 'At a tender age religious schizophrenia has set in and we keep telling Uncle George how much we love him and how good he is and that we want to do only what pleases him. We observe what we are told are his wishes and dare not admit, even to ourselves, that we loathe him.'[20]

If I am honest, when I begin to pray with Psalm 139, I too struggle to hide from myself the negative feelings of resentment and maybe even revulsion that rise up in me. Like David, I feel as if God has become a dangerous stranger and is refusing to be placated by my professions of humility and love.

> You hem me in, behind and before,
>   and lay your hand upon me.
>
> (Ps. 139.5)

---

[18]Edward M. Cook, *The Psalms Targum: An English Translation*, www.targum.info/pss/tg_ps_index.htm (accessed: 4 March 2020). All references to the Targum are from Cook's translation.
[19]Gerard W. Hughes, *God of Surprises* (London: Darton, Longman and Todd, 2008), 3.
[20]Hughes, *God of Suprises*, 3.

Again, the Targum translation suggests a startling deviation from the idea that this is a simple devotional psalm. Verse 5 reads, 'From behind me and in front of me you have confined me, and you have inflicted on me the blow of your hand.' In Christl Maier's feminist analysis of the language of the body in Psalm 139, she suggests:

> The 'behind and before' makes it impossible for the psalmist to move horizontally, renders him incapable of going on, to go on his way, and to rest as he sees fit. The laying on of hands in this context is not a gesture conveying blessing, but prevents the psalmist's movement in vertical direction: YHWH's hand rests heavily on him, even presses him down.[21]

David is trapped in the panopticon, weighed down by the burden of God's demands, battered by this omniscient, omnipotent disciplinarian.

Alter's commentary reveals a peculiar reticence here. His translation reads,

> From behind and in front You shaped me,
> and you set Your palm upon me.

He observes that the first line 'could also mean something like "besiege", "bring into straits"', but, explains Alter, 'the sense of shaping or fashioning like a potter seems more likely here, especially as the poem moves ahead to the imagining of the forming of the embryo in the womb. In this understanding, "You set Your Palm upon me" is not a menacing act but rather the gesture of the potter'.[22] I am not persuaded, since the sense of menace has begun building through the psalm. David flies in despair from this pursuing and vengeful God, but God still besieges him.

Francis Thompson's poem, *The Hound of Heaven*, expresses this sense of being hunted by God more eloquently than many devotional interpretations:

> I fled Him, down the nights and down the days
> I fled Him, down the arches of the years
> I fled Him, down the labyrinthine ways
> Of my own mind; and in the midst of tears
> I hid from Him, under running laughter.[23]

---

[21]Christl M. Maier, 'Body Imagery in Psalm 139 and its Significance for a Biblical Anthropology', *Lectio Difficilior: European Electronic Journal for Feminist Exegesis* 2 (2001): 1–17 (7).
[22]Alter, *The Psalms*, 480.
[23]Francis Thompson, *The Hound of Heaven* (Harrisburg, PA: Morehouse Publishing, 1893).

The psalmist at this point begins to give up on his attempt to praise God:

> Such knowledge is too wonderful for me,
>   it is so high that I cannot attain it.
>
>   (Ps. 139.6)

David's God is not only all-knowing, he is also remote, at a great height from the vulnerable human being who trembles before him with no hiding place. Maier makes the point that the adjective translated as 'wonderful' in verse 6 might better be rendered in this context as 'too difficult, not intelligible', so that 'read from verse 5, the first section of the psalm does not end in wonder but in despair'.[24]

Prayer is too hard for me, and God is too far away. My attempt to fake a sense of wonder has opened me up to despair. I want to give up. I feel like running away. Maybe I even want to die.

Prayer on the Threshold of Death

> Where can I go from your spirit,
>   Or where can I flee from your presence?
> If I ascend to heaven, you are there,
>   If I make my bed in Sheol, you are there.
>
>   (Ps. 139.7-8)

As David flees in terror before the God who is high in heaven, his thoughts turn to the chthonian depths. God is also there in Sheol, but what kind of God inhabits the realm of darkness with its intimations of the womb and the tomb?

Despair drags me down and I slump into a state of distraction. My imagination begins to lure me away from the futile attempt to fulfil my duty to pray to the Almighty. What is this darkness I am edging towards? What is this body weighing me down and laying claim to my thoughts? It has the kiss of death about it, but something else as well – something forbidden, warm, mysterious and enticing.

David's psyche may not have been shaped by Greek philosophy with its dualistic associations between paternal form and maternal matter, the abstract rationality of the masculine *logos* and the chaotic lure of the feminine flesh, but he lived at a time when the people of Israel were setting in motion their own version of that dualism. They were being chosen by

---

[24]Maier, 'Body Imagery in Psalm 139', 7.

God, set apart from the maternal and oedipal cults of the ancient world, circumscribed and circumcised by the Law which divided the world in two. On the one side were purity, holiness and right worship; on the other side were pollution, profanity and idolatry. All of these divisions were materially inscribed on the individual and social body, and they revolved around bodily substances associated with sex, birth, food and death. The language of the Hebrew Bible does not lend itself to abstraction. Christian translations obscure the significance of the body when they use the language of the soul and salvation. The faith of ancient Israel was a faith that mapped the body in all its functions to signify a people set apart by God through corporeal practices and rituals dictated by the Law.

Modern European cultures with their Christian inheritance are positioned within a continuous history which begins with that ancient process of cultic separation. This formative human story has navigated a tortuous path away from its roots in the corporeal customs of ancient Israel through its entanglements with Greek philosophy, from the patristic era through the Middle Ages to the Reformation, the Enlightenment and secular modernity. With that in mind, I want to ask how psychoanalytic insights can help a Christian today to understand how she might be unconsciously conditioned by this enduring narrative with its many cultural and religious variations.

Psychoanalytic theory does not offer a scholarly account of the history of religions and it should not be read as such. It seeks to explain its discovery of the unconscious and the architectonics of the soul by reflecting on how religious and theological influences have shaped Western culture and language. To quote Derrida again: 'psychoanalytic theory itself is for me a collection of texts belonging to my history and my culture. ... In a certain way, I am *within* the history of psychoanalysis'.[25] This is certainly true for me, having engaged extensively with Lacanian psychoanalysis in my reading of theological texts. It is from this vantage point that I begin to see a pathway through Psalm 139, as ambivalence, flight and fear breach the barrier of prohibition to enter into a brief space of pleasurable respite in the tomb/womb of the forbidden flesh.

The early church violated the Jewish purity laws, not least in its proclamation of an incarnate God who was identified with the most polluting aspects of bodily life – the womb and the corpse – but this incarnational language was filtered through the rationalizing and dualistic influences of Greek philosophy. Thus Christian theology emerged as an unresolved compromise between the scriptures of ancient Israel and the philosophy of ancient Greece, and the Christian body became encrypted with complex desires and prohibitions bearing the traces of both. Psychoanalysis claims

---

[25]Derrida, *Of Grammatology*, 160.

to reveal the ways in which the Western soul has been formed through this process.

Sigmund Freud traces the phenomenon of the unconscious back to the pre-oedipal relationship and the intrusive paternal rupture of the infant's total dependence upon the maternal body. The resolution of the Oedipus complex produces a turbulent psychic hinterland of repressed emotions – erotic desire and murderous rivalry – associated with the earliest parental relationship. Freud turns this family drama into a metanarrative about the development of Western culture by locating its origins in the oedipal father gods of the ancient cults and tracing it through the law-giving God of Hebrew monotheism and later the God of Catholic and then Protestant Christianity, up to the emergence of modern scientific rationalism. This progressive momentum would, he thought, put an end to religion by exposing its illusory claims to the scrutiny of science and reason.[26]

Freud's account with its Jewish influences privileges the patriarchal relationship, but Catholic Jacques Lacan introduces a more maternal dimension into psychoanalysis. Lacan developed Freudian psychoanalysis as a theory of language, because it was through the language of the analysand that Freud arrived at his theory of the unconscious. Influenced by his studies of Thomas Aquinas as well as of Freud, Lacan recognizes that the forbidden desire associated with the maternal body which haunts the speaking subject is also the desire for God. In place of Freud's vanquished Father God, Lacan offers us a vanquished m(O)ther and invites us to navigate a space of habitation for our desires in her nihilistic depths, without the illusion of there being any divine source or *telos* who would constitute the ultimate satisfaction or resolution to the problem of desire. In this sense, Lacan offers us a Thomist theology of desire without God.[27]

Gender theorists such as Judith Butler, Hélène Cixous, Luce Irigaray and Julia Kristeva bring different critical perspectives to bear on Freud and Lacan, but all draw on psychoanalytic and Marxist theories to analyse the formation of the modern masculine subject and his feminized other within the essentially heterosexual economy of late capitalism. As a form of resistance they seek to bring into discursive play the voice of the marginalized maternal feminine other, seeking forms of linguistic expression which can accommodate the

---

[26]See Sigmund Freud, *The Future of an Illusion* (1927) and *Moses and Monotheism: Three Essays* (1939) in vol. 21, 1–56 and vol. 23, 1–138, respectively, of *The Standard Edition of the Complete Psychological Works of Sigmund Freud*, trans. and ed. James Strachey (London: Hogarth, 1953–74).

[27]See Tina Beattie, *Theology after Postmodernity: Divining the Void – A Lacanian Reading of Thomas Aquinas* (Oxford: Oxford University Press, 2013).

body with all its erotic and maternal impulses, its gendered fluidities and its material relationships and dependencies. Though different in the theories they propose, each of them asks what would happen if we sought to loosen the weave of language in order to allow the repressed desire associated with the pre-oedipal maternal relationship to show through, redolent as it is with infantile hauntings of yearning and mourning.

Kristeva suggests that the social and bodily taboos of ancient Israel are internalized and give rise to the guilt and shame of the Christian soul. Christ's violation of taboos associated with flesh, death and blood could have opened the way for a reconciliation between the maternal cults and the laws of Israel. However, this compromise was never fully realized, and Christianity inflicts upon the subject a burden of guilt and forbidden desire no longer enacted in external separations and purity laws but linguistically mediated in the language of the sinful flesh and the life of the spirit. 'Maternal principle, reconciled with the subject, is not for that matter revalorized, rehabilitated. Of its nourishing as much as threatening heterogeneity, later texts, and even more so theological posterity, will keep only the idea of sinning flesh.'[28]

A postmodern Christian seeking to pray the Psalms is poised on the cusp of these competing and conflicting narratives. Philosophical dualisms and haunting theological prohibitions wage war on the desiring flesh. Divine majesty, omnipotence and omniscience wrestle with the incarnate vulnerability of the birthed and crucified God. Into this conflicted space comes the pray-er herself, bearing her own complex entanglements of guilt and longing, hope and mourning, motivated by a desire and perhaps a duty to pray, but also held back by confusing feelings of reluctance, inhibition and doubt that constitute the shadow side of prayer.

Incarnating Desire

Psalm 139 moves beyond failed attempts at conventional praise, to enter darker and deeper psychological territory. The praying body begins to hunger for God by way of its persistent urgings and instincts that insinuate themselves into the blood and marrow of fleshy human existence. This is the body that longs to be known, accepted and loved in its utmost depths by God, and yet it is also the body that cowers before the omnipotent and distant God in shame and fear.

---

[28]Julia Kristeva, '… *Qui Tollis Peccata Mundi*', in *Powers of Horror – An Essay on Abjection*, trans. Leon S. Roudiez (New York: Columbia University Press, 1982), 117.

Imagination is the medium by way of which suppressed bodily desires pass from silence into speech. Metaphors of transcendence, abstraction, rationality and power associated with God begin to sink into the imaginary depths of the body's yearnings, and creative forms of expression emerge from that dark underworld. To probe the depths as well as the heights of God's presence in prayer is to surrender to the downward tug of bodily desire, so that with the psalmist we find ourselves standing on the threshold of Sheol, with some forbidden longing luring us towards the maternal.

Perhaps the most vivid account of the theological quest to navigate a linguistic structure capable of expressing rather than repressing maternal desire is Kristeva's 'Stabat Mater', in which the rationalizing language of Mariology is set alongside a visceral account of childbirth. Here, the body that speaks is not the pre-oedipal infant but the birthing mother, retrieving her own fleshy discourse from the abstractions of theology and philosophy:

> Words that are always too distant, too abstract for this underground swarming of seconds, folding in unimaginable spaces. Writing them down is an ordeal of discourse, like love. ... Let a body venture at last out of its shelter, take a chance with meaning under a veil of words. WORD FLESH. From one to the other, eternally, broken up visions, metaphors of the invisible.[29]

Maier points out that, in Hans Walter Wolff's influential 1973 study titled 'Anthropology of the Old Testament', 'women are explicitly spoken of only under the topic of sexuality and human reproduction. Speaking about the inner parts of the body, a mother's womb is mentioned en passant whereas Wolff concentrates on all the words that are euphemistically applied to the male genitals.'[30] This serves as a reminder that, for a woman to pray with the scriptures, some contortions may be necessary if she stops running away from God and remains still for long enough to become the body that she is.

The medieval female mystics (now better recognized as vernacular theologians) tell us that contemplation awakens erotic and maternal desire. Their language is redolent with the seductions and consummations of the nuptial bed, but also with the maternal body of Christ which is open to receive them and offers them a union of the flesh before and beyond sex and before the linguistic subject is inserted into the gendered binaries of the status quo. The pre-oedipal imaginary is a boundless fluidity of being unconstrained

---

[29]Julia Kristeva, 'Stabat Mater', in Tales of Love, trans. Leon S. Roudiez (New York: Columbia University Press, 1987), 235.

[30]Maier, 'Body Imagery in Psalm 139', 3.

by laws and prohibitions, groaning and gasping with a desire too deep for words. The thirteenth-century Flemish beguine Hadewijch writes with erotic abandonment of the exquisite torment of fearing that 'I should not satisfy my Lover and my Lover not fully gratify me, then I would have to desire while dying and die while desiring. ... The state of desire in which I then was cannot be expressed by any words or any person that I know.'[31]

Desire for God is heaven and hell. It leads us towards Sheol and beyond, into a wordless abyss where we 'desire while dying and die while desiring'.

The Womb of God

If I take the wings of the morning
    and settle at the farthest limits of the sea,
even there your hand shall lead me,
    and Your right hand shall hold me fast.

(Ps. 139.9-10)

Alter translates this as 'Your right hand seizes me' which is closer to the Targum: 'Also there your hand will guide me, and your right hand will seize me.' Let us note the subtle conflict in the psalmist's relationship with God at this point, what Maier describes as a fluctuation 'between the feeling of security and the fear of persecution'.[32] The imagery implies that it is God's left hand which is guiding David, while the right hand is seizing him. In the body imagery of the Hebrew Bible, the left hand is associated with inferiority and sometimes with weakness and betrayal, while the right hand signifies superiority and is associated with strength and blessing.

God's left hand is guiding David towards Sheol while the right hand is holding him back. Deeply conflicted, David nevertheless follows where his desire leads and allows his imagination to be guided by the hand of the maternal deity which lures him towards the forbidden cults of his pagan neighbours. He must risk death by desire.

Sheol, the territory of the dead, is also the territory of the womb, the enfolding darkness of the maternal body which precedes the coming into being of the individual self. David begins to indulge in a pre-oedipal fantasy of the all-encompassing bliss of the omnipotent maternal presence.

Let us return to that suggestion that the psalmist is alluding to the first human creature, the *golem* which covered the earth before acquiring

---

[31]'Hadewijch, Vision VII', in *The Essential Writings of Christian Mysticism*, ed. Bernard McGinn (New York: The Modern Library, 2006), 102–4.
[32]Maier, 'Body Imagery in Psalm 139', 7.

individual human form. Alter proposes a 'vividly mythological' reading of the reference to taking 'wing with the dawn' and dwelling 'at the ends of the sea'.[33] The psalmist extends to cover the face of the earth.

> If I say, 'Surely the darkness shall cover me,
>   And the light around me become night',
> Even the darkness is not dark to you;
>   The night is as bright as the day,
>   For darkness is as light to you.

(Ps. 139.11-12)

Alter observes that 'this fantasy of being enveloped in darkness picks up the idea of bedding down in Sheol, the underworld'. He continues, 'The location in the womb is associatively triggered by the idea of being enveloped in darkness.'[34]

God the m(O)ther has arrived on the scene. The darkness of the womb is no longer the threatening darkness of God's absence in the depths of Sheol. It has become the maternal God of erotic desire and enfolding warmth.

> For it was you who formed my inward parts;
>   you knit me together in my mother's womb.
> I praise you for I am fearfully and wonderfully made.
>   Wonderful are your works;
> that I know very well.
>   My frame was not hidden from you,
> When I was being made in secret,
>   Intricately woven in the depths of the earth.
> Your eyes beheld my unformed substance.
> In your book were written
>   All the days that were formed for me,
>   When none of them as yet existed.

(Ps. 139.13-16)

Alter explains that 'at this point there is an archetypal association between womb and the chthonic depths'. He points out that the reference to 'innermost parts' (in his translation) is a translation of the Hebrew for 'kidneys', which in this context is 'a synecdoche for all the intricate inner organs of the human creature'.[35] Maier offers a close analysis of the ways in

---

[33] Alter, *The Psalms*, 480.
[34] Alter, *The Psalms*, 481.
[35] Alter, *The Psalms*, 481.

which body imagery informs the reversals and paradoxes of the psalmist's discourse with God. She suggests that 'Psalm 139 combines the formation of a human body in the womb, which can be physically experienced, with the theological tradition of God's primeval creation known from Genesis 1 to 2'.[36]

David has breached the boundaries of the law-bearing self to dissolve into the cosmic oneness of being before any individual creature came to be. He has violated the taboos of separation and arrived at that state of unformed being which constitutes the unwinding of the self all the way back to conception. This idea resonates with the words of a poem attributed to Hadewijch, in which she describes the sense of union that comes from the complete satisfaction of her desire to be united through and through with Christ:

> In the intimacy of the One, Those souls are pure and inwardly naked, without images, without figures, As if liberated from time, uncreated, Freed from their limits in silent latitude.[37]

Rage and Reconciliation

David's awakening from his dream of the maternal body brings with it a return to reality and an eruption of rage.

> How weighty to me are your thoughts, O God!
>   How vast is the sum of them!
> I try to count them – they are more than the sand;
>   I come to the end – I am still with you.

(Ps. 139.17-18)

Alter translates the last line as 'I awake, and am still with You'. The Targum overlays the Hebrew with a highly elaborated interpretation: 'And how precious to me are those who love you, the righteous, O God; and how mighty have their scholars become! I will number them in this age; they will be more numerous than sand; I awake in the age to come and still I am with you.'

As David returns to reality he finds that other God waiting for him – the God whose right hand seizes him, the God of the scholars, the God of the righteous whose wrath is turned against the idolaters and worshippers of

---

[36]Maier, 'Body Imagery in Psalm 139', 9.
[37]'The Mengeldicthen (Poems in Couplets)', in *Women in Praise of the Sacred: 43 Centuries of Spiritual Poetry by Women*, ed. Jane Hirshfield (San Francisco, CA: HarperCollins, 1995), 25–9.

false gods. He has emerged from the boundless now into this age and the age to come, both of them presided over by the Almighty.

Now, rather than fleeing from God, David's anxiety turns to rage. He puts on a mask of self-righteous anger to hide from God his own transgression in the realm of the forbidden.

> Would You but slay the wicked, God –
> O men of blood, turn away from me! –
> Who say Your name to scheme,
> Your enemies falsely swear.
> Why, those who hate You, Lord, I hate,
> and those against You I despise.
> With utter hatred I do hate them,
> they become my enemies.[38]

The 'men of blood' are the idolaters of the cults, the children of Israel who have turned to the worship of false gods and who have been contaminated by the impure blood of pagan sacrifices. We know that the maternal cults never lost their capacity to seduce the people of ancient Israel. David's own son Solomon stirred up God's fury and vengeance when in old age he began worshipping the gods and goddesses of his foreign wives (1 Kgs 11.1-13).

But who is David really raging against? As he emerges from the depths of all-consuming bliss to face the God he has been fleeing, his hatred is stirred up. Is it the enemies of God who rouse such anger, or is it God? Does David protest too much?

I want to reflect on this question by returning to Basset's study of anger. She describes anger as 'an engine capable of transforming a potential devastating energy into the violent life force that accompanies every birthing process. We must be attentive to the true anger that lies hidden beneath the false words of a feigned peace. Underlying the outburst of anger, we will discern the desperate quest for justice.'[39]

Basset explores these arguments through the stories of biblical figures who rage against their enemies and against God. In each case she argues that, when a person stops running away, hiding their anger and avoiding confrontation, a true encounter with God – a face-to-face encounter – becomes possible. Anger feeds on a sense of injustice, but ultimately in Basset's reading this means that anger can be faced as God's own anger rousing our longing for

---

[38]Alter, *The Psalms*, 481.
[39]Basset, *Holy Anger*, 16.

justice and seeking a response. To arrive at that point of turning to face God, we need to go through a painful but cathartic process of acknowledging and expressing our anger. We have to face the urge to kill or be killed, and that means confronting our own fear of death.

Basset situates her analysis in the context of two complementary traditions in the Hebrew Bible: 'According to the more ancient of the two, we cannot see God without dying; according to the other, the worst trial is when God hides his face, for to see the face of God is to be secure in the joy of his presence.'[40] She attributes this ambivalence to there being '"something of the OTHER" at work in us'. She goes on, 'We always have to overcome a certain fear of death when we face this OTHER that is within us and knocks us around, works us over and wounds us. For we have no proof at all that he is well-disposed towards us and thirsts for justice as well, at least as much as we do.'[41] This, I am suggesting, is the process that unfolds in Psalm 139.

That something of the other is, in my psychoanalytic reading, something of the m(O)ther. The ambivalence arises out of an image of God which is dirempted between the womb/tomb of the maternal body, and the distant all-seeing gaze of the heavenly divine. In Western thought, the former is associated with the feminized chaos of incarnate desire and the latter with the masculinzed order of abstract rationality. In this context, it is interesting to note Maier's suggestion that the language of Psalm 139 'expresses an intimate relationship with God focusing on body parts and their function and it shows that the two areas which are separated in the Protestant tradition, thinking and feeling, can be expressed synthetically and in a body-related language'.[42]

As Kristeva suggests in 'Stabat Mater', the cult of the Virgin Mary in Catholicism offers a sublimated form of incarnate maternal desire but it is overlaid by the rationalizations of the theological tradition, eviscerated in favour of an abstract ideal of virginal purity.[43] Basset and Maier suggest in different ways that the ethical God of Israel and the maternal God of the cults can be reconciled if we are honest in prayer and diligent in study. This means allowing prayer and theology to impregnate one another and also to deconstruct one another in order to be birthed anew in the continuous spiral of flight and fear, encounter and embrace which constitutes the human quest for God.

---

[40]Basset, *Holy Anger*, 82.
[41]Basset, *Holy Anger*, 82.
[42]Maier, 'Body Imagery in Psalm 139', 4.
[43]See Tina Beattie, *God's Mother, Eve's Advocate: A Marian Narrative of Women's Salvation* (London: Continuum, 2002).

For Basset, when we finally acknowledge that the source and target of our rage is God, we can come face-to-face with God in vulnerability and trust, for we come to recognize that the justice we long for is God's justice: 'God is our demand for justice, even before he is the just God we long for.'[44]

Psalm 139 leaves us on the threshold of this face-to-face encounter between David and God, but we have been present at the birth of the integrated self from the conflicting oppositions of divine transcendence and maternal immanence. These oppositions play out differently upon Jewish and Christian bodies, through texts which open themselves to many interpretations and ritual and ethical incarnations.

Conclusion

Today we are experiencing many forms of religious extremism which are infecting different traditions. These emerge out of the kind of rage that David feels towards the enemies of God and they constitute a state of arrested theological development. The immature believer, angry with a God who pursues him with overwhelming demands, turns his fury on those who seem less constrained by these rules and prohibitions. The violent rhetoric of some Christians who rage against feminists and homosexuals is one example of this, and of course there are many stories of the most aggressive homophobes being people in denial of their own homosexual desires. When we deflect our fear and anger away from God and project it onto those we deem enemies of God, we become the most deadly and dangerous of believers. As Freud feared, when we are our own worst enemies, we end up hating others as we hate ourselves.[45]

We cannot remain like infants in the womb of God, for we must be birthed into a world where love of neighbour confronts us with the complex demands of justice and ethics. That is why I want to end with Catherine of Siena's caution against the narcissistic seductions of spiritual perfection. This, according to Catherine, is the ultimate idolatry and the ultimate offence against God. God complains vociferously to her about those who ignore their neighbours' needs in order to pray:

> They are deceived by their own spiritual pleasure, and they offend me more by not coming to the help of their neighbors' need than if they had abandoned all their consolations. For I have ordained every exercise of

---

[44]Basset, *Holy Anger*, 85.
[45]See Beattie, *Theology after Postmodernity*, chapter 11.

vocal and mental prayer to bring souls to perfect love for me and their neighbors, and to keep them in this love. So they offend me more by abandoning charity for their neighbour for a particular exercise or for spiritual quiet than if they had abandoned the exercise for their neighbor.[46]

In the end, I shall never pray 'properly', but through the linguistic fumblings and frustrations of honest prayer and the disciplined demands of theological study I can learn to love myself as God loves me, and out of that love I can learn what it means to love my neighbour as myself.

---

[46]Catherine of Siena, *The Dialogue*, trans. Suzanne Noffke, CWS (New York: Paulist Press, 1980), 131.

INDEX